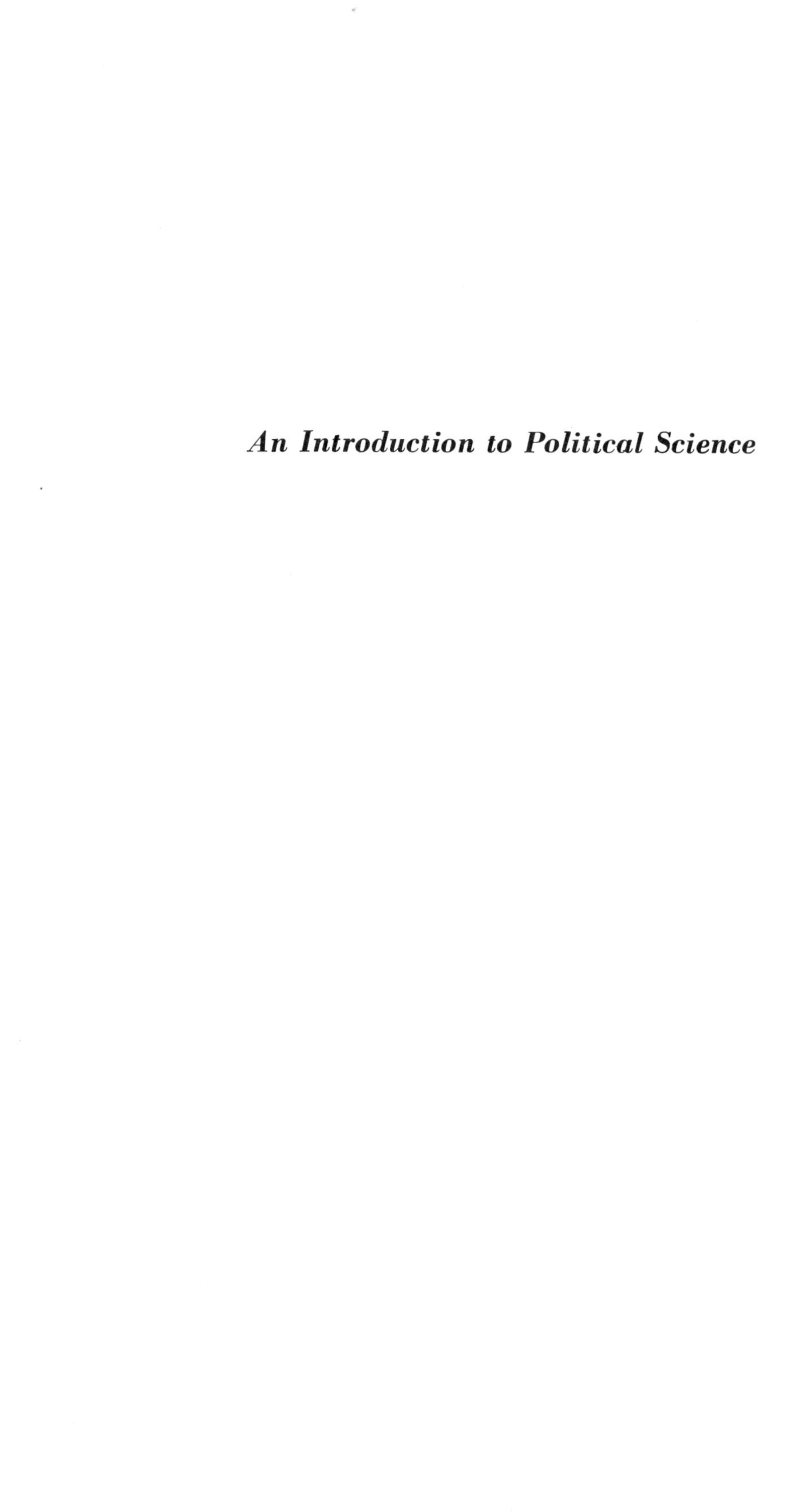

An Introduction to Political Science

An Introduction to Political Science

Rais A. Khan
Associate Professor of Political Science
The University of Winnipeg

James D. McNiven
Associate Professor of Political Science
University of Western Ontario

Stuart A. MacKown

1977   Revised Edition

IRWIN-DORSEY LIMITED Georgetown, Ontario L7G 4B3

Revised Edition

6 7 8 9 0 MP 5 4 3 2 1

ISBN 0-256-01785-9

Printed in the United States of America

Preface

THE FAVOURABLE ACCEPTANCE given to the first edition of this book
has prompted us to attempt to improve it even further. However, we
continue to believe that students in an introductory political science
course must first be exposed to the major concepts and analytical
tools of the discipline so that their initiation to the discipline is broadly
based. As the individual student goes along, it is then possible to
progressively narrow down the field of study to his or her particular
area of interest and analysis.

In this revised edition, we have tried to reorganize our basic
framework somewhat to tighten its logic. We have integrated the material on theories and ideologies, which previously occupied a single
chapter, into different parts of the new Chapters 1, 4 and 5. We have
moved most of the old chapter on types of systems to immediately
follow the discussion of the systems approach in Chapter 2. We hope
that these changes will provide a more coherent progression of material through to the chapters on international affairs. The problem of
integrating the three chapters on the "isms" is not insoluble. But the
mass of material is quite indigestible within our framework and we
have, therefore, elected to retain our original nonsolution. Some in-
structors have indicated to us that they have effectively used these
chapters in conjunction with the material on political culture, public
opinion, and political parties.

This revised edition is the product of many minds. We received
much valuable advice from all parts of the country. We are especially
grateful to Hugh Thorburn of Queen's University, Roman March of
McMaster University, Joseph Jabbra and his colleagues at St. Mary's

University, William Matheson and his colleagues at Brock University, and Richard Vernon of the University of Western Ontario. Our publishers assisted by soliciting comments from others across the country concerning the logic and material incorporated in the text. As far as possible, we have attempted to incorporate the suggestions we received. The resulting mix is obviously of our own making and, therefore, all sins of omission and commission must be attributed to us.

We would also like to thank Margaret Zubal Lott who assisted in typing parts of the manuscript. Professors Khan and McNiven gratefully acknowledge the financial assistance extended by their respective universities, the University of Winnipeg and the University of Western Ontario. They owe special thanks to their wives, Marilee and Jane, for their patience and understanding, without which this revision would not have been possible.

December 1976   RAIS A. KHAN
                                   JAMES D. MCNIVEN
                                   STUART A. MACKOWN

Contents

1. Nature and Scope of Political Science 1

What Is Political Science? Politics and Political Science. Fields of Specialization: *Political Theory and Methodology. National Government and Politics. Comparative Government and Politics. Public Administration. International Relations.* Political Science and Other Social Sciences. Studying Politics: *Normative Politics. Scientific Politics.* Approaches to the Study of Political Science.

2. The State and the Political System 16

Essential Elements of the State. The Origins of the State. The Political System: *Roles, Structures, and Functions.*

3. Types of Political Systems 33

Type A. Type B. Type C. Type D. *Modern Authoritarianism. Totalitarianism.*

4. Political Culture and Socialization 53

Political Culture. Political Socialization.

5. Interest Articulation 76

Passive Interest Articulation. Formation of Public Opinion. Factors Influencing Public Opinion: *Family. Religion. Education. Peer Groups. Economic Factors. Mass Media.* Measuring Public Opinion: *Polling*

viii   *Contents*

Techniques. Interpreting Techniques. Meaning of Public Opinion. Active Interest Articulation: *Informal Interest Articulation. Organized Interest Articulation.* Techniques of Interest Articulation.

6. Interest Aggregation 107

One-Party Systems. Two-Party Systems. Multiparty Systems. Canadian Party System. Party Organization. Party Leaderhip. Party Finances. Electoral Process.

7. Constitutions and Constitutionalism 140

Written and Unwritten Constitutions. Amending the Constitution. Development of Constitutional Principles and Practices: *The Monarchical Principle. The Democratic Principle.* Constitutionalism: Some General Features: *Fundamental Rights. Representative Government. Distribution of Political Power.* Unitary and Federal Governments: *Federalism. Quasi-Federal Constitutions. Right of Secession.*

8. Rule Making 175

Rules, Decisions, and Policies: *Policy Analysis. Policy Process.* Rule Making Structures: *Head of State. Privy Council. Head of Government. Cabinet. Administration.* Legislatures: *Canadian Parliament. American Congress.*

9. Rule Implementation 231

Subfunctions: *Communication. Facilitation. Enforcement. Role Conflict and Effectiveness.* Implementation Structures and Processes: *Head of State. Cabinet. Administration. Administrative Structures. Administrative Controls.*

10. Rule Adjudication 254

Theories of Law: *Natural Law. Positive Law.* Modern Study of Law. Legal System: *Functions. Structure and Process.*

11. Change and Revolution 282

Feedback and Change. Violent Change. Turmoil. Conspiracy. Rebellion. Revolution: *Mechanics of Revolution. Classical and Modern Revolution.*

12. International Relations 307

National Determination of Foreign Policy: *Role of the Legislature. Role of the Executive. Ministry of Foreign Affairs.* Techniques of Promoting

Foreign Policy: *Diplomacy. Propaganda. Economic Techniques. Foreign Aid.* Basic Objectives of Foreign Policy: *Territorial Integrity and Political Independence. National Security. National Interest.* Conditioning Factors of Foreign Policy: *Geographic Factors. Population. Economic Resources. Nationalism and Internationalism. Ideology. Imperialism and Colonialism. International Law.* Power in International Relations: *Balance of Power. Balance of Terror.*

13. Towards an International Political System 335

Collective Security: *Main Principles and Assumptions.* International Organizations: *The League of Nations. The United Nations Organization.* Regionalism and Regional Organizations: *The Commonwealth.*

14. Liberalism and Conservatism 355

Liberalism: *Reform Liberalism. Canadian Liberalism.* Conservatism: *Classical Conservatism. Romantic Conservatism. Canadian Conservatism.*

15. Socialism 386

Utopian Socialism. Marxian Socialism. Soviet Communism: *Leninism. Stalinism.* Chinese Communism. Reform Communism. Anarchism. Syndicalism. Democratic Socialism: *Fabian Socialism. Continental Democratic Socialism. Internationals.* Canadian Socialism: *Communism. Democratic Socialism.*

16. Nationalism 427

European Nationalism: *The Socialist Reaction.* Radical Nationalism: *Italy. Germany.* American Nationalism. Asian and African Nationalism: *China. India. The Middle East.* Canadian Nationalism.

Name Index 463

Subject Index 467

1

Nature and Scope
of Political Science

POLITICAL SCIENCE as a discipline is concerned with the study of one of
the most significant areas of human affairs: people's existence as members of organized human society. Philosophers, statesmen, and politicians in all ages and all civilizations have concerned themselves with
finding answers to questions pertaining to the political facets of a society's existence.

Western political tradition originates with Greek civilization. The
foundations of political thought and analysis were first explored by
Socrates, Plato, and Aristotle. Subsequent writers expanded upon
these foundations in their own ways and in response to the needs and
problems of their particular societies. One of Rome's prominent
statesmen, Cicero, was also its foremost political commentator. Religious thinkers such as St. Augustine and St. Thomas Aquinas, though
not basically oriented toward politics, nevertheless found it necessary
to deal with the subject. Niccolo Machiavelli, a product of the Italian
Renaissance, addressed himself to political problems of his time. The
various stages of the evolution of the English political structure were
the setting for the works of Thomas Hobbes and John Locke in the
17th century and Jeremy Bentham and John Stuart Mill in the 19th.
These centuries also witnessed a variety of intellectual responses to
political developments on the European continent, some prominent
examples being Rousseau, Hegel, and Marx.

Non-Western civilizations have also had their political commentators. The Indian political tradition was enriched by the spiritualism
of Guatama Buddha and the political realism of Kautilya. Chinese
political ideas were influenced by Confucius and Mencius, while the
Arabs, whose contribution to the growth of Western civilization cannot

1

be minimized, can rightly boast of such names as Ibn Sina (Avicenna), Ibn Rushd (Averroes), and Ibn Khaldun. While they developed independently of each other, one nonetheless discovers remarkable similarity of ideas between the Western and the non-Western traditions. The "Philosopher-King" of Plato and the "Middle Kingdom" of Confucius operate on similar planes of justice, fair play, and morality. Political realists like the Italian, Machiavelli, and the Indian, Kautilya, recommend to leaders similar patterns of ruthlessness, egoism, and disdain for ordinary standards of morality in politics.

The essential nature of the problems examined by political scholars of the past is not significantly different from that which preoccupies modern political scientists. For instance, the nature of the relationship between economic classes, wealth, and political stability, which so occupies the attention of contemporary political scientists, was discussed by Plato and Aristotle. Political scientists also deal with such question as: the nature and role of authority and power, the characteristics of political ideas and behaviour; the requisites for political stability; and the causes of political change and revolution.

What Is Political Science?

Political scientists do not agree on a common view of the nature of their discipline. Instead, there exist a number of competing schools and subschools of thought concerning the nature of political science. Some have argued that a rigid definition of the discipline would restrict its natural growth, and political science should include whatever the political scientist desires to bring within its scope.

Contemporary attempts by political scientists to arrive at a generally acceptable definition underscores this problem. Alfred de Grazia maintains that political science is the study of "the events that happen around the decision-making centres of governments."[1] Charles Hyneman argues that the focus of attention in political science "is that part of the affairs of the state that centres in government, and that kind or part of government which speaks through law."[2] Political science has also been defined as the "study of government," that is, the study of "the control, distribution, and use of power over human activities in society," or as the "art of the possible" in human affairs.

Existing definitions of political science may be divided into two major types. The first type focusses on the structure of government and thus refers to forces that constitute and shape the government's

---

[1] Alfred de Grazia, *Political Behavior* (New York: The Free Press, 1965), p. 24.

[2] Charles Hyneman, *Study of Politics* (Urbana: University of Illinois Press, 1956), p. 26.

policies and actions. The second type refers to the nature of these forces and concentrates on the concepts of power and influence. *Government may be defined as the totality of those structures which act in the name of the society to promote and safeguard its interests. Power, on the other hand, may be defined as the relations of men, in association and competition, submission and control, through which they seek to influence the behaviour of others.*[3] Clearly, neither of the two types of definition of political science comprehensively reflects the nature of political science. For, to confine political science merely to the study of government would be as erroneous as to emphasize "power" as the focus of political enquiry. "Power" is the central organizing factor in politics, while "government" is its basic operational structure. Political science, thus, is the study of "power" and of "government".[4]

POLITICS AND POLITICAL SCIENCE

The term politics is generally used to refer to those activities which revolve around the decision-making organs of the state and involve the concepts of power, authority, command, and control. Some political scientists would also extend "politics" to cover any activity at all levels of human relationships which involves power and authority. Conflict, they argue, is an indispensable characteristic of any human relationship, and when conflicts are resolved and the solution imposed through the use of power and authority, the activity becomes political. Thus, politics exists within trade unions, families, corporations, and wherever human beings indulge in group activity.

Our discussion thus far has demonstrated the very wide dimensions of the study of politics. Practically every member of society is involved in some kind of activity which can be legitimately designated as political. The activities are discernible at all levels of society. It is true that some individuals and groups in society are more directly involved in political activity than others. These are designated "political actors." Such individuals and groups, however, constitute at best a small segment of all those involved in the political process. They are primarily spokespersons for the vast number of less active citizens and purport to represent their interests. They seek and control political power in the name of the citizens, on their behalf and to promote their interests. But it would be erroneous to say that other members of the society are not political beings. To them the importance of political science lies in the

---

[3] See Harold Lasswell and Abraham Kaplan, *Power and Society: A Framework for Political Inquiry* (New Haven, Conn: Yale University Press, 1965), pp. 74–102.

[4] Also see Robert A. Dahl, "What is Political Science?" in Paul Fox, ed., *Politics Canada*, 3d ed. (Toronto: McGraw–Hill, 1970).

fact that it provides knowledge about the intricacies of the political process, enlightens them about the various political organizations in society and the appropriate process through which their interests may best be promoted. The relevance of political science for a practitioner of politics is that it may equip him or her with generalized knowledge about the use of power and provides an acquaintance with the structure and dynamics of political organizations.

It may appear, superficially, that a student of politics would be ideally suited to indulge in the practice of politics. There are many instances in history where a student of politics has served as an advisor to a politician or has become one. Both Plato and Aristotle reportedly performed this role; Plato is said to have served the ruler of Syracuse, in Sicily, in 367 B.C., and Aristotle served as advisor to Alexander the Great. Machiavelli served as secretary of the Republic of Florence for 14 years. Woodrow Wilson was a political scientist who became the 28th president of the United States. Then, there is the contemporary example of Pierre Elliot Trudeau, who became an active politician after his earlier work as a scholar in political economy and international law. These are, however, atypical examples, indicating only that a political scientist may become a practitioner of politics. As a rule, engaging in politics is not the same as studying politics. It requires different skills and orientations.

FIELDS OF SPECIALIZATION

Political science has been divided into a number of separate, though overlapping, fields. A brief examination of each field will demonstrate the relationship among them and also illustrate the broad dimensions of the discipline.

Political Theory and Methodology

The normative and speculative component of political science is known as political theory. Political theorists attempt to understand the nature of political organization and formulate principles designed to impose order and meaning on chaos. Guided by these, the political scientist sets about analysing problems such as the foundations of political authority, the determination of individual and collective responsibility, and the ideal basis of political organization and its role in society.

Courses of instruction in political theory include theories of government, state, and law, dating from the early years of the Western political tradition as well as theories of liberalism, conservatism, socialism, communism, and nationalism which inspire and motivate contemporary political behaviour.

National Government and Politics

This very broad field of political science is often the most interesting to students, for in many cases it is the study of the politics of their own country. Courses of study in this area are structured depending upon the way in which a country is organized and the way in which those teaching the course see the situation. In many universities the course which introduces students to political science is a general course in the politics of their own country. Such courses include discussions of the basic structure of the country, the basic political units inside and outside of the government, and at least some aspects of the country's history and development. More specialized courses in Canada concentrate on such things as the various components of the national government (legislature, administration, courts and legal systems), provincial and local governments, political parties and interest groups, and the nature of the federal system.

However, if all attention is focussed on one particular country, the result is likely to be a rather parochial outlook at a time when countries are being drawn into increasingly intricate relationships because of modern economic and technological interdependence. Students will fail to gain insight into other countries, their political behaviour and organization, and the extent to which these aspects of one's own country are similar to, and different from, others. For example, if students were to concentrate on Canada alone, they would miss such important points as the manner in which other countries have solved or are attempting to solve problems such as those posed by the presence of different language groups and the need for economic development. Many political scientists believe that in order to understand the politics of one's own country it is also necessary to develop an insight into the operation of other countries.

Comparative Government and Politics

The use of the comparative method in studying political phenomena is commonly traced back to Aristotle, who made a study of the Greek city-states of his time. On the basis of this material, Aristotle formulated a classification of governments which remains useful even today. The contemporary field of comparative government has grown out of the desire of students to compare their domestic political processes with those of other states. Their objective is, in part, to discover and understand the similarities and differences between them. Originally, comparative government was restricted to the classification of political institutions in Western European and North American countries. Since the 1950s there has been an increasing tendency to include African, Asian, and Latin American countries as well.[5] The comparative, or the cross-national, aspects of political attitudes and behaviour, policy making and public administration are now major areas of concern to political scientists.

Public Administration

The study of the behaviour of organizations which implement policy decisions has been necessitated by two developments: the growth of governmental activity and industrialism. Over the last 150 years the responsibilities of governments have expanded beyond the minimal needs of internal and external national security to encompass educational, health, welfare, economic, and other social needs. These additional responsibilities have resulted in an expansion in the size of governmental bodies to a point where they are often the largest organizations in any society. The implications of this growth for the policy-making process, personal freedoms, and economic prosperity have prompted increasing concern over and study of their structures and processes.

Industrialism, at the same time, has encouraged the development of theories of organizations in general. Human motivation and behaviour have been investigated in order to discover methods of increasing productivity and efficiency. These theories, developed primarily for large private corporations, have been adapted to the public organization. Techniques of planning, control, and decision making have also been harnessed to the public service.

The study of public administration has been further enriched by the incorporation of analytical ideas from other areas of political science. Political scientists are increasingly viewing governmental organizations as contributors to policy making and as subjects of organized pressure and lobbying. Comparative public administration, an outgrowth of comparative politics and government, has been developed as a means of understanding the nature of public organizations throughout the world.

International Relations

The scourge of two world wars in this century aroused statesmen and scholars to intensify their understanding of the tensions among

---

[5] One of the earliest works in this area was Gabriel A. Almond and James S. Coleman, eds., *The Politics of the Developing Areas* (Princeton, N.J.: Princeton University Press, 1960).

states. Their aim was to develop a set of propositions which would enable states in the increasingly interdependent world of modern technology to unite for the common purpose of promoting the survival and progress of mankind. A major concern has been to articulate common values which transcend such often divisive factors as nationalism and chauvinism. Thus, there was room for the development of the study of international relations to gather, classify, and integrate data and formulate generalizations on international behaviour, focussing insight from all relevant fields of knowledge.

Courses of study in international relations include international law and organization, the principles and practice of diplomacy, comparative foreign policy, foreign aid, and conflict resolution.

POLITICAL SCIENCE AND OTHER SOCIAL SCIENCES

Political science as a discipline which focusses on the behaviour of man in society is thus one of the social sciences, some others being psychology, economics, and, for our purposes, history. In order to appreciate just what political science is, one must reflect on its relation with other social sciences and understand the way in which it is parallel to and different from them.

The lines of distinction between the various social sciences is, like the divisions within political science, an arbitrary attempt to fragment a vast field of study into more manageable and meaningful segments. It would be incorrect to assume that the distinctions between social sciences have any validity except as organizational tools. Human problems and attempts to resolve them are multifaceted, some being basically political, others basically economic, and so on. All of them possess overtones that influence or are influenced by several facets of human life at once. In order to understand and resolve these problems, the analyst has to draw upon several social science disciplines.

History's close relationship with political science should be apparent. History is an accounting and interpreting of the events in society. This accounting, usually presented in a chronological fashion, serves to illuminate the origin and consequence of events. This allows the researcher to understand the factors that led to the events of interest. For example, if a student of politics were to prepare a detailed outline of the current formal governmental powers in Canada, the result would be an incomplete picture of reality. This would stem directly from the fact that such an outline could not explain how these powers developed. In other words, sensitivity to the traditions and long-term forces which shape contemporary society would be lacking.

Psychology has been called the science of human behaviour. It deals with the complexities of human nature and personality. If political science is the study of political behaviour, then psychology must be of importance to the study of politics. For example, an understanding of psychology helps the political scientists to appreciate why individuals vote in certain ways and how the personality of a leader affects the manner of that leader's exercise of power. Two of the most fundamental desires in human beings are those of self-preservation and self-expansion. The desire for self-preservation may impel a human being to resort to any and all action that is necessary for the accomplishment of this purpose, including the surrender of individuality to an organized group. A direct manifestation of this desire is the conceptualization of a "state of nature" in which life was "nasty, selfish, brutish, and short" and its transition into organized society governed by laws. The manner in which members of a modern society react towards civil rights, individual freedoms, police powers, capital punishment, and electronic eavesdropping, is, in one way or another, motivated by the psychological desire for self-preservation. These reactions are reflected in the laws and institutions of government in society. Similarly, the psychological desire for self-expansion also motivates the individual to attempt to influence colleagues and associates.

The first impulse in primitive societies is to organize. Whatever might be the method of this organization, the motivation was the desire to devise means (through collective action) which would preserve society as well as the individuals within it. Once people have organized into communities, the question of leadership arises. People seek power as a means to an end. They also seek power as an end in itself—to display superiority over others, to command esteem, or to satisfy their own egos. Though the manner of achieving power is largely culture-bound, all societies have members who aspire to political leadership and the exercise of political power. Many political scientists have attempted to develop a whole science of politics based upon such psychological forces as desire for power and self-interest.

Sociology is the branch of the social sciences concerned with the study of human behaviour in groups. It explores such questions as why groups form, how they form, and what kinds of relationship exist within and between groups. Sociology is also interested in the dynamics of change in society. As political behaviour is usually also group behaviour, it is quite obvious why political scientists are interested in what sociologists are doing. The political activities of various groups that sociologists study are important to a political scientist as are the values, customs, and traditions of these groups. The action of groups produces an ever-changing pattern of relationships in society. These changes result in pressure for further changes in policies or structures in the political world. The attitudes and values of groups may also have a decisive impact on political actions. Here again we have two disciplines which are intimately related.

Economics and political science are also closely related. Many of the most crucial political decisions made are questions of economic policy. Such matters as tax policy, tariffs, labour relations, inflation, wage and price controls, and energy supplies are politically important, not just as economic questions but because of their larger social and political implications. Various groups and alignments of political importance emerge around economic issues. The interplay between these groups is often of great importance in the making of political decisions, as reflected by the concern of Canadians about the consequence of extensive American investment in Canada.

Other disciplines also interrelate with political science. For instance, the relationship between *geography* and politics is explicit in the study of geopolitics and urban planning. *Anthropology* has enriched our knowledge of the relationship of culture, political process, and political institutions.

STUDYING POLITICS

To this point our discussion has centered upon the scope of the discipline of political science and its relationship with the other social sciences. It is now necessary to examine the ways in which one may go about gaining an understanding of political phenomena.

Throughout most of human history knowledge about any phenomena, physical or human, has relied primarily upon individual experience, intuition, and insights passed on from earlier generations. Science, of any sort, is a relatively recent development. For millenia, people accepted their physical environment and assumed that it was simply nature operating upon the basis of some unknown general law, or, more commonly, a manifestation of the will of God or the gods. Knowledge that is called science was often stoutly resisted as a threat to the natural order of things or an affront to the gods. However, progress in the physical sciences has been markedly faster than in the social sciences, and it is still quite safe to say that by and large the understanding of the physical sciences is far more complete and verifiable than is the case with social sciences.

Normative Politics

Until the mid-20th century there was little writing about politics that was of a scientific character. The development of ideas about the values and beliefs which underlay political organization was impressionistic and historical. The questions about the goals of political activity and the ethics of the means to achieve them are designated as political philosophy.

The relation of contemporary political science to the heritage of political philosophy has been the subject of considerable debate in recent years. Some political scientists have argued that because of its overemphasis on moral and normative principles, political philosophy overlooks the empirical elements which lie at the base of contemporary political science and hence is largely irrelevant. While it is difficult to deny that emphasis on the normative aspect could lead to a neglect of the scientific basis of contemporary political science, it is equally difficult to accept the thesis of irrelevance.[6]

The political organization of a society is an instrument for the accomplishment of certain goals. The determination of these goals necessarily introduces the problem of value judgments, or normative considerations, since the goals of society are an amalgam of a wide variety of beliefs and desires. In one sense all political systems aim to promote the welfare of their inhabitants—to lead them to a better life. What in fact constitutes this higher level, or a better life, has been a main concern of political thinkers and actors since the advent of political organization. While the nature of these goals is important, of equal importance are the questions of who shall define these goals, how should they be achieved, and who is responsible for their achievement. The question of values in politics thus involves judgments as to the true and desirable nature of the relationship between the rulers and the ruled. In simplest terms, a political theory is a frame of reference which enables an individual to identify political phenomena and to evaluate their significance.

All political theories are based upon a set of broad philosophical concepts concerning the basic nature of people, society, and politics. Plato, for instance, believed that reality was to be found in the world of ideas and that the objective, physical world was an imperfect reflection of this "reality." For him it followed that the only really effective way to reach a truer understanding of reality was through a method which would emphasize logic rather than empirical observation.

Other theories have looked to one aspect or another of the natural world for a pattern of relationships that could be transferred by analogy to the political world. For instance, people may be seen as essentially competitive animals, and it is often suggested that from this competition comes the force which creates change and progress in society. Thus, it is suggested that though the vision of the ultimate form of society may be obscure, the only way for people to reach it is to continue to be competitive. It thus becomes the function of the society's political organization to protect, and if possible nurture, this competitive instinct while, at the same time, preventing it from becoming destructively violent. This attitude underlies the theories of most contemporary conservatives and liberals. Often they diverge as to

---

[6] Sheldon A. Wolin, "Political Theory as a Vocation," *The American Political Science Review* 63, no. 4 (December 1969).

the best means while not being in disagreement over the basic processes involved in people's progress.

It is quite possible, on the other hand, to view people as essentially cooperative. Such an assumption underlies the rationale for the political organization designed to curb competitiveness and encourage cooperative or communal enterprises. It is felt by these theorists that competitiveness is an inherently wasteful method of achieving progress and that it encourages a waste of resources and hostile attitudes toward other people. This approach is found in most socialist theories.

A related area of theoretical concern is the role of the individual in a larger sense. Are individuals to be valued for themselves? Is society and government organized primarily to protect individuals, to free them from unnecessary fear of other people and of the elements? If so, though the ultimate society may be a dimly seen vision, certain methods are indicated and others proscribed. For instance, some theorists have argued that because people subordinated themselves to government in exchange for security, they could not be compelled to surrender that security unless they had violated the laws. In other words, such an undertaking as military conscription would be unthinkable since it would force people to jeopardize their lives, something they have a perfect right to do as a matter of choice. If the government does so jeopardize a person, then by definition it is no longer providing security and thus loses its legitimacy. By the same token, steps that would promote or enhance the abilities of the individual could be regarded as desirable. For theorists of this school, the maintenance of individualism also included the judgment that the biggest threat to the individual comes from government, not from the power of some people over others. Thus the expansion of governmental power and influence was regarded as something to be resisted unless all other alternatives had proven fruitless. Others of an individualist bent have argued that the main threat to people does indeed come from other people, not from government. Government is the only organization capable of resisting the encroachments of large and powerful private organizations, such as big business and labour unions, in the name of the individual. Thus, government intervention becomes a necessity, not necessarily desirable, but possibly the lesser of two evils.

There are a bewildering number of variations of these and other central themes which will be explored as specific theories in later chapters.

Scientific Politics

The term "science" is generally applied to the acquisition of knowledge where, on the basis of systematic and orderly analysis of collected data, predictive and reliable propositions can be formulated. This process of gaining knowledge, of course, has been more fully developed in physical sciences. Political scientists, like their colleagues in the other social sciences, are concerned with human behaviour which is inspired by a complexity of motives and is difficult to predict. They are also concerned with social forces which are in a constant process of change and modification and cannot be readily controlled. With this in mind, then, how justifiable is it to designate the study of political behaviour as a "science"? The answer lies more in the extent to which political enquiry follows the scientific method than in the success enjoyed by political analysts to date.

By and large, any scientific method consists of four fundamental components:

1. Observation and collection of data.
2. Classification of the data in significant and meaningful categories.
3. Formulation of generalizations and predictions.
4. Verification of the stated generalizations as laws, trends or tendencies.

To simply assert that political science follows the scientific method and thus is a science would be to minimize the many problems faced by political scientists which detract from the scientific nature of their methodology. Clearly, political scientists can follow the first three stages of the scientific method with relative ease. They can observe the political phenomena they wish to examine and collect the data pertaining thereto, classify their data into significant and meaningful categories, and then formulate their generalizations and predictions. When they arrive at the fourth stage of the scientific method, namely the verification of their generalizations, the political scientists run into their most serious problems. They deal primarily with the highly inconstant human variable. They are further faced with inadequate means for a quantitative measurement of social forces and the conceptual difficulty of delineating the various other forces which contribute to the complexity of social life. Political scientists cannot manipulate people the way chemists manipulate chemicals.

Finally, and perhaps most important, there is the element of personal and social bias and prejudice in human beings which works in different ways. First, bias in the individual may spark behaviour which defies logical and rational explanation. Second, the political scientist, being human, cherishes personal convictions, beliefs, preferences, and values, which tend to influence his or her analysis and conclusions. Third, the political scientist's cultural background may tend to cloud objectivity. These factors compound the difficulties of studying political phenomena scientifically.

Unable to overcome, at least for the present, the inherent difficulties in verification, political science has not yet reached the level of predictability which is the hallmark of physical sciences. The possibility of error in prediction among political scientists is infinitely greater than it is among physical scientists. This, of course, is not to say that the latter are by any means infallible. However, political scientists may frequently arrive at conclusions and generalizations which are not verifiable through laboratory experiments. Encumbered by these difficulties, political science has not succeeded in constructing "an all-encompassing body of theory that relates the laws to each other and provides the basis for explaining all operations, data and the relations within the field of the science in question."[7]

It could be said that the use of the term "science" as a suffix to "political" is an expression of intent. The problem of the ability to generalize conclusions is further compounded by the inability to develop a common approach in the discipline. Political scientists often cannot agree upon the questions to ask, let alone the answers to them. Thomas Kuhn has argued that an examination of the literature of physical optics before Newton shows that it was not quite "scientific" even though the practitioners in the field considered themselves to be scientists. In the absence of any existing common approach, each student of optics sought to create his own. Motivated by a common desire to discover the truth behind physical optics, they also developed a dialogue among themselves. The dialogue facilitated new discoveries and eventually led to a common approach to optical questions.[8] Political scientists work under somewhat similar conditions. Faced with the absence of an agreed upon approach, they develop their own. Despite apparent divergences in their pattern of enquiry, they are all, nonetheless, motivated by a common desire to discover the "truth" behind politics.

APPROACHES TO THE STUDY OF POLITICAL SCIENCE

In the course of its growth, the discipline of political science has been exposed to revolutionary additions in the number and sophistication of approaches to its study. An approach is the name given to *the perspective adopted by the analyst engaged in the study of political phenomena*. At different periods scholars and thinkers have developed new insights and contributed new perspectives into hitherto unrecognized vistas of social and political life.

---

[7] J. Roland Pennock and David G. Smith, *Political Science: An Introduction* (New York: Macmillan, 1964), p. 9.

[8] Thomas S. Kuhn, *The Structure of Scientific Revolutions*, 2d ed. (Chicago: University of Chicago Press, 1970), p. 13, also chapters 1 and 2.

From the days of Plato and Aristotle, the development of new approaches to political science has rested upon both the normative and scientific aspects of the discipline. However, because the preponderant interest of scholars until recently lay heavily toward the establishment of prescriptions rather than the investigation of behaviour, scientific studies of politics have been the exception rather than the rule.

The successful application of scientific approaches to the understanding of the physical world influenced the study of politics. New approaches became increasingly scientific in their orientation, with a growing emphasis on the collection and classification of data. Nevertheless, all approaches possess certain common denominators. All of them start with some basic assumptions which establish a framework for political analysis. All of them lead to formulations, though normally only details are verifiable. Approaches may be used to create new hypotheses which then form the basis for further analysis. Alongside these common denominators there are significant differences between them which determine their utility and adequacy for political analysis. Some of them are more highly developed and refined, while others are simplistic and crude. Some are broadly conceptualized; others focus on one or two basic concepts.

The selection of an approach for the study of political phenomena is based on utility. It allows the analyst to organize his data in a fashion that is meaningful to himself and to others. Motivated by this desire, the authors have adopted one form of the *systems approach* in this book. A more detailed discussion of this approach is presented in the next chapter.

RECOMMENDED READINGS

Almond, Gabriel. "Political Theory and Political Science." *American Political Science Review* 60, no. 4 (December 1966).

Bell, David V. J. *Power, Influence and Authority*. Toronto: Oxford University Press, 1975.

Bluhm, William T. *Theories of the Political System*. Englewood Cliffs, N.J.: Prentice–Hall, 1965.

Charlesworth, James C., ed. *Contemporary Political Analysis*. New York: The Free Press, 1967.

Cobban, Alfred. "The Decline of Political Science." *Political Science Quarterly*, 68, no. 3 (1958).

Cox, Richard, ed. *Ideology, Politics and Political Theory*. Belmont, Calif.: Wadsworth Publishing, 1969.

Dahl, Robert A. "What Is Political Science?" In *Politics: Canada*, edited by Paul Fox. Toronto: McGraw–Hill, 1970.

———. *Modern Political Analysis*. Englewood Cliffs, N.J.: Prentice–Hall, 1959.

Duverger, Maurice. *The Ideal of Politics.* London: Methuen & Co., 1964.

Easton, David. "The New Revolution in Political Science." *The American Political Science Review* 63, no. 4 (December 1969).

Eulau, Heinz. *The Behavioral Persuasion in Politics.* New York: Random House, 1963.

Greene, Thomas H. "Values and Methodology of Political Science." *Canadian Journal of Political Science* 3, no. 2 (June 1970). See also, comment by Cooper, Barry, "Values and Methodology in Political Science." *Canadian Journal of Political Science* 4, no. 1 (March 1971).

de Grazia, Alfred. *Political Behavior.* New York: The Free Press, 1965.

Hacker, Andrew. *Political Theory: Philosophy, Ideology, Science.* New York: Macmillan, 1961.

Kuhn, Thomas S. *The Structure of Scientific Revolutions.* Chicago: University of Chicago Press, 1970.

Lasswell, Harold, and Kaplan, Abraham. *Power and Society.* New Haven, Conn: Yale University Press, 1965.

Lasswell, Harold. *Politics: Who Gets What, When, and How?* New York: World Publishing, 1958.

McClosky, Herbert. *Political Inquiry.* New York: Macmillan, 1969.

Sabine, George. *A History of Political Theory.* 3d ed. New York: Holt, Rinehart & Winston, 1961.

de Sola Pool, Ithiel, ed. *Contemporary Political Science: Toward Empirical Theory.* Toronto: McGraw–Hill, 1967.

Somit, Albert, and Tanenhaus, Joseph. *The Development of Political Science: From Burgess to Behavioralism.* Boston: Allyn & Bacon, 1967.

Sorauf, Frank J. *Perspectives on Political Science.* Columbus, Ohio: Charles E. Merrill, 1966.

Storing, Herbert, ed. *Essays on the Scientific Study of Politics.* New York: Holt, Rinehart & Winston, 1962.

Strauss, Leo. *What is Political Philosophy?* New York: The Free Press, 1959.

Van Dyke, Vernon. *Political Science: A Philosophical Analysis.* Stanford, Calif: Stanford University Press, 1960.

Wolin, Sheldon. *Politics and Vision.* Boston: Little, Brown & Co., 1960.

————. "Political Science as a Vocation." *The American Political Science Review* 63, no. 4 (December 1969).

2

The State and the Political System

A SOCIETY is a collectivity of individuals living and working together for the satisfaction of their mutual needs. These needs, however, may often conflict, and society needs an orderly process to accommodate and decide between the possible courses of action. Decisions primarily related to an individual's daily life, which do not significantly impinge upon others in the society, are generally left to his or her discretion. These decisions are shaped by the manner in which the individual views the situation based largely upon the type of values which he or she has been brought up to believe. The sources of these values are the family, school, associates, neighbours, and religion. Thus, the bulk of individual decisions are a matter of habit, custom, or morality and, so long as these values do not interfere with the overall operation of society, are of little concern to it. The individual is free to accept or reject any of them.

If, on the other hand, the potential effects of any act are widespread and likely to involve other individuals significantly, then society as a whole begins to concern itself with these decisions and their outcome. Decisions of such scope are relatively few as compared to the totality of decisions made in a society, but they are crucial to social life.

The individual, therefore, acts within a broad framework of socially approved decisions. He or she is not free to commit murder, to rob, or to assault a fellow citizen. Society, in the interest of providing a minimal degree of certainty and security for its members, has decreed that such conduct is proscribed. It has gone even further and removed such prohibitions from the level of the mundane by calling them *laws* and labelling transgressions as acts hostile, not just to the individuals directly affected, but to the society as a whole. When society acts in concert in this manner—that is, when it organizes to make political decisions—it identifies itself as a *state*. The formal institution within the state making decisions is generally known as the government. The state may be defined as *a conception of a people inhabiting a territory* while the government is the *rule-making organization for these people*.

ESSENTIAL ELEMENTS OF THE STATE

All states contain four elements which are necessary for their existence: *population, territory, government* and *sovereignty*. The importance of *population* is obvious. The size of the population is not as important as the degree to which it is willing and able to work for the furthering of its cumulative interests. Thus we have such extremes as China with its nearly 800 million people and Nauru in the South Pacific with a population of slightly over six thousand.

Territory is also indispensable to the existence of a state. For a people to organize itself as a state, it is necessary that they be permanently settled in a territorial area to which they hold perpetual claim. The Bedouins of Arabia and the gypsies do not have states because they have neither permanently settled down in a territory nor organized to develop those institutions, laws, and procedures with which a state is identified. The Jewish people continued to maintain strong community feeling through history, although they were widely dispersed. When they laid claim to Palestine and were able to make it a permanent abode for Jews, they created the state of Israel.

As with population, states vary in the size of their territory. While states with large territories do have political, economic, and geographical advantages, there are many states with very small territorial areas. The Union of Soviet Socialist Republics (U.S.S.R.), for instance, covers one sixth of the land surface of the globe while there also exist such tiny states as Nauru with 8 square miles and Malta with 95 square miles.

Government is the agent that acts in the name of the state to promote and safeguard the interests of its population and maintain its territorial boundaries. Thus it is essential to the existence of the state. It is not identical or coterminous with the state since the state is usually permanent and continuing while its government may be changed, altered, modified, or totally obliterated. Canada has had 15 different Prime Ministers since 1867; Germany moved from a monarchy until after World War I to republican democracy (the Weimar Republic) until Hitler established his National Socialist dictatorship; France vacillated between monarchy and republic since the Revolution of 1789 until the Third Republic was firmly in place in 1875; but in none of these cases did the end of the government bring about an end to the state as well. On the other hand, the governments have associated their identity, authority, and actions with the state.

International law recognizes states rather than governments as international persons having rights and obligations. In the United Nations, membership is given to a state and not to any particular government. Once a state becomes a member, it continues as such, unless it withdraws or is expelled, irrespective of the frequency of or the manner in which the government changes. In essence, the government is considered only an agent and an instrument of the state.

The fourth element necessary for the existence of the state is *sovereignty*. Sovereignty implies that the government of the state has absolute and final legal authority over all matters and is not subject to any power outside of itself. This supreme power applies both to domestic as well as to foreign affairs. Sovereignty allows the government, in the name of the state, complete independence of action.

The first notable proponent of the concept of sovereignty was the 16th-century French philosopher Jean Bodin. He posited that the state was held together by law and that there should, therefore, be some power from which the laws emanate and which itself was above the law. This power is the state, which has absolute and supreme authority over its subjects and can wage war or make peace unrestrained by any other power. Despite its absolute and supreme power the state would, nonetheless, be restricted by such things as divine law, natural law, and international law. Bodin's concept of the absolute sovereignty of the state has been transformed by modern theorists into a concept of the sovereignty of the people, or democracy. This implies that the state acts within the confines of its power as determined by the people.

The concept of sovereignty of the state is, however, not a reflection of political reality as no state has unqualified, unrestricted, and unrestrained power either in external or internal matters. Policies in both areas are influenced not only by political forces within the society but also by such external factors as world public opinion, attitude of allies and friends, international obligations, and the fear of reprisals from other states. Even the most powerful states are obliged to take these factors into consideration.

THE ORIGINS OF THE STATE

Historical and anthropological evidence indicates that states emerged from a variety of circumstances in different physical settings.[1]

---

[1] See Lawrence Krader, *Formation of the State* (Englewood Cliffs, N.J.: Prentice-Hall, 1968).

The precise origins are shrouded in the seemingly impenetrable past of prehistory. As a result of the lack of precise knowledge various theories have been developed over the years by a number of social scientists, theologians, and political philosophers.

Under the influence of Platonic and Aristotelian ideas, the early Greeks believed that the state was a *natural*, inevitable, and dynamic institution. Plato asserted that people could find fulfilment only as member of the state. Aristotle posited that the state is natural and prior to the individual, who has no existence outside of the state. Although this theory was later replaced by others, the Greek influence was reflected in the thinking of some late 19th-century scholars.

In medieval Europe the belief prevailed that the state was a divine creation. It was, in part, responsible for the papal claims to substantial authority and power over temporal matters. It also contributed to the growth of the theory of divine right of kings. The rationale for this theory was that if the state was of divine origin then its rulers were naturally vested with divine authority and sanction to rule. Later conflicts between the papacy and some of the ruling monarchs of Europe, the upheavals of the religious Reformation, and the intellectual Renaissance led to the acceptance of more rational theories about the origin of the state which tended to discount the religious theory.

Another popular theory, particularly among the German thinkers of the 19th century, was that the state originated as the result of *force* by the strong over the weak. Strong and powerful individuals established their sway over the weak, settled them in a specified territory and arrogated to themselves the power of governing. The concept of 'might makes right' underlies the force theory of the state. The influence of this theory in the 20th century is evidenced, for instance, by the belief of Hitler that

. . . All development is struggle. Only force rules. . . . Only through struggle have states and the world become great. If one should ask whether this struggle is gruesome, then the only answer could be: For the weak, yes, for humanity as a whole, no.[2]

Perhaps the most rational and widely accepted theory concerning the origin of the state is that of the *social contract*, or *compact*. While many versions of this theory exist, it was mainly popularized by three 17th- and 18th-century scholars—Thomas Hobbes, John Locke, and Jean Jacques Rousseau. It proceeds from the basic assumption that a state of nature existed where people possessed absolute natural rights without states or governments. People were free from any kind of restraints on their activity. There was unfettered freedom but, as a

---

[2] From a speech by Hitler, Essen, November 22, 1926; quoted in Carl Cohen, ed., *Communism, Fascism and Democracy* (New York: Random House, 1969), pp. 406–7.

consequence, there were no guarantees of safety and security for people and their possessions. Total anarchy and chaos prevailed, and the strong possessed and exploited the weak. Tiring of this state of unorganized and insecure existence, people entered into a mutual contract or agreement with others to form a state and establish a government to which they agreed to surrender their freedom in return for security.

It must be borne in mind that the social contract covers two different forms of contract. The first is what may be called the social contract proper or that part in which people in the state of nature decided to establish an organized society or the state. The second form may appropriately be called the contract of government, in which people prescribed the conditions under which the government of the state will operate.[3]

While it is possible to discuss the state in terms of its origins and its common elements, it is, however, too ambiguous a concept to be of real use as a unit of political analysis. Its central deficiency is that the state as a concept relates to existence rather than process. In legal terms the state may be said to "act," but in terms of actual behaviour, it simply exists. It is there. Groups of people who inhabit the territory of the state are empowered to act on its behalf.

As the focus of analysis, the government is also inadequate, since it really encompasses only part of the political activity found in a state. It is perhaps the critical or most important part of the wider political process, but politics is not exclusively a governmental activity. There must be a concept which allows us to discuss in a logical fashion the political behaviour of the population in any given state, including that of the government.

THE POLITICAL SYSTEM

In the previous chapter, the usefulness of adopting an approach for the study of social and physical sciences was noted. "Reality" is too large and complex for any human being, or group of them, to comprehend all at once. Our minds tend to resemble our eyes, in that they look at a phenomenon, social or physical, from basically one perceptual vantage point at a time. Much of the task of scientists in any discipline consists in finding the most useful vantage point. Needless to say, this point, or the perceptual approach which comes with it, changes as ones more suited to the needs of the times are found. No approach is

---

[3] See Chapters 3 and 5. For a detailed and comprehensive analysis of the social contract, see J. W. Gouch, *The Social Contract* (London: Oxford University Press, reprinted 1967).

absolute truth, nor is it the final one ever to be discovered. Reality is too complex to support such an arrogance.

The approach commonly labelled as the systems approach is no more or less than this. At the present, it seems more useful than other ways of looking at political phenomena. It helps to explain more things in a logical fashion than the other approaches known to date.

Curiously, the systems approach is not just a single formulation. It is, in fact, an umbrella term which shelters a number of systems approaches. All of them share similar notions: (1) that reality consists of things or phenomena which are constantly interacting and interdependent, (2) that these interplays are variable in intensity, which allows the observer to arbitrarily distinguish certain parts of reality as "separate" entities, (3) that these entities often try to maintain their individuality by building up internal interplays while downplaying those with the outside environment. Anyone who has driven swiftly across provincial borders in Canada only to be halted in a long waiting line at a border crossing into the United States can see the ready applicability of this approach to political phenomena, including the state.

Among systems approaches, there are three which are of particular use to political scientists. One is rather rudimentary and concentrates on the interactions and relationships within a state based upon the functions which various structures carry out in order to maintain it. This simple balancing, or equilibrium, model was put forward by Gabriel Almond in 1960[4] and is the one adapted for this text. A more sophisticated version of the systems approach has been developed by David Easton.[5] It also focusses on the balancing act, or equilibrium points, in a society's effort to maintain its political operations, but the structure of his model more closely reflects that used by scientists in other disciplines to understand systems of phenomena important to them. It is therefore more difficult to use and to understand. Richard Van Loon and Michael Whittington's text on Canadian government uses this variation to some degree.[6] The third variation of the systems approach is still little used by political scientists, partly because of its conceptual difficulty and also because of the lag time which always occurs between the introduction of a new approach and its adoption. This is the cybernetic-systems approach suggested by Karl Deutsch.[7]

---

[4] See the introduction to Gabriel A. Almond and James S. Coleman, eds., *The Politics of the Developing Areas* (Princeton, N.J.: Princeton University Press, 1960).

[5] See especially David Easton's *A Systems Analysis of Political Life* (New York: John Wiley & Sons, 1965).

[6] Richard Van Loon and Michael Whittington, *The Canadian Political System* (Toronto: McGraw–Hill, 1971).

[7] Karl Deutsch, *The Nerves of Government* (New York: The Free Press, 1963, 1965).

Its main concern is with the measurement of communications within the political system and the control mechanisms used to modify the behaviour of the system as a whole as it interacts with other such systems. Deutsch borrowed his concepts from those who explained the operations of modern computers, cybernetics being the basis of their technology.

Let us turn to the political system itself. The first step in explaining this approach is to define the word *system*. It is normally used to indicate any situation in which various elements, physical or human, are related to each other in a significant way. A simple gathering of people does not constitute a system; for a human system to exist it is essential that a group of individuals establish relationships with each other. Such systems can be established for a variety of purposes: to win a hockey game, build an automobile, or to form a political organization. Our interest is in the *political system* which may be defined as *a network of individuals, groups, and organizations whose relationships help to determine, enforce, and interpret rules governing the behaviour of society.*

The systems approach is quite versatile when used in political analysis and allows for the study of organizations and patterns of behaviour at a variety of levels. Any system is composed of a number of subsystems, each of which can be considered as a system in itself. Canada, for instance, can be considered as a system composed of many subsystems, the most obvious example being the several provinces.

The national government itself is divided into various organizations (or subsystems), and there are also many nongovernmental but political organizations that are subsystems. Each one of these subsystems can be further broken down into subsystems right down to the community level. At all levels the use of this approach helps to focus attention upon the relationships between these components and their internal processes.

Canada can also be considered a subsystem of several larger systems including the United Nations and the Commonwealth of Nations. In fact, Canada, being a member of the general community of nations, could be considered a subsystem of this all-inclusive political system.

The systems approach is complicated as a form of analysis in that the subsystems are related to each other in a variety of ways. First of all, the individual subsystems at the same level are not all the same (the various provinces, for example). Each of the subsystems is unique in the sense that they all have different components and varied internal relationships. Thus it would naturally follow that each of the subsystems at the same level would be related to others in different ways, reflecting their different natures. It would also follow that these subsystems would be related to the general system (Canada) under the same conditions.

In order to discuss political systems, it is necessary to define their limits or boundaries. Political systems exist in complex and limiting environments. In a discussion of the elements of a state, several of these limits were noted, such as size of population and territory. These physical and geographic elements have substantial influence upon a system as the presence or lack of natural resources, favourable climate, and proximity of other political systems are all important in determining what a political system can and cannot do. The political aspects of this setting are known as the political culture. More specifically, *political culture* refers to the political attitudes, skills, and values of the members of a community. The political culture is the basis of any political system; and any system that is substantially out of harmony with the culture upon which it is based is in danger of being altered or replaced. The political culture is connected to the political system through public opinion and interest articulation. *Public opinion* emerges from the political culture and is the raw material which the political system uses to determine the shape of policies and rules of the community. The process of converting public opinion, as articulated or perceived, into policies and rules is known as the *conversion process*. The results of this conversion process alter the environment and the political culture of the community. This altered environment provides the basis for a new public opinion, and the process repeats itself. Those factors which go into the making of decisions are called *inputs* and the results are the *outputs*. The process by which the outputs affect the culture and environment is known as *feedback*. The following diagram illustrates the overall relationships as outlined above:

The political system, then, is bounded on the one side by the inputs and on the other by the outputs. The actual structures and the func-

FIGURE 2–1
The Political System and Its Environment

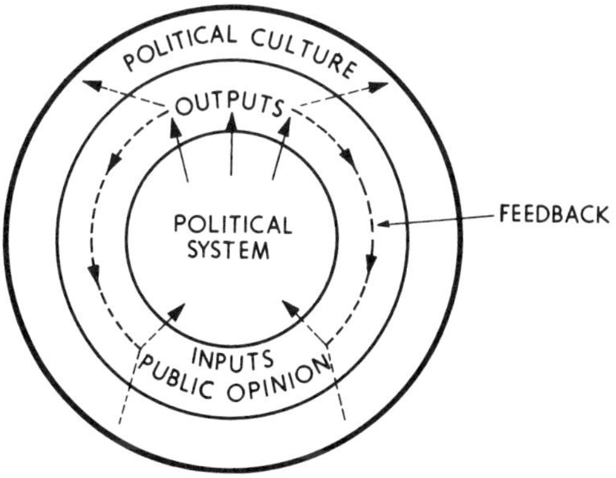

tions they perform in the conversion process constitute the pattern of relationships known as the political system.

Roles, Structures, and Functions

An approach intimately linked with the systems approach is structural-functional analysis. This form of analysis is based on the assumption that there are certain functions that must be performed in any political system for it to be able to survive and that as a result of this necessity various structures have been created to perform these functions.

The purpose of structural-functional analysis is to determine how these functions are performed, by what structures, and with what effect on the overall system. Though the functions appear to be the same in all political systems, the structures created to carry them out and the manner in which they do so differ from one system to another and from one period to another in the same system. In other words, it is quite possible that a given structure, a political party, for example, may play its role in the political system in one way at one time and in another at a later date. The concept of role playing in politics can be utilized to explain the changes in the behaviour of structures and individuals in a political system.

The concept of *role* identifies the relationship between a particular social function and the individual or group performing that function. Individuals play a variety of roles in an average day and shift from one role to another quite readily, and usually automatically. For example, there is a certain pattern of behaviour that is accepted as being appropriate for students in their relations with a professor; a different pattern of behaviour may well exist between a student and a fellow student, and still another pattern between the same student and his or her father. In fact, the roles individuals play tend to be tailored to the specific situation; a student will not necessarily behave the same way with all professors, or with all fellow students. He tailors his behaviour in the light of several considerations: what he thinks others expect of him, what he thinks is appropriate to the occasion, and the results he wishes to gain from the relationship. This series of judgments is usually based on past experience in similar situations and it can be quite unsettling to get a result different from that intended. Such failure could result from the inability to judge the other person or persons properly, or a lack of understanding of how others in fact see the individual. The complex of roles that people play can be called a *role system*, and probably the only persons who do not operate within such a complex of roles are hermits.

A factor which complicates both role behaviour and its understanding is that the wide variety of roles played by individuals lead to situations of *role conflict*. An example of this would be the conflict of roles imposed upon a legislator. According to the norms and expectations of colleagues in Ottawa, a member of the House of Commons is expected to subordinate his or her personal views to the goal of party unity. By the same token, the constituents of an individual legislator may feel very strongly that he or she is there to represent their interest. The individual legislator caught in such a crossfire of conflicting perceptions of his or her role is in a difficult position. It is permissible for a member of the House of Commons to deviate from the party line in the rare situations where this conflict is exceedingly strong.[8]

The idea of role conflict applies to structures as well as individuals. It is possible to trace the origins of many debates within a political structure to a difference of opinion over the role it should play. For instance, some individuals and groups clearly regard the role of the Canadian Senate as little more than honorific. From the behaviour of some of the senators, it would appear that they share this view. Others clearly wish the Senate to play an active role as a decision-making structure, and various proposals have been made to bring this about.

Role conflict is also important in understanding why political actors or structures may or may not be effective. If a structure operates in a setting where its role within the system is generally agreed upon, then it is fairly easy for that role to be carried out. However, if such role consensus is lacking, it is quite possible that more time will be spent trying to define the nature of the role than in carrying it out. An example of this is the continuing debate over the authority of the national and provincial governments in tax matters. Until this role conflict is settled, it will be difficult for either level of government to be fully effective in this area. It is clearly important that such role conflicts be settled quickly and amicably as failure to do so may cause either a split in the system or a structural paralysis which could render the system inoperative in critical situations.

In outlining a political system it is useful to think of it in functional terms, that is, in reference to those things which are done in any political system which help to maintain the system over time.[9] The degree to which these functions are performed in similar or dissimilar fashion in different systems is the measure of the extent to which the systems

---

[8] For a discussion of role playing in the House of Commons, see Allan Kornberg, *Canadian Legislative Behavior* (New York: Holt, Rinehart & Winston, 1967), pp. 105–17 and 129–36.

[9] See Gabriel Almond and G. Bingham Powell, Jr., *Comparative Politics: A Developmental Approach* (Boston: Little, Brown & Co., 1966), pp. 27–33 and Alan C. Isaak, *Scope and Methods of Political Science*, rev. ed. (Homewood, Ill.: The Dorsey Press, 1975), pp. 217–25.

themselves are alike. To assess the actual performance in a political system, the focus is on behaviour and relationships, not on formal groups or organizations. These functions can be broken down as follows:

1.   Political socialization and recruitment.
2.   Interest articulation.
3.   Interest aggregation.
4.   Rule making.
5.   Rule implementation.
6.   Rule adjudication.

Political socialization is defined as ". . . the process of induction into the political culture. Its end product is a set of attitudes . . . toward the political system."[10] A wide variety of structures are involved in this process, including family, schools, and the media, in addition to governmental structures. This process is both covert and overt in all systems, though systems vary both as to the means used and the manner in which they are used. The extent and content of political socialization is not consistent from one group to another within a political system. In an authoritarian society, a concerted attempt may be made to socialize the population in a carefully controlled manner. In a more open society, the accepted existence of subcultures may mean considerable variation in socialization patterns. In some systems the differences between the subcultures may be small, and the consequences of the different patterns of political socialization may be inconsequential. In other systems the differences may be so great as to be potentially disruptive. Examples of this type of disruption are secession movements by religious or ethnic minorities or revolutionary movements designed to alter the fundamentals of the system in question.

Political socialization prepares the way for a more specialized subfunction—that of *political recruitment.* This subfunction serves to develop a more specialized set of values, skills, and goals of the sort needed to orient the individual towards the more specifically political roles in the system. One of the means of distinguishing between more and less advanced political systems is the way in which they recruit their political personnel. In traditional systems there is a tendency to rely upon such criteria as family and kinship ties as the basis for selecting political actors to fill a political role; in more modern systems such considerations as level and type of education and merit are emphasized as the basic criteria. Those recruited are not a uniform group in spite of often rigorous selection processes, since they have been

---

[10] Almond and Coleman, *Politics of the Developing Areas,* pp. 27–28.

recruited from various subcultures. They then bring to their new roles at least some of the values learned in the earlier, more generalized, socialization process.

It was pointed out previously that public opinion emerges out of the political culture of a system. That the public, or a portion of it, has an opinion on some matter means little unless that opinion finds a means of expression. The various opinions found in any political system must be made intelligible to the rest of the public and the decision makers if they are to have meaning. The process by which claims are made and interests expressed is called *interest articulation*. This is a crucial input function and the way in which it is performed is important to the system. Complex political systems not only have numerous interest groups, but several types as well. As the level of complexity of the system increases, so will the variety and mixture of methods used to press an interest. In an authoritarian system an effort is made to limit the potential diversity by restricting the number of legitimate articulators and the means that they may use. Democratic systems, while imposing some limits on articulation, are far more generous and place a high value on diversity of interests and methods of expression.

Interest articulation is followed by *interest aggregation*. This is the function of sorting and combining the numerous specific interests promoted in the articulation process with the objective of formulating more inclusive programs that will form a simplified basis for political decision making. Interest aggregation is primarily a responsibility of the political parties in modern democratic systems. In clarifying the issues for the decision makers, the parties also clarify the issues for the electorate. Given the wide diversity of competing interests in most democratic systems, the electorate would otherwise be overwhelmed by a cacaphony of claims and the decision makers bewildered by the conflicting demands pressed upon them.

The boundary line between the interest articulation process and the interest aggregation process is vague. The theoretical distinction between the two functions can be drawn far more clearly than the practical one. The interest articulation process is that of the expression of specific interests; the interest aggregation process is that of the assimilation of many of these specific interests into larger common interests.

One of the most persistent problems facing students of politics has been that of proper identification of the different functions of government. It has been conventional to divide government into three parts: the legislative, executive, and judicial. The basic problem with this tripartite conception of government and its functions was that it was tied, in theory, to specific structures. In other words, the function of making laws was the business of the legislature; the function of implementing them was the responsibility of the executive; and the function of adjudicating disputes was the duty of the courts. Gradually it became obvious that each of the branches was to some extent involved in the function of the other branches. As political scientists began to appreciate this, they looked for other suitable means of explaining the relationships. In the systems approach the tripartite conception of governmental functions is retained, but the assumption that each branch of government had one of the functions as its own private preserve was dropped. To reflect this change in orientation, there has been a subtle change in terminology. The tendency now is to talk in terms of rule making rather than law making, underscoring the fact that the process is more extensive than the simple enactment of laws—rule implementation and rule adjudication instead of law enforcement or interpretation.

The function of *rule making* is as old as organized society itself, but people's awareness of the extent to which they could alter their circumstances by restructuring their society or economy through conscious effort is a relatively recent development. In the words of two writers, ". . . rule making in traditional and primitive systems tends to be either a charismatic process or a slow, incremental process of the accumulation of tradition. . . ."[11] As modern political systems evolved, the various structures involved in rule making became more distinct, and as these structures became more effective in shaping people's environment, they became increasingly self-aware rule makers. In democratic systems, the rule making function is traditionally identified with the legislature, but much of the inspiration and direction comes from other components of the political system and most of the detailed rule making is done by the administration.

The *rule implementation* function is primarily carried out by the various governmental structures known collectively as the executive. In modern systems these structures are numerous and complex and are concerned with such diverse activities as law enforcement, tax collection, food and drug inspection, provision of welfare benefits, and military security. In carrying out these responsibilities, the various agencies taken as a group are in far more consistent contact with the public than either the legislative or judicial bodies. To the student of such matters the executive and its pattern of relationships is as diverse and complex as any in the political world.

The pervasiveness of the rule implementation structures is an unsettling thing to many. Such novels as *1984* and *Brave New World* reflect the fear of some that the combination of modern bureaucracy and ideology may mean the end of individual freedom. Such concern has given rise to many schemes to restrict the scope of the executive or

---

[11] Almond and Powell, *Comparative Politics,* p. 133.

to increase the power of the public over it. As the public does not have as much control over the executive as it does over its legislators and other elected officials the task of making it responsible and responsive is difficult in the extreme. Even political leaders in totalitarian systems have difficulty in managing the structures they have constructed to apply the rules they make.

The political scientist concerned with the executive faces a number of other problems. One of them is to identify the structures and the extent of their involvement. Another is the relationships between the administrative bodies and the politically accountable leaders on the one hand and the public on the other. The relationships between administrative bodies is yet another area of concern. As the rule implementation structures are the ones most involved with the public, their efficiency and responsiveness is of vital concern to any political system. Their day-to-day activities shape the consequences of the rules made and the attitude of the public toward these rules.

The *rule adjudication* structures are also of importance to the political system, but in a manner different from that of the rule implementation structures. This segment of the political system is also involved with the outputs, but it is especially organized to deal with two questions: has a rule been violated, and, if so, what are the penalties that are appropriate to the occasion? In democratic countries with elaborate constitutional structures, it is often possible, and by no means uncommon, for the implementation of rules to be taken to the courts and contested on grounds of the violation of rights of one sort or another. The United States, with its influential Supreme Court, is the clearest example of this. Some democratic systems lack such prepared avenues of appeal, but all systems have some means of settling such questions. The court system can also be used to settle disputes between governmental organizations. In Canada, however, the major disputes over the jurisdiction of the national and provincial levels of government are generally reserved for settlement at federal-provincial conferences because of constitutional and political complications arising from the use of the courts.[12]

It can be seen from the discussion that the rule implementation and rule adjudication structures are not only important to the system, but are also inextricably related to each other. Good rules can be rendered useless by poor implementation, and an ineffective forum for adjudication will simply compound the bad effects.

In this discussion of the conversion process we have been describing the complex identified as the political system. In order to make it easier to comprehend, Figure 2–2 is presented.

---

[12] See Chapter 7.

FIGURE 2–2
The Structure and Functions of the System

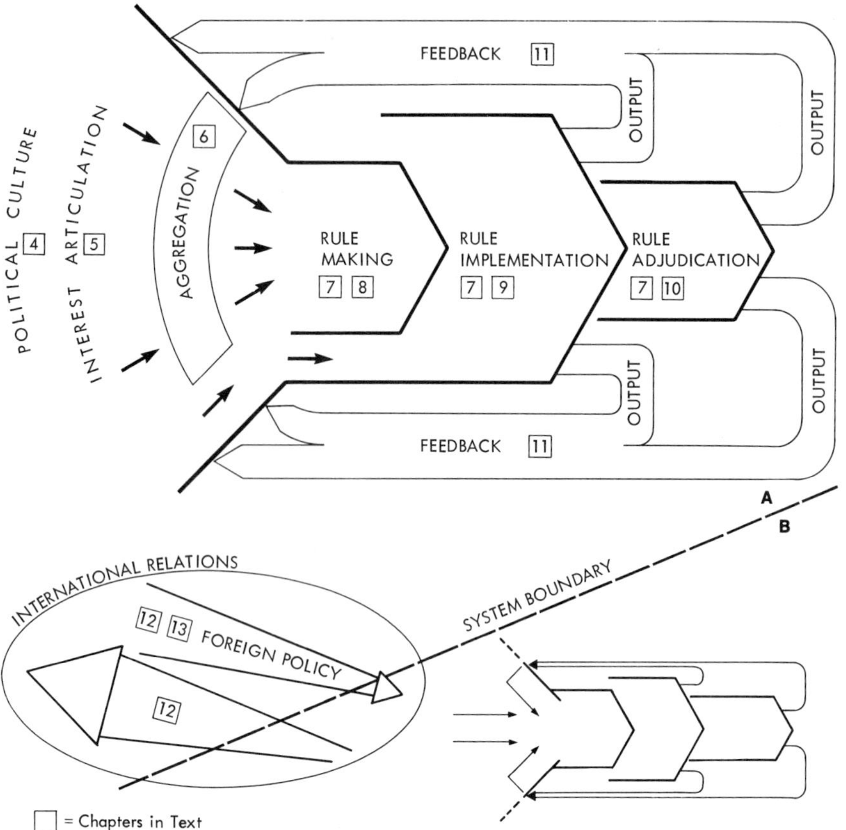

The boxes inside Figure 2–2 indicate the order of the following chapters and suggest how they are logically related to one another. Chapters 4 through 11 attempt to describe the operation of the political system in a step-by-step fashion. While this model is appropriate for any state, our main focus will be on the modern democratic variety, such as Canada. The only complication in this presentation occurs with Chapter 7, which deals with constitutions. Depending upon the state, a constitution may deal minimally with the legal makeup and operations of the formal institutions of government, or maximally with some of the elements comprising the entire political system. Here, the discussion of constitutions, and the position of the chapter in the framework, is oriented toward the minimal approach.

Chapters 12 and 13 complete the discussion of the political system by outlining some of the interactions between systems. Chapter 12 discusses these relationships at the system-to-system level, while Chapter 13 probes the existence of an international system, of which the separate political systems discussed earlier are but parts. This completes the outline of systems and subsystems at four levels, as shown in Figure 2–3. Depending on the level at which an observer

FIGURE 2–3
Examples of Systems and Subsystems in Politics

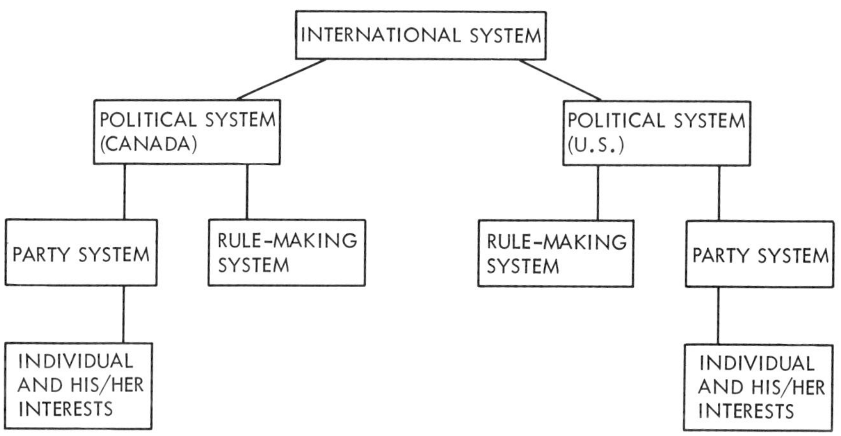

wishes to begin investigation, systems, subsystems, and "super" systems may be identified. The terminology, as has been noted previously, is relative to the level under discussion. It is not absolute.

The final three chapters do not fit the scheme of the system, as they are concerned with the development of political ideas rather than with action. They could be fitted logically into Chapters 3, 4, or 5. The material has been singled out for special emphasis, however, which requires that they be removed from the progression through the system. The development and the breadth of influence of liberal, conservative, socialist, and nationalist ideas is therefore treated separately. Neatness is sacrificed, but a better perspective on politics is gained.

RECOMMENDED READINGS

Almond, Gabriel, and Powell, G. Bingham, Jr. *Comparative Politics: A Developmental Approach.* Boston: Little, Brown & Co., 1966.

Butz, Otto. *Of Man and Politics.* New York: Holt, Rinehart & Winston, 1956.

Campbell, Angus. *Essays on the Behavioral Study of Politics.* Urbana: University of Illinois Press, 1962.

Charlesworth, James C., ed. *Contemporary Political Analysis.* New York: The Free Press, 1967.

Dahl, Robert.   *Modern Political Analysis.* Englewood Cliffs, N.J.: Prentice–Hall, 1959.

Deutsch, Karl W.   *The Nerves of Government.* New York: The Free Press, 1963, 1965.

De Jouvenel, Bertrand.   *Sovereignty.* Chicago: University of Chicago Press, 1957.

Easton, David.   *A Framework for Political Analysis.* Englewood Cliffs, N.J.: Prentice–Hall, 1965.

———. *A Systems Analysis of Political Life.* New York: John Wiley & Sons, 1965.

Eulau, Heinz.   *The Behavioral Persuasion in Politics.* New York: Random House, 1963.

Gouch, J. W.   *The Social Contract.* London: Oxford University Press, reprinted 1967.

Isaak, Alan C.   *Scope and Methods of Political Science.* rev. ed. Homewood, Ill.: The Dorsey Press, 1975.

Krader, Lawrence. *Formation of the State.* Englewood Cliffs, N.J.: Prentice–Hall, 1968.

Laski, Harold.   *The State in Theory and Practice.* London: Allen & Unwin Ltd., 1967.

MacIver, R. M.   *The Modern State.* London: Oxford University Press, 1926.

Mitchell, William C.   *Sociological Analysis and Politics.* Englewood Cliffs, N.J.: Prentice–Hall, 1967.

Wolin, Sheldon.   "Political Theory as a Vocation." *The American Political Science Review* 63, no. 4 (December 1969).

Young, Oran. *Systems of Political Science.* Englewood Cliffs, N.J.: Prentice–Hall, 1968.

Young, Roland.   *Approaches to the Study of Political Science.* Evanston, Ill.: Northwestern University Press, 1968.

3

Types of Political Systems

IN BOTH POPULAR AND PROFESSIONAL LITERATURE there is a great deal of discussion about the different types of political systems. To the professional this discussion may mean one thing, to the public it often means another. The objective here is to outline what political scientists mean when they discuss the variety of political systems.

In general, two standards are used to distinguish between types of political systems: the degree of modernity of the system and extent of democracy within it. The more advanced a society becomes in skills and technology, the greater the need for more elaborate political structures. As society evolves, it also becomes increasingly difficult for the decision makers to make decisions on their own. Thus the administrative structures become increasingly complex and the decision makers find themselves in need of more support from outside the formal government in order to maintain their positions against rival claimants. Such developments, especially in England, gradually forced the monarch to regularize consultations with outsiders and thus established the logic of a parliamentary body. Ultimately, the system evolved to the point where real power shifted to the Parliament and the monarchy was reduced to a symbolic institution.

All modern political systems, democratic or not, exhibit this same pattern of increasing complexity, differentiation of functions, and a broadening of the decision-making base. Many of the developing nations are in the process of evolving from traditional political systems to a more modern variety—from a situation where the population was largely passive and uninvolved to a point where the population is mobilized for political and other activities in ways consistent with the needs of a society in the 20th century. There are a few political systems that are holdovers from the traditional patterns (Nepal and Saudi Arabia, for example), but most of the developing systems are modern in their objectives and at least have partially evolved in this direction.

In the contemporary media, reference is often made to the differences between democratic and nondemocratic systems as well as references to capitalist, socialist, and communist ones. If one wishes to use these terms correctly, however, such words as *capitalist* or *communist* cannot be used to describe political systems. These terms refer to economic rather than political arrangements. There is no necessary correlation between democracy and either capitalism or socialism, neither is there any correlation between totalitarianism and either capitalism or socialism.

In order to determine the type of a political system, it is necessary to reflect upon its central objective; it is organized to make decisions concerning policy for the community and to carry out these policies. Implicit in this is the goal of perpetuating the political system and the society it protects. The definition of democratic or nondemocratic should logically be based upon the way in which the community makes its decisions and enforces its policies, not on the policies themselves. In other words, it is not the nature of a decision to order the economic system a certain way that makes a political system democratic or undemocratic, but the manner in which the decision is made and carried out. If such a decision is made with the observance of the rules of free discussion and majority rule, and due respect for human rights and fundamental freedoms, then it is difficult to argue that the system is nondemocratic.

The specific criterion used to distinguish between democratic and nondemocratic systems is known as subsystem autonomy. In a system where this autonomy exists, the various subsystems, be they governmental, or nongovernmental, usually have the opportunity and freedom to pursue their own objectives in their own way. In such a system the various subsystems can seek alliances with others, recruit members, and attempt to persuade those in and out of government that their ideas are the ones which the community as a whole should follow. It should be stressed that this autonomy implies more than a technical freedom. A newspaper, for example, that is technically free to say what it wishes can hardly be considered really free if the government can withhold the necessary newsprint.

An illustration of this concept of subsystem autonomy can be provided by comparing Canada with the Soviet Union. In Canada there are so many groups trying to gain governmental and public approval that it would take a book just to list their names. Each of these groups, in its own way, seeks to persuade the public, party leaders, and governmental officials that it has the answer to at least some of the problems facing society. In this environment, labour unions organize and strike; farmers hold protest meetings and marches on tractors and confront their prime minister; students picket and protest; newspapers praise or damn the government. It is difficult to imagine such a series of events in the Soviet Union. Farmers, labour, students, and media also exist there; but their activities are coordinated to support the communist party. Expressions of particular interests are, at best, covert. Clearly, then, such functions as interest articulation and communication are handled differently in Canada and in the Soviet Union.

Every political system differs from all others in certain respects. Analytically, these differences may be discussed in terms of patterns of behaviour corresponding to the broad division of functions and structures noted above. Two political systems, for instance, may closely resemble each other in their judicial and party subsystems while widely diverging in their political culture and legislative apparatus. By observing specific similarities and differences, it is possible to determine the obvious fact that overall differences exist between systems.

The process of distinguishing systems may be carried onto a more generalized plane by looking for common overall patterns by which to group them. The two dichotomous typologies identified above, the democratic-nondemocratic and the traditional-modern, are far from being the only typologies, but at present they are the most widely used and discussed.

The simplest method of depicting the system types which are implied by these dichotomies is to look at the possibilities which arise out of a superimposition of one pair upon the other. The result is the four-celled diagram in Figure 3–1. The diagram suggests four types of

FIGURE 3–1
Types of Political Systems

	Traditional	Modern
Democratic	A	B
Nondemocratic	C	D

systems: Type A, which is both democratic and traditional at the same time; Type B, modern and democratic systems; Type C, traditional and nondemocratic; and Type D, modern and nondemocratic.

TYPE A

The existence of Type A systems may be open to question. If the major criterion for a democratic system is assumed to be a relatively high level of subsystem autonomy, the very primitiveness of the subsystems in a traditional system militate against their autonomous existence. An exception to this logic may be said to exist where a traditional society is so fragmented by class, caste, and ethnic divisions that traditional structures openly compete against each other. This competition maintains a facade of democratic institutions and practices. India, for instance, calls itself the "world's largest democracy." Indian society is far from modern but it is sufficiently fragmented to allow democratic practices to take root.

TYPE B

A democratic system exists when the process of making community decisions is potentially open to all citizens and their interests. The actuality of this participation is in fact limited in every case, either by the apathy of citizens or by rules which allow for the maintenance of the system itself. The traditional American ideal, for instance, that any person can be president does not mean in fact that all will be. For one thing, the chaos resulting from this absurdity would destroy the political system.

A democratic system, then, is the expression of an unworkable ideal. It is a practical compromise between the goal of a wholly open system, responsive to the concerns of all citizens, and the necessity to impose some structuring, or limits, on this participation in order to assure the continuity of the system over time.

The connection between modernity and democracy is very close. The most common indicator of a modern society is the sophistication and wealth of its economy. An economically developed society must also support an institutional structure of great diversity, not only to produce and distribute wealth, but to govern and enhance the society. Development has generally meant that social institutions of all types have become more diverse and specialized. Democracy cannot exist without this diversity of social institutions. Even in the case of a Type A traditional democratic system, the diversity of traditional racial, religious, caste, and linguistic units is critical to its continued existence.

While modernity is normally a necessary condition for a democratic system, it is nevertheless not sufficient for its existence. The existence of Type D systems indicates that a diversity of subsystems is not in itself a guarantee that democratic procedures will be adopted by a society.[1] The key to modern democracy lies in the relationship of these institutions, groups, and organizations with each other. There must be some degree of natural congruency between the relationships with families, political parties, businesses, and churches, for instance, and those between the official institutions of government and the governed. An absence of such congruency leads to an unstable political situation and it is likely that the democratic political system will falter in the face of social pressure.[2] The power to make decisions must be shared to some degree in all social institutions if a lasting democratic political system is to survive.

The term *subsystem autonomy* is used to identify this major characteristic of democratic systems. In Type A systems, this autonomy exists *between* traditional sects, castes, and ethnic groups, while it does not exist *within* them. This simply reinforces the proposition that such systems are a special case.

Within modern systems, subsystem autonomy describes a condition where institutions, groups, and even individuals possess a significant degree of freedom in determining their relationships to each other and in deciding upon their respective goals. That they are not completely free is obvious from our use of the word *autonomy*. There must be limits to the freedom of one subsystem if the freedom of other subsystems is to be maintained. This also extends to the subsystems which make up the government. There must be limited government—some things that officials cannot do.

Naturally, if the political system is to be open to all citizens and their interests, democratic politics will be characterized by a clash of ideas and by eventual compromise. Subsystem autonomy encourages social and individual differences, and these differences are expressed politically in the form of various interests and proposals. In order to arrive at any decisions by which interests are to be met or given priority, some rationalization must be done. The vast variety of interests must be limited in number. Since many people are likely to have the same ideas, this job is not as impossible as it sounds. Further, many are apathetic and refrain from expressing interests. By contrast, in a nondemocratic system, potential interests are cut down by restricting those who are heard (nobody counts but the dictator and his or her friends), or by filtering the interests through a religious belief or set of political ideas (does this proposal serve the revolution?). Most often in

---

[1] Duane Neubauer, "Some Conditions of Democracy," in *Empirical Democratic Theory*, ed. Charles Cnudde and Duane Neubauer (Chicago: Markham, 1969) pp. 224–35.

[2] Harry Eckstein, *A Theory of Stable Democracy* (Princeton, N.J., Princeton University Press, 1958).

a democratic system, competing organized groups, or parties, are used for this purpose.

The way in which a democratic system decides upon issues is crude, but effective. Instead of choosing among issues directly, however, this choice is normally tied to the selection of people to operate the decision-making subsystems. In this way democratic systems allow for decisions to be made while overcoming the problem of deciding who is to make these decisions. The issues are decided indirectly through the choice of a small number of citizens who are empowered to act on behalf of society as a whole. In short, the political parties support competing candidates for positions in the rule making subsystem. A more-or-less regular series of choices, or elections, provides for change in the subsystem and maintains a degree of responsiveness between the representatives and the citizens.

Where other types of systems may stress the maintenance of certain traditional ways or the obverse, rapid change, the primary concern of a democratic system is one of process. Great care is taken to limit the roles of people in power so as to keep decision making within certain bounds. Government activities are scrutinized with care to ensure that the entire process of election, decision making, implementation, and adjudication is conducted fairly and that all people enjoy relatively equal influence. Equality is a necessary adjunct to freedom in the continued operation of a democratic system.

The major values of a democratic system are that (1) it provides for a peaceful and socially accepted means of settling disputes; (2) it ensures peaceful change; (3) it allows an orderly succession of rulers; (4) it minimizes coercion, and (5) it encourages a measure of diversity within society.[3] To sum up, a democratic system permits a society to react to change in a variable fashion, at one time slowly and at another quickly, without destroying itself or inflicting unnecessary degrees of uncertainty and fear upon its citizens.

Type C

Historically, traditional nondemocratic systems have predominated among the world's societies. Such systems are noted for their longevity, based upon the generally unchanging nature of the social structures which supported them. Since the beginning of the 20th century such systems have come under increasing pressure from two sources. Economic and social development introduced by the imperial powers struck against the traditional attitudes and beliefs which underlay

---

[3] Henry B. Mayo, *An Introduction to Democratic Theory* (New York: Oxford University Press, 1960) pp. 218–24.

these systems. Also, revolutionary ideologies from France, England, the Soviet Union, and the United States were introduced into these countries. The results of this two-pronged attack thus far have been a measure of chaos. Neither democracy nor modernity has triumphed in Asia, Africa, or Latin America, but the traditional nondemocratic systems have been effectively undermined. Thus much of the world is in a state of political instability.

The ubiquitous and durable Type C system was based upon a particular basis of social relations. Guy Hunter has labelled these social relationships as "peasant society."[4] Though differing in many aspects, such as language and religious beliefs, peasant societies are basically similar in their social structure and activities. Commentators as long ago as 800 B.C. noted these fundamental parallels just as modern anthropologists have. The peasant society is the most common and stable form of human community created since people began herding flocks and cultivating fields.

Peasant society is characterized by particular sets of geographic, economic, and social relationships which combine to produce a particular type of political system. Geographically, peasants are concentrated into small villages or clusters of dwellings. Interspersed among these villages are market towns and administrative centers. The economy of a peasant society is focussed upon subsistence agriculture. The peasants are both unable and unwilling to produce sufficient surpluses which could be used for further investment and consequent prosperity. They are unable to do so because of the low level of technical knowledge available to them and unwilling because of the nature of the social system in which they exist. To understand the nature of the social relationships which encourage peasants to remain at this constant level of subsistence living, one must look to a theory of personality relevant to their situation.

E. E. Hagen, a development economist, turned to the investigation of personality after noting that the economic situation of the peasant was an integral part of the wider social system in which the person was involved.[5] He suggested that the peasant has been brought up in such a fashion as to have taken on an "authoritarian" personality. The key to this type of personality is the realization that the world is both arbitrary and unknowable. In such a world the concept of progress is nonsense; since progress suggests that the world is knowable. Instead, one copes and survives.

---

[4] Guy Hunter, *Modernizing Peasant Societies* (London: Oxford University Press, 1969), chapter 1.

[5] Everett E. Hagen, *On the Theory of Social Change* (Homewood, Ill.: The Dorsey Press, 1962), Part II.

The rigid morality designed for use in a western universe of fixed ethics is often replaced in Asia by a flexible causistry more suitable for an eastern Cosmos in a constant state of change. . . . The westerner on his solid philosophical ground believes he can manage his universe, while the oriental knows he must give way to tides and currents.[6]

An arbitrary world is countered by a stable social system. Family structures are broad and include several degrees of relatives, all of whom are morally bound to assist each other through times of hardship. The redistribution of resources works to prevent any capital accumulation and hence development; however, this is logical since people never know when they might need the help of those who needed them earlier. The subsistence nature of the economy is thus maintained.

Outside of the family another form of predictable security is formed within the village. Close attention is paid to status and respectability since often whole villages must cooperate if their society is to survive. Deviancy from accepted social norms, including those regulating family roles, property, religion, and technical knowledge cannot be permitted because they threaten the precarious survival of the village as a whole. Again the subsistence nature of the economy is maintained.

Above this village society exists a narrow elite which holds sway over a large area of land. This elite is both the result of, and bound to, the peasant society. Status relationships in the villages and between them result in the creation and maintenance of certain families who deal with the outside world and regulate internal village affairs. This elite provides, at the same time, the social, economic, political, and military leadership of the area.

The inputs into the traditional nondemocratic system are of two types. First, interests are formulated by the same individuals who are involved in decision making. Secondly, there is the unspoken desire of the villagers to be left in peace of some sort. Consequently, political opinions are neither sought nor expected from the villagers, although outputs of the system must provide some degree of security and/or satisfaction for them.

The outputs are, like the village society as a whole, designed almost solely for the maintenance of the system. The concept of providing social services to the society is alien to such a mode of governing. Paradoxically, though, this orientation bears out what was implied in the earlier discussion of the modern democratic system—that those who express and aggregate interests tend to be the recipients of out-

---

[6] Dennis Bloodworth, *An Eye for the Dragon* (London: Secker and Warrburg, 1970), p. 252.

puts. In the traditional nondemocratic system any expenditures not made for the survival of the society are devoted to the well-being of the elite. The rest of society is "invisible."

The expenditure of resources in many states is concentrated upon the physical surroundings of the ruler and upon the military. The military is the only disciplined organization existing above the village level, save for some trading concerns. As such it becomes the "government" itself, with generals serving as governors and the armies acting as occupation forces. Their major function is to put down local revolts, eliminate bandits, and repel incursions by neighbouring powers. They may also be used to collect taxes, where this duty is not contracted or "farmed out" to professional tax collectors. The rudimentary levels of services provided by states is emphasized by the fact that even European cities did not enjoy organized police protection until the beginning of the 19th century.

One form of traditional system went beyond this primitive pattern of government. Karl Wittfogel in his *Oriental Despotism* described the existence of "hydraulic societies" in Asia and Latin America.[7] These societies were greatly dependent upon the management of water resources for survival and consequently required a degree of mobilization of the peasants. Workers were needed to dig irrigation works, and construct and maintain flood control facilities on the Nile, Tigris and Euphrates, and Yangtze rivers. Other labour armies were needed to erect the Great Wall of China, the Pyramids of Egypt, and the fabled Hanging Gardens of Babylon. All of this effort required the existence of extensive bureaucracies and professional labour organizers.

The biggest threat to any form of traditional society is internal division. Consequently, the political system is concerned, above all, with maintaining itself in the face of centrifugal forces. Like the extended family and the village structures, the traditional system is oriented toward survival in an unknowable world. Internal division results from the nature of village society and from the lack of statewide organizations other than the army. Village society is characterized by considerable ignorance on the part of the peasants about the rest of the country since the emphasis on survival found in the village leads logically to a fear of and antipathy toward strangers. Communications between villages are limited to contacts in neutral market towns, contacts between village headmen and the regional administration, and contacts with traders as they move from village to village. In the latter two instances, external contact involves part of the social and political

---

[7] Karl Wittfogel, *Oriental Despotism* (New Haven, Conn.: Yale University Press, 1957).

elites, thus reinforcing the dependence of the peasant upon these people.

The lack of organizations which operate across the boundaries of such systems requires a concentration of political and economic power in the military. Army commanders become regional political commanders and their forces exercise, in effect, all forms of power there. Often these regional "warlords" aspire to higher office and, in order to forestall local revolts and palace coups, the rulers attempt to reduce the bases of power under the regional commanders by posting them to strange areas, preventing them from meeting with their counterparts from other regions, regularly reassigning them to new commands and areas, and by instituting a relatively rapid turnover in the incumbents. Provincial governors in Thailand, for instance, were forbidden, as late as 1920, under penalty of death to meet each other privately.

A final method has been to appoint less ambitious members of the ruling family to these posts or to entrust them to men of humble station who are dependent upon the ruler for the maintenance of their status. The result of this narrow, fused, military-politico-administrative arrangement is a world of constant intrigue and insecurity which contributes to the reinforcement of the authoritarian personality.

Revolts in the traditional society take the form of peasant uprisings and military coups. Peasant uprisings are normally reactions to threats to survival in the form of heavily oppressive or corrupt landlords and administrators. They may also take the form of pogroms against minority groups in the area where they hold a monopoly on trade and credit. North African Jews and the Chinese of Southeast Asia have both suffered such attacks through the past thousand years. Military divisions are normally provoked by the ambitions of local commanders to usurp the central power of the system. The success or failure of such moves does not result in any real change in the nature of the relationships within the system but only in the personnel.

The low-level capability of the traditional systems could not meet the pressures exerted from outside by the arrival of the Europeans after 1500. Increasingly, over the next 400 years, the outsiders reduced these systems to dependencies and colonies except where the mutual jealousies of the European states themselves acted to prevent takeovers. The nominal independence of Ethiopia, Turkey, China, and Thailand was maintained in this fashion. Japan avoided falling to the imperial states by undertaking a program of rapid modernization in the late 1800s, and becoming an imperial state itself.

The most striking result of the imperial era, which to all appearances may be said to have ended in the 1960s, was to graft onto the traditional society an economic and political replica of Europe and America. What are described as "modernizing" societies are, in fact, amalgams of two types of society, the traditional and the modern, thrown together within the bounds of a newly independent state. As might be expected, this dualism has produced great problems in these countries, not the least of which is an aggravation of the already existing centrifugal tensions. These were formerly papered over by virtue of the military potential of the colonial power, but its withdrawal left the newly independent countries face to face with the age-old problem of unity.

The dualistic nature of these countries has produced curious mixtures of modernity and traditionalism within their political systems. In the countryside, politics is left to the elite, and the peasants are content to look to this group for political direction. Where a form of democratic process had been superimposed over this arrangement, the result has been one of massive electoral majorities for the candidates of parties approved by the traditional elites, thus allowing them to dominate the politics of the country. In the cities, new values have tended to supplant traditional ones. Labour interests are especially articulated and are reflected in the creation of left-leaning democratic and revolutionary parties. The new urban population—merchants and manufacturers whose political concerns only partly reflect those of the older groups—challenges the traditional elite for political power. Where democratic apparatus has been adopted, the conflict between urban and rural interests generates intense frustration accompanied by terrorism and riots.

The divisions in society are also transposed onto the military. The local bureaucracy was strengthened with the coming of imperial rule, but military force still constituted the centre of power throughout these years. After independence the new national armies acquired the role played by colonial detachments earlier, but they could not reestablish the traditional nature of their power. True, the military in most of these systems has once again reassumed political and, to a great extent, economic power, but the nature of modern military organization and training thrust it into the role of modernizer. The army has become in many states the real agent for change, thus undercutting the traditional basis for its own power.[8]

The traditional basis for power in most modernizing countries has caused a regression in modernization since independence. At independence most of these systems included a number of specialized institutions for political activity which paralleled those of modern systems. Political parties, labour unions, and specialized interest groups

---

[8] D. Lerner and R. D. Robinson, "Swords and Ploughshares: The Turkish Army as a Modernizing Force," *World Politics* (October 1960), pp. 19–44; also Morris Janowitz, *The Military in the Political Development of New Nations* (Chicago: University of Chicago Press, 1964).

all contended for power with the colonial rulers. In part this was due to the fact that in their dealings with the colonial power local politicians had to adopt the types of institutions suited to the system of the rulers, in much the same manner as they had to learn and use the language of the imperialists in order to communicate with them. Once independence was achieved, these tools were no longer useful. For instance, the Convention Peoples' Party in Ghana organized the population of the country for political action against the British before independence, but its rural bases withered after independence in 1957. When its leader, Kwame Nkrumah, was ousted from power by the military in 1965, the party was little more than an urban organization with scattered support elsewhere. It hardly contested the overthrow of Nkrumah and was virtually ignored by the military, a sure sign of its political impotence. In sum, it might be said that imperialism resulted in the forced growth of modern political institutions. The attainment of independence resulted in a more accurate portrayal of the nature of power in these systems. Only where interest groups and parties have managed to "colonize" the bureaucracy and limit the size and power of the military have even the vestiges of such institutions remained.

TYPE D

One of the most attractive political myths generated during the 19th century was that of the inevitability of social progress and, with it, the growth of democracy. The English, American, and French revolutions all seemed to point towards the modern democratic system as the ultimate state of political life. This myth reached the peak of popularity during World War I, which was ostensibly fought "to make the world safe for democracy."

The experiences of the decades of the 1920s and 1930s in Europe and East Asia cruelly shattered this myth. One after another the democracies created in central Europe following the war collapsed and were succeeded by nondemocratic systems. The first Russian revolution, which ended the Czarist regime and brought a coalition of liberals and social democrats to power, collapsed even before the war was ended and was succeeded by a communist regime.[9] Italian democracy, which was never very strong before the war, fell before Mussolini's fascists in 1922–23. The Weimar Republic, established on the ruins of the defeated German Empire, was only a democratic façade when Hitler erased even these vestiges in 1933. By 1935 the fascist dictatorships could boast that they were "the wave of the future."[10]

---

[9] See Chapter 16.

[10] See Chapter 17.

This prediction seemed to be confirmed when the democracies stood aside while Italy overran Ethiopia in 1935–36, the fascists in Spain destroyed the Republic in the Civil War (1936–39), and Hitler was permitted to consolidate his power and begin his conquests. Similar failures in the face of Japanese expansion in the Far East from 1931 on also helped to strengthen the image of fascism as irresistible and invincible. After the sacrifice of dozens of millions of lives in a second war, the fascist myth was disproven, but that of democracy could not be revived. It is increasingly clear that there is no necessary correlation between modernity and democracy and there is thus no guarantee that a modern democratic system will inevitably remain democratic.

Modern nondemocratic systems may be divided into two classes, the authoritarian system, which resembles to a degree the traditional nondemocratic variety and the totalitarian system which makes use of modern technology to remould all social relationships.

MODERN AUTHORITARIANISM

The modern authoritarian system is characterized by an emphasis on social stability and upon a limited repression of autonomous political structures. Ideologies or systems of political beliefs are sometimes proposed as underpinnings for such political systems, but they are rarely of critical importance to the operations of the structures. The major supports for such systems have been the military and established conservative interests.

The assumption of power by the military in a modern system is generally due either to the political orientation of military leaders or to the fact that the political system has ceased to be responsive to the needs of the population as perceived by the military leaders. In the former case, officers may adhere to a political orientation which serves as a catalyst for action in situations where they fear that partisans of an opposing orientation may take control of the system. Thus the military may intervene to prevent the victory of a popular movement at the polls. In 1970, the chief of staff of the Chilean army was assassinated apparently by right-wing opponents of the Marxist President-elect Salvador Allende in the hopes that this action would be interpreted by the army as emanating from Allende's sympathizers, thus provoking a *coup d'etat* against the leftist parties. While this ruse did not work, continual pressure to overthrow Allende resulted in the assumption of power by the Chilean military in 1973.

Military leaders may also participate in overturning a political system in which the parties and interest groups no longer operate effectively. The parties in the French Fourth Republic became effectively paralyzed after 1956 over the question of Algerian independence.

They were unable to form any coherent majority because of their differences over Algeria and the war being waged there to retain it as a French dependency. The increasing preoccupation with colonial policy undermined the ability of the system to make decisions in other policy areas, thus exacerbating the already existing tensions and hostilities within the system as a whole. The army, noting the evaporation of government authority, began after 1956 to pursue its own policies in Algeria independent of government direction. Finally, acting from the fear that a new cabinet might be formed by a weary national assembly to negotiate with the rebels, the army took over control of Algeria in May 1958 and moved to assume power in France itself. The country was spared from a right-wing authoritarian regime only because the Gaullists were able to steal the coup from them. During 1959 and 1960 DeGaulle managed to isolate and crush resistance in Algeria and in the army.

The emphasis on restoration or maintenance of the system's relationships desired by the military demonstrates one form of stability which is promoted by modern authoritarian regimes. A second form arises out of the concern of members of some economic groups or classes over rapid urbanization and industrialization and the political changes which accompany these factors. Those regimes which have adhered to a fascist concept of a political system (other than Nazi Germany) are examples of this form.[11] Italian, Spanish, Japanese, Argentinian, and Portuguese "fascisms" have been based upon the desire of certain classes to retain power. Only the Italian went beyond authoritarianism and became a totalitarian system. Originally, in these countries, large landowners maintained a traditional nondemocratic system (Type C), but the rise of an urban manufacturing and trading elite and a politically active urban work force constituted a real threat to their position. At the same time the new urban elite felt threatened by both the conservative landlords and the urban workers. In the end, both segments of the upper classes in these countries combined in the face of purportedly revolutionary urban and rural political movements to support an authoritarian nationalist group. The new government appeals to national unity in the face of an "international socialist threat" and to law and order which would both preserve the security of the upper classes and discourage the workers from resorting to rebellion and violence. The authoritarian nature of such a movement eliminates the only strong card in the hands of the workers—their numbers—by doing away with competitive elections. The opportunist nature of such class alliances explains why fascist ideas have rarely been consistently and coherently outlined. There are as many fascist ideas as there

---

[11] A. F. K. Organski, *The Stages of Political Development* (New York: A. A. Knopf, 1967), chapter 5.

are such groups. Though it is today out of fashion to refer to a regime as fascist, except in condemnation of it, there is little doubt that the above model applies to some of the so-called socialist or nationalist governments found around the world.

The most obvious characteristic of the modern authoritarian system is the restrictions placed on the number and autonomy of political input structures. Normally all political parties are suppressed except the one which the leadership may have used as a vehicle to gain power. The reasons given for this action are varied; the need for national unity, the threat posed by foreign powers or ideologies, and antiquated and unrepresentative nature of the old-time parties.

Trade unions and agricultural organizations are also affected, normally by transforming them into "fronts" controlled by the governing elite, either directly or through a single party. Structures which are not closely tied to the political system, such as churches and professional associations, are not directly controlled. They, and other similar potential political input structures, are subject to minimal restraints so long as they limit their political activity to measures of support for the regime. Only when there is deviation from this rule does the regime act to control them.

The conversion and output structures are likewise "streamlined." Legislatures are retained but serve only as sounding boards and supports for policies of the leadership. Depending upon the strength of the dictator, cabinet members may or may not exercise individual initiative, but, regardless of this possibility, the entire group is committed to a program quite similar to that of its leader. The administration, faced with the necessity of devoting considerable energies toward the control of public opinion, quite naturally is obsessed with policing functions, hence the term "police state." The independence of the judiciary is curtailed in order to add its prestige and authority to the support of government activities.

The modern authoritarian system is neither completely politicized nor does it allow more than a small measure of openness and autonomy in the political structures. This ambiguous position stems from the reason for the existence of such regimes; they are attempts to halt the social evolution which must accompany economic development, without preventing development itself. This contradiction means that such regimes are necessarily temporary. It would appear that modern authoritarian systems must take on other forms as the process of development continues. These may be either democratic or totalitarian, depending upon the orientations of the successors to the regime. The successors to the right-wing military government in Greece, which was overthrown in 1974, opted for a civilian parliamentary regime. In national elections, moderate groups won a majority of seats and took control of the government. In Portugal, in the same year, a left-wing military group overthrew a civilian fascist regime. It allowed elections, which right-wing groups were prohibited from contesting, and the socialists won. The Armed Forces Movement, however, was more radical than the socialists and did not allow them any measure of power, viewing itself as the true expression of Portuguese national will. Thus parliamentary democracy eluded Portugal.

TOTALITARIANISM

Conservative interests in modern systems are not alone in their promotion of authoritarianism. Others who would change the system in order to make it more in keeping with their particular ideas have not been overly reticent about the use of force to do so. The difference between the conservatives and such groups is that the latter tend to go beyond the stability-oriented authoritarian model to the use of coercion on a total societal scale.

The word *totalitarian* entered common usage after Mussolini employed it as a description of the Italian fascist state in the late 1920s. The rise to power of Hitler and Stalin during this period added to its popularity as a description of an extreme form of authoritarian government. Totalitarianism is in many ways similar to authoritarianism but the differences outweigh the similarities. Whereas an authoritarian regime is one which encourages social stability, the totalitarian is concerned with the remaking of society. It is concerned with the total destruction of the former social relationships and the construction of new ones on a principle which hitherto existed only as an utopian myth.[12] The totalitarian movement attempts to create a permanent social revolution and to control the end results of their creation.

Except for technology, the ingredients for the creation of a totalitarian state have existed throughout history. It is, first of all, an authoritarian form of rule. Totalitarianism usually involves what purports to be a meaningful ideology, a set of coherent ideas about how people and society should be, if they were perfect. The leadership is committed to using all the means at its disposal in order to reach this utopia. Perhaps the means of violence could be monopolized. However, the control of communications and ideas necessary for the erection of a totalitarian system could not be maintained with the methods then available. Technology is the essential factor underlying modern totalitarianism. Modern weapons give relatively few soldiers the means to control large populations and mechanical transportation provides the means for moving populations and soldiers at will. Modern com-

---

[12] See Chapter 11 on revolution.

munications give organized people an advantage over masses of disorganized people and provide the means for the political leadership to manipulate the thoughts of the population. The development of complex organizations allows governments to perform intricate tasks with relatively few men and to control the behaviour of large numbers through an efficient bureaucracy.

Concurrent with the development of modern technology came the realization that the state of humanity could actually be changed by people themselves. The realization that traditional society was not the only form of society, or even a desirable one, led to the propagation of new ideas about the best forms which society could take. Ideologies and revolutions have been the result of this realization and, subsequently, so has totalitarianism. At the core of the totalitarian system is a leader who is supported by two major institutions, the party and the administration. The function of the leader in the totalitarian state is to formulate policy. Having the closest connection with the forces affecting society, the leader commands without responsibility. Only he or she can see the full reality spelled out in time and space and his or her policies are the levers which will move and conduct society towards its appointed end. Hitler dreamed of the *Herrenvolk* or master race, which would stride through the world purifying it with fire and blood. Mussolini saw the Italian nation resurrecting the ghost of the Roman Empire, bearing the fruits of a superior civilization to the Mediterranean basin. Stalin could see the march of history towards the final overthrow of capitalism and the institution of the communist utopia. Constitutions and legal forms could not hold these men: they saw themselves as servants of the highest law, of a reality that must be made. Stalin could deal with Hitler and Hitler with Stalin in 1939, because each saw that the arrangement would favour the movement towards their respective "truths." When Pastor Niemoeller, who was one of the leaders of a Christian movement opposing Nazi ideas, was freed by a court in 1934, Hitler is said to have exclaimed that "this is the last time a German court is going to declare someone innocent whom I have declared guilty."[13] Guilt, innocence, right, and wrong are all dependent upon the immediate needs of the state which reflect the leader's present view of the ultimate reality.

The leader's view of reality is translated to the general public by means of an official ideology. An *ideology* consists of a critique of the former society, or a definition of the enemy, a vision of the society to come, and a prescription for attaining it. Contrary to the traditional authoritarian state, the totalitarian state insists that its citizens move

---

[13] Carl Friedrich and Zbigniew Brzezinski, *Totalitarian Dictatorship and Autocracy* (New York: Praeger, 1965), p. 35.

psychologically. It is not enough that they acquiesce; they must believe, participate, and build the new reality. The institution responsible for the fostering of belief is the party. The party disseminates the official ideology, relates it to the events of the day, provides for a single-minded political conformity and continually probes for deviations in thought and deed from the accepted party line. Everything is related to the transition from the political evil of the past to the heaven on earth of the future. To quote a Nazi agitator:

> We don't want lower bread prices,
> We don't want higher bread prices,
> We don't want unchanged bread prices,
> We want National Socialist bread prices![14]

The new reality was not the reality of dollars and cents but that of National Socialism.

The party also acts to provide personnel for the system. In contrast to the methods used in systems where competitive elections predominate, the totalitarian party provides personnel through a process of cooption, where personnel already in the system choose colleagues after the party organization has verified their loyalty to the ideology and the leadership. Since there is but one party there are no competing sets of personnel, only individuals striving through demonstrations of fidelity to prove their worthiness in the selection process.

The administration is the second pillar supporting the totalitarian state. To a great extent the mix of functions performed by the administration differs from that in other systems:

We have learnt history more thoroughly than the others. We differ from all others in our logical consistency. We know that virtue does not matter to history, and that crimes remain unpunished; but that every error has its consequences and venges itself unto the seventh generation. . . . Each wrong idea we follow is a crime committed against future generations. Therefore we have to punish wrong ideas as others punish crimes: with death.[15]

In order to purge society of its wrong ideas the state must create revolutionary conditions, yet, paradoxically, a fundamental condition in revolutions is the collapse of the existing order, including the state. Totalitarians create conditions approximating revolution when they turn the political institutions against the society. Instead of creating the terror that comes to people when there is no system of decision making, it turns the rule implementing system against them. A political system exists but functionally it has gone mad: it does not protect society but attempts to destroy it, at least at the level of the individual.

---

[14] Peter Drucker, *The End of Economic Man* (London: Basic Books, 1940), p. 13.

[15] Arthur Koestler, *Darkness at Noon* (New York: Macmillan 1940), p. 99.

The attack on the individual is total. Organized economic, social, and political life is subordinated to ideology. There are no jobs without political indoctrination, no clubs without political purposes, no politics without ideology. A normal social life is impossible without political participation—directed, enthusiastic participation. Personal life is invaded as well. Guilt by association is pronounced on the relatives of political deviants and family ties are threatened by the intensive political indoctrination of young children.

The individual is subjected to the pressure of terror, created in the totalitarian state by the secret police and other parts of the bureaucracy. This leads to an obsession for security. Job tenure, fear of informants in all aspects of life—including the family—and the inability to predict the twists and turns of ideological tactics, which at any moment may place an individual outside the law, all contribute to this continual search. Security is only to be found in the party and the leader. When National Socialist bread prices become more important than the price itself, the individual has found security. The individual is secure in that he or she is an instrument of race or of history.

Totalitarianism is a product of the 20th century though its roots are as old as society. As a political style it promises much to those who are lost in the complex world of today. The equipment is ready for its installation and all that stands between today and the *1984* of George Orwell are the individuals who constitute any political system.

RECOMMENDED READINGS

Apter, David.   *The Politics of Modernization.* Chicago: University of Chicago Press, 1965.

Arendt, Hannah.   *The Origins of Totalitarianism.* New York: World Publishing, 1966 (first published 1951).

Beer, Stafford.   *Designing Freedom.* Toronto: CBC Publications, 1974.

Barker, Ernest.   *Reflections on Government.* New York: Galaxy, 1958, Part IV (first published 1942).

Burch, Betty, ed.   *Dictatorship and Totalitarianism.* Princeton, N.J.: Van Nostrand, 1959.

Buchanon, James M., and Tullock, Gordon.   *The Calculus of Consent: Logical Foundations of Constitutional Democracy.* Ann Arbor: University of Michigan Press, 1962.

Carsten, F. L.   *The Rise of Fascism.* Berkeley: University of California Press, 1969.

Cohen, Carol.   *Democracy.* Athens: University of Georgia Press, 1971.

Cohen, Ronald, and Middleton, John, eds.   *Comparative Political Systems.* Garden City, N.Y.: Natural History Press, 1967.

Dahl, Robert.   *A Preface to Democratic Theory.* Chicago: University of Chicago Press, 1956.

Ebenstein, William. *Totalitarianism: New Perspectives.* New York: Holt, Rinehart & Winston, 1962.

Eisenstadt, S. N. *The Political Systems of Empires.* New York: The Free Press, 1962.

Fickett, Lewis. *Problems of the Developing Nations.* New York: Crowell, 1966.

Friedrich, Carl, and Brzezinski, Zbigniew. *Totalitarian Dictatorship and Autocracy.* New York: Praeger, 1965.

Friedrich, Carl, ed. *Totalitarianism.* New York: Grosset & Dunlop, 1964.

Hunter, Guy. *Modernizing Peasant Societies.* London: Oxford University Press, 1969.

Kautsky, John, ed. *Political Change in Underdeveloped Countries.* New York: John Wiley & Sons, 1962.

Koestler, Arthur. *Darkness at Noon.* New York: Macmillan, 1940.

Latey, Maurice. *Tyranny.* London: Macmillan, 1969.

MacPherson, C. B. *The Real World of Democracy.* Toronto: CBC Publications, 1965.

————. *Democratic Theory: Essays in Retrieval.* Oxford: Clarendon Press, 1973.

Mayo, Henry B. *An Introduction to Democratic Theory.* New York: Oxford University Press, 1960.

Neumann, Sigmund. *Permanent Revolution.* 2d. ed. New York: Praeger, 1965 (first published 1942).

Organski, A. F. K. *The Stages of Political Development.* New York: A. A. Knopf, 1967.

Parkinson, C. Northcote. *The Evolution of Political Thought.* New York: Viking Press, 1960, Part I and IV.

Pye, Lucien. *Aspects of Political Development.* Boston: Little, Brown & Co., 1966.

Riggs, Fred W. *Administration in Developing Countries.* Boston: Houghton Mifflin, 1964.

Wittfogel, Karl A. *Oriental Despotism.* New Haven, Conn.: Yale University Press, 1957.

4

Political Culture and Socialization

IT WAS STATED in an earlier chapter that political life is but one facet of the overall life in the community and that every political system exists within a socioeconomic setting. The political aspect of this setting was labelled the *political culture,* which may be more specifically defined as *the political attitudes, skills, and values of the members of the community.*

POLITICAL CULTURE

A community's political culture is the basis for its political system; it is the constantly shifting backdrop for political activity with the specific directions of this change differing from one society to the other. If the political structures and processes do not reasonably reflect the actual state of the political culture, then an unstable, and potentially revolutionary, situation tends to arise. The history of France following the Revolution of 1789 is a reflection of the frustrations caused by the inability of an overly rigid political system to respond to the rapidly occurring social and economic changes. The revolution itself was a traumatic affair which left the country more divided at its end than at its outset. Not all of France was in sympathy with the social changes or with the revolution caused by them. The terror and counterterror of the next few years left the political culture of France fundamentally divided. Subsequent changes in French society since the revolution have caused further fragmentation of the political culture. The result is that no specific set of political structures and processes have gained general long-term acceptance. The Fifth Republic,

53

formed in 1958, appears to have been more successful in overcoming these divisions than its predecessors.

The congruity of the political culture with the structures and processes of the political system is critical since ultimately all political systems, if they are to achieve any degree of stability and security, must be acceptable to the bulk of the population. In other words, the system must be seen as *legitimate* by its citizens. It is possible for a government to maintain itself in power by sheer terror and brute force, but it has been repeatedly demonstrated that such methods may generate forces which will sweep away the incumbent government and destroy the existing political and social relationships. The wide diversity in types of government, and the longevity of many of these systems, makes quite clear that for a political system to be acceptable to the population, and thus to be legitimate, it need not be of any particular type. There is nothing in either logic or reality that precludes an authoritarian government of a type highly repugnant to most Canadians from being acceptable to its own population.

Each political system is based upon a different political culture that incorporates the society's history, traditions, and experiences. Neighbouring political systems may be characterized by very divergent historical and cultural backgrounds. Europe, for instance, is a relatively small part of the land mass of the world and has less than 20 percent of its population (including European Russia). Yet Britons, Frenchmen, Italians, Germans, Poles, and Swedes are very different people, in spite of the fact that there are few distinguishing physical characteristics between them. Attempts to establish recognizable differences have led to innumerable discussions of "national character" and racial and ethnic traits. From these discussions, and from both pleasant and unpleasant contacts, images, or stereotypes, of the various national groups have emerged. The British are supposed to be a reticent "stiff upper lip" people, the Italians voluble and excitable, the Germans ruthlessly efficient and lovers of authority, and the Swedes promiscuous. Such stereotyping obscures far more than it reveals, for as with all stereotypes and caricatures, it depends upon catchy labels rather than facts. That there are differences between peoples is obvious, but, as any investigation into culture will show, the differences and similarities form a complex and ambiguous pattern. Thus, the study of cultures, and in our case political cultures, is an attempt to systematically identify these differences and evaluate their significance for the political life of the community.

The gathering of accurate information in this area is difficult and depends on a type of in-depth questioning called an opinion survey. There is no general agreement about the most suitable questions for this type of survey or even about the best way of administering and interpreting it. In spite of serious theoretical, methodological, and practical problems, such surveys are the best tools at hand to do the work of delineating the nature of a political culture.

The difficulties which face the student of political culture are compounded by the fact that political cultures are in a constant state of flux, and thus any survey reflects conditions over restricted time periods only. This situation is complicated by the fact that such surveys deal with an intertwined collection of subcultures rather than one homogeneous culture. For example, a political culture survey of Canada is automatically also a survey of French Canada, the Atlantic region, the Prairies, and so on, and all the differences in attitudes and outlooks that that entails. Canada would make an interesting country in which to conduct such a survey given the diverse origins of its population and the widely varied physical, economic, and historical settings in the various parts of the country. To date, only a limited number of such studies have been carried out.[1]

In order to examine the concept of political culture in detail, it is important to discuss the manner in which people are oriented towards the political system. All political orientation can be broken down into three components at the individual level: individual perceptions of the political system and its personalities and structures; his or her feelings about these aspects of the system; and the conclusions and opinions she or he draws about them.

The way in which a member of the community sees the political system is called his or her *perception* of it. What one perceives as the reality is what is important, not necessarily what is real. It is quite common for people to hold incorrect views about their political system, or related or competing systems. Since people act upon these perceptions, accurate or otherwise, it is to these that one must turn. *Feelings* about the political system are manifested by such emotions as affection and loyalty, distrust and alienation. These are labels for the emotional reactions of people towards the political world as they know it. Finally, *evaluation* of the political system refers to the judgments that are made about political phenomena. Implicitly or explicitly, these judgments are based upon a set of values, or beliefs about what is right and proper. These beliefs, which are often based on religious or philosophical concepts, are not necessarily political. For example, many people in Western society are brought up to place a high value on human life, individually and collectively. Such an attitude can

---

[1] John Wilson, "The Canadian Political Cultures," *Canadian Journal of Political Science* 7 (September 1974). Also see Richard Simeon and David J. Elkins, "Regional Political Cultures," *Canadian Journal of Political Science* 7 (September 1974); John Meisel, "Political Culture and Politics of Culture," *Canadian Journal of Political Science* (December 1974); Donald Smiley, "Canada and the Quest for a National Policy," *Canadian Journal of Political Science* 8 (March 1975).

easily influence judgments of political institutions and activities when such matters as capital punishment and war are concerned. Many white South Africans are brought up to believe, as a matter of religious principle, that their culture is specially blessed and must be preserved at all costs. This provides the justification for the racist and highly repressive policies of government, policies generally condemned outside of South Africa.

A hypothetical example may further illustrate the above ideas. In a survey of political culture it may be found that a group of respondents perceive the politics of their system as being primarily a game between people of wealth and power who manipulate the system to their own advantage. As they perceive it, the system is one of bribery, influence peddling, favouritism—a world where money and connections bring success and the little person is simply a pawn. Given such negative perceptions of the political reality, it would not be surprising to find a low degree of attachment to the political system among these respondents. Such a low emotional commitment to the system could result in apathy, alienation, or outright hostility. If these feelings about the system are combined with a set of religiously or philosophically based values emphasizing honesty and equal treatment of all citizens, then this group of respondents is faced with a situation in which their political culture and the perceived realities of the system are out of harmony. This is a potentially revolutionary situation.[2]

In one of the earliest studies of political cultures, Almond and Verba set forth three basic categories of political culture: parochial, subject, and participant.[3] A *parochial culture* is defined as one in which political institutions are not clearly separated from the economic or the religious and where the individuals involved are not aware of the existence of political processes and structures. Individuals in such cultures generally have little political knowledge and no explicitly political skills. It is quite possible for such a culture to exist within a larger political culture, as is often the case with tribal groups in Africa or Latin America. A *subject culture* is one in which the individuals are aware of the political world and identify with it, but primarily as passive observers. Such persons are "output" oriented; that is, they recognize the rules, policies, and agencies of the system but do not consciously attempt to influence them.[4] A *participant culture* is distinguished from a subject culture by a higher level of political awareness among the individuals and at least a minimum of positive involvement

---

[2] See Chapter 11.

[3] Gabriel Almond and Sydney Verba, *Civic Culture* (Boston: Little, Brown & Co., 1965), pp. 11–26.

[4] Ibid., pp. 17–18.

aimed at influencing some of the activities of the system. Individuals in a participant culture are "input" as well as "output" oriented. They are aware of at least some of the possible benefits of political activity and have acquired some of the political skills that can be used to affect the system.

National political cultures are, in fact, mixtures of these three types and it is highly unlikely that one would find a culture that is completely of one type. In theory the Canadian political culture is a participant one, and elaborate electoral and representational structures have been developed to make it possible for the citizens to participate. This does not mean that all will participate, or that the theoretically dominant culture pervades all parts of the system. Indeed, it is possible to find in the Canadian political culture examples of subcultures of each of the other two types. Remote Eskimo groups would be an obvious example of the parochial and many of the Indian groups an example of the subject culture.

Just as any given political culture may contain within itself multiple subcultures, the individuals within the culture may have different orientations in different circumstances. For example, a person brought up in a family which is pessimistic about and hostile toward politics may at the same time be subjected to the influence of an educational system which stresses optimism and participation. She or he may well acquire the values of both and exhibit this conflict by acting out her or his roles as a student and as a family member in very different ways.

Any attempt to assess what type of political culture is dominant in a particular political system requires the political scientist to enquire into the degree to which the population is aware of political affairs and of the institutions involved in them. Table 4–1 indicates the proportion

TABLE 4–1

Perceptions of the Effect of National and Local Governments (in percent)

	U.S.	*U.K.*	*Germany*	*Italy*	*Mexico*
National government has:					
A great effect	41	33	38	23	7
Some effect	44	40	32	31	23
No effect	11	23	17	19	66
Other and don't know	4	4	13	27	4
Local government has:					
A great effect	35	23	33	19	6
Some effect	53	51	41	39	23
No effect	10	23	18	22	67
Other and don't know	2	3	8	18	3

Source: Gabriel A. Almond and Sidney Verba, *The Civic Culture: Political Attitudes and Democracy in Five Nations* (copyright © 1963 by Princeton University Press) Tables 1, 2 pp. 80, 81. Reprinted by permission of Princeton University Press.

of those interviewed who felt that the national and local governments of their country had an effect upon their lives.

The data indicate that Americans, Britons, and Germans generally believed that their national and local governments affected their lives; Italians were substantially less cognizant of this, while only a relatively small minority of Mexicans believed this. Since one of the critical differences between political cultures is the degree of awareness among citizens of political institutions and their activities, it appears that Mexicans and Italians were less participant-oriented than the other peoples studied. This interpretation is reinforced by the responses to an additional question designed to measure the extent to which those interviewed followed political and governmental affairs. Eighty percent of Americans indicated that they followed these matters at least occasionally, while in Germany 72 percent did so and in Britain, 68 percent. Italians had the lowest response with 37 percent and Mexicans reported 55 percent. The relatively high proportion of the respondents in the United States, Britain, and Germany who were aware of the impact of governments was matched by a fairly high rate of observation of political activity. A majority in Italy was aware of the impact of governments, but only a small number actually followed political affairs. In Mexico the reverse was true, few perceived the effects of governmental activity, but a fairly high number followed politics anyway. Further questioning established that Americans and Germans were best informed about political personalities and organizations and Mexicans the least. When questions were asked to find out how willing they were to express political opinions, the Italians expressed the most reluctance, while the Mexicans appeared to be very willing to discuss such matters. The authors came to the conclusion that the Italian and Mexican political cultures were both essentially parochial, but the Italians showed distinct signs of alienation from the political system whereas the Mexicans had a far more positive attitude toward politics even if the level of their political information was low.

It should be noted that the data of the Almond and Verba study has undoubtedly been made somewhat obsolete with the passage of nearly two decades. Both Italy and Mexico have undergone increasing urbanization and industrialization with an accompanying increase in literacy and availability of information through an expanding mass media. Public opinion surveys, while not related directly to the questions addressed in the Almond and Verba study, suggest that political information may be more widely dispersed in Italy, but a high degree of alienation and cynicism still persists. While data concerning Mexico is less available, it also suggests a greater degree of political awareness and an ingredient of frustration with the system as it struggles to cope with the many problems facing it.

To this point we have been concerned primarily with the way the respondents saw their political systems. Available data for Canada shows a fairly high level of interests in government, but not a particularly high level of accurate information about political institutions and processes.

A second major aspect of political culture is people's feeling toward the political system. One way to assess these feeling is to ask what features of the society are generally regarded as its outstanding characteristics. Table 4–2 presents some findings on this subject.

TABLE 4–2
Characteristics of the Nation Producing Pride (in percent)

	U.S.	U.K.	Germany	Italy	Mexico
Political institutions	85	46	7	3	30
Economic system	23	10	33	3	24
Character of the people	7	18	36	11	15
Contribution of the arts	1	6	11	16	9
Physical attributes	5	10	17	25	22
Social legislation	13	18	6	1	2
Other	20	30	23	32	26
Nothing or don't know	4	10	15	27	16

Note: The responses added up to more than 100 percent as respondents were allowed to cite more than one characteristic.

Source: Gabriel A. Almond and Sidney Verba, *The Civic Culture: Political Attitudes and Democracy in Five Nations* (copyright © 1963 by Princeton University Press) Table 1, p. 102. Reprinted by permission of Princeton University Press.

Certain contrasts emerge between these findings and those discussed earlier. There is a consistency in the cases of the United States and Britain between the high level of affection or positive feelings toward the system, the levels of information, and a willingness to discuss politics. The Germans, however, appear to have considerable interest in politics but exhibit little affection for their political system. The Italians are even more emphatic in this respect while the Mexicans, who saw themselves as least affected by political activity and were least informed, demonstrated a relatively high regard for their system. Finally, the Italians exhibit a consistently negative attitude—poorly informed, generally reticent about politics, and quite clearly lacking in affection for their political system.

The inconsistencies in the German and Mexican responses may be best explained in the context of their history, a good demonstration of the need for a degree of historical sensitivity on the part of political scientists. Contemporary German attitudes have been shaped by a generally unsatisfactory experience with politics in the last 60 years. Pre–World War I Germany was an autocratic system with very little scope for significant political input by the public. The Weimar Republic, created after the collapse of the monarchy at the end of World War I, proved to be incapable of dealing with the problems facing Germany in the early 1930s. The resultant rise of Hitler brought a temporary reprieve to many Germans, but in the end the Nazi regime proved to be an illusory success that brought defeat, world condemnation, and a divided Germany. The continuing division of the country has made it difficult for a new and strong political attachments to develop since both regimes were, until recently, officially regarded as "temporary."[5]

Mexico has, in the last 60 years, changed from a chaotic, fragmented, and underdeveloped nation to a united, relatively well-developed, and respected member of the community of nations. It has the enviable reputation in Latin America of having brought about a major revolution (which predates the Russian Revolution) and achieved a substantial degree of independence from the United States. Thus, while it is still a nation with a high rate of illiteracy and extensive poverty, it also enjoys a political tradition of progress and stability in which citizens could take pride even if they knew very little about politics or the working of their political system.

A survey of Canadian youth made for the Royal Commission on Bilingualism and Biculturalism includes some information relevant to the question of affection toward the political system. Respondents were given an opportunity to identify the characteristics of Canada which came most readily to mind by drawing or writing them on a blank map of Canada. Natural terrain and geography were the most frequently identified characteristics, though this is perhaps due to the form in which the question was put. However, it revealed some interesting information when comparisons were made between Anglophone and Francophone Canadians. This is shown in Table 4–3.

TABLE 4–3
Most Identified Characteristics (in percent)

	Anglophone	Francophone
Natural terrain or geography	75	66
Economic resources or industries	67	44
Form of government or way of life	27	13
Political subdivisions (regional, provincial, local)	37	96
Social environment	30	21
Other	44	16

Note: Total is more than 100 percent as respondents were allowed more than one answer.
Source: John C. Johnstone, *Young People's Images of Canadian Society.* (Ottawa: The Queen's Printer, 1969), p. 2. Reproduced with the permission of Information Canada.

---

[5] Elizabeth Noelle and Eric Peter Neuman, *The Germans* (Allensbach: Verlag fur Demoskopie, 1967), pp. 214–16, 227–28, 231.

Young English-Canadians were most likely to think in geographic and economic terms when thinking about Canada, whereas French Canadians were most likely to think in political terms, with special reference to provincial (Quebec) government. Traditionally the majority of French Canadians are Québecois, and the provincial government has been looked-up to as an instrument for protecting the French language and culture. It would also appear that the primacy of interest in political institutions found in the United States is not found in Anglophone Canada because Canadians are more deferential toward politicians than their American counterparts.

Another important aspect of political culture is the popular attitude toward political participation. The Almond and Verba study included such questions as whether a citizen would participate in community affairs, if it would be possible for an individual to do something about an unjust national regulation, and what means should be used for this purpose. Table 4–4 outlines the answers they received.

TABLE 4–4
Political Activity and Competence

	U.S.	U.K.	Germany	Italy	Mexico
Percentage who say:					
Citizen should be active	51	39	22	10	26
Could do something about an					
unjust national regulation	75	62	38	28	38
Would act alone	42	40	18	18	18
Would seek the aid of others	32	22	19	10	20

Source: Gabriel A. Almond and Sidney Verba, *The Civic Culture: Political Attitudes and Democracy in Five Nations* (copyright © 1963 by Princeton University Press) Table 3, p. 176, Table 1, p. 185, and Table 6, p. 203. Reprinted by permission of Princeton University Press.

Americans and Britons seemed to place a high value on political activity; Italians valued it the least. They also felt less able to effect changes. Respondents were further asked whether they felt that they would get equal treatment and consideration from the police and bureaucrats when they expressed their points of view. Americans, Britons, and Germans were relatively optimistic in these matters, whereas the Italians and Mexicans were pessimistic. Those of higher educational attainment in all cultures felt that they were more likely to be fairly treated and that they could have some influence upon governmental actions.

These questions were explored in a Canadian survey in 1968 when respondents were asked whether or not they thought they could influence Parliament, the civil service, and the government in general.[6] The result would seem to indicate a degree of detachment and reservation about the efficacy of political activity. For instance, 69 percent agreed with the statement that "politics and government seem so complicated that a person like me can't understand what's going on." Another 47 percent felt that they did not have a say in what the government did and 56 percent agreed with the proposition that members of Parliament soon lost touch with the people. As far as actual participation in the political process was concerned, 76 percent agreed with the proposition that voting was the only avenue available to them to influence the government. This relates very closely to data on the actual extent of political participation in Canada.

The Almond and Verba study also enquired into attitudes toward voting and election campaigns. The authors found that Americans were most satisfied with their system, that they were most optimistic about the treatment they would receive from the system and the most confident about the usefulness of political activity in general. In spite of this, or perhaps because of it, they still tend to have one of the lowest voter turnouts among democratic political systems. Results of many public opinion polls in the aftermath of the Vietnam War and the Watergate scandals suggest a measurable increase in cynicism about politics.

The British tend to fall into the same pattern as the Americans, but they have a less positive relationship to the political system in almost every instance, although in both cases the political culture is significantly participant-oriented. On the other hand, Germans appeared well equipped for political activity in economic and educational terms, were politically informed, and paid attention to politics, but were reluctant to discuss or participate in political activity. Italians had a very negative view of their political system and a very low sense of political efficacy. Mexicans, in spite of their social and economic problems, exhibited a more positive attitude toward the political system, even though political awareness and activity were at a very low level.

A further aspect of political culture explored was the extent to which partisanship, or a strong feeling for a particular party or faction, influenced respondents' attitudes toward those not of the same political persuasion. Americans and Britons who identified with a particular party were the least likely to have strong negative feelings about those of opposing parties; the most intense antagonism existed between the supporters of the Italian Christian Democratic and Communist parties. Obviously, in a political system where parties are ideologically oriented, one would expect to find a high level of hostility. In the

---

[6] See R. M. Morris et al., *Attitudes Toward Federal Government Information,* Institute for Behavioural Research (Toronto: York University, 1969).

Italian culture, where citizens are already alienated, such interparty hostilities only serve to further fragment the political system.

In Canada, the Johnstone survey of Canadian youth approached the question of intergroup hostility obliquely through a series of questions which asked whether the respondents felt that Canadians could agree with each other on questions of the country's future. A positive picture emerged. Relatively few felt that agreement of some sort was unlikely. This series of questions did not deal with partisanship *per se*, but the results suggested a relatively low level of intergroup hostility of the type found in Italy. Canada would appear to have more in common with Britain or the United States, and, in fact, if overt activity in the form of mass demonstrations and violence in any guide, Canada has a lower level of intergroup hostility than either of those nations.

Another aspect of Canadian culture surveyed, though not explicitly political, was the attitude of young Canadians concerning the factors essential for future personal success. A number of interesting differences between Anglophones and Francophones emerged. These are shown in Table 4–5. Francophones tended to put more emphasis upon

TABLE 4–5
Important Factors in Getting Ahead

	Percentage Citing Factor		
Factor	*English*	*French*	*Other*
Good grades in school	95	69	94
Hard work	94	47	90
Good personality	85	69	77
University education	80	49	83
Knowing the right people	50	51	61
Being bilingual	39	75	45
Coming from the right family	23	27	27
Coming from right religious group	11	32	35
Being born in Canada	10	22	2
Having parents with money	6	11	11

Note: This survey was taken in 1965. Political developments since may have altered the findings somewhat.

Source: John C. Johnstone, *Young People's Images of Canadian Society*, p. 8. Reproduced with the permission of Information Canada.

characteristics related to the family or groups into which one is born rather than upon those that one might acquire. Francophones regard the Canadian setting as one in which they were not likely to be rewarded for education and hard work. This contrasts with the prevalent attitude among Anglophones.

The attitudes of French Canadians correspond to those found in more traditional societies where little class mobility exists and where important and prestigious jobs are handed out largely on the basis of family connections rather than merit. The political culture in such areas is apt to be subject or parochial rather than participant, with the centre of attention being family and group rather than the larger society. It is quite possible that the many forms of discrimination practiced against French Canadians over the years have created the impression that the kind of open opportunity which the English Canadians are so fond of stressing is really intended only for English Canadians and certain favoured immigrant groups. Reactions to such subtle, and not so subtle, forms of discrimination have occurred among members of minority groups in other societies, most notably among the American blacks. It should be pointed out that the Johnstone survey was taken only a few years after the flowering of the "Quiet Revolution" in Quebec in 1960 and its resultant explosion in the scope of educational opportunities but before the implementation of many programs designed to enhance the position of the Francophones, especially in the federal civil service. What impact these developments may have had, or are having, upon attitudes of the people in Quebec is still quite unknown.

Although the survey data used as the basis for the above discussion dealt directly with career opportunities, it is not difficult to demonstrate the significance of such attitudes upon political culture. If one has little faith in education, hard work, and merit as avenues to personal success, there would be little reason to prize education, experience, or proven abilities as virtues in elected officials. Rather, the emphasis might well fall on the ability to keep up appearances and care for one's relatives and associates. English Canadians have often been critical of the substance and style of Quebec politics on the grounds that it is too extravagant with funds and flamboyant in style. Given what appear to have been general sociopolitical attitudes among French Canadians, these political habits are understandable. Yet the substance of political life in English Canada is not necessarily of better quality; perhaps only different. There is a fair amount of evidence that English Canadians do not always practice the political virtues they preach. Accusations of electoral bribery, irregularities in awarding government contracts, conflict of interest, inadequate supervision in the disbursement of public funds, have all been levelled and in some cases proven, in the other provinces of Canada. Charges of tampering with the electoral machinery and the use of public funds as patronage to maintain party organizations have been laid against more than one government in the Atlantic Provinces. Situations of conflict of interest have been apparent in such diverse governments as that of Premier

Davis of Ontario and Premier Bennett of British Columbia, while the possibility of a lack of proper supervision of public funds has been a central part of the still unresolved Churchill Forest Industries affair in Manitoba.

The Johnstone survey also attempted to investigate the orientation of youth toward the various levels of government. Table 4–6 illustrates the differences of opinion with respect to government activity that exist between those who are from English-speaking homes and French-speaking homes.

TABLE 4–6
Orientations to Levels of Government by Language (in percent)

	Government Doing Most for the People		Government Doing Least for the People	
	English	*French*	*English*	*French*
Municipal	23	23	30	21
Provincial	33	40	12	13
Federal	32	22	26	34
Not sure	13	15	31	32

Source: John C. Johnstone, *Young People's Images of Canadian Society*, p. 18. Reproduced with the permission of Information Canada.

It is clear that Anglophones are more complimentary in their assessment of federal government activity than the Franchophones. The responses of the two groups in their assessment of the provincial governments is predictably the reverse. As Figure 4–1 shows, when the results are broken down into smaller categories, regional variations among both linguistic communities become apparent.

The only Canadians to exhibit a strongly profederal bias were those from the Atlantic Provinces and Quebec Anglophones, while the Québecois and Anglophone British Columbians exhibited a strong proprovincial bias. The only group to show an antiprovincial government bias, and by a very small margin, was the Anglophone Quebecers. In general the prevailing attitudes of young Canadians appeared to be negative toward the federal government and positive toward the provincial. The municipal level of government was considerably less well regarded than the federal. The same question, dealt with in a different survey in 1968, suggested a moderately positive feeling toward the federal government, with the French Canadians ranking slightly higher than the English.

This data tends to confirm the general perception of Canadian polit-

FIGURE 4–1
Regional Variations in Orientations toward Levels of Government by Language

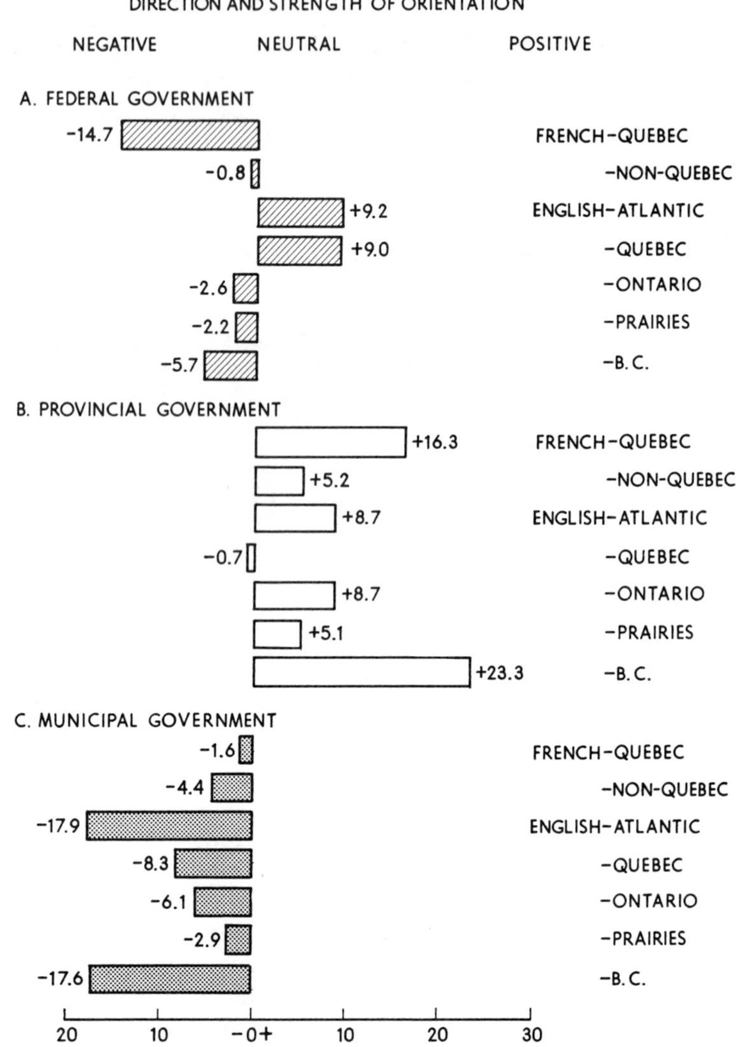

Source: John C. Johnstone, *Young People's Images of Canadian Society*, p. 19. Reproduced with the permission of Information Canada.

ical culture as one encompassing two fundamentally distinct entities: the French and the English. This view of Canadian political culture, however, tends to obscure the existence of significant differences in the perceptions, expectations, and evaluations of the Canadian political system by people in different parts of English Canada. In recent years, a number of studies have acknowledged the existence of these differences.[7]

Mildred Schwartz has suggested that "the crisis of our national existence is expressed in three distinct but related confrontations: Canada versus the United States, Ottawa versus the provinces and English Canada versus French Canada."[8]

There exist considerably divergent perceptions of the nature of Canadian–United States relations. These arise from the ambivalence created by the fear of the American domination of the Canadian economy, on the one hand, and the need for investment capital and trade outlets conveniently available across the border, on the other hand. Similar divergence exists in the perception of the role of the Federal Government. The Atlantic Provinces look to the Federal Government as an indispensable instrument for the amelioration of regional economic disparities. In contrast, even though they have grudgingly accepted the measures involved in interprovincial revenue equalization, the attitude of the more prosperous provinces has vacillated from ambivalence to outright opposition. Ontarians tend to believe that their province is treated as the "milch cow of Confederation." Albertans seem to feel that their province's energy resources are being siphoned off to the rest of the country at the cost of maximizing benefits for Albertans themselves. Premier W. A. C. Bennett of British Columbia once accused the Federal Government of treating his province as a "goblet to be drained" and even threatened judicial action to test the constitutionality of federal powers concerning equalization payments.[9]

A different hypothesis about the fragmentation in the Canadian political culture has been developed by John Wilson.[10] He argues that the significant factor in the determination of political culture is not historical tradition but economic and political development. He prefers to use the terms "underdeveloped" and "developed," instead of the customary "subject" and "participant," though the terms denote essentially the same set of conditions.

According to Wilson, the more economically and politically developed a society is, the more developed or participant its culture would be and, *vice versa*, the less developed a society, the more subject its culture. Economic and political development take place on a time scale and not all societies, or even segments therein, cover the

---

[7] S. D. Clark, *The Developing Canadian Community*, 2d ed. (Toronto: University of Toronto Press, 1968).

[8] Mildred A. Schwartz, *Public Opinion and the Canadian Identity* (Berkeley: University of California Press, 1967). See also, her *Politics and Territory: The Sociology of Regional Persistence in Canada* (Montreal: McGill–Queen's University Press, 1974).

[9] Donald Smiley, *Canada in Question: Federalism for the Seventies* (Toronto: McGraw–Hill Ryerson, 1972) p. 66.

[10] John Wilson, "Canadian Political Cultures."

time scale at identical speed. Thus the position occupied by a society, or its segment, on the time scale determines the nature of its political culture. This hypothesis does not regard the French fact as significantly contributing to the fragmentation of Canadian political culture.

Wilson establishes that the provinces of Canada constitute independent political systems, since each of them exercises autonomous legislative jurisdiction in such areas as health and welfare which are crucial to the economic and social life of its inhabitants. Assuming that many of the differences between provinces may be attributed to their relative level of development, he attempts to show the possible relationship between these levels and the political cultures of these provinces. In this way, Wilson shows that the Atlantic Provinces are in the very first stages of development; that Quebec, Ontario, Manitoba, and British Columbia are crossing the transitory phase, and that Alberta and Saskatchewan have reached an advanced level of development.

Wilson finds that these conclusions are supported by the data collected in a Canadian survey (1968), an Ontario survey (1967) and a Manitoba survey (1974) as well as by a study of the socioeconomic characteristics of the candidates for provincial legislatures. He concludes that more than two political cultures exist in Canada.

We must therefore either abandon the search for national unity altogether or redefine its meaning in a way which recognizes that our "limited identities" constitute the essence of what it is to be a Canadian. If we can accomplish that, and yet remain a nation, we will have taught the world a lesson it sorely needs to learn.[11]

As political cultures, national or regional, are not static, it is possible for events and personalities to influence their future development. Success of particular policies in dealing with pressing issues can have the effect of changing peoples views about their society and can encourage a greater degree of integration within the political system. Conversely, the example of separatist groups and parties in Quebec has spread to other parts of the country. Small "nationalist" or separatist groups, such as the Western Canada Party, the Brothers and Sisters of Cornelius Howatt in Prince Edward Island, and provincial movements in Cape Breton Island and Northern Ontario, all reflect a renewed interest in regional differences being expressed through different political arrangements.

---

[11] Ibid., p. 483. Detailed findings of the surveys are included in Wilson's article.

POLITICAL SOCIALIZATION

The process by which the values, attitudes, and skills that constitute political culture are diffused throughout the society is known as political socialization. It is essentially a specialized aspect of the general socialization process which teaches a person how to relate to his or her social environment. The study of political socialization is concerned with those aspects of socialization that are of political import, though not always explicitly so in content.

Basically, one may classify the sources and instruments of political socialization into two groups: those found in the wider society and those found specifically in the political system itself. The former includes the family, the educational system, the occupational environment, and peer groups.

The first analysis of the sources of political values and attitudes emphasized childhood experiences as the most important factor, and most specifically those provided by the family. It was often argued that if the family relationships were authoritarian, then the later political attitudes of the children were apt to be authoritarian; conversely, if the family was one in which decision making involved participation of the child, then the result was apt to be a democratic orientation in later life. In more recent years a different view has emerged, and the argument is often made now, that while these early experiences are important, the experiences that take place closer in time to actual or potential political activity are more influential. It appears that what is most important as a socializing agent may differ from person to person, but the process itself is continual from childhood through adolescence to the adult years.

The importance of the family does not necessarily lie in any deliberate political socialization, but in providing a consistent exposure to the political attitudes of adults. If, for example, parents regard politics as a dirty business and politicians as evil, and if, in their behaviour and discussions within the family, they communicate these attitudes to the children, then it is likely that the children will, at least initially, have the same attitudes. If the parents are totally apathetic to politics and rarely discuss it, evidence indicates that this apathy will be transmitted to their children. If, on the other hand, parents are active and articulate, the children will tend to acquire a positive attitude toward political affairs.

Recent assessments of the socialization process in Canada suggest that in Quebec the tradition has been one of an hierarchical and paternalistic family structure complemented by similar structures in other social organizations. The result, until the recent explosion of educational and occupational opportunities at least, was a hierarchical and paternalistic political structure. The suggestion was also made that for somewhat different reasons the same was true of English Canada. In the latter it is possible to make the observation that democratic values are to some extent passed on within the family, but that an active role in politics is not a high priority.

When a child enters school, he or she is exposed to another major source of socialization. A recent study has indicated that the most critical period in shaping the attitudes of young adults is the period from age 11 to 15, a period which coincides with some decline in the influence of the family, an increase in the influence of peer groups, and the presence of a reasonably advanced level of formal education.[12] The Johnstone survey, dealing as it did with the age group 13 to 20, gives some insight into this critical period as it applies to Canada. When the question of orientations toward the levels of government was broken down into age groups [see Table 4–7] it was shown that different orien-

TABLE 4–7
Young People's Perceptions of Government
(Quebec; in percent)

Government Perceived in Terms of:	French	English
Persons	59.0	51.6
Institutions	10.4	11.7
Processes	5.3	5.1
Norms (Values)	4.2	8.9
Symbols	.7	3.2
Other and not sure	20.4	19.5

Source: Jean Pierre Richert, "Political Socialization In Quebec," *Canadian Journal of Political Science* 6, no. 2 (June 1973): 307.

tations were related to different age groups. Many of the orientations found in the younger respondents probably reflect the attitudes of home, while those of the oldest age group reflect the additional impact of school, peer groups, and early adult experiences. The survey indicates that attitudes of Anglophone Canadians towards the Federal Government shift from mildly positive to mildly negative, among Francophone Canadians from moderately negative to very negative. At the same time the attitudes of both groups toward the provincial governments shift from moderately positive to very positive. The municipal level of government is not well regarded by the younger group surveyed and becomes less so as the survey moves on to the

[12] Elizabeth Noelle and Eric Peter Neumann, *The Germans*, p. 21.

older groups. There is, according to this survey, considerable consistency in the pattern of development of the orientation of young Canadians as they grow older; only the starting points differ.

There is somewhat conflicting information on this point in a more recent survey of the attitudes of young people in Quebec.[13] This survey is geographically more limited, and administered differently, but presents the rather interesting data of Table 4–7 on the question of children's perceptions of government.

The data suggests that Francophones tend to see government in terms of the persons involved while Anglophones tend to emphasize the institutions, norms (such as democracy, freedom), and symbols. This data is complemented by that in Table 4–8 which indicates that English Quebecers have an input orientation.

TABLE 4–8
Young Quebecers Perceptions of the Functions of Government (in percent)

Functions	French	English
Policy agency (input orientation)	41.8	49.1
Distribution agency (output orientation)	45.1	37.9
Other, not sure	13.1	13.0

Source: Jean Pierre Richert, "Political Socialization in Quebec," *Canadian Journal of Political Science* 6, no. 2 (June 1973): 308.

When the above data is distributed by age throughout the survey group, it appears that the orientation of the English Quebecer becomes increasingly policy-oriented while that of the Francophones remains predominantly distribution-oriented. This is tentatively attributed by Richert to the more authoritarian family, social, and business structures among the French.

The influence of the educational system in shaping those values and skills which lead to a participatory attitude toward politics can be positive or negative, depending in part upon whether political and social questions are treated in the curriculum. If they are largely ignored, then by implication they are not important things to know and the student is likely not to pay attention to such matters. Most political systems, democratic as well as authoritarian, insist upon a considerable amount of instruction in order to foster a positive image of the system and create a set of attitudes and skills compatible with the way it operates or the way in which its leaders would like it to operate. The curriculum of American secondary schools is peppered with courses in

---

[13] Jean Pierre Richert, "Political Socialization in Quebec," *Canadian Journal of Political Science* 6, no. 2 (June 1973): 303–13.

American history, civics, and related social studies, just as the Russian educational system includes a considerable amount of material on its history, institutions, and ideology. The Canadian public school system has been sharply criticized for not providing the student with an interesting and stimulating curriculum in social studies in general and political studies in particular.[14] In this respect Canada is well behind the United States; in fact it is common for state governments to require university students to take a basic course in American government and, in many cases, even courses in state government!

While the family and the schools may shape basic character and personality as well as political attitudes, experiences with peers and exposure to a wide variety of social influences extend the process of political socialization throughout the active life of most individuals. It is well known that religious groups and political parties, especially those exhibiting an authoritarian bias, attempt to provide ancillary organizations that can keep the members involved in controlled activities. By establishing labour, cultural, social, athletic, and educational organizations, a party or church can, if its recruiting is successful, limit the possibilities of defection or doubt. Such diverse entities as the Communist Party and the Catholic Church have shown, by the extent to which they support such organizations, that they are well aware of the continuing nature of the socialization process.

There are a number of ways in which adult experiences may affect political values and attitudes. For example, an individual who takes employment in a unionized industry may find that his or her attitude toward unions changes and that his or her political orientation moves closer to that of the union. The individual is likely to hear numerous stories of the difficult days before unionization, often vivid descriptions of the struggles to establish an effective labour organization, and a running commentary upon the many grievances outstanding against current management. He or she may then conclude that "his" or "her" union at least, has merit and, therefore, he or she may begin to look at issues involving unions in a different light. The same process may work in reverse when a union member is promoted to a managerial position.

Adult attitudes may be formed in settings that are essentially social but where politics is a subject of discussion. Exposure to other points of view and experiences may alter previously held views. Obvious causes of such changes are traumatic events such as an unexpected war or economic disaster. A classic example of this was the depression of the 1930s, which was such a traumatic event for many that they changed lifelong political allegiances. In Canada the depression

---

[14] A. B. Hodgetts, *What Culture? What Heritage? A Study of Civic Education In Canada* (Toronto: Ontario Institute for Studies in Education, 1968).

formed the backdrop for the creation of two major political movements: the Cooperative Commonwealth Federation (CCF), now the New Democratic Party, and the Social Credit Party. For many, the apparent inability of the existing parties to cope with the depression demonstrated the need for new forms of political organization. In the United States, the Democrats successfully campaigned against the Republicans for the next 20 years by recalling the depression and reminding voters of "Hoovervilles," the shanty towns that sprang up in many parts of the country as a result of extensive migrations of unemployed workers. Such social trauma does not necessarily mean an overnight reorientation of values and skills, but it does open the way for people to abandon old and trusted values which seem to be no longer efficacious. This presents new groups with the opportunity to recruit these disaffected persons. If one of these new groups comes to power and appears successful, then a more fundamental and continuing reorientation of values may begin.

The major political source of socialization is the government itself. All governments are involved in the socialization process to the extent of encouraging loyalty and promoting observance of the law. The socialization process as carried on by governments is an application of the "carrot and stick" approach wherein "good citizens" are rewarded and "bad citizens" are punished. Some governments engage in coordinated efforts at political socialization, especially those that are ideologically oriented, such as the Russian and Chinese governments. Other governments enter into this process less directly, and, in most democratic systems, much of this type of activity is left to nongovernmental organizations such as parties and interest groups. The end result of this less coordinated approach to political socialization is often the development of a more diverse and conflicting set of political attitudes.

A specialized form of the socialization process is the recruitment of political actors. The *recruitment* process is the means through which individuals enter into the various roles and structures of the political system. Every system must employ some method of renewing leadership over time in order to maintain itself. History is replete with examples where leadership groups were small and restricted and the death of a central figure produced a crisis. Hierarchical and hereditary systems attempt to transfer power automatically upon the death of a monarch to a predesignated heir. Democratic systems have attempted to avoid the rigidity of the hereditary method by resorting to such devices as elections, prescribed terms of office, and specific procedures for appointment to produce a predictable and peaceful turnover of governments.

The recruitment process in a democracy most often begins with attempts to encourage individuals to become politically active. The success of this form of recruitment is determined largely by how well the socialization process has created a favourable disposition to political activity in the first place. Some groups whose ideas are closer to the values of the majority of the community are apt to be more successful because the prospect of gaining power constitutes a lure in itself.

All those brought into the lowest levels of political involvement cannot be advanced, but much of the success of the recruitment process rests upon the extent to which it does in fact advance those with commitment and ability. One of the disadvantages of the recruitment process in ideologically oriented systems is that the emphasis on ideological orthodoxy may in fact attract and advance the mediocre rather than the brilliant and capable. A dilemma arises when an incumbent leadership tries to assure an orderly succession among competing groups which are not tolerated in the electoral process. While they may want to advance the most able under them, there is danger that those intended successors may conclude "too soon" that they can perform better than the incumbent leadership. The possibility exists that the proteges might try to take control ahead of schedule. This encourages the incumbents to advance those who, because of a lack of ability, will not pose such a threat.

The methods of recruitment may be used as one measure of the differences between democratic and nondemocratic systems. Traditional political systems tend to rely upon family and kinship group ties as a means of selecting office holders. Modern systems, with characteristically larger numbers of positions to fill, rely heavily on methods which may be loosely characterized as being based on merit. What constitutes merit may be based on a very flexible definition; in government bureaucracies it may be the ability to pass a given test, in other structures it may be party affiliation and/or ideological orthodoxy, and in still others a mixture of both. The extent to which recruiting reaches into all segments of society may be used as a rough guide to the openness of the political system. No system is entirely open. This is demonstrated by the existence of security checks and personal investigation of candidates for some government positions in Canada, and especially in the United States.

RECOMMENDED READINGS

Almond, Gabriel, and Powell, G. Bingham, Jr. *Comparative Politics: A Developmental Approach.* Toronto: Little, Brown & Co. (Canada) Ltd., 1966.

Almond, Gabriel, and Verba, Sidney. *The Civic Culture.* Boston: Little, Brown & Co., 1965.

Boissevain, Jeremy. *The Italians in Montreal: Social Adjustments in a Plural Society.* Ottawa: The Queen's Printer, 1970.

Clark, S. D. *The Developing Canadian Community*. Toronto: University of Toronto Press, 2d. ed., 1968.

Elkins, David J. "Regional Political Culture." *Canadian Journal of Economics and Political Science* 28 (1962).

Johnstone, John C. *Young People's Images of Canadian Society*. Ottawa: The Queen's Printer, 1969.

Meisel, John. "Political Culture and the Politics of Culture" *Canadian Journal of Political Science* 7, no. 4 (December 1974).

Morris, R. M., et al. *Attitudes Toward Federal Government Information*. Institute for Behavioural Research. Toronto: York University, 1969.

Porter, John. *The Vertical Mosaic*. Toronto: University of Toronto Press, 1965.

Richert, Jean Pierre. "Political Socialization in Quebec." *Canadian Journal of Political Science* 6, no. 2 (June 1973).

Pye, Lucien, and Verba, Sidney. *Political Culture and Political Development*. Princeton, N.J.: Princeton University Press, 1965.

Russell, Peter H., ed. *Nationalism in Canada*. Toronto: McGraw–Hill of Canada, Ltd., 1966.

Schwartz, Mildred A. *Public Opinion and Canadian Identity*. Berkeley: University of California Press, 1967.

———. *Politics and Territory: Sociology of Regional Persistence in Canada*. Montreal: McGill–Queen's University Press, 1974.

Smiley, Donald. "Canada and the Quest for a National Policy." *Canadian Journal of Political Science* 8, no. 1 (March 1975).

Wilson, John. "The Canadian Political Cultures." *Canadian Journal of Political Science* 7, no. 3 (September 1974).

5

Interest Articulation

THE STUDY of political culture and socialization leads into a discussion of how these basic attitudes and values are transformed into expressions of interest or opinion on specific issues, events, and personalities. This transformation is of great importance to the system, as general cultural attitudes would be an impractical basis upon which to make decisions on matters of policy and law. What political decision makers need to know is how the public interprets these values in relation to specifics. For instance, it is generally felt in Canada that murder is not justifiable. At a more specific level the public might be willing to condone, as recent opinion polls have shown, the taking of life in self-defence and the taking of life by the state as punishment for the commission of a serious offense. Thus, it is not the general value of the sanctity of life that is important to decision makers, but rather the specific conditions under which the public would feel that an exception is warranted.

In a democratic system especially, it is assumed that what the

FIGURE 5–1
Forms of Interest Articulation

	Passive	*Active*
Unorganized	Public opinion polls	Anomic representation Personal representation Proxy representation
Organized		Interest groups —Nonassociational —Institutional —Associational

public wants is important. The difficulty is that it is not possible to determine exactly what the public *does* want. This chapter will explore the ways in which specific public attitudes are made manifest. The process by which the individuals and groups in society make their opinions known to their fellow citizens as well as to the formal decision makers is known as *interest articulation*. This process is carried out in a wide variety of ways. Basically, there are two types of interest articulation—passive and active. The interest articulation process in depicted in its basic form in Figure 5–1.

PASSIVE INTEREST ARTICULATION

Passive interest articulation consists of those attitudes about specific issues and personalities which must be sought out by others in the political system. This is more commonly referred to as public opinion and is quite distinct from active interest articulation, which is the expression of attitudes by individuals or groups in some public or organized manner. Public opinion may be defined *as the attitudes held by individuals about specific issues and personalities in politics*, in contrast to political culture, which consists of basic attitudes about the political system as a whole and its environment. Public opinion is largely conditioned by a combination of political socialization and direct experience. The basic attitudes about politics and the political system largely determine the limits, contexts, and contents of public opinion.

The difficulty with understanding public opinion lies in the fact that it is dispersed in erratic patterns amongst the population. Partly for this reason, interest groups and political parties have been developed to channel the expression of opinion and to serve as a medium of contact between political leaders and the public at large. In all societies, a voluntary organization primarily attracts only those people who are most interested in its objectives and policies. Given the fact that large parts of the public are not intimately involved in political organizations, some other means must be found to discover their opinions and desires. Further, as societies became more complex and as the leaders inevitably became more removed from direct contact with the public, the need for a more regular and systematic method of ascertaining public opinion became obvious. As a result, organizations were established for the purpose of developing and conducting surveys of public opinion. Since the 1930s such surveys, or opinion polls, have become increasingly scientific and reliable and have gained widespread acceptance in academic, commercial, and political circles. Thus in democratic systems, at least, any discussion of public opinion must include a discussion of polls.

Public opinion is also important in nondemocratic systems. The elaborate network of political institutions established by authoritarian governments are designed to do more than simply control the public. They are intended to serve as lines of communication, for it is important that the leaders know the mood of the public. An authoritarian government that is not effectively informed about public attitudes may find that in a crisis it lacks public support, thereby imperilling the regime.

FORMATION OF PUBLIC OPINION

Throughout much of Western history it has been argued that opinion could be formulated rationally through an objective appraisal of reality. Cases of irrational opinion were ascribed to faulty knowledge or insufficient education. The rise of the natural sciences led many to believe that a similar process of reasoning could be used eventually to solve social problems.[1] This belief has led to efforts to make education generally accessible, to extend voting rights as a vehicle for the expression of opinion, and to an emphasis on opening of channels of communication. Many of the provisions dealing with freedom of speech, press, and assembly represent attempts to keep the lines of communication open. Increasingly, this view has been tempered by the realization that such improvements in communication do not eliminate irrationality from the process of opinion formation.

Existing ideas about the impact of background factors and irrationality on opinion formation may be divided into two basic categories: deterministic and conditioned. The former is most widely found in the various forms of Marxism,[2] which postulate that economic factors determine social, cultural, and political behaviour and attitudes. This explanation finds little favour today in its more rigid and ideological forms except among more orthodox Marxists. A modification of this theory centres on the proposition that the main function of social and political organizations is to provide a degree of security and predictability in life. As society has moved to an openly materialistic attitude, money has emerged as the measure of security and a means of satisfaction of want and needs. It follows logically that real or imagined threats to economic security can exert a powerful influence upon the political opinions of the citizenry.

Considerable emphasis has been placed upon sociological and psychological conditioning in the formation of political culture and as part of the socialization process. This line of reasoning may be extended to

---

[1] The liberals have always felt this to be important; see Chapter 14.

[2] See Chapter 15.

cover the formation of public opinion as well. Such factors as childhood and family experiences emerge, though evidence suggests that the specifics of public opinion are greatly affected by adult experiences as well. As might also be expected, studies have indicated that individuals vary greatly in their responses to the same adult experiences.

The process by which individuals form the specific preferences that constitute public opinion is subtle and complicated. They continually receive information about themselves and their environment, including the political. This information is selectively retained and ranked according to the individual's basic attitudes and his or her previously held opinions about what is important. In many cases the individual will react to new information both automatically and unpredictably. The source of information, the manner of its presentation, the agreeableness of its contents, the state of mind and circumstances of the recipient at the moment will all shape the nature of the response. Information regarded as useful will be selected for retention and a value attached to it. The fact that the opinion formation process is an individual matter means that while the general process may be described, great care should be taken in evaluating individual cases.

It is impossible to talk of uniform opinion formation for all the people in any group. Many people reach similar opinions by very different routes, all perfectly intelligible if not logical. An attempt to unravel the sources of opinion at the individual level is frustrated by one's inability to recall all the experiences that have influenced basic outlook or to accurately describe the process by which the individual became aware of the issue and acquired knowledge about it. There are so many factors influencing an individual's opinion on any given matter that only the probable influences and their relationships with each other may be posited.

FACTORS INFLUENCING PUBLIC OPINION

Family

Family influence has been widely noted in the study of opinion formation. For example, many polls have indicated that the majority of voters follow the same partisan lines as their parents. At the same time, it is not uncommon for members of a family to differ, a natural reflection of the varying experiences they have as individuals. Changes from one generation to another in economic and social status often affect political attitudes, probably more so than is revealed by overt changes in partisan allegiance. There is nothing to prevent members of a family from belonging to the same political party while, at the same time, holding differing views on specific issues or personalities. Differences of opinion in some families may be encouraged by the way in which disputes within the family are handled, or even allowed to be discussed at all. As was pointed out in the discussion of political culture, family structures in some countries are more democratic than in others, thus the nature of this influence will vary from country to country.

Religion

In societies where most members adhere to the same faith, the impact of religion on public opinion may be comparatively straightforward. But in a polyglot society such as Canada, the multiplicity of religions and the values they seek to maintain complicate this relationship. There is a tendency for certain religious groups to act politically *en bloc*, in some cases out of a general sense of group solidarity, in other cases out of a sense of special group interest in a particular issue.

In terms of involvement of a religious group in larger social and political questions, the traditions of North America are ambiguous. Some churches actively attempt to solve various economic and social problems through the political process; others have opposed this involvement. Some religious groups so involved have had a liberal, others a conservative influence. Surveys have shown that only the Jews are consistently liberal on social and political questions, while the Protestants and Catholics tend to be more conservatively oriented.[3] The influence of religion appears to be contradictory to individualistic values in a pluralistic society; regular churchgoers have been found to be less tolerant of nonconformist behaviour than those who are not. The only major religious group to deviate from this was the Jewish.

The relationship between religion and politics has been shaped in North America and some European countries by the concept of an operational, if not legal, separation of church and state. This means that although citizens may express their religious values in political terms where relevant, church organizations as such are expected to remain aloof from direct involvement in political activity. Conversely, the state is expected to refrain from interference in religious affairs. This separation may break down if the public and church authorities come into conflict over government involvement in matters which the church considers to be within its area of moral concern. In other parts of the world, religious groups are overtly active and may constitute an integral part of the political establishment. The status of the Christian

---

[3] Bernard C. Hennesey, *Public Opinion* (Belmont, Calif.: Wadsworth Publishing, 1965), pp. 206–15.

Democrats in Italy as the party publicly favoured by the Catholic Church is well known as was the collaboration of the Catholic Church in Spain with the Franco regime. Such a close connection is not always approved of by all religious leaders in the countries involved, and there has been a conspicuous effort on the part of some of the younger clerics in Italy, Spain, and the Latin American countries to break this tie on the grounds that it inexorably links the church with the fate of transient political regimes.

Education

The relationship between religion and political opinions is reasonably well documented, but such is not the case with respect to educational institutions. In most instances the educational system fosters impressions of the world and reinforces certain basic cultural values. Higher education generally appears to encourage somewhat more tolerant attitudes than the primary or secondary levels, but higher education is still an option open to only a minority in all countries. An educational system that stresses independent work and thought is likely to create a generation of more independent and tolerant individuals.

Survey evidence indicates that the higher one's educational achievement the higher the level of political knowledge, opinion holding, and activity. It also appears that a higher degree of confidence in the political process and the efficacy of one's participation in it also accompanies advanced education. A higher level of education enhances the willingness and ability of individuals to think about political issues and to hold and express opinions about them.

Peer Groups

Most individuals associate with a variety of groups in their daily lives and most of these groups have no political origins or intentions. However, individuals tend to develop or accept the norms of the groups to which they belong. These norms may have political implications, and fear of group disapproval may dictate behaviour the individual might not exhibit if she or he were a member of another group. This is an extension of the concept of role playing, where the individual anticipates certain behaviour by her or his associates and believes that they expect her or him to exhibit similar behaviour. One group situation might require aggressive behaviour, another passive. As individuals move from one setting to another, they adapt their behaviour in order to minimize or eliminate the possibility of being ostracized.

The implications of the presence of group norms for politics are quite clear. Many essentially nonpolitical attitudes, such as ethnic or religious prejudice, may be created, reinforced, or diminished, depending upon the circles in which the individual moves. When overtly political questions arise, the reaction may be based upon group values and attitudes.

Economic Factors

Certain important conclusions emerge from extensive surveys of opinion related to economic factors. First, economic interests do not dictate a given point of view for all members of a given economic group; there is diversity in all such groups. Second, the influence of economic interests is strongest where they are clearly involved in a given issue. Frequently, opinions expressed may be contrary to what may be in one's economic interest, often because the interest is not clearly understood. Other factors may also prevent unanimity within the affected group; the presence of a competing standard of judgment such as religious beliefs and the existence of differing opinions on how to best promote its interests. It is not illogical for people in business to be in favour of measures which provide a guaranteed minimum income for everybody in society, for they might believe that they will be better off when everybody has at least some money to spend. The fact that this may not be consistent with business attitudes which are hostile to government involvement in the economy would probably be overlooked, or perhaps not even perceived as a conflict of values. Third, issues which are not economic in implication seem to be little affected by an individual's economic group status.

Mass Media

The mass media deserve special attention as a factor in the formation of opinion because of the immediacy of their impact. This imparts to the media considerable influence over the intensity and direction taken by public opinion.

It is ironic that, by and large, the mass media in North America are nonpolitical. Even the prestige newspapers devote less space to strictly political matters than to such matters as sports or social notes, to say nothing of advertising. Much of the content of the electronic media in particular is geared to the statistically largest group, and its essentially nonpolitical nature apparently reflects the inclination of the average listener toward entertainment at the expense of more serious matters. This sentiment is demonstrated in the oft-heard criticism of news broadcasts because of their concentration on "bad" news as opposed to "good" news.

The lack of political content in the media in no way diminishes their potential influence in forming opinions. Intense reaction caused by programs on radio and television bear witness to this potential impact. A near-panic ensued as a result of the 1937 dramatization of H. G. Wells' novel *The War of the Worlds*. It is doubtful that such a broadcast would fool the average first-grader brought up on television, but the portrayal of the invasion of Earth from Mars in documentary form on radio was realistic enough to many who missed the opening of the program which announced that it was only a dramatization. Television has undoubtedly contributed to a deglamorization of warfare by bringing the tragedies of Indo-China and the Middle East into peoples' living rooms. The possibilities of a heightened impact of events when reported by radio was magnified immensely by television. Dramatic events such as the assassination and funeral of President Kennedy, the near-tragedy of Apollo XIII, and the first landing on the moon illustrate the immediacy that a television camera and transmitting system can provide.

Studies of the effect of the media on public opinion indicate that people have more confidence in television than in the printed word. They can, after all, see it for themselves. This credibility has been undermined in recent years by the feeling that television reporting may be subject to as much bias in editing and reporting as newspapers or magazines.

The relationship between the electronic media and the government varies between countries and produces differing results. In countries where the media are largely under the control of private enterprise, the profit motive is naturally present. Thus the emphasis is on reaching wide audiences so as to be able to attract sponsors who will be willing to underwrite the programs and to some extent subsidize the usually unprofitable public-service broadcasts. This has led to criticism of private broadcasting for devoting insufficient attention to public affairs, just as government networks are often criticized for not providing sufficient "popular" programming. There is evidence to suggest that, in both public and private broadcasting in North America, reporters and editors in news and documentary programs have gone beyond objective reporting and indulged in editorializing and the expression of personal views. There is also the demonstrated danger in private broadcasting that pressures from sponsors of public affairs programs may alter their content or even prevent certain material from being aired at all.

In countries where the electronic media are largely under the control of government, the need to cater to advertisers is not so pressing so long as the political leadership is willing to use sufficient public funds to provide for programming. The recent trend in Canada has been to reduce, and ultimately eliminate, advertising from the government network, the CBC. At the same time it has come under increasing pressure to provide more Canadian programming of quality which would require yet more public funds. The rulings of the Canadian Radio and Television Commission (CRTC) on the proportion of "Canadian content" in broadcasting has put pressure on private as well as public broadcast networks to get away from the tradition of relying upon United States private network programs or imports from Britain. In addition, the spread of cable television in Canada has meant that even wider dispersal of American programming is now possible. Tighter regulation governing cable operations have been announced to discourage these trends. A revision of the taxation laws has been undertaken to discourage Canadian advertising on U.S. border stations.

In any country the use of electronic media is a specially sensitive subject. In France during the De Gaulle years, for instance, the government network permitted opposition political groups, even during elections campaigns, the most minimal access to radio and television. The United States was treated to a variation of this phenomenon, particularly during the years of the Nixon administration. Some rather obvious efforts were made to use the federal regulatory agencies to discipline the television networks for their critical reporting of the government's policies. Such efforts at monopolization or control of the media in a democratic system are a threat to the system itself, as democracies can operate properly only if the channels of communication are open, whereas it is expected in authoritarian systems that the media would be controlled as an instrument of propaganda and socialization. As a result, alternative sources of information and ideas are limited to clandestine channels: the "grapevine," foreign radio and television broadcasts, illegal newspapers such as the current *Samiszdat* in Russia, and illegally imported books. In many Eastern European countries after 1947 it was illegal to listen to foreign radio stations such as the Voice of America or the BBC.

Direct ownership or control over the organs of communication is not the only way in which the government may influence what is presented to the public. In every democratic system complaints have been made that government officials have "managed" the news in one way or another by either simply not providing information or explanation of events to the media or by presenting it in such a way as to create favourable impressions of the government's actions. The sheer size of many modern governments makes it difficult for outsiders to get accurate information, even when the bureaucrats are inclined to be cooperative, and much less when they are determined to frustrate enquiry. An example of this was the effort by the Nixon administration in the United States to prevent the publication of the so-called

"Pentagon Papers" in 1973. These documents were leaked to the press by an employee of a research group under contract to the U.S. Department of Defense and revealed a picture of American policy in Vietnam quite at variance with the public posture. The government sought, and got a temporary restraining order against the *New York Times* and *Washington Post,* who had initiated publication. The U.S. Supreme Court overturned the injunction and publication continued. The relations between the government and the media took an even more bizarre and momentous turn when it was revealed that the Nixon Administration had been involved in a number of illegal and unethical practices during the 1972 presidential campaign. Again, an effort was made to prevent disclosure, but the "Watergate Affair," as it came to be known, could not be swept under the carpet. Ultimately the media, the congress, and the courts all became involved in a struggle to pry the truth out of a reluctant administration. This developed into the constitutional struggle of the century and led to the initiation if impeachment proceedings against the president. Government official after official was forced to resign, some to face prosecution and conviction for a wide variety of offences from tax evasion to illegal wiretapping. This process involved cabinet members, the vice president, and finally forced the president himself to resign. It is quite safe to say that without an enterprising and aggressive media these events would never have come to pass.

MEASURING PUBLIC OPINION

The only way to discover the nature of public opinion on a given subject is to ask a sample of the public directly. Such enquiry, to be useful, must include information concerning both the distribution of attitudes and the intensity with which they are held.

A number of impressionistic polls have been in common use for years, such as the "straw" poll often used to predict elections. In such polls a few general questions will be asked of a group of indiscriminately selected persons. Such polls are unreliable, as the group which is actually polled may not be representative of anything that would lend itself to reasonable projections. Telephone polls are unreliable as they must be brief. People are also reluctant to talk to total strangers about controversial matters over the phone. Many poor people do not have phones of their own, thus compromising the representativeness of the poll. Polls conducted by mail suffer from a different failing; they must rely on the respondent to fill out the questionnaire and return it. The return rate is normally low and those returned have the natural tendency to reflect the attitudes of the more committed and articulate members of the community. By contrast, a scientific personal interview survey, though time-consuming, expensive, difficult to manage, and subject to a variety of errors, is a far more precise instrument for determining public opinion.

Polling Techniques

The first factor that must be considered in making a survey of this type is the nature and limits of the group to be studied. This group is referred to as the "population" and the actual individuals to be queried as the "sample." This is an important distinction as the population is normally far larger than is practical to interview. The researcher, after defining the population to be studied, must then decide how large a sample is necessary. Many people become confused about polls at this point, for they fail to understand how a survey involving perhaps only 2,000 persons could possibly say anything accurate or significant about public opinion in a society the size of Canada. What is not generally understood is that the sample is very carefully selected so that it is reflective of the population in all its identifiable characteristics. Even a very complex population can be reconstructed in matters of age, sex, ethnic origin, religious groupings, and occupational and income categories. Experience has shown that a degree of accuracy in measuring attitudes may be reached with a sample considerably smaller than 1,000 respondents, while samples that run larger than 2,000 present a situation of diminishing returns. Accuracy is improved with a larger sample but the added time, expense, and effort involved is far greater than the improved accuracy can justify. There are sources of possible error other than sample size so that once the sample has passed an optimum size the degree of inaccuracy created by these errors may be as great as that resulting from a smaller sample. Polling results are normally reported in terms of a margin of error of plus or minus a given percentage.

Having chosen the population and sample, it is necessary to determine the content of the poll. It may be a poll commissioned by a detergent manufacturer to determine the most appealing brand name for a new product or by an automobile manufacturer to determine what kind of car the public may want. A good case of a misapplied poll was that used by the Ford Motor Company which resulted in a decision to bring forth the ill-fated Edsel. The market research survey was taken in the usual fashion and opinions favourable to the idea of the Edsel were discovered. However, several years elapsed between the initial poll and the introduction of the car, and by the time the Edsel was introduced, public opinion had changed substantially. The resulting failure of the car did not invalidate the earlier poll, but the lapse in time did.

Proper timing in polling must be accompanied by proper construction of the questionnaire. For the results to be valid, the questionnaire used must be standardized and those doing the interviewing must follow the same format. The actual questionnaire should be carefully prepared and any words or phrases that might confuse, offend, or intimidate the respondents must be left out. Leading questions must be avoided as a certain percentage of respondents is likely to be looking for clues as to what they are expected to think or know. They then reply, saying not what they feel but what they think the interviewer wants to hear. Many people are defensive about their lack of extensive knowledge when confronted by a professional interviewer and they must be put at ease, as must those who are afraid to discuss controversial subjects. Political polls are, by their nature, controversial and the defensiveness or fear on the part of the respondent must be minimized by cautious wording and careful selection of interviewers. It is as important to have interviewers who know how to ask difficult questions inoffensively and without apparent prejudice as it is to phrase the questions properly.

Most major polling efforts are prefaced by a test poll where the questions to be used and the interviewing techniques are tried out. The results are then analyzed for any signs that important questions have been omitted or improperly worded. Researchers generally begin constructing a questionnaire with a long list of questions they would like to ask and then reduce this number to a manageable size. An overly long and complicated poll results in inaccuracies; it may bore or confuse the respondent and thus distort the result.

The common form of questions are close-ended and open-ended. Close-ended questions are similar to questions on a multiple-choice examination and limit responses to a narrow range of choices. This type of question seriously limits the amount of data which can be collected and assumes that the person constructing the questionnaire has anticipated all the useful responses. The open-ended questions resemble those on an essay examination in that the responses may take a wide variety of forms. Open-ended questions give the respondents a chance to express themselves accurately and, though such answers are extraordinarily hard to analyse, a method of classification can be devised to accommodate these answers.

The open-ended approach has another advantage in that the questions allow people to demonstrate more fully their degree of commitment and emotional involvement. A knowledge of the depth of attachment is necessary if the analyst is to be able to offer any predictions concerning the impact of future events upon opinion. During the last days of the 1964 presidential election campaign in the United States, it was revealed that one of President Johnson's personal aides had engaged in homosexual acts in a public place. As Johnson's opponents had made an issue of morality in government, such a revelation in a society heavily influenced by restrictive sexual attitudes could have a major impact. However, the polls taken for President Johnson had indicated that while the voters were concerned about morality in government they were more concerned with other issues. The obvious implication was that a calm demeanor was in order. Without the foreknowledge of this general attitude, it is quite possible that the disclosure could have created a panic in the Johnson camp, compounding the problem and turning it into a major and dangerous issue.

The analysis of public opinion polls is a time-consuming process in spite of the assistance of sophisticated computer techniques. For purposes of analysis, a questionnaire comprised of close-ended questions requires only that all answers be tabulated, sorted, and distributed into predetermined categories. The population and sample are broken down into a large number of categories known as cells. For example, if we assume that a sample of 2,000 respondents is distributed into 50 cells and that the questionnaire contained 50 questions with four options each, the dimensions of the sorting job become clear. In order to quickly transform the data into a usable form, a computer must be used for sorting and compiling the answers. Computers have another advantage in that they can relate the survey data to information gained from previous ones stored in its memory. The extent to which the current survey deviates from the earlier survey is a check against major errors in the current effort.

The analysis of open-ended questions presents a different problem. Giving respondents the opportunity to answer a number of questions at length creates a problem of classification of the answers into categories that the computer can handle. The need for classification of the answers requires that the researcher interpret their meaning, thus introducing an element of subjective error. Once these problems are overcome, the process is generally similar to that used for close-ended questions. Though the processing of analytical data gained from open-ended questions is more time-consuming than is the close-ended type, it is a more accurate form of survey in spite of the possibilities of error in interpreting the individual answers.

Interpreting Techniques

The following pair of survey results may help to illustrate the problems involved in the interpretation of polls. Table 5–1 is a series of three polls by the Gallup organization in the United States asking for an evaluation by the public of the overall performance of the supreme court.

TABLE 5–1
Public Opinion on Supreme Court Performance, U.S. (percent)

	Excellent/Good	*Fair/Poor*	*Don't Know*
July 1967			
Republicans................ 39	52	9
Democrats 48	42	10
College educated.......... 54	45	1
Grade school 34	44	22
June 1969			
Republicans................ 28	61	11
Democrats 35	51	14
College educated.......... 43	52	5
Grade school 25	51	24
July 1973			
Republicans................ 40	50	10
Democrats 35	51	14
College educated.......... 45	51	4
Grade school 28	46	26

Source: *Public Opinion Quarterly* 38, no. 4 (Winter 1974–75): p. 628.

One of the points that emerges from the data is related to the discussion of political culture and opinion formation, where the effect of education upon the willingness or ability to express an opinion was noted. In all three survey years the college-educated group was quite willing to express an opinion while one quarter of the grade school group was not. The survey question was designed to elicit an evaluation of a rather remote governmental institution with which the average citizen has no contact. The other point which emerges is that the fluctuation in responses by the sample is greater when the variable considered is party preference rather than education. This suggests that responses may be tied to some extent to the impact of the court's activity on partisan interests. In Table 5–2, the Gallup organization reports on a series of surveys about opinion on a particular issue rather than an organization.

The death penalty was effectively abolished in June 1972 when the U.S. Supreme Court ruled that it was a capriciously used penalty. Data on executions showed quite clearly that most were carried out in the southern states and that a majority of those then under sentence were blacks or Spanish-speaking and poor. In this situation, the court did not pay much heed to public opinion as the survey indicated that the trend for nearly a decade was in favour of capital punishment.

The issue of capital punishment, as is known from the debate in Canada, is highly emotionally charged. In comparing this survey with the one on the supreme court, it is apparent that the differences of opinion between the college- and the grade-school-educated respon-

TABLE 5–2
Public Opinion on the Death Penalty, U.S. (in percent)

	Favour	*Oppose*	*Don't Know*
January 1965			
Republicans	49	40	11
Democrats	42	46	12
College educated	43	48	9
Grade school	43	44	10
February 1969			
Republicans	55	36	9
Democrats	50	40	10
College educated	52	43	5
Grade school	48	42	12
November/December 1972			
Republicans	62	29	9
Democrats	51	37	12
College educated	57	36	7
Grade school	49	34	17

Source: *Public Opinion Quarterly* 38, no. 4 (Winter 1974–75) p. 631.

dents is much less pronounced on the policy issue than on the institution of the supreme court. The difference between the two groups in
the Don't know/No opinion category ranged from 19 to 22 percent in
the surveys on the supreme court. They fluctuated in the much nar-
rower range of from 4 to 10 percent in the capital punishment survey.
Clearly, the grade-school-educated group found it easier to form an
opinion on capital punishment, which is a very specific issue that can
be perceived in personal terms, than on the more abstract question of
supreme court performance. At the same time the college-educated
group appears to have had more difficulty in making a determination
about capital punishment than about the court. It is possible that this
group suffered from a conflict between humanitarian values that are
likely to be stressed in advanced education and visceral response to a
very emotional issue.

The most prevalent use, and abuse, of survey research occurs during election campaigns. Surveys are commissioned by candidates and
party organizations to determine what the potential voters are thinking. Candidates and their advisors then use this information to help
determine the content of their campaigns. At the same time the media
also commission polls as part of their efforts to keep abreast of the
election as it develops. The media's polls are generally widely reported while the candidates polls are usually treated confidentially.
The publicly reported polls are often badly handled by newswriters
and editorialists who are often out to prove a specific point. Information as to the form and number of the questions, the size of the sample,

the margin of error, and timing are usually not reported. A poll which reveals that in a given area one party will receive 45 percent of the vote, another 40 percent, with 15 percent undecided, is likely to be used to predict impending victory for the leading party. If the margin of error and the relatively large number of "undecided" were taken into account such a prediction would obviously be hazardous.

Public opinion polls play an important role in contemporary political systems. Though their faults are numerous and well known, they are the best available means for measuring opinions. Their relatively high degree of accuracy is attested to by their repeated use by commercial as well as political clients. Those who reject polling methods do so, in many cases, because the polls reveal facets of public opinion they do not wish to believe.

MEANING OF PUBLIC OPINION

If polls are accurate, what should the attitude of the political leadership be toward them? To what extent should the leadership allow its actions to be determined by the results of opinion polls?

The public opinion poll is a better instrument for gauging the attitudes of the public on specific issues than are elections or the activities of interest groups. In any given election, the issues and personalities will be diverse and the reasons the voters use for voting one way or the other even more diverse. Elections measure single aggregates; they are only an indication of the summary conclusions of the voters. They are not summaries of opinion on specific subjects. Proof of this lies in the highly varied interpretations that political commentators put upon the results of any election. This does not negate the value of elections, but it does emphasize the fact that measurement of public opinion in its specifics is not one of the functions of an election.

At the same time, the activities of interest groups and those who petition the government by letter, demonstration, or other direct means are also misleading indicators of public opinion. Such actions are usually the activity of the committed and, on most issues most of the time, the proportion of those holding an opinion and sufficiently motivated to engage in such activity is quite small. It is easy to say that because most "letters to the editor" or calls to "talk shows" run in a given direction that they must reflect public opinion. Such an interpretation overlooks both the possibility that a large proportion of the communications may come from a small number of highly motivated fanatics and that some interest groups can mobilize their members to engage in such efforts.

The usefulness of polls for political leaders is limited by a number of factors in addition to simple technical errors. Polls may inaccurately reflect the degree of commitment of the opinion holders. Intensity of feeling is often as important as its direction. There is a wide range of potential distribution of opinion when one takes into account both direction and intensity. Probably the most dangerous configuration of opinion is that of two relatively equal groups passionately committed to contrary and mutually exclusive objectives. A good example of this kind of polarization would be the seemingly intractable situation in Northern Ireland.

The need to evaluate the intensity of opinion raises serious practical problems. If a poll reveals that 70 percent of the respondents are in favour of a proposition and 20 percent are opposed, while 10 percent do not care, an immediate reaction could be that the majority should rule. However, if the majority is one without much enthusiasm, while the minority is passionately committed, such a conclusion might be an erroneous interpretation. A fundamental political question arises as to whether a passionate minority should have its way against the wishes of the silent majority. Denying the wishes of such a minority risks its alienation and the possibility that it may become a source of serious discontent. At the same time a thwarted majority may turn aggressive as the result of its being denied its "rights." Since there is, of course, no reason why the public's wishes need correspond to what the system is capable of delivering, policy makers may be placed in impossible situations. Both sets of actions clearly fly in the face of an increasingly hostile public opinion. Where do the decision makers' responsibilities lie? Should they conform to public opinion as best as it can be deciphered or use their admittedly superior sources of information as to the actual nature of the situation and their own consciences as their guide? This is a question that has bedeviled political leaders for centuries.

Thus a knowledge of the content of public opinion does not relieve the decision maker of the responsibility for making decisions. It can perhaps indicate what the public will tolerate as well as what it wants, and in many cases the former may be as useful as the latter. Public opinion as measured in polls is essentially a passive input into the system since it must be sought out. The organized expression of opinion by interest groups is the basic active input of opinion into the political system. To the extent that the activities of such groups correspond reasonably well to the general distribution of opinions in any society, the task of the decision maker is made a little easier.

ACTIVE INTEREST ARTICULATION

Thus far the discussion has centered on how opinions, or interests, may be sought out in what can be characterized as passive interest articulation. The various measures of public opinion and interests such as public opinion surveys are largely passive as they merely seek out opinion. When individuals and groups attempt to make their presence felt by their own activity, one enters into a different phase by which the attitudes of the community are revealed.

The processes by which individuals and groups make their interest known to the decision makers are quite varied and are an indispensable part of all political systems. The central feature of a democratic political system is the degree to which individuals and groups in the society are allowed to press their respective interest without undue censure or reprisal from the authorities. This is a manifestation of the extent of subsystem autonomy, for the complex of interests formed by active individuals and groups may be considered as a subsystem of the overall political system. The effectiveness of the articulation process as a whole is directly related not only to this autonomy but also to its diversity, that is, to the extent that the interests presented reasonably approximate the actual diversity within the society. If significant groups are prevented from expressing their interests freely, they may resort to disruptive or revolutionary activity. The importance of interest articulation to political stability is recognized even in authoritarian systems, although the emphasis there is placed upon the articulation of support rather than the proliferation of demand.

Restricting the scope and influence of interest articulation to the extent that it seriously distorts the existing patterns of public opinion may result in *anomic interest articulation*. This term refers to spontaneous, unpremeditated demonstrations or acts of political violence. Such action may be taken either by an individual or a group. The assassination of political leaders by individuals, such as that of U.S. President John F. Kennedy in 1963 (assuming the validity of the official version of this event) or of D'arcy McGee in Canada are examples of this form of behaviour. The assassination of civil rights leader Martin Luther King in 1968 has more of the characteristics of an organized event, though much of the evidence is open to debate. In Canada the kidnapping and subsequent murder of Quebec Labour Minister Pierre Laporte in 1970 was an organized act, albeit of a very small group, rather than an instance of anomic behaviour. On a larger scale, many of the major race-related riots in the United States during the 1960s and the Montreal riots during the 1970 police strike appear to have been largely anomic in origin.

Riots and demonstrations, no matter how disorderly, may be planned by a group or groups interested in promoting dissension for their own ends. It is also quite possible that such events may begin without any structure or leadership but acquire them as developments unfold. One should not confuse the later posturings of political opportunists with the reality of the situation, for it may be expedient for the leaders of some groups, surprised by the outbreak of a riot or demonstration, to claim responsibility for them to enhance their own image and power. Naturally, if such claims arise, those who were the targets of the events may find comfort in having an identifiable enemy and thus be eager to accept such posturing at face value.

This confusion indicates one of the most critical problems concerning anomic events: the difficulty in assigning a realistic meaning to them. Due to their disorganized and spontaneous character, they offer few clues as to what the participants want. This type of behavior arises when individuals or groups feel that their needs are not being met, that their interests are not being served, and that the normal political or other channels of influence are not effective for them. It is not necessary that they be in fact so treated but only that they believe themselves to be. The gap between the alienated and the leadership (and, by implication, the rest of the community) may be so great that the leaders really believe that they are being responsive. Such situations demonstrate the existence of inadequate articulation structures, for if the leadership believes that it is responding and the groups involved are equally convinced that it is not, then communications must be distorted.

Anomic activity is a highly visible and dramatic form of interest articulation which, by its nature, has several disadvantages from the standpoint of those using it. The initial shock value may be useful, but it is one thing to use such means to get attention and another to repeat the events so often that shock and alarm turn into hostility and repression. Anomic behaviour is quite likely to be counterproductive if indulged in too frequently, but, of course, its disorganized nature means that no one can control its frequency. Its highly ephemeral nature means that it will be difficult for even the most well-intentioned leadership to understand the issues involved. Extended repetition may induce the leaders to emphasize "law and order" at the expense of the issues involved. The resultant frustration may encourage such groups to either lapse into apathy or begin organized activity. Assuming that the intent of the participants is a redress of their grievances, it is difficult to imagine a form of interest articulation less suited to success. There is very little evidence that such activity is of benefit to the protesting groups to any significant degree.

Informal Interest Articulation

Probably the oldest and the most ubiquitous form of interest articulation is *self-representation*, where demands and supports are communicated on a personal basis.[4] In such circumstances the effectiveness of articulation depends on the nature of the relationship between the individuals involved. This form of interest articulation is found in all political systems and is dominant where decision making is in the hands of a small elite, such as in traditional political systems and in modern dictatorships. In political systems with a complex of highly organized groups, such as Canada or the United States, this form plays a less significant role.

A political system that relies heavily upon this type of interest articulation operates under a number of handicaps. Such interest articulation may amount to little more than an interaction among the decision-making elite itself and a circle of immediate friends and associates. This method will satisfy moral conditions so long as the rest of the population remains passive and uninvolved. However, the inevitable isolation of the elite from the rest of society may lead to a situation where the interest of the citizenry are seriously neglected, resulting in stringent demands for political reform.

Many regimes that have fallen into this condition have contained leaders of a reformist character who, given the opportunity, might have saved much of the old system. What is usually required in this situation is a broadening of the base of the decision-making structure, a condition which an entrenched elite is often unwilling to accept.

As government grows increasingly complex, it becomes dangerous to rely heavily upon self-representation as a major source of information about the needs and desires of the public. It is difficult for a small elite to be truly competent in all matters of state and for them to restrain those members of the elite who would abuse their positions. Such personalized systems have a history of feuds between families and cliques. A narrow base of interest articulation is also likely to result in necessary information not reaching the decision makers, handicapping them in assessing present situations and future problems. Inappropriate decisions may go uncriticized for lack of any recognizable means of doing so or from the fear of criticizing the elite. However annoying it may be at times, the saving grace of the complex of interest articulation structures found in a modern democracy is that few, if any, policy decisions are likely to remain unchallenged. It is implicit in democratic theory that decision makers should not be allowed to evade public scrutiny lest they forget whose interests are supposedly being served. Even misdirected and invalid criticism can be regarded as having some value.

---

[4] The classification of interest articulation is derived from Gabriel Almond and G. Bingham Powell, Jr., *Comparative Politics: A Developmental Approach* (Boston: Little, Brown & Co., 1966), pp. 74–79.

A variation on personal representation is *proxy representation*, the representation of a group by a sympathetic member of the decision-making organizations who is not himself or herself a member of the group represented. Elected politicians may retain close connections with groups outside the government and, though not being either members of or formally employed spokespersons (lobbyists) for the group, nevertheless may be counted upon to represent their interests. Through such sympathizers, groups such as the blacks in the United States and the Indians and Metis groups in Canada have had their interests made known in periods where they were not politically organized enough to speak with any force for themselves. In such situations these advocates are not necessarily responding to electoral pressure, at least not from the group they are representing, but rather to their own beliefs and sense of justice. Without the backing of a strong, organized group such a form of representation is obviously far less desirable than a more organized form. In addition, it has all the vices of personal representation plus the added disadvantage of a possibility of error or misunderstanding on the part of a well-intentioned spokesperson. It can only be regarded as a temporary form to cover the phase in the development of an interest that lies between a passive, inarticulate stage and a self-aware, organized stage where the group in question can speak for itself.

Organized Interest Articulation

A discussion of organized interest articulation is concerned with the activities of organized interest groups that have developed regularized patterns of contact with the political decision makers. There is a great variety of patterns of relationships between the groups and the political leaders, amongst the groups themselves, and in the internal structures and relationships of the various groups.

The least important type of interest group, from the political point of view, is the *nonassociational interest group.* Its primary focus is upon family, religious, ethnic, or linguistic matters, so it is rarely likely to feel the need to be politically active. It may, however, become politically active if it feels threatened. An example would be the response of a religious group which decides to protest an easing of abortion laws or drinking regulations by sending a delegation to meet with officials, or even organizing a public demonstration.

A group such as this faces a number of problems in relating effectively to the political leadership. The more politically sophisticated interest groups will have long since worked out their relationship within the political system and come to an understanding with certain elements of the leadership. The nonassociational group has little, if any, of the intimate knowledge of the workings of the system. As such it is likely to be given little consideration unless it finds some gimmick to attract sufficient public attention to force the leadership to deal with them. Even so, lacking a network of contacts and significant experience, such a group may quickly lose its newfound advantage through an inability to exploit its initial gains. It takes resources, organization, and, most importantly, credibility with the leadership, to sustain influence. In order to gain this influence, an organization must orient itself to the long-term build up and husband its political resources. The likelihood that a nonassociational group will be able to do this is not great. The political leadership and the other interest groups in the system know this only too well.

An *institutional interest group* is made up of individuals who, by occupation, are members of one of the formal organizations of the society, including the government. Such groups arise as common interests emerge among people who hold positions in the same organization. For example, a group of military officers may act in concert to strengthen the position of the military within the country. Given their responsibility for defence, these officers are likely to have specific views concerning the organization, policies, manpower, and materials necessary for the discharge of their responsibilities. These also have social, political, and economic implications which are of concern to the civilian leadership. Thus, differences between the military and civilian leadership are almost certain to arise, and this inherent tension will inevitably become a part of the political scene. Oftentimes one finds both the military and civilian leadership internally divided on issues, with some civilians supporting one faction of the military, some the other. This sort of conflict occurred during the long debate over the unification of the Canadian armed forces, a move favoured by many civilian leaders in the name of overall efficiancy and economy and opposed by most military leaders because of its possible effects on morale and the logistical problems it entailed. Many of the widely publicized discussions on equipment acquisition by the military, in Canada and elsewhere, often puts one faction of the military and civilian leaderships against other military and civilian factions.

Institutional interest groups are found in all parts of society. Among the more vociferous civilian institutional groups in the last few years have been the organizations of police officers. They have been involved in quests for pay raises and improvements in working conditions, but the most notable aspect of their involvement in the political process has been their agitation for the implementation of capital punishment for murderers of police officers and prison guards and their advocacy of tighter bail and probation policies. As they see it, the relaxation of judicial penalties and the freer use of bail and parole has seriously handicapped them in their fight against crime. The forces which led to the present policy were generated by other groups who felt that the traditional system was inadequate and inhumane. The political leadership has been forced to choose between the importunings of a specialized group with a specific task to perform and the wishes of a broader range of groups interested in reforming specific features of the overall legal system.

An institutional interest group is, by its nature, likely to be important. Its members are among the administrators and decision makers of the system. They are in a favourable position to influence other decision makers and often also to influence public opinion, either directly, or through the time-tested device of the information "leak" from a "usually reliable source." In situations where a high degree of technical knowledge is necessary for decision making, these groups often have access to the information resources of the political system not normally available to those outside the government. They are also in a position to frustrate the efforts of outside interest groups to gain needed information from governmental sources. The political leadership can, in fact, be put into a difficult situation, as it must rely upon its experts to assess the validity of information or policy options. This presents an issue critical to the political system; namely, to what extent should a political leader rely upon experts as opposed to his or her own common sense, intuition, or the apparent desires of the general public? There are enough examples of the errors of "experts" to make it a plausible question, just as there are good examples of what happens when a political leadership ignores its experts.

Two excellent examples of this dilemma can be found in World War II. In the spring and summer of 1940 the French army disintegrated in the face of German attack in spite of the fact that on paper the French army and air force were the equal of the Germans, and the French were operating from the presumed advantage of a strong defensive position. The French General Staff had learned the lessons of World War I so well that they refused to learn any new ones regarding the use of aircraft, armour, and modern communications.[5] The political leadership operated through the 1930s on the assumption that the experts knew what they were doing. In contrast as the war drew to a close, Hitler, and his staff, consistently refused to listen to the information and advice of their experts.

The most obvious and generally recognized interest articulation structures are the *associational interest groups*. These groups are specifically organized to represent group interests to the other organizations in the political system. Examples of such groups would be

---

[5] William L. Shirer, *The Fall of the Third Republic* (New York: Simon & Schuster, 1969), chapter 12.

labour unions, business groups, and permanent political organizations set up by consumer and civil right interests. They are distinct from the other forms because they are formed specifically to articulate interests in a political manner. They normally have professional staff, and regularized methods and channels of communication. As they are explicitly interest articulators, they tend to be treated as a part of the political system and accepted as legitimate political bodies by other political groups and the society as a whole.

In assessing the role of associational interest groups, one caveat should be offered. Most political systems have some organizations which superficially share the characteristics of associational interest groups, but lack one essential ingredient—true independence. For example, it is common for a communist party to establish "interest groups" under different names as an extension of the party organization. These groups do not promote their own interests but rather the goals and values of the parent organization. Similarly, the Catholic Church in France and Italy has promoted its own labour organizations, although a comprehensive and effective articulation process probably does not exist. This condition is often perceived by potential members of interest groups, thus encouraging cynicism or apathy among them. These "common fronts," therefore, do not adequately fulfill the information and communication functions normally associated with interest groups. It is characteristic of totalitarian political systems that all interest groups are fronts controlled by the elite party. The extent to which interest groups are independent is one of the measures of the degree of freedom in any political system.

TECHNIQUES OF INTEREST ARTICULATION

There are a variety of articulation techniques open to interest groups, the most obvious of which are demonstrations and violence. It was pointed out earlier that such expressions were characteristic of anomic interest articulation and were likely to be counterproductive. There are numerous examples of structured interest groups using these techniques but normally only in the case of the failure of other, less controversial, methods of expression. Having exercised positive influence in the past, most structured groups prefer to use the tried and traditional methods rather than resort to such risky techniques. In political systems where the channels of influence are deliberately restricted or where the political structures are incapable of processing the inputs, demonstrations and violence may become a regular occurrence, being the only readily available means of influencing the decision makers in the system.

The avenues of influence chosen by an interest group are dependent upon a number of factors. Of obvious importance is the perceived centre of decision making, which may vary from system to system. In the Canadian system the tradition has been to focus upon the Cabinet and the civil service as the primary points of contact. This is partly because they are intimately involved in devising and implementing policy. Also, the relationship between the legislature and the Cabinet is such that the latter dominates, and is informed and advised primarily by the bureaucracy. It is, therefore, logical to concentrate on the advisors and the decision makers rather than upon the party organizations or upon the legislature itself. The nature of the object of interest articulation then conditions the techniques likely to be effective. Accessibility to the decision makers also limits interest group activity. In Canada it is quite difficult to develop continuous and deep ties with the Cabinet because of its extensive, time-consuming responsibilities. So a premium is placed upon long-standing relationship with specific bureaucrats which enables the interest group to generate an input directly into the information system of the government and provides the bureaucrats with a means of generating an input into the interest group. In the long run the interest group needs its bureaucratic allies more than they need the interest groups, and evidence suggests that to a considerable extent the relationships between interest groups and bureaucracy in Canada have been dominated by the latter.[6]

Having cultivated a workable, if not ideal, relationship with the relevant administrators, the interest group would be reluctant to pursue alternate methods of exerting influence if such a course is likely to offend their allies. Thus demonstrations, publicity campaigns, electoral efforts, and so forth all have to be evaluated on the basis of not only their intrinsic value, but also in terms of the impact upon the bureaucracy.

A recent study of the role of interest groups in Canada reached the conclusion that by and large their tactics were fairly uniform. As shown in Table 5–3 the belief that the civil service was the focus of this activity seems to have been confirmed.

From Table 5–3 it is obvious that economic and occupational interest groups (mostly of the associational type) focused their interests and activity initially on the civil service, and then upon the Cabinet and their executive assistants. The only exception to this pattern was the behaviour of the labour groups who chose the legislature as their primary focus. Given the fact that they have been in many cases allied with what has to date been an opposition party, the New Democratic Party, it is quite possible that they feel unwelcome at both the ad-

---

[6] Helen Jones Dawson, "Pressure Groups in Canadian Bureaucracy: Farm Organizations in Canada", in *Bureaucracy in Canadian Government,* ed. W. D. K. Kernaghan (Toronto: Methuen and Co., 1969), pp. 105–11.

TABLE 5–3
Primary Targets of Interest Group Activity, in Canada (in percent)

Target	*Prof.†*	*Lab.*	*Bus.*	*Ed.*	*Wel.*	*S-R†*	*Rel.*	*F-S*
		*Economic/Occupational Interest Groups**				*Other Groups**		
Civil service	23	32	51	46	50	50	31	21
Cabinet and executive assistants to Cabinet	32	9	27	31	23	11	31	21
(Subtotal)	(55)	(41)	(78)	(77)	(73)	(61)	(62)	(42)
Legislature and legislative committees	34	51	19	16	21	11	19	57
Other	8	7	2	7	5	26	19	—

* Agricultural and ethinic groups not included due to insufficient data.

† Prof.: Professional   S-R: Social-Recreational
   Lab.: Labour   Rel.: Religions
   Bus.: Business   F-S: Fraternal-Service
   Ed.: Education
   Wel: Welfare

Source: Adapted from Robert Presthus, *Elite Accommodation in Canadian Politics* (London: Cambridge University Press, 1973), p. 153.

ministrative and Cabinet levels. It is also possible that, given the history of early hostility to union organizations, which has been replaced by grudging acceptance in more recent years, union leaders still do not feel part of the decision making elite. They may feel that they must resort to more public forums to make their case. The "other groups," include many nonassociational interest groups, which would be likely to have only sporadic interest in political issues. In the matter of tactics, the same study provides the data in Table 5–4.

It is clear that the most preferred tactic is to enlist the membership of the organization in a campaign to influence the decision makers. This can be done by a variety of means, the best known being letter writing campaigns to bureaucrats, Cabinet ministers, MPs, and the passing of resolutions at official meetings of the organizations. Personal visits to the decision makers is a high-priority tactic and one whose effectiveness clearly depends upon ready access to and credibility with them. This underscores the importance of developing long-term relationships between the spokespersons for the interest groups, bureaucrats, and politicians. It is also clear that there is a general reluctance to rely primarily on alternate devices, such as publicity campaigns that take the groups' case to the public or on the formation of alliances with other groups. The exceptions are the labour unions, again probably for the reasons noted in connection with their variance

TABLE 5–4
Primary Tactics of Interest Groups, in Canada (in percent)

| | *Proportion Ranking Each Tactic First* | | | | | | | |
| | *Economic/Occupational Interest Groups** | | | | | *Other Groups** | | |
Tactic	*Prof.†*	*Lab.*	*Bus.*	*Ed.*	*Wel.*	*S-R†*	*Rel.*	*F-S*
Enlist membership	46	27	33	34	23	26	17	44
Personal visits to politicians, civil servants and cabinet	23	22	33	43	27	34	21	17
Publicity campaigns	18	22	12	11	23	6	17	33
Other	14	29	22	12	27	34	37	6

* Agricultural and ethinic groups not included due to insufficient data.
† Prof.: Professional   Wel.: Welfare
  Lab.: Labour   S-R: Social-Recreational
  Bus.: Business   Rel.: Religions
  Ed.: Education   F-S: Fraternal-Service
Source: Adapted from Robert Presthus, *Elite Accommodation in Canadian Politics* (London: Cambridge University Press, 1973), p. 157.

in primary targets and the welfare groups. This latter exception may be a result of the fact that these groups by and large are relative newcomers to the political scene and may not have had sufficient time to establish their contacts and their credibility.

Clearly, interest groups perceive the need for intensive relationships with governmental agencies and the civil servants who work in them. It should be kept in mind that senior civil servants, in their capacity as advisors to the Cabinet, are in a position to influence many important inputs into the policy-making process. In addition, once a decision is made, it is these same bureaucrats who are entrusted with the job of implementing the policy. If a group wins its case at the policy-making level, it is prudent to continue its work and ensure that the policy is properly implemented. As for the losers in the policy-making process there is the opportunity to ameliorate the effects of that loss by persuading those implementing it to take a more "generous" view of their case. In some instances, it may even be possible to frustrate the implementation altogether. All of this manoeuvring requires individuals well versed in the subject matter and with the contacts and knowledge about the power relationships to act effectively. Such persons, usually paid professionals, are referred to as lobbyists. Lobbying is a very highly developed activity at the federal level in the United States and in some of the larger states, but it has not been as well developed in Canada at either the federal or provincial levels.

Lobbyists are a much criticized group of political actors. Their collective reputation is based on experiences from the latter 1800s and early 1900s when they regularly engaged in the outright vote buying of legislators and bribing of administrative and judicial officials. These practices still remain, but they are risky and politically damaging if discovered and publicized. The fate of many associates of President Richard Nixon as a result of the Watergate scandals or the embarrassment to the Trudeau government caused by the suspicion that officials were involved in underhanded dealing with the Seaman's International Union (SIU) are examples of risks involved in underhanded practice. The ability of the lobbyist to provide useful information to decision makers about the effects of policy alternatives and express accurately public attitudes on the issues appear to be his most useful technique. A conscientious lobbyist is probably more effective in serving his or her client's interests in the long run, since political leaders can be reasonably certain that they will not be publicly compromised by the lobbyist's activities and that they can rely upon him or her for accurate information.

If the commonly used tactics of lobbying, such as letter writing and personal contacts, fail, it is always possible to take the issue to the public via the media. The media in a democratic system have the responsibility of informing the public about issues and personalities in politics. This is not easy, due to the volume of information to be communicated and to the fact that governmental and nongovernmental personalities are often not quite candid about their ideas and their activities. From the point of view of the interest group the media's coverage of events may well result in a wider dissemination of information about their particular interests and activities. The extensive coverage of the public debate over the White Paper on Taxation in 1970 and the Green Paper on Immigration in 1975 are examples of this. Some groups enjoy easier access to the media than others because they are among the major or most prestigious groups in the community. Others enjoy access through the "newsworthy" tactics they use in illustrating their concerns.

The least-used technique for utilizing the media as an access channel is direct advertising. Few groups can afford the finances required for an effective advertising campaign. It is often possible, however, to use sponsorship of television programs as a means of creating favourable impressions. Much of the advertising done by private and public monopolies, such as telephone and power utilities, fall into this classification. So also do other corporations which do not deal directly with the public.

Several other factors affect a group's decision as to the tactics to be used in promoting its interests. As was pointed out earlier, whether or not the group is already a recognized part of the political system is critical to its success. If it is not, and if it is experiencing difficulty in gaining recognition as a legitimate group, it may resort to more aggressive methods than are normal. A small organization composed of wealthy and respected members of the community could be expected to rely primarily upon discreet personal contacts and direct lobbying. A mass organization, such as a labour union, is likely to find demonstrations more useful. A show of numerical strength offsets the disadvantage, at least in North America, of being one of the less-respected interest groups.

The activities of interest groups may be limited by their internal composition. Most groups are made up of individuals with varied interests who may belong to several groups. Members join a particular group for a variety of motives and many view the organization from different perspectives. There is, thus, considerable potential for conflict within most interest groups, and it is unlikely that any interest group leader can realistically claim to speak for every member of the organization. The political leaders that the groups try to impress know this and, depending upon their assessment of the state of affairs within the group, may discount their presentations. Most political leaders have themselves been members of such organizations and have learned from experience the possibility of internal disagreement even on issues central to the groups' existence. The inability of the leadership of the interest groups to lead all its members down one path is illustrated with every election when a certain percentage of labour union members vote Conservative or Liberal rather than New Democratic Party or when some business and professional people opt for the New Democrats rather than the Liberals or Conservatives.

This lack of unanimity within interest groups in many instances is compounded by a degree of apathy or alienation among the members. The average member attends few meetings and seldom votes either on policies or officers. The incumbent leadership of such groups often remains in office for long periods, and any elections are simply *pro forma* legitimizations of their rule. This comes less from design than from the fact that most members simply do not get involved sufficiently in the groups to which they belong to know what happens on a day-to-day basis. As a consequence, much of what a group does officially takes little account of the members. The extent to which the leadership speaks for the bulk of the members is then determined largely by its sensitivity and conscientiousness. The leadership, in order to maintain its long-term effectiveness and credibility, may try to overcome this natural inclination of the membership to lapse into apathy. It feels that it must find ways of involving its members and, most of all, show that it is able to deliver results to them. An interest group that cannot protect its members' interests is quite likely to be abandoned by them for one that can.

The low level of involvement of the membership in organizational affairs increases the likelihood that the incumbent leadership will dominate the recruitment process. Their choice of successors could fall upon their supporters, preferably those who have helped to carry the burden of running the organization while holding a lower office in it. Thus, many interest groups are characterized by a leadership selection process that emphasizes continuity. The phenomenon of choosing from among "office boys" is not confined to interest groups, but applies to other organizations as well.

Interest groups are often initiated and then built up by men of imagination and energy. Frequently this spirited and individualistic leadership gives way to bureaucratic types in the process of succession. The history of many trade unions in North America provides examples of this, as does the succession to power in the Soviet Union, where leaders of the calibre of Lenin and Trotsky were replaced by organization men such as Stalin whose main virtues seem to be reliability and orthodoxy.

Interest groups, in attempting to carry out their function in the political scheme of things, are thus faced with a number of problems as well as prospects. They are highly varied and their behaviour is influenced considerably by their environment. The following chapter will focus on the ways by which the various specific inputs expressed through public opinion polls and interest group activity are aggregated into policy alternatives.

RECOMMENDED READINGS

Almond, Gabriel, and Verba, Sidney. *The Civic Culture.* Princeton, N.J.: Princeton University Press, 1963.

Eckstein, Harry. *Pressure Group Politics.* Stanford: Stanford University Press, 1960.

Ehrmann, H. W. *Interest Groups on Four Continents.* Pittsburgh: University of Pittsburgh Press, 1958.

Fox, Paul, ed. *Politics: Canada.* Toronto: McGraw–Hill Company of Canada, Ltd., 1970.

Hennessy, Bernard C. *Public Opinion.* Belmont, Calif.: Wadsworth Publishing, 1965.

Key, V. O. *Public Opinion and American Democracy.* New York: A. A. Knopf, 1961.

Lijphart, Arend. *The Politics of Accommodation.* Berkeley: University of California Press, 1969.

Lipset, Seymour M.; Trow, M.; and Coleman, James S. *Union Democracy.* Glencoe, Ill.: The Free Press, 1956.

Parry, Geraint. *Political Elites.* New York: Praeger, 1969.

Porter, John. *The Vertical Mosaic.* Toronto: University of Toronto Press, 1965.

Presthus, Robert. *Elite Accommodation in Canadian Politics.* Cambridge: Cambridge University Press, 1973.

Pross, A. Paul, ed. *Pressure Group Behaviour in Canadian Politics.* Toronto: McGraw–Hill Ryerson, 1975.

Schwartz, Mildred A. *Public Opinion and Canadian Identity.* Berkeley: University of California Press, 1967.

Zeigler, Harmon. *Interest Groups in American Society.* Englewood Cliffs, N.J.: Prentice–Hall, 1964.

6

Interest Aggregation

THE AGGREGATION OF INTERESTS lies between the articulation of interests and the rule making functions in a political system. It is the process by which the multiplicity of articulated interests is reduced to a smaller number of policy alternatives that are amenable to decision making.[1] The vast number of interests articulated in a modern and complex society would quickly overwhelm the most competent decision-making apparatus unless these inputs were processed and filtered by the political system. Some interests may be shunted aside as irrelevant, unimportant, or simply not of high enough priority; the remainder are aligned into aggregates or combinations that have some basic underlying relationships.

The aggregation of interests, like other functions, is found in all systems and is performed by a variety of structures. Interest groups themselves are aggregations of highly specific interests. An example would be a situation in which the various specific components of the labour movement—craft, industrial, and service unions—combine to rationalize their particular interests in order to increase the likelihood that their generalized objectives will be more readily attained. The unions will have to compromise among themselves and, in so doing, perform a low order of interest aggregation. The combined labour interests then become some of the many interests competing for the attention of the political decision makers, requiring further aggregation at this level.

The primary focus of aggregation is the political party, especially in modern democratic systems. The *political party* is an organization designed to gain and hold the major decision-making positions in a

---

[1] Gabriel Almond and G. Bingham Powell, *Comparative Politics: A Developmental Approach* (Boston: Little, Brown & Co., 1966), pp. 98–100.

107

system and to recruit leaders. In democratic systems the acquisition of power is gained through competition between parties, designated as the electoral process.

The political party is involved in socialization and recruitment and interest articulation as well as interest aggregation, but its primary function is the aggregation of interests. There is a considerable interlocking of party, legislative, and administrative leaders in political systems and the functions of all of these structures overlap; nevertheless, the need to arrange the very large number of articulated interests into sets of policy alternatives tends to be of primary concern to party members and officials. The existence of parties creates a series of relationships within the political systems known as the *party system*, a subsystem of the larger unit. This party system acts to collect and process most of the interests of the society, with different parties giving priority to different combinations of them. There are three basic types of party systems: one-party, two-party, and multiparty. Each performs the aggregation function in somewhat different ways.

ONE-PARTY SYSTEMS

It is common to think of one-party systems as being all of a kind, but there are a number of variations on this structural theme. The image that comes first to mind is usually the one-party system of the type found in the Soviet Union or in Nazi Germany. Such parties as the Communist Party of the Soviet Union (CPSU) and the National Socialist German Workers' (Nazi) Party are ideological in their outlook and authoritarian in structure. If it is in power, this type of party will usually not allow other parties to function legally. The party and its ideology are the chief determinants not only of governmental policy, but of the style, content, and even the very existence of the media and interest groups. The party will require that important government officials be members of the party or of satellite groups and will expect their behaviour to conform to the policies and ideologies.

In ideological one-party systems, the decision makers and political party leaders are the same. Thus the top positions of the party, from the standpoint of the ambitious, are the most important positions in the political system. Additionally, those who have interests to express must focus their attentions on this same group of people. The fact that ideological one-party systems expect obedience does not mean that the various interests in the system do not press their points of view upon the decision makers. What it does mean is that the decision makers exercise considerable, if not total, control over how these representations are made, by whom, and when. The interest groups in this type of party system serve primarily to link the party with the people in smaller and more specialized groups. It is not a one-way communication process and even in the most monolithic party systems certain groups are sufficiently crucial as to be able to retain some autonomy.

There have been attempts in recent years in some ideological one-party systems to decentralize authority and decision making while still maintaining ideological consistency and one-party dominance. The most successful of these experiments has taken place in Yugoslavia. In the early post World War II years the regime of Marshal Tito was as rigid and repressive as that of Stalin's. Not only was the party faced with the necessity of establishing itself; it also had to deal with deep-seated hostility between several subcultures and pressure from the Soviet Union to conform to the pattern laid down by Stalin. By rigidly enforcing party unity at home and appealing to such Yugoslavian nationalism as existed among the welter of regional and ethnic sentiments, Tito was able to form a regime strong enough to resist these outside pressures. With the passage of the years since the early 1950s the regime has slowly relaxed its control. By utilizing a federal structure to give scope to regionalism, some of that pressure has been contained while strenuous efforts to build a new economy were undertaken. As the economy developed, it became apparent that the rigid centralization of authority characteristic of the Stalinist version of Marxism was in many ways a hindrance to more rapid progress. Various programs were proposed to allow for decentralization, attempting the potentially contradictory objective of the maintenance of the party as aggregator and decision maker while avoiding the logjam of decisions to be made at the centre. The dilemma of the Yugoslavian Communist party is illustrative of the difficulties of the ideological one-party system where an attempt is made to avoid the problems of overcentralization. Such decentralization is an invitation to factionalism of a type closer to that found in democratic systems, and very few ideologically oriented parties wish to see that come about.

The Yugoslav and Russian Communist parties are illustrative of another dimension of the problem associated with their ideological one-party status. It was noted by Milovan Djilas in his book, *The New Class*, that the party leadership in Communist systems tends to evolve into a new upper class of privileged individuals.[2] Djilas, at one time the heir apparent to Marshal Tito, spent considerable time in prison for his views but, with an irony often found in political life, his point has been implicitly accepted by the regime. In fact, a subsequent heir apparent of Tito's, Vice President Aleksander Rankovic, was ousted from power in 1966 allegedly because he was engaged in obstructing the decentralization program. A number of other party officials were

---

[2] Milovan Djilas, *The New Class* (New York: Praeger, 1957).

also ousted as part of a housecleaning of those who were committed to the doctrine of centralized decision making. At the same time, similar voices were heard in the Soviet Union urging its leaders to decentralize the system there. For a period in the early 1960s it appeared that this might be done, but the contradiction between the ideological and practical roles of the party was resolved in favour of continued centralization and ideological orthodoxy. The proponents of change in the U.S.S.R. have gradually been ousted from power and the intellectual critics have been called to account and silenced. Thus, whereas Yugoslavia opted for a less central role for the party, the reverse is the case in the Soviet Union.

Ideological one-party systems are also prone to severe leadership conflicts. For example, the leadership style of the Communist party in Czechoslovakia could have been characterized as centralist until the fall of 1967. The high degree of centralization and a tendency to promote loyal rather than capable men led to an economic crisis. As a result of pressure from within the party, President Antonin Novotny was deposed as party leader in January 1968 and, two months later, forced out of the presidency. The new party boss, Alexander Dubcek, initiated a series of reforms involving both the decentralization of the party and a relaxation of party controls over interest articulation, which led almost immediately to demands for further changes. A power struggle within the party between the old and the new leadership emerged into public view. Party bosses long used to dictating what the media would say found themselves in the embarrassing position of having to answer pointed questions and having their failures openly discussed by the party press. Labour unions, long an arm of the party, began to openly express their interests and, in fact, appear to have been encouraged to do so by the new leadership. Such groups and the media were apparently being used as a weapon against a resurgence of the old leadership. The latter was steadily eliminated from power during the spring of 1968 and a party congress was called for later in the year to ratify these actions, but before it could meet the armies of the Soviet Union and its allies invaded Czechoslovakia and put an end to the liberalization movement. The Russians expected to restore the previous state of affairs without difficulty. Due in part to their inadequate planning and the subtle evasions of the Czechs, the Russians were unable to gain effective control quickly. The country and the rest of the world were treated to a televised spectacle of the invasion and occupation, reported by the Czech news services themselves. Though this peculiar situation did not last long, the reinstated centralist leadership experienced difficulty in subjecting the media and the various interest groups, to say nothing of the party itself, to the former controls.

There are two other types of one-party systems besides the ideological. These are the authoritarian and democratic one-party systems. The difference between the authoritarian and the ideological types is that in the former the party is an auxiliary to the group or groups who are the decision makers. The party serves as a disseminator of information, a recruiting group for future leadership, and a means of organizing the supporters of the regime. The party does not necessarily control the governmental institutions, though it will usually be the only recognized party. In Spain, the *Falange,* generally thought of by outsiders as being similar to the Nazi party and the Italian Fascist party, was established as the single party with foreign fascist help during the Civil War (1936–39). In fact, the party was seldom more than an auxiliary of the government. It has managed to maintain some independence of action, but the leaders of the party have at times been barely able to conceal their disappointment at not being in a position to more substantially influence events.

The nondemocratic one-party system should, at first sight, possess certain advantages over other methods of interest aggregation. The centralization of authority and control should permit more coherent policies and make long-range planning significantly easier since there need be no concern over the vagaries of an electoral process. The chosen nominee will always be "elected." Such a party naturally restricts the number and variety of interests that may be considered for aggregation. Therein lies the defect, for if the authoritarian or totalitarian party is unable to maintain rigid and restricted access to the decision makers in government, it is liable to collapse. So many claims will be pressed upon the party that establishing priorities and making rational decisions will become impossible. This was one of the problems of the Nazi party in Germany. A postwar examination of this supposedly monolithic organization has revealed the existence of a morass of intra-party conflicts accompanied by vicious infighting that led to an erratic pattern of party discipline and inconsistent, often contradictory, decision making. All key decisions were so dependent upon Hitler's judgment that matters were often decided on the basis of his personal feelings and intuitions, or not decided at all if he could not bring himself to face an unpleasant situation. Decisions could also be reversed by him or subverted by his subordinates as part of their continuing jockeying for power.

The third variation on the one-party theme is that of the democratic or one-party dominant system. If this seems to be a contradiction in terms, it should be pointed out that there is nothing illogical about a system in which one party so predominates that no other group in the system can be compared to it. The party acquires such a broad basis of support that it faces no real competition in elections or in any other arena. An example of this would be in Mexico where the Institutional

Revolutionary Party (PRI) has such prestige that it regularly wins elections, normally with overwhelming majorities. In this case the party has the prestige of involvement in and leadership of the Mexican Revolution.

TWO-PARTY SYSTEMS

The two-party system as found in the United States has often been idealized in many countries in North American and elsewhere. It is argued that the system provides the citizenry with a choice of policies and leaders while at the same time guaranteeing governmental stability. The mechanics of the electoral arrangement in such a system assure a majority for one party or the other, thus ensuring that one will have the power to carry out its election promises.

The United States has historically supported two major parties since the Civil War (1861–65). There have been a number of third-party movements protesting the unwillingness, or inability, of the two major parties to accommodate certain interests. The most notable of these movements was the People's Party of the 1890s, the Progressive Party of the then ex-President Theodore Roosevelt in 1912 and the Progressive Party of Senator LaFollette in 1924. The People's Party and the 1924 Progressive Party were in large part agrarian protest movements, while the 1912 Progressive Party was a reform movement with a more middle-class orientation. None of these survived as viable parties. Generally, third parties have catered to ideologically oriented factions with very limited support. Since the turn of the century, several socialist parties, most of them Marxist in orientation, have contested elections, but they have never had any significant impact.

The most recent and widely publicized third-party effort was made in support of the presidential campaign of Alabama Governor George Wallace in 1968. The American Independent Party was established solely for the purpose of providing a vehicle for his presidential aspirations and was never intended by him to be a permanent political party competing with the established parties. The formation of third parties, either as an attempt to replace the existing major parties or as personal vehicle for individual candidates, is a frequently discussed option in the United States though little comes of such discussions given the many practical as well as cultural and psychological barriers to success.

The two-party pattern in the United States is not evenly distributed around the country. There are many states, and parts of states, that habitually give overwhelming support to either the Republicans or the Democrats. The number of electoral districts that are truly competitive is relatively small; for example, only about one quarter of the seats in the House of Representatives are considered likely to change hands in any election and normally about 10 percent actually do. The most conspicuous example of a one-party region used to be that of the "solid South." After federal forces occupying the southern states following the Civil War were withdrawn, the party system moved gradually to a single-party type and the South remained loyal to the Democratic Party almost without exception until the 1950s. This consistent preference for one party concealed the fact that certain regions of several of these states were normally Republican; in many cases these were areas which had been Unionist strongholds in the Civil War. A very loose parallel would be the persistence of strong pro-federal sentiment found in parts of Quebec.

The utility of the two-party system as a vehicle for choice rests on their being perceived as promoting clearly contrasting alternatives. Given that the two-party system is not uniformly distributed within the United States, it is clear that many areas have little choice between parties. This is compensated for by the existence of "primary" elections in which voters can select party candidates to stand in the general election. Thus even though a particular party may hold an overwhelming position in a given area, the voter has the ability to choose from among persons aspiring to be the party's candidate and thereby influence the aggregation patterns of that party. By contrast, primaries to select minority party candidates are usually uncontested and the party often has to "draft" a candidate lest the office go completely uncontested in the general election. A voter in a two-party region can vote both for the potential candidates of one's choice in a party primary and then vote for or against the party's candidates in the general election. There are numerous examples of voters, frustrated in the primary by the defeat of their favourite, who then vote for the opposition party candidate in the election.

Part of the flexibility of the two-party system of the United States lies in the fact that it can offer prospects of success to any individual or faction possessing the right combination of organization, capital, and charisma. Examples of maverick candidates and dissident factions taking control of political organizations in the various states and at the national level are numerous. The most obvious were the "capture" of the Republican national machinery by Barry Goldwater in 1964 and the Democratic "capture" by George McGovern in 1972. The evolution of George Wallace from third-party candidate in 1968 to Democratic presidential hopeful in 1976 is another example of a "capture" at work. This relative openness combined with the structural bias of the system itself has quite effectively blocked the path of third-party movements since the establishment of the Republican Party in the 1850s.

There are other political systems organized along two-party lines, the most obvious being the United Kingdom. Though there are other parties operating in competition with the Labour and Conservative parties, they have in the past played a minor role. As the British system is organized on the parliamentary style, there is the possibility that a third party, such as the Liberals or Scottish Nationalists, may hold the balance of power between the two major parties as was the case during the minority government of 1974. The party system in West Germany appeared for a time to be moving in the direction of a two-party alignment with the Social Democrats and the Christian Democrats as the major parties. In the 1969 general election neither party won a majority, thus the Free Democrats played the role of balance wheel and they have been able to maintain enough presence since then so as to continue to be a significant factor in federal and Lander (provincial) politics.

The two-party system is relatively uncommon, most political systems being organized along either one-party or multiparty lines. The origins of many one-party systems are obvious; but the question often arises as to why some modern countries function as a two-party system when these societies are so complex that it should be impossible for two parties to aggregate all the interests present and still stand for anything. This, in fact, is the source for complaints often voiced about the major parties in a two-party system; that they have no recognizable ideology or clear-cut program, that they are parties of compromise and bargain.

The presence of a two-party structure in the United States, for instance, conceals the fact that many "parties" exist under Republican and Democrat labels. These local and state parties form the "national" party mainly for the purpose of electing a president and for organizing the congress. Other than that, the national party organizations serve as little more than a forum for discussion and a vehicle for financing and publicity. The factions within the parties go their own way most of the time, dividing on some issues and uniting with their so-called opponents, at other times combining with their fellow party members. These alignments are issue- and time-oriented and no particular dishonour is involved in crossing party lines. In effect, the party system is so decentralized that national parties hardly exist.

MULTIPARTY SYSTEMS

Most democracies contain a multitude of parties, all of which serve to aggregate narrow ranges of interest. The economic, religious, social, and historical diversity in these countries have created a social setting where a multiparty arrangement is a reasonable answer to the need for aggregation. Since each party aggregates a narrow range of interests, it generally fails to command a majority of seats in the legislature. The aggregation process is then completed by forming a coalition of two or more parties. Some multiparty systems are fairly simple in their structure, with four or five major parties, while some have over a dozen. Such large numbers can obviously complicate the process of forming a government. Probably the ultimate in party proliferation occurred prior to the 1955 general elections in Indonesia when 169 separate political groups were formed to contest 257 seats. Twenty-seven of them elected candidates.[3]

The major weakness of the multiparty system arises from the fact that it may be a reflection of irreconcilable divisions within the political culture that preclude the possibility of a stable government. This condition prevailed in France after World War I when significant elements within the society, determined to bring down the political system, gained strength. A splintered party structure made it difficult for those who wished to preserve the system to form a strong and stable government. A variation of this pattern was repeated after World War II with a large Communist party on the left and various right-wing parties determined to undermine the system. Again, no nonrevolutionary party acquired a working majority, and weak coalition governments were the result. The political system as a whole lacked a strong decision-making centre and as the country's unsolved problems accumulated, it collapsed.

The party system of the Fourth Republic (1946–58) contained a number of contradictions. Its largest party, the Communist Party, was consistently and systematically excluded from office since it was regarded as hostile to the system and subordinate to a foreign power. The party's popular support was seen as being largely a protest against economic conditions. Whatever the reasons for its extensive support, its strong centralized organization and extensive network of ancillary groups made it a formidable force. The Socialist Party was neither as popular nor as highly organized or centralized as the Communist Party. The vote of the non-Communist left was shared between the Socialists and the Popular Republicans (MRP), the latter reflecting a Catholic concern for social issues. The right of centre elements in the society were represented by the Radical Socialist Party, the Conservative Independents, and the Gaullist French Popular Rally (RPF). The right was generally as lacking in centralized organization as the left was in possessing it. The Radical Party was in fact a conservative movement with a sizable following among small business leaders. It

---

[3] Dennis Bloodworth, *An Eye for the Dragon* (London: Secker and Warburg, 1970), pp. 40–41.

was often said that it was neither radical, socialist, nor a party. It was an electoral organization and, in its degree of decentralization and local autonomy, resembled an American party more than most European ones. The Conservative and Independent parties were really collections of vague groups centered around a number of important politicians. The RPF began as a highly organized antisystem party, but it splintered when some of its members in the National Assembly began to support the centre parties against the wishes of its leader, General DeGaulle.

The basic issues that created these divisions were: the republican system itself opposed by the Communists and many of the rightist groups; the question of church influence in politics which separated the Communists, Socialists, and Radicals from the MRP, Conservatives, and Gaullists; and the question of social reform which separated Communists, Socialists, and MRP members from the rest. Figure 6–1 illustrates these divisions.

FIGURE 6–1

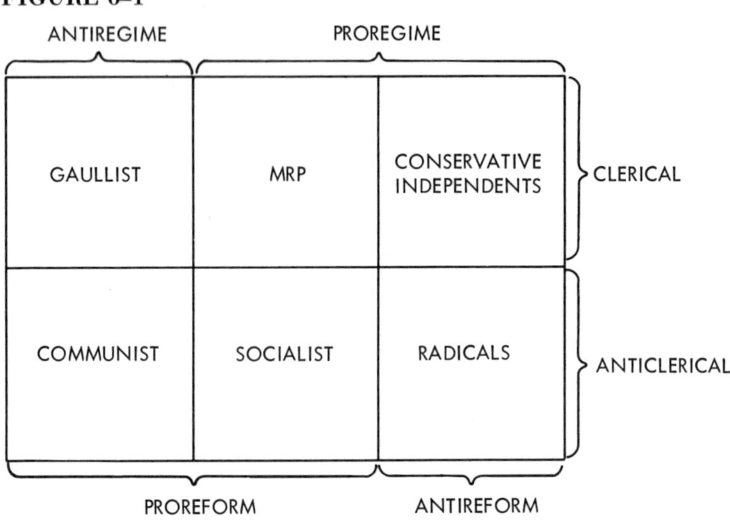

Italy also has a multiparty system. The largest party in the system is the Christian Democratic Party, an assemblage of conservative and moderate elements. The second largest party is the Communist Party which, though similar in structure and organization to the Communist Party in France, exhibits a higher degree of independence from the influence of outside Communist movements. It displays greater flexibility in ideology and program than its French counterpart. The third largest party is the Socialist Party, a Marxist group that has retained its independence from the Communist Party, but, like it, operates largely on a working-class base. For many years after World War II it collaborated with the Communists, but for most of a decade, it has been involved in an alliance with the Christian Democrats and the Social Democrats, a small, less radical, socialist group. This new alignment was designed to produce reforms to alleviate the conditions that have maintained Communist support and, by uniting the two Socialist parties, to create a working-class party capable of meeting the Communists on their own ground. This loose coalition has, in turn, split the Christian Democratic Party as the conservatives in it regard the proposed reforms as unwise. The coalition is also debated within the Socialist Party, where many members feel that by collaborating with the party of the conservative and church interests they will undermine their own basis of support. The resultant infighting within the two major partners in this coalition has meant a succession of governmental crises and growing paralysis of decision making similar to that which afflicted and destroyed the Fourth Republic in France. It was pointed out in the discussion of political culture in the preceding chapter that Italy is a country with a high proportion of alienated citizens who are quite cynical about politics. The party system may be seen as both a contributor to and a result of this alienation.

A deliberate effort was made in France to reshape the party system into simpler arrangements by creating larger and more stable aggregating units. The Gaullist Democratic Union for the Fifth Republic (UDR) has consistently held a plurality or a majority of the national assembly seats. The leftist opposition has been forced into a coalition situation where the Communists and the Socialists may be said to constitute a very loose "party."

It should be pointed out that there are a number of political systems that operate along multiparty lines and yet exhibit none of the instability of the French or Italian cases, the Scandinavian systems being good examples of this. Part of the explanation for their stability may lie in the fact that Sweden, Norway, and Denmark do not face serious political threats from within in the form of large revolutionary parties and that many reforms of a social and economic type that are still controversial in most countries have already been carried out. The standard of living in these countries is high and there are virtually no ethnic or religious minorities to complicate the picture. Thus, some of the possible sources of discontent are not present and, as these countries have had multiparty systems for some time, they have grown accustomed to coalition governments and have found a way to make them work.

In an evaluation of the merits of the different types of party systems, a number of features stand out. A two-party system guarantees government stability barring a party-splitting issue, while multiparty systems tend to produce minority or coalition governments. The two-party system offers a simple choice of broadly based aggregators, while a multiparty system offers a more complex choice of several less-generalized aggregators. The options in a multiparty system are generally wider and more clear-cut, but there is also the risk that unless the many parties are able to work out a durable means of forming governments, the system may suffer paralysis at the centre. By the same token, the broad aggregations of the two-party system may conceal serious divisions within the system that may be potentially dangerous. No one system is *the* answer to the need for stable and effective interest aggregation; each is an outgrowth of the history and culture of a given political system and in turn tends to perpetuate the system and its institutions.

THE CANADIAN PARTY SYSTEM[4]

The party system in Canada presents an interesting problem of classification. Though it is traditionally thought of as a two-party system, the major parties together have normally received less than 80 percent of the vote in federal elections since the formation of the Commonwealth Cooperative Federation (CCF) prior to the 1935 general election. Minor parties have been consistently represented in the House of Commons for the last three decades. A further contradiction of the two-party image is that various provincial governments have been, or are presently, directed by parties other than the Liberals and the Conservatives.

The Canadian party system is, for all practical purposes, a multiparty system even if it has yet to result in a formal coalition government in Ottawa. The existence of a federal system including strong regional governments with their own responsibilities has produced a situation where voters select one party at the provincial level to serve their interests there and to support a different party at the federal level. This divergence is represented in Table 6–1, which indicates which parties hold the largest blocs of seats for federal and provincial legislatures.

The classic two-party pattern can only be found consistently in the Maritimes. The voters there may not grant the same party majority status at both the federal and provincial levels, but they generally opt for one or the other, third parties seldom gaining more than 5 percent of the vote. The political patterns outside of the Maritimes are less consistent, and though many areas in the rest of the country are two-

---

[4] An extensive discussion of the theoretical principles underlying Canadian parties may be found in the "Canadian" sections of Chapters 14–16.

TABLE 6–1
Representation of Major Parties in Canada, July 1976

| Province | House of Commons | | Provincial Legislature | |
	First Party	Second Party	Government	Official Opposition
Newfoundland	Liberal	PC	PC	Liberal
Prince Edward Island	PC	Liberal	Liberal	PC
Nova Scotia	PC	Liberal	Liberal	PC
New Brunswick	Liberal	PC	PC	Liberal
Quebec	Liberal	Cred.	PQ	Liberal
Ontario	Liberal	PC	PC	NDP
Manitoba	PC	Liberal	PC	NDP
Saskatchewan	PC	Liberal	NDP	Liberal
Alberta	PC	—	PC	SC
British Columbia	PC	Liberal	SC	NDP

Note: The following abbreviations have been used: PC—Progressive Conservatives; SC—Social Credit; NDP—New Democratic Party; Cred.—Ralliément Créditiste; PQ—Parti Québecois.

party, the provinces as a whole are not. The reasons for these odd distributions lie in the nature of the parties themselves and the electorate they seek to reach.

The contemporary Liberal Party continues to play a long-established role as the bridge between the francophones of Quebec and the rest of Canada. The early Liberal Party was a marginally successful coalition of radical Québécois and West Ontario "True Grits." Wilfred Laurier succeeded by 1896 in reorienting the Quebec branch of the party to appeal more successfully to the electorate by downgrading the party's anticlerical attitudes and building up its appeal outside of Quebec. Quebec has generally been a Liberal stronghold and the problem the Liberals have had to face is how to gain and retain favour in at least one other region of the country—the Maritimes, Ontario, or the West. Without support from outside of Quebec the Liberals fall far short of the votes needed in the Commons to sustain a government. The large bloc of seats available in Ontario has especially tended to draw the interest of all parties, the Liberals included.

The Liberals have avoided the trap of being purely a Quebec party in recent times by tailoring a program designed to appeal to urban and reform-minded voters. There has been a fairly consistent attempt to downgrade the traditional ties with Great Britain, exemplified by the flag debate in 1964, the recent decision to remove the Queen's portrait from some currency, and the absorption of the "Queen's Printer" into "Information Canada." While embarked on a policy of loosening the ties with Britain, which may appeal to the non-English immigrants as well as the French Canadians, the Liberals have also followed a so-called continentalist economic policy which has resulted in the Canadian economic progress and growth being tied to the economy of the United States. Such a policy has allowed vast quantities of American capital into the country for development purposes, certainly the easiest route to economic development, if not necessarily the best in other ways. This program has appealed to those living in the area that would logically become industrialized, that is, the provinces closest to the American industrial heartland, Ontario and Quebec. The Liberal Party has also tended to emphasize the role of the intellectual and the technocrat in government.

The strengths and weaknesses of the Liberal Party can be further illuminated by contrasting it with its major competitor, the Progressive–Conservative Party. Federally, the main areas of Conservative strength are the Maritimes, where they hold 17 of the 32 Commons seats and the Prairies, where they hold 36 of the 45 seats. These 53 seats comprise over one half of the 93 seats they now hold. The regional distribution of party strength is confirmed by Table 6–2.

TABLE 6–2
Percentage of Voter Support by Region, 1974 Federal Election

Region	Liberals	Conservatives	NDP	Others†
Atlantic*	44.2	41.9	9.9	4.0
Quebec	54.4	20.8	6.7	18.1
Ontario	43.3	36.0	20.0	0.7
Prairies*	27.2	51.1	18.7	3.0
British Columbia	33.1	41.8	23.0	2.1

* The Atlantic region consists of Newfoundland, New Brunswick, Nova Scotia, and Prince Edward Island. The Prairies consist of Alberta, Manitoba, and Saskatchewan.
† The bulk of the "others" is Ralliément Créditistes in Quebec and Social Credit elsewhere.
Source: Compiled from Report of the Chief Electoral Officer, *Thirtieth General Election*, 1974.

The position of the Conservatives in the Atlantic Provinces has deteriorated in the 1972 and 1974 elections from that held following the Diefenbaker victories in 1957 and 1958. Prior to this the region had generally been Liberal territory, but apparently as a result of a feeling in the area that the Liberals were too concerned with Quebec and not enough with the Atlantic area, the Conservatives achieved considerable success. The party has pressed this feeling in Ontario and the Prairies where its Anglophone background is felt to be an asset. They also have appealed to the other minority groups by pointing out that the Liberals support a special status for the Francophones while not providing similar consideration for other non-English groups. What was needed, they felt, was a nation of "unhyphenated Canadians."

Part of the appeal of the Conservatives lies in their relative lack of enthusiasm for the economic continentialism of the Liberals and thus, by loose implication, greater identification with Canadian nationalism. In many respects, however, the differences between the parties relate to the detailed content of social policies rather than to their nature. As with the American party system, the difference between the major parties is to a considerable extent one of style and emphasis.

The third largest party in Canada, the New Democratic Party, plays a rather different role in the system as it has a more specific and distinctive program and a somewhat more clearly defined clientele. Born in the depression of the 1930s as the Cooperative Commonwealth Federation (CCF) and based upon farmer organizations in the Prairies and labour in British Columbia, it has constantly sought the role of a major national party but has yet to achieve it. The CCF was able to govern Saskatchewan from 1944 to 1964 and has at various times had representatives in Ottawa from five of the provinces. Of late its successor, the New Democratic Party (NDP), represented in the legislatures of six provinces, governs one (Saskatchewan) and is competitive in two (Ontario and Manitoba). The CCF/NDP has historically appealed to elements in the farm community of the West and labour circles of Ontario and the West. Except for an occasional success in Nova Scotia it has little impact in the Atlantic region and even less in Quebec.

The agreement between the CCF and the Canadian Labour Congress (CLC) which resulted in the formation of the NDP in 1961 has had the effect of stereotyping the party as a labour party in a country where labour unions enroll fewer than one third of the workers and a class party in a country not greatly class conscious. The formal links between the CLC and the NDP are more in the British tradition of alliance between labour unions and a political party rather than in the North American tradition where, typically, unions or their leadership take positions on individual candidacies. The main challenge to the NDP is to break away from its restricted clientele, make itself more appealing to other groups, and especially to sink some roots east of Ontario. A glance at the electoral map of Canada shows that the Atlantic Provinces and Quebec contain nearly half of the seats in the House of Commons. Without seats from this area the NDP would have to elect 133 members (the current minimum for a majority) from the 158 seats in Ontario and the West to form a government in Ottawa! This situation will not change materially even with the new reapportionment[5] (expected to go into effect at the next federal election) in which 142 seats out of the 175 from Ontario and the West would be required.

The program of the federal NDP departs from that of the Conservative and Liberal parties in that it openly favours increased government

---

[5] See Chapter 8.

involvement in economic planning and public ownership of some industrial and service organizations. It is increasingly sensitive to the growth of American economic and cultural influence. Whereas the major parties have little concern with ideology as such, the NDP, with a more specific and somewhat ideological approach, has difficulty in attracting voters from the varied segments of society. The continuing success of the Manitoba and Saskatchewan NDP parties under avowedly nonideological leadership demonstrates that the party can shed its minority status but only at the cost of its ideological purity.

Minority party status does not necessarily mean that the party has no influence upon events. Many CCF/NDP proposals, such as old-age pensions and many welfare programs, originally have been popularized by the party and subsequently adopted by Conservative and Liberal governments at all levels. Besides, as the minority government situation of 1972–74 showed, a third party which controls the balance of power in the House of Commons can force a vulnerable governing party to alter its priorities and programs. These are not insignificant contributions to the political process, but there is a substantial difference between this kind of influence and that which the party would have if it were to govern or be the official opposition.

The Social Credit movement, represented in the West by provincial parties in Alberta and British Columbia and in the East by Ralliément Créditistes, has even less claim to the status of a national party than the NDP.[6] Social Credit in Canada first gained attention as a Western protest movement in the wake of the same depression which also brought about the birth of the CCF. It was founded by an evangelist, William Aberhart, who already had a substantial following in Alberta. He was able to utilize preexisting farmer organizations to quickly establish a political party capable of taking control of the province in 1935. The government of Alberta remained in the hands of the Social Credit Party until 1971 when it was defeated by the Conservatives led by Peter Lougheed. The Party also controlled most of Alberta's seats in the House of Commons from the 1930s until the Conservative victory under Diefenbaker in 1958. The only other Social Credit government in Canada was formed by W. A. C. Bennett in British Columbia in 1953 following the collapse of the provincial coalitions of Liberals and Conservatives. This government was ousted by the NDP, led by David Barrett, in 1972.

It is unclear what the long-term future of the party in either province is. In Alberta the Social Credit suffered a second humiliating defeat in 1975. However, later in the same year, it regained power in British Columbia as the result of a backlash against the controversial

---

[6] Maurice Pinard, *The Rise of a Third Party* (Englewood Cliffs, N.J.: Prentice–Hall, 1971).

decisions and policies of Premier David Barrett. Whatever the future holds for this party, the passage of time has resulted in it changing from a party of protest to one of conservatism rooted in the middle class. It is, in effect, the "conservative party" in the two provinces.

The most recent extension of Social Credit strength has been in Quebec where a branch was formed in the early 1960s to contest federal elections. Differing from the Western branches in that it is largely a rural lower-class party, it developed its own character as the Ralliément Créditiste. Its success in gaining federal seats has far outstripped that of the Western party. The Rally entered into provincial elections for the first time in 1970, and, while it achieved some temporary success, it has been overshadowed by the emergence of Parti Québecois (PQ) strength. Efforts by the Rally to extend its influence outside of Quebec have been singularly unsuccessful.

In addition to the above parties, there are a number of smaller parties which so far are significant only at the provincial level. Two of these, the Parti Québécois and the Union Nationale (UN), operate in Quebec. The UN has been a force in the province since 1935 and, until recently, was the only credible alternative to the Liberal Party.[7] The program and clientele of the UN have been basically conservative with a mixture of federalist and nationalist sentiments. The Quebec provincial election of 1970 saw the Union Nationale government of Premier Bertrand caught between a new threat to its conservative clientele in the form of the Ralliément Créditiste and a threat to its nationalist wing created by the newly formed Parti Québecois. The Liberals swept the majority of seats in the National Assembly and the PQ emerged with the second largest percentage of votes. Between that and the following election in 1974 the party was rent with internal feuds and it was then shut out entirely from the National Assembly by the electorate.

The emergence in the November 1976 elections of the Parti Québecois as government party in the province has shaken Quebec politics severely. Formed from an amalgam of small separatist groups and led by a former Liberal, René Lévesque, it has taken an unequivocal stand for the secession of Quebec from Canada. It has maintained that it seeks to do so only by democratic means, and it presents the image of a socialist reform party as well as a nationalist one. It contains within it a variety of groups espousing competing economic and social policies and may well have difficulty maintaining its cohesiveness. It has undertaken the difficult job of trying to persuade the Quebec electorate to abandon all it has known in politics and to embark on a political adventure.

---

[7] Herbert F. Quinn, *The Union Nationale* (Toronto: University of Toronto Press, 1963).

PARTY ORGANIZATION

One of the most important factors in the success of a political party as an aggregator of interests is its internal structure. The major North American parties have a very loose structure with a great deal of local autonomy. They are often called *caucus parties*. Their loose structure makes it possible for a variety of interests to become involved in the party and, given the lack of ideology, find an acceptable place within the party system. The basic element of organization is the constituency unit, whose active membership is usually composed of individuals who choose to identify themselves with the party. Party meetings are used in Canada to select candidates for election, develop and transmit policy proposals to the party executive, and provide the campaign organization. In the United States most party candidates are chosen in primaries, thus leaving the local organizations with only electioneering and platform-writing functions.

One of the factors contributing to this decentralized pattern of party organization in North America is the presence of a federal system in both Canada and the United States. The existence of two levels of government whose officials have different responsibilities, and frequently different election cycles as well, means that there must be two sets of party organization, one geared for national politics with a program appropriate to that level, and the other geared to the provincial or state politics with programs appropriate to them. It is not surprising in this situation that national and provincial/state organizations of the same party often do not see eye-to-eye on policies.

Parties in Canada and the United States are well suited to the task of broad interest aggregation. They lack any rigid ideology, party membership is self-defining, and the organizations are decentralized. Many shades of opinion may be found within the ranks of any of the parties. The resultant ambiguity and confusion makes it difficult to distinguish between them in the same way that more tightly organized and ideological parties may be distinguished from each other. The very virtues that make them successful aggregators, however, make them rather poor vehicles for sweeping changes or rapid action. They contain such a variety of elements that complete unity on any issue of consequence is highly unlikely.

The second type of party organization is that of the *mass party*. The rationale behind the mass party is that the mobilization and manipulation of large numbers of followers results in the creation of a powerful political weapon. Mass membership is seen as a way to counter the inherent power of the establishment parties whose leaders are drawn from the same social strata as the other economic and political decision inherent power of the establishment parties whose leaders are drawn from the same social strata as the other economic and political decision makers in the society. The mass party style has been particularly attractive to nationalist, socialist, and, on the surface at least, communist movements which have generally found themselves in the position of opposing more traditional parties or governments. All the major parties in North America like to consider themselves as mass parties, but though they may have masses of supporters at election time they do not have equally large numbers of active and participating members.

There are a number of advantages and disadvantages to a mass party structure. As a result of the principle of majority rule, democratic systems place considerable emphasis upon the value of numbers; thus, a psychological advantage accrues to a party that can legitimately claim a high proportion of voters as its bonafide members. The size of the party also provides a source of power for recruiting candidates and providing them with a campaign organization. A large and committed membership can also form the basis for a complex of organizations which act as extensions of the party, such as labour unions and student groups. It is also practical in such a context to establish a network of newspapers and magazines to further the cause and to reinforce the socialization of party members.

The mass party as an aggregator is likely to be less successful in the long run than a caucus party, especially when the former's existence is based on a strong ideology. For a party to be effective as an aggregator requires that it be open to people and ideas. An ideologically oriented mass party will screen out ideas which conflict with its ideology and with the needs of its own captive interest groups. Thus, a closed system is likely to result, and the party will likely reinforce divisions within the society rather than break them down. If a goal of the political system is to reduce the division among its groups to form a cooperating society, then, with all its failings, the caucus party is a better device.

In addition to caucus and mass parties, another type of party organization is represented by *militia* parties. Militia parties are characterized by a tightly organized central structure and a highly dedicated group of supporters. They maintain a para-military organization to be used as an instrument for overthrowing an existing political system or maintaining a totalitarian regime. Nazi and fascist parties are examples of this type of party organization.

PARTY LEADERSHIP

A problem common to all political parties regardless of their organizational arrangements is that of maintaining a useful degree of responsiveness among the leadership. It was noted earlier that a tendency exists for the leadership in interest groups to become distant from the membership and also for the leadership element to be self-perpetuating. The same holds true for political parties. The decentralized nature of the organization of caucus parties makes sweeping changes difficult to effect with any rapidity. A desire for a change in policy or leadership may arise in one region or among one or more subgroups, but large parts of the organization may be generally unaffected by these forces. Given the relatively small number of active party members, it is not difficult for a small group to take over a specific segment of the organization, but a very extensive and well-organized campaign will be required to take over the party as a whole. By contrast, a mass party with a more centralized organization would be easier to renovate provided the requisite power for replacing the leadership is available. If not, then it will be difficult to significantly alter any of the components of the organization, as those trying to make the changes will have to contest with an entrenched and organized leadership element. Thus, the caucus party form has certain advantages in this area as well, for though its leadership may seek to perpetuate itself, name its own successors, and maintain party policy largely unchanged, the nature of the organization renders it difficult to keep other individuals and groups from making their presence felt. A mass party, especially one with a strong ideology, may not be as amenable to the entrance of new interests, and ideological purity can be used as one of the weapons to beat back challenges from party malcontents. This is not to say that such parties do not change their policies or leadership, for inevitably they must or they cease to function, but such changes are not as easy to initiate from the "grass roots."

The procedure in the two major Canadian parties for chosing leaders is to hold leadership conventions when necessary, whereas the NDP uses a more rigid system of biennial review of its leadership.[8] The latter is apparently more democratic as it gives the members an opportunity on a regular basis to change the leadership. In practice, contests have developed only when a leader has stepped down, as did T. C. Douglas who led the party from its founding in 1961 to 1971. His successor, David Lewis, retired following his personal defeat in the general election in 1974 and was replaced by Edward Broadbent in an "acting" capacity. Neither Douglas nor Lewis were seriously challenged during their tenure, while Broadbent was able to overcome his opposition at the 1975 leadership convention held in Winnipeg.

The practical effect of using a convention for leadership review is to

---

[8] John C. Courtney, *The Election of National Party Leaders in Canada* (Toronto: Macmillan, 1973).

increase the likelihood of the leadership becoming entrenched since it normally controls the convention. Using conventions for the selection of political leaders has been imported from the United States where it is used to choose presidential and vice-presidential candidates at a time reasonably close to an election. Unless a convention is unusually divisive, it is a good tactic to hold it close to the beginning of a political campaign as it generates a great deal of publicity. The timing of the Liberal Party leadership convention in 1968 close to the election date, which was also set by the party, contributed somewhat to Trudeau's electoral victory. A more conclusive example of the importance of timing is provided by the experience in Manitoba in 1969. The Conservative government suddenly dissolved a legislature in which it had a small majority and timed the election to fall just prior to the scheduled provincial NDP leadership convention and only short weeks after a divisive Liberal leadership convention. It would appear to have been an attempt to put the NDP in the position of having to fight an election campaign with an outgoing leader and the Liberals with an unsatisfactory leader. The NDP confounded these calculations by moving the date of its convention to a couple of weeks before the election, and conducted the contest for the leadership in a spirited but gentlemanly fashion, thereby generating a great deal of favourable publicity for the party. The impact of this convention and the election of a leader who caught the imagination of the public helped to create an atmosphere favourable to the NDP which contributed to an unexpected victory at the polls.

Studies suggest that leadership conventions in Canada are less tightly organized than the United States presidential conventions.[9] The common American practice of "favourite sons" who present themselves as candidates mainly to bind the delegates of their own states for bargaining purposes is a ploy that has not been adopted to any great degree in Canada, where the tactics of the candidates and their backers is to be oriented more towards individuals than blocs of delegates.

The most critical problems faced by leadership candidates in North America is the rising cost of a leadership campaign. Such a leadership campaign in the Conservative or Liberal parties federally would cost a serious candidate upwards of $100,000.[10] A campaign for a

---

[9] D. V. Smiley, "The National Party Leadership Convention in Canada," in *Canadian Journal of Political Science* 1, no. 4 (December 1968), pp. 373–97.

[10] The total expenditure by 10 candidates in the 1976 Progressive-Conservative leadership convention has been computed at $1,598,556. Individual expenditures ranged from a low of $9,336 to a high of $294,107. Joseph Clark, the eventual winner, spent $168,354. Two candidates have refused to disclose their expenditures; see *The Winnipeg Free Press*, June 22, 1976.

presidential nomination of the Republican or Democratic party in the United States is a multimillion dollar affair, and a senatorial or gubernatorial nomination in a given state can cost over $1 million.

PARTY FINANCES

The cost of operating a major political party has become a serious problem in recent years. Financing a continuing organization is the least of the difficulties. The cost of election campaigns can be truly staggering. In democratic countries where *mass* parties exist or where parties have established integral links with labour, church, or other organizations, some automatic sources of funds are available. For *caucus* parties, fund raising is a largely individual matter; specific groups and individuals must be induced to contribute funds or other resources. In such a situation the possibility of corruption is obvious, as the sordid Watergate affair in the United States demonstrated.

To meet this problem, a number of approaches have been suggested. One is that the media, at least that directly under government control (radio and television), should be required to provide a certain amount of free time to parties and candidates as part of their public service obligation. There have also been numerous laws passed to limit the amount a candidate or organization may spend, but there appears to be a tendency for the cost pressures to be so severe as to make such limits impractical. The most recent innovation in North American politics is to establish a system whereby a certain amount of campaign expenses are provided by the government itself in exchange for observance of some of the other rules of campaign financing. In the United States, for example, this takes the form of a direct subsidy, both for presidential nomination and election campaigns. There is even some provision for the funding of third-party efforts.

In Canada, the major party organizations apparently spend, on an average, upwards of $10 million each on a federal election. This figure includes the support given by the national organization to individual candidates, but not the funds the candidates raise locally. It also does not include the cost to the public of the expenses incurred by the government in administering the election itself. One conservative estimate suggests that the total cost of the 1972 federal election exceeded $31 million.[11]

Traditionally the funds for such campaigns have come from individuals and corporations. Many of these contributors play both sides of

---

[11] Khayyam Z. Paltiel, "Party and Candidate Expenditure in the Canadian General Election of 1972," in *Canadian Journal of Political Science* 7, no. 2 (June 1974). For a general review of party financing in Canada, see K. Z. Paltiel, *Political Party Financing in Canada* (Toronto: McGraw-Hill, 1970).

the street by making contributions to both parties, tending to favour the party in power. It appears that the Canadian business community and wealthy individuals account for 90 percent of the contributions, while the general public supplies the balance. In contrast, the minor parties have more limited sources of revenue and rely heavily upon the general public. The NDP, for instance, derives much of its funding from the labour unions through a self-imposed per capita levy on the membership.

The abuses to which a system such as this is subject finally brought about a new law, the election expenses act of 1974.[12] The act is based on the principle that political parties must be officially recognized and held responsible for the collecting and spending of funds. An effort is made to equalize the financial capacity of the parties by requiring the federal government to extend certain services to them as well as to provide subsidies. A tax deduction is allowed for individual contributions in an effort to reduce the reliance of the parties on wealthy organizations and individuals. A limit is also placed upon the amount candidates and party organizations may spend. Both are further required to make public disclosures of the amounts received and spent and their sources. The act defines a party for legal purposes as any organization represented in the House of Commons on the day before dissolution or any organization that had, 30 days prior to election day, officially nominated candidates in at least 50 electoral districts. In 1975 six parties qualified under the ruling: the Liberal Party, the Progressive Conservative Party, the New Democratic Party, the Social Credit Party of Canada, the Communist Party, and the Communist Party (Marxist–Leninist).

ELECTORAL PROCESS

The end result of the activities of a political party is its participation in the electoral process. As the agent designed to organize and channel resources for acquiring control of the decision-making positions, it must persuade the people that its candidates and programs are the right ones.

The electoral process ties together all of the structures and functions discussed in this and the preceding chapter. Basically, elections are a means of providing the system with accepted decision makers. The society, or a part of it, chooses those who will make the decisions. Along with this choice, political parties also provide a means of allowing society to choose, in a rough sense, between general philosophies

---

[12] Bill C203, *an Act to amend the Canada Elections Act, the Broadcasting Act and the Income Tax Act in Respect to Election Expenses, 1974.*

of government. Elections also provide a focus for interest groups since the policy orientation of the parties must be developed if the party's candidates are to act as a coherent and credible group. Interest articulation reaches a peak in intensity and quantity at election time. Finally, elections provide a form of feedback to the political culture in that they function everywhere as a socialization device. They demonstrate the system at work at the local level and also call for a minimum of participation in the political process by most of society.

These functions of elections can be divided to distinguish between those relevant to the various types of party systems. An election in authoritarian and totalitarian one-party systems is not designed to provide the voter with a choice between parties and programs. The election acts primarily to give the party or government a chance to socialize the public and gauge to some extent their feelings. Elections in such situations are part of the socialization process and the penchant for reporting election results in terms such as 98 percent vote in favour of the party helps to reinforce the notion of the party as a popular instrument. By closing off all alternatives, the party can create an aura of invincibility which will help persuade the doubters within the system of the strength and legitimacy of the regime. Besides, by holding elections the leadership can counter the charges of its critics that it is not responsive to the wishes of the people. The important characteristic that distinguishes democratic from nondemocratic systems is not whether the processes or groups exist but whether they are autonomous. In a nondemocratic system, such as that of the Soviet Union, elections, like the interest groups, are all under tight party control. It is not accurate to say that such elections are not significant, but it is fair to say that they do not mean the same thing as they do in competitive party systems.

The function of elections in competitive systems is in part one of socialization but in a broader sense than is the case in closed systems. Elections provide an opportunity for the parties and interest groups to make contact with the public and to give the public an opportunity to make choices between the parties. By involving citizens in this process, elections bind them a little closer to the system so long as the voter believes the process to be fair and has sufficient evidence that his or her interests can be served. Except for those systems which legally require citizens to vote, such as Belgium and Australia, the act of voting is a minimal act of affirmation for the system, and consistently low-voter turnout reflects degrees of alienation or apathy. Thus an emphasis is put on voting as part of one's civic obligation.

The efficacy of elections as a vehicle of choice for the voter depends to a large extent on the type of parties in the system. Broadly based institutions such as the traditional parties in North America provide a choice, but usually for a very blurred choice. This can be frustrating for the voter who is looking for specific results. By the same token, the fact that the parties are loosely organized and little encumbered by ideology means that whatever the choice the majority makes, those in opposition are unlikely to see their loss in a particular election as catastrophic. If the members of one party are so committed that defeat seems to pose a real threat to their interests, then they are not as likely to accept the election results. If they are forced by circumstance to accept them, they are likely to resent this and to regard the system as rigged against them. This suspicion reinforces their sense of separateness from the rest of the system and diverse groups in the society are driven further apart. Such a condition is not healthy for the long-term prospects of the overall system.

The content and style of the election campaigns have an impact upon the utility of the election process. Election campaigns require large amounts of money and manpower. The party must raise money to pay for publicity and candidate expenses, maintain extensive networks of workers to seek out the voters, confirm that they are registered, attempt to get them involved in the campaign, and, above all, make sure they get to the polling stations. To organize such an effort on a national scale requires thousands of people possessing a wide variety of skills, especially those related to public relations. Speaking tours must be arranged, reporters accommodated, advertising campaigns arranged, and a myriad of other tasks performed. As seen by the public, the campaign is only a few weeks long. But the period actually devoted to the task of picking the candidates and creating the necessary organizations is much longer. In the United States and Canada much of the party organization lies dormant between elections since it would be much too expensive to maintain a large standing organization. Much of the manpower is therefore composed of short-term volunteers.

The relative brevity of the electoral campaign in Canada and United Kingdom coupled with its complexity, makes very heavy physical and psychological demands upon the party activists. It is a hectic affair which leaves many people financially, physically, and psychologically impoverished. It is a measure of the challenge, the exhilaration, and the magnetic attraction of the political process that many active workers, candidates included, swear off politics when a campaign is over, but most will recover from the ordeal and return to the political arena at the next opportunity. There is, for some people, a tremendous appeal in participation in what is one of the most critical acts in society: the act of choosing decision makers for the political system. In spite of the often overdone emotionalism and the sometimes seamy qualities of politics, the vast majority of the rank-and-file activists gain little that is tangible for their efforts.

The satisfaction comes through active participation. Personnel and finances are of little value to a party if it lacks the means to present its case to the public. This freedom of access is restricted in all political systems in various ways. In some cases the government, through its ownership of the electronic media in particular, may discriminate against the opposition. It should be remembered that in most countries all radio and television is government owned. In countries where the electronic media are privately owned the same issue exists, as there is nothing to prevent private interests from discriminating as well. Additionally, the incumbent public officials by virtue of their status and power have greater access to such media even when they are controlled by hostile private interests. It would be unthinkable for the private networks in Canada or the United States not to broadcast, live if possible, a major speech by the prime minister or the president. Such speeches may receive extensive network coverage and, even in cases where the speech has clear political overtones, the opposition does not receive equal treatment.

The access to the public through the other media is less subject to governmental control in democratic systems, but they are subject to a considerable amount of private bias. It is difficult to find a major newspaper in Canada that has any visible sympathy for the NDP. Though most readers may not consult the editorial pages, the fact remains that newspaper editors can, and do, influence the content of the news and thus use them to propagandize the public. A case in point would be that of *The Winnipeg Free Press* and its handling of news relevant to the NDP government first elected in Manitoba in June 1969. *The Free Press* took the editorial position that the election of a "socialist" party was inimicable to the interests of Manitobans and that the party did not have a real right to govern as it did not poll a majority of the votes (the vote being divided between the NDP, Conservative, Liberal, and Social Credit parties and several Independents). The paper did not mention that the outgoing Conservative government had run the province on the basis of an identical proportion of the voters which it had received in 1966. *The Free Press* then proceeded to publish as front-page news any developments in business or politics that could be regarded as reflecting upon the ability or judgment of the government while frequently reporting any favourable news in the inner recesses of the newspaper.[13]

Such a situation is not so serious if there are comparable alternative sources available. Unfortunately, the media are generally run solely as businesses and few Canadian communities have two newspapers under different ownership. Perhaps the most publicized example of

---

[13] Alvin Finkel, "The Winnipeg Free (Enterprise) Press," in *Canadian Dimension* 7, nos. 1–2 (June–July 1970).

this state of affairs arose from the recent prosecution of companies controlled by the Irving interests in New Brunswick. These interests had gained control of the English language newspapers on a province-wide basis and were subsequently charged with unfair practices. Newspaper control may often be combined with control of radio and television stations in the same area. Thus groups with ideas unacceptable to the media managers must create their own means of reaching the public. This means resorting to meetings, marches and demonstrations, use of handbills and fliers, and, if the money is available, the purchase of advertising time or space. Thus the structure of the media favours the established parties and interests so that other groups need a particularly dramatic or compelling cause or unusually charismatic leader to overcome these disadvantages.

If one combines this situation in the media with the fact that the basic structure of the electoral system in Canada tends to favour the two traditional parties, it is not surprising that the NDP, which aspires to be a national party, has considerable difficulty in doing so. The strength of the NDP tends to be concentrated where it can maintain its contacts without great expenditures in time or money and without much need to rely on the mass media. Its situation is somewhat ameliorated by the fact that the broadcast networks frequently seek out the opinions of the NDP leaders in Ottawa on major issues instead of interviewing only the leaders of the government and the leaders of the official opposition.

Party fortunes in election campaigns are affected by such factors as demography, organization, and the response of the media. The structure of the election process has a significant bearing on these outcomes as well. The first of these structural factors is the method of representation. The most popular form in North America is called the *single-member district*, wherein one person is elected from each geographic region or constituency. The seat is awarded to the person attaining the highest number of votes of all the candidates, that is, a plurality. It is not necessary that the winning candidate receive an absolute majority and where there are often three or four candidates competing in a given constituency, it is not uncommon for the winner to gain less than 40 percent of the vote.

The members of the House of Commons are elected on the basis of single-member districts. This tends to create a bias in favour of a two-party alignment within the constituency. Part of the reason for this is what has often been referred to as "bandwagon psychology"—voters do not like to feel they are wasting their votes on candidates who have no chance of victory. It also creates pressure on the various interest groups to align themselves with a party that has a chance of success. Thus minor parties tend to get squeezed out as the major parties strive to outdo each other by reaching out to the various interests, and the interests seek out a party that may have the opportunity to enact some of its ideas. In many parts of Canada individual constituencies are basically two-party even if the province as a whole is not. Canadian parties have not yet succeeded in aggregating as wide a variety of interests as parties in the United States. For example, neither of the two traditional parties has gained the allegiance of the blue-collar class in areas in Ontario and the West, whereas the NDP has not been successful in extending its strength outside of labour or farm areas. The 1969 victory of the NDP in Manitoba was a breakthrough in this respect, as the party won significant numbers of voters away from the traditional parties and greatly increased its strength outside its main base in Winnipeg.

There is another way in which the use of the single-member district election system hurts minor parties. If they are similar in ideology to the NDP, with strength in a variety of places but few large concentrations of supporters, the dominant parties will gain a disproportionate number of seats. The 1974 federal election is a good example of this as the NDP polled 16 percent of the popular vote but gained only 6 percent of the seats in the Commons. A minor party whose strength is geographically concentrated will probably be more successful. This is indicated by the experience of the Créditistes, who polled 5 percent of the vote and gained 4 percent of the seats. The situation that faces the NDP is that it has not been represented in the House of Commons in numbers proportionate to its percentage of the vote. This creates an image of being more of a minority party than it is. The Créditistes are faced with a different problem; with their main base in one province, they are regarded in much the same light as the western Social Credit Party, as simply a regional party and not as an alternative to the traditional parties. Analysis of the election results indicates that at the national level if a party polls 30 to 35 percent of the vote it may receive its "fair" share of seats; if it goes over this range it will gain a disproportionate number, and if it falls below it will receive fewer seats than its percentage of votes justify. In the 1974 federal election the Liberals polled 41 percent of the vote and won 55 percent of the seats.

The alternative to the single-member district is called the *multimember* district, wherein a constituency is geographically broadened to include what would be several constituencies in a single-member system. In this enlarged constituency several identical offices are available. The winning candidates may normally be determined on the basis of the proportion of the votes they received. This, hopefully, would result in a distribution of these offices which accurately reflect the partisan allegiances of the voters. This form of distribution of seats is commonly known as *proportional representation.*

There are a number of methods of proportional representation, but the basic features of all of them is that they guarantee a better opportunity for a minor party to gain its "fair" share of seats in the legislature. Had a simple proportional representation system been applied to the 1974 federal election (on a provincewide basis), the Liberals would have won 120 seats instead of 144 and the NDP 37 instead of 15. In this particular instance the Conservatives would not have benefited. The differences at the provincial level would have been striking. For instance, the 3-man Conservative delegation from Quebec would have been enlarged to 15 and even the NDP would have gained 3 members from that province. While these gains would have enhanced the national image of both parties, the gains would have been at the expense of the Liberals, but the Conservatives would lose seats in the West to the NDP and the Liberals. Psychologically, this would have been of greater benefit to the Liberals as their elected representation from the West was very small after both the 1972 and 1974 elections. The greatest psychological benefit would probably have accrued to the NDP, for the party would have acquired greater overall status and would also have had a broader base and experience. Thus the NDP would have become a more credible alternative to the traditional parties. The question of whether to use a single-member or multimember constituency is determined in part by the desirability of establishing an electoral system that will more accurately reflect the voters' desires as opposed to one that will tend to create a situation of clear-cut majority-minority party dichotomy.

A second structural factor in elections which can influence party fortunes is the relationship between the constituency boundaries and the population. Until 1965 it was possible to have one MP representing 12,000 people and another 233,000.[14] While democratic practice presumes that all voters are equal, such malapportionment gives some voters greater influence than others simply because of where they live. Such a situation can have a serious effect upon the political system if a group of voters is consistently unable to gain effective voice, not because they lack the votes, but because the parties in power refuse to set up an equitable system of seat distribution. The boundaries of Canadian House of Commons constituencies were redrawn before the 1968 election and the worst inequalities were eliminated.[15] There is a new reapportionment for the 1978 elections.[16] It is difficult, and probably not too important, to reach absolute mathematical equality.

---

[14] Report of the Chief Electoral Officer, *The Twenty-Seventh General Election, 1965* (Ottawa: The Queen's Printer, 1966), pp. xiv and xv.

[15] For a general discussion of reapportionment in Canada, see William E. Lyons, *One Man—One Vote* (Toronto: McGraw–Hill, 1970).

[16] See Chapter 8.

The inaccuracies of a census and the mobility of the population render such accuracy impractical, but it is feasible to reduce the inequalities to an inconsequential level. In many countries, fair reapportionment has been avoided, as the status quo favoured the incumbent majority and they were reluctant to give up their advantage.

A third use of electoral arrangements to gain partisan advantage is the practice known as "gerrymandering." This involves drawing constituency boundaries in such a manner that one party is assured of more seats than its voter support would justify even though the population of the constituencies may be reasonably equal. This is accomplished by dividing up areas of opposition strength so that they are included as minority areas in districts otherwise favourable to the party in power. By spreading the opposition party's strength among many districts, its votes are so diluted that it may fail to gain any seats. A reverse process can be applied where the constituency boundaries are drawn in such a way as to include as many opposition strongholds as possible, thus concentrating its strength in a very few constituencies. Such a manipulation of constituency boundaries, when superimposed on a map, can create some very weird-looking works of political art.[17]

The process of registering voters can also influence the result of elections. The normal procedure in Canada is for the residents of areas in which a federal or provincial election is to be held to be canvassed prior to the election to ascertain if they are eligible to vote and, if so, to register them. The success of this depends in part upon the thoroughness of the canvassers, but it is more likely to attain a higher number of registered voters than the system commonly used in the United States, where individuals must appear in person before a registrar at specified times in order to be put on the voters' list. An alternate system used in many countries is that of permanent voter lists which are periodically checked to prevent persons who have moved or died being used as a cover for illegal voting. The efficiency and honesty of the registration process and the relative ease of registration can all have an influence upon the numbers who are eligible to vote.

Modern democratic practice generally presumes that all adult citizens who are mentally competent and not imprisoned, are eligible to vote. In North America, as elsewhere, there were originally property qualifications for voting, property holding being considered a sign of trustworthiness and responsibility. There was also a fear on the part of the property owners that the numerous propertyless people might use their political power, if they were enfranchised, to expropriate private

---

[17] For a general discussion of electoral mechanics in Canada, see Terence H. Qualter, *The Election Process in Canada* (Toronto: McGraw–Hill, 1970).

property. While property qualifications were generally eliminated as a barrier to manhood sufferage in the United States by the 1840s, such was not the case in Canada until 1898. It would appear that the 19th-century political leaders of Canada were a good deal more conservative in their interpretations of democracy than those of the United States. Property qualifications have generally gone out of style and now are usually found only in local elections where property taxes figure prominently in political decisions.

The timing of an election can affect the performance of the political parties in both presidential and parliamentary systems. In the former it is common for the elections to be held at fixed intervals. In the United States, an election must be held on a given date irrespective of the circumstances. It is hypothetically possible for the United States to be attacked with nuclear weapons on one day and constitutionally obliged to hold elections on the next. Most parliamentary systems specify that elections must be held within a certain period, such as every four or five years, but the actual timing is not dictated. It is common for elections to be called by the head of state on the advice of his or her ministers, who will usually try to pick the time best suited to their own electoral strategy. Britain provides an example of the possible flexibility in a parliamentary system where elections were suspended for the duration of World War II. Had the House of Commons elected in 1935 been dissolved at the end of its normal term, an election would have been called during such epic events as the fall of France and the Battle of Britain. Instead, the elections originally scheduled for 1940 were not held until the spring of 1945.

In Canada, as in most parliamentary systems, the legislature rarely lives out its full term, not because the government is necessarily in difficulty but because its leaders wish to choose the most advantageous time; if they wait too long, they will reach the point where they *must* hold the election. Of course, elections may also be forced if the government loses the confidence of the House. In several of the multiparty systems of Europe, however, the fall of one coalition government is normally followed by the institution of another. It is not considered necessary or wise to go to the electorate too frequently lest they become annoyed with the recurrent crises and opt for groups not normally involved in coalitions (such as the Communist Party in Italy or France).

There are a number of other factors which affect the efficiency of the electoral process. To varying degrees efficiency is hampered by the fact that elections take place in many systems on weekdays when most voters are at work. Canada does not have a particularly good provision for absentee voting, though this has improved recently. Registration procedures and residency requirements vary from one province to another for provincials elections though not for federal. Such factors as the weather can affect the voter turnout. It is also alleged that the early reporting and predicting of election results by the television network may affect the voting in the western parts of the country where the polling stations close several hours after those in the east. Therefore, in assessing the results of an election, a number of relatively mundane matters must be considered as well as the more dramatic ones of policy, personality, and efficiency of organization.

RECOMMENDED READINGS

Alford, Robert R. *Party and Society.* Chicago: Rand McNally, 1963.

Beck, J. M. *Pendulum of Power: Canada's Federal Elections.* Scarborough, Ont.: Prentice–Hall, 1968.

Christian, W., and Campbell, C. *Political Parties and Ideologies in Canada.* Toronto: McGraw–Hill Ryerson, 1974.

Courtney, John C. *The Election of National Party Leaders in Canada.* Toronto: Macmillan, 1973.

Dahl, Robert, ed. *Political Opposition in Western Democracies.* New Haven: Yale University Press, 1966.

Duverger, Maurice. *Political Parties.* New York: John Wiley & Sons, 1954.

Englemann, F. C., and Schwartz, M. A. *Canadian Political Parties: Origins, Character, Impact.* Scarborough, Ont.: Prentice–Hall, 1975.

Key, Vladimir Orlando. *American State Politics: An Introduction.* New York: A. A. Knopf, 1956.

———. *Southern Politics.* New York: Random House, 1949.

Leiserson, Avery. *Parties and Politics.* New York: A. A. Knopf, 1958.

Lyons, William C. *One Man—One Vote.* Toronto: McGraw–Hall, 1970.

McKenzie, R. T. *British Political Parties.* 2d ed. New York: Praeger, 1963.

Meisel, John. *The Canadian General Election of 1957.* Toronto: University of Toronto Press, 1962.

———. *Papers on the 1962 General Election.* Toronto: University of Toronto Press, 1970.

———. *Working Papers on Canadian Politics.* Montreal: McGill–Queen's University Press, 1973.

Michels, Robert. *Political Parties.* London: Jarrold and Sons, 1915.

Newman, Peter. *Renegade in Power: The Diefenbaker Years.* Toronto: McClellan and Stuart, Ltd., 1963.

Paltiel, Khayyam Z. *Political Party Financing in Canada.* Toronto: McGraw–Hill, 1970.

Pinard, Maurice. *The Rise of a Third Party.* Englewood Cliffs, N.J.: Prentice–Hall, 1971.

Rae, Douglas. *The Political Consequences of Election Laws.* Englewood Cliffs, N.J.: Prentice–Hall, 1971.

Qualter, Terence H. *The Election Process in Canada.* Toronto: McGraw–Hill, 1970.

Quinn, Herbert F.   *The Union Nationale.* Toronto: University of Toronto Press, 1963.

Scarrow, Howard.   *Canada Votes.* New Orleans: Hauser, 1962.

Schattschneider, E. E.   *Party Government.* New York: Rinehart and Co., 1942.

Schwartz, Mildred A.   *Public Opinion and the Canadian Identity.* Berkeley: University of California Press, 1967.

Thorburn, Hugh.   *Party Politics in Canada.* 2d ed. Toronto: Prentice–Hall of Canada, Ltd., 1967.

Winn, Conrad, and McMenemy, John.   *Political Parties in Canada.* Toronto: McGraw–Hill Ryerson, 1976.

Zakuta, Leo.   *A Protest Movement Becalmed: A Study of Change in the C.C.F.* Toronto: University of Toronto Press, 1964.

7

Constitutions and Constitutionalism

The three preceding chapters have discussed those aspects of a political system concerned with the generation, expression, and organization of inputs. The core of the system, however, is that set of institutions which receives these inputs. It has been noted that these institutions have assumed a special degree of importance in the political culture of all societies because they are the only institutions which make decisions that are binding upon the whole society. The special degree of importance is summed up in the term *official,* which is used to describe governmental institutions, whereas parties, interest groups, and other socializing agents are considered to be *unofficial* bodies.[1]

The importance of the official bodies to the existence of the society has led to a concern for their stability. From the time when the first clans and tribes accepted political leadership with a monopoly over decision making, these bodies have been surrounded by ceremony and bounded by laws, taboos, and traditions which have served to regularize the activities and limit the scope of official powers. As societies became more complex, considerable attention was devoted to the establishment and maintenance of these rules through the development of *constitutions,* or bodies of fundamental principles, laws, and conventions according to which the country is governed. A constitution, in any form, describes the types of decisions which may or may not be made by official institutions and prescribes the processes through which legitimate decisions may be made. Society is

---

[1] Neil A. McDonald, *The Study of Political Parties* (New York: Random House, 1955), p. 83.

140

thus given some certainty about the extent of the power of these institutions. Former Prime Minister Lester Pearson, in a discussion of constitutional revision observed:

If we are to be sure that we have the best arrangements we can devise to order and govern the relationship between Canadians in the Canada of the future, we must be willing and concerned to examine all of the facets of our legal framework.[2]

The practice of adhering to a constitution is called *constitutionalism*. It emphasizes that politics should be conducted non-violently and according to rules which spell out the role of the groups and individuals in society. Constitutionalism is sometimes confused with democratic practices, but its real essence is that a measure of certainty is given to the relationships within the official institutions and between these institutions and society. The significance of a constitution in the operation of a political system is reflected in the intense and often spirited debate in Canada since the Constitutional Conference of February 1968.

Thomas Paine, who considerably influenced the formation of the American Republic and contributed to the French Constitution of 1793, likened the importance of a constitution for a political system to the importance of grammar for a language. According to him:

A Constitution is not the act of a government but of a people constituting a government; and a government without a constitution is power without right.[3]

The nature of the structures designated as constitutional varies among political systems. Some political systems may operate on the basis of a very detailed document (India); others operate on the basis of a more general document (United States). There are still other political systems which have no single document as the key to their constitution (Britain and Israel).

WRITTEN AND UNWRITTEN CONSTITUTIONS

Ever since the inauguration of the United States Constitution in 1789, it has been thought that the government is the creature of a special document which is the conscious act of a people. This has been the dominant theme of constitutional thought since the beginning of the 19th century. The British North America Act in Canada, the constitutions of the Weimar Republic of interwar Germany, the Fourth and Fifth Republic of France, the governments of the U.S.S.R., the Federal Republic of Germany (West Germany), and India, to mention

---

[2] Lester B. Pearson, *Federalism for the Future* (Ottawa: The Queen's Printer, 1968), p. 4. Reproduced with the permission of Information Canada.

[3] Thomas Paine, *Rights of Man* (London: Freethought Publishing Co., 1883), p. 86.

only a few, bear testimony to this dominant thought. Current activity surrounding the attempts at revising the Constitution of Canada emphasizes the belief in the values of a consciously formulated and written constitution. Political systems which operate on this basis are said to possess a *written constitution*.

The process of enacting a written constitution is comprised of two separate activities: the formulation of a draft and its ratification by the people. These activities can be carried out by several different methods. The creation of a draft constitution may be entrusted to the executive, the legislature, or specially convened bodies. Ratification may be performed by these bodies as well or through popular referenda. In most cases there is an attempt to associate the constitution with the whole of society. A constitution may be enacted by the people through their chosen representatives as were the Indian Constitution of 1949 and the now defunct constitution of Pakistan of 1956. The special feature of the process in the two countries was that while the same body acted as a constituent assembly when it discussed the provisions of the proposed constitution, it became a legislative body when it performed the rule making function for the interim government. Some other constitutions, after being formulated by a representative assembly, sought to secure tacit popular acceptance. Such was the case with the United States Constitution of 1789, which was initially formulated by the representatives of the 13 states gathered together at the Constitutional Convention of 1787. The draft was then submitted for ratification by the population of the 13 states through special conventions in each state comprised of representatives elected specifically for that purpose. The Irish followed a similar process in 1937 when the Irish Parliament approved a draft constitution which was then submitted to the people and came into force only after it had received their approval by a majority vote.

Quite often a constitution may be prepared for the people by an executive commission, as was that of the French Fifth Republic in 1958. The draft constitution was then put to a popular referendum. The 1962 Constitution of Pakistan was created as the result of a similar process. It was drafted by a Constitutional Commission appointed by the military regime of Field Marshal Ayub Khan and was approved by the people in a referendum.

The British North America Act (BNA Act) came into existence as an act of the British Parliament, which was the ruling power over Canada at the time. Popular support for it may be considered to have come from two sources. First, it came from the fact that it had been formulated by the tacit consent of the representatives of the people of Canada at the Charlottetown and Quebec Conferences. Second, some element of popular support may be construed from the sentence in the preamble which says:

Whereas the Provinces of Canada, Nova Scotia, and New Brunswick, have expressed their desire to be federally united into one Dominion under the Crown of the United Kingdom of Great Britain and Ireland . . . .

It was not considered necessary or prudent at the time, however, to seek the explicit acceptance of the people by submitting the BNA Act to a referendum.

Table 7–1 illustrates the ways in which some written constitutions have been created and ratified.

TABLE 7–1
Creation and Ratification of Constitutions

Country	Creating Body				Ratifying Body			
	a	*b*	*c*	*d*	*a*	*b*	*c*	*d*
Canada (1867)	x				x			
India (1949)		x			x			
Ireland (1937)		x				x		
France (1946)		x				x		
(1958)			x			x		
Pakistan (1956)		x			x			
(1962)			x			x		
Japan (1947)			x				x	
West Germany (1949)				x			x+	
United States (1789)				x				x+

a—Imperial legislature.	*a*—None.
b—Legislature.	*b*—Popular vote.
c—Executive commission.	*c*—Legislature.
d—Special convention.	*d*—Popularly elected convention.
	+—State bodies.

The acceptance and approval of a constitution by the people, irrespective of the form it might take, is what makes it an "act of the people." Most modern constitutions emphatically assert their origin in "an act of the people." The Irish Constitution of 1937 declares: "We, the people of Eire, do hereby adopt, enact and give to ourselves this constitution." The Constitution of India begins in the same vein: "We, the people of India . . . in our Constituent Assembly . . . do hereby adopt, enact and give to ourselves this constitution." And, then, there are the famous words which constitute the Preamble of the Constitution of the United States:

We, the people of the United States in order to form a more perfect Union, establish justice, insure domestic Tranquility, provide for the common defence, promote the general Welfare, and secure the Blessings of Liberty to ourselves and our Posterity, do ordain and establish this Constitution . . .

The people, then, prescribe the form of their government, delegate and legitimize its powers, and impose limitations on them. Once again, the BNA Act deviates from this generally recognized principle of modern constitutionalism. Though it may be argued that the BNA Act was formulated by the representatives of "Canada, Nova Scotia and New Brunswick," the actual enactment was performed by a sovereign external to the Canadian people, that is, the British Parliament.

The acceptance of a constitution "by the people" does not guarantee the workability of the prescribed relationship. Popular endorsement of a constitution may be necessary in order to avoid open disregard of its provisions by society, but only the test of time can establish whether these relationships will be positively accepted by society and incorporated into the political culture. Constitutional experience in Latin America, for example, hardly suggests that the constitutional relationships have become ingrained in the thinking of these societies. (See Table 7–2.)

Written constitutions cannot be expected to provide for every single aspect of government operations. Almost all governments operate in some measure on the basis of unwritten rules called *conventions*. When a government operates in a certain fashion over a prolonged period, the practice gains acceptance as if it were a part of the constitution. For example, the U.S. Supreme Court's power of judicial review is not mentioned in the U.S. Constitution. Yet, as the highest judicial authority in the land, it has pronounced judgment upon the constitutionality of numerous executive and legislative actions.

Another example of a political system with a written constitution operating on the strength of political conventions is that of India. Constitutionally, the prime minister of India holds office during the "pleasure of the President." This provision has, however, been linked to a political convention borrowed from Britain which results in the prime minister holding office as long as he or she enjoys the confidence of the majority in the Lok Sabha, the lower house of the Indian Parliament.

In essence, then, no constitution can be wholly written. A political system is designated as having a written constitution not because all conceivable aspects of its constitutional practices are specifically provided for in the written document but because most or a very large part of them are.

TABLE 7–2
Latin American Constitutions

Country	Number	Dates of Constitutions
Argentina	5	1811, 1819, 1826, 1853, 1949 (1957, back to 1853)
Bolivia	17	1825, 1831, 1834, 1839 (two), 1843, 1851, 1861, 1868, 1871, 1878, 1880, 1931, 1938, 1945, 1947, 1961
Brazil	5	1824, 1891, 1934, 1937, 1946, 1967
Chile	9	1811, 1812, 1814, 1818, 1822, 1823, 1826, 1833, 1925
Colombia	6	1821, 1843, 1853, 1858, 1863, 1886
Costa Rica	7	1825, 1844, 1847, 1859, 1869, 1871, 1917, 1949
Cuba	4	1901, 1934, 1935, 1940
Dominican Republic	21	1844, 1854, 1865, 1868, 1872, 1874, 1875, 1877, 1878, 1879, 1880, 1881, 1887, 1896, 1908, 1924, 1927, 1934, 1942, 1947, 1963
Ecuador	16	1820, 1825, 1843, 1845, 1851, 1852, 1861, 1869, 1878, 1884, 1897, 1906, 1929, 1945, 1946, 1967
El Salvador	12	1824, 1841, 1864, 1871, 1872, 1880, 1883, 1886, 1939, 1945 (back to the 1886, 1950, 1962)
Guatemala	6	1839, 1851, 1879, 1945, 1954, 1956, 1967
Haiti	13	1801, 1805, 1806, 1843, 1849, 1867, 1879, 1889, 1918, 1935, 1946, 1957, 1964
Honduras	11	1825, 1839, 1848, 1865, 1873, 1880, 1894, 1904 (restored 1894), 1924, 1936, 1957
Mexico	6	1824, 1835, 1837, 1843, 1857, 1917
Nicaragua	7	1826, 1838, 1858, 1893, 1905, 1911, 1939, 1950
Panama	3	1904, 1941, 1946
Paraguay	4	1813, 1844, 1870, 1940
Peru	17	1823, 1826, 1827, 1828, 1834, 1836 (two), 1939, 1855, 1856, 1860, 1867, 1868, 1879, 1880, 1920, 1933
Uruguay	4	1830, 1918, 1934, 1951
Venezuela	22	1830, 1857, 1858, 1864, 1874, 1881, 1891, 1893, 1901, 1904, 1909, 1914 (two), 1922, 1925, 1928, 1929, 1931, 1936, 1947, 1953, 1961

Source: Alexander T. Edelmann, *Latin American Government and Politics*, rev. ed. (Homewood, Ill.: The Dorsey Press, 1969), p. 388.

The most notable exception to the pattern of written constitutions is that of Britain. The British Constitution is based largely on political conventions which are the result of an evolutionary process. This type of constitution is often classified as an *unwritten constitution*. Though this term is not literally correct in so far as documents such as the Magna Charta and the Bill of Rights are, in fact, written, it is true that Britain has no organic laws or practices which cannot be changed by Parliament. Unlike states which have written organic laws superior to statutory (legislatively enacted) law, Britain has none.

The Canadian Constitution may be classified as either a written or an unwritten constitution, for, whereas some aspects of it are written, many significant aspects are based on political conventions. The BNA Act prescribes a federal structure for Canada, allocates power between the federal and provincial governments, establishes the offices of the governor general and the provincial lieutenant-governors and spells out their power and authority, specifies the structure of the federal legislature—House of Commons and Senate—and of the provinces, and makes various other provisions. On the other hand, the act makes no mention of such facets as the office of the prime minister and its constitutional position within the political system; the structure, position, and functions of the cabinet and its individual members; the relation between the prime minister, cabinet, and the Governor General; the relation between the cabinet, privy council, and Parliament; and several other significant matters.

In other words, the BNA Act does not provide for the structure of the federal government except in relation to the Governor General, the privy council, and the Parliament. The normal operational and functional pattern of the federal government is based on the somewhat ambiguous phrase occurring in the preamble which says that Canada shall have a "Constitution similar to that of the United Kingdom." Thus British political conventions have been borrowed to arrange the various structural and functional segments of the government. The ambivalence results from the lack of clarity inherent in this mixture of relatively equal portions of prescribed organic laws and transplanted political conventions.

Amending the Constitution

Where a constitution is a reflection of a society's basic values and traditions, there is an inherent resistance to changing and modifying it. However, values and traditions underlying it are constantly changing and, therefore, if the system is to operate smoothly, constitutions should be amendable.

There are two general ways in which amendments may be enacted. Some constitutions, such as that of Britain, can be amended by resort to the normal legislative procedure requiring the approval of a majority of the members of Parliament. In such cases the guarantee against hasty and insufficiently considered change is inherent in the conventions surrounding the constitutional machinery. In contrast, change in other constitutions has been made relatively difficult to obtain procedurally.

Constitutions may also be classified according to the process by which they are amended. Those that can be amended procedurally by the legislature are classified as *flexible constitutions*. Constitutions of Britain and New Zealand are two of the few examples of this kind. Most others prescribe their own method of amendment and are classified as *rigid constitutions*. Examples of rigid constitutions, besides that of the United States, may be found in the constitutions of Switzerland and the Federal Republic of Germany.

Unlike flexible constitutions, there is no uniform method of amending rigid constitutions. The element of rigidity arises not from their immunity from amendment but from the fact that such political systems accept the supremacy of the constitution over the legislature so that it cannot be amended through the ordinary legislative process. Different constitutions prescribe different method of amendment. Article V of the U.S. Constitution, which deals with amending procedures, prescribes two methods of amendment. The U.S. Congress with two-thirds majority of both houses may propose an amendment which shall then be ratified by legislatures of three fourths of the several states. Or, the U.S. Congress, on the request of the legislature of two thirds of the several states, shall convene a convention for proposing amendments which shall then be ratified by conventions in three fourths of the several states. In the case of the 26 amendments made to the U.S. Constitution so far, the first method has been followed. The Swiss Constitution provides separate and detailed procedures for a total revision and a partial revision. In either case, the Swiss voters are called upon to approve the principle or the text of the revision; the federal assembly then formulates the amendment, which is submitted for approval by popular vote.

There are some constitutions which, though not amendable through normal legislative procedure, may still be amended by the legislature without requiring the approval and consent of outside bodies as do rigid constitutions. The Indian Constitution may be amended by a two-thirds majority of the members present and voting in both houses of the Indian Parliament. Similarly, the Constitution of the U.S.S.R. can be amended by a two-thirds majority of each house of the Supreme Soviet.

The Canadian Constitution is neither flexible nor rigid because the BNA Act did not prescribe any procedures whereby it could be amended. It was generally assumed that as an act of the British Parliament, it could only be amended by the Parliament. As a result, the question of amending the Constitution has become a controversial subject. The controversy centres around the role of the federal government in the amendment process and the need for federal-provincial agreement over amendments to be made.[4] The procedure followed so far has been that the British Parliament passed amendments upon a request by the federal government. In ten instances, in 1871, 1875,

---

[4] For a more detailed analysis of constitutional amendment in Canada, see Guy Favreau, *The Amendment of the Constitution of Canada* (Ottawa: The Queen's Printer, 1965). Also, Donald V. Smiley, *The Canadian Political Nationality* (Toronto: Methuen & Co., 1967), pp. 24–26.

1886, 1895, 1915, 1916, 1943, 1946, and twice in 1949, amendments were enacted without any consultation with the provinces. In 1930 an amendment was sought and obtained following consultations with only those provinces directly affected by it. Five amendments—those in 1907, 1940, 1951, 1960, and 1964—were made following federal-provincial consultation and agreement.

The most significant step toward devising a method for the amendment of the Constitution was the passage by the British Parliament of the British North America Act (No. 2) in 1949. This act confers the power of amending the Constitution, relative to some provisions, in the Parliament of Canada, though power relative to certain other provisions was reserved to the British Parliament. The Canadian Parliament can amend any provisions of the BNA Act of 1867 following normal parliamentary procedure except:

1.   Matters relating to provincial jurisdiction and rights and privileges of provincial governments.
2.   Privileges granted to denominational schools.
3.   Status of the English and French languages.
4.   Provisions relating to the five-year term of the House of Commons and the requirement of at least one annual regular session of Parliament.

Amendments to these provisions can be made only by the British Parliament. To the extent, then, that it can be amended by the Parliament of Canada through normal parliamentary procedure, our Constitution can be classified as flexible. In those matters which may be amended only by an outside body, that is the British Parliament, it is a rigid constitution. The Constitution is unique in that certain portions cannot be amended in Canada; in other words, Canada does not have complete control over its own Constitution. This inability has led to a wider discussion on the adequacy of the Constitution as a whole.

There are three main trends of opinion on the subject. Some would like the Constitution patriated; that is, they would like the power to amend all aspects of the Constitution vested in the Canadian people and exercised through our own institutions. Others go further and advocate patriation and a total revision of the Constitution so as to make it more relevant to the needs of the country. The underlying motive of both these groups is to make the Constitution distinctly Canadian, unencumbered by external control. Finally, there are those who hold that the present setup has worked quite satisfactorily over the years and that the constitutional question should be deferred until more important social and economic problems have been resolved.

It is inconceivable that the British Parliament would deny a request from Canada for amending any or all provisions over which it has power or even conferring the power to do so on the Parliament of Canada or any other Canadian institution. However, these are matters of crucial importance affecting the basic structure and operation of the political system, and a decision on specific amendments or on the amending procedure should have the agreement of the federal and provincial governments. This agreement has been difficult to secure.

Between 1927 and 1964 five dominion-provincial conferences attempted to develop a formula for constitutional amendment. Hopes were raised that a method may finally have been found when the 1964 conference devised the Fulton–Favreau formula.[5] The apparent success reflected in the agreement over the formula was short-lived, as the Quebec government of Premier Jean Lesage reversed its position shortly afterwards and rejected it. In 1967 Premier John Robarts of Ontario convened the Confederation for Tomorrow Conference, in which the provincial premiers deliberated upon the constitutional question without federal participation. Subsequently, the Liberal government of Prime Minister Trudeau constituted an all-party parliamentary committee to look into the matter.[6] The February 1970 Dominion-Provincial Conference revealed a general consensus among the participants about the need for constitutional revision and, when the 11 first ministers of the country reassembled at Victoria in June 1971, they agreed upon a draft amending formula entitled Constitutional Charter, 1971, commonly referred to as the Victoria Charter.

The charter was a lengthy and complicated document which, besides providing for the patriation of the Constitution and prescribing an amending formula, dealt with such other provisions as certain basic political and language rights, regional disparities, the Supreme Court of Canada, federal-provincial consultation, and repeal of the federal powers of reservation and disallowance. It was agreed, when the charter was accepted by the conference on June 16, that the 11 first ministers would report the charter as a whole to their respective governments for acceptance by June 28, which would then recommend it to their legislative assemblies and, in the case of the federal government, to both houses of Parliament. If all ten provincial assemblies and both houses of Parliament were to endorse the charter, the necessary action would be taken to patriate the Constitution "so that the power to amend and enact constitutional provisions will rest exclusively with the Canadian people." Appended to the draft charter were three pages comprising a schedule of outdated sections of the BNA Act which would be repealed.

-----

[5] For details of the Fulton–Favreau formula see Guy Favreau, *The Amendment of the Constitution of Canada,* p. 28 and Appendix 3.

[6] See, The Special Joint Committee of the Senate and of the House of Commons on the *Constitution of Canada: Final Report* (Ottawa: Information Canada, 1972).

As far as the amending formula itself was concerned, the charter prescribed that amendments to the Constitution of Canada can be made by resolutions of the Senate and the House of Commons and of the legislative assemblies of:

1.   Every province which at any time before the passage of such a resolution had, according to any previous general census, a population of at least 25 percent of the population of Canada—in plain terms, Ontario and Quebec.
2.   At least two of the Atlantic Provinces (Nova Scotia, New Brunswick, Newfoundland, and Prince Edward Island).
3.   At least two of the western provinces (Manitoba, British Columbia, Saskatchewan, and Alberta) who, according to the then latest census, have a combined population of 50 percent of the population of all western provinces.

Amendments relating to the position of the crown in Canada, the Governor General and the provincial lieutenant-governors, annual sessions of Parliament and provincial legislatures, the term of the House of Commons and provincial assemblies, powers of the Senate, provincial representation in the Senate and the House of Commons, and the status of the English and French languages would be made according to this procedure. Where amendments to the Constitution would concern one or more, but not all, provinces, they could be made by resolution of the federal Parliament and the legislatures of the provinces concerned.[7]

Amid the enthusiasm and hopes generated by the adoption of the charter by the first ministers, there was an undercurrent of pessimism arising from the stand of Quebec. Premier Bourassa of Quebec insisted throughout the conference that his province desired exclusive or special position in the disbursement of income security and social welfare benefits in return for endorsement of the charter. The charter failed to provide for this exclusive jurisdiction with the result that on June 23, five days before the expiry of the deadline, the Quebec government rejected it.[8] Subsequently, Prime Minister Trudeau announced that discussions concerning constitutional amendment would be suspended for the time being to allow the provincial and federal governments to take a fresh stock of the situation. Since then, nothing noticeable has been done in this area. However, at the opening of the 30th Parliament in September 1974, the Prime Minister expressed the hope, on October 2, that an agreement on the amending formula would be reached within four years. He indicated that he would attempt to

---

[7] For text of the constitutional charter, see *The Winnipeg Free Press*, June 21, 1971.

[8] Six provincial governments—Ontario, Manitoba, Alberta, British Columbia, Nova Scotia, and Prince Edward Island—and the federal government had up to that point signified their acceptance of the charter. The remaining provinces were expected to do the same.

seek the agreement of all provincial governments in achieving this end and, if no better formula could be found, he would propose the adoption of the formula of the Victoria Charter.

DEVELOPMENT OF CONSTITUTIONAL PRINCIPLES AND PRACTICES

People have long had an interest in the relationship between the political system and the society. This has given rise to a number of ideas concerning the structures and practices of the official institutions of the system. An interest in these was shown by the early Greeks, and Plato devoted considerable attention to such questions as the right form of government, the most desirable qualities of a ruler, and the appropriate methods of selecting and appointing rulers and officials of state. Plato was also concerned that the ruler should govern in the general interest of society.

> . . . there is no one in any rule who, in so far as he is a ruler, considers or enjoins what is for his own interest, but always what is for the interest of his subject or suitable to his art; to that he looks and that alone he considers in everything which he says and does.[9]

Aristotle's ideas on these subjects are much closer to contemporary constitutional philosophies. He recognized that the relationship between ruler and ruled could take several forms, and developed a system of classification based on two criteria: (1) governments that ruled in the interest of the community and those that did not, and (2) the number of individuals involved in community decision making (one, a few, or many). He concluded that governments controlled by one, a few, or many which endeavour to promote the interests and welfare of the community as a whole are right constitutions. On the other hand, governments controlled by one, a few, or many who seek to promote their selfish interests are perversions. In this fashion Aristotle arrived at the six-fold classification as shown in Table 7–3.

The Monarchical Principle

The idea that the general welfare may be best served through decisions made by a single individual is as old as social organization. Historically, it has been the most common method of government. Originally, the authority of the ruler was based upon a belief that he or she possessed a special connection with the forces which affected society, either that he or she enjoyed some form of control over them or

---

[9] Plato's *Republic in Five Great Dialogues*, trans. B. Jowett (New York: Walter J. Black, 1942), p. 242.

TABLE 7–3

No. of Citizens Entitled to Rule	Rulers Rule in Interest of	
	All	*Themselves*
One	Kingship (Monarchy)	Tyranny
Few	Aristocracy	Oligarchy
Many	Polity	Democracy

Source: Robert A. Dahl, *Modern Political Analysis*, rev. ed. (Englewood Cliffs, N.J.: Prentice–Hall, 1970), p. 49.

that he or she had a unique contact with whatever beings or spirits did. In some societies the ruler was revered as a god incarnated on earth; in others he or she was considered as the representative of higher powers.

This traditional concept was explicitly revived towards the end of the Middle Ages by the European kings who used it in their attempts to form and maintain large nation-states on the ruins of the decentralized feudal system. Monarchy was allied with Christianity in such a way that believers were required to accept that the political authority of the kings was of divine origin. The Reformation, stressing the role of the individual in spiritual matters, lent indirect support to the concentration of political authority under religious aegis as Christianity dissolved into warring sects which allied themselves with different monarchs. The alliance of religious authority with political power lent physical support to the sects and spiritual support to the rulers.

The developments led to the growth of the divine right theory, which posited that the right of a king to rule was a direct result of his birth and that it was a divinely sanctioned right. His only obligations were to God, and his authority could not be challenged by anyone but the Divine Power itself. The king could not be subjected to human judgment. Law was supposed to reside in the person of the king. Thus the king, being above ordinary people, was wholly irresponsible and could do as he pleased. The logical and natural extension of the divine right theory was the establishment of such despotic and authoritarian monarchies as those of Louis XIV of France and James I of England.[10]

The theory of divine right collapsed under the impact of the English, French, and Russian revolutions, but its fundamental tenet, that the enlightened mind of one person can best serve the general welfare, has been resurrected in another form from time to time. During the 19th century, a number of theories were advanced about the great

---

[10] See G. H. Sabine, *A History of Political Theory*, 3d ed. rev. (New York: Holt, Rinehart & Winston, 1961), pp. 391–97.

forces underlying human society. One school of philosophers considered the idea of the nation, a large group of people united by a common past and culture, to be the driving force in history. Others saw the economic class, a large group of people bound by their common lot in life, as the motivating force. The interplay of nations or classes served as the substitute for the will of God. The 20th century has seen the rise of leaders who have based their authority upon the special vision of this interplay which they alone possessed. Mussolini and Hitler saw visions of national struggle; one wished to revive the glorious Roman Empire and the other saw the barbarian German *volk* once more on the move. Others computed the movements of class struggles; Lenin, Stalin, and Mao have all claimed a superior connection with the flow of history and have ruled in accordance with this mission.[11]

The constitutionality of the monarch's rule differs greatly from that found where the collective will is supposed to function. The difference lies in the nature of the authority or right to rule found in each type of government. The monarch, as a single individual, exercises sole authority, and as long as his or her decisions are in keeping with his or her perception of the forces surrounding people, he or she is ruling constitutionally. Where the society rules itself, many conflicting visions exist and the procedure for determining whose vision prevails takes on great importance. Decisions are bound not only by the correctness of their content, but by the manner in which they are carried out. Procedure is of lesser importance in the monarchical constitution.

The Democratic Principle

In contrast to the principle of rule of the monarch is that of the rule of the society by its members. Such a principle assumes that no one person or group of people enjoy a special contact with the nation, history, or God.

The justification for democratic constitutions has its roots in diverse theories and practices. Popular sovereignty, the vesting of political authority in the people, was known in Rome. Cicero, the most outstanding of the Roman intellectuals and political observers, maintained in his *On the Commonwealth* that Rome would eventually degenerate into a tyranny unless it revived the earlier practices of the republic when the people enjoyed the right of political participation. The basis of early Roman constitutionalism was the concept of *lex* or legislation by the people. As Charles McIlwain has observed, in Rome, "the state as a bearer of rights is the whole of the citizens, the civitas; it is not abstraction apart from the people, and therefore rights

---

[11] See Chapters 15 and 16.

inhere in the people themselves and, what is more, in each of them individually."[12]

The idea that government was a contracted service performed by part of the society in the interest of everybody was implicit in the feudal relationship. The main characteristic of feudalism was the existence of a contractual relationship of reciprocal obligations between individuals of different social classes based upon a system of land tenure. Political power was decentralized, obedience to central authority was nominal, and effective political power was exercised at the level of feudal lords and barons. As the Middle Ages came to a close, the contractual nature of feudalism was increasingly subordinated to the concept that political authority emanated from God and that political rulers were responsible to the Deity alone. This concept was adopted especially by the kings who were concerned with the amalgamation of feudal domains into centralized political systems.

The continuing attempts of British monarchs to effectuate their claims to divine right produced a strong reaction which ultimately resulted in the growth of the concept of popular sovereignty. The conflict began during the Middle Ages and continued for a period of 500 years. The Magna Charta (1215) was an enumeration of certain demands made by the rebellious nobles of King John which he was forced to accept and, by putting his signature to the document, made it a landmark in the progressive development of British constitutionalism. Its significance lies in that it imposed restrictions on the arbitrary exercise of power by the king. For example, a provision in the Magna Charta underscores the concept of *due process of law* by iterating the principle that the king cannot arbitrarily punish anyone until a case has been duly made out against him according to law. The nobles were also given the right to petition the king and to be consulted in matters of taxation. A further provision established a committee of 25 barons who,

together with the community of the entire country, shall distress and injure Us (the King) in all ways possible . . . until they secure redress. . . .

This was the beginning of Parliament.

The imposition of these constraints on royal authority was the beginning of a prolonged process which resulted in the shifting of political power from the will of the king into the hands of the people. Parliament did not immediately become the authoritative legislative body which it has been since the 17th century. It was relegated to the side lines during the reign of the strong-willed Tudor monarchs

---

[12] Charles McIlwain, *Constitutionalism: Ancient and Modern*, rev. ed. (Ithaca, N.Y.: Great Seal Books, 1958), pp. 46–47.

(1485–1603) who eclipsed the Parliament by establishing a strongly centralized government.

The most intense struggle between the divine right theory and the right of the people in the progressing course of British constitutionalism occurred during the reign of the Stuart Kings (1603–1714). This period witnessed the erosion of divine right through such developments as a civil war, establishment of Cromwell's republican Commonwealth, the Restoration, and framing of the Bill of Rights (1689). The Bill of Rights put an end to the divine right principle in England by establishing the supremacy of the Parliament and reinforcing the concepts of popular sovereignty and the rule of law. The process was further refined by the various suffrage acts, the Parliament Acts of 1911 and 1948, and the Statute of Westminster of 1931. These political developments were intellectually supplemented by the introduction of new concepts such as the principle of sovereignty enunciated by Jean Bodin (1629), the theory of social contract of John Locke (1690), doctrine of separation of power in Montesquieu's *Spirit of Laws* (1748), and the concept of individualism expounded by Adam Smith in his *The Wealth of Nations* (1776).

U.S. constitutionalism, unlike the British, was the product of a constitutional convention convened exclusively for this purpose and its principles are embodied in one document, the U.S. Constitution of 1789. It prescribed a structure for their political system completely different from that of the British. It gave to the president substantial real power which was, however, checked by the legislature (the U.S. Congress). It borrowed the idea of a bicameral (two-house) legislature from Britain but made the upper house (the Senate) an elected body with far more powers than those enjoyed by the hereditary House of Lords. In contrast to the British principle of supremacy of the legislature, the United States adopted the principle of constitutional supremacy in which the courts are normally the final arbiter of the Constitution and ultimate protector of fundamental rights. And, above all, due to the pluralistic nature of American society and deep-seated local and regional loyalties born during their colonial experience, the Americans discarded the unitary structure of Britain's political system and established a federal structure.[13]

CONSTITUTIONALISM: SOME GENERAL FEATURES

Modern constitutionalism represents people's perennial efforts to discover a viable relationship between liberty and authority. The elu-

---

[13] The unitary and federal systems are discussed later in this chapter. Two houses of legislatures, the head of government, and the head of state are discussed in Chapters 8 and 9.

sive nature of this relationship has resulted in endless arguments over whether liberty implies voluntary obedience to authority or whether authority in any form is incompatible with liberty. Constitution making is an attempt to create authority acceptable to society and, at the same time, to guarantee liberty to the individual. For, despite the conflict between them, some element of authority is indispensable for maintaining the order without which liberty becomes meaningless. Authority can provide a predictable environment in which an individual may exercise liberty, secure in the knowledge that the excesses of others will be constrained.

Fundamental Rights

Many constitutions seek to establish liberty within the society by instituting fundamental guarantees and protections for its citizens. The concept of fundamental rights has grown out of the early ideas about "natural law" and "natural rights." One of the features of the philosophy of "natural law" suggests that human beings are endowed with the capacity to reason. The concept of "natural rights" implies that human beings have the inherent right to enjoy certain basic freedoms underlined in the phrase, "life, liberty and the pursuit of happiness," which grow out of the rational nature of people. These concepts have been endorsed in both thought and action during the course of the growth of Western political tradition. Natural law is considered as unchangeable, eternal, valid for all nations and for all times, and above laws of human origin, or "positive law." Rights granted by positive law are regarded to be subordinate to natural rights.

The process of translating these ideas into practice can be said to have started in England with the signing of the Magna Charta. The strength of the guarantees for the rights of Englishmen incorporated in the Magna Charta, the Habeas Corpus Act of 1679, the Bill of Rights, and other documents does not lie in their being embedded in a written constitution and thus being above normal legislative action. It lies in the fact of their having become so firmly rooted in British political tradition that they carry the same force as guarantees in a written constitution.

The practice of providing written guarantees for the basic rights of citizens became established as a constitutional practice with the American Revolution. The Declaration of Independence (1776) begins with the words which have since formed the basis of guaranteeing human rights:

We hold these truths to be self-evident, that all men are created equal, that they are endowed by their Creator with certain inalienable Rights, that among these are Life, Liberty and the pursuit of Happiness. That to secure these rights, Governments are instituted among Men, deriving their just powers from the consent of the governed. . . .

When the U.S. Constitution of 1789 was framed, however, it contained no positive guarantees for the rights of citizens in consonance with these principles. Such guarantees were considered unnecessary since that Constitution was established by the people and it explicitly limited the power of the government. Thomas Jefferson represented a significant portion of popular opinion when he took strong exception to the omission of a bill of rights. He reacted to the new Constitution by saying that a people are entitled to a bill of rights against every government and that no government should refuse it to them. He declined to give his endorsement until he received a commitment from George Washington, the first president of the United States, that the congress in its first session would be called upon to pass an appropriate series of amendments to the Constitution. The first ten amendments were passed in 1791 and are commonly known as the Bill of Rights.

In France the Declaration of the Rights of Man and Citizens (1789) sought to achieve the same purpose. It asserted that:

Men are born and remain free and equal in rights . . . the aim of every political association is the preservation of the national and imprescriptable rights of man. These rights are liberty, property, security and resistance to oppression.

These developments in Britain, the United States, and France have been subsequently used as models in the creation of many constitutions.

Some of the rights guaranteed in these constitutions relate to the freedom of conscience, speech, assembly, press, religion, the privacy of person, home, and correspondence, protection from illegal search and seizure, sanctity of private property, and the right to fair trial according to law. The 1936 Constitution of the U.S.S.R. goes beyond the enumeration of the traditional rights and provides guarantees for employment, rest and leisure, medical services, and social insurance. These rights have been granted not so much in recognition of the concept of natural law and natural rights but as an outgrowth of the ideological foundation of the Soviet government. For instance, the Soviet constitution recognizes the right of antireligious propaganda—which is an extension of the atheistic nature of Communism—while passing over recognition of the right of religious propaganda. Again, freedom of speech, press, and assembly are closely tied with the strengthening of the Socialist system and cannot be exercised to criticize or condemn it.

Canada is one of the rare Western political systems which does not provide a list of constitutional guarantees for basic human rights as found in the constitutions of France, the United States, Australia, Switzerland, West Germany, and many others. However, when the assertion is made that the BNA Act does not contain a bill of rights, one should not forget that it provides some explicit as well as implicit guarantees. Explicitly, it recognizes the equality of the English and French languages in the federal Parliament, courts, and statutes, and in the province of Quebec. It guarantees protection to denominational schools and prohibits legislatures from interfering with these rights as they existed at the time of the founding of the confederation. Implicitly, it grants to Canadians the conventional and statutory fundamental rights enjoyed by Englishmen as paragraph 2 of the preamble prescribes that Canada shall have a Constitution similar in principle to that of the United Kingdom.

Both the federal and provincial governments have attempted at different times to provide more explicit guarantees for the basic rights of Canadians. Most provinces have provided additional guarantees for some of these rights but the laws are not comprehensive and are limited to the jurisdiction of the respective provincial governments. In 1960, the government of John Diefenbaker piloted the Canadian Bill of Rights through the Parliament. This measure promulgates various legal, egalitarian, and political rights and stipulates that these rights shall not be infringed by federal legislation. The act, however, falls short of a comprehensive bill of rights because its applicability is limited to federal jurisdiction. Besides, since the bill is a parliamentary statute and not a constitutional provision, it may be changed, modified, or even abrogated by a simple majority in Parliament. This fact is reflected in the provision that gives to Parliament the authority to declare any law operative notwithstanding the Bill of Rights. Finally, the bill fails to establish any machinery to enforce the rights it guarantees.

There was a general tendency in the judiciary at first to assume that it was not the intention of Parliament to superimpose the Bill of Rights upon preexisting statutory laws inconsistent with its provisions. It was considered to be little more than a rule for the construction of federal statutes. This position was reversed by the Supreme Court's decision in *Her Majesty the Queen* vs. *Joseph Drybones* in November, 1969. Joseph Drybones was an Indian trapper who was fined $10 and costs for being drunk off a reserve in violation of section 94(*b*) of the Indian Act. By a six-to-three decision, the Supreme Court ruled that section 94(*b*) was inoperative because it was contrary to section 1 of the Canadian Bill of Rights, which guarantees "the right of the individual to equality before the law . . . without discrimination by reason of race."

This was the first time the Bill of Rights was used to invalidate federal legislation. It is predicted by some that the Court's decision to invalidate part of the Indian Act is the beginning of a more activist role of the Court as the guarantor of fundamental rights. However, subsequent decisions of the Supreme Court in cases invoking the Bill of Rights have cast a shadow of doubt on these expectations.

Despite the Bill of Rights, the basic rights and freedoms of Canadians still lie at the mercy of a transient legislative majority. As Christian Bay says:

. . . majorities are never sacred; nor are laws—fashioned and accumulated in the name of majorities—sacred or even necessarily legitimate. Democracy and the "rule of law" are means, in need of criticism and at times, perhaps, resistance. What is sacred is human rights.[14]

The same concern also motivated Lester Pearson and Pierre Elliott Trudeau to further endeavours in this area. In his statement of policy to the 1968 Dominion-Provincial Conference Lester Pearson said:

This (adequate guarantees) can be achieved only by placing a Charter of Human Rights in the Constitution of our country. Such a Charter . . . would not involve a transfer of legislative power from one government to another. It would not, for instance, affect provincial jurisdiction over criminal law and procedure in criminal matters. Instead, it would involve a common agreement to restrict the power of all governments.[15]

As Minister of Justice in the Pearson government, Pierre Elliott Trudeau presented a detailed proposal for a Canadian charter of human rights to the conference.[16] After becoming Prime Minister, he reiterated the principle of his proposal before the Dominion-Provincial Conference of February 1969:

The need for freedom of thought and action, for protection of liberty and security by fair laws, for equal treatment without prejudice and for the means of expressing oneself in the official language of his choice—these are basic to all our people. It should be a primary purpose of government to secure these things, for without them man loses the peace, dignity and power of self-expression which should be part of his unique heritage.[17]

Provisions of an entrenched constitutional bill of rights could not be changed through ordinary legislative process by either federal or pro-

---

[14] Christian Bay, "Needs, Wants and Political Legitimacy," *Canadian Journal of Political Science* 1, no. 3 (September 1968), p. 242.

[15] Lester B. Pearson, *Federalism for the Future*, p. 20. Reproduced with the permission of Information Canada.

[16] See Pierre Elliott Trudeau, *A Canadian Charter of Human Rights* (Ottawa: The Queen's Printer, 1968).

[17] Pierre Elliott Trudeau, *The Constitution and the People of Canada* (Ottawa: The Queen's Printer, 1969), p. 14. Reproduced with the permission of Information Canada.

vincial legislatures. The federal government, for instance, could not have invoked the War Measures Act in October, 1970, and suspended the civil liberties of Canadians, including the Canadian Bill of Rights, had the bill been entrenched in the Constitution. The suspension of civil liberties, irrespective of the circumstances, would require some form of constitutional sanction. Technically, it amounts to subordinating the hitherto recognized supremacy of the Parliament to constitutional guarantees of civil liberties and elevating the position of the courts as the arbiter of disputes concerning these liberties.

These proposals are by no means the reflection of a uniform feeling in the country. There are those who see no need for a constitutional bill of rights.[18] They argue that Canadians fared well with respect to basic rights in spite of occasional transgressions. Donald Smiley maintains that "Canada is relatively free" and he does not expect such rights as he enjoys.

at the continuing pleasure of Parliament and the Legislative Assembly of British Columbia to be in jeopardy . . . .[19]

Serious reservations about entrenched rights also exist at provincial government levels.[20] In view of this wide disparity of views, the answer as to whether Canada will have a constitutional bill of rights lies in the womb of future.

Representative Government

It is one thing to institute a bill of rights in a constitution, but another to create reasonable assurances that its principles will be respected and its provisions enforced. An indispensable prerequisite to a bill of rights is that it be complimented with institutions which control the exercise of political power in a manner so as to honour these rights. Historical experience in England under the Tudors and Stuarts demonstrated the dangers of entrusting the rights of citizens in the hands of authoritarian governments. So far, the most common means found of assuring that fundamental rights are honoured and protected is representative government.

---

[18] See, for instance, Peter Russell, "Mr. Trudeau's Bill of Rights," *Canadian Forum,* March 1969.

[19] Donald V. Smiley, "The Case Against the Canadian Charter of Human Rights," *Canadian Journal of Political Science* 11, no. 3 (September 1969), p. 277–91. Italics ours.

[20] Three provinces—Newfoundland, New Brunswick, and Prince Edward Island—supported the Trudeau proposal. Manitoba, Alberta, and British Columbia were, in principle, opposed to constitutional entrenchment of basic rights. Ontario, Nova Scotia, and Saskatchewan accepted in principle, provided it covered only fundamental political rights. Quebec also accepted in principle, subject to an overall redistribution of powers between the federal and provincial governments. There has been no apparent indication of a change of attitudes since.

The principle of representative government implies that the people's representatives are responsible for their actions to the electors. The rationale is that the citizens decide who should govern them, for what period of time, and under what manner of responsibility and accountability. If the chosen representatives in government fall short in the fulfillment of their delegated responsibility and tamper with or deny basic rights, the citizens could replace them.

The French and American interpretation of representation requires that representatives reside in the areas they seek to represent so as to remain in contact with their electors. The traditional British theory, expounded by Edmund Burke and John Stuart Mill, is that the holder of representative office has a wider responsibility; once elected, the representative is concurrently the custodian of the interests of the electors as well as of the entire society. If these responsibilities conflict, the representative should exercise his or her judgment as to which of the two is of greater importance. Burke, for instance, maintained that a representative body was not an assembly of ambassadors representing conflicting interest, but a "deliberative assembly of one nation"[21] serving the interests of the whole, and the representative would thus be justified in acting contrary to the wishes of the electors if such action served the interests of the nation. Burke's insistence that he follow his own judgment rather than the wishes of his electors once cost him an election.

The traditional British view makes it unnecessary for the representative to reside in his or her constituency and this practice is followed in Canada. Members of Parliament (MPs) and Members of (provincial) Legislative Assembly (MLAs) who live outside their constituencies have developed means of maintaining contact, such as periodic visits, establishing a temporary office, or even moving their residence into the constituency following the electoral victory. The NDP leader, T. C. Douglas, who was once the premier of Saskatchewan, defended and lost his seat from the Burnaby-Seymour constituency in British Columbia in the 1968 federal elections. When the NDP member from Nanaimo-Cowichan-the Islands, also in British Columbia, died, Tommy Douglas was given the party nomination and he won the by-election. There is the other example of the former Manitoba Premier Duff Roblin, who failed in his bid for the seat of Winnipeg South Centre in the 1968 federal election. Leaders of the Progressive Conservative party then tried to persuade him to contest a "safe" seat in some other province. Roblin declined it in favour of a business offer in Montreal. However, in the 1974 elections he unsuccessfully contested an Ontario seat.

---

[21] Edmund Burke, "A Speech to the Electors of Bristol," in *The Works of Edmund Burke* (Boston: Little, Brown, & Co., 1897), p. 95; also, pp. 89–98. John Stuart Mill, *Representative Government* (London: J. M. Dent & Sons, 1968).

Distribution of Political Power

In absolute monarchies, all legislative, executive, and judicial power was vested in the person of the monarch. This concentration of power encouraged arbitrary and irresponsible actions. Various principles and devices have been developed to restrain such arbitrary and irresponsible government.

Fusion of Power and Parliamentary or Cabinet Government.   The most common principle in use today is that of *parliamentary* government where official functions are vested in a body whose members are responsible to the society for their actions. The final outcome of the struggle between the king and his subjects in England was that the representatives of the people, the Parliament, became the decision-making body in the name of the crown and its leaders also came to be known as ministers of the crown.

Parliamentary government is based on the principle of *legislative supremacy* in which all political power rests in the legislature. The principle of legislative supremacy is far more pronounced in Britain than it is in Canada. In the famous words of Walter Bagehot:

The ultimate authority in the English constitution is a newly elected House of Commons. No matter whether the question upon which it decides be administrative or legislative . . . whether it concerns high matters of the essential constitution or small matters of daily detail . . . whether it be a question of making war or continuing a war . . . whether it be the imposing of a tax or the issuing of a paper currency . . . a new House of Commons can despotically and finally resolve.[22]

A reflection of the constitutional and political powers of the British Parliament, on a less serious note, is found in the saying that the Parliament of England can do anything except change a man into a woman and a woman into a man. In Canada, the "supremacy of the Parliament" is restricted by two factors, the federal nature of the Canadian political system and restrictions imposed by the BNA Act (No. 2) of 1949 on the ability of the Parliament to change certain provisions of the Constitution.

The other institutions of government derive their power and authority from the legislature. They are responsible to it for their actions and the legislature in turn is responsible to the people. This is known as *responsible government*.

The rise of parliamentary leaders to executive positions meant that the legislative and executive powers were "fused" in one body. This is known as the principle of *fusion of power*. The ministers retain their

---

[22] Walter Bagehot, *The English Constitution and Other Essays* (New York: D. Appleton & Co., 1889), pp. 289–97.

positions as long as they enjoy the confidence of the legislature by controlling a majority of votes. The cabinet operates on the principle of *collective responsibility,* that is, the cabinet as a whole is responsible for the actions of its individual members. A repudiation of one member of the cabinet by the legislature may result in the resignation of the entire cabinet. In such cases either a new cabinet is formed or fresh elections are called. Although legislatures are normally elected for a maximum term of three, four, or five years, elections may be held at the discretion of the prime minister.

Parliamentary systems have two chief executives, the head of state and head of government. The head of state is the personification of national unity and the fountain of all executive authority. The head of government exercises *de facto* political power in the name of the head of state. Official designation of the head of state varies from king or queen, as the case may be, in Britain, Belgium, and Denmark and in the dominions of Canada, Australia, and New Zealand to president in most other countries. A head of state in parliamentary systems succeeds to the position in two different ways: by heredity in constitutional monarchies and by election, as in republics such as India, Israel, and West Germany. In Canada and some other Commonwealth countries, the governor general is appointed by the king or queen on the advice of the prime minister to act as his or her personal representative.

The head of government is generally known as the premier, prime minister, or chairman of the council of ministers. The last is a more correct reflection of the prime minister's legal role in government. Parliamentary government is found in Canada, Britain, Australia, New Zealand, India, Israel, and most of the Western European countries. With operational differences, these governments adhere to the principles of legislative supremacy, fusion of power, and collective responsibility.

Separation of Power and Presidential Government.   The alternative to the fusion of powers principle is the *separation of powers* principle. This idea was first popularized by Montesquieu in his *Spirit of the Laws* (1748). Montesquieu came to the conclusion that individual freedom could best be assured by separating governmental structures into three functional categories: the legislative, to make the laws; the executive, to enforce them; and the judiciary, to settle disputes concerning them. In order to prevent these theoretically separated structures from combining to form a new absolutism, it was proposed that each of these structures be given different sources of power and at the same time be empowered to prevent the other structures from acting unilaterally. This principle is known as *checks and balances* and was used as the basis for the U.S. Constitution. The U.S. Constitution has subsequently served as an example to many states in Latin America and several of the newer nations of Asia and Africa.

The style of government based on these principles is often called *presidential government* in order to distinguish it from the more common parliamentary style. The most notable feature of such a system is the role played by the chief executive, the president. Whereas the parliamentary system normally has a nonpartisan monarch or president as national symbol or ceremonial head of state, the president in a presidential system is both the ceremonial head of state and the head of government. The president is elected for a fixed term of office and, barring resignation, impeachment, death, or mental or physical disability, stays in office for the duration. The parliamentary system operates in the context of an intimate connection of the legislative and executive branches because the prime minister and his cabinet are also normally members of the legislature. Thus the prime minister and his followers may make as well as oversee the enforcement of the laws as long as they maintain a majority. In a presidential system, the president and his cabinet are barred from membership in the legislative body, thus guaranteeing that the body that makes the laws will be different in personnel from the body that enforces them. This separation in personnel is usually supplemented by such devices as the power of the president to veto unwanted legislation and the power of the legislature to prevent executive actions by refusing to grant either legal authority or the necessary funds. The president is elected by the population at large (directly or indirectly) whereas the members of the legislature are elected by much smaller local constituencies. Thus the same forces that combine to elect a president may be unable to elect a majority in the legislature. As there is no necessary connection between the presidency and the legislative leadership even if they are of the same party, the practical result is a decentralized party system without the discipline characteristic of parliamentary systems. Thus practical politics reinforces the constitutional separation of powers and checks and balances.

UNITARY AND FEDERAL GOVERNMENTS

Modern constitutions provide two patterns for the organization of government—unitary or federal. A *unitary* government is characterized by a single level of government for the entire country. There are no provincial, municipal, or local governments acting independently of the national government. The national government usually delegates specific powers to locally constituted bodies or functionaries who are responsible to the national government for their action. This delegation of authority is made through statutory law rather than through the constitution and can therefore be revoked at will.

The most familiar example of this form of government is that of Britain, and the most emulated is that of France. Other countries such as Sweden, Japan, Sri Lanka, and Tunisia have also structured their governments on the unitary principle. In Britain, for instance, all authority is vested in the Parliament. The Parliament, for purposes of administrative convenience, delegates responsibility to local bodies. Thus, while the Parliament derives its authority directly from the people, local bodies operate on the power delegated to them by the Parliament.

It is sometimes suggested that centralization of power in unitary governments discourages wide popular participation in civic affairs. However, the working of unitary governments in Britain, New Zealand, France, and other countries does not provide substantial evidence to suggest this. There is little in the structure of a unitary government to make it any less democratic and representative than any other form of government. Representativeness and political participation is contingent upon several factors quite distinct from the structure of government. It is worth noting that a consistently larger percentage of voter turnout has been recorded in Britain with a unitary government than in the United States, which does not operate on that basis.

A unitary government has certain political and administrative advantages which make it desirable. The existence of a strong national government may discourage divisive tendencies within society from coming to the fore. It may generate a greater sense of national unity since all citizens are subject to only one political authority. It prevents the growth of regional and local loyalties and leaves little room for the development of jurisdictional and other political disputes that are commonly found in federal governments. Administratively, the centralization of power results in greater uniformity of laws, regulations, and administrative practices throughout the country and leads to a high degree of consistency of procedure.

Federalism

In contrast to the centralization of power inherent in the unitary form, federal government or *federalism,* as the practice is commonly designated, is characterized by the decentralization of power. Federal governments are more suited for countries with a relatively vast expanse of territory and for a population marked with religious, cultural, ethnic, or economic diversity.

Federalism is a method whereby political power is exercised at two levels: national and regional. Separate political entities may decide to join together in a political partnership, or an existing unitary government may decentralize. In the first instance, a common rationale for federalism is that a pooling of resources will facilitate the achievement of common goals. In the second case, a federal system may be created in order to accommodate the demands of particular groups for control over particularly sensitive local concerns. Powers attributed to the national government relate to matters common to all the constituent units which can be best exercised nationally, while regional governments retain powers relating to regional and local matters. Each level of government then operates autonomously of the other. K. C. Wheare describes federalism as the ". . . method of dividing powers so that the general and regional governments are each, within a sphere, coordinate and independent."[23] Another scholar defines federalism thus:

On the one hand each of the members of the union must be wholly independent on those matters which concern each other only. On the other hand, all must be subject to a common power in those matters which concern the whole body of members collectively . . . . Each member is perfectly independent within its own sphere; but there is another sphere in which its independence or rather its separate existence vanishes.[24]

Federalism is an American contribution to modern political thought and practice. The U.S. Constitution of 1789 organized a federal form of government for the first time and many political systems since have used it as a model for their governmental organization. James Madison, one of the American founding fathers, gave expression to the sense of novelty then inherent in American federalism. Referring to the framers of the U.S. Constitution, Madison said: "They accomplished a revolution which has no parallel in the annals of human society. They reared the fabrics of governments which have no model on the face of the globe."[25] Besides the United States, some notable examples of federal constitutions are Canada, Australia, Switzerland, West Germany, and the U.S.S.R.

Characteristics of a Federal Constitution. In a federal system, each citizen is subject to two governments: the national or federal government, and the regional, state, or provincial government. Federalism is characterized by a written constitution which distinguishes the powers of the national and regional governments so as to

---

[23] K. C. Wheare, *Federal Government* (Toronto: Oxford University Press, 1963), p. 10.

[24] E. A. Freeman, *History of Federal Government* (London: Macmillan, 1893), pp. 2–3.

[25] James Madison, "The Federalist No. 14," in Alexander Hamilton, John Jay, and James Madison, *The Federalist* (Washington, D.C.: National Home Library Foundation, 1937), p. 85.

ensure that each will operate within its prescribed jurisdiction. Ambiguity in the distribution of power leads to jurisdictional disputes between the different levels of authority and can, at best, hinder its smooth and effective operation and, at worst, jeopardize the stability of the system. With the exception of Canada, which can be classified as having neither a wholly written nor a wholly unwritten constitution, all federal systems operate on the basis of a written constitution.

The power of amending the federal constitution is of crucial importance since amendments may affect the distribution of powers between the levels of government. In some federal political systems, such as India, the power is given to the federal legislature, though in others the agreement of the federal legislature and a majority of legislatures at the lower level is required. In Canada this issue has hampered the repatriation of the amending process from Britain because no procedure acceptable to both levels of government has so far been devised.

In many federal systems, the judiciary or some other nonpartisan body is given the power to interpret the provisions of the constitution, resolve jurisdictional disputes that may arise between the different levels of government, evaluate and pass judgment upon the constitutionality of legislative or executive action of the various governments if and when called upon to do so.[26]

Division of Power in Federalism. The successful operation of a federal state is dependent upon a clear division of powers between the national and regional governments, and the maintenance of proper balance to ensure that one level of government does not become so powerful as to compromise the autonomy of the others. Though it is generally possible to allocate most political powers between the national and regional governments, there are, nonetheless, certain subjects which have an importance for both levels. Since the laws of a regional government are enforceable only within its own jurisdiction, it becomes necessary that the national government look after those aspects which are of national importance. To facilitate this, almost all federal constitutions classify political power in three categories:

1. A federal list consists of powers granted exclusively to the national government. Section 91 of the BNA Act enumerates the powers of the Canadian federal government.
2. A provincial list enumerates the powers of the regional governments. Sections 92 and 93 of the BNA Act describe the powers of the provincial governments.
3. A concurrent list includes those powers over which both the national and regional governments have authority, with the provision

---

[26] Wheare, *Federal Government*, chap. 4.

that in case of conflict between a national law and a regional law, the latter will be invalid to the extent of conflict with the former. Concurrent jurisdiction in Canada is small and includes only agriculture and immigration as prescribed in section 95 of the BNA Act. In Australia and the United States the concurrent jurisdiction is broad and includes certain aspects of interstate and foreign commerce, bankruptcy, copyrights and patents, census and statistics, and weights and measures. The most comprehensive list of concurrent jurisdiction is found in the Constitution of India, which includes 47 subjects over which both the union and provincial governments may legislate.

Cooperative Federalism.   A recent trend in many federal states is known as *cooperative federalism*. Frequently regional governments find themselves unable to perform the functions for which they are responsible due to a lack of resources, planning, or sheer inertia. In such situations a cooperative partnership may be developed between the national and regional governments, as a result of which the former participates in matters of the latter's jurisdiction. This partnership generally takes the form of "shared-cost programs," where assistance and general guidelines are issued by the national government for specific projects which are administered by the regional governments. Sometimes the national government may simply provide financial aid without any conditions attached and the regional government then uses those funds as a part of its overall budget.

Education and Medicare are two examples of the working of cooperative federalism in Canada. In terms of the BNA Act, education is a provincial matter, but due to rising costs caused by the rapid pace of advance in modern technology, increasing demand for post-secondary education, and the need for modifications in the educational system to keep pace with the changing needs of society, provincial governments are increasingly hard put to raise adequate funds. As the result of an understanding between the federal and provincial governments, the former makes a substantial annual grant to the provinces for education. Also, the federal government meets up to 50 percent of the cost of provincial Medicare plans, provided these conform to the guidelines provided in the Federal Medicare Act of 1966. Cooperative federalism is reflected in many other aspects of government activity, such as the use of the RCMP as provincial police in most provinces, highways, and agricultural programs. Cooperative federalism tends to downplay the element of "independence" of the different levels of government from each other and emphasizes their "interdependence."

Several attempts have been made to indicate the extent of federal-provincial efforts in the area of cooperative federalism. One source lists 67 federal-provincial committees in 1957.[27] Using a different criteria, the Institute of Intergovernmental Relations of Queen's University listed the existence of as many as 190 federal-provincial and interprovincial committees in 1967.[28] Other estimates vary between these two extremes. Although not a very dependable source of analysis, the figures are indicative of the broad scope of cooperative federalism in Canada.

Quasi-Federal Constitutions

Although constitutions are generally classified as either unitary or federal, there is a hybrid form which may be designated as quasi-federal. There are a number of constitutions which, though apparently federal in character, are in fact closer to the unitary form because they contain provisions which tend to give prominence to the national government over regional governments to an extent that the system operates as unitary. Some of these powers are written in the constitution; others may result from political conventions. The Constitution of India, for an example, provides that the president, on the advice of the cabinet, if convinced that constitutional machinery has broken down in a province, may dissolve its legislature, dismiss the cabinet, suspend the constitution, and place the province under the control of the national government until such time as fresh provincial elections may be held. The government of India has resorted to this measure on a few occasions, thus deviating from the principle of constitutional autonomy of the constituent units of the federation. The Swiss Constitution also has a provision which deviates from the strict federal principle. It requires the courts to treat all laws passed by the national legislature as valid even though they may relate to subjects under the jurisdiction of cantonal governments. In effect, such laws, when passed and enforced, would tend to modify the constitutional distribution of powers between the national and regional governments by the unilateral action of the national legislature.

The BNA Act, providing a federal base for the Canadian political system, has several features of a unitary constitution. The Governor General has the right to disallow any act of a provincial legislature dealing with provincial matters. The provincial lieutenant-governors are appointed by the federal government and have the authority to withhold assent from a bill and "reserve" it for the consideration of the

---

[27] K. W. Taylor, "Coordination in Administration," in *Proceedings of the Ninth Annual Conference, 1957* (Toronto: Institute of Public Administration of Canada, 1957) p. 253.

[28] As quoted in Donald Smiley, *Canada in Question: Federalism in the Seventies* (Toronto: McGraw–Hill Ryerson, 1972) p. 58; also, chap. 3.

Governor General. All major judicial appointments in the provinces are made by the federal government. In all these matters, provincial authority vanishes. Speaking of the Canadian Constitution, K. C. Wheare expresses the opinion that ". . . it is hard to know whether we should call it a federal constitution with considerable unitary modifications or a unitary constitution with considerable federal modifications."[29] Therefore, he calls it a quasi-federal constitution.

The presence of such constitutional provisions does not necessarily mean that they are indiscriminately and unscrupulously used by the national government to undermine the authority and independence of regional governments. In fact, these powers are sparingly used; no provincial legislation in Canada has been "reserved" for the perusal of the Governor General since 1943.

Right of Secession

One of the unresolved questions of federalism is whether one or more constituent units of a federation have the right to unilaterally secede from the union. No generally acceptable principle governing this question has been devised. The Civil War in the United States (1861–65) was an attempt on the part of the southern states to secede from the Union. The issue was settled when the secessionists were defeated. This established a precedent that in case of unilateral secession by one or more constituent units the national government has the authority to maintain the integrity of the federation by the use of force. Other than this precedent, no provision exists in modern federal constitutions governing the unilateral right of secession except in the Constitution of the U.S.S.R., which, in Article 35, gives the constituent units the right to secede from the union. Of course, whether the government of the U.S.S.R. would permit the constituent republics to exercise this right is another question. The precedent set by the American Civil War has been reinforced by the civil wars in Nigeria in 1966–69 and Pakistan in 1971 prior to the invasion by India.

Besides unilateral secession, federal ties may be dissolved through common agreement between the different levels of government. Federations of former colonial countries have been particularly prone to this tendency. The British-inspired federation of Rhodesia and Nyasaland and that of the West Indies both collapsed. The French federations of West and Equatorial Africa did so as well.

Strains in Canadian Federalism.   In its preliminary report, the

---

[29] Wheare, *Federal Government*, p. 19.

Royal Commission on Bilingualism and Biculturalism expressed the opinion that Canadian federalism

. . . without being fully conscious of the fact, is passing through the greatest crisis in its history. The source of the crisis lies in the province of Quebec . . . Although a provincial crisis at the outset, it has become a Canadian crisis because of the size and strategic importance of Quebec, and because it has inevitably set off a series of chain reactions elsewhere.[30]

The "crisis" in Canadian federalism, though more acute in recent years, is as old as Canada. Ever since its establishment, the nature of the Canadian confederation has been disputed and subjected to at least two contradictory interpretations. There is the usual political interpretation that the confederation was originally a partnership between New Brunswick, Nova Scotia, Ontario, and Quebec subsequently enlarged by the admission of the other provinces who, for certain common purposes, delegated some of their authority to the central government while retaining jurisdiction in matters of regional interest. Then there is the interpretation that the confederation was a contract between two communities, English and French, each with its distinct linguistic and cultural background. The two communities had agreed to form one state for the pursuit of mutual interests and satisfaction of mutual ambitions. Ever since, the French Canadians have complained that they are treated as second-class citizens by a government dominated by Anglophone Canadians. They argue that this group, by virtue of its numerical majority, dominates the federal government and treats Francophone Canadians as a minority group rather than equal partners. The argument goes that Quebec represents and speaks for most of this latter group and therefore cannot be treated as just another province.

The accumulated grievances, real or imaginary, over the past hundred years are reflected in the development of French-Canadian separatism. The separatists argue that the partnership between the two communities set up by the BNA Act has not worked satisfactorily for French Canadians. It has led to constant bickering between Ottawa and Quebec City. The only way out of this, they suggest, is for the two communities to part ways, with Quebec becoming an independent state.

The French-English-Canadian question has been exacerbated in large measure by the complications that arise from the lack of a clear definition of authority between the federal and provincial governments. For example, education and matters pertaining to it are under

---

[30] A *Preliminary Report of the Royal Commission on Bilingualism and Biculturalism* (Ottawa: The Queen's Printer, 1966), p. 13. Reproduced with the permission of Information Canada.

provincial jurisdiction. The Quebec government has argued that educational television is related to education and thus falls under its provincial jurisdiction. By extension, the argument also goes that international conferences on education and conclusion of international treaties relating to education and cultural matters also "implicitly" fall under provincial jurisdiction. The argument over whether such provincial jurisdiction is implied in section 93 of the BNA Act[31] has caused some spirited debate between the federal government and the government of Quebec. The federal government maintains that educational television falls under its general powers of control over broadcasting, and international conferences on education and conclusion of international treaties on educational and cultural matters is a part of the general field of the country's international relations and is, therefore, under federal jurisdiction.[32] Besides Quebec, other provincial governments have their own jurisdictional disputes with Ottawa. These and other jurisdictional disputes can be settled only if the constitution is amended so as to remove the ambiguities.

A unique feature of Canadian federalism is the use of informal operational agreements between the different levels of government to circumvent jurisdictional and constitutional disputes. This is done through the dominion-provincial conferences in which the first ministers of the various governments attempt to promote cooperative federalism unhampered by constitutional ambiguities.[33]

In the final analysis constitutions are documents prepared by people. The political ingenuity of people is restricted by their inability to see far enough into the future and to take into account all the possible transformations that a community may pass through. People are, therefore, unable to produce a comprehensive, all-encompassing, fool-proof document which anticipates all possible future eventualities. Besides, capricious and unscrupulous persons, in the promotion of their own vested interests, may exploit the loopholes and weaknesses found in all constitutions. The successful operation of a constitutional system depends in large measure on the sense of constraint and responsibility of those who exercise political power.

---

[31] Section 93 of the BNA Act deals with the issue of provincial jurisdiction over education.

[32] For the federal government's position on international conferences on education and international treaties relating to educational and cultural matters, see Mitchell Sharp, *Federalism and International Conferences on Education* (Ottawa: The Queen's Printer, 1968) and Paul Martin, *Federalism and International Relations* (Ottawa: The Queen's Printer, 1968).

[33] Kenneth McRae, ed., *Consociational Democracy: Political Accommodation in Segmented Societies* (Toronto: McClelland and Stewart, Ltd., 1974). For a detailed analysis of federal-provincial interaction and negotiation, see Richard Simeon, *Federal-Provincial Diplomacy: The Making of Recent Policy in Canada* (Toronto: University of Toronto Press, 1972).

RECOMMENDED READINGS

Bay, Christian.   "Needs, Wants and Political Legitimacy." *Canadian Journal of Political Science* 1, no. 3 (September 1968).

Black, E. R. and Cairns, A. C.   *A Different Perspective on Canadian Federalism*. Ottawa: University of Ottawa Press, 1968.

Cheffins, R. I.   *The Constitutional Process in Canada*. Toronto: McGraw–Hill, 1969.

Favreau, Guy.   *The Amendment of the Constitution of Canada*. Ottawa: The Queen's Printer, 1965.

Forsey, Eugene.   *Freedom and Order: Collected Essays*. Toronto: McClelland and Stewart, Ltd., 1974.

Friedrich, Carl J.   *Constitutional Reason of State*. Providence, R.I.: Brown University Press, 1957.

————.   *Constitutional Government and Democracy*. New York: Ginn & Co., 1949.

————.   *Trends of Federalism in Theory and Practice*. New York: Praeger, 1968.

Hockin, Thomas A.   *Government in Canada*. Toronto: McGraw–Hill Ryerson, 1976.

Jennings, Sir Ivor.   *Cabinet Government*. Cambridge: Cambridge University Press, 1969.

Johnson, A. W.   "The Dynamics of Federalism in Canada." *Canadian Journal of Political Science* 1, no. 1 (March 1968).

Loewenstein, Karl.   *British Cabinet Government*. New York: Oxford University Press, 1967.

McIlwain, C. H.   *Constitutionalism: Ancient and Modern*. rev. ed. Ithaca, N.Y.: Great Seal Books, 1958.

McRae, Kenneth, ed.   *Consociational Democracy: Political Accommodation in Segmented Societies*. Toronto: McClelland & Stewart, Ltd., 1974.

Meekison, J. Peter, ed.   *Canadian Federalism: Myth or Reality*. Toronto: Methuen & Co., 1969.

Ormsby, William.   *The Emergence of the Federal Concept in Canada 1839–1845*. Toronto: University of Toronto Press, 1969.

Paine, Thomas.   *Rights of Man*. London: Freethought Publishing Co., 1883.

Pearson, Lester B.   *Federalism for the Future*. Ottawa: The Queen's Printer, 1968.

Schmeiser, D. A.   *Civil Liberties in Canada*. London: Oxford University Press, 1964.

Smiley, Donald V.   *The Canadian Political Nationality*. Toronto: Methuen & Co., 1967.

————.   "The Two Themes of Canadian Federalism." *Canadian Journal of Economics and Political Science* 31, no. 1 (February 1965).

————.   *Canada in Question: Federalism in the Seventies*. Toronto: McGraw–Hill Ryerson, 1972.

Simeon, Richard.   *Federal-Provincial Diplomacy: The Making of Recent Policy in Canada*. Toronto: University of Toronto Press, 1972.

Tarnopolsky, Walter.   *The Canadian Bill of Rights*. Toronto: Carswell, 1966.

Trudeau, P. E.   *Federalism and the French Canadians*. Toronto: Macmillan of Canada, 1968.

————. *A Canadian Charter of Human Rights*. Ottawa: The Queen's Printer, 1968.

————. *The Constitution and the People of Canada*. Ottawa: The Queen's Printer, 1969.

Varcoe, Frederick.   *Constitution of Canada*. Toronto: Carswell, 1965.

Vaughan, Frederick; Kyba, Patrick; and Dwivedi, O. P., eds.   *Contemporary Issues in Canadian Politics*. Scarborough, Ont.: Prentice–Hall, 1970.

Wheare, K. C.   *Modern Constitutions*. London: Oxford University Press, 1951.

————. *Federal Government*. 4th ed. London: Oxford University Press, 1963.

8

Rule Making

NEITHER THE BASIC PATTERN of official structures nor their ostensible functions vary appreciably from system to system. There are four basic governmental structures found in political systems: the legislature, cabinet, administration, and judiciary. Taken together these structures convert the demands articulated and aggregated by the unofficial structures into prescriptions for future social behaviour, generally called laws or rules.

RULES, DECISIONS, AND POLICIES

A *rule* is *a prescription for the future behaviour of groups and individuals in society*. Rules may be broken down into two major categories, decisions and policies, and may be distinguished by their relationship to actual behaviour. *Decisions,* simply stated, *are choices made between alternatives by an individual or group.* They normally involve choices between specific alternatives in specific situations. The process of governing involves the making of a vast number of decisions both simultaneously and over time. There exists the probability that these decisions will be mutually contradictory and inconsistent since the individual backgrounds of the decision makers, their limited sources of information, and the peculiarities of specific situations affect the choices they make, even where the problem is generally widespread. Without a coordination of decision choices, governments or human society as a whole could not continue to function.

In order to avoid the terrible uncertainties of a government full of individual decision makers, an attempt is made everywhere to impose order and consistency upon political decisions. A hierarchical order is imposed in which the broad sets of individual decisions are subordinated to a higher, more abstract, set called policies. *Policies* are *deci-*

175

sions about decisions: they are the guides or parameters to decisions about specific cases. The difference between policies and decisions in government is very important. Generally the central governing institutions are concerned primarily with policies and with the development of effective controls to ensure that the decisions made by administrators correspond to these policies. The process of forming policies is the core of the rule making function and the translation of these broad decisions into decisions affecting specific situations and groups is called rule implementation.

During the past few years, considerable effort has been devoted to the study of policies. What kinds of policies are made is the subject of *policy analysis,* while the study of the *policy process* concerns the way in which policies are arrived at.

Policy Analysis

Policy analysis is both a practical and an academic subject. As the nature of modern society has become more complex, governments have become increasingly interested in developing techniques which would lead to the formulation of more effective policies. For one thing, the technical nature of many parts of society elude the comprehension of policy makers. Specialists in such areas as agriculture, energy production, and armaments have had to be employed. Their advice must necessarily be tendered in ways that would allow legislators and cabinet members to reconcile it with political necessities. It must be comprehensible and contain alternatives, so that the power to choose remains in political hands.

The rapidity of change also puts pressure on political systems to develop practical means of policy analysis. Simply to meet crises as they occur would, sooner or later, lead to political disaster. Attempts have to be made to anticipate problems, to understand them, and to develop contingency plans. A *plan* may be defined as *a comprehensive set of related policies.* Planning is a fact of life in all modern political systems today, and also in many which are moving toward more complex societies. For ideological reasons, countries such as Canada and the United States have rejected the idea of a formal national comprehensive plan, but such planning goes on informally within the cabinet and bureaucratic structures.[1]

If types of policies cannot be analyzed within a planning framework, which is often the case, then the analyst is forced to adopt different criteria. Perhaps the most popular method of categorizing

---

[1] At the subnational level, only Prince Edward Island has a comprehensive plan. All other provinces and states in the two countries depend upon informal projections.

policies is on the basis of their expected outputs. In this way policies may be divided into four types: (*a*) distributive, (*b*) regulative, (*c*) redistributive, and (*d*) emotive-symbolic.[2] Distributive policies are those which allocate resources or privileges to various groups in society. Those involved in the making of such policies are individuals and groups which stand to benefit from these allocations. Regulative policies, in contrast, provide for both "winners" and "losers." They add resources or privileges to some while denying them to others. For example, licensing of television broadcasting is primarily a regulative policy in that it may give very few applicants for station licenses in a given geographic area the authority to broadcast, while denying it to others. Redistributive policies constitute direct attempts to take resources from one segment of the society and give them to another. Guaranteeing minimum annual incomes to all citizens is an example of a redistributive policy. The financing of such a scheme must necessarily come from taxpayers, who, by definition, would already earn more than the minimum income. They would pay for it, but not benefit from the scheme. Finally, emotive-symbolic policies deal with the intangibles of a political system—its loyalties, symbols, and concepts of right or wrong. Such policies do not really affect the material aspects or the privileges of citizens but, instead, alter their perception of society and, to some degree, change the political culture. The decision to phase out the designation "Dominion" for Canada (with its traditional royal emblems) in favour of a "Canadian" state, with its distinctive emblems, flag and institutions, is a result of a series of emotive-symbolic policies.

A third aspect of policy analysis consists of developing tools to measure the impact of policies, without regard to their overall intent or their substantive output. A vast number of analytical tools have been devised. Most of these are mathematical in nature, such as planning-programming budgeting systems (PPBS), operations research, and economic and social indicators.[3] These tools attempt to put policies into frameworks which can be monitored and where outputs can be measured, thus providing some indication as to preferable alternatives and possible impacts of different alternatives. Most of these tools lend

---

[2] This categorization originated with Theodore Lowi. See Peter Aucoin, "Theory and Research in the Study of Policy-Making," in *The Structures of Policy-Making in Canada* ed. G. Bruce Doern and Peter Aucoin (Toronto: Macmillan of Canada, 1971), pp. 19–22. See also T. Alexander Smith, "Toward a Comparative Theory of Policy Making," *Comparative Politics* 1, no. 4 (July 1969), pp. 498–515.

[3] See, for instance, the Economic Council of Canada, *Eighth Annual Review: Design for Decision Making* (1971); *Ninth Annual Review: The Years to 1980* (1972); *Tenth Annual Review Shaping the Expansion* (1973); and *Eleventh Annual Review; Economic Targets and Social Indicators* (1974) (Ottawa: Information Canada).

themselves especially to forms of planning, and may be considered as strategic and tactical planning aids. Policies may also be considered on the basis of the decision style in which they were arrived at. The planning-mathematical approach to policy making tends to encourage innovative, broad-scale policies, as analysts find themselves able to manipulate large quantities of information through the help of computers. Less technical methods result in the necessity of making decisions on the basis of smaller quantities of information. These decisions are more conservative and are based upon past behaviour. They are incremental in nature, that is, their impacts vary only marginally from those of previous policies. They are also disjointed in that new policies will be formulated to meet specific problems, with little thought being given to the connections or contradictions between various policies.[4]

Policy Process

Paradoxically, the policy process is different in all systems, and yet it is also generally the same. It is different in that the various institutions of the governments may become involved in different ways with policy making. For instance, in Canada the committees of the House of Commons are rather unimportant in terms of policy making while the opposite is the case for congressional committees in the United States. The importance of the cabinets in these two countries also offers a contrast, with the Canadian body being much more influential. Differences between systems may also reflect the style of decision making used in the development of policies. Where great emphasis is laid on planning and its related techniques, policies may be made through somewhat different structures and processes than when the policies are determined in a disjointed-incremental style. Finally, differences may exist in the methods by which various types of policies are made. Distributive and regulative policies, for instance, may be handled in different ways, depending upon the makeup of the political system.

The major similarity in the policy process of most countries is due to the fact that the problems to be solved are extremely complex. In order to develop appropriate policies, the problems have to be broken down into manageable components. This has led to a hierarchical system of policy making, especially where elements of planning have been involved.

At the highest level of the policy-making structures, normative planning is done. Normative planning is concerned with the goals to be achieved by the government; what "ought" to be accomplished.

---

[4] David Braybrooke and Charles Lindblom, *A Strategy of Decision* (New York: The Free Press, 1963).

This is generally a function of cabinets, chief executives, and legislatures. Strategic planning tends to come out of an interaction between cabinets and subdivisions or departments of the administration. It is concerned with the translation of normative goals into concrete objectives and general concepts for meeting these objectives. While these departments are primarily concerned with the implementation of policy, they are also used to gather information and develop alternatives for cabinet consideration. Finally, tactical planning deals with the construction of specific programs within strategic limits which will accomplish the stated objectives.[5] Tactical planning tends to be largely a function of the departments and, in terms of its political ramifications, of the cabinet. An example of these three types of planning may be seen where a government establishes that the citizens "ought" to be able to live comfortably. This normative judgment may be fulfilled by concentrating on the development of a service package (public housing, health care, and food distribution) or on augmenting money incomes (guaranteed annual income). Strategic planners may opt for the latter, in which case tactics are devised for distributing funds to only those who need them.

In general, legislatures and cabinets are primarily concerned with the higher levels of policy making, though it must be noted that their relative influence in the process varies from system to system. The concern of the bureaucracy is primarily with techniques of accomplishing these goals, whether as part of a strategy or tactic. These similarities will be further explored below in the context of the rule making (decisions and policies) function.

The actual process of making policies begins normally as a definitional one. In a planning context, the defining of issues and policy types is intimately tied up with the normative aspects of a plan. Where policies are disjointed and incremental, the definition of the issue at hand is determined through bargaining and political manoeuvre. Depending upon the perceived nature of a future policy decision, various governmental, interest group, and party personnel will become involved. Thus it becomes a matter of political tactics for a specific party or interest group to define an issue in such a manner as to maximize its own strength. Distributive policy decisions are normally made in bureaucratic or legislative committee milieux. In Canada, legislative committees are likely to be unimportant in this context, except perhaps for the majority party caucus, which is not really an official legislative committee.

Regulative policies are normally subject to legislative approval, though this is often a formality in Canada. Much regulative policy is

---

[5] Ibid.

made under a device known as delegated legislation, where the legislature passes a broad law which is then put into effect by cabinet and administrative bodies. Redistributive policy issues tend to be directed at the political leadership of the country and are decided at the executive level. Since much of this type of policy involves forms of taxation, there must be some involvement of legislatures as well. The people involved in the contest over redistributive issues are normally the same each time a problem arises. Leaders of business, labour, and ideological groups tend to consistently take important roles in this particular issue arena.

Emotive-symbolic policies are normally left for legislatures to decide, if they are not decided by the general public in plebiscites or referenda. The reason why political leaders refrain from directing battles over them is because the issues are divisive, making the stakes too high to risk forcing an issue and losing. Where policy is made in legislatures on emotive-symbolic issues, it is not uncommon to see the prime minister declare a "free vote" on the issue. Legislators are not obliged to vote with their party or their leaders in this case. Even referenda may be accompanied by temporary party splits as in the 1975 referendum campaign in Great Britain over Common Market membership. The ruling Labour Party caucus was permitted to divide over the question for purposes of the referendum, with the prime minister and others favouring membership, while some Cabinet members and many of the backbenchers opposed it. The adoption of the Maple Leaf as the national flag and the abolition of capital punishment are examples of two emotive-symbolic issues which involved Canadians in the 1960s and 1970s respectively.

An example of the importance of defining a policy issue may be seen in a civil service strike. The union itself may simply wish to secure a better settlement from the government for its members. It looks for a distributive policy solution and insists that the strike is a matter between the union and the "employer," in this case the government. Citizens and business leaders hurt by the strike may argue in favour of a regulative decision, one which would presumably favour their interest at the expense of the strikers. A political party may denounce the government for not helping the low-paid wage earners in the country and for catering to the rich. Part of a change of philosophy, it claims, would be a fair settlement for the union. This would herald a new redistributive policy. Finally, a group of extremists denounce the strike as part of a plot to destroy the government and the existing political system and call for the arrest and imprisonment of the strike leaders in order to "show who is boss," an obvious emotive-symbolic policy. Depending on the success of the various groups, the issue and its resolution could be defined as anything from a form of business deal to an attempted revolution. It could engender almost no public interest or, at the other extreme, lead to violence.

In the sense that policies are a type of rule, and perhaps the most important type, the rule making process and the policy-making process must of necessity overlap in any system. While the political structures discussed in this chapter are in fact the primary generators of policies, they are also involved in more specific decisions as well. Thus it is necessary to return to a discussion of rule making in its broadest sense, keeping in mind that the critical rules to be set down are generally policies.

RULE MAKING STRUCTURES

The conversion of inputs into outputs is accomplished through the coordinated performance of three functions: rule making, rule implementation, and rule adjudication. Traditionally, these functions have been associated with the legislature, the executive (cabinet and administration taken together), and the judiciary, in that order. The actual performance of these functions is not always fulfilled in accordance with this formal division, for, as with other aspects of the political system, there is a pattern of informal relationships that often deviates from the formal pattern.

The function of rule making can be fulfilled either in an authoritarian manner—where a single leader makes most decisions or retains effective power to oversee the decisions of others—or in a democratic manner—through a parliamentary system in which the leadership of an elected legislature makes the decisions, or a presidential system—where the legislature ostensibly makes decisions on its own which are then implemented by the executive. The difference between the two latter forms can be briefly outlined as in Figure 8–1.

This diagram illustrates the fact that a parliamentary system is based upon a fusion of powers wherein the cabinet consists simultaneously of the leadership of the majority party or coalition of parties in the legislature and the leadership of the administration. The cabinet is thus in a position to coordinate the activities of both the legislature and the administration while being accountable to the legislature upon which it is based. A presidential system is based upon the premise that the concentration of power existing in a parliamentary system is undesirable and dangerous and that rule making and rule implementing should be separated from each other by prohibiting the overlap of key personnel.

These complex arrangements are characteristic of modern political systems and have evolved over many centuries. Diverse circumstances in each case have resulted in a wide variety of patterns. Though the

FIGURE 8–1
Legislative-Executive Relations

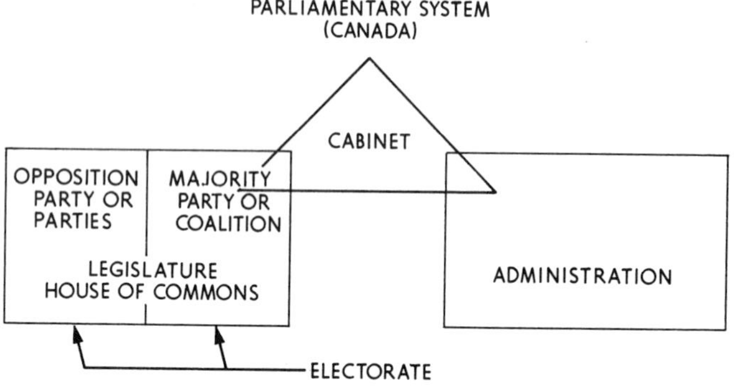

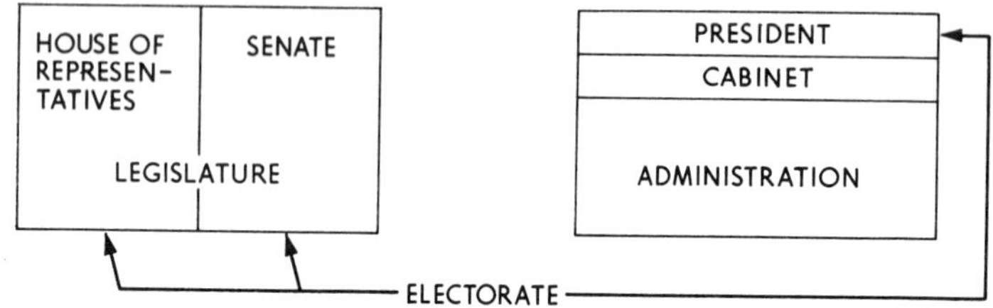

governmental structures generally perform similar functions everywhere and the institutions created have considerable superficial similarity, each arrangement is unique and presents its own problems of analysis.

Head of State

For much of history, leadership, including the political, has been associated with age, strength, and a presumed ability to influence events. Leadership associated with age is accepted—even today—because of the assumption that experience is the best insurance against future mistakes. Such leadership was of great importance to the primitive societies of food gatherers, since their existence was so precarious that mistakes could be fatal to the group. Leadership associated with mental or physical strength reassures a group against subjugation by other people and gives some control over the forces of nature to the society. Leadership associated with influence over events has been the most pervasive form existing in large, settled communities. The merger of religion and political authority in Egypt and Mesopotamia brought forth a long era where special powers over nature and people were attributed to specific individuals on the basis of their claims to a special relationship with the regulating force of the universe, be it God or the gods. The continuing influence of this form of leadership offered new life to the institution of monarchy at the end of the Dark Ages in the form of the divine right of kings. This conception of a special contact between king and God has given way in more recent times to the notion of king as the embodiment of the nation, or special contact between the king and society.

As the basis for the singular leaders in a society has changed in most political systems, the forms surrounding the leader have also been changing. In some systems, titles and authority were left unchanged while power was deleted; in other systems the title of the leader was also changed: the president succeeded the king. Power was in some cases restored or added to the newly titled leaders. In all cases the singular leader has remained to represent the whole of the people or to cement their ties to the Supreme Being. This leader, regardless of title, may be called the head of state.

The common practice in most political systems, including that of Canada, is to separate the offices of the head of state and the head of government. The head of state holds authority while rarely exercising power, whereas the head of government normally exercises the power. *Authority* may be defined as *the right to influence the behaviour of others*, and *power* is the *ability to do so*. Authority is often found without power, and vice versa. In contrast, the merger of power and authority in a single executive post is found in the presidential systems of the United States, most countries in Latin America, and others in Africa and Asia. The French political system also includes a head of state who may exercise considerable power, though in this case power is shared with the prime minister. There are also systems such as Morocco and Saudi Arabia, where a monarch exercises both authority and power.

There are three basic reasons for the continued existence of the office of head of state in a modern country: the value of the traditional aspects of the office, the legitimizing function the office performs within the political system, and the role of personification played by the incumbent. Examples of these reasons may be seen in the Queen as the head of state in Canada.[6] This office has a traditional aspect which is of value to the society and to the political system. It is a historical link with the origins and growth of the country as well as the

---

[6] It should be noted that all the Queen's legitimizing authority was delegated to the Governor General in 1947.

legal tie to the British past. The stolid existence of such an office amid the short-term wrangling of parliamentarians and cabinet ministers also evokes the idea of a society which has existed and will exist regardless of any single crisis or issue.

The concept of the head of state as the embodiment of society has resulted in the retention by that office of certain legitimizing functions. Legitimacy, in the modern political system, implies the conformity of an action to the ethical norms of the society as generally expressed through convention or law. Society sees some actions as "right" and others as "wrong." In the political system some actions may not be performed until the head of state gives his or her approval, that is, makes them "right."

In Canada, as elsewhere, the use of this legitimizing authority is complicated by the lack of power in the office of head of state. Such authority has generally been acquired or, as in the case of the Queen and the Governor General, retained through a formal constitution or by tradition. In both cases the possessors of power in the system may legally divest the head of state of his or her authority. In Canada, as in most other systems with similar offices, the Governor General must play a passive role with respect to the use of his or her authority. Paradoxically, the Governor General may keep that authority only by never, or rarely, exercising it independently of those who hold power. The value of such authority lies in the relative rarity with which it is exercised independently of the prime minister, since politicians know that an instance where it is so used will be the equivalent of a ringing alarm to society that something is drastically wrong in the political system. In effect, the Governor General can help keep the game of politics relatively "honest."

The exercise of the authority of a head of state normally revolves around three actions. First, the head of state may choose a candidate for the office of prime minister. If the candidate is accepted, or given a "vote of confidence" in the legislature, he or she then takes office. If the candidate is rejected, then another candidate may be chosen. A modification of this practice exists in England and the Commonwealth where the prime minister is formally appointed by the head of state, rather than first being a candidate. This provision means that if the Governor General's choice is rejected by Parliament, the prime minister has the right to ask for dissolution of Parliament and new elections. Such a situation led, in part, to the last Canadian constitutional crisis known as the King–Byng affair, involving the Governor General in 1926.[7]

---

[7] For information on the King-Byng affair, see Eugene A. Forsey, *The Royal Power of Dissolution of Parliament in the British Commonwealth* (1943; reprint ed., Toronto: Oxford University Press, 1968).

The second activity reserved for the head of state is the dissolution of Parliament, which leads to new elections. This is done at the request of the prime minister, and not always in conjunction with the defeat of a cabinet on a confidence vote in Parliament. In France, for instance, the dissolution of the National Assembly by Premier Faure in late 1955 was considered an unusual event, since most assemblies in the Third (1871–1940) and Fourth (1946–58) republics had seen a number of cabinets fall without affecting the normal term of parliamentary office. The request for dissolution is rarely turned down by the head of state. Constitutionally, the governor general may do so in Canada; however, the 1926 crisis and decisions made by the Privy Council in 1935 lay this question open to debate.

Third, the head of state also exercises authority in two other related fashions. He or she gives royal assent to bills passed by Parliament before they can become law and must approve orders and decrees issued by the cabinet before they can have legal effect. Refusal or the vetoing of a bill or decree is almost unknown where the head of state has little power, though in Canada the provincial lieutenant-governors have "reserved" 70 bills for the perusal of the Governor General since 1867. Most of these actions were taken before 1900, the latest occurrence being in 1961. Even where the head of state exercises power, as in the United States or France, the vetoing of a bill or order is a relatively rare occurrence.

If there is a common thread running through the ways in which the head of state exercises authority, it is to legitimize the existence and decisions of the formal decision-making bodies in the political system. When the head of state performs this legitimizing action with the concurrence of the elected representatives of the society, all is well. When the head of state acts independently to dissolve the legislature, choose the prime minister, or reject a bill, society is warned that a malfunction may exist in the political system.

The role of personification played by the head of state also serves a useful purpose. The ceremonial or binding-together role of the head of state is demanded in every society, and its association in most countries with a nonpartisan office serves only to make it more meaningful. One sees this demand satisfied by the amount of formal ceremony surrounding the Queen or the Governor General, and by the tendency, where the head of state is appointed or elected, to choose a dignified older man for the position. In Canada, the nation-binding aspect of the Governor General's office is ironically attested to by the demands for the formation of a republic either in Quebec or Canada as a whole by certain elements of Canadian opinion. The republican structure would, of course, also include a head of state, but this office would not have its ties to the past military defeats and cultural allegiances which exist around the present form of the office.

Privy Council

Most countries over the last two centuries have managed through revolution or constitutional change to sweep away many archaic political institutions in favour of the set of standard bodies known as head of state, head of government, cabinet, legislature, and administration. Many governments patterned on the British tradition have retained at least one complicating formality: the Privy Council. Originally, when the king or queen exercised both authority and power, he or she gathered a set of advisors who, as a body, eventually became known as the privy (private, close) council. The rise of the cabinet as the wielder of power in Great Britain marked the decline of the Privy Council in terms of influence, though not in a legal sense. To the present day, in Great Britain as well as Canada, the authority of the Queen and the Governor General is exercised "in council." Though the Cabinet in Ottawa or in any provincial capital is the subject of constant discussion and analysis, it has no legal existence whatsoever. The cabinet is a committee of the Privy Council. This does not, of course, mean that there is no such thing as the cabinet; just that the cabinet, as it is, has no legal authority or existence. The realities of power, or the ability to command obedience, are such that in terms of behaviour the cabinet exists while the Privy Council is little more than a shell.

The reasons for this informal arrangement of the central institutions of governments lie in tradition and the desire to adapt institutions rather than rebuild them. The Privy Council in Canada is made up of all former cabinet members, regardless of party, and other persons whom the Governor General, at the request of the prime minister, may wish to appoint. Members are appointed for life, though the Governor General may dismiss whomsoever he or she wishes. In England especially, the Privy Council is a large and unwieldy group.

The full Privy Council rarely meets, and then only on ceremonial occasions. Conventions or traditions govern the attendance of the councillors at committee (Cabinet) meetings. The prime minister calls the meetings and he may invite those council members whom he pleases. Of course, this means that usually only Cabinet members attend Privy Council meetings. The quorum necessary to enact council business is very small, so that the Cabinet, in effect, acts for the Privy Council. In this way, the Cabinet is able to act with power equivalent to the cabinet in any other country which employs the parliamentary method of government.

There are two important policy-making bodies besides the Cabinet which are formally attached to the Privy Council. They are the Treasury Board and the Privy Council Office. The Treasury Board is formally a committee of the Privy Council, like the Cabinet itself, but because of the central position of the Cabinet, it in fact acts as if it were a Cabinet committee.

The role of the Treasury Board in policy making has undergone major shifts during the past decade. Its original task was to oversee the expenditure of government funds, ensuring that money was spent only on authorized projects. It also acted to verify the budgetary requests of the various administrative departments and to control the expenditures on civil servants, thereby keeping down the budgets and the number of administrative staff. Its jurisdiction over such matters naturally gave it considerable influence in the areas of financial and budgetary policy.

In the 1960s, the Treasury Board staff was separated from that of the Department of Finance, and its role became that of the management arm of the Cabinet. Its autonomy was symbolized by the granting of cabinet status to the President of the Treasury Board. It was to supervise the actions of the administrative departments as they developed programs to implement policies; establish procedures for measuring the costs of these programs; and make sure that adequate personnel with the right qualifications were on hand to carry out programs.

The second policy-making organization attached to the Privy Council is the Privy Council Office (PCO). Originally the PCO was responsible for the occasional formalities related to the Privy Council itself. During and since World War II, it has been transformed into what might more appropriately be called a "Cabinet secretariat." The present role of the PCO is to provide the Cabinet and prime minister with assistance and technical advice on policy alternatives; to coordinate various policies so that overlapping and contradictory efforts are eliminated, and to inform various departments of policy decisions so that they can begin the implementation process.

The PCO has been the subject of continuing press and legislative interest since Prime Minister Trudeau began to emphasize its role in policy planning and advice to the Cabinet. From 1968 to 1972 the most influential PCO advisors were dubbed the "supergroup" because of their emphasis on planning and the use of modern technological aids, such as computers and operations research. After the 1972 "nonvictory" election, the Liberal minority government took a more political stance and some PCO technocrats were relegated to a less important role. Trudeau's victory in the 1974 election signalled the rise of the PCO again and, as the press seems to feel, the creation of a new "supergroup."

Head of Government

The prime minister as the head of government is a single individual who exercises power and leadership over the system. The office developed out of the preference of the monarch for the advice of one minister over others, the prime minister thus being given special access to the legitmizing agent of the system. In terms of the government, the prime minister functions as a directing and coordinating agent, requiring the individual ministers to act in a coherent, cooperative manner.

The relationship between the head of government and head of state has evolved from the position of the prime minister as the chief advisor to the monarch. In some systems, the monarch still exercises the powers Canada assigns to the prime minister, controlling the cabinet; in other republics, the president is both head of state and head of government. The President of the United States, for example, acts as the head of state in signing bills passed by the Congress, pardoning criminals, and signing treaties, while acting as the head of government by calling cabinet meetings, approving budgets, and appointing officials to positions in the administration.

In most systems, however, the head of government is a separate individual from the head of state. In Canada, the prime minister is chosen by the Governor General from the party commanding the "confidence" of the House of Commons. Once he has been appointed, he chooses the other ministers of the Cabinet, who then serve during his pleasure. The prime minister exercises power in a number of ways:

1. The link between the Cabinet and the Governor General is the prime minister. He, therefore, controls the dispensing of legitimacy.
2. As Cabinet leader, the prime minister determines the agenda of its meetings, thus controlling the range of decisions to be made.
3. As party leader, the prime minister is the central link between the electorate and the rule making process.
4. As the link between the Parliament and the Governor General, the prime minister controls the former's existence and sessions.
5. As the link between the administration and the Governor General, the prime minister controls appointments and finances.

Being the centre of power in the political system, the prime minister is also subjected to a variety of limitations and influences. By controlling access to the legitimizing agent, he becomes responsible for its conservation in the person of the Governor General. As the party leader he must use his power so as to maintain the position of the party between elections. Since he determines the nature of the policy decisions to be made, he becomes identified with the program of the Cabinet as a whole. Finally, his influence in administrative matters renders him somewhat responsible for the actions of the whole administration. The very qualities which make the prime minister powerful serve to render him vulnerable to political shifts.

The functions of the prime minister within the Cabinet are of special importance. It was noted that the prime minister sets the agenda for Cabinet meetings. This task reflects the primary functions of the prime minister: leadership and coordination. Some form of final screening of aggregated interests must be made in order to ensure that the Cabinet uses its time efficiently. By setting the agenda, the prime minister both ranks and screens questions. Secondly, he concentrates upon the work of the Cabinet itself rather than on any particular administrative duties. Though sometimes a system may include a number of administrative duties in the prime minister's office, these usually pertain to general policy matters.

The head of government, whether a prime minister or a president, normally has a large staff at his or her disposal to aid in these complex tasks. In the United States, the office of the president tended over the years to combine the roles of cabinet secretariat (such as the Canadian PCO) with that of the personal office of the president. The high point of this development came under President Nixon, and the confusion of domestic policies with party and election politics led to the bungled burglary at the Watergate complex and the eventual fall of Nixon as president.

The Prime Minister's Office (PMO) in Canada provides the prime minister with political advice and support. Its original function was to handle his correspondence and appointments. During the past 40 years its role has expanded, basically into the area of providing political advice on policy matters. While the PMO and the PCO do overlap to a degree, attempts are made by both bodies to delineate separate jurisdictions. The PCO concerns itself with the more technical aspects of policies while the PMO considers their political ramifications. However, the potential for disastrous confusions continues to haunt observers of the growing influence and interdependence of these two bodies.

Cabinet

Evolution.   In any group larger than a small clan, the task of making political decisions tends to outstrip the capabilities and energy of a single person. The leader then begins to entrust other people with part of his or her power in certain areas. This process of delegating authority to subleaders has led, in our day, to the institution known as the cabinet. Though they may have varying powers and names, every political system in the world contains this key committee of decision makers.

The evolution of the cabinet in Europe and Asia began with the institution of formal positions for certain services performed in the household of the king or queen. Two of the most important were treasurer and secretary. The treasurer originally was a highly trusted servant who watched over the crown's money and property. In time, the treasurer might be given the duties of collecting and spending this wealth. The technical job of accounting for funds formed the embryo of what is now in most countries the ministry of finance. To minister to someone is to help or serve and the term "ministry" itself indicates the archaic origins of the institution.

The secretary to the king or queen was naturally responsible for the royal correspondence. This position gradually evolved into at least three separate jobs. These secretaries were called secretaries of state, a term still used in Canada, France, the United States, and elsewhere. One secretary of state was in charge of correspondence with other countries—the foreign secretary or minister. Another secretary of state prepared the royal laws and decrees and became known as the home secretary in England and the minister of the interior in France. A third secretary communicated the royal decisions concerning the punishment of criminals and civil disputes, eventually becoming the minister of justice. Another member of the early cabinets was the general of the armies, who eventually became known as the minister of war or defence. Besides the ruler then, the initial divisions of the cabinet were five: finance, foreign affairs, interior, justice, and defence.

Size.   The size of the cabinet varies greatly throughout the world. If a cabinet is considered as the sum of all the ministers appointed to direct the administration and others appointed "without portfolio," the number ranges from less than a dozen in Switzerland to over 90 in the U.S.S.R. Membership in the Canadian Cabinet typically numbers over 20. The number changes when ministries are consolidated, created, or headed by a minister holding more than one portfolio.

The legal or formal size of the cabinet often conflicts with reality, since groups larger than 20 are unwieldy as policy-making bodies. A compromise between the coordinative value of a small group of ministerial policy makers and the large group of ministers necessary to control the burgeoning apparatus of the modern administration has been the formation of "inner" cabinets. In England, for instance, most ministers are excluded from the inner cabinet, which contains about 20 members, unless an issue is brought up in a meeting of that body which pertains directly to the excluded minister's portfolio. He then attends at the times when this issue is discussed. A second method of reconciling size with efficiency is through the formation of superministries. In France, during the Fourth Republic, the defence minister exercised authority over the ministers of the army, air force, and navy.

The large size of the cabinet in many countries is due to two factors: the first is the increased specialization of the tasks of the ministry of the interior, which at one time handled most domestic government matters. In some countries such as Canada and the United States, this position has either not existed or the title has been used for only a specific part of its former scope. The Secretary of the Interior of the United States government has powers similar to those of the Canadian Minister of Indian Affairs and Northern Development, whereas the interior ministry in France reflects tradition in that it controls the police and a large part of the local government powers. Some of the ministries which have "spun off" from the ministry of the interior concept are: education, health and welfare, transportation, mines and resources, and manpower and immigration. In Canada the adoption of a federal system has meant that certain functions such as education and highways have been taken out of the national context and included in provincial cabinets.

The increase in governmental responsibilities has also prompted the enlargement of cabinets. The growth of the welfare state and the consequential involvement of the government in the economy have required the creation of ministries of labour, consumers' affairs, services and supply, and housing. Special historical conditions gave rise to a ministry of Indian affairs. The wholesale nationalization of industry and agriculture in communist countries has led to the creation of a phalanx of specialized ministries. There are 45 ministries alone in the Soviet Union to handle various aspects of industry, construction, transport, and agriculture.

Specialization. The existence of a cabinet is, in itself, an indication of the need to divide the work load of decision making among a number of people. One may distinguish three forms of specialization: the formation of administrative and functional divisions called ministries; the division of ministries included in and excluded from the cabinet or inner cabinet; and the formation of cabinet committees.

Ministers are normally given portfolios, or the responsibility for particular ministries called "departments." However, in many cabinets, provision is made for the inclusion of ministers without portfolio. These ministers are often appointed to seal political bargains in coalitions where the demands for cabinet posts outstrip their availability. In other systems, such as the Canadian, ministers who lack experience but who represent a necessary geographical balance in the Cabinet may be appointed without portfolio. A third reason is the need for a minister to handle a pressing political problem which cuts across administrative boundaries.

A second form of specialization is the division between ministries as a whole and the cabinet. Where the number of ministries is too large to allow for manageable meetings of the full cabinet, an inner cabinet may be formed from the most important ones. An alternative to this procedure is the formation of quasi-ministerial posts which allow for a difference of status among cabinet and noncabinet members. In Canada, the practice of raising certain positions to ministerial rank without calling them ministries has been infrequent, but the existence of special assistants and undersecretaries is common in the United States and Great Britain. Still another variation, which is practiced in Canada, is the cooption by the Cabinet of a number of aides from the House of Commons who assist the ministers in their parliamentary duties. These aides are called parliamentary assistants, and the positions are considered to be good "stepping stones" to Cabinet membership.

A third form of specialization consists of the formation of cabinet committees. The pressures of World War II led to the formation of ten Cabinet committees in Canada, though only one survived the war. Later other committees were formed, but it was not until the Liberal victory in 1963 that a working system of formal Cabinet committees began to operate. By the early 1970s there were at least 10 Cabinet committees. These have been divided into operational or activity committees and coordinating committees as is shown in Table 8–1. An extra committee called Special Committee of Cabinet handles tasks which do not readily fit into the standing committee structure.

TABLE 8–1
Cabinet Committees

Activity	*Coordinating*
1. External Policy and Defence	1. Priorities and Planning
2. Economic Policy	2. Treasury Board
3. Social Policy	3. Legislation and House Planning
4. Science, Culture, and Information	4. Federal Provincial Relations
5. Government Operations	*Other*
6. Security and Intelligence	1. Special Committee

Source: Gordon Robertson, "The Changing Role of the Privy Council Office," *Canadian Public Administration* 14, no. 4 (Winter 1971), p. 492, and Marc Lalonde, "The Changing Role of the Prime Minister's Office," *Canadian Public Administration,* 14, no. 4 (Winter 1971), p. 514.

The importance of the committee system, like that of the PCO and PMO, has been increased since 1968. The committees have been given the power to make a wide range of decisions, which are then ratified or, rarely, rejected by the Cabinet as a whole. Normally, Cabinet meetings include few matters which require a decision of the whole body. Far more decisions are made in the committees and these are then referred to the body as a whole. This procedure allows the ministers more time to attend to work which involves their specific areas of responsibility and also to fulfill other political and legislative duties. The number of full Cabinet meetings dropped nearly in half between 1966–67 and 1970–71 while the committee meetings tripled.

The key committee in this structure appears to be the Priorities and Planning Committee which is chaired by the prime minister.[8] The committee works to integrate the policy recommendations of the Economic Policy and Social Policy committees into some form of long-range plan. This plan is then translated into financial terms by the establishment of expenditure guidelines for the administrative departments. The tactical allocations are then worked out between the Treasury Board and the departments before the introduction of new budget proposals to the House of Commons.

Membership.   A crucial question in any political system is, who becomes a member of the cabinet.[9] Although the choice of ministers in any cabinet is always the result of careful and detailed bargaining, the process of constituting a cabinet is relatively simple. The head of state designates a prime minister who, in turn, selects the other ministers. Where the head of state is also the head of government, the initial step is eliminated. Conflicts in the criteria for selecting ministers transforms this relatively simple task into one demanding delicacy and artistry.

There are several criteria basic to the selection of members of a cabinet. The power inherent in a cabinet attracts the attention of the society as a whole and leads to demands for representation by specific minorities and interests, and intraparty factions. Some combination must be represented so as to achieve a relatively permanent acceptance of the cabinet's right to exist on the part of a majority of these groups. In most countries, geographical representation in the cabinet is a subject of some concern, especially in federal systems where regionalism is high. Such representation has been achieved in Canada by means of a formula wherein a certain number of Cabinet posts have been allotted to politicians from each area of the country:[10]

1. Each province will generally have one representative in the Cabinet.
2. Ontario has at least four representatives.
3. Quebec has at least two.
4. The West normally has at least four.

---

[8] Khalid B. Sayeed, "Policy Analysis in Washington and Ottawa," *Policy Sciences* 4, no. 1 (March 1973), pp. 92–93.

[9] This is a modification of formula stated in R. M. Dawson and N. Ward, *The Government of Canada*, 4th ed. (Toronto: University of Toronto Press, 1963), pp. 194–95.

[10] Ibid. See also William Matheson, *The Prime Minister and the Cabinet* (Toronto: Methuen, 1976).

This formula means that no Canadian Cabinet will normally number less than 14 posts and, in fact, no Cabinet in the 20th century has numbered less than 15. This theoretical minimum increases to 17 if the French-English quotas are included (see below). These rules, all of which are only customary, have required the occasional appointment of unqualified or politically undesirable people to Cabinet posts over the heads of some of their potentially more able colleagues.

Another form of geographical representation is also found in the federal Cabinet. Certain ministries are allotted to individuals on the basis of which provinces they represent. The Prairie provinces tend to receive the ministry of agriculture; the Maritimes, the fisheries portfolio; and eastern Canada, the finance portfolio.

The representation of specific interests or interest groups in the cabinet is generally expressed in a negative fashion, that is, care is exercised that an individual is *not* appointed to a ministry whose "clientele" would find the incumbent objectionable. An appointment not conforming to this convention may cause the near collapse of a cabinet, as was demonstrated by the appointment of Walter Gordon to the finance ministry in 1963. Opposition from commercial interests and the civil servants in his own ministry threatened the Cabinet as a whole and soon ended his Cabinet career.

A third criterion is the representation of race and religion. In Canada the linguistic division between "French" and "English" has produced another customary formula which requires that the Quebec representation be divided between a Roman Catholic French majority and a Protestant English minority of posts. The Ontario or New Brunswick representation may also include a French Canadian.

A more extreme form of religious representation existed in Lebanon, prior to the recent civil war, where a "national pact" between the country's religious denominations apportioned not only cabinet but parliamentary and high administrative posts among the Christians and Muslims. In Malaysia, certain cabinet posts are generally allotted to Chinese and others are exclusively reserved for Malays. Cabinets in the United States in recent years have tended to include "token" women, blacks, and Jews.

Party factions constitute a fourth criterion. When choosing a cabinet, the head of government must take into account the strength of the more powerful members of his or her own party and unify it by a judicious distribution of the rewards of victory. Where party factions remain relatively stable, such as in the Japanese parties or the West German Christian Democratic Union, the prime minister or chancellor must allocate posts on the basis of the perceived strength of each faction, unless political advantage might be gained by favouring one faction over another. In Canada the election of Pierre Trudeau in

1968 resulted in the elevation to Cabinet status of nearly all of his major and minor rivals to the leadership of the Liberal Party. On the other hand, in a system where the president is elected for a fixed term, the need to accommodate rivals is less pressing. Neither of Richard Nixon's major opponents in the campaign for the Republican nomination for the presidency in 1968 received cabinet posts, although this could possibly be attributed to the fact that both were in possession of strong centres of power outside the federal government and were reluctant to give them up.

The cabinet makeup becomes quite complex once these criteria are acted upon, and one wonders where room is left for valuable and talented supporters of the head of government. Often some of these people may fit other criteria and are then included. Where this is not possible, these supporters may be placed in new posts added to the cabinet or in the personal advisory staff of the prime minister or president. In general, three circles may be distinguished in most cabinets. The inner circle around the head of government is composed of his or her close political allies and advisors. Next come the party notables who have been incorporated into the cabinet in the name of unity, and an outer circle is formed of ministers chosen on other criteria, including technical competence and future potential. Once these general criteria have been met, a second set are used to evaluate individuals for promotion to the cabinet. These may be called personal criteria.

Probably the most important personal requirement is that of integrity. Since the ministers will be under close scrutiny by the same media which report their policy decisions, character faults such as dishonesty and immorality are easily connected with the correctness of political decisions. Politics and personality are closely related in the minds of the public.

Another personal requirement for a cabinet post is political experience. Experience, in terms of political longevity, is of great importance in a parliamentary system where cabinet members must be members of the legislature. Party influence, essential in cabinet selection in the former case, is most often a direct result of longevity: Diefenbaker, for instance, was a conservative member of Parliament for almost 17 years before succeeding to party leadership. On the other hand, Trudeau entered the Liberal Party ranks and moved quickly to its leadership on the strength of his experience with the crucial question of Quebec's place in the confederation.

Technical competence as a requisite for a cabinet post is a desirable quality, though of relatively low priority. For the most part, the structuring of the decision-making process at the cabinet level does not require technical competence. Important qualities are those related to sensitivity to political opinion and management ability. The technical details related to decision alternatives are the responsibility of the administration and are expected to be presented to the minister and cabinet in a fashion which allows them to judge their political acceptability.

The turnover of cabinet ministers is, to a great extent, dependent upon the speed with which cabinets rise and fall. In parliamentary systems this rate varies widely: between 1941 and 1952 Iran saw 26 cabinets take office while England saw four. In Canada, West Germany, and the U.S.S.R., among others, cabinets with rare exceptions remain in office from one election to the next. In most presidential systems, a cabinet does not fall since its term coincides with that of the head of government. A more common phenomenon is a change in individual ministers during the tenure of a cabinet. These changes occur frequently in all systems, some at a faster rate than others. In Japan, for instance, prime ministers have tended to reshuffle their cabinets at least once a year. Deaths and resignations affect the composition of cabinets, as does the continual struggle for position and power between cabinet factions.

One would expect that this continual turnover would eventually bring a great number of politicians to cabinet status, but such is not the case because many of the same people tend to be included in each reshuffling of the cabinet and in successive cabinets. This repetitiveness may be seen by comparing the number of cabinet posts over time with the number of different individuals who have occupied them. For instance, a system which contains ten cabinet seats and which has ten cabinets over a period of time may be said to have produced 100 posts. In Iran the 26 cabinets mentioned above opened up 400 posts, but 18 people filled 133 of these and only 144 people filled all 400. About the same proportions may be discovered by studying the cabinets of the French Fourth Republic. Such persistence at the cabinet level is also found in North America. Phillip Williams notes that the six highest government posts were held between 1944 and 1958 by 48 men in Paris, 27 in London, and 30 in Washington.[11] Lester Pearson was associated with the federal Cabinet or its opposition counterpart (the "shadow cabinet") for 20 years. The relative stability or instability of cabinets as bodies is not closely related, then, to the stability of their membership.

The cabinet has become the focus of political activity in parliamentary systems because it combines the legislative and executive leadership, thereby being in the position to both formulate policies and oversee their execution. As a group, it is representative of many of

---

[11] Phillip Williams, *Crisis and Compromise* (London: Longmans, Green, 1964), p. 216.

the forces within the society and is the focal point of the bargaining process that is a part of policy formulation. The cabinet receives the various inputs which have been already filtered and ranked in preliminary fashion by parties and other groups and decides which of the various possible alternatives is desirable. Various interest groups, the political parties, and the media may suggest any variety of options and the departments may accumulate and process volumes of data, but the cabinet has the responsibility of deciding what is to be undertaken and under what circumstances. The prime minister, as the primary figure in this group, would normally set the pace and tone of the deliberations and, depending upon his strength vis-à-vis his cabinet colleagues, be in a position to exercise the most individual influence. Cabinet meetings must of necessity involve discussions of an issue, the various feasible alternatives, and the best means for getting them accepted by the rest of the government party and, hopefully, by the parliament. Individual cabinet ministers are responsible for presenting the proposals concerning their departments. The measure of a cabinet minister is how well he or she acquits himself or herself in his or her public role, the political forces he or she represents, and his or her effectiveness within the meetings of the cabinet and its committees.

Administration

The role of government departments and agencies in the rule making process is normally a significant one, but, it may vary depending upon the informal relationships between the official political structures. Where there are strong policy-making bodies surrounding the cabinet, as in Canada or the United States, the role of bureaucrats at this level of rule making may be quite restricted. It may be enlarged where there are significant government-owned enterprises or where there are a large number of autonomous regulatory agencies. Crown corporations and agencies, such as the Canadian National Railways and the Bank of Canada may constitute relatively important policy-making centres.

The role of bureaucrats may also vary according to the political makeup of the cabinet. If a political system is continually involved in the process of forming coalition governments, and especially if these governments tend to rise and fall very rapidly, the initiative for most policy making will pass to the departments. If decisions taken by cabinets are unwelcome, the bureaucracy can stall implementation until a new cabinet comes to office and then try to bury the original policy.

On the other hand, where governments are stable and are dominated for long periods by one party, there is a tendency for senior bureaucrats to reflect the party's ideological orientations. This has been noted as a by-product of the long Liberal tenure in Ottawa between 1935 and 1957. Similarly, the defeat of the NDP in Saskatchewan in 1964 led to a migration of "NDP" civil servants out of the province and into federal service. Some of these later returned west with the NDP victories in Manitoba (1969), Saskatchewan (1971), and British Columbia (1972).

In modern nondemocratic systems and in traditional systems, the administrative bodies may also enlarge their sphere of policy-making influence. Bureaucrats in the party, military, and administrative hierarchies become the politicians. In communist systems this tendency to translate politics into bureaucratic terms has led to administrators being called "the new class" in what are ideologically proclaimed to be classless societies. In more traditional regimes, the expertise of military and administrative bureaucracies appears to give them a particular advantage in the policy process, since they are virtually the only points in society with clear access to the techniques of running the modernizing sectors of these countries.

Where the role of the administration is more restricted, its main function is to provide information for the use of policy makers. Otherwise, it is restricted to the levels of decision making involved in rule implementation. The information provided may be of two types: data or policy alternatives. Data is, simply, aggregated bits of information on subjects of interest to policy makers. Policy alternatives consist of programs of structure and action which might be used to achieve certain goals. Normally, these alternatives will be devised within certain limitations imposed by policy makers, such as monetary restrictions, problems of timing, or the identification of a particular target group in society as the main proposed beneficiary of a policy.

Such information may be provided directly by the departments concerned, or it may be provided by auxiliary groups, such as advisory committees and royal commissions. While advisory committees may be found attached to the bureaucracy at all levels, including those just below the cabinet, royal commissions are created by the Governor-General-in-Council, that is, the prime minister and Cabinet, to look into particular problems which the Cabinet feels could be best investigated impartially. Due to the nature of such commissions, and the length of time needed to finish deliberations (one survey of provincial royal commissions reported an average duration of 19 months),[12] criticism of this method of policy investigation has been continual. It

---

[12] Hugh R. Hanson, "Inside Royal Commissions," *Canadian Public Administration* 12, no. 3 (Fall 1969), p. 363, note 1.

would appear that the greatest value of such commissions is their contribution to the reform of structures and practices which are functioning badly in the political system. Reports on the organization of the administration and the tax system have been instrumental in encouraging reform, even if not along lines identical to those proposed.

LEGISLATURES

Legislatures in the modern sense could come into existence only after society had developed a clear differentiation of governmental functions and a high level of political sophistication leading to demands for popular participation in political decision making. Modern legislatures provide a vehicle for such participation when, as the duly elected representatives of society, they assemble to perform the rule making function. Though it is generally correct to say that legislatures propose, alter, and make laws, in fact they do not monopolize the rule making function. The other structures of the government participate in it to varying degrees just as legislatures participate in activities that cannot be classified as rule making.

The earliest movement for popular participation in rule making led to the growth of the powers of the British Parliament. This evolutionary process has left behind an accretion of obsolete institutions and practices that have sometimes been confused with the essentials of the system. The collection of advisors to the crown that were the original "legislators" gradually developed into a two-chamber Parliament, one house largely hereditary and the other wholly elected. As the political system was gradually opened to participation by wider segments of the population, increasing emphasis was placed upon the elected house, the House of Commons, at the expense of the largely hereditary and appointive House of Lords and the crown itself. The House of Commons became paramount in the sense that it was now necessary for the crown to gain parliamentary acceptance for its policies. For some time the crown was in a very strong position to influence, and even subvert, the proceedings of the legislature because of the ability of the king or queen to distribute favours and patronage. The widening of the franchise, the reform of electoral boundaries, and the extensive social and economic changes of the 19th century reduced this extraparliamentary influence and all effective power gravitated to the House of Commons. Within the legislature the role of the cabinet shifted from that of supposed advisors to the crown to the effective collective government, empowered by the majority party and, so long as it retained that support, the actual legislative and administrative leadership.

In presidential systems, such as the United States, where the legislature and the executive were deliberately separated rather than fused, it was intended that the U.S. Congress, composed of the House of Representatives and the Senate, should determine policy and the president, his staff, and administration should implement it. This effort to insure legislative primacy in rule making has been undermined by circumstances to the extent that though it is still possible for the U.S. Congress to determine policy independently of the executive, it is not common for it to do so. It, instead, normally confines its activities to passing upon the advisability of policies recommended by the executive. The power of the American legislature to publicly reject an executive proposal is frequently exercised, whereas in Canada or Britain the unlikely event of such a rejection would abruptly terminate the life of that particular government, and probably the tenure of that particular legislative body as well.

There are four basic structural patterns for legislative systems, two based upon the nature of the relationship with the executive and the others determined by the type of representation desired. In the former case the pattern is determined by whether the executive and legislative functions are arranged according to the separation of powers principle or the fusion of powers principle. In the latter, the pattern is determined by the number of legislative houses and the method of selecting their members.

Executive-Legislative Relations. There are a number of consequences which follow from the choice of relationship between legislature and executive. The parliamentary system, if it is in fact to be both responsible to the people and be effective, requires a stable party structure. The various parties should be aggregators of a reasonably wide range of interests and they should be sufficiently united internally that if one or a coalition of them is charged with the responsibility of governing, it will be able to do so. The major executive officers, or cabinet, will have to reflect a majority of opinion in the legislature in order to function, and for policy to be coherent there must be a relatively low rate of turnover of cabinet personnel. The Canadian and British systems, rather similar in nature, are able to provide stable governments so long as the ruling party can maintain its internal unity. The need for this unity is inherent in the tradition that members of a party must vote together. In the absence of party discipline, the government majority in the House of Commons might well fragment, resulting in the passage of little legislation and unstable governments.

The French, who supported such a system from 1871 to 1958, called it "immobilisme." The lack of a system of broadly based and disciplined parties led to situations where the most durable leaders were those who successfully avoided making difficult decisions. Politics in

France also had a highly personalized character and the combination of coalitions, personal ambitions, and crisis management virtually guaranteed that no government could last more than a few months. The current problems of Italy are similar. These examples are often taken as evidence that parliamentary systems characterized by more than two parties are inherently unstable. The Scandinavian countries, though, have developed both a multiparty system and a tradition of interparty cooperation that makes stable government possible, suggesting that stability may be more the result of specific circumstances than party structures.

A presidential system, on the other hand, does not require party unity to be effective. The president deals with the legislature as an outsider and so long as there are sufficient means for him or her to influence the members in normal political bargaining it does not matter whether party unity exists. In fact, it is possible for a legislature to be dominated by a party different from that of the president, an impossible situation in a parliamentary system. In addition, the president and the legislature are elected separately and serve fixed terms, so that the ultimate weapon of the government in a parliamentary system, the power to dissolve a recalcitrant legislature and call new elections, is unavailable in most presidential systems, the French system being one exception.

The parliamentary system also operates on the premise that there is an official governing party, or coalition, usually referred to as the *government*, while the other party or parties not so included are usually styled the *opposition*. In the latter case many systems, the Canadian included, make provision for the largest of the nongovernment parties to be considered as the "official" opposition and provide certain amenities for it at public expense. The official opposition is also considered to be the group which would form a new government if the incumbent government were to fall. It is common for certain members of the opposition to assume an interest in specific policy areas which parallel the cabinet posts of the government, creating a "government-in-waiting," or "shadow cabinet." In countries where multiparty coalitions are common, the distinction between government and opposition is less clear-cut as shifts of political fortunes may dictate that one of the government parties leave the coalition and one of the opposition parties join it.

The mechanism for changing governments in parliamentary systems is twofold. The electorate, by altering its preference in an election, may dictate which party or parties must be included in any legislative majority. In parliamentary systems that are basically two-party in nature the presence of a majority and minority party immediately establishes which party will be the government. The only likely grounds for alteration is a split in the majority party, a sudden crisis which creates a demand for a "grand coalition" of the two parties for the sake of national unity, or a new election. In multiparty parliamentary systems where the alliances between certain parties are stable, a long-term coalition is possible. When such interparty stability does not exist, such as in Italy at present, governments may come and go with considerable rapidity as factions within the parties coalesce and split in response to specific issues or personalities. It is common for the government in such a system to revolve around one of the parties and for others to be added or subtracted as the circumstances dictate.

There is no such thing as a government party or an official opposition in the American presidential system. The government is usually referred to by the partisan allegiance of the president, but as there is no necessary party connection between the executive and the legislature, the term opposition has much less meaning. In the case where the U.S. presidency is occupied by a Republican and the U.S. Congress is controlled by the Democrats, both congressional parties could be considered as in opposition depending upon whether one meant opposition to the party controlling the congress or opposition to the president. The congress elects its own officers on the basis of disciplined party voting, one of the few occasions where such unity occurs. Otherwise, many congressmen of both parties see it as their task to oppose, or at least closely supervise, the president. The formal separation between the branches of government has thus been reinforced by tradition.

Legislative-executive relations are affected by structural considerations in another sense. The cabinet in a parliamentary system is both the political leadership of the legislature and the administration; it is made up of members of the legislature and deals with it as a group of colleagues. In the presidential system the political leadership of the administration, the president and the cabinet, must deal with the legislature as outsiders. This means that the "we-they" attitude necessary to competitive situations is formed along party lines in the legislature in a parliamentary system but is likely to result in a legislative-executive division in the presidential system. It is quite true that the government in a parliamentary system may be a very close-knit group in which the cabinet makes the decisions and simply informs the party's parliamentary delegation of their tasks in the party meeting, or *caucus*, but such highly centralized leadership is possible only if the cabinet is well aware of how far it can go before provoking rebellion. In any event, political influence, fame, and fortune are to be found in honouring and supporting the party. In a presidential system, especially that of the United States, these rewards are gained by being able to drive hard bargains as an individual or as a recognized leader of a group of colleagues. If this means supporting the party as a whole, so much the better; if it means open defiance of the party's leadership in both branches of the government, so be it. Except in the situation where a "doublecross" is involved, there is seldom any political dishonour incurred, though the benefits and potential drawbacks of too rigid a position must be carefully weighed.

Type of Representation.   The second set of fundamental structural considerations centre upon the number of houses in the legislature. Most political systems have two houses, as is the case in Canada and the United States. This arrangement is known as *bicameral* in contrast to *unicameral,* one house, arrangement such as found in Israel and Sweden. There is a variety of rationale underlying both systems, but only in presidential systems has the bicameral arrangement, where real political equality between the houses may exist, been effectively used. It is illogical for a government in a parliamentary system to be equally responsible to two different legislative houses.

In parliamentary systems, most of which are bicameral, one house has assumed primacy and the other has become largely vestigial. This fate has befallen the Canadian Senate, which on paper possesses considerable political power. Effective power and emphasis have been increasingly placed upon the popularly elected house. In many systems the so-called upper house is appointive or hereditary, or both. Being divorced from direct contact from the population, it was originally intended to act as a brake against possible rash acts of a popularly based lower house. As this fear receded in the 19th and early 20th centuries, the upper houses became increasingly irrelevant. Their formal powers were either taken away, as was the case with the House of Lords, or fell into disuse. Whatever the original rationale for a bicameral arrangement in a parliamentary system, it has been largely superseded by an arrangement in which the popularly elected house is dominant. In the Canadian provinces where such upper houses existed, they were eventually abolished, so that all provincial legislatures are unicameral.[13]

Presidential systems may also divide the legislative powers between two houses which are designed to reflect different realities within the political system. One of the reasons for instituting a separation of powers arrangement is to provide protection for minorities. It is felt that the more power is diffused the greater the possibilities that any minority might find a position in the system from which it may defend itself.

The rationale for a bicameral system in the United States and Canada was somewhat different from that of most similar systems in

---

[13] A curious exception was in Prince Edward Island where the upper house was not really abolished but merged with the lower house in an expanded unicameral legislature.

Europe. In the latter, the upper house was often populated by nobility, on a hereditary as well as an appointive basis. As such it had a distinct and intentional class bias, a bias based on the belief that the lower classes were inclined to passion and bad judgment. In North America, where the same feeling existed and much the same arguments were advanced, an additional and ultimately more critical consideration was added. This is the fact that the systems are organized on federal rather than unitary bases. Geographic units were considered important and an upper house based on them rather than population seemed to provide a safeguard against the more populous provinces or states seriously infringing upon the interests of the rest. In the United States the original formula was simple; two senators from each state were elected by the state legislatures. It was common to think of them as being ambassadors from the state governments to the federal government. In Canada the formula was based upon regional considerations, equality being sought between the Senate delegations from the Maritimes as a region, Quebec, and Ontario. The original Senate had 72 members, 24 each from these three "regions." The addition of the western provinces led to additional seats being created and in 1915 these provinces were made a fourth region and given 24 seats, each province being represented by six members. Six more seats were created to accommodate Newfoundland when it entered Confederation in 1949. Unlike their American counterparts, the senators are appointed by the Governor General, in effect by the incumbent government. The appointive system in the United States was changed to one of statewide direct popular election in 1912, thus giving the American Senate something the Canadian Senate has never had, a popular basis from which it could exercise power. Canadian senators may have been expected to defend upperclass and regional interests, but the fact that they have no direct connection with or accountability to any constituency has left them largely bereft of the political influence and prestige necessary for them to fulfill the role of an independent component of the rule making apparatus of the system. Thus, the rather substantial powers of the Canadian Senate lie largely unexercised. There are additional reasons why it has evolved as it has, but the lack of any tangible constituency and the fact that its members are appointed by a government based on the House of Commons have proven critical.

Functions of the Legislature.   Legislatures in contemporary democratic systems, be they organized along parliamentary or presidential lines, are less involved in the formulation of rules than in their ratification. They, in effect, legitimize policies and actions of the executive. This is an important function, for legislative *legitimization* is an indication that society's representatives have found these policies acceptable. This constitutes one of the main rationales for creating legislative institutions, even in nondemocratic systems.

The legislature in all systems performs an equally important *communication* function by providing the government with an opportunity to speak to the citizens, to indicate its intentions and the rationale for its decisions. In Canada, for example, the government speaks to the nation at the opening of each session in the "throne speech." Technically, the crown is speaking, but in fact the speech is drafted by the government and by tradition is read as written. By doing so, the crown legitimizes the proposals in the speech as well as communicates them. The crown has the power to refuse to do this, but such an action would immediately raise constitutional questions and seriously embarrass the government. Like many residual and largely symbolic powers, this power is retained by not exercising it. One is thus assured that if such a refusal were to occur it would indicate a serious malfunction in the system. In this context it is no longer curious that the crown can make one throne speech for one government and a contradictory one for its successor. It is not the specific policies that are being approved of by the crown, but rather the right of the government to make the proposals.

In democratic systems, the communication function also works in reverse when the opposition parties exercise their right to criticize the government proposals. Traditionally in Britain and Canada it is difficult to defeat them, given party unity. It is possible, however, to harass and embarrass the government to the point that it loses credibility with the voters and they reject it at the next election. Often governments create their own difficulties through errors of omission or commission which the opposition, if it is alert and assertive, will exploit. This attack may be carried on either in the context of the debate over specific proposals or by raising questions concerning the manner in which the proposals were enacted into law. The most famous such example is the "Great Pipeline Debate" of 1956 when the Liberal majority, acting under pressure from certain cabinet ministers and gas and oil pipeline companies, forced enabling legislation through the House of Commons over bitter opposition by means of cloture. John Diefenbaker led the Conservatives to their first victory since 1930 in the general elections held the next year, largely on the theme that the Liberals had so abused the parliamentary process in forcing the pipeline bill through that they were unfit to remain in power.

The opposition may also use daily question periods in which members are free to make virtually any inquiry of the government they wish. Such queries may be in response to complaints from constituents or arise from information that the opposition has received concerning some government activity. The government, however, may decline to answer some questions.

Related to the communication function is that of *catharsis*. Inevitably, in any political system there are a multitude of minor and major grievances against the operations of governmental organizations. The maintenance of stability of the system requires that these grievances find a means of expression, and the legislative arena is well suited to this need. The opportunity that a legislature in a democratic system provides for the questioning and criticizing of governmental policies and actions constitutes tangible evidence to those who are aggrieved that they have a means of making themselves heard and of potentially influencing the type and nature of political decisions. If the legislature can make perceptible changes in the decisions, its success as a cathartic agent may be even greater, since extended criticism without tangible effect may also lead to alienation and hostility. French legislatures since 1870 have excelled in criticism and aggressive partisan activity, but due to their consistent inability to resolve serious problems, they ultimately came to be regarded by many as bad political jokes. The present cynicism and hostility revolving about the Italian parliament stems from much the same source—the inability of this body to convert the varied demands and criticisms into effective and responsive policies. Thus, the very openness which is necessary for a legislature to perform a cathartic function effectively may be counterproductive if no possibility of satisfaction is perceived by those who would use it.

The legislature in a nondemocratic political system may also serve a cathartic function, but in a different way. The legislative sessions, which are called simply to ratify the decisions of the government, provide an opportunity for the members to voice support and, perhaps, limited criticism of these decisions. Though such expressions are carefully regulated, the spectacle can give both participants and onlookers some measure of participation—especially if a government, at the same time, keeps close track of the state of public opinion and responds with promising policies.

A fourth function is that of *information gathering*. One of the critical inputs into the legislative apparatus is the data it needs to make decisions. In nondemocratic systems the legislature is usually provided with little data since the government expects speedy ratification. The legislature in a democratic system is faced with the need for gathering a wider range of information, since it is generally assumed that it is entitled to have at its disposal any information that might affect the nature of its decision making. In both parliamentary and presidential systems the government is the primary source of such data but, as an interested party in most deliberations, the data it provides will seldom be considered as wholly satisfactory by all parties. The difficulty in a parliamentary system is that the maintenance of a useful alternate source of information would require an act of parliament and continuing appropriations. It is not surprising that opposition parties regularly ask for greater powers for committees of Commons and for provision of research staff, and it is not any more surprising that government parties are reluctant to finance an extensive apparatus which would be used to criticize them. In the U.S. system the independent legislature can, and does, maintain an extensive network of committees and research staff designed to fill this information gap. In spite of this, it is a common complaint of congressmen that they do not have proper information.

A classic activity of a legislature associated with the concept of that body as a decision maker is the performance of the *deliberative* function. It is implicit in a legislative body that to come to a decision it must not only gather information and be a recipient of interest group and party inputs, but it also must find its way to that decision by a process of discussion. The debates and other means of exchanging opinion within legislative bodies are a part of this process, but in parliamentary systems, operating on the basis of party unity, discussions are more likely to involve a presentation of only as many views as there are parties and the actual decisions as to how the parties vote is not seriously affected by such debates. The extent to which this is true is a partial explanation for the frequent lack of decorum and enlightening debate often noticed by disappointed visitors to the legislatures. In fact, the debate is often important not because an impassioned speech is going to directly alter the probable outcome but because well-organized and well-presented opposition to a proposal may, as it is communicated to interested groups outside the legislature, arouse such adverse reaction that the government will be forced to alter or abandon its proposals. An example of this phenomenon was the withdrawal in 1970 of a bill to alter the powers of the auditor general as Parliament's watchdog of the public purse. The bill was widely assailed as a measure intended to gag an official who occasionally embarrassed the government by publicizing inefficiency and waste in administrative activities. The opposition parties criticized the government for attempting to prevent such disclosures in the future. The media joined in the fray and sufficient interest was generated that the issue of the bill itself turned out to be a severe embarrassment to the governing party. Thus, though many of the discussions and enquiries that are part of ordinary parliamentary activities may not be inspiring or earthshaking, and much of it is often petty, the floor of the House is an open forum and the debates themselves are an integral part of the deliberative as well as the cathartic and communication functions of the legislature.

In a system of separation of powers and weak party ties, such as that found in the United States, individual legislators have far greater scope in fulfilling the deliberative function. The proceedings may be influential in changing individual members' attitudes as well as arousing public interest in the issue, though again much of congressional debates are conducted in a manner conducive to sleep rather than to excitement in the public gallery. Most of the important discussions and enquiries take place in committee or subcommittee meetings. Traditionally, many of these sessions were closed to the public though, as part of the reform movement that has changed many congressional practices, an increasing number of these sessions are now open.

A fifth function of the legislature is that of *administrative oversight* or supervision of the activities of the executive. This function is tied into the others and is important for maintenance of a high level of bureaucratic responsiveness and credibility in the system as a whole. By its nature this is an after-the-fact function and is usually carried out by exposing problems, seeking to compensate for poor performance and to ensure against their repetition. Besides certain of its committees, the House of Commons has created the offices of the auditor general and the Public Service Commission to carry out this function. The legislatures in nine provinces have appointed an ombudsman to act in a similar capacity. These are discussed in Chapter 9.

The function most commonly associated with legislative bodies is that of *representation*. The representative function is satisfied when the legislature reflects with reasonable accuracy the general community on the basis of a generally acceptable criterion. Generally this basis is that of population. Chapter 6 presented the various ways in which electoral systems are affected by the drawing up of political boundaries and by the machinery of elections. These factors were important for their impact on the election process, but since the primary importance of the electoral process is that it results in a government reflective of popular sentiment, their impact upon the legislature is equally profound. Democratic practice presumes that all citizens will be treated equally in the sense that each legislator represents approximately the same number of people. Since it is not possible to gain absolute equality of representation, our concern is therefore directed more at this point to the question of other impediments to this ideal and to other methods of representation than that based on population.

It was once a practice to base the franchise upon the ownership of property, irrespective of the method of drawing up constituency boundaries.[14] It is, of course, quite possible for such boundaries to

---

[14] For a fuller discussion of property and similar restrictions on franchise, see Terence H. Qualter, *The Election Process in Canada* (Toronto: McGraw–Hill, 1970).

meet the criteria of equal population and still not be representative if only a portion of the adult population is enfranchised. Such a qualification means that only a selected elite may vote and such a system will be reflective of the attitudes of the general population only to the extent that this elite takes it upon itself to do so. This is, for all purposes, a means of institutionalizing elite representation. Other restrictions upon the franchise, involving qualifications such as literacy, age, sex, have a similar effect upon representativeness.

There are two major alternate methods of representation, one based upon specific social characteristics, the other upon geography. It is possible to construct constituency boundaries on the basis of ethnic, religious, class, or occupational criteria. This method has been styled as corporatist and enjoyed popularity among fascist theorists before World War II. Corporatism requires that various classes or groups in society select representatives irrespective of geography. The best example of a corporatist representational system was that found in Lebanon prior to the recent civil war, where the 99 seat parliament was apportioned among the various religious groups—30 seats going to Maronite Christians, 11 to Greek Orthodox, 6 to Greek Catholic, 4 to Armenian Orthodox, 1 to Armenian Catholic, 1 to Protestants, 20 to Sunni Muslims, 19 to Shi'ite Muslims, 6 to the Druze, and 1 to "minorities."[15] To insure that this apportionment is maintained, only members of the same religion may run against each other for a given seat, though the voters of all groups have a say as to which member of that religious group is elected. This rather cumbersome system was based on the assumption that religion is the critical criterion, and in the context of Lebanese history this is not a necessarily inaccurate assessment. Such an electoral and representational system both reflected and helped to maintain the highly distinctive subcultures of Lebanon, until it completely broke down under the impact of the divisions within the general society.

The geographic alternative to the equal population method is embodied best in the Canadian and American senates. Here territorial units are equally represented regardless of their population. This method was adopted because the Canadian regions and the American states were seen as having distinct identities which needed protection. In both cases such protection for regions was an essential part of the bargain which made the new political arrangements, the BNA Act of 1867 and the U.S. Constitution of 1789, possible. The importance of geographical representation declined in Canada because the Senate has not used its political power, though in the United States it remains

---

[15] Michael W. Suleiman, "Lebanon," in *Government and Politics of the Contemporary Middle East*, ed. Tareq G. Ismael (Homewood, Ill.: The Dorsey Press, 1970), pp. 232–33.

important because the U.S. Senate is very much the equal of the U.S. House of Representatives. U.S. Senate seats are apportioned on the basis of two to each state, but the senators themselves are elected by popular vote. Since they represent a state as a whole and are far less numerous than the representatives (100 as opposed to 435), they can claim to have a larger constituency and by implication a broader mandate than do the members of the lower house. Such a situation does not obtain with the appointive Canadian Senate.

The Canadian Parliament

The Canadian Parliament operates in an essentially two-party context and in the presence of a strong executive. It is based upon a pattern of relationships in which the Cabinet, acting with the information and assistance provided by professional civil servants, is predominant. The Parliament consists of two houses: the House of Commons and the Senate.

House of Commons.   The House of Commons does not normally originate legislation, but, rather, is the recipient of inputs usually generated by the Cabinet. As the Cabinet is in power because it represents a majority of the House, the legislature is normally in the position of ratifying policies proposed by it. Thus, it does not fulfill the classic role of a legislature, that of deliberating upon ideas largely of its own creation and selecting a particular policy. Should the legislature in fact exercise such independence in the face of contrary recommendations from the Cabinet, the Cabinet would be forced to resign, having "lost the confidence" of the House. The control of the House of Commons by the Cabinet does not mean that the former is not important, for it performs a variety of functions for the political system which were outlined earlier in this chapter.

The House of Commons is the primary legislative body in the political system and was given wide powers under the BNA Act. It is composed of 264 members elected simultaneously from constituencies relatively equal in population. A legislative body of this size, too large to be intimate and completely personal in its internal relationships, is, nonetheless, small compared to the House of Representatives in the United States (435), the British House of Commons (630), and the lower house in the U.S.S.R., the Soviet of the Union (767).

The composition of the House of Commons is redistributed following every decennial census in order to accomodate shifts of population between provinces. Thus, provinces which experience a decline in population also suffer a reduction in the number of their members in the House. Following the 1971 census, Newfoundland, Nova Scotia, Quebec, Manitoba, and Saskatchewan would have lost seats through redistribution. The objection was raised that all of these provinces except Quebec already have relatively small representation in the House and any further reduction in the number of their members would deprive them of the opportunity to effectively articulate their interests in the federal legislature. As a result, redistribution was suspended by Parliament until a new formula could be devised.

In December 1974 the House of Commons passed a new reapportionment law to become effective with the next federal elections, normally expected in 1978.[16] The new formula is based on a projection that the present population of 22 million will become 30 million by the year 2001 and it guarantees that no province would have fewer seats than at present. Table 8–2 indicates the projected representation by province subsequent to each new census.

TABLE 8–2
Composition of the House of Commons

	Present Situation	Decennial Redistribution (projected)			
Provinces	*1961*	*1978*	*1981*	*1991*	*2001*
Newfoundland	7	7	8	10	10
Prince Edward Island	4	4	4	4	4
Nova Scotia	11	11	11	11	11
New Brunswick	10	10	10	10	10
Quebec	74	75	79	83	87
Ontario	88	95	101	113	127
Manitoba	13	14	15	15	15
Saskatchewan	13	14	14	14	14
Alberta	19	21	22	25	28
British Columbia	23	28	30	37	46
Territories					
Yukon	1	1	1	1	1
Northwest Territories	1	2	2	2	2
Total	264	282	297	325	355

Source: The Representation Act, 1974.

The House is large enough and based on sufficiently varied constituencies to include a membership which contains the variety of talents needed if a government is to be drawn from it and a coherent opposition is to exist at the same time. Cabinets normally number over 20, and the opposition's potential, or "shadow," cabinet, is generally of

---

[16] See, Andrew Sancton, "The Application of the 'Senatorial Floor' Rule to the Latest Redistribution of the House of Commons," *Canadian Journal of Political Science* 6, no. 1 (March 1973), pp. 56–64; also, Andrew Sancton, "The Representation Act, 1974," *Canadian Journal of Political Science* 8, no. 3 (September 1975), pp. 467–69.

the same size so that a minimum of 40 talented members are needed. The problem can be put in some perspective by noting that the provincial legislatures average 64 members. Even though provincial cabinets are smaller than the federal Cabinet, it is obvious that for their cabinets and opposition leadership groups to be competent a far higher proportion of talented members is required than is true of the House of Commons. To put it another way, the House of Commons can afford to have more members who are not especially talented or interested in its proceedings than can the provincial legislatures.

Patterns of formal relationships and procedures emerge in every legislative body, especially at the national level where the number of members often reach into the hundreds and members represent sharply conflicting groups. The legislature must develop means for channeling and controlling these inherent conflicts so that its functions may be adequately fulfilled. These typically take the form of a set of fairly rigid rules concerning the processing of legislative proposals and the development of a set of committees for carrying out certain time-consuming aspects of this process. Since the major function of the House of Commons is to ratify the proposals of the government, its procedural rules are biased in favour of expediting the business before it. The government controls the matters to be brought before the House of Commons by determining its agenda, thus effectively limiting individual members' ability to initiate legislation. By such procedures the government ensures that its proposals will be accepted by the House without inordinate delay.

Each legislature differs in the precise manner in which it treats matters before it, but there is a degree of commonality of procedures in systems based upon the British tradition. A bill, once drafting is finished, is placed on the order paper. A motion for permission to introduce the bill, which is nondebatable, is made at an appropriate time. At a later sitting the bill is given first reading, when it is accepted or rejected for consideration—normally, only a formality. The second reading occasions the first real debate and the bill must pass this stage before amendments may be made; in other words, the House must agree with the principle of the bill while reserving judgment as to its details. The opposition may move to sidetrack the bill to committee or delay its consideration for six months. Once the bill passes second reading, it goes to committee with the exception of supply and ways and means bills, which are referred to the Committee of the Whole (the whole House sitting under more relaxed rules as a "committee"). In committee, a bill is open to extensive challenge and amendments. Once committee work is finished, the bill, however amended, is reported back to the House, when debate and amendments are permitted. Members of the House then address themselves to the particular points of the bill which may trouble them before it is moved to the third and final reading. Once this last hurdle is passed, the bill goes to the Senate (unless the latter has already dealt with it) and if approved there, as it normally is, it is presented for royal assent.[17] It takes effect as law only after the Governor General gives his assent and it is published in the *Gazette*.

The rules of the House permit extensive debate, especially during second reading. The fact that every member has the legal prerogative to speak on each amendment and subamendment, as well as on the bill itself, would create a situation of paralysis if there were not a system of time limits on speeches at various stages and usually an agreement among the party leaders as to who will speak. At the same time the government holds in reserve the power to enforce tighter restrictions on debate, the most drastic of these being closure—the power to shut off debate altogether.

House of Commons Committees.   The inherent limitation upon the ability of the House of Commons as a whole to consider all aspects of the business presented to it has resulted in the multiplication of committees to which the various proposals may be submitted for detailed examination. In Canada the committees are tied to specific subjects, such as defence and external affairs, whereas in Britain committees have no specific areas of competence. In this sense the Canadian committees are similar to those in the United States though they lack the independence of their American counterparts. At present there are 18 standing committees and two joint committees consisting of members both from the House of Commons and the Senate. The number of members of Commons committees varies from 12 to 30 and the membership is chosen to reflect the party distribution in the House as a whole. Only in the case of their fiscal watchdog, the Committee on Public Accounts, is the chairman not of the government party. Appointment is based upon the expressed interests of the members where possible and a committee assignment is usually for the duration of that particular Parliament. Individual members are usually members of more than one committee.

The role of the committee has been enhanced in recent years by the increasing practice of assigning the government budgetary estimates to the standing committees, thus giving them a direct influence upon expenditures and taxes. The committees have access to a limited amount of funds for research purposes, but not in quantities comparable to those available to the government. The fact that they can consult interested groups outside the House is of importance from more than the standpoint of simply aggregating public opinion, since such presentations may also be a good source of additional information.

Committees suffer from more encumbrances than the question of

---

[17] J. R. Mallory, *The Structure of the Canadian Government* (Toronto: Macmillan, 1971) pp. 272–74.

availability of information. Since they are controlled by the government party, a committee will be able to exercise independent discretion to the degree which the government allows it, or to the degree to which it is able to force the issue in a situation of government division or indecision. The fact that most members of the Commons have five or less years experience in the House means that tenure on committees is relatively short-lived and the possibility of a committee acquiring influence through the recognized expertise of its members is thereby limited. Tenure is often shortened by shifts in committee assignments as well. This contrasts sharply with the situation in the U.S. Congress, where a member may sit on a committee for decades, often resulting in his or her acquiring a much greater expertise than other legislators, and even greater insight into specialized government business than the political appointees in the various departments of the government.

There is also provision for the establishment of special committees in the Commons and the Senate for the express purpose of dealing with specific issues or problems. As the membership is drawn from the House, there is no guarantee of expertise; thus their investigations are not usually the equivalent of those conducted by royal commissions whose members are supposed to possess special qualifications for their appointment. Such special committees, however, can serve a very useful purpose and may become the centre of considerable controversy if their report and recommendations strike sensitive areas, as was the case in the Senate with the Davey committee's report on the mass media in 1970.

Legislative Restraints.   There is a variety of occasions in which the opposition may make its presence felt and there are numerous examples of this presence being influential. There is in the Parliament a sense of what is acceptable and what is not in the way of possible policies, and a government that ignores these often unspoken limits runs the risk that its own members will abandon it. Party discipline is firm, and the fear of social and political ostracism is a potent weapon in the hands of the party leaders. There are, however, limits to the use of such power and for this reason a party will occasionally allow one or some of its members to abstain or even oppose the official position if the issue is such that it is a serious matter of conscience or elemental political survival.

The restraints upon Canadian governments and their legislative majorities are normally more subtle than an outright rejection of a bill or a vote of no confidence. The government is concerned with the relatively long-range objective of attaining reelection as well as the short-term goal of gaining parliamentary acceptance for a particular proposal. The government is restrained from asking its members in Parliament for support on measures which would be politically suicidal and from asking the Parliament as a whole to accept proposals which will arouse the opposition as well as the electorate and thus risk defeat in the next election. Any government is obliged to make decisions which are unpopular and which may be unsuccessful, but the calculations which go into the choice of policies are based upon the fundamental political law of survival.

To fully appreciate the operations of the rule making process, it is important to recall that the primary function of Canadian political parties is to aggregate interests. This means there is automatic competition within the governing party between various interests which sensitizes the leadership to at least a portion of the electorate. The fact that its proposals must openly compete with those of the opposition groups tends to sensitize the government to those claimants and it further attempts to estimate the reactions of the public. The natural unwillingness to jeopardize its position frequently creates a degree of governmental hesitancy when faced with a difficult choice. There is a tendency to procrastinate in hopes that somehow the choice will become less painful or that delay may permit political bargaining to proceed towards an easier solution to the problem. There is no guarantee, though, that delay will help matters and, in the case of serious and growing problems, it is more likely to aggravate them. Nevertheless, since a democratic system is based upon the aggregation and evaluation of different interests, when complex issues are involved, the rule making process is naturally time-consuming—even if the government is determined to expedite matters. The size and complexity of the rule making apparatus conceals most of the actual process from public view, thereby creating the impression of even less efficiency in the process than actually exists.

Senate.   The basic operation of the legislative process in Canada is fairly straightforward, though the large amount of business and the complexity of much of the subject matter makes the overall legislative process a complicated undertaking. It is further complicated by the fact that Canada, like most countries, uses a bicameral system and the Senate as the upper house still retains, on paper, its power to amend or reject a bill passed by the House of Commons. Outright rejection is rare, and amending is not common; but should the latter occur, then it is necessary for the differences to be adjusted, either by the House of Commons accepting the amendments or through a conference of the leaders of the two houses to adjust the difference. There is also provision for the prime minister to advise the crown on the appointment of a limited number of additional senators so long as the regional distribution formula is not violated. There have been several instances where prime ministers have considered doing this, but so far it has not been implemented. It is assumed that grounds for such a move would have to be serious, involving either an outright deadlock between the two houses or some serious deficiency in the composition of the membership of the Senate. Though the Senate was given the power to amend or reject legislation from the lower house, it was barred from originating money bills, the most important single class of legislation in any democratic system. It was never envisioned as the equal of the lower house, but rather as a guarantor of provincial rights and as a review body to prevent unwise legislation. It seldom has exercised any substantial powers, however.

The Senate was designed to assure a calm arena for review of acts of the lower house but it has turned into a political graveyard, a titled retirement for party loyalists of earlier years. The average appointee is approaching retirement age and is guaranteed tenure until the age of 75.[18] There has been little more than talk devoted to any substantial changes in its composition. It still retains on paper its considerable powers but, being cut off from the body politic, it is not possible for it to exercise any appreciable influence. The hope has been expressed that the opportunity afforded by the relatively leisurely pace of Senate activity would allow it to undertake extensive studies of current problems that are beyond the power of a harassed Commons, independent of the government control. One of the more notable investigations in recent years has been the report of the Davey committee on the state of the media in Canada, a report uncommonly blunt in its assessment of the media and of official policies which have encouraged certain trends within the industry. Senate investigations may come to serve as alternatives to the royal commissions created by the government, which monitors appointments to them and defines their nature and scope. A Senate committee may be, and is, struck at the behest of a senator or senators regardless of whether the government is happy with the idea or not. Any political system needs an institution that can investigate matters which the government, powerful interest groups, and possibly even the opposition, might want to see swept under the political rug. The Senate could perform such a role in Canada.

Whatever the contribution the Senate may make to the rule making process, it is likely to remain as indirect and primarily one of information gathering. So long as it has no popular base and substantial role in the Cabinet, it will be circumscribed in what it can do in the normal rule making operations. Thus, one returns to a consideration of the House of Commons, and, to better understand its collective behaviour, it is necessary to take a close look at the kinds of people who are its members, what they bring to that body, why they are there, and what they feel they are accomplishing.

---

[18] Prior to 1968, appointments to the Senate were for life.

Canadian Legislators. Political scientists and other observers have been intrigued with the social characteristics of the members of legislatures. Historically, Canadian legislators, like their American, British, and continental counterparts, are from the older, more established groups with higher levels of education and income and professional or managerial occupations. This contrasts sharply with those societies in which the vast majority of people belong to less well-endowed social and economic classes. Many critical observers have inferred from this that a legislature cannot be truly representative, and some, such as the Marxists, argue that these structures are a sham created by the established and propertied classes for their benefit and to the disadvantage of those whom they exploit.

The first point of these observations is well taken; the House of Commons, for instance, is usually composed of about one-third lawyers, one-quarter businessmen, and one-sixth other professionals.[19] Farmers, blue- and white-collar employees normally comprise less than one quarter of the membership. One of the reasons for this is that persons with better education and a participation-oriented political socialization are better equipped to both perceive possibilities in political activity and to successfully compete for political office. A second reason is that professionals and managers have a more flexible work schedule, whereas the average blue- or white-collar employee is confined to a set schedule with limited free time. Third, the professional or managerial people have a higher income and are better able to afford the costs of political participation for which they are not compensated and, through occupational connections with other high-income groups, they find it easier to raise funds for a political campaign. Finally, certain highly competitive occupations such as law, real estate, or insurance can often be advanced by the free publicity that participation in politics brings. It is thus far easier for a person of higher occupational and social status to enter into politics and to devote enough time to it to be successful.

These considerations are distinct from the question of specific motivations for entry into political activity; motivations that may allow the well off and the less well off to ignore the hardships and inconveniences of public life. An important factor is the socialization pattern a person has experienced. Allan Kornberg, in a study of the members of the House of Commons, found that those who were politically socialized in a positive sense by family and associates at a young age tend to have initiated their own political careers, whereas those whose political socialization was more importantly affected by adult experi-

---

[19] Allan Kornberg, *Canadian Legislative Behaviour* (Toronto: Holt, Rinehart & Winston, 1967), pp. 43–49.

ences frequently had to be induced into politics by others.[20] It would appear from his data that about one half of the members of the Commons were induced to run by a party and that the rest found their way into politics by other routes. The data also suggest that previous involvement and position within a political party is common among members of Parliament.

A political party, in order to induce people to run, must be able to offer something in return. One of the benefits is naturally that electoral success offers the opportunity for the exercise of leadership and influence. Economic reward is another benefit, although less persuasive, as the costs, direct and indirect, are quite likely to exceed all legitimate income that might be gained from the office. Probably more persuasive is the consideration that success brings the individual to "where the action is." Besides, for some political parties, ideological commitment may be a major motivation, especially for Marxists and other distinctly ideological parties.

One of the major considerations in an assessment of the potential representativeness and responsiveness of a legislative body is that of the motives for seeking such an office. It is unlikely that financial reward is an inducement, for even though members of Parliament receive upwards of $20,000 in salary and fringe benefits, one should remember that they come primarily from professions and businesses where such salaries are common and where the kind of burdens that go with being a member are not required. In fact, it is not uncommon for legislators to have earned far more when privately employed. Kornberg's data suggest that about one quarter of the members became candidates for Parliament very reluctantly and that roughly equal groups (23 percent and 21 percent, respectively) hoped to participate in furthering certain policies or a specific ideology. Approximately one third appear to have been motivated to contest an election for essentially personal reasons.

When motivations are analyzed on the basis of party membership, some interesting contrasts emerge, as shown in Table 8–3. According to the data, the most ideologically motivated members of Parliament appear to be among the Social Credit and the least among the Conservatives. It is noteworthy that the primary motivation among Liberals is personal, neither policies nor ideologies being important. The New Democrats, often stereotyped as an ideological party, appear to be more ideologically inclined than the Liberals and Conservatives, but, even so, almost as motivated by interest in policy and service as by ideology. Given that approximately 80 percent of the House of Commons is made up of Liberals and Conservatives, and assuming that

---

[20] Ibid., pp. 49–55 and 66–70.

TABLE 8–3
Motives for Candidates (in percent)

Motives	Conservative	Liberal	New Democrat	Social Credit
Not motivated	24	23	22	8
Interest in policy and service	29	15	31	22
Ideology	10	16	39	65
Personal reasons	37	46	8	5

Source: Allan Kornberg, *Canadian Legislative Behaviour: A Study of the 25th Parliament.* Copyright © 1967 by Holt, Rinehart and Winston, Inc., pp. 74–75. Reprinted by permission of Holt, Rinehart and Winston, Inc.

the types of members have not changed radically since 1962 when the data were collected, it would appear that personal motivations dominate the members of the major parties; that nearly a quarter of them were recruited rather than sought a nomination on their own; and that policy and ideology are not especially important factors. As the major parties are aggregators of a wide range of interests, it is probably best that this be so since if the members of the governing and official opposition parties were highly ideological in their approach, then the bargaining process that characterizes much of their relationships could not proceed.

A further consideration is that of the goals of the legislators once they are in office. The Kornberg study suggests that they become primarily interested in influencing policies rather than representing specific interests or constituencies as such.[21] As the Canadian parliamentary system is not designed to encourage a large public role for the average member, the party caucus must provide the bulk of the satisfaction for these goals. If the caucus did not provide an adequate outlet for the various policy goals and preferences of its members, it would then be difficult for the party to retain its unity in Parliament and even more difficult than it already is to induce incumbents to run for office again.

It is also important to consider precisely what the members think they should be doing in reference to their role as a representative. In a landmark study of legislatures carried out in several states of the United States in 1957, it was posited that there are three basic orientations in reference to the role of a representative: those of trustee, delegate, and politico.[22] The trustee orientation takes its justification from

---

[21] Ibid., pp. 79–83.

[22] John Wahlke et al., *The Legislative System* (New York: John Wiley & Sons), pp. 267–86.

the philosophy that a representative is in office to consider the interests of all the citizens, that they cannot know all that is needed to make a decision themselves, and that therefore the representative should exercise his or her own judgment. If the constituents do not care for the representatives judgments, they are free to replace him or her, but until then he or she is an essentially free agent. The delegate orientation is essentially the reverse, that the representative is in office to represent his or her constituents as faithfully as possible regardless of whether he or she personally favours their judgment. This assumes that a representative can know these sentiments exactly, just as the trustee orientation assumes that the representative's wisdom is best. The politico orientation is based on the assumption that it is the representative's duty to seek to reconcile the conflicting views in the community as reflected by the attitudes of his or her fellow members. Thus, the politico orientation is well suited to a political system based upon compromise. The Kornberg study suggests that though the delegate role is the most commonly favoured by the members of Parliament, a sizable proportion see themselves as politicos.[23] Given the fact that the members are bound by party unity and that the critical decisions are usually made within the party, it is clear that so long as the members are not especially ideological or parochial in their view, they may play the delegate role with satisfaction only so long as they continue to believe that the party is the best available vehicle for the advancement of their particular interests. Clearly, in such a situation a fair number of those of politico orientation would be needed as the catalytic agents necessary for the attainment of a suitable balance of interests. The predominance of such attitudes and orientations mesh well with the requirement that the major parties play the role of aggregators.

Though many voters may express the feeling that the differences between the two major parties are not significant, the members of Parliament feel that party is very important. Party unity is the recognized norm of behaviour, but a variety of circumstances exist where a member may deviate from party unit. This, however, is an option not frequently exercised.

It would seem that as a result of bargaining and negotiation between an individual and his party it is possible for the former to contract out of supporting a caucus decision, or even a public position, taken by the latter. Also, it appears that there are times when the parties will adjust their decisions out of consideration for the possible unfavourable effects these decisions may have upon individual party members. In particular, they apparently hesitate to act in ways that impinge adversely upon the personal values of party members.[24]

---

[23] Kornberg *Canadian Legislative Behaviour*, pp. 107–15.

[24] Ibid., pp. 131–32.

Actual behaviour indicates that this freedom is more theoretical than practical, and it may well be similar to many other "powers" in the political system that retain their usefulness so long as they are not actually exercised. The data suggest that the bulk of the members of Parliament accept party unity as a norm because they value the party as an instrument and feel that without this unity they would not be able to achieve as much as they can with it.

There is another sense in which the constitution and organization of the Parliament militates against an effective role for the average member in most situations. The formal and informal limits upon debates, the limited time for speeches, the lack of adequate research and administrative assistance, the discipline of the party all contribute to a sense of futility on the part of many members. Added to this is the burden that most of them must bear if they are to retain their roots in their constituencies—the numerous trips back and forth, the catering to the needs of individual constituents, the expense of maintaining two homes, the disruption of the regular career, probably in law or business, and the expenses above and beyond official compensation all make being a member of the House of Commons a less satisfactory occupation than it might be for many of its members. One recent suggestion, designed to make it easier to maintain constituency and personal relations, was that the House of Commons should be reorganized so as to be in session the year round, as in the U.S. Congress. As compensation for the extended session, actual meetings might be scheduled on a three weeks in session and one week away basis. One of the possible side benefits would be the avoidance of the typical last-minute rush at the close of each session when many bills are quickly passed without any serious discussion. Another benefit would be the time available to MPs each month to maintain their constituency contacts and get out of the hot-house atmosphere of Ottawa on a regular and predictable basis. The frustrations of the job at present are such that upwards of 40 percent of the incumbents do not return to the House for a second term, a majority of them retiring rather than being defeated. The resulting high percentage of freshmen members in any particular Parliament exacerbates the problem of maintaining a strong legislative position vis-à-vis the Cabinet.

The situation of the Canadian Senate is an interesting contrast. Made up primarily of semiretired or retired party officials, it has not exercised any substantial authority for some time and, though party ties can be assumed to be strong, given that they are the main reason for appointment, the fact that the Senate is regarded as largely irrelevant by most other actors in the political system limits its role severely. It can, and sometimes does, play an informational role, but as a representative body it is a failure. Not being usually concerned with, or seriously consulted about, policy formation, it cannot play a significant rule-making role. Thus, though the fact that it is indeed a body of relatively elderly politicians and business leaders is interesting, it probably does not matter. It may be important to try to foster some degree of diversity of class in the House of Commons, but until the Senate plays a more active role it is of little consequence who its members are.

The situation in the provincial legislatures is far less well documented. It would appear that these bodies are also made up of the same types of people as the House of Commons and share most of the same procedures and behavioural norms. Their much smaller size means that individual members may have greater scope for promoting their interests, if for no other reason than that a higher proportion of the members of the government party must be members of the Cabinet and the official opposition must parcel out official roles to a higher proportion of its members. Whether this has an appreciable effect upon lowering the attrition rate or heightening the member's sense of political efficacy remains to be investigated and documented.

The American Congress

The legislative bodies of the United States, as the ostensible rule makers of the political system, are constructed in ways very different from the parliamentary idiom so common elsewhere. The first, and most fundamental, difference is that they are constitutionally separated from the executive. It is forbidden for one to hold a post in the Congress of the United States and an executive position at the same time. It is thus impossible for a member of the legislature to be in the cabinet. In fact, to a degree not found in parliamentary systems, federal legislative office is a career in itself and many members of Congress, especially senators, would regard most cabinet posts as a demotion.

The mere fact of the separation of powers alone does not explain the attraction of congressional office. The powers and privileges of the office itself are important. Since party unity is largely imaginary, the individual member of Congress has wide latitude in the issues he or she may pursue and the relationships he or she may build with colleagues. The lack of party influence in the United States, the fact that an average member reaches the Congress in large part on his or her own initiative, and the support of associates he or she has gathered together also result in an inclination to act independently. There is also a rivalry between the two houses of Congress, the Senate and the House of Representatives, which often influences the way the members of Congress behave. Finally, unlike most parliamentary systems where both logic and practice dictate that power be concentrated in one house even if the other has considerable powers on paper, the Senate and the House of Representatives are essentially equal.

To better understand the Congress in relation to the other components in the political system, its formal relationship with the executive should be considered. First, all measures to be considered must be presented to the Congress by a member. Second, there is no compulsion that the Congress consider any proposal made to it, and, except for moral authority and political leverage, the executive must await developments. Too overt an interference in the process may cause the legislators to react in a hostile way. Third, except for a few areas of exclusive senatorial jurisdiction, both houses must agree, literally, on a proposal before it can become law. A proposal accepted by the Congress as a whole must then have the signature of the president, which he may withhold or may reject the bill outright by vetoing it. Congress can initiate legislation diametrically opposed to the known wishes of the president and, if it can gain a two-thirds majority in both houses, override his veto. Unlike a parliamentary system in such a situation, there is no necessity for the president or his cabinet to resign and it is not within the powers of the president to dissolve a troublesome Congress, though many presidents have wished they could do so. On the other hand, more than one Congress has toyed with the idea of trying to remove a president, but only one unsuccessful attempt has been made in the almost 200 years the system has been in operation.

The resignation of President Nixon in 1974 illustrates the significance of the impeachment process, and of the difficulties inherent in activating that process. Discussions of possible impeachment of the president originally centred upon the question of the legitimacy of many of his actions in the Vietnam war. Then, the publicity given to the bungled Watergate political espionage efforts aimed at the Democratic presidential campaign in 1972 shifted the focus of his opponents. More investigations led to revelations concerning other questionable practices within the administration. Repeated denials of involvement by the president were shown to be false. The discovery of the so-called Nixon tapes of White House conversations led to even more extensive investigations. The initial investigations were made by the press followed by a special Senate Committee. By the end of 1973 so many questions had been asked, so many indictments had been drawn, and so many admissions made relative to the president's own conduct, that a special House of Representatives committee was set up to determine whether or not the formal process of impeachment should be begun against the president.

Constitutionally, the process is that the House of Representatives acts as a grand jury to draw up an indictment (articles of impeachment) of the president. The Senate then conducts a trial to determine whether or not the president should be removed. In 1868 the Senate conducted just such a trial against the then president, Andrew Johnson, but failed to establish the two-thirds vote necessary to remove him. In 1974 a special House committee presented articles of impeachment which the full House approved. The battle lines were drawn. The president, unable to conceal his tapes and other documents, as a result of several court decisions, found himself forced to make even more damaging admissions. Apparently convinced that the struggle was hopeless, the president resigned. Nixon was neither impeached (formally indicted) nor convicted, though both appeared to be inevitable had he remained in office.

The powers of the Congress vis-à-vis the executive extend beyond the simple passage of legislation. The executive must rely upon the Congress for the authorization and the funds to implement any policy. All presidential appointments to the cabinet, the diplomatic service, the federal courts and sundry boards and commissions must gain the approval of the Senate and it may, and occasionally does, refuse to confirm nominations. On the other hand, the Congress is dependent upon the president for the implementation of the policies it prescribes.

Given the size and complexity of the executive branch of the government and the wide variety of policies in force, it is not difficult for the president or his assistants to frustrate the will of the Congress if it suits their purpose. In addition, the Congress is heavily dependent upon the executive for the information it needs to formulate policy and, in many areas where much of the information is classified as secret, the Congress must simply take the president at his word that the situation requires a given policy or appropriation. The elaborate formal and informal checks and balances built into the American system would appear to militate against effective action, but stalemate has been avoided by the creation of an atmosphere where political bargaining predominates.

The Legislative Process.   The elaborate network of relationships between the Congress and the executive is compounded by an even more elaborate structural arrangement within the Congress itself. Both of the houses conduct most of their meaningful work within committees, and most committees have subcommittees. These committees have specific jurisdiction such as agriculture, defence, judiciary, and others, and these jurisdictions are jealously guarded. For an appreciation of the difficulty of gaining legislative approval for a proposal, an outline of the mechanical process is provided in Figure 8–2.

The path any bill must take through the Congress is complicated by a number of additional considerations. At no stage are any of the committees, subcommittees, or houses in general obligated to act, and all

FIGURE 8–2
The Congressional Labyrinth

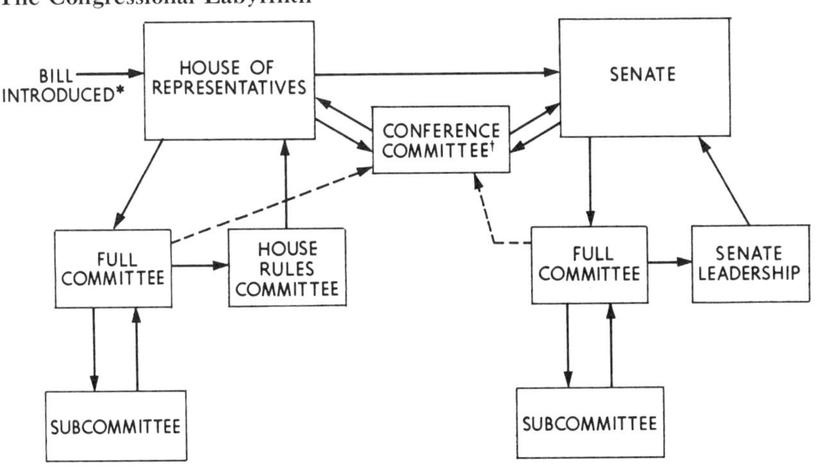

* All bills may be introduced in either house, separately or concurrently, except for tax and appropriation bills, which must be introduced first in the House, and treaties and confirmation of appointments, which are the sole responsibility of the Senate.

† The conference committee is ad hoc and deals only with the disputed bill. It is composed of members of the House and Senate committees which originally dealt with the matter at hand. The committee's recommendations are not binding on either house.

may freely amend what has been presented to them. For instance, a proposal may be put that the United States establish a new foreign aid program to Latin America. For such a program to be authorized, it must go through the appropriate committees, in this case the House Foreign Affairs Committee and the Senate Foreign Relations Committee. Each will probably refer the proposal to a standing subcommittee that is responsible for overseeing United States relations with that part of the world. If one of these subcommittees refuses to act, there is little even other members of Congress can do except attempt persuasion. By the same token, the subcommittee may radically alter the proposal and the full committee may alter it yet again. Except for tax and appropriations bills which must originate in the House of Representatives, proposals may originate in either house and it is quite possible for committees of the two houses to be working on the same proposal, but at cross purposes. Further, none of their work is immune to amendment by either house meeting as a whole. A final complication is provided in the House of Representatives where the Rules Committee, which is charged with arranging the agenda of the House as well as determining whether a bill will be debated under rules that permit amendment or lengthy speeches, may not schedule it for debate at all! There is no rule which says that amendments need have anything to do with the substantive matter of the bill. It is possible to attach a civil rights amendment to a foreign-aid bill or any other combination that members of Congress might imagine. Such nongermane amendments are referred to as riders and, as the president is required to accept a bill *in toto*, it is a favourite device for forcing the president to accept something he does not wish in exchange for receiving something he feels he must have. Finally, in many instances, bills emerge from the two houses in different forms and neither house will accept the other's version. A conference committee composed of members of the committees of the two houses originally involved in the legislation will then have to be called and a compromise negotiated which either house may accept or reject. The legislative system is thus constructed in a manner which allows several different groups of legislators to exercise a veto over any particular piece of legislation. This increases the scope of activity for an individual member, especially among senators who may be members of many committees and several subcommittees at the same time. This also means that any interest group can influence legislation which affects it if it can establish a friendly relationship with one of the committees dealing with its area.

American Legislators.   The behaviour of American legislators at the national level is one of the more discussed topics in American politics. Their rationality is often obscured by circumstances and much of their behaviour is predictable, though not to the extent that is possible in Canada or Britain where party discipline prevails. The basis of what predictability exists is found in the background of the individual member and the electorate he or she represents.

The average member of the U.S. Congress does not differ greatly in general background from his or her Canadian counterpart. He or she commonly belongs to a business of professional occupation, and is a middle- or late middle-aged person of upper- or middle-class socio-economic background. A member is likely to have been a resident of the area he or she represents for a considerable period and, on average, stays in office for about a decade. He or she usually has independent financial resources and maintains some outside business or professional contacts while in office. He or she is normally white, married with children, and belongs either to the Protestant or the Catholic religion. Prior political experience is common, especially among the group drawn from the legal profession.

It was pointed out earlier that the national parties in the United States have little real power as organizations, and the party as such has little influence over members of Congress. The national party may or may not have assisted them in their election campaigns, but they consider themselves as either free agents or as part of a local party group. This does not mean that party means nothing to them. There is, however, more than one "party" involved. Party leaders in the Congress, such as majority or minority leaders, party whips, and their aides, are elected in caucus. Traditionally, committee chairpersons were chosen on the basis of seniority, but, as part of a recent internal reform movement, especially in the House, chairpersons are now subject to election by the members of the committee. In addition, the traditional practice of the leadership controlling committee assignments has been replaced by a process in which they are now controlled by the caucus itself, at least among the Democrats. The Democrats have been far more inclined to press for internal reform than have been the Republicans.

Most members of Congress behave quite rationally once one accepts the fact that they are relatively autonomous and are likely to respond to constituency interests and to their own political philosophies as they see them. A variety of studies using a wide range of techniques has revealed that both parties contain members who are conservatives or liberals on various issues. Factions and key personnel in each are easily recognizable. For instance, on several occasions, Presidents Kennedy and Johnson, both Democrats, assiduously cultivated the then Republican leader in the Senate, the late Senator Dirksen of Illinois. They would look to Dirksen to persuade some of his more conservative Republican colleagues to support them on civil rights matters to offset the opposition from Southern Democrats. He would naturally exact a political price for his support, but on more than one occasion he was able to bring with him enough Republicans to allow the passage of an important measure. After 1968, both Presidents Nixon and Ford had to work with congresses dominated by the Democratic Party. Since the Democrat legislators were generally unable to muster the vote necessary to override presidential vetoes of their legislation, the Democratic leadership in Congress and the President had to bargain over each contested issue.

One of the phenomena that makes the Congress somewhat difficult to understand is that though each party has elected leaders who are expected to oversee the party's efforts in the two houses, on specific issues there may be members of Congress who are considered so knowledgeable in certain areas that, even though they hold no leadership position, they are consulted by others and their advice taken. It is also common for members to rely on the judgment of other members when matters with which they are relatively unfamiliar come up for discussion and decision. Thus a senator or representative who is primarily interested in labour matters, for instance, may well ask a colleague, not necessarily of his or her own party, what he or she should do on a tax bill or a resources measure. This is a reasonably safe way to get around the problems posed by the overwhelming bulk and complexity of the material the members of Congress must consider. Such a system, of course, works only so long as the rules and practices of the houses effectively muffle the always threatening and potentially disruptive personal and political rivalries. Thus rules governing courtesy are far more rigidly observed than is the case in Canada and the kind of personal exchanges common in the House of Commons and the provincial legislatures are seldom indulged in and almost always suppressed as soon as they occur.

Part of the reason for this sensitivity is that the individual members have great procedural powers, especially in the Senate. Legislative bodies in the United States and Canada accept for consideration before first reading only those matters that are officially brought before them by unanimous consent. Opposition to a bill forces those seeking to introduce it either to withdraw it, make some bargain with the objector, or begin the time-consuming process of introducing it in spite of opposition. The use of such opposition is a more potent force in the hands of the autonomous member of Congress than in those of the Canadian legislator bound by party discipline. Further, any American senator may mount a filibuster, that is, he or she may hold the floor indefinitely, thus preventing matters he or she does not wish discussed from being considered and voted upon. As in Canada, there are procedures for ending overly long debates, but they too are clumsy and likely to produce hard feelings that increase the possibility of another filibuster. The process in the United States is far more complex than in Canada and the filibuster's potency has meant that the threat of one is usually enough to cause the various parties to try to resolve differences in advance. Like the "unanimous consent" rule on introduction of matters, the filibuster remains useful because it is infrequently exercised. The rules of procedure induce the members of the Congress to cooperate and bargain. Members who prove too difficult, or unresponsive to the needs and sensitivities of their colleagues, usually have little influence no matter how important they may appear to outsiders. While it is not common, the Congress will occasionally ostracize a member whose behaviour has become intolerable. Such an individual is likely to find himself or herself bereft of meaningful committee assignments and unlikely to be consulted on matters of interest to him or her. Such a lack of cooperation from a member's colleagues will quickly render him or her ineffective as a legislator. The late Senator Joseph R. McCarthy (Republican of Wisconsin) was censured by the Senate in 1955. He died in 1957, just prior to the expiry of his term, and thus the electorate did not get an opportunity to respond to this situation. The Connecticut Democrat, Senator Dodd, was censured in 1966 and, when his term ended in 1970, he was rejected by the Connecticut Democrats as a nominee.

The U.S. Congress, with its many formalities and its high group *espirit de corps,* is a good example of socialization at work at a very high level of the political system. Each member of Congress has considerable individual power. He or she is encouraged to respect, or at least tolerate, even difficult and irrascible colleagues. And, as part of the "code," members become quite sensitive to outside criticism of the institution and quite jealous of its prerogatives, especially if a conflict with the president is involved.

RECOMMENDED READINGS

Albinski, Henry S. "The Canadian Senate: Politics and the Constitution." *American Political Science Review* 57 (June 1963): 378–91.

Cheffins, Ronald I. *The Constitutional Process in Canada.* Toronto: McGraw–Hill, 1969.

Courtney, John C. "In Defence of Royal Commissions." *Canadian Public Administration* 12 (Summer 1969): 198–212.

Dawson, R. W. *The Government of Canada.* 5th ed. Toronto: University of Toronto Press, 1970.

Dawson, W. F. *Procedures in the Canadian House of Commons.* Toronto: University of Toronto Press, 1962.

Doern, G. Bruce, and Aucoin, Peter, eds. *The Structure of Policy Making in Canada.* Toronto: Macmillan, 1971.

Doern, G. Bruce, and Wilson, V. S., eds. *Issues in Canadian Public Policy.* Toronto: Macmillan, 1974.

Epstein, Leon D. "Cohesion of British Parliamentary Parties." *American Political Science Review* 1 (June 1956): 360–77.

Finer, S. E. *Anonymous Empire: A Study of the Lobby in Great Britain.* London: Pall Mall, 1958.

Forsey, Eugene. *Freedom and Order.* Toronto: McClelland and Stewart, Ltd., 1974.

Gibson, Frederick W. *Cabinet Formation and Bicultural Relations.* Ottawa: The Queen's Printer, 1970.

Goodwin, George. *The Little Legislatures: The Committees of Congress.* Amherst: University of Massachusetts Press, 1970.

Hockin, Thomas A. *Apex of Power: The Prime Minister and Political Leadership in Canada.* Scarborough, Ont.: Prentice–Hall of Canada, 1971.

Hutchinson, Bruce. *Mr. Prime Minister: 1867–1964.* Toronto: Longmans Canada, Ltd., 1964.

Jackson, Robert J., and Atkinson, Michael M. *The Canadian Legislative System.* Toronto: Macmillan, 1974.

Jantsch, Erich. "From Forecasting and Planning to Policy Sciences." *Policy Sciences* 1, no. 1 (Spring 1970); pp. 31–41.

Jennings, Ivor. *Cabinet Government.* 3d ed. Cambridge: Cambridge University Press, 1969.

Jewell, Malcolm E., and Patterson, Samuel. *The Legislative Process in the United States.* New York: Random House, 1966.

Kelson, Robert N.   *The Private Member of Parliament and the Formation of Public Policy: A New Zealand Case Study*. Toronto: University of Toronto Press, 1964.

Kornberg, Allan.   *Canadian Legislative Behavior*. Toronto: Holt, Rinehart & Winston, 1967.

————.   "The Rules of the Game in the Canadian House of Commons." *Journal of Politics* 20 (1964): 358–80.

————, **and Thomas, Norman.**   "The Political Socialization of National Legislative Elites in the United States and Canada," *Journal of Politics*, 27 (1965): 761–75.

Kunz, F. A.   *The Modern Senate of Canada, 1925–1963: A Reappraisal*. Toronto: University of Toronto Press, 1965.

Lalonde, Marc.   "The Changing Role of the Prime Minister's Office." *Canadian Public Administration* 14, no. 4 (Winter 1971).

Lindblom, Charles E.   *The Policy Making Process*. Englewood Cliffs, N.J.: Prentice–Hall, 1968.

Mackay, R. A.   *The Unreformed Senate of Canada*. rev. ed. Toronto: McClelland and Stewart, Ltd., 1963.

Mallory, J. R.   *The Structure of Canadian Government*. Toronto: Macmillan, 1971.

March, Roman R.   *The Myth of Parliament*. Scarborough, Ont.: Prentice–Hall, 1974.

Matheson, William A.   *The Prime Minister and the Cabinet*. Toronto: Methuen, 1976.

Newman, Peter C.   *Renegade in Power: The Diefenbaker Years*. Toronto: McClelland and Stewart, Ltd., 1963.

Parkinson, C. Northcote.   *The Evolution of Political Thought*. New York: Viking Press, 1960. Introduction and Part I.

Ranney, Austin.   *Pathways to Parliament*. Madison: University of Wisconsin Press, 1965.

Robertson, Gordon.   "The Changing Role of the Privy Council Office." *Canadian Public Administration* 14, no. 4 (Winter 1971).

Sayeed, Khalid B.   "Public Policy Analysis in Washington and Ottawa." *Policy Sciences* 4, no. 1 (March 1973): 88–101.

Smith, T. Alexander.   "Toward a Comparative Theory of Policy Making." *Comparative Politics* 1, no. 4 (July 1969): 498–515.

Wahlke, John et al.   *The Legislative System*. New York: John Wiley & Sons, 1962.

Walker, Patrick Gordon.   "On Being a Cabinet Minister." In *Policy Making in Britain*, ed. Richard Rose pp. 115–27. London: Macmillan, 1969.

9

Rule Implementation

IN EVERY POLITICAL SYSTEM, once decisions are made concerning the demands registered by society, they must be implemented. The implementation of these decisions involves informing society of the behaviour expected, mobilizing the governmental facilities to encourage such behaviour, and maintaining subsidiary organizations to enforce the expected behaviour. To take an example from everyday life, let us assume that a city council has decided upon a speed limit for a particular street in town. The speed limit is posted in the area and the police are instructed to enforce it. The courts are authorized to assess all cases where offenders have been detected and impose the penalties prescribed by the city council for violating the rule. The subfunctions of communicating, facilitating, and enforcing behaviour expected as a result of political decisions are collectively called the rule implementation process.

SUBFUNCTIONS

Communication

The communication of decisions is accomplished informally by the media as some of the decisions are being made; however, the selectivity of newspapers, radio, and television requires that more comprehensive publicity be given to political decisions, especially the more technical and less dramatic ones. Also, the legitimizing act performed by the head of state on many political decisions must logically be announced to the society for which he or she speaks.

The political system publicizes its decisions by the distribution of a gazette, an official magazine which lists the laws, decrees, and regulations enacted since the previous publication date. Decisions are unenforceable until they are officially published, since it is assumed in most systems that illegal activities may be defined as such only when a person contravenes a published regulation. Other methods of publicity are used in all situations where contact is made with groups and individuals especially affected by certain decisions. Information Canada was an example of a government organization designed to provide information concerning government policy. At the local level one may see publicity devices such as building permits, newspaper accounts of zoning changes, traffic and road construction signs, and postal and tax regulation posters being used.

The major problem with the communication subfunction is the deliberate restriction or selection of communications—administrative secrecy. Information about the content of decisions is communicated regularly, since expected norms of behaviour must be explained. However, the process and ideas used in making a decision are only rarely divulged. The reason for this secrecy would appear to be the desire of official bodies not to expose their internal relationships to the view of society as a whole. By not exposing the decision-making process, the system is able to regulate the "gateways" into the rule making arena in such a way that the evaluation and selection of alternative policies may be made and implemented in relative peace. Were the bureaucracy to be open to continuous and strong influences from society, the function of implementing decisions already made would be compromised. Implementation involves making specific decisions within the limits permitted by a general policy, but intense political pressures on the bureaucracy can force a breakdown of these limits.

The crux of the problem with regard to the acceptable limits of administrative secrecy lies in the dual nature of the bureaucracy. In all countries, to greater or lesser degrees, it helps to make policy as well as implement it. As a policy formulation agent, the bureaucracy must necessarily be as open to society as are political parties and legislatures. As the organization entrusted with the implementation of policy, it must also be insulated from a great deal of social pressure in order to guarantee that its methods of implementation achieve the ends desired by the policy makers in the cabinet and legislature.

The tension between secrecy and openness exists in all societies and any solution reflects only the relative levels of policy formulation and implementation found in a given administration—with one reservation. The key to bureaucratic efficiency is the limitation and patterning of communications and, as such, a bureaucracy will tend to prefer more secrecy than is warranted by its need for insulation from outside pressure. In order to preserve the ideal of a well-informed electorate and to expose bureaucratic policy experts to social concerns, a constant effort must be made to maintain and broaden the openness of the administration. The prescription is especially valid where a "responsible" cabinet system exists, since the concept of collective responsibility of cabinet members reinforces the natural tendency towards secrecy in the bureaucratic organization responsible to it. One of the results of the Watergate scandals in the United States has been the passage of legislation requiring some agencies to open their meetings to the public and press. Other agencies have been required to produce a wide variety of internal documents on request by the public.

Facilitation

The administrative departments are involved in myriad ways in the provision of support for the decision-making bodies. Most obviously it must make available the organization and resources necessary for the implementation of policy.

In 1974, for instance, the federal government spent over $7 billion on goods and services, including civil service salaries, equipment, and transportation, among other things.[1] One third of this expenditure was for military purposes. Included in this type of expenditure in 1973–74 were military and civilian expenses of $66 million for the repair and overhaul of government aircraft and engines, $15 million for ship repairs and refits, $104 million for petroleum products, and $4 million for office furnishing. For the convenience of travelling civil servants, the government maintained its own Central Travel Service, which arranged 125,000 trips in 1973–74. The government spent $24 million on security police in the same year.[2] Capital expenditures for 1973–74 included the provision of such facilities as an Indian Reserve school in Alberta, a wharf in New Brunswick, an RCMP aircraft hangar in the Northwest Territories and a harbour wall in Toronto.[3]

Most government expenditure, however, is not concerned with the provision of facilities, though that is the common assumption. In fact, only about 12 to 17 percent of federal expenditures have been for nondefence goods and services. The fastest growing areas of government spending have consisted of simple transfers. The federal government collects taxes and then passes the money back to taxpayers and others through such programs as family allowances, pensions, and unemployment insurance. Over 30 percent of federal government

---

[1] Canada, Department of Finance, *Economic Review: April 1975* (Ottawa: Information Canada, 1975), taken from Table 54, p. 161.

[2] Preceding figures taken from Canada, Department of Supply and Services, *Annual Report, 1973–74* (Ottawa: Information Canada, 1974).

[3] Preceding figures taken from Canada, Department of Public Works, *Annual Report 1973–74* (Ottawa: Information Canada, 1974).

monies in 1974 were given to individuals. Another 21 percent was transferred directly to other levels of government while 10 percent was transferred to individuals and corporations as interest on the public debt.[4] While it may seem odd that over 60 percent of federal expenditures consisted of a reshuffling of tax money from one individual or company to another or to another level of government, it is important to remember that control over the use of resources is a vital part of politics. Even if the federal government does not actually spend the money, it does strive to influence those who spend it and for what purpose.

The bureaucracy is also involved in the provision of facilities to society in general, as part of the implementation of policy decisions. At the federal level such services include communications (mail service, airports), conservation of resources, scientific research, and product and quality regulation. Besides such social services, the administration, by being accessible to the public, can act as the instrument for transmitting public views to the decision makers.

There are two reasons for such a service. First, the method of implementing decisions already made can affect their social acceptance. Thus the cabinet and bureaucracy are concerned with gaining preliminary advice and assistance from those interest groups most directly involved. Second, access to decision makers in all systems depends to some degree upon channels of communication provided by the administration. Where the efficacy of normal "input channels" is low, influencing the bureaucracy and, through it, the political leadership, is a popular alternative. The tendency of cabinets in Canada to resist the modification of bills presented in the House of Commons leads interest groups to try to influence bills in advance, that is, when civil servants are in the stage of formulating their details.

The provision of access facilities for interest groups varies in detail from system to system. One possible arrangement is the creation of advisory boards which include members of interest groups specifically affected by the activities of the particular branches of the bureaucracy to which boards may be attached. Such boards act as communications links in the formation of policy, as publicizing bodies after policy has been decided, and as coordinating bodies between those affected by policy and those implementing it.

Advisory boards in Canada are found attached to federal departments as well as to provincial and municipal administrations. There exists a problem of role conflict in that the members of advisory boards are often faced with the choice of becoming "rubber stamps" for pol-

---

[4] Preceding figures derived from Canada, Department of Finance, *Economic Review: April 1975*, p. 161

icy decisions or of taking a more active role in the implementation of policy and overstepping their "advisory" role.

Another method of providing access in influencing implementation of decisions is through informal consultations. Contacts of this nature depend, to a great extent, upon interpersonal relationships between civil servants and representatives of interest groups. Contacts based upon ethnic and school ties have been noted in the U.S.S.R.; the retention of retired military officers by defense-related industries in the United States has been criticized in recent years. In Canada the formation of "public relations" agencies based in Ottawa by former ministerial executive assistants represents a similar trend. Such contacts are primarily used in influencing policy choices; however, their potential use in situations where implementation and enforcement of policy are in question is obvious.

Enforcement

Whereas the subfunction of the provision of facilities relates partially to interest articulation and aggregation, that of enforcement carries us into an area related to rule adjudication. Enforcement may be defined as the utilization of various sanctions to reduce the incidents of noncompliance with the decisions made in the political system. Enforcement, for the most part, is a subfunction which deals with the margins of society—the exceptions.

The administration delineates deviations from expected behaviour and uses its facilities to discover transgressions or crimes. Facilities for enforcement are employed in the investigation and the apprehension of persons suspected of committing crimes. There are many more investigatory bodies than apprehension ones. Besides the regular civil police there may be tax agents, security police, secret police, military police, and licensing agents such as those handling the operation of restaurants, race tracks, liquor establishments, and even elevators. People are also officially employed to check for infraction of policy decisions in building construction, electrical wiring, automobile driving, water pollution, truancy, quality in food and meat production, securities and bond sales, treatment of children by parents, immigration, import and export goods, motion pictures, and radio and television programming.

With regard to the formal enforcement bodies such as the police, the number of formal civil police in most societies appears to be about 1 to 2 persons per 1,000 population. Estimates for countries widely separated in economic and cultural terms are rather close as shown in Table 9–1.

TABLE 9–1
Ratio of Civil Police and Population

Country	Year	Police per 1,000 People
Canada.............	1961	1.4
Senegal	1957	1.3
United States	1962	1.9
West Germany	1961	1.7

Source: Compiled from Seymour M. Lipset, "Revolution and Counter-Revolution in the United States and Canada," reprinted Orest Kruhlak et al., eds., *The Canadian Political Process* (Toronto: Holt, Rinehart & Winston, 1970), p. 18; U.S. Army, *Area Handbook for Germany* (Washington, D.C.: U.S. Government Printing Office, 1960), pp. 86–87, 605; U.S. Army, *Area Handbook for Senegal* (Washington, D.C.: U.S. Government Printing Office, 1963), pp. 53, 437.

While urban areas may be said to have higher police-to-population ratios, Canadian cities such as London, Saskatoon, and Winnipeg still ranged between 1.3 and 1.7 police officers per 1,000 population in 1974. This similarity is further emphasized by contrasting these ratios with that for a totalitarian society, where the enforcement of a substantially greater range of economic and social laws and regulations requires more personnel.

The structure of civil police forces throughout most of the world is national in character. Ordinary police operations (criminal and traffic) are coordinated by a ministry of interior or its equivalent, and directed at the lower levels by a *prefect* or other local government officials. In federal systems such as Canada, the United States, and West Germany, most civil police are employees of the province or state. The Royal Canadian Mounted Police (RCMP) is an exception in that it is a federal police force which operates at local levels in many areas of the country. Ontario and Quebec possess their own provincial police forces, however, and the cities and towns across Canada employ local forces. Besides civil police, the most obvious forces are those engaged in security and border investigations. These are invariably attached to national bureaucracies. Other investigating agents are attached to territorial and local divisions which are empowered to enforce pertinent decisions. Apprehension of criminals is generally the function of the civil police, except in security or border cases. Since the RCMP handles security as well as a significant portion of civil and criminal police cases in Canada, its scope of operations is very broad.

Role Conflict and Effectiveness

Administrative personnel are subjected to a role conflict because as members of society they are entitled to participate in the activities of society, including the political; yet, as members of the administration they are required to publicize, facilitate, and enforce expected behaviour. Most political systems which allow for the existence of more than one political party have taken steps to neutralize the civil service by the adoption of regulations prohibiting overt political activity. In Canada, the Civil Service Act of 1918 prohibited civil servants from engaging in any political activity other than voting, and entrusted the enforcement of this provision to the Civil Service Commission. Similar regulations were adopted in all the provinces. With the rise of technical specialization and a "business" orientation in the Canadian bureaucracy in the 1960s, certain restrictions on party membership and official leave for civil servants who wish to run for office have been relaxed. Some provinces such as Saskatchewan and Quebec have also relaxed prohibitions on civil servants' political activity. Reforms have also taken place in the British civil service and to a lesser extent in the United States. France has always had to cope with the problem of party "colonization" of different ministries. In the Fourth Republic especially, leaders of different parties would specialize in certain cabinet posts in each new cabinet so that, over time, their political sympathizers became strongly entrenched in these departments.

In ideological one-party states, the problem takes on another dimension. Rather than encouraging political neutrality, the political system demands that the civil service must be politically committed. As in other types of systems, the aim is to encourage reliability of the agents of implementation, though the lack of alternative parties eliminates the value of political neutrality.

IMPLEMENTATION STRUCTURES AND PROCESSES

A common method of representing a complex organization diagrammatically is to portray it as a pyramid. This pyramid, when applied to the executive, is divided into three parts, representing the major divisions of power and authority. These parts represent the head of state, the cabinet, and the administration, as in Figure 9-1.

The head of state is legally the holder of authority in the executive. The cabinet consists of his advisors, who also individually oversee the many departments of the administration. The administration does the actual work of communicating, facilitating, and enforcing the decisions made in the political system.

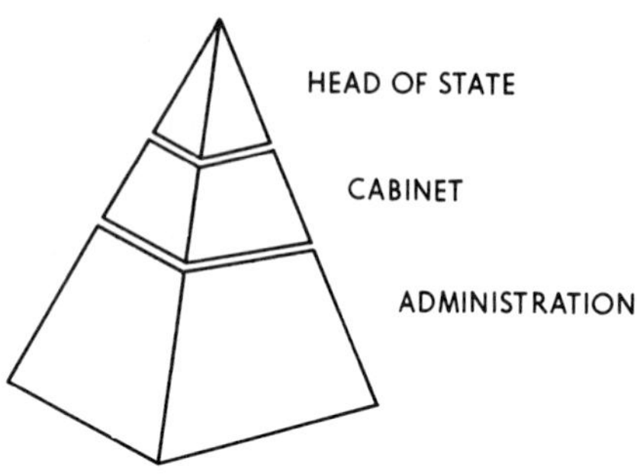

FIGURE 9–1
The Executive Pyramid

Head of State

The executive functions of the Governor General, as head of state, are largely symbolic, since he exercises his authority only on the advice of the Cabinet. All civil servants are considered as agents of the crown, that is, they are hired by and are accountable in theory to him.

Cabinet

The cabinet is involved in both the rule making and rule implementation functions. The first has been dealt with in Chapter 8. The second will be considered in this chapter.

Coordination.   The most important rule implementation function of the cabinet as a whole is the coordination of the various departments, agencies, and other bodies of the administration into the service of the structures which make political decisions. The parallel structures in the administration, called "departments," are normally in little contact with each other, and it is unlikely that they would pursue an integrated policy without some form of high-level coordination. Cabinet meetings and committees serve to impress upon ministers their particular roles in the implementation of policy decisions and to make known the problems and needs of each department so that an integrated policy may be followed.

Successful coordination is dependent in part upon the personalities of the ministers, their relative positions of power in the cabinet, and their political strength outside of it. Ministers who are antagonistic toward one another may end up moving in opposite directions. A weak prime minister, or one who is uninterested in "administrative details," may inadvertently encourage a lack of coordination in policy implementation. Some ministers may force coordination upon the cabinet: finance and defence ministers often hold power second only to the prime minister and may be able to impose agreement where others find it impossible. Where the president or monarch appoints and runs the cabinet, the problem of disintegration may be less. This is especially the case in France, the United States, and such countries as Nicaragua, Morocco, and the communist states.

The political strength of ministers outside the cabinet may provide them with levers for forcing coordination or for protecting their independence. Coalition cabinets in France before 1958 were characterized by groups of politicians who controlled parties or blocs in the National Assembly joining together so that they were relatively immune to pressure. Phillip Williams has noted the effects of coalitions upon French premiers:

. . . . the British premier could weather any but the most extraordinary tempest . . . while in France the captain was more vulnerable than the crew to shifts in the parliamentary wind.[5]

The task of keeping a cabinet coordinated is one of the crucial problems facing any executive, since it is the cabinet which gives direction to the administration and thus the society. When the helm is untended, the ship will either drift or be guided from some other source.

Insulating the Administration.   The acceptance of the supremacy of the legislature in most democratic systems has brought about a common form of control function on the part of legislatures over the behaviour of the administration. When actions of the administration result in public criticism, the cabinet in a parliamentary system has to defend or revise these actions. If the criticism is valid, the minister involved will correct the situation and report to the legislature that, in good faith, he or she was unaware of the undesirable behaviour until it was brought to his or her attention. In an extreme situation, the opposition may try to censure the minister or express "no confidence" in the government. The legislature in presidential systems may use or threaten to use its power to reduce budget estimates, reject important executive proposals, or initiate investigations to force the executive to comply with its wishes.

Exercise of Administrative Powers.   Once policy has been decided, the cabinet minister undertakes the task of setting administrative goals and parameters of action. Generally, this function is only vaguely attended to; though, with the gradual incorporation of "program-planning and budgeting" techniques into North American and European executives, this function is assuming an important place in

---

[5] Phillip Williams, *Crisis and Compromise* (London: Longman's Green, 1964), p. 216.

cabinet business. In a system employing "program budgeting," the activities of the administration are broken down into personnel and financial needs over time, so that the cabinet has a relatively accurate understanding of what may be accomplished with the available resources.

Besides the managerial control exercised by the minister, the cabinet provides other major controls. One is the power of appointments. This power in many systems has been restricted voluntarily by the cabinet to only the most important posts in the administration. In most systems where responsible cabinet government exists, there are few departmental appointments made by the cabinet, with the exception of political coordinators sometimes referred to as the ministers' staff, executive assistants, or, as in France, his own "cabinet." In systems where the cabinet is not responsible to the legislature, more officials are appointed. In the United States as many as 30,000 new appointments are made when a new president assumes office.

Appointments to agencies of the administration not directly under departmental control are quite common. Regulatory boards, public or mixed ownership corporations, autonomous agencies, and other independent bodies are managed by boards whose members are appointed by the cabinet. Such appointments allow the cabinet to ensure that these bodies will be managed by people whose political views are generally acceptable to the ministers. The terms of office of these appointments are important in that many board members are appointed for a long period and may exercise influence contrary to that desired by a new cabinet. Such an obstacle is often overcome by stipulating that appointees serve at the pleasure of the cabinet. As an alternative, a tradition of formal resignation at the investiture of a new government may also be encouraged.

The exercise of administrative powers by cabinets has been the subject of intense investigation by royal commissions in Canada and Great Britain and special congressional and presidential commissions in the United States and France over the last 15 years. Probably the most comprehensive was that instituted by the Canadian federal government in 1960. The Royal Commission on Government Organization, called the Glassco Commission after its chairman, the late J. Grant Glassco, published its report in 1961–62 on desirable changes in the organization of the administration. The central recommendation was that a new style of management and control, similar to that found in modern business organizations, be instituted. Basically departmental power and responsibility were to be encouraged within a system of well-defined goals and financial programs. This would allow for more efficient and effective implementation on the part of the departments. Cabinet control would be restricted to general aspects of policy implementation. Many of the recommendations of the Glassco Commission have been implemented by the Cabinet, notably the delegation of more power and responsibility to lower levels of the bureaucracy, the simplification of some personnel and financial controls, and the movement towards program budgeting. The Glassco Commission report has influenced several provinces. Saskatchewan, Ontario, and Manitoba have conducted similar enquiries into the nature of their bureaucracies and effected reforms designed to make cabinets more effective policy-making and control bodies.

Administration

For much of the period of human existence the administration has been represented by the soldier, the tax collector, and the diplomat; other activities are of comparatively recent origin. The rise of the large and complex administration which typifies both modern and developing political systems today may be traced to the twin impulses of war and welfare. The demands of warfare after the consolidation of nation-states and the development of gunpowder technology led to a reinvention of a classical organizational method known as bureaucracy. With a bureaucratic organization, armies of the 18th and 19th centuries were able to integrate large masses of men and machines into effective fighting forces. The requirements of total war during the Napoleonic period (1795–1815) forced the adaptation of this type of organization to parts of society other than the military.

Concurrently with its application as a method of organizing society towards goals of war and conquest, bureaucracy was being increasingly used as the agent for internal social reform. The possibility of efficient implementation of political decisions meant that reformers and revolutionaries could envision the control of the policy-making process as a method of effecting lasting social change. Most theories of social change since the 18th century have been based in some fashion on human equality, which logically leads to a consideration for general human social and economic welfare. Laws affecting voting rights, working conditions, health, education, and income equitability are meaningful only when there is sufficient control over society to implement them.

In Canada, the administration, measured in terms of finances and personnel, grew slowly from 1900 to 1914, jumped during World War I, declined slightly by 1920, and remained stable until 1939, whereupon it jumped once again until 1946. The postwar period has seen a steady growth after an initial decline until, by 1969, the administration at all levels had far surpassed in size that which was mobilized to fight World War II. The personnel figures for the federal government in

Table 9–2, though they do not show the size of the civil service (government personnel, not including military) during the two war periods, illustrate the impact of war and the postwar welfare state on the size of a bureaucracy.

TABLE 9–2
Canadian Federal Civil Service
(per 1,000 people)

Year	*Personnel*
1913	23
1920	47
1939	46
1948	118
1950	127
1955	137
1960	152
1969	230
1974	260

Sources: *Report of the Royal Commission on Government Organization* (Ottawa: The Queen's Printer, 1962), p. 305, and personal communication from the Public Service Commission.

Representative Bureaucracy. The size of government bureaucracies has led to some controversy about their effectiveness in dealing with social problems and a suspicion that the monies spent by them might be put to better use in other ways. Apart from these concerns, an internal problem of serious import has arisen since the end of World War II. This is the problem of establishing a "representative bureaucracy."

The major continuing reform of civil services in all countries during the past century is the movement from a bureaucracy staffed through political patronage and family ties to one which respects only technical ability and intelligence; the merit principle. Today, even the merit principle has come under attack as being insufficient to open the ranks of civil service to all citizens who might wish to compete for positions. The demand for civil service positions has intensified as the scope of government activity has increased and salary scales have improved. The criticism of the merit principle centres around the obvious statistical preference of government employees for middle-class, educated males from a nation's dominant ethnic group. "Merit," it appears, has been too-narrowly defined.

The response of many governments to criticism that their civil services are not representative of the ethnic, religious, sexual, and class mixtures of the population has been to consciously redress the imbalances. The most commonly used device is the quota, where employers are directed to favour specific types of people, when they qualify through civil service examinations. While quotas may quietly be expressed in terms of percentages of new recruits, these may also be simple directives or programs to enhance the qualities of potential candidates. In this direction, for instance, the Canadian government sponsors training programs for natives in the Yukon and the Northwest Territories, who are underrepresented by a factor of ten in the local bureaucracy. Other programs train women to gain managerial skills so that they can more effectively compete for executive positions, in which they are greatly underrepresented.

In Canada, the most extensive attempt to implement representation in the civil service has been in terms of linguistic groups. The federal government hopes to install bilingual officials in about 54,000 positions by 1978, about 17 percent of the total establishment and including most senior posts. This goal is being pursued through a number of devices. Bilingual personnel are being hired, while others are being trained to develop skill in the other official language—French. The aim of the linguistic-administrative reforms is, in part, to provide services to all parts of the country in both official languages. It also has a representative intent: to strengthen national unity by making governmental communication between the two main national groups easier and to provide a sense of belonging to a group of citizens heretofore underrepresented within the federal bureaucracy. The seriousness of the effort is underlined by its cost: an estimated $345 million from its inception to 1978.[6]

Administrative Structures

An organization is a group of people consciously united in the pursuit of a common goal. This goal may be profit, pleasure, political power, or, as in this case, public service. As an organization, the administration follows patterns of behaviour which are similar to those found in all other organizations. The study of organizations centres around the identification and the analysis of these patterns and their relationships to the individuals operating inside them.

Organizations can be divided into two types, "simple organizations" and "complex organizations." This distinction is based upon the number of layers of authority in an organization. A simple organization has very few of these layers. A class in session and a football team are examples of simple organizations. The class, regardless of size, has one

---

[6] *Toronto Globe and Mail,* November 25, 1974.

teacher presiding over a group of equal students; likewise, the football team has a quarterback who calls plays and 11 other men who assist in the execution of his decisions. A complex organization has many layers of authority. Figure 9–2 illustrates the two types of organizations.

FIGURE 9–2
Simple and Complex Organizations

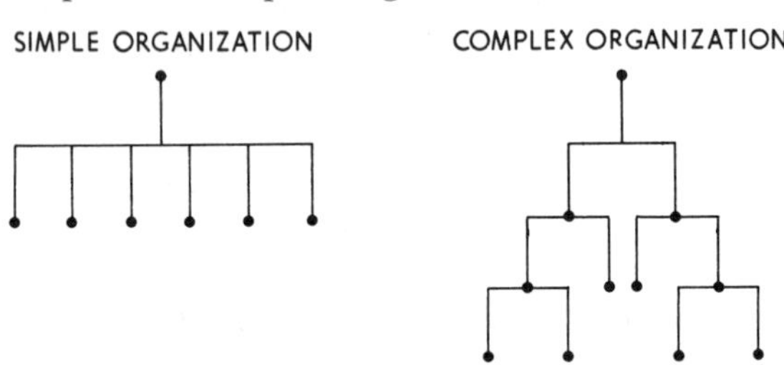

The administration, like all large organizations which have varied and difficult tasks to perform, is a complex organization. The advantage of a complex organization is that its members can engage in coordinated, specialized operations on a large scale.

A bureaucracy is a common form of complex organization. The term "bureaucracy" entered the language as a result of the studies by Max Weber of the German administration before World War I. Weber set down what he considered to be the characteristics of a model or "ideal-type" bureaucracy:[7]

1. A continuous organization of official functions bound by rules.
2. A specified sphere of competence for each official.
3. Hierarchical organization.
4. Officials are trained in job functions, rules, norms.
5. The office and the incumbent are separate entities.
6. Activities are proposed and reported in writing.
7. Officials exercise legal authority.

Weber's list of characteristics say a great deal about the nature of bureaucracy. It is, first of all, continuous, that is, its operations do not start and stop, organize and fall apart, on a sporadic scale. The organization is also tightly structured. Each person has his or her own "function," or role to perform and these roles have specific limits put on them. These limits, or rules, set out the area in which a given official is competent to act. Competence here is a legal term and does not refer to the mental capabilities of the bureaucrat.

---

[7] Summarized from Max Weber, "The Essentials of Bureaucratic Administration: An Ideal Type Construction," in *Reader in Bureaucracy*, ed. Robert K. Merton et al. (New York: The Free Press, 1952), pp. 19–21.

Hierarchy is the relationship of one role in the organization to another. The "higher levels" include roles which have wider limits than those farther down in the hierarchy. In order to understand their place in this graduated system of roles, bureaucrats must be trained. Among other things, they must come to realize that no one "owns" his or her job. If a bureaucrat leaves his or her position, then someone else must be found to fill his or her role. No one is irreplaceable, often not even the organization.

Returning to the idea that a bureaucracy is continuous in operation, it must be noted that this requires some method of accurately transmitting decisions taken by predecessors, superiors and subordinates through space and time. This is why files of documents and other written material are collected and stored by a bureaucracy. It is a relatively permanent mode of communication. One of the ironies of archaeology is that most of the Babylonian clay tablets and Egyptian scrolls which have been unearthed are simply bureaucratic records. Scientists know a lot about the price of wheat in ancient Babylon but comparatively nothing about its music and literature.

Finally, Weber noted that the duly appointed and trained officials in any bureaucracy, public or private, exercise legal authority while on their jobs. A civil servant may hold a position as a result of budgetary approvals in the annual financial law. He or she may have been appointed under a civil service act, and his or her operational role is circumscribed by the law creating the department and by the laws which he or she is supposed to implement. If, in the execution of duties, a civil servant steps outside these boundaries he or she can be dismissed, arrested, or otherwise disciplined. Within them, though, the civil servant is quite powerful.

Weber saw bureaucracy as encompassing a different type of leadership from those discussed in the preceding chapter. A bureaucracy depends upon leadership which is designated from above. Leadership does not then depend so much upon the person in a bureaucracy as upon the position of the office in the authority structure. Such an organization is stable, long term, and capable of efficient action on a growing scale.

With few exceptions, the administrations of political systems today are bureaucratic in nature. As a type of complex organization, one of its most obvious features is specialization. The organization is structured in such a way that it is divided into various parts, each producing a portion of the whole output. Specialization in the bureaucracy means that political decisions are implemented by a coordinated effort on the part of various departments, divisions, agencies, and offices.

Though the departments of the administration which follow from the discussion of cabinet posts constitute the most important specialized bodies, they are not the only ones. Departments or ministries may be referred to as *operational divisions.* Other types of divisions have been encouraged by many governments in order to make the implementation of political decisions more effective. These are territorial and systemic divisions.

Territorial divisions of the bureaucracy are common throughout the world and are often associated with the territorial divisions of the policy-making bodies. Most decisions are made at the central level and specialized departments are entrusted with implementing them at local levels. The common form of territorial division is the prefectoral system of administration developed by Napoleon which is found throughout much of Europe and the non-Western world. A single local authority, the *prefect,* supervises the actions of the central departments where they enter his geographic area. The prefect may be assisted by a local council which assures that some local influence may be brought to bear on the central bureaucracy. Two other widely used methods are the formation of local or municipal administrative bodies and the formation of federal states. Local government in Canada is a creature of provincial legislatures and may be considered to be another type of territorial division. In federal systems where the central government exercises preponderant constitutional and political power, provinces may be considered as a type of territorial division of the central administration. This is the case in federations such as Argentina and Brazil, though not in Canada.

Systemic divisions occur where agencies which are actually a part of the administration are placed on the periphery of the political system. The most common examples are independent regulatory agencies and nationalized companies, or crown corporations—agencies such as the Canadian Wheat Board and companies like the Canadian Broadcasting Corporation, Renault in France, and the many state-owned airlines around the globe. For purposes of efficiency or honesty, these agencies and corporations are given an autonomous status and subjected to only minimal supervision by the administration, cabinet, and legislature. This separation exists in fact most of the time, though decisions made by these bodies may subject them to temporary direct political interference. CNR rail schedules, labour unrest in Renault, and kosher foods on El Al flights have all been carried into the political arena by virtue of the companies' ties to the governmental apparatus.

Personnel policies in systemically divided bodies often differ from policies in those operationally and territorially divided. The top managements of these corporations and agencies are appointed by the cabinet or head of state for specific terms or "during pleasure." Regulations concerning the hiring, firing, and promotion of workers or staff members are generally not the same civil service regulations which affect the operationally or territorially divided bodies, and frequently resemble more closely those used in the private sector. Systemic divisions are often established to give some public bodies a private character so that they may compete in the economic sector.

Administrative Controls

The problem of assuring that the rules which are made are faithfully implemented is one of the most critical facing any political system. The use of a complex, hierarchical bureaucratic organization structure is, in itself, an attempt to limit the possibilities of administrative error. More deliberate than this is the creation of specific procedures and structures by rule making bodies to control the behaviour of bureaucrats.

Financial controls are probably the oldest known and are instituted in order to guarantee to the decision-making apparatus that the resources allocated for the implementation of policy are used for their designated purposes. The most important of these is the budget. Funds are normally allocated a year at a time. This period, which in many countries does not coincide with the calendar year, is called a fiscal year. Before the beginning of each fiscal year (April 1 in Canada) the cabinet, as the directing body of the executive, is required to submit budgetary papers for the approval of the legislature. The Canadian budgetary process described below is similar to that found in most countries.

Approximately a year before the fiscal year for which a new budget is to be prepared, the Treasury Board issues general directives to the various levels of each administrative department, outlining the expected overall financial position of the executive with projected departmental allocations. With this policy document in hand, the various levels of the administration begin to compile their estimated needs, each level passing its estimates to the next highest one, until the departmental estimates are placed in the hands of the minister. At this point the estimates are merged into the overall budget estimate. Throughout this process of consolidation, all departments keep close contact with the Treasury Board in order to coordinate their estimates with the financial policy laid down at the beginning. The role of the Treasury Board is similar to that played by the Office of Management and Budget attached to the Office of the President of the United States, and similar bureaus in the finance ministries of other countries.

The Treasury Board forwards the budget estimates to the cabinet for final adjustments and approval. They are then sent to the Governor General for acknowledgment and subsequently presented to the House of Commons by the Minister of Finance. While the estimates are normally revealed well before the budget debate begins, the government's tax proposals are kept secret until they are presented to the House.

The control aspects of the budgetary process are evident. The administration commits itself to a certain level and scope of performance in the estimates, which are concomitant with the general policy set down by the cabinet. If the implementation of a certain policy requires a given amount of funds and these funds are not forthcoming, then the policy cannot be carried out. By restricting or withholding funds, the cabinet and the legislature directly control the implementation of policy.

With the 1969–70 budget, the federal government began to use a new process of budget formation called the planning-programming budgeting system (PPBS). It requires the departments to draw up their estimates in line with an overall five-year financial projection or plan. This plan allows the decision makers to control not only the specific policies decided upon that year, but also the overall trend of spending and activities during each plan period.

Another financial control is the audit, a check made to determine whether money allocated was spent for the purpose for which it was intended and whether this money allocated was spent efficiently. Regulations are issued by the Treasury Board concerning the methods of spending and accounting for funds. Infractions of these rules are subject to severe penalties. Audits are conducted by a separate agency which in Canada is the Auditor General's office. The Auditor General, in contrast to almost all other functionaries, reports directly to the House of Commons, thus assuring that the policies approved in the budget are implemented honestly.

Personnel controls such as loyalty investigations and entrance examinations may be traced back to the early Chinese Empire. The modern civil service system found throughout the world was instituted first in Europe and then North America as a method of selecting and promoting qualified personnel required by the expanding bureaucracies. In the late 19th and early 20th centuries this technical rationale was paralleled by a growing feeling that a politically dependent civil service was impairing the efficiency and the status of the bureaucracy in the political system and in the society in general. A system of controls was devised to insure the selection and promotion of only those people who were best qualified for positions in the administration. In Canada, as a typical example, laws were passed in 1908 and 1918 creating and strengthening a control agency, the Civil Service Commission. The Civil Service Commission was empowered to examine candidates for hiring and promotion, investigate and correct personnel decisions based on political connections, supervise disciplinary measures, and hear appeals. The competence of the Commission over the years was not extended to bodies in the territorial and systemic divisions of the administration, with the result that many government employees did not fall under its jurisdiction. These personnel were either placed under provincial civil service commissions or were treated in accordance with practices in private industry. The original aim of the Civil Service Commission (now the Public Service Commission) was to "depoliticize" the civil service so that the administration could serve as the implementation agent for the decision-making process and not as the executive arm of any particular political party. Taking the bureaucracy out of partisan politics did not eliminate its role in policy making, but it did restore faith in the administration as a relatively neutral enforcing organization. A related discussion is presented in the section on role conflict in the administration.

Ministerial responsibility for administrative actions and the ombudsman, an agent of the legislature who investigates complaints about bureaucratic behaviour, are the most obvious forms of *activity* control. Cabinet members in all political systems are responsible to someone for the conduct of their individual departments. Ministerial responsibility has traditionally meant that in a parliamentary system the cabinet members are responsible to parliament in the sense that parliament may force their resignation. However, the influence of the idea of collective responsibility is such that this action could be achieved only through the drastic measure of rejecting the entire cabinet. In effect, the individual minister is responsible first to the prime minister, who may remove the minister from his or her duties if a scandal should break, thus avoiding an embarrassing confrontation in the parliament. A similar situation exists in presidential systems even though the cabinet cannot be rejected by the legislature. The political costs of public legislative investigations or antagonistic resolutions are great enough to warrant the dismissal of a minister whose department is guilty of contradicting policy decisions. The precariousness of the minister's position is, in turn, then transmitted downward into the administration through the managerial structure to the lowest levels. The ability of a minister to assert himself in his or her ministry depends heavily upon the minister's personality and understanding of the general means and ends he or she wishes subordinates to pursue. A political system which exhibits a high turnover of cabinets or a chronic rapid reshuffling of ministerial posts will tend to be governed as well as administered by the civil service. The rapid turnover of political leadership may mean that there is no consistent policy to be implemented and the subordinate levels of the administration may be forced to make decisions as well as to implement them. Where orders from the legislature and cabinet are not acceptable to the administration, the leadership vacuum encourages the administration to delay their execution until new leaders assume power. There is a tendency at this point to forget the old orders.

Another form of control is a special agency reporting to the legislature which investigates allegations of improper conduct within the administration and in its relations with the general public. The most common names for this type of agency are the parliamentary commissioner and the ombudsman, (from the Swedish title) who supervises such an agency. Ombudsmen are found today in the Scandinavian countries, Great Britain, New Zealand, and the West German army, and in most of the provinces of Canada. Variations of this agency are found in France, the United States Army, the U.S.S.R, Yugoslavia, Tanzania, and Japan. Many other political systems are in the process of adopting this technique of control.

The first ombudsmen were established in Sweden (1809), Finland (1919), and Denmark (1953–54). The duties of the Swedish ombudsman were to "supervise the observance of laws and statues as applied . . . . by the courts and public officials and employees" and to "institute proceedings . . . . against those who, in the execution of their official duties, have through partiality, favoritism, or other cause committed any unlawful act or neglected to perform their official duties properly."[8] Over time, the emphasis in the ombudsman's work has come to lie in the relationship between the administration and the public.

The powers of the ombudsman vary from system to system, ranging from the right to initiate court proceedings against civil servants in Sweden to the obligation of the English parliamentary commissioner to accept complaints from and report only to members of Parliament. The scope of investigation also varies as some ombudsmen enjoy the right to investigate nearly all administrative activities, while others are barred from significant segments of the administration. The case loads of ombudsmen are small relative to the number of administrative actions taken in political systems, yet large enough to justify the existence of the office. The office is more active in systems where it has been in existence longest and where its powers of investigation are greatest. The results emanating from the ombudsman's office are roughly similar in most countries. About one third of the cases prove to be outside the jurisdiction of the office and, at most, one fifth require remedial action.

Variations of the office of ombudsman generally take the form of a

---

[8] Geoffrey Sawer, *Ombudsmen*, 2d ed. (Melbourne, Aust.: Melbourne University Press, 1968), p. 8; Donald Rowat, ed., *The Ombudsman: Citizen's Defender*, 2d ed. (Toronto: University of Toronto Press, 1968).

commission or an agency set up inside the administration for the purposes of investigating complaints. The most venerable of these is the French *Conseil d'Etat* (Council of State), which provides a separate court system wherein complaints against the actions of the administration may be registered by private citizens and civil servants. West Germany and the Soviet Union have similar arrangements. The major drawback to such arrangements is that they may be ineffective because of their continuing connection with the particular administration or administrative body which they are expected to investigate.

In addition to financial, personnel, and activity controls, the bureaucracy is subject to the direct organizational control of the cabinet. Through various psychological techniques, the cabinet and levels of bureaucratic managers subordinate to it attempt to further control the implementation process.

The major psychological problem facing a bureaucratic organization is what Anthony Downs calls "authority leakage."[9] As policies are transmitted down the hierarchy for application in specific situations, there is a tendency to distort the original intent and to supplement intended bureaucratic behaviour with personal actions and priorities. If the authority leakage between levels is very great, the bottom levels of the bureaucracy may be found administering "policies" which are contradictory to what was intended, and doing so with the best of intentions!

One of the ways of avoiding such a situation is to select for offices people who share the same general values as the rule makers and who have had extensive training in understanding and following orders. Personnel tests are devised to filter out those who through character traits or social and political activities would not fit into the bureaucratic mould. The training process itself is used to shape new civil servants properly. The traditions and history of the bureaucracy and its role in the overall political process are stressed. Finally a continuous process of evaluation of job activities by superiors, which is an essential part of the promotion process, provides a general check on the behaviour of bureaucrats and helps to ensure that only the most competent and trustworthy people are placed at higher levels of authority.

A very popular and somewhat sophisticated method of controlling behaviour is the management-by-objectives (MBO) technique. MBO is basically goal-oriented, in that superiors in a bureaucracy are expected to set down policy objectives clearly. Then subordinates are evaluated on the accomplishment of these objectives, leaving the means to these ends up to their superior's discretion. Previous man-

---

[9] Anthony Downs, *Inside Bureaucracy* (Boston: Little, Brown & Co., 1967) p. 134–36.

agerial techniques have stressed the need to control and guide all aspects of bureaucratic behavior. MBO simply concentrates on objectives.

The MBO technique consists of the setting of objectives, an agreement between superiors and subordinates on the feasibility of accomplishing them, and a continual evaluation of the subordinates' progress in meeting these agreed-upon goals. This approach to management was accepted by the Canadian Cabinet in late 1971 and the Treasury Board was instructed to begin revising managerial procedures throughout the bureaucracy.[10]

The problem of control brings us close to the focus of the last three chapters of this text. In the preceding pages the administration has been outlined and its structures and functions discussed. It is, in most countries, fairly effective in that it carries out the tasks assigned to it. What shall these tasks be? An organization is an instrument like a knife. Like a knife, a bureaucracy can be used for purposes of good or evil. William Shirer, in his *Rise and Fall of the Third Reich*, quotes from suppliers' letters to the administrators of the concentration camp at Auschwitz:[11]

To: the Central Construction Office of the S.S. and Police, Auschwitz.
Subject: Crematoria 2 and 3 for the camp.
We acknowledge receipt for your order for five triple furnaces, including two electric elevators for raising the corpses and one emergency elevator. A practical installation for stoking coal was also ordered and one for transporting ashes.

The tone is very bureaucratic . . . and very terrifying.

The use to which the bureaucracy is to be put is one of the central problems of society. It is often confused with the supposed problem of "controlling" the bureaucracy; however, the problem of control, as one has seen, is technical and is amenable to solution. What is done with this instrument after it is controlled is a matter for philosophers and the general public.

Recommended Readings

Brown-John, C. Lloyd. "Party Politics and the Canadian Federal Public Service." *Public Administration (London)* 52, no. 1 (Spring 1974): 79–93.

Cheffins, Ronald I. *The Constitutional Process in Canada*, chap. 3. Toronto: McGraw–Hill, 1969.

---

[10] J. S. Hodgson, "Management by Objectives—The Experience of a Federal Government Department," *Canadian Public Administration*, 16 no. 3 (Fall 1973): 422–31.

[11] William L. Shirer, *Rise and Fall of the Third Reich* (New York: Simon and Shuster, 1960), p. 971.

Civil Service Commission, Organization Division. *The Analysis of Organization in the Government of Canada.* Ottawa: The Queen's Printer, 1964.

Cutt, James. "The Program Budgeting Approach to Public Expenditures: A Conceptual Review." *Canadian Public Administration* 12, no. 4 (Winter 1970): 396–426.

Dawson, R. M., and Ward, N. *The Government of Canada.* 4th ed., part 4. Toronto: University of Toronto Press, 1963.

Downs, Anthony. *Inside Bureaucracy.* Boston: Little, Brown & Co., 1966.

Fougère, Louis. *Civil Service Systems.* Brussels: International Institute of Administrative Science, 1967.

Heady, Ferrell. *Public Administration: A Comparative Perspective.* Englewood Cliffs, N.J.: Prentice–Hall, 1966.

Hodgetts, J. E. *The Canadian Public Service: A Physiology of Government, 1967–1970.* Toronto: University of Toronto Press, 1973.

Hodgetts, J. E., and Corbett, D. C., eds. *Canadian Public Administration.* Toronto: Macmillan, 1960.

Jay, Antony. *Management and Machiavelli.* Hammondsworth, England: Penguin Books, 1970.

Kernaghan, W. D. K., ed. *Bureaucracy in Canadian Government.* 2d ed. Toronto: Methuen & Co., 1973.

Kernaghan, W. D. K., and Willms, A. M., eds. *Public Administration in Canada.* 2d ed. Toronto: Methuen & Co., 1971.

Krislov, Samuel. *Representative Bureaucracy.* Englewood Cliffs, N.J.: Prentice–Hall, 1974.

Macridis, Roy C., and Brown, Bernard E., eds. *Comparative Politics,* 4th ed. Homewood, Ill.: The Dorsey Press, 1972.

Marini, Frank, ed. *Toward a New Public Administration.* Scranton, Pa.: Chandler, 1971.

Rowat, Donald C., ed. *The Ombudsman: Citizen's Defender.* 2d ed. Toronto: University of Toronto Press, 1968.

Royal Commission on Government Organization. *Report of the Royal Commission on Government Organization,* vol. 1 (abridged). Ottawa: The Queen's Printer, 1962.

Schultze, Charles. *The Politics and Economics of Government Spending.* Washington, D.C.: Brookings Institute, 1968.

United Nations, Department of Economic and Social Affairs. *A Handbook of Public Administration.* New York: United Nations, 1961.

Waldo, Dwight. *The Study of Public Administration.* New York: Random House, 1955.

White, W. L., and Strick, J. C. *Policy, Politics and the Treasury Board in Canadian Government.* Don Mills, Ont.: Science Research Associates, 1970.

Wilson, V. S. "The Relationship Between Scientific Management and Personnel Policy in North American Administrative Systems." *Public Administration* (London) 51, no. 2 (Summer 1973): 193–205.

10

Rule Adjudication

IN ORDER for a political system to be effective, the members of society must incorporate its decisions into the fabric of their lives. They must obey, and most people do so voluntarily most of the time. As a result, the greater part of the work of the administration is concerned with the publicizing of decisions and facilitating compliance. The process of deciding if an activity has, indeed, transgressed the dictates of the system is of crucial importance since it reflects the authority of the system over the society, demonstrates its power, and serves to reinforce the political culture.

A *law* in the political system is the "package" which contains an important, unique decision. It prescribes the general behaviour and orientations which the government expects to be incorporated into society. To this end the agents of the government are instructed to publicize, support, and enforce these laws. The subsystem performing rule adjudication, or the legal system, includes this legislation in its inputs and considers specific actions of individuals and groups in the light of these commands from the government. Law, then, is a device for defining and clarifying, over time, decisions made by the government.

Law is a human artifact used to manipulate reality. It is not reality nor does it necessarily have to reflect it, since it helps to create new realities. The artificial nature of law is often forgotten when law and justice are compared. Law attempts to orient social relationships so that a just or equitable situation is created, but its first requisite is to attain certainty rather than justice.

The fact that law is a human artifact invented in prehistoric times from diverse social experiences does not mean that its value is any the less or that it does not perform any real functions in society. Modern society would be unable to function without it if only because of the numbers and variety of people which populate a country. The size of a country like Canada, for instance, would prohibit the propagation of uniform cultural norms without the aid of a singular norm-setting body. Modern technology would give the deviants, even though few in numbers, a large advantage over their fellows unless the rest of society concentrated on personal defense. In short, without law and the legal process, society today would revert to barbarism, at the least. Law thus performs an integrative function; it knits together the individuals making up a society.[1]

THEORIES OF LAW

Natural Law

The concept of natural law is a refinement of the traditional notion of the primacy of the supernatural. Though the concept has gone through successive stages of interpretation, it may generally be defined as law which is based upon the recognition of traits in human nature which are common to all people.

One of the ideas of early people was that their social, as well as individual, existence depended upon the goodwill of supernatural entities. Law was seen as the prescribed forms of placation. For many ancient societies, this marked the endpoint in philosophical considerations along this line, but in the Mediterranean world the Jews and the Greeks carried the religious-legal connection one step further.

The Jews were monotheistic; that is, they believed in a single God rather than the historically more common plurality of gods. Monotheism led to the consideration that God had a plan, or end purpose, for things. This was suggested throughout the Old Testament and especially in the nomination of the Hebrews as "chosen people." While the Jews developed the notion of purpose, the Greeks began to see order. As they observed their natural surroundings, the early Greek philosophers noted the regularities that occurred around them. The motions of the sun, moon, and stars, the life cycle of plants and animals, the nature of gravity, and other physical phenomena were seen as operating according to relatively fixed rules. It was logical to assume that people as individuals and societies as a whole also operated according to some natural order.

Plato suggested that the existing social relationships were an imperfect reflection of the ultimate social ideal. Its outlines could be perceived by wise people employing the proper philosophy or framework for analysis. The best society would then be guided by these wise men,

---

[1] J. Salmond, "Jurisprudence," in E. Adamson Hoebel, *The Law of Primitive Man* (Cambridge, Mass.: Harvard University Press, 1964), p. 275.

the "philosopher kings," whose decisions would in turn be guided by their vision of the ideal reality. Aristotle took a different approach by suggesting that people and society, like natural phenomena, have a purpose in existence. Like the Jews, he saw some wider plan behind reality and wrote that people act justly when they act in accordance with it. He distinguished between conventional or man-made justice and natural justice, which applies to all human beings regardless of their condition. The Stoic philosophers expanded upon Aristotle's views by emphasizing that people were bound to live in accord with nature. This condition was fulfilled when they were governed by their most important faculty—their reason. The inclusion of reason into the theory of natural law is sensible as reason is the problem-solving faculty in people. Reason implies a goal to be attained and consists of an evaluation of the various means of arriving at that goal, based on some desirable criterion.

During the Roman era, the Stoic philosophy encountered Christianity, which was heir to the Jewish concept of divine purpose. The two philosophies merged with regard to natural law—a merger which has been maintained to this day. Christian natural law saw the ultimate reality of Plato, the purpose of Aristotle, and the nature of the Stoics as various conceptions of divine purpose. The plan of God included nature as well as people and a correct use of reason would allow people to see and follow this plan. For more than a thousand years natural law was tied to religious doctrine.

During the Renaissance a movement began to secularize the concept of natural law. Hugo Grotius saw natural law as arising out of human nature rather than directly from divine inspiration. Moral rules could be discovered through the use of reason applied to human nature. This approach predominated through the next centuries, reaching a high point in the thought of the rationalists of the 18th century. Natural law was used to justify both the American and French revolutions.

The rationalists' interpretation of natural law resulted in the development of a number of important concepts. Among them were the identification of fundamental rights and the invention of judicial supremacy. Through an analysis of human nature the rationalists saw that people, in order to use their reason, must be equipped with certain freedoms since where there is no choice of behaviour or thought there is no reason involved. People cannot be truly people unless they are free to decide their fate; therefore they must enjoy certain "inalienable" rights with which government may not interfere, if it is to remain in accord with natural law. If it does interfere with them, people have an obligation as human beings to alter or overthrow the government.

The idea of judicial supremacy also arises from natural law. If one accepts the idea that there is an order of law which is superior to government and which is supposed to guide political activity, it follows that some method must be devised to ensure that government is effectively prevented from acting against reason and contravening natural law. This idea has been most thoroughly carried out in the United States where the Supreme Court has assumed the right to declare acts of government unconstitutional, on the assumption that the constitution is in conformity with natural law. This approach has never been incorporated into either the British or Canadian constitutions because of a different notion of law.

Natural law as a general theory has been de-emphasized in the 19th and 20th centuries; however, it has not died out, nor is it likely to do so. It has remained as a basis for the political philosophy of the Catholic Church, influencing a large proportion of the people in Western countries. It has also enjoyed academic and a populist revival in recent years.

The return of academic thought to natural law theory was stimulated by some of the research of social scientists, especially anthropologists and sociologists, into the nature of primitive order and society. Certain constant concerns in these societies have been discovered by these researchers. These concerns are related in a general fashion to such concepts as personal security and property relations which are found in the modern framework of law. Within very broad limits it can be said that societies have similar methods of maintaining human relationships.

The convergence of social science theory and natural law was paralleled by a concern over the status of totalitarian dictatorships. The general repugnance felt for the laws passed by these states prompted many thinkers to review their conceptions of morality and law. Regardless of the legality of Nazi anti-Semitic legislation, for instance, there was doubt as to its legitimacy since the source of legitimacy, the people, was effectively controlled by the government. An appeal to a higher source of legitimacy, humanity itself, had to be formulated. Nazi laws were considered legal in the Aristotelian sense of conventional justice, but were adjudged illegal in terms of natural or human justice.

The revival of natural law has not been confined only to the academic scene. After World War II the major powers took the step of instituting war crimes trials against German and Japanese officials. These men were tried for "crimes against humanity," not for acting contrary to established German and Japanese law. This largely unconscious revival of natural law thinking led to diverse protests against such "immorality" as racial segregation and apartheid, the Vietnam war, the occupation of Czechoslovakia, and the depreciation of the environment by big business interests. As the world becomes increasingly interdependent, there appears to be a growing need "for a standard of justice by which to evaluate the positive law, a standard firm yet not subject to the criticism which destroyed the older natural law doctrines."[2]

Positive Law

It can be argued, and rightly so, that positive law has existed since people first created organized societies. It may be simply defined as people-made law. Positive and natural law are related by some natural law theorists who argue that positive law must be oriented toward or congruent with natural law. It was not until after the Renaissance and the rise of secular rationalism that people began to see law as a concept not being necessarily connected with morality, implying, *in extenso,* that law itself could be studied free from the prescriptions of human nature. The separation of natural law and positive law in theory was based on the difference between fact and value, separating "is" from "ought." It was felt that existing phenomena could be profitably studied without reference to the moral use for which they were intended, if any.

Attempts to posit the underlying rationale of positive law free from the confines of natural law has resulted in a continuing relationship between the two major theories, in spite of attempts to separate them. The major theory of positive law relevant to the Canadian context is that based upon utility. Jeremy Bentham's successful advocacy of utilitarian law reforms in 19th century Britain (see Chapter 14) led to a divergence between Anglo-Canadian and American perspectives on law.

Utility means usefulness, which implies the existence of a purpose for the thing being analyzed. The importance of utility was argued on the basis that people were basically guided by an urge towards pleasure and away from pain. Law, like other social inventions, could be analyzed from the point of view of utility, that is, whether laws gave the greatest pleasure to the greatest number or not. Laws could be divided into good and bad on this principle and new laws devised to promote the common good. In one form or another utilitarian principles have survived to this day though the language of analysis has changed.

MODERN STUDY OF LAW

The two most important methods for studying the role of law in society today are analytical and sociological jurisprudence. Jurispru-

---

[2] Carl J. Friedrich, *Philosophy of Law in Historical Perspective,* 2d ed. (Chicago: University of Chicago Press, 1963), p. 188.

dence may be simply defined as *the formal study of positive law.*[3] Analytical jurisprudence is derived from the utilitarian principle which perceives law as a self-contained body of rules which can be examined in a logical, if not scientific, manner. The analytical "school" of jurisprudence includes a number of prominent jurists who drew inspiration from development in linguistics and the rising prestige of science. Linguistics, the study of the use and function of words, enabled these jurists to see the principles of law in a new light. As a result, the methods of legal reasoning and the internal complexity of laws have been more thoroughly studied.

Since 1930, analytical jurisprudence has also been influenced by the attempt to formulate a "pure science of law." Rather than discuss law as a part of human affairs or social science, scholars have sought to establish a logical system more akin to mathematical thinking. They have limited jurisprudence to the study of a hierarchy of norms descending from the highest legal authority in the society. These attempts have been criticized as having deprived the study of law of its relevance by restricting it to a set of abstract principles; however, an engineer could just as easily criticize a person who deals in pure mathematics. Increasingly, then, jurists who have been included in the "school" of analytical jurisprudence have tended toward a more abstract, scientific, analysis of law.

Sociological jurisprudence developed alongside the analytical approach but it emphasized the relation of law to society. It combines sociological research with legal studies. Sociological jurists advocate going outside the formal system of law to discover the behavioural rules of society. Their concern is with social processes rather than abstract norms or principles.

Sociological jurisprudence was most readily accepted in the United States after the turn of the century. It proposed a relativist notion of law. In this view, the jurist has no special insight into eternal truths or correct norms; he or she can only affect temporary compromises over the intent of the law; compromises based on the views of the community at a given time. Sociological jurisprudence further suggested that the study of law should include an evaluation of its social effects. Laws should serve the particular ends for which they have been written; if they do not, they should be changed.

This trend of thought has been carried further by the "realist" school of jurisprudence which emphasizes relativism and tends to see law as decisions or actions rather than rules or norms. The rules have no meaning apart from their application:

---

[3] T. E. Holland, "Jurisprudence," chapter 1 as quoted in George W. Paton, *A Textbook of Jurisprudence*, 3d ed., ed. by David P. Derham (Oxford: Clarendon Press, 1967), p. 2.

What we are accustomed to describe as "legal rights," then, apparently grow out of specific law suits and are to be found in specific court-orders, judgments, or decrees. If no court-order has as yet been entered with respect to any of your legal rights or mine, then those rights are not yet known, but can only be guessed. Maybe you have some particular right, maybe you haven't. The only way you can find out definitely is to see what a court will do about it.[4]

The realist school, above all, reflects a number of developments in Western society over the last century. The rise of positivist social sciences has given an emphasis to the behaviour of people rather than to legal principles. Technological, political, and social change has disrupted philosophies oriented toward stable and unchanging values and beliefs. "Truth" does not flourish when there are many "truths." Consequently there has been a willingness to accept a behaviourally oriented, skeptical, relativist viewpoint towards law which did not exist in the past. The realist school stands at the boundary between the study of law and of the social sciences, resulting in an increasing number of joint studies by social scientists and jurists.

The connections between law and political science are historically older and more intimate than between it and the other social sciences. Both political and legal theory have long been concerned with the common good. At times law has been considered as the medium in which politics operates, and at other times politics has been seen as the medium in which law functions.

THE LEGAL SYSTEM

The patterns of behaviour which surround the utilization of law are analogous to those found in the political system. There are social structures which perform certain actions which contribute to the maintenance of these structures and to the operations of society and the political system. Hence, one may speak of a *legal system,* which may be considered here as a political subsystem. The legal system derives its most important inputs, formal structures, resources, and personnel from the political system and depends upon the administration for the transmission of much of its output into society.

Functions

If law is considered as performing an integrative role in society, then the legal system must be considered as the mechanism which

---

[4] Jerome Frank, *Courts on Trial* (1949; reprint ed., New York: Atheneum, 1963), p. 9.

translates the potential of the law into actuality. Either bad law or a bad legal system may prevent law from being effective. The overall role of the legal system is to *apply* political decisions, as expressed in laws, to specific instances of social behaviour. It does this normally by deciding upon the appropriateness or legality of a particular case. Often people conform to laws only if they know that nonconformity will be punished. Punishment requires the willingness of both the administration and the legal system to present and demonstrate an example of wrong behaviour. The legal system may also indicate expected behaviour by eliminating uncertainties about the intent of a law. Legislation to a great extent is couched in vague terms, since it is designed to cover a variety of situations. The legal system is then expected to *interpret* the law in terms of specific behaviour.

Another function of the legal system is that of *reinforcing* the political culture. The process of applying the laws is conducted in such a manner that the legal system and, through it, the political system are associated in the minds of citizens with the society itself. Consider Captain Vere's reply to his lieutenant in Melville's *Billy Budd:*

Lieutenant, were that clearly lawful for us under the circumstances, consider the consequences of such clemency. The people (meaning the ship's company) have native sense; most of them are familiar with our naval usage and tradition, and how would they take it? Even could you explain to them— which our official position forbids—they, long molded by arbitrary discipline, have not that kind of intelligent responsiveness that might qualify them to comprehend and discriminate. No, to the people the foretopman's deed, however be it worded in the announcement, will be plain homicide committed in a flagrant act of mutiny. . . . Your clement sentence they would account pusillanimous. They would think that we flinch, that we are afraid of them. . . . What shame to us such a conjecture on their part, and how deadly to discipline.[5]

The ship's company expected a harsh sentence and, regardless of circumstances, tempering the law would mean the disintegration of the bonds which made the sailors a fighting team. Billy Budd was sacrificed for the common good.

Structure and Process

The legal structures vary from country to country, but the basic nature of the process is the same. An official structure is empowered to decide upon the facts of a case, evaluate them, compare them with the intentions and wordings of laws, and reach a decision as to the correct-

---

[5] Herman Melville, *Billy Budd, Foretopman*, ed. Harrison Hayford and Merton M. Sealts, Jr. (Chicago: University of Chicago Press, 1962), pp. 112–13.

ness of the action which was disputed. In conformity with its role as a contributor to social integration, the legal system must present an appearance of permanence and certainty. As a result, its structure and process are highly detailed and subject to a plethora of internal rules. The most familiar method of its operation is through a form of ritualized verbal battle called a trial.

The trial requires three inputs: the relevant laws and the information provided by two opposing parties. The law input consists of an appropriately authorized written communication which may be called a *positive law* or a *statute*. In the English system, which is used in Canada, except for a part of Quebec law, there also exists a body of law which has evolved through historical practice called *common law*. This form of law has been increasingly supplanted by positive law, but it still forms a vital part of the law as a whole. In Quebec, *civil law*, as opposed to *criminal law*, is derived from a *code* or compilation of laws. Legal codes have been known since the time of the Mesopotamian King Hammurabi, who lived over 4,000 years ago. The most influential code of laws today is the Napoleonic Code, compiled in France shortly after 1800. It has served as a model for codes in Eastern and Western Europe, including the U.S.S.R., the Middle East, and South America. Besides the civil code in Quebec, Canada, since 1892, also has codified criminal law, which is entirely under federal jurisdiction.

Essentially two conflicting pictures of reality are presented by the plaintiff and the defendant. The relative merits of these pictures are evaluated and the resulting interpretation is used as a basis for applying appropriate laws. In spite of the appearance of solidity and certainty, the legal process deals primarily with contradictory and uncertain materials. The reinforcing function is fulfilled by the process, not by the contents of the decision. Here one returns to the point made earlier: that the certainty of a legal decision is more important than its contents.

At best, it [reality] is only what the trial court—the trial judge or jury—thinks happened. What the trial court thinks happened may, however, be hopelessly incorrect. But that does not matter—legally speaking. For court purposes, what the court thinks about the facts is all that matters. . . . The court usually learns about . . . (the) real, objective, past facts only through the oral testimony of fallible witnesses.[6]

The two "pictures" are generally transmitted to the legal decision-making structures, or courts, by professionals, called attorneys. The plaintiff makes a complaint that a particular law has been contravened, while the defendant denies that this is so. The trial consists of psychological instead of physical combat and the judge acts as a

---

[6] J. Frank, *Courts on Trial.*, p. 15.

referee as well as decision maker. Where the state itself is involved in a controversy it employs its own legal specialists. Each level of government in Canada includes attorneys who direct the legal operations for the particular government. At the federal level the chief attorney is the minister of justice who is assisted by other lawyers who in fact carry on the legal business of the department. The minister of justice is the chief legal advisor to the crown who also recommends candidates to fill vacancies on all but the lowest levels of courts. The duties of the provincial attorneys-general resemble those of the federal minister of justice in that they assist in provincial legal matters, the drafting of legislation, and in the selection and appointment of local magistrates and other legal officials.

In addition, another group of lawyers, called prosecutors or crown attorneys, serve the government. They are appointed in Canada by the provincial attorneys-general to handle all criminal cases, recommending changes in charges, determining the scope and nature of the evidence to be presented (thus, perhaps, limiting the "picture" presented to the court), and advising to some extent on the sentences, or punishments, served on convicted individuals. In the United States the prosecutor or district attorney is the rough equivalent to the crown attorney. But, unlike the latter, prosecutors are elected (except in four states) and enjoy legal independence from the state attorneys-general. In both countries the crown attorney or prosecutor has tended to be a part-time governmental employee. Due to the elective nature of the office in many parts of the United States, the prosecutor's office has been seen as a stepping stone to higher political office. This perception of the office encourages a more political attitude towards justice; the prosecutor is more vulnerable to pressures—to prosecute in some cases and not in others.

The court is the official decision-making unit in the legal system. It is composed of decision makers, called judges or magistrates, and supporting personnel who assemble the evidence presented in court, maintain order in proceedings, and aid the judge in his or her own research and correspondence. Judges are assisted in some countries by a panel of citizens called a jury, which is chosen at random to hear and evaluate the alternative versions of reality.

The staffing of the courts is usually by appointment, though judges are elected in some states in the United States and in Switzerland. In the United States' federal hierarchy, the president nominates all the federal judges including the members of the Supreme Court. The U.S. Senate then is asked to approve these appointments, and it normally does. A major political crisis arose in 1969–70 as a result of the rejection of two successive Nixon nominees by the U.S. Senate, a situation that had no precedent in this century.

A variant on the executive appointment of judges is found in many countries which adhere to continental European political and legal traditions. In France and West Germany, for instance, a judge is considered as a member of a judicial profession. A judge is academically trained and enters the judicial profession much as a person might enter the civil service. The staffing of courts then becomes a matter of promotion within the profession and court hierarchy, rather than a quasi-political act.

Criticisms have been leveled against the various methods of appointment, though little is known about the effects of these methods on the administration of justice. Both election and political appointments are criticized on the grounds that political ties tend to be given more importance than legal ability in the selection of judges. In one of the few pieces of research on the subject, Stuart Nagel has noted that, of a sample of U.S. state supreme court judges, elected judges tended to vote on cases more along the ideological positions of their parties than did their appointed counterparts.[7] The most common problem, however, appears not to be ability or fairness on the bench, but that of conflict of interest. Unlike civil servants, North American judges are not required to be politically neutral or uninvolved with concerns outside their courts. As a consequence, situations occasionally arise where judges are attacked for involving their positions in business schemes or in the promotion of party interests. Dishonest or incompetent judges are of great concern because their actions affect the political culture by calling into question the fairness of the political system. The continental approach has also been criticized in that it leads to an isolation of judges from political and social realities, which are always changing, and encourages legal rigidity and conservatism.

The use of juries, or groups of laymen, as decision makers in the courts has a long history. In England the use of juries began in medieval times and has been transplanted to all English-speaking countries. The most extensive use of juries is found in the United States, where virtually all important civil and criminal cases must be jury trials. England and the rest of the Commonwealth have agreed to retain jury trials in criminal cases, but the practice has declined in civil cases. In Canada the use of juries in civil cases has all but disappeared, except in Ontario. Criminal offenses are divided into serious or *indictable* offenses and minor or *summary* offenses. The latter are tried before a judge or magistrate, whereas in the remainder of cases the accused may elect a jury trial.

Juries consist of a group of 12 citizens (six in Alberta, Yukon, and the

---

[7] Stuart S. Nagel, *Legal Process from a Behavioral Perspective* (Homewood, Ill.: The Dorsey Press, 1969), pp. 193–97.

Northwest Territories) chosen from the voters lists of each province. In Manitoba, for instance, each municipality, town, or city must furnish a list of eligible jurors, not exceeding 5 percent of the electorate. Prospective jurors in each judicial district are then selected by lottery to serve in one of three sessions, or assizes. One third of the group, called a panel, reports for each session. The members of the panel are then chosen by lot to sit on specific cases.[8]

Criticisms have been made that jury trials take too much time out of already overcrowded court sessions, since a jury trial is significantly longer than a trial before a judge. Juries, by their very nature, lack technical legal competence and to those most concerned with this aspect of trials this is a major weakness. It is also alleged that jury decisions are inconsistent and often not related to the complexities of the case. Jury duty is not a very popular civic obligation because of the disruption it causes in an individual's daily life, the low pay associated with the task, and the nature of the work itself. Exemptions are granted to certain professional and religious groups and to others who can show cause. Evasion of jury duty means arrest and some form of punishment, normally a fine or a sentence to attend court sessions for a number of days. On the other hand, jury trials have been defended as institutions which help keep the law simple and in touch with the people, since it must be made intelligible to a panel of laymen. It has also been seen as a bulwark against interference in the courts' business by means of political pressure being placed on judges.

Cases presented before a court may be classified by their relationship to the state, as cases involving the government as one party in the trial and cases where both parties are unofficial groups or individuals. The former class of cases may be divided into those involving criminal law, administrative law, and constitutional law.

Cases involving the government and/or private parties are generally handled by the same system of courts. There are, however, a number of important exceptions. Cases relating to military personnel, whether the charge laid concerns criminal law or internal military regulations are normally handled by military courts, or courts-martial. Some countries such as France and West Germany have separate courts to decide upon cases involving administrative law. These courts are open to citizens who have been the victims of unfair administrative action as well as to administrators who are seeking redress from actions taken by their superiors. Most political systems have also special courts dealing with administrative matters such as taxes and tariffs. Further, a number of countries, such as West Germany, have developed special courts to handle only constitutional issues. A special constitutional

---

[8] *Winnipeg Tribune,* March 7, 1970, p. 4.

court to handle such cases in Canada has been proposed as a method of overcoming the suspicions of the provinces, especially Quebec, about the centralizing influence of the Supreme Court.

Courts are arranged in hierarchies, with higher courts being concerned with more serious cases or reviewing the decisions made by lower courts. In unitary states there is but one hierarchy, reaching from localities to the national level. Federalism has affected this structure in that the constituent units of the federal system have their own courts, whereas national courts are restricted to federal law and to final review of some cases decided in the provincial courts. The court hierarchies in Canada and the United States are different, yet similar, as illustrated in Figure 10–1.

FIGURE 10–1

Court Hierarchies in Canada and the United States

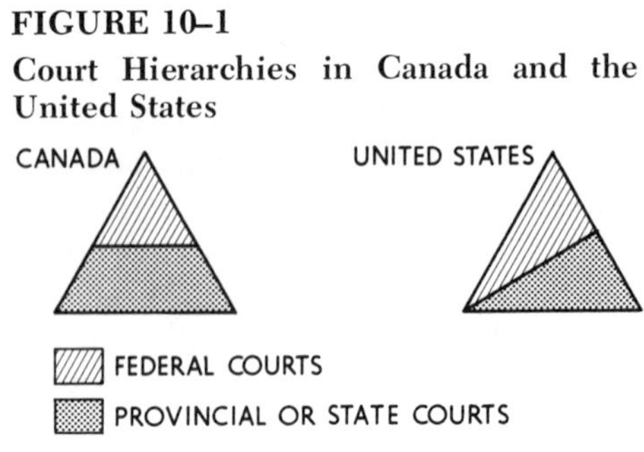

Both countries have federal and provincial (or state) courts, but in the United States some levels of state courts are paralleled by federal courts, whereas in Canada federal courts exist only at higher levels of the hierarchy. In both systems the supreme court is a federal body which sits at the apex of the court hierarchy.

The creation and staffing of courts in the Canadian hierarchy often requires action from both levels of government. At the lowest levels, the provinces have sole jurisdiction over the creation and staffing of courts. The most common forms are magistrates' courts and justices' courts, which deal primarily with minor criminal offenses, small claims courts, family and juvenile courts. Since each province has sole jurisdiction at this level, the types, nomenclature, and powers of these courts differ across the country.

In most provinces there exists a second level of courts called district or county courts. These courts and their jurisdictions are the responsibility of the province, but the staffing and remuneration are federal responsibilities. A third level, the provincial superior courts, including courts of Queen's Bench or provincial Supreme Courts, are also created and staffed in the same fashion. This level serves primarily an appellate function; that is, they hear appeals on cases which have been decided in lower courts in order to guarantee that a fair trial was given.

Federal courts consist of the Supreme Court of Canada and the Federal Court of Canada. The Supreme Court is the highest appellate court in the country and is concerned with points of law, rather than with the substantive matter of a case, or, in criminal cases, the severity of the sentence. The Supreme Court relates decisions of the lower courts to constitutional (BNA Act) provisions and investigates questions of proper procedure in the appealed cases. It also acts as the legal advisor for the cabinet on matters of impending legislation. The federal government has exclusive jurisdiction over the Supreme Court.

On December 3, 1970, the Federal Court of Canada was created by reorganizing and expanding the jurisdiction of the former Exchequer Court. Created in 1887, the Exchequer Court was given authority to hear complaints and appeals against actions of the federal government and disputes over patents, trademarks, and economic regulations. The new Federal Court consists of 12 judges, of which four must come from the Quebec judiciary or legal profession. The Federal Court is designed to relieve the Supreme Court of the pressure of many appeals, notably in those arising from administrative tribunals and some interprovincial disputes. Its orientation, therefore, is primarily towards conflicts involving businesses, economic matters, and administrative actions.

One of the important functions of the Federal Court is the supervision of most of the federal administrative tribunals by hearing appeals from their decisions. Administrative tribunals are much more common than courts, and their decisions tend to have a greater impact on the daily life of the average man than do those of the courts, with the probable exception of the adjudication of traffic offenses. Yet little is known about their numbers, their activities, and the magnitude of their impact. Some federal tribunals are, or are associated with, the following: the Atomic Energy Control Board, the Board of Grain Commissioners, the Board of Transport Commissioners, the Immigration Appeal Board, the Labour Relations Board, the National Energy Board.

Hierarchically, the courts in other countries resemble those of Canada; there are local courts whose jurisdiction is generally limited to minor criminal offenses and civil actions, intermediate courts which handle more important cases and hear appeals, and a supreme court which is generally an appellate court concerned with points of conflict in the application of laws or with procedural questions.

Social scientists have been mainly concerned with two aspects of court activity: the incidence of crime and criminal conviction and the nature of supreme court decision making. The first is of special concern to politicians because insecurity of person and property lend themselves to political controversy, "law and order" being a well-known and frequently used political rallying cry. Secondly, decision making at the highest level of the courts is important because it approximates political decision making. This is especially apparent where the concept of judicial review of legislation to determine its constitutionality is accepted. The decisions of supreme courts are also important in that they establish attitudes in the judges of the lower courts towards the interpretation of laws. One decision enunciated in the highest court on a particular law will then affect subsequent decisions in a multitude of cases at lower levels. Such influence constitutes political power.

Criminal Justice.   Crime may be defined simply as an act or omission which violates the provisions of criminal legislation.[9] Criminal laws are laws which provide penalties for noncompliance with designated instructions or prohibitions. As this legislation changes from time to time, so does any substantive definition of crime. Jurisdiction over criminal law in Canada is difficult to determine since, according to the BNA Act, all criminal legislation must be passed by the federal Parliament, yet many of the functions of the provinces could not be carried out without the use of laws which are, to all intents and purposes, criminal legislation.

Crime in Canada has been the subject of serious study by jurists, sociologists, and corrections officers. To a great extent their statistics depend upon official sources, whose figures depend in turn upon the reliability of the general public in reporting crimes. For instance, it is obvious from nearly everyone's personal experience that official traffic crime rates are lower than the real rate. Official statistics, however, can give some indication of the incidence of crime in the country.

The number of convictions for crimes per 100,000 people over 15 has risen from 1,236 in 1901 to 32,010 in 1965.[10] This alarming statistic suggests that Canada is well on its way to becoming a nation of criminals! In 1965 there was one criminal in about every three people in the country. Fortunately (if that is the appropriate word), 99 percent of the 1965 convictions were for summary offenses, 90 percent of these being for traffic violations; while 1 percent of all convictions were for indictable offenses. While the rate of convictions for summary offenses grew 25 times between 1901 and 1965, that for indictable offences grew only four times.[11]

---

[9] W. T. McGrath, "Crime and Correctional Services," in *Crime and Its Treatment in Canada*, ed. W. T. McGrath (Toronto: Macmillan, 1965), p. 1.

[10] *Report of the Canadian Committee on Corrections* (Ottawa: The Queen's Printer, 1969), p. 23.

[11] Ibid., pp. 23–27.

Convictions for indictable offences have grown about 6.5 percent faster than has the population between 1950 and 1966 and affect about .07 of 1 percent of the adult population each year. To a great extent crime is related to age, primarily involving those under 30. Men have traditionally been involved in much more crime than women, though female convictions doubled between 1950 and 1973 while, the male rate has remained stable. Women were mainly involved in certain criminal activities such as petty theft, murder, manslaughter, prostitution, and drug offenses. See Table 10–1.

TABLE 10–1
Charges for Indictable Offenses

	Ratios (male to female)	
Charges	*1966*	*1973*
Theft		
Under $50	3 to 1	—
Over $50	10 to 1	—
Under $200	—	4 to 1
Over $200	—	13 to 1
Automobile	50 to 1	31 to 1
Robbery	32 to 1	12 to 1
Fraud	8 to 1	5 to 1
Offenses against the person		
Murder	5 to 1	7 to 1
Attempted murder	20 to 1	9 to 1
Manslaughter	3 to 1	7 to 1
Wounding	6 to 1	4 to 1
Sex offenses (excluding rape)	80 to 1	70 to 1
Assault (not indecent)	16 to 1	11 to 1
Other		
Relating to prostitution	1 to 1	1 to 4
Narcotics	3 to 1	7 to 1
Total charges	6.7 to 1	6.4 to 1

Source: Data compiled from *Report of the Canadian Committee on Corrections* (Ottawa: The Queen's Printer, 1969), pp. 405, 474. Reproduced with the permission of Information Canada and from *Crime and Traffic Enforcement Statistics* (Ottawa: Information Canada, 1974).

As Table 10–1 indicates, the overall distribution of charges for indictable offenses by sex has not changed significantly from 1966 to 1973. What appears to have happened is an increase in the proportion of robberies committed by females, but a decrease in the murder and manslaughter categories. It would also appear that there is a marked shift in narcotics charges, though it should be noted that the emphasis has generally shifted from prosecution for any form of involvement to an interest primarily in those involved in drugs for profit. It should also be noted that there is an increase in the proportion of females involved in assaults and woundings.

Other statistics on crime in Canada suggest that certain crimes seem to run in seasonal cycles, with assaults and sexual offences being more prevalent during the summer season. Conversely, robberies and attempted murders peak during the Christmas season. Of even greater interest, however, is the disposition of reported crimes. Typically, from 5 to 10 percent of reported crimes are judged to be unfounded and are not pursued further. The major exceptions are auto thefts, with 13 percent regarded as unfounded, and rape complaints with 37 percent regarded as unfounded. The handling of rape complaints by the police has come under considerable criticism, as have the laws of evidence applicable in rape trials. This data would suggest that there is something amiss in the way these complaints are handled.

Another interesting aspect of the crime statistics is the disposition of complaints regarded as legitimate. This is indicated in Table 10–2. In approximately three quarters of the cases involving murder, attempted murder, and manslaughter, the original charges were upheld, while only one quarter of the rape and one third of other sexual offence charges were so disposed. Additionally, as the seriousness of the original charge decreased, the percentage of convictions was also reduced. For example, only one quarter of the breaking and entering complaints were upheld. Only about one quarter of the cases involving auto theft and theft of under $200 in value were brought to trial. The evidence is pretty clear that with the exception of rape, reported crimes involving violence were pursued by the police with considerable success, but that crimes involving property alone were not.

As Table 10–2 shows, Canadians violate a wide assortment of laws, not counting traffic violations. Yet crimes involving violence are a relatively small proportion of the total picture. The impression possibly conveyed by the overall crime statistics may be one of a very lawless nation but, in reality, Canada is one of the more peaceful and safe countries of the world.

In attempting to assess the full meaning of statistics such as these, certain additional factors should be kept in mind. Many crimes, especially minor ones, may not be reported. For example, very few people are prosecuted for littering or jaywalking, even when it is done within sight of a police officer. Police forces, like most organizations, operate on the basis of priorities, and crimes of violence or potentially violent situations take precedence. Minor infractions will often not be pursued by most police organizations since they have enough paper work, court appearances, and other administrative tasks related to serious crimes, and the courts would not have time to spend on minor offences, anyway.

TABLE 10–2
Crimes Reported in Canada, 1973

Category of Crime	Number of Cases	Disposition, by percent			
		Unfounded	Convicted as charged	Convicted otherwise	Not convicted
Violence					
Murder	496	5	69	12	14
Attempted murder ...	507	5	78	5	12
Manslaughter	71	7	84	1	8
Wounding	2,058	9	52	20	19
Assault	97,568	8	31	45	16
Subtotal	100,700				
Sexual					
Rape	2,530	38	24	14	22
Other Sexual	11,415	9	32	17	41
Subtotal	13,945				
Property					
Robbery	13,958	6	27	5	62
Break and enter	210,511	6	16	7	71
Theft-Auto	82,189	13	16	6	65
Theft Over $200	68,189	7	10	6	77
Theft Under $200 ...	434,608	5	14	10	71
Possession stolen					
goods	14,434	4	85	7	4
Fraud	76,552	6	55	13	36
Subtotal	900,903				
Morals					
Prostitution	3,663	3	93	2	2
Gambling	3,414	12	75	8	5
Subtotal	7,077				
Drugs	58,042	9	71	8	12
Other criminal code ...	364,883	7	24	16	53
Federal statutes	49,436	13	61	14	12
Provincial and					
municipal laws ..	423,773	2	67	26	5
Total	1,918,759				

Source: *Crime and Traffic Enforcement Statistics* (Ottawa: Information Canada, 1974).

Added to the administrative difficulties is the attitude of the public. Many crimes that should be reported are not, either because the individuals do not wish to become involved, or they presume that a minor matter would simply end up in the police files. There is also a tendency, among minority groups, to fear involvement with the police, no matter how justified their complaint. The history of police-minority relations in North America is not good and crime statistics in urban areas reflect this.

Finally, many laws that are on the books are simply not respected by the people, so infractions are unlikely to be reported. A contemporary example of this is the attitude of many people toward the laws on so-called "soft" drugs. Very few infractions are reported and even fewer prosecuted.

Trials are handled at the magistrates' level in the court hierarchy. Over half of these trials are heard by a jury. This places a further load on the lower levels of the courts since a jury trial normally takes about twice as much time as a trial solely before a judge.

An appeal is made to a higher provincial or territorial court in about 6 percent of the cases tried. About 30 percent of these appeals result in some change in the conviction or sentence. Far more appeals are made by the accused than by the crown and most are for changes in sentences rather than in convictions, since appeals are only concerned with points of law. It appears that if the Supreme Court hears an appeal, chances of a favourable judgment are better than even. Only about one case in 1,800 reaches this level, however.[12]

Serious crimes are committed by about 1 percent of the population, primarily by male teen-aged youths. Taken in itself this could not be considered as reasonable grounds for political controversy or agitation; however, the criminal has an important role to play in society—his or her crimes keep the rest of society honest and unified. The function of criminal law, according to Professor J. D. Morton of Osgoode Hall Law School, is to preserve the normal citizen from the breach of society's criminal law.[13] The trial and incarceration of a criminal is in fact a morality play which confirms the noncriminal in the righteousness of his or her ways and shows him or her the potential danger of not conforming. The criminal is tried and convicted, not for his own good but for the common good.

Political Justice.   Criminal law and the courts are of special interest to political scientists because of the possible political uses to which they may be put. The use of the legal system in pursuance of political ends is called political justice.[14] Both the established government and its opponents may employ the courts as a political device. Those in power may seek to stifle opposition and change by equating or associating them with criminal activity. Opposition elements, including revolutionaries, may seek to use the legal process to embarrass the government or to disseminate propaganda and mould public opinion, but

---

[12] Data computed from Ibid., pp. 158–70.

[13] J. D. Morton, *The Function of Criminal Law in 1962* (Toronto: Canadian Broadcasting Corporation, 1962), p. 52.

[14] Otto Kirchheimer, *Political Justice* (Princeton, N.J.: Princeton University Press, 1961), preface.

official neglect of the political or social implications of an individual offence may serve to exacerbate the crisis rather than solve it.

The government may also elect to convict a political enemy for a crime which is specifically political in nature. Political crimes are generally classed as treason, a definite attempt to overthrow the existing government, or sedition, which consists of spreading dissatisfaction and discourtesy towards the government and its leaders. The use of these weapons, however, may serve only to provide the opposition with a ready-made platform in the form of the court. The trial of the "Chicago Seven," resulting from the riots during the Democratic National Convention in 1968, ended with more people becoming familiar with radical propositions. The sentences meted out to the defendants were the price paid for weeks of national exposure.

The use of treason and sedition charges have been relatively rare in democracies because of this "soapbox" effect. The Canadian treason law is part of the Criminal Code and comes to us from Britain. It is basically the same law which was formulated in 1351 covering attacks on the person of the Monarch and his or her high officials and family, war against the crown, and other attempts to overthrow the government.[15] Only one treason trial has been held in Canada—that which resulted in the conviction and execution of Louis Riel in Regina in 1885. Sedition is a relatively more common basis for prosecution; it has been used against accomplices to Communist espionage and to punish the leaders of the 1919 General Strike in Winnipeg.

The political trial is a distortion of the normal procedure of justice. Both the prosecution and defence are concerned with the citizen audience, not with the crime or the accused. The prosecution attempts to discredit the accused either by insisting that his or her crime was no more than a common offence or that it was such a heinous offence as to threaten the very fabric of society. He or she is either a common thug or a danger to all people. Meanwhile, the defence attempts to demonstrate the idealism and purity of motive of the accused, implying that his or her accusers are no more than a group of unscrupulous politicians. The court is no longer an arbiter in such a case. The judge owes his or her position to the government in power, so conviction is not usually an issue. Conviction serves to demonstrate that the accused is a victim of official persecution. It may also serve as a credential of loyalty to a cause, resulting, as times change, in political acceptability. Lenin and Trotsky in Russia, Nehru and Gandhi in India, and Hitler in Germany served prison terms as a result of their political beliefs and activities. Socrates and Christ were other victims of political justice.

---

[15] Royal Canadian Mounted Police, *Law and Order in Canadian Democracy*, rev. ed. (Ottawa: The Queen's Printer, 1952), pp. 127–31.

A government which succeeds in its attempt to reduce its real or potential enemies through the legal system may afterwards grant pardons or amnesties to political prisoners. This has the effect of psychologically tying the convicted leaders to the existing system, in that they are either considered to be of small consequence or it is felt that such a release would place them under suspicion by their comrades. Clemency also acts to reassure possible defectors from the opposition as to the humaneness of the present rulers. In any case, clemency serves to build support for the existing regime.

Judicial Review and Court Behaviour.   The idea that courts and judges reflect the values underlying the political system has formed the basis for an investigation of court behaviour by political scientists. Two areas of court behaviour have been under study: the use of judicial review and the behaviour of the judges as individuals and as small groups.

Constitutional law, like any other law, requires application if it is to become "living" law. Courts interpret a constitution in two ways. First, they may use the directives or laws made by bodies with constitutional authority as the basis for judging correct behaviour. This is the normal mode of operation in the court hierarchy. Second, the courts may consider the validity of these laws and directives in the light of known constitutional provisions. This is called *judicial review* and is only found in some systems which have a written constitution. Judicial review of legislation, because of its importance in relation to the political system, is done by the highest court of a nation. Some of the Commonwealth countries (Britain excepted), West Germany, and the United States are examples. The practice has become more commonly accepted in the United States than elsewhere because of its relevance to natural law.

Judicial review in Canada is tied up with the provisions and status of the BNA Act. Section 101 of the act provided for the establishment of a general court of appeal for Canada. There was no mention of its powers, structure, or personnel. The status of the BNA Act, that is, its formulation as a common legislative act in the British Parliament, meant that its ultimate interpreters were the Houses of Parliament and, in particular, the Privy Council of Great Britain. In 1833, long before the BNA Act, a judicial committee of the Privy Council had been formalized and empowered to review all colonial legislation so as to harmonize it with British statutes. Therefore, at the time of Confederation, the power of judicial review lay in London. From 1867 to 1949 conflicts arose over the desirability of having the interpreters of the BNA Act reside outside Canada.

These conflicts were gradually settled as Canada acquired independence. The Statute of Westminster (1931) opened the way for the

Canadian government to vest final jurisdiction over Canadian legal issues in the Supreme Court; however, this power was not finally used until 1949. The Supreme Court now has the ultimate power to review legislation in the light of constitutional provisions. Similar evolutions took place in Australia, South Africa, and India.

As in the countries of the Commonwealth, there is no provision in the U.S. Constitution for judicial review by the U.S. Supreme Court. It has become a practice because of the initiative of certain early court justices and because of its practical necessity. The Supreme Court has been called the guardian of the constitution, though it is probably more accurate to say that it is a "legal tailor," refashioning the cut of the constitutional garment to fit the style and needs of the times.

This refashioning may be described in terms of constructionism, or the relationship (construct) between the words of the document and the intent of the writers. Strict constructionism implies a close, literal interpretation of the constitution, whereas loose constructionism implies a willingness to interpret the constitution in the light of the intent of the framers applied to the problem of the day. The battle over appointments to the U.S. Supreme Court in 1969–71 was to some extent between a President who desired a Supreme Court which would be strictly constructionist and a Senate dominated by people opposed to this. The supreme courts of the Commonwealth, where judicial review is exercized, have traditionally been strict constructionist:

. . . We must face up squarely to the question of whether judges legislate, in the sense of making conscious choices between conflicting policy alternatives. Although since . . . 1937, few in the United States would hesitate to answer this question in the affirmative, the theory of the judicial slot-machine is still powerful in a country whose jurisprudence is dominated, as Canada's is, by the worst rigours of Austinian formalism.[16]

The scope of judicial review differs in ways other than in the construction of interpretations. A supreme court may choose to judge legislation on the basis of its relationship to the value orientations of the constitution, or it may be concerned with the jurisdictional powers of the various governmental bodies. The U.S. Supreme Court, for instance, has frequently exercized judicial review in cases involving individual rights; the Canadian Supreme Court has been primarily concerned with legislation which oversteps constitutional bounds in terms of the jurisdiction of either federal or provincial bodies. Until very recently the Canadian Supreme Court restricted its scope to such cases but its judgment in the *Drybones* case (1969) suggested a more active political role for the Court which has yet to be realized. Joseph

---

[16] Edward McWhinney, *Judicial Review,* 4th. ed. (Toronto: University of Toronto Press, 1969), p. 69.

Drybones was convicted and fined $10 in Yellowknife, N.W.T., for being drunk while off a reservation, under a provision of the Indian Act. The Supreme Court eventually decided that this part of the act contravened the federal Bill of Rights and invalidated the conviction. This was considered a form of judicial review in that a provision of one federal law was invalidated because it conflicted with the provisions of another federal law. The BNA Act was not involved in this case, however. This example of court activism has encouraged speculation on the future role of the Supreme Court. As a federal institution it is rightly seen as a centralizing body, so that increased activism may threaten the provincial autonomy built up so carefully by the British Privy Council in the first half of the 20th century. There is also a question of the appropriateness of judicial review in a system based upon parliamentary supremacy. The two concepts are to a great degree incompatible.

Court behaviour may be seen as formalistically determined, that is, that judges exercise what McWhinney calls a "slot-machine" function, or it may be seen as a result of a number of factors which have influenced judicial thinking—the case, the manner of presentation of the issues, the law, and the multitude of personal factors which enter into any decision. This latter interpretation has been emphasized by political scientists in order to account for changes in court activism, constructionism, sentencing, and variations in judicial review. Again the supreme courts have been the focus of emphasis. Court behaviour may be analyzed by describing the impact of cultural factors on legal systems, comparing court attitudes towards official bodies, and analyzing the regional, ethnic, and political orientations of individual justices.

Carl Baar has outlined some of the differences between the U.S. and Canadian supreme courts in terms of their activism or the willingness of the courts to review action by public officials. Canada's Supreme Court is far less active and more restrained in terms of invalidating these actions. See Table 10–3. Both supreme courts are centralizers in that they tended to support federal action to a greater extent than state or provincial action. The Canadian court was also more supportive of both federal and provincial actions than its counterpart in the United States.

Within a given country, the activities, decisions, and orientations of the courts may change as personnel change. This possibility has been of continuing concern in Canada in spite of the overt attachment of Canadian judges to Austinian or analytical jurisprudence. Since the debates preceding Confederation, concern has been voiced by French Canadians over the possibility that a Canadian supreme court might use its powers to deprive a great deal of Quebec civil law of its vitality, substituting English common law for the Quebec code. Consequently, the 1875 Act establishing the Supreme Court required that two of the

TABLE 10–3
Rulings on Public Action in Constitutional Cases—Since 1950

1. Provincial or state action*

	Canada		United States	
	Number	*Percent*	*Number*	*Percent*
Valid	29	54.7	140	34.6
Partially valid	4	7.6	1	0.2
Invalid	20	37.7	264	65.2
Total	53	100.0	405	100.0

2. Federal action*

	Canada		United States	
	Number	*Percent*	*Number*	*Percent*
Valid	29	93.5	109	63.7
Partially valid	0	0	2	1.2
Invalid	2	6.5	60	35.1
Total	31	100.0	171	100.0

* U.S. Cases extend from October 1950 to June 1969, Canadian Cases from January 1950 to July 1972.

Source: Carl Baar, "Judicial Behavior and Comparative Rights Policy" in *Comparative Human Rights*, ed. Richard P. Claude (Baltimore: Johns Hopkins University Press, forthcoming).

six justices to be appointed must come from the Quebec courts or bar. The numbers were eventually changed to the present three of nine justices. Representation of the other provinces was not provided for in the legislation, but a general balance was established in line with the importance of the regions of the country. See Table 10–4.

TABLE 10–4
Regional Representation on the Supreme Court—1875–1975

Year	Quebec	Ontario	Maritimes	West
1875	2	2	2	0
1903	2	1	2	1
1924	2	3	0	1
1932	2	2	1	2
1949	3	3	1	2
1968	3	3	1	2
1975	3	3	1	2

Source: G. Adams and Paul Cavalluzzo, "Supreme Court of Canada: A Biographical Study," *Osgoode Hall Law Journal* 7, no. 1 (November 1969): p. 70 and *Canadian Parliamentary Guide*, 1975.

The political and ethnic backgrounds of Canadian Supreme Court justices have also been studied, since these characteristics may be reflected in the justices' orientations toward policy issues in cases brought before the Court. Successive Conservative and Liberal governments appointed 20 justices between 1930 and 1968. While a certain regional balance was maintained on the Court, Table 10–5 also suggests that this balance is coupled with very definite party and ethnic considerations. Both the Liberals and Conservatives favoured their own ranks in the search for prospective justices, and the ethnic characteristics of the appointees reflect party support in the two major ethnic groups. Both parties passed over possible appointees from other ethnic groups. Party affiliation tended to remain a strong characteristic over time, whereas judicial rather than political experience was stressed in the choice of justices since at least 1930. Justices do not only reflect the culture of the political system as a whole but also the dominant party values of the period in which they were selected.

TABLE 10–5
Party and Ethnic Characteristics of Justices, 1930–1968

	Conservative Appointments	Liberal Appointments	Total
Total	8	12	20
Party affiliation			
Conservative	4	2	6
Liberal	—	8	8
Unknown	4	2	6
Ethnic background			
British Isles	8	9	17
French	—	3	3
Other	—	—	—

Source: Compiled from G. Adams and Paul Cavalluzzo, "Supreme Court of Canada: A Biographical Study," *Osgoode Hall Law Journal* 7, no. 1 (November 1969): 72, 76, 78, 81, 83.

The most common method of studying judicial behaviour has been to analyze the actions, background, and ideologies of the individual justices in order to formulate some general ideas on their decision-making criteria. This form of study lends itself very well to statistical analysis though it suffers from the fact that relative differences between justices can be perceived only when they publicly disagree among themselves on given decisions. Unanimous decisions among the members of the panel sitting on the case (a quorum is five justices in the Canadian Supreme Court) are quite common.

The most popular method for studying individual behaviour is to analyze the nonunanimous decisions and rate the judges over time on scales corresponding to a generally defined "conservatism," "liberalism," "dogmatism," and "pragmatism." Justices' attitudes toward economic, political, and criminal cases may also be compared. This method of studying judicial decision making was pioneered by C. Herman Pritchett, who analyzed the U.S. Supreme Court's decisions during the Roosevelt era (1937–47). Glendon Schubert, among others, followed with studies extending Pritchett's in time and in sophistication. These methods were applied to the Canadian Supreme Court by S. R. Peck and Peter Russell. J. T. Holmes and E. Rovet published a similar study of the Ontario Court of Appeals.[17]

Once the dissensual, or nonunanimous decisions, are separated from the rest, a number of statistical tools may be employed to analyze the general orientations of Supreme Court justices towards issues of the times. S. R. Peck, in analyzing the Canadian Supreme Court actions from 1958 to 1966, found variations and similarities in justices' attitudes according to the nature of the case presented. See Table 10–6.

TABLE 10–6
Canadian Supreme Court Justices' Attitudes on Case Types

	Highly pro- affirmative	Pro- affirmative	Neutral	Pro- negative	Highly pro- negative
Taxation		C	T R S M H	A F	J
Negligence	H	S C T	J M F R	A	
Criminal	C	H S	R	M A	J T F

Note: The initials are those of the Supreme Court justices.

Source: S. R. Peck, "The Supreme Court of Canada, 1958–1966: A Search for Policy through Scalogram Analysis," *Canadian Bar Review* 45, no. 4 (December 1967): 723.

Justices rated "affirmative" consistently stood for the individual against the crown in taxation and criminal cases and for the plaintiff (usually an individual) in cases of negligence, which normally involved suits against insurance companies. "Negative" attitudes signified the opposite tendencies in voting.

The study of judicial behaviours has only recently begun in Canada, but the findings of such scholars as S. R. Peck and Peter Russell will

---

[17] See list of recommended readings at the end of this chapter.

add to our knowledge of the interconnections between politics and the judiciary and may indirectly modify the traditional concept of "slot-machine" justice castigated by McWhinney.

RECOMMENDED READINGS

Adams, G. and Cavalluzzo, Paul. "Supreme Court of Canada: A Biographical Study." *Osgoode Hall Law Journal* 7, no. 1 (November 1969).

Beaudoin, Gérald A. "Le système judiciare canadien." in *Le système politique du Canada* edited by Louis Sabourin, chapter 24. Ottawa: Editions de l'Université d'Ottawa, 1968.

David, René and Brierley, John. *Major Legal Systems in the World Today.* London: Stevens and Sons, 1968.

Dawson, R. MacGregor. *Government of Canada,* 4th ed. Toronto: University of Toronto Press, 1963.

Evan, William M., ed. *Law and Sociology.* New York: Free Press of Glencoe, 1962.

Frank, Jerome. *Law and the Modern Mind.* Garden City, N.Y.: Doubleday Books, Anchor, 1963.

Friedrich, Carl J. *Philosophy of Law in Historical Perspective.* 2d ed. Chicago: University of Chicago Press, 1963.

Hoebel, E. Adamson. *The Law of Primitive Man.* Cambridge, Mass: Harvard University Press, 1964.

Holmes, J. and Rovet, E. "Ontario Court of Appeal: Some Observations on Judicial Behaviour." *Osgoode Hall Law Journal* 7, no. 1 (November 1969).

Kirchheimer, Otto. *Political Justice.* Princeton, N.J.: Princeton University Press, 1961.

Lederman, W. R. *Courts and the Canadian Constitution.* Toronto: McClelland and Stewart, 1964.

Lang, O. E. *Contemporary Problems of Public Law in Canada.* Toronto: University of Toronto Press, 1968.

Lloyd, Denis. *The Idea of Law.* Harmondsworth, Engl.: Penguin Books, 1964.

————. *Introduction to Jurisprudence.* New York: Praeger, 1965.

McGrath, W., ed. *Crime and its Treatment in Canada.* Toronto: Macmillan, 1965.

McWhinney, Edward. *Judicial Review.* 4th ed. Toronto: University of Toronto Press, 1969.

Morton, J. D. *The Function of Criminal Law in 1962.* Toronto: Canadian Broadcasting Corporation, 1962.

Nagel, Stuart S. *The Legal Process from a Behavioral Perspective.* Homewood, Ill.: The Dorsey Press, 1969.

Peck, S. R. "A Behavioural Approach to the Judicial Process: Scalogram Analysis." *Osgoode Hall Law Journal* 5, no. 1 (April 1967).

————. "The Supreme Court of Canada, 1958–1966: A Search for Policy through Scalogram Analysis." *Canadian Bar Review* 45, no. 4 (December 1967).

Pritchett, C. Herman. *The Roosevelt Court.* New York: Macmillan, 1948.

Reid, Robert F. *Administrative Law and Practice.* Toronto: Butterworth's, 1971.

Report of the Canadian Committee on Corrections. Ottawa: The Queen's Printer, 1969.

Russell, Peter H. *The Supreme Court of Canada as a Bilingual and Bicultural Institution.* Documents of the Royal Commission on Bilingualism and Biculturalism, #1. Ottawa: The Queen's Printer, 1969.

Schubert, Glendon, ed. *Judicial Behavior.* Chicago: Rand McNally, 1964.

————. *Judicial Policy Making.* Chicago: Scott, Foresman and Company, 1965.

————. *The Judicial Mind.* Evanston Ill.: The Northwestern University Press, 1965.

11

Change and Revolution

IT IS AXIOMATIC that the only constant in human affairs is change itself. In implicit or explicit recognition of this, modern political systems endeavour to cope with the phenomena of change. Political systems seek to establish acceptable patterns of relationship within the society and to create a predictable environment in which the inhabitants can feel some degree of security. Yet, while political systems are expected to provide stability, they must at the same time allow for change. A dilemma is thus created; a system which overly restricts change may provoke its own dissolution at the hands of a frustrated citizenry, while a system that cannot control the rate of change may disintegrate as the result of a collapse of support generated by an increasing feeling of insecurity and uncertainty on the part of its inhabitants. It would appear that the ideal political system is one which provides for an acceptable balance between stability and change. Such a system would be assured of longevity. It should also be clear, based upon what has been said about political culture earlier, that acceptability is a relative matter.

FEEDBACK AND CHANGE

There are basically two sources of change in a political system—changes resulting from its physical or human environment and the changes which the system itself generates with each response to the environment. The system must then respond to these changes, as it is expected to balance and harmonize expectations and protect the community against disorder. As the political system responds to these *inputs* in the form of such things as disaster relief, new housing, new regulations on labour management, or the adoption of new symbols or enforcement of the old, it has an impact on society. These new realities will then shape future inputs as they have altered the system's environment. This process of the system's *outputs* affecting *inputs* is known as *feedback*. As long as there is balance between the two, people are reasonably content; they get from society and life in general what they expect of it. This may be very little or very much.

If a change is introduced into either values or environment, an individual will try to restore the balance. This may be done in two ways: The individual may either reject the change or may alter the unchanged factor so as to create a new balance between the two. The attempts to maintain a balance may lead to demands being placed upon the political system.[1] Homeowners who thought their drains were adequate to handle any storm (value) encounter flooded basements one spring (environmental change) and as a result complain bitterly about the inefficiency of the city council, perhaps going so far as to change the personnel of the council at a subsequent election. The reverse may also happen; for instance, a low-paid Asian factory worker (environment) sees a film about labour standards in the U.S.S.R. which suggests that he or she too is entitled to such benefits (value change) and as a consequence joins a local communist party.

Value changes may be prompted by a variety of factors. New ideologies or religious beliefs may be developed or imported from abroad. Communications from other societies demonstrating the existence of higher standards of living may disrupt traditional values. The collapse of local authority as a result of conquest may lead to a rejection of traditional values or their resurgence in a more puritanical form. These changes in values are often translated into political action.

Changes are also caused by variations in the physical environment. The most immediate of such changes are natural disasters. Flooded prairie towns or areas devastated by forest fires hold portions of society which quickly inject their demands into the political system to seek favourable decisions from appropriate authorities on financial assistance for rebuilding. Economic disaster in the 1930s on the prairies led to the creation of the Social Credit movement and the Cooperative Commonwealth Federation (CCF) which demanded the reforming of the formal relationships in government at all levels. Conversely, the sudden rise in value of petroleum supplies in 1973–74 led to fierce squabbling between the producing provinces in Canada and the federal government. This in turn led many Albertans to question the economic benefits of Confederation.

Environmental changes have also resulted from the advance of technology. Increased manufacturing productivity has led to greater

---

[1] Chalmers Johnson uses the term "synchronization" in this context. See his *Revolutionary Change* (Boston: Little Brown & Co., 1966), pp. 63–80.

influence of business in political circles, often at the expense of traditional agricultural interests. At the same time, the organization of labour in the factories has created a new set of interests. Technology has also created new problems for the political system to resolve. Environmental pollution, for instance, was not an issue before 1968. Since 1970, political leaders in all parts of the country have devoted a great deal of time moralizing over the pollution of the Great Lakes and defending the policies of their parties with respect to its control. In one case, that of control over Arctic waters, the threat of pollution created the demand for changing international formal relationships with respect to territorial jurisdictions.[2]

Recent research has established that economic changes associated with development are among the major causes of political violence in the world's nations. Figure 11–1 is a plotting of 119 societies according to their per capita income in 1962 and their propensity for civil violence (TMCV, or Total Magnitude of Civil Violence) in these societies. The trend is a roughly curved line. Very poor societies, that is, those with little economic change, and very rich societies are freer from civil violence than those which are undergoing improvement in their economic situations.

FIGURE 11–1
Economic Wealth and Civil Violence

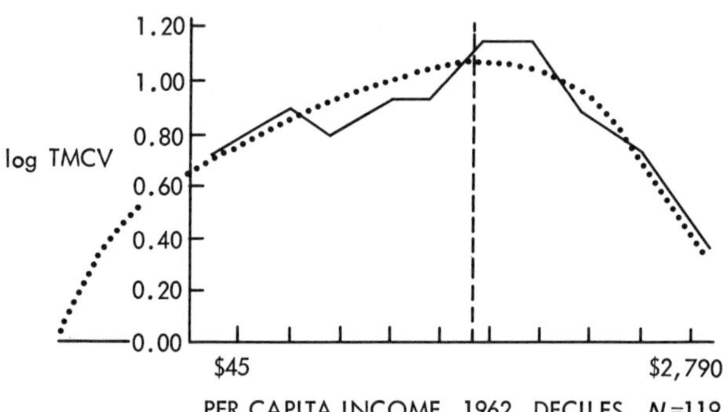

Source: Ted Robert Gurr, unpublished paper, adapted by D. P. Bwy, "Political Instability in Latin America: The Cross-Cultural Test of a Causal Model," *Latin American Research Review* 3, no. 2 (Spring 1968): p. 23.

Three important ingredients in a political system are affected by these changes in inputs. These are the formal relationships between

---

[2] For an interesting discussion of the rise and fall of issues, see Anthony Downs, "Up and Down with Ecology—The Issue–Attention Cycle," *Public Interest* 28 (Summer 1972): pp. 38–50.

people in the system, their informal relationships and, of course, the substantive matter under consideration.

In Chapter 2 we saw that clusters of roles, which are called structures, exist in the political system. The relationships between these structures are generally well-defined and constant over time so that the activities of the system may be repeated, and the system maintained. These are called formal relationships, as the limits of expected behaviour are prescribed so that the people in such structures know what is expected of them and people outside the structures know how to deal with them. Formal relationships, like those in a bureaucracy, apply to an office regardless of the individual occupying it.

Change in these relationships is carefully controlled. It is generally achieved only slowly and with difficulty so that any uncertainties generated by new relationships are minimized. The long controversy over the reform of the amending process for the BNA Act demonstrates the importance which is attached to a stable and predictable method of altering formal relationships inside the political system.

The connection between feedback and the formal relationships within the system is especially close. When frustration is experienced by groups whose interests are not satisfied, they may shift their focus of attention from the substantive matter of the decision to the formal relationships in the system. This may occur when policy decisions are made which reject their claims, when decisions are made in a manner which is offensive to these groups, or, when the demands made exceed the ability of the system to meet them. For instance, one of the arguments advanced by the Parti Québécois for the secession of Quebec from Confederation is that the federal system is unable to meet the needs and aspirations of Quebec and English Canada simultaneously. Separation, it is proposed, would allow both communities to further their own interests without competing for the attention of one national government.

The fact that frustration relating to a specific interest may be translated into a call for system reform has not escaped the notice of revolutionary critics. Excessive demands may be deliberately made upon a system not with the expectation or even the desire to have them satisfied but to cast doubt on the value and legitimacy of the system itself. The rejection of the demand "exposes" the nature of the existing political relationships and "heightens the consciousness" of others with respect to the "fundamental immorality" of the system as presently constructed. There was a glimmer of this logic in the FLQ demands in return for the release of their kidnap victims in 1970. These demands were so extreme (release of 23 prisoners, $500,000 in gold, and transportation to a country of their choice) that their acceptance by either the Quebec or the federal government would have "exposed their weakness," leading others to doubt the legitimacy of these structures.

Informal relationships are dependent upon the people involved, not upon their positions. Even though individuals may conform to the formal requirements of the structures in which they operate, they cannot completely submerge their personalities. Individual initiative, likes and dislikes, personal relationships, and political opinions affect the actions of people within the system. These factors create a set of informal relationships which parallel the formal. Often these exist in a complementary fashion and sometimes in conflict with each other. As individuals enter or leave the political system the configuration of these relationships changes, sometimes abruptly and often unpredictably.

The substantive matter in the political system, or the interests which clamour for resolution, is also in constant flux. Some interests are part of the personal orientations of political actors and their importance is directly related to the position of these individuals in the system. Other interests depend upon the formal relationships between political structures and endure regardless of the passage of time or the actors involved. For instance, every opposition party expresses its concern over honesty in government, administrative secrecy, and high taxes. However, the shoe is on the other foot when the position of the parties is reversed.

The term *system maintenance* refers to the continuing attempt by a political system to remain in a stable state. A system is initially formed to minimize uncertainty by maintaining stable patterns of relationships. One of the most essential of such relationships is that between the system itself and society. Its existence must be maintained in the face of external and internal pressure. Security from external threats normally takes the form of military defence; however, there are other forms. Increasingly, system maintenance has come to mean a protection of existing values rather than a protection of the country from physical invasion. The Union of South Africa, for instance, in an attempt to reduce the impact of ideas brought in from outside by the media, prohibited television until 1975. Since the late 1960s, Burma has virtually cut itself off from outside contact after its political leadership resolved to develop the country solely on the basis of indigenous values and resources.

The capability of a system to respond to change is determined by a wide range of factors. Some of these are the resources available to the system, the willingness of the political actors in power to act on demands, the support commanded by decision makers from other parts of the system and society in general, and the personalities and general value structures of the major politicians. The pattern in which these factors emerge dictates capability.

The quantity of new inputs and the intensity with which they are promoted combine to form the *load* placed upon the system. When the load exceeds the capability, the system breaks down and a new leadership, forming a new pattern and a new level of capability, takes over. On the other hand, the willingness of the administration to use force in dispersing revolutionary organizations, controlling interest articulation and political communication, may result in the reduction of the load. Partial reforms may also make the load tolerable.

FIGURE 11–2
Germany—1915–1936

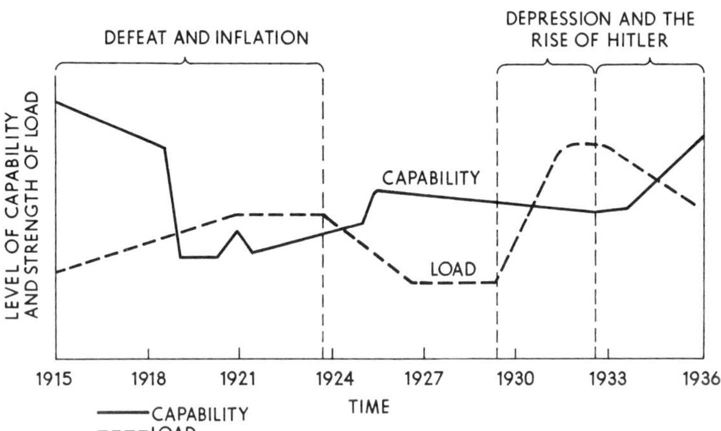

Figure 11–2 depicts how the Weimar Republic broke down in two periods, 1919–23 and 1931–33. Revolutionary chaos was avoided in the first instance by the presence of foreign troops and the inability of antigovernment forces to unite, so that the system was able to weather the crisis. In the 1930s it again succumbed to a heavy load with the result that Hitler came to power, reorganized the system, and through repression and redirection of interests, greatly increased its capability.

Over the long run the relationships within a system are patterned upon the load which is normal for that society. A low level of changes in relationships and interests may be satisfied by a system with a low capability. The Turkish governor of Aleppo at the turn of this century who could boast that he did not spend any tax revenue on administering his province could survive only so long as the level of demands placed upon him was nil. Conversely, a system of high capability is able to absorb a heavier load, as in Canada, where diverse values of ethnic groups and a wide territorial distribution of population contribute to a variety of interests and relationships within the system. Even so, the system has its limits, notably in the accommodation of French–Canadian demands.

There are times, however, when the normal load exceeds that which the system is designed to accommodate. Values and environment become increasingly out of harmony with each other and the number and intensity of demands increase, while the structures for evaluating and converting these demands into policy adapt too slowly to accommodate them. As these pressures mount, it becomes necessary also to alter the formal relationships between the structures so as to enhance the capability of the system for coping with these demands through accommodation, repression, or both.

As long as change is carried out within these capabilities it is possible to speak of *evolutionary* change. Issues, actors, and relationships alter over time in a manner slow enough or predictable enough so that the fundamental loyalties of the vast majority of the society remain stable. The New Deal in the United States—a set of political and economic changes proposed in 1933—came as a result of the election of a new party with new personnel put into positions of power. Identification with the system was maintained while change was introduced. Similarly, the rise of Adolf Hitler to power in Germany in the same year came as a result of political maneouvrings which were acceptable within the context of the Weimar Republic, but Hitler immediately proceeded to use the structures and practices to destroy the republic and establish his "New Order."

If modern, economically developed societies are less prone to civil violence than are others (see Figure 11–1) part of the reason may be due to their willingness to experiment with new methods of increasing the responsiveness of government to citizen demands. In many democratic states this has taken the form of increased citizen participation.

Citizen participation may be defined as involvement on the part of citizens in the governmental processes through means which are different from previously accepted structures and processes. In a democratic society, people may normally participate in politics through voting, running for office, joining an interest group, a political party, or becoming a member of a government advisory board. While these are participatory activities, they are not usually designated as citizen participation, because they are parts of the normal political process. Citizen participation has something of the unique and unordered about it. It is also most closely associated with the process of feedback to government policies.

The most common participatory activity is the formation of a citizens' group to oppose some economic or political change which is initiated or sanctioned by government. Opposition and reaction are not the sole activities of citizens' groups, but it appears that these are easier to generate among people than others which might support or propose new changes.

Citizen participation has become most obvious at the municipal level across Canada, as opposed to the more senior levels of government. Groups tend first to try to generate pressure on behalf of their causes. This may take the form of petitions or demonstrations, and, in extreme form, riots. Where these fail to achieve results, the groups may begin to use their numbers to try and replace government decision makers, by acting as new political parties. Participation may then run the gamut from a simple process of becoming more informed about policy to one of dictating it. Sherry Arnstein has devised the best-known spectrum of citizen participation activity in her "ladder of citizen participation" (Figure 11–3). The ladder is divided into three parts with eight rungs in total. The two lowest rungs, therapy and manipulation, are not really indicative of participation, though activities which may be designated as being on these rungs often are called that. Manipulation consists of engineering support for a change or proposal by playing on the emotions or ignorance of citizens. Therapy is a device whereby citizens' groups are used to control or improve the behaviour of their members. There is no question of involvement in decisions, but only of self-improvement. An example of therapeutic participation is the use of public meetings to generate a spirit of community or neighbourhood improvement. The aim of the meeting is not to involve citizens in decision making but to teach them to be better people.

The middle rungs of the ladder constitute a token approach to participation. People are informed of decisions, often after the fact. It is assumed by those in power that this courtesy will help to eliminate problems. A higher rung is consultation, where people are asked their opinions about changes, but not necessarily given any means to make their opinions felt. The power still rests with the officials. Finally, as a token gesture, citizens may be placated on certain points or occasional decisions when opinion runs very strong, but by and large overall control remains with those who had it in the first place. The decision of the Government of Ontario to halt the construction of Toronto's Spadina Expressway is an example of placation. There was no shift in decision-making powers; simply a response by the authorities to heavy public pressure.

Real participation begins when citizens or citizens' groups are given some measure of power and responsibility. Partnership implies the

FIGURE 11–3
The Ladder of Citizen Participation

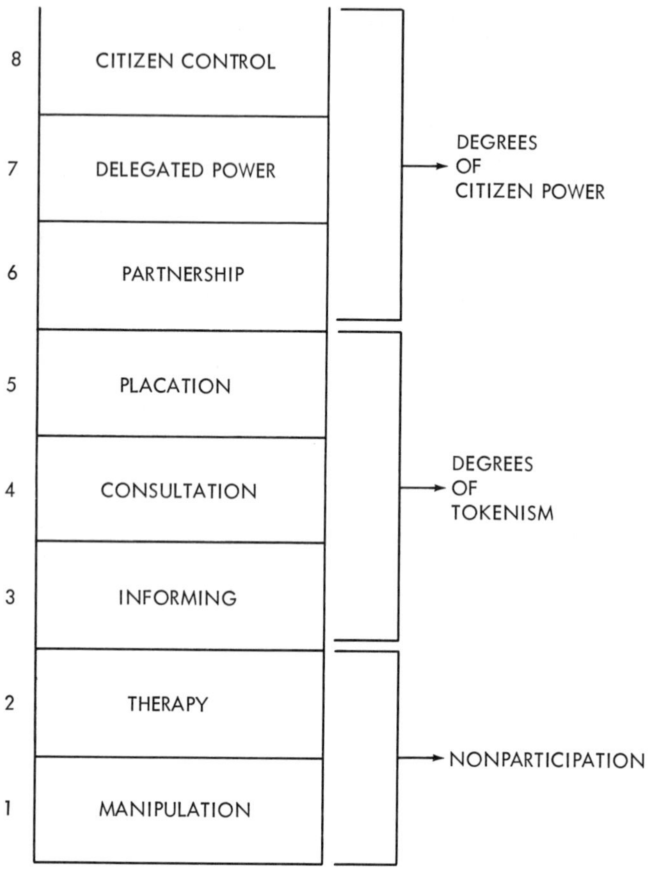

Source: Sherry Arnstein, "A Ladder of Citizen Participation," *Journal of the American Institute of Planners* xxxv (4), July 1969, p. 217.

sharing of this power by the officials with the people affected by change. Delegated power is a variation, where certain issues or types of change may be considered and decided upon by local groups, though the ultimate power to act still remains with the officials. Finally, when citizens' groups take on the power to run their own affairs, the top of the rung is reached, citizen power.

It must not be felt that this ladder constitutes an inevitable or even a wholly desirable progression. The top of the ladder in fact implies a new government, which in all probability would resemble the old one in its approach to decision making, thus requiring people to begin the same process again. Instead, the expansion of citizen participation must be seen as a safety valve which prevents the pressures of change from exploding into violence. Rather than some perpetual process of power struggles, it is probably more useful to see citizen participation as expanding or contracting as change and its impact fluctuate. The ability of a democratic system to expand and contract with pressures for citizen participation is one of the measures of its ability to maintain itself.

VIOLENT CHANGE

When the capability of a system to change in order to meet social pressures is not equal to the task at hand, new methods of effecting change are introduced by those who are discontented. The essential ingredient of these alternatives is violence. For our purposes, *violence may be defined as those actions taken on the part of interest groups or the system itself which tend to heighten an individual's uncertainty over his or her environment.* Violence may take physical forms as in warfare or psychological forms as in racial discrimination. Assassination, riots, sabotage, and the activities of secret police are examples of political violence.

The disposition to collective violence depends on how badly societies violate socially derived expectations about the means and ends of human action. . . . . . Civil violence can occur in the context of any kind of political community. It is most likely to occur in societies that rely on coercion to maintain order in lieu of providing adequate patterns of value-satisfying action.[3]

Generally, the use of violence by either the agents of the political system or by its opponents contributes to a further weakening of the system, since it heightens the disparity between the existing values and the environment which surrounds the individual. Unless the system is capable of using violence to successfully alter the values of society, resorting to violence will only add to the load placed upon it, since the disparity between values and environment will continue to grow.[4] A recourse to violence by any of the political actors indicates that society is moving back towards Hobbes' "state of nature," in preparation for a reconstitution of the decision-making mechanisms. The extreme result of this process is revolution; however, in the overwhelming majority of cases the entire process is never followed through.

---

[3] Ted Robert Gurr, *Why Men Rebel* (Princeton: Princeton University Press, 1970), p. 317.

[4] William H. Flanigan and Edwin Fogelman, "Patterns of Political Violence in Comparative Historical Perspective," *Comparative Politics* 3, no. 1 (October 1970): 29–33.

The *incidence* of political violence in the world has been intensively studied during the past few years. There seems to be general agreement that the quantity of violent activity short of international warfare has been continually increasing since World War II. One count of violent incidents suggests that such activity in the period 1946–66 was about 30 percent greater than in 1919–39.[5] During this period, an average of just under seven governments a year changed hands as a result of political violence.[6]

Between evolutionary change and utter chaso lies a wide range of violent solutions to the problem of political change. These may be divided into four categories: turmoil, conspiracy, rebellion, and revolution. All of these solutions include some form of violence and all address themselves to the need to increase the capability of the system to respond, positively or negatively, to an increased load.

TURMOIL

Turmoil may be defined as violent political activity which has a wide degree of popular participation, a relatively low degree of organization, and objectives that are either limited or unformulated.[7] It is very close to the anomic interest articulation discussed in Chapter 5. The most common forms of turmoil are riots, strikes, and demonstrations. Often it may be difficult to tell where one form begins and another leaves off. For instance, following the publication of the Cliche Report (1975) on corruption in the construction unions, the Quebec government moved to place those most implicated under trusteeship. A group of union members met to plan strategy about a strike to oppose the government's action. The meeting moved into the streets where it became a demonstration against the government. Then the demonstrators moved on an aircraft plant where another strike was in progress and, by then, the demonstration turned into a riot which resulted in the occupation of factory buildings and the kidnapping of hostages.

Turmoil may be simply a result of frustration, that is, anomic behaviour, or it may be tactical. Riots and strikes may be fomented by agitators in order to force governments into repressive activities

---

[5] Arthur S. Banks, "Patterns of Domestic Conflict: 1919–39 and 1946–66," *Journal of Conflict Resolution* 16, no. 1 (March 1972): p. 42.

[6] See I. Kramnich, "Reflections on Revolution: Definition and Explanation in Recent Scholarship," *History and Theory* 2, no. 1 (1972): p. 29.

[7] Ivo K. Feierabend, Rosalind L. Feierabend and Ted Robert Gurr, eds., *Anger, Violence and Politics: Theories and Research* (Englewood Cliffs, N.J.: Prentice–Hall, 1972), p. 264.

which, they hope, will then drive more people into opposition. This would precipitate a deepening of the crisis.

Crise de regime, the most serious form of turmoil, has no real equivalent in the English language. The term means a crisis or critical period in the functioning of the system itself, as compared to any single cabinet or government. Such crises are often provoked by riots or demonstrations which are contained only with difficulty by the forces of the government or not at all. In Canada, such crises have been rare. The Winnipeg General strike of 1919 may be considered an approximation, even though the federal government in Ottawa was not directly threatened. The system as a whole reacted as though it were threatened, by repressing the strike and enacting discriminatory legislation against European immigrants who might be similarly involved in the future.[8]

In the long run, some of the strike leaders were elected to legislative offices and the interests of the strikers were accommodated to some extent. The FLQ kidnappings in Montreal and the invocation of the *War Measures Act* in 1970 may be interpreted as a crisis. France has been plagued with such crises, especially because of the centralized nature of its government. Strikes and riots in Paris in 1936–7, 1947, and 1968 and in Algiers in 1958, 1960, and 1961 strongly affected the existing regimes. Other well-known crises have occurred in Poland in 1956 and in Italy in 1923 when Mussolini came to power.

CONSPIRACY

The second category of political violence is generically labelled as conspiracy, which may be defined as relatively *"small-scale clandestine uses of force for specifically political purposes, usually to seize or enhance political power."*[9] The most common forms of conspiratorial violence are, assassination, terrorism, and the *coup d'etat.*

Assassination is a selective form of violence where political leaders are killed in order to weaken or destroy a political system. The effectiveness of this tactic depends on the centralization of power in the regime, and the provisions for the replacement of political leadership. If power is concentrated in one or a few people and there is no peaceful method of transferring power, the result of an assassination can be chaos. On the other hand, as the assassination of U.S. President John F. Kennedy in 1963 demonstrated, where power is more dispersed and where there are adequate provisions for the succession of new leader-

---

[8] See "Canadian Socialism" in Chapter 15.

[9] Ivo K. Feierabend, et al., *Anger, Violence and Politics,* p. 265. Italics ours.

ship, the system as a whole is unlikely to be affected. Except in occasional instances, assassinations are likely to be isolated phenomena. More commonly it is a tactic used in conjunction with another form of violence, such as a coup d'etat, riot, or terrorist attack.

The use of terror, or a heightened degree of uncertainty about one's physical or psychological safety, has become more popular in recent years among conspirators. This is partially due to the theatrical value of terrorist attacks—they make good news copy. It is also due to the spread of modern technology and to the increasing importance of public opinion in influencing domestic and foreign policies. Terrorism has also gained impetus as the lessons of successful nationalist guerrilla struggles are learned.

Since 1970, terrorism has taken on an international aspect. Small groups of activists had formerly confined themselves to domestic operations, especially in Northern Ireland, Uruguay, and Israel. Their main tactics were kidnapping, random shootings, and bombings. After the debacle of the 1967 Israeli–Arab War, Arab countries began to give more concrete support to Palestinian terrorist groups. These groups acquired significant financing and began building a web of terrorist groups throughout the world. Counter-terrorist activities also took on international aspects, with suspected Arab terrorists being assassinated in Lebanon and Norway. The most glaring example of international terrorism was the Lydda airport massacre in Israel in 1972, when 27 people, mostly Puerto Rican pilgrims, were machine-gunned by members of the Japanese Rengo Sekigun (Red Army). The Japanese were brought to the Middle East by a Palestinian group, trained and then sent to Europe for a "cooling off" period before boarding a plane for Lydda.

The failure of a terrorist group to achieve its aims over time leads to a different tone of violence. In the first five years of terror in Northern Ireland (1969–74), 223 terrorists were killed. This largely decimated the ranks of the fanatics with the result that:

The armed killer, the free-lance gunman often owing allegiance to no particular organization, who is determined to even the score on a football-match basis after each Catholic or Protestant death, has taken over from the bomber acting under instructions.[10]

The *coup d'etat* differs from the previous tactics in that it almost exclusively involves the military. Coups are not necessarily related to social discontent, though the interests of the military, or part of it, must definitely be taken into account. Violence in a coup is often psychological; many coups are bloodless and sometimes known well in advance

---

[10] *The Economist*, November 30, 1974, p. 23.

to the victims. The traditional style of a coup consists of a quick seizure of the means of communication, capture of the main political actors, and neutralization of any forces which might oppose the new regime. In spite of the number of coups reported in the media, this activity is not a guaranteed success. Timing, secrecy, and planning are of vital importance and miscalculations are critical. The escape of General Nasution from his assassins resulted in the failure of a Communist coup in Indonesia in 1965, costing the losers an estimated half-million lives.

The results of successful coups are unpredictable. Some have increased the capability of political systems to respond to the needs of the society while others have contributed to an increasing malaise as coup and counter-coup destroy the network of political relationships. Some have in fact been little more than violent alternatives to elections. In Latin America they are often consummated by the exiling of the major political figures of the overthrown regime. The losers are escorted to an airport and, with some ceremony, placed in a chartered plane, usually bound for Europe.

Not all coups end so quietly. A coup in the African republic of Chad in 1975 ended in the death of its president, as did that in Chile in 1973. Coups may lead to new political stances as well. The Chilean coup replaced a left-wing Marxist executive with a right-wing military dictatorship. A coup in Portugal in 1974 replaced a right-wing fascist government with a left-wing military regime. A series of bloody coups in Nigeria in the mid-1960s led to the secession of the eastern part of the country and then to the tragedy of the Biafran War, otherwise known as the Nigerian Civil War.

REBELLION

A more intense form of reaction against the existing political system is a rebellion. A *rebellion* is a *violent, protracted effort on the part of a relatively large number of people designed to effect a measure of change in the political system.* It represents an extreme form of crisis because of its protracted nature. Unlike a riot, which contains a great measure of spontaneity and has a narrow geographic and chronological scope, a rebellion includes a strong measure of rationality in the use of violence and a great deal of organization and communication over distances. Leadership tends to develop as the rebellion continues and the situation becomes one of "internal war."

The difference between rebellion and the two previous categories lies not only in the scope of violence and disruption but in the fact that in a rebellion the development of leadership means that an alternative ruling group rises to confront the existing rulers. In a *crise de regime,* leadership may be passed from one part of the ruling group to another. In a coup d'etat, people who are nonleaders suddenly assume the positions of power within the system. There are "ins" and "outs" in both cases. Where there is a state of internal war, a civil war, the rebels constitute a rival government, holding sway over whatever area their forces are able to control. There are two governments, each claiming legitimacy and a monopoly over force.

Historically, many rebellions have arisen in order to preserve or restore traditional relationships. Revolts against corrupt and cruel officials have been common; their main objective has been to demonstrate to the ruler, or the society, the extent of the depredations of such officials. Anticolonial rebellions are often tinged with such sentiments. The U.S. Declaration of Independence presented the argument that the colonies had to secede because the king and parliament had taken away liberties to which the Americans were entitled. The declaration of Louis Riel, in the Rebellion of 1870, was modelled after the U.S. Declaration of Independence and expressed much the same sentiment. Arab nationalists extolled the glories of the early Arab empires and used the appeal of Islam in the rebellions in North Africa. Gandhi and his colleagues adroitly mixed modern organization and appeals to traditional values in the long struggle of the Congress Party to free India from British rule. The appeal to traditional values, past glories, and liberties has been used successfully in order to provoke rebellion among rural populations; however, once such a rebellion succeeds there has been a near-universal trend to submerge much of this sentiment in favour of a more widespread program of modernization. In the end, many of the things for which the peasant fought are denied by the nationalists more stringently than they had been by the imperialists.

Rebellions, like coups and crises, occur when the load exceeds the capability of a system and a malfunction develops. There is no assurance that the malfunction will result in a new set of personnel or different formal relationships within the system; however, the opportunity for such changes does exist. The ruling group may be able to stave off such changes by a program of drastic reforms, or the opponents of the regime may be disorganized and lack effective leadership. Moreover, the extent of the changes instituted by either the old regime or by new leadership may not be of a far-reaching character; in fact, the changes may constitute a restoration of earlier relationships.

REVOLUTION

The term *revolution* is today widely used both inside and outside the political sphere. There are industrial revolutions, revolutionary detergents, revolutions of rising expectations, and an innumerable host of other processes, products, and human conditions which are seen as incorporating revolutions of some sort. In commenting upon this ubiquity of revolution, Eugene Kamenka has written that:

. . . the twentieth century is notable not as the era that gave the world political revolutions, but as the era that successfully institutionalized society's passage from one nonpolitical social or economic revolution to another.[11]

Revolution, then, is the normal state of things today.

Pressure for change affects the political system in a variety of ways. Normally new demands are accepted or rejected according to a process which is acceptable to the vast majority of citizens and the system thus maintains itself. However, there are times when demands may exceed the capacity of the system to cope with and instigate violent activity. Certain variations of this violent activity and its effects upon the equilibrium and the maintenance of the system have been discussed. The overloading and collapse of an entire political system is one of the preludes to a revolution. Kamenka defines a *revolution* as:

. . . a sharp, sudden change in the social location of political power, expressing itself in the radical transformation of the process of government, of the official foundations of sovereignty or legitimacy and of the conception of the social order.[12]

Kamenka offers only one of a host of definitions for revolution. The topic has attracted the attention of political scientists, historians, philosophers, and psychologists for three centuries. If one includes a discussion of the other forms of violence against the political system in this framework, it is possible to trace concern over political upheaval into antiquity.

It is generally agreed that the term revolution was taken from the lexicon of Renaissance astronomers, who used it to describe the rotation of the planets. At first the term was used to indicate the process of upheaval and reestablishment common to rebellions, where a king or queen might be overthrown and replaced by another. After the English upheavals of 1640–88, the term gradually came to emphasize only the changing of the established order, since revolutions such as the English, the American (1775–83) and the French (1789–1815) did not include a basic return to prerevolutionary relationships in the political system.

Each of these revolutions added depth to the concept as well. The French Revolution in particular involved a thorough-going restructur-

---

[11] Eugene Kamenka, "The Concept of a Political Revolution" in *Revolution*, ed. Carl Friedrich (New York: Atherton Press, 1966), p. 123.

[12] *Ibid.*, p. 124.

ing of roles in the political system as well as the wider society. The revolutionary ideas which came to dominate the political realm were translated into policies which deeply affected social relationships. The political slogan, "Liberty, Equality, Fraternity," implied the destruction of the French social hierarchy, the redistribution of national wealth, and the forging of nationalist bonds. The entitling of the revolutionary manifesto as a "Declaration of the Rights of Man," gave the ideals of the revolution international scope and constituted a threat to the maintenance of traditional social order in all parts of Europe. The adoption of a new calendar and the metric system of measurement extended the revolution into science and engineering as well. The revolution was meant to be a total transformation of society.

Mechanics of Revolution

Revolution, like other forms of political upheaval, is a product of the disharmony between the ways in which people see reality and the ways in which they think reality should be. The resultant demands overload the political system and new relationships are created to satisfy or repress them. Revolution differs from other forms of violent change in that it is more pervasive in its effects upon the political system and upon society itself.

The drama of revolution, destruction, and reconstruction has been of great interest to political analysts.[13] Attempts have been made to distinguish the stages through which a revolution passes. There are five discernable stages in a revolution:

1.   The *preconditions* for revolution.
2.   The *collapse* of the old system.
3.   The *destruction* of old relationships.
4.   The *construction* of new relationships.
5.   The *stabilization* of a new system.

While all of these stages may be discerned, their relative importance and timing is determined by the particular circumstances of the event. A certain degree of overlapping exists between them.

The *preconditions* for revolution are similar to those for other forms of disruption. Change being endemic in society, discontent with its institutions is always present, though it is at times greater in intensity or better articulated. General discontent is dangerous but not of overriding concern as long as it is not focussed.

One of the critical requirements preceding a revolution is the

---

[13] See, for instance, Crane Brinton, *Anatomy of Revolution* (New York: Vintage Books, 1959).

development and propagation of values to supplant those supporting the existing political system. This set of values is the creation of what Eric Hoffer calls "men of words," men who are disenchanted with society and government. They try to give the ruling elites and the people as a whole an explanation for their dissatisfaction, which generally consists of an indictment of the existing values, and a vision of the future which satisfies the unspoken needs of the society.[14] Probably the most influential man of words has been Karl Marx, whose ideas have served to inspire the great revolutions of the 20th century. As the ideas of the people of words spread among the intellectuals and leadership groups, the quantity and intensity of demands upon the system increase. Concentrating discontent through the creation of a revolutionary ideology increases the load placed upon a system.

Revolution depends upon the breakdown of relationships in the system, the nature and style of the existing political leadership, and the resources at the disposal of this leadership. In short, revolution is the result of decline in a system's capability relative to its load. A society governed by structures which are financially bankrupt, mismanaged, or prone to illogical decision making is ripe for revolution. Popular discontent is, at most, a necessary contributing factor. Most revolutions are sparked by poor political management, not correct revolutionary theory.

The second stage, that of the *collapse* of the old system, follows as the alienation of leadership groups increases and misfortunes continue to plague the government. Often this stage is not reached until a great reformer has arisen to try to rescue the old system. Turgot and Necker attempted to strengthen the French monarchy before 1789, and Stolypin attempted the same task in Russia before World War I, but both efforts failed. Leon Blum may have been cast in a similar role in 1936 when the French Popular Front brought him to power but again radical reform failed to renovate a decaying system—in this case democratic—and it collapsed under the shock of war in 1940. Someone once noted about the French Third Republic that "it was dead by 1934, but it was not buried until 1940." The same could be said for many systems which have fallen to revolutions, coups, and rebellions.

The essential difference between a revolution which destroys an existing political system and coups and rebellions is the extent of the collapse and disorganization. All of these forms of sudden change are precipitated by a single or a series of violent acts and, if successful, lead to a change in personnel. A coup is a substitution of one part of the ruling group by another while a successful rebellion results in the replacement of the entire ruling group. Neither a coup nor rebellion

---

[14] Eric Hoffer, *True Believer* (New York: New American Library, 1951), pp. 119–30.

necessarily changes the basic features of the existing political system. A revolution, on the other hand, is an attempt to create *a new system on the ruins of the old.* A successful revolution requires a more complete collapse and greater disorganization than either of the other forms. It is possible to discover instances where coups and rebellions have led to revolution but they do not inexorably do so.

The importance of a coup or a rebellion in the development of a revolutionary situation lies in the act itself and not in the intent of those who may perform it. A successful coup or rebellion indicates that the leadership of the country was unable to maintain its position. This stroke of violence may also act as a catalyst which precipitates collapse of all types of social and political relationships. The leaders of the coup or rebellion then find that they have unleashed forces which they are unable to control. They are overshadowed by fanatics. The end of the second stage comes when the social order collapses and rebels, revolutionaries, and elements of the old regime all move to establish some sort—any sort—of order.

The *destruction* of old relationships, the third stage of revolution, has its beginnings in the prerevolutionary conditions when popular acquiescence in, or support for, the old order falters. The changing pattern of personnel and the recourse to violence in the second stage further contribute to the disintegration of structural relationships and the predictability of roles known previously. Up to this point the old order is said to have experienced a collapse but, like an old house which has a collapsed roof, much of the value foundations and the major structures for interest articulation, political decision, and, above all, policy implementation remain intact. The complete destruction of the old order becomes a necessity for the revolutionaries in order to prevent a reconstitution of the political system along earlier lines. A modern example of the revolutionary destruction of the old order was the total evacuation of Phnom Penh, the capital of Cambodia, after it fell to Khmer Rouge troops at the end of the civil war in 1975.

> Perhaps as many as three or four million people, most of them on foot, have been forced out of the cities and sent on a mammoth and grueling exodus into areas deep in the countryside, where . . . they will have to become peasants and till the soil.
>
> No one has been excluded. . . . .
>
> In sum the new rulers . . . appear to be remaking Cambodian society in the peasant image, casting aside everything that belonged to the old system, which was generally dominated by the cities and towns, and by the elite and merchants who lived there.[15]

---

[15] Sydney Schanberg, *New York Times,* May 9, 1975, p. 1.

Terror is perhaps the ultimate political weapon. It is more useful than other forms of force because of its psychological effects. Terror destroys certainty; the knock on the door in the middle of the night is far more frightening than the ultimate result. Many people throughout history have gone to certain death calmly and bravely, but few have withstood the awful anxiety of not knowing whether they will be taken, for what reason, and to what kind of an end. The creation of a state of terror in a population causes people to throw off their values and relationships if by so doing they may achieve greater certainty. The terrified person will be alone before the wielders of force in that he or she will mistrust neighbours lest they be informers, desert organized comrades in order to become inconspicuous, and recite the new values in order to demonstrate utter loyalty. In the rush to acquire certainty about life and death, all social and political relationships except those desired by the new rulers are abandoned. This is the ultimate feedback within the political system; by denying the desired certainty, the decision makers are able to create the demands upon the system they wish to see articulated and suppress at the outset all that they consider undesirable. In a reign of terror all policies are acceptable to the society and all demands receive the blessing of the rulers *before* they are articulated. It is during this third stage that most of the personnel of the old order and of the previous revolutionary ruling groups, if any, are eliminated from society. Some escape abroad and others are liquidated.

Once the destruction of the old order is underway, the fourth stage of the revolution begins; the *construction* of a new order based on the values created by the "people of words" (who by this time have often been liquidated if they were not dead before the revolution). There is never an exact relationship between the concepts that sparked the revolution and those implemented in this stage, since there are likely to be competing sets of ideas, such as those of the Liberals, Social-Democrats, Mensheviks, and Bolsheviks in Russia in 1917. Also, the circumstances under which the new order is set up condition the forms of the structures and the needs for which the system must be organized. France in the 1790s faced primarily external enemies; the U.S.S.R. in 1917 faced primarily internal foes; Hitler's Germany had to contend with an economic depression; and the Vichy regime in France after 1940 had to contend with defeat and occupation. The new order becomes a hybrid of ideals and necessity.

This combination of ideals and necessity perpetuates the political instability which began with the collapse of the old order. People of action conflict with fanatics over the structures and the demands to be included in the new system. Either ideals or action must be subordinated to the other. Whichever dominates, it uses idealism to rout the adherents of the losing faction. The ideals, the new values, are enshrined regardless of whether they are applied. They constitute a test of political morality and those who err in relation to them are treated in the same manner as those who had rejected these values earlier; they are condemned as traitors. The ideological connection between policy decisions and ultimate ends results in policy conflicts being treated among the revolutionaries as conflicts over "truth" and the losers are treated accordingly. As Rubashov, in Arthur Koestler's *Darkness at Noon,* wrote in his diary:

> We have learnt history more thoroughly than the others. We differ from all others in our logical consistency. We know that virtue does not matter to history, and that crimes remain unpunished; but that every error has its consequences and venges itself unto the seventh generation. . . . Each wrong idea we follow is a crime committed against future generations. Therefore we have to punish wrong ideas as others punish crimes: with death.[16]

A rash of treason trials and purges, such as those in Cuba after 1959, China after 1949, and throughout much of the history of the U.S.S.R., attest to the usefulness of this practice in resolving policy questions within the new system. Also, such trials contribute to the maintenance of the regime by demonstrating its strength symbolically to the society.

The final stage of a revolution consists of the *stabilization* of a new system. The construction of the new system may begin during earlier stages when changes in personnel are abrupt and experimentation with roles and structures abounds. As the reign of terror continues, the quest for order increases until the society is prepared to accept the value of present stability rather than to continue struggling over past glories and future utopias. Sometimes the process is drawn out, as in France in the 1790s, or it may be preshortened as in Germany after 1932. The length of the period of consolidation appears to be a function of the strength and position of the revolutionary groups. Lenin's Bolsheviks were but one faction among many at the time the Czar abdicated in 1917 and the consolidation of the Communist system took most of four years. Hitler, on the other hand, used his political organization to put himself at the helm of the old system; when the appropriate time came, he was able to compress the stages of revolution into a very short period using the authority of the old system to destroy it and refashion his own.

The system which ends the revolutionary struggle is different in many respects from the one whose collapse touched off the process but it also contains elements of the earlier one. These remnants are most often parts of the administration since the fanatics, in order to attack

---

[16] Arthur Koestler, *Darkness at Noon* (New York: Macmillan, 1941), p. 99.

and destroy their enemies, are often forced to call upon the remnants of the old administration since it is still a repository of force and direction. Consequently, there is a tendency to leave the "reorganizing" of the bureaucracy until a later date—which is seldom reached.

The disintegration of the core values of the old political culture during the revolution weakens the degree of support any new regime might logically expect. In order to remain in existence, the new regime must prove its viability. This is most often done through the use of military force and it is not uncommon to find post-revolutionary regimes headed or controlled by their generals. The rise of Napoleon Bonaparte in French political circles after successes in Italy in 1795 is the classic case, while both Hitler and the leaders of the U.S.S.R. managed to manipulate and subordinate the military.

The political leadership of the new regime also attempts to heal the wounds caused by years of uncertainty by incorporating a few of the surviving leaders and certain of the old institutions into the new system. For instance, the Bolsheviks adopted the forms and tactics of the Czarist police organization (Okhrana), renaming it the Cheka. Both military force and the inclusion of former leaders serve to dissipate the revolutionary fervour and restore some measure of certainty and continuity to the country. In effect, the post-revolutionary leadership establishes emotional ties with both the revolution and the old regime and claims to have extracted the best from them.

Classical and Modern Revolutions

While the process discussed above applies in general to all revolutions, there are differences between those which happened before the middle of the 20th century and those which occur after this approximate date. The earlier revolutions, such as those in the United States, France, and Russia, came about in a manner which might be called classical. The classical revolution was from the start one where the governing powers of the country were seized by the revolutionaries, either by a decision in a national congress (U.S.), through a crisis brought on by riots (France), or through a series of coups (Russia). The revolution in classical cases was, in a sense, conducted from the top down. As of this writing, what appears to be a revolution in the classical sense, is taking shape in Portugal.

Modern revolution operates from somewhat different principles, though eventually the same process works itself out. The difference between the two types appears to be that the seizure of the governing power is a more protracted effort requiring a greater degree of sacrifice and effort than in the classical model. While the seizure of power is relatively quick in the classical model (the collapse of the old order), in the modern model, the political system must be methodically reduced and destroyed. The overthrow of the old system becomes a major subgoal of the revolutionaries, where in the classical model it is but the opening round of the process.

Modern revolution must begin as a subversive process. Rather than wait for a collapse which may never come, modern revolutionaries must attempt to destroy the effectiveness of a system which may be functioning adequately. The general outlines of this subversive method were developed first in China by Mao Tse-tung and the communist revolutionary army. Variations were later employed in the two Vietnamese wars (1946–54, 1963–75), in the Algerian War (1954–62) and in Cuba (1957–59).

This method of gaining power is called revolutionary war. It opens with the organizing of a disciplined, reliable group into a revolutionary or subversive party. The party widens its support among the people, especially peasants. It gradually moves into guerrilla warfare and selective terrorism. As parts of the country are detached from the control of the government, the party and its "front" organizations set up an alternative government and the guerrilla bands expand into regular army units. Finally the government's army is defeated by the revolutionary army and the party takes complete power. While revolutionary changes may have begun earlier in "liberated zones," once the seizure of power is complete, more radical changes are instituted and the larger process of revolution goes on its way.

A revolutionary war does not have the same objective as conventional warfare—the acquisition of territory or position in order to force an opponent to surrender. It is instead a political one, to weaken the will of the government so as to precipitate its complete collapse. Mass support is the primary need of any guerrilla movement. It must try to alienate people from their government, primarily through appeals to popular morality. The desire for land among a peasant population is a critical factor in many cases, and great inequalities in ownership have been consistently related to government instability in poorer countries.

Once support is gained, it must be maintained. This means that the guerrillas must not only outfight the government but they must also out-administer it. They must provide a more responsive and effective political system. No revolutionary war can be won without popular support, and this support must be earned. Terror can neutralize opposing forces, but it cannot generate the consistent popular backing which is necessary for a revolutionary war to succeed.

While revolutionary war has its appeal to those wishing radical change, its fruits have been most difficult to gather. During the period 1964–69, an average of 12 guerrilla wars were under way at any given time, yet only one, in the desert land of South Yemen (formerly the British protectorate of Aden), succeeded in its aims.[17] Needless to say the recent fall of South Vietnam, Laos, and Cambodia to revolutionary armies will have restored the lustre to this method.

RECOMMENDED READINGS

Ahmed, Eqbal. "Revolutionary War and Counterinsurgency." *Journal of International Affairs* 16, no. 3 (September 1972): 383–96.

Arendt, Hannah. *On Revolution.* New York: Viking Press, 1965.

Banks, Arthur S. "Patterns of Domestic Conflict: 1919–39 and 1946–66." *Journal of Conflict Resolution* 16, no. 1 (March 1972): 41–50.

Brinton, Crane. *Anatomy of Revolution.* New York: Vintage Books, 1959.

Daniels, Stuart. "Weathermen." *Government and Opposition* 9, no. 4 (Autumn 1974): 431–59.

Davies, James. "Toward a Theory of Revolution." *American Sociological Review* 27, no. 1 (February 1962).

Chapman, Phillip C. "Stress in Political Theory." *Ethics* 80, no. 1 (October 1969): 38–49.

Eckstein, Harry, ed. *Internal War.* New York: Free Press of Glencoe, 1964.

Feierabend, Ivo, Feierabend, Rosalind, and Gurr, Ted Robert, eds. *Anger, Violence and Politics: Theories and Research.* Englewood Cliffs, N.J.: Prentice–Hall, 1972.

Hagopian, Mark. *The Phenomenon of Revolution.* New York: Dodd, Mead, 1974.

Hoffer, Eric. *True Believer.* New York: New American Library, 1951.

Hutchinson, M. C. "The Concept of Revolutionary Terrorism." *Journal of Conflict Resolution* 16, no. 3 (September 1972): 383–96.

Johnson, Chalmers. *Revolution and the Social System.* Stanford, California: Hoover Institution, 1964.

————. *Revolutionary Change.* Boston: Little Brown & Co., 1966.

Kraemer, J. S. "Revolutionary Guerrilla Warfare and the Decolonization Movement." *Politics* 4, no. 2 (Winter 1971): 137–58.

Kramnic, I. "Reflections on Revolution: Definition and Explanation in Recent Scholarship." *History and Theory* 2, no. 1 (1972): 26–63.

Lefevre, Georges. *The Coming of the French Revolution.* Translated by R. R. Palmer. New York: Vintage Books, 1957.

Leiden, Carl, and Schmitt, Karl. *The Politics of Violence: Revolution in the Modern World.* Englewood Cliffs, N.J.: Prentice–Hall, 1968.

Manzer, Ronald. *Canada: A Socio-Political Report,* chap. 3. Toronto: McGraw-Hill, Ryerson, 1974.

Meisel, James. *Counterrevolution.* New York: Atherton Press, 1966.

Moss, Robert. "International Terrorism and the Western Societies." *International Journal* 28, no. 3 (September 1973): 418–30.

---

[17] J. S. Kraemer, "Revolutionary Guerrilla Warfare and the Decolonization Movement," *Polity* 4, no. 2 (Winter 1971): p. 156.

Neumann, Sigmund. *Permanent Revolution.* 2d ed. New York: Praeger, 1965.

Starrs, Catherine, and Steward, Gail. *Gone Today and Here Tomorrow: Issues Surrounding the Future of Citizen Involvement.* Ontario Committee on Government Productivity. Toronto: The Queen's Printer, 1971.

Springer, Phillip, and Truzzi, Marcello eds. *Revolutionaries on Revolution: Participants' Perspectives on the Strategies of Seizing Power.* Pacific Palisades, California: Good Year Publications, 1973.

Toffler, Alvin. *Future Shock.* New York: Random House, 1970.

12

International Relations

IT WAS NOTED in Chapter 2 that the human community is politically divided into nation-states which operate according to the principle of sovereign equality. This principle implies that all states, at least in theory, are politically equal to one another irrespective of differences in territory, population, resources, wealth, and military power. Moreover, as sovereign political entities, each state is free to act as it wishes in both external and domestic affairs. The principle of sovereign equality, if taken literally, is fraught with dangers. If each nation-state insists on a strict and literal adherence to this principle and acts solely in its own interests, it could well disrupt the fabric of human society.

The use of the doctrine of sovereign equality has ramifications for the study of the relations between states. A national society is politically integrated, with one set of legitimate authorities who govern the entire community and whose actions are legally enforceable. The international society is characterized by its disintegrated nature. It is devoid of relatively uniform values and incentives, and its structures are characterized by a voluntarism which is not to be found at the national level. Paradoxically, though, this is an age of interdependence of states in which even the wealthiest and most powerful of them depend in some measure upon goods and services supplied by others. This helps to mitigate some of the inherent dangers in the principle of sovereign equality and obliges states to discover and agree upon areas of common interest.

Many factors foster this interdependence. Modern technology, for instance, has no national label. The release of atomic energy was engineered by the Americans but a large part of the earlier research was done by Italians, Scandinavians, and Germans. Atomic reactors which generate energy for peaceful uses operating in many developing na-

307

tions were manufactured in the United States or Britain. The nuclear explosion by India in 1974 was facilitated by the use of a CANDU reactor manufactured in Canada. Modern techniques of production and marketing, irrespective of the source of discovery and invention, are becoming increasingly universal. Probably the most dramatic example of this increasingly technological convergence was the 1969 moon landing watched on television by hundreds of millions of people around the world. In these days of the spectre of nuclear annihilation, perhaps the most overpowering interest of all nations is the desire for peace. While all states may be equally concerned about peace, they have not been able to agree upon the most desirable approach for bringing it about. Governments pursue policies which they consider to be most conducive to peace even though these policies do not always coincide with the thinking of others. All want peace, on their own terms.

International relations, then, arises from the interplay of foreign policies promoted by governments resulting in mutual cooperation or conflict. A *foreign policy* involves the prescription and formulation of a set of objectives, priorities, and procedures to guide the behaviour of a government in its external affairs.

NATIONAL DETERMINATION OF FOREIGN POLICY

The primary responsibility for the formulation and implementation of foreign policy in all states, federal and unitary, is vested in the national government. Constituent units in a federal state may make their needs, requirements, and views on matters of special interest to them known to the national government; however, wisdom and common sense require that, in the interest of political effectiveness and national unity, final decisions must be left to the national government.

The constitutional allocation of power over foreign policy depends on the structural pattern of the government. Presidential governments, operating according to the separation of powers principle, divide authority over foreign affairs between the executive and legislative branches of government. In parliamentary governments, authority over foreign policy is technically vested in the legislature but politically exercised by the cabinet. In either case, the executive tends to dominate the conduct of foreign policy.

Role of the Legislature

There are a number of ways in which the legislature in a political system can help to determine the foreign policy of the government. The most obvious of these, though the least used, is for the legislature to deny to the government the power or authority to carry out a proposed or current policy. In a parliamentary system, this can mean the ousting of the government if its majority collapses, or the creation of such pressure as to force the ministers responsible for the policy to leave office. The latter situation arose when the British Conservative government of Prime Minister Anthony Eden became embroiled in the Suez Crisis in 1956. Opposition to the invasion of Egypt within the governing party was so strong that it undermined the government's authority to the point that the prime minister resigned soon afterwards. In a presidential system, the legislature cannot force the government to resign, but it may make the position of certain officials so difficult that they will either have to modify their policies substantially or, in extreme cases, step down.

Another option before the legislature in any democratic system is to refuse the necessary funds for the implementation of policy, thus effectively crippling it. Such a refusal in a parliamentary system would probably cause the government to resign, while in a presidential system the government would either simply abandon the policy or look for a means of getting approval. Cutbacks, and even outright denials, of funds are common in the United States and, while inconvenient, seldom constitute a major crisis.

The checks upon government policy are usually effective only if a majority of legislators are willing to confront the executive. This is seldom the case. It is possible, however, for individual members of the legislature to question the government's actions and to protest or denounce them from the floor of the legislature. This serves to focus public attention on the matter and may result in the mobilization of opinion which will ultimately force a change in policy. The question period in a parliamentary system affords the legislators the opportunity to question the minister responsible, while in a presidential system the legislative committees may examine government policies and solicit evidence from the government as well as from its opponents.

There are other weapons available to the legislature in the presidential system of the United States. Constitutionally, no treaty with another government is valid without the approval of the U.S. Senate, which also has the power to approve or reject appointments to executive positions in the State Department. The most notable example of the use of the Senate's power was the rejection of the Treaty of Versailles following World War I, which kept the United States out of the League of Nations. Such difficulties have led presidents since Franklin Roosevelt to arrange "executive agreements" which have a somewhat vague legal status and are binding only so long as a president wishes them to be. For instance, after the Paris Accords of 1972, President Nixon made a secret agreement to support the former South

Vietnamese government in the case of an attack. This came to light after the collapse of South Vietnam in 1975, but Nixon's successor, President Ford, chose to ignore the pledge. The power to declare war resides with the U.S. Congress, though, again, there are a number of factors which have limited this power in recent years. In certain situations, existing treaties and executive agreements, as well as the nature of intercontinental nuclear war, have made a formal declaration of war an academic question.

Role of the Executive

The role of the executive in the formulation and conduct of foreign policy is politically more pronounced. This is attributable to a number of factors. Legislatures consist of transient politicans who, by and large, are not only unaware of the intricacies of foreign policy formation and implementation but also lack most of the information required for this task. The conduct of foreign affairs is a specialized job. The executive has at its disposal a wide variety of national agencies which collect and analyse relevant information on which foreign policy is ultimately based. This is not to say, however, that information supplied by these agencies is always correct and trustworthy and that a foreign policy based on it always effective.

Then, too, members of the legislature, other than those who serve on legislative committees, which often meet *in camera,* are not bound by an oath of secrecy. On the contrary, they are normally obliged to keep their constituents informed of government activity. There are several aspects of foreign policy—such as military strategy, stockpiling of armaments, and negotiations between states—whose divulgence to the public is considered as a risk to national security. Members of the executive and the bureaucratic infrastructure involved in foreign affairs are bound by an oath of office obliging them to maintain the tight-lipped secrecy which has become the hallmark of many a foreign service employee.

Executives are often criticized for wielding too much power in foreign affairs. There has been a substantial growth in executive authority over foreign affairs in most political systems, resulting from the nature of international politics rather than the greed of the executive for more power. Much of this growth in executive authority is extra-constitutional in nature. Twice since the end of World War II, the armed forces of the United States have been involved in full-fledged wars; in Korea from 1950 to 1953 and in Indochina between 1963 and 1975. These involvements were considered by many to be unconstitutional since the U.S. Congress in neither case issued a formal declaration of war. The presidential argument has been that a congressional declaration of war was not necessary since these were not wars in the usual sense but only an attempt on the part of the United States government to fulfill UN and SEATO obligations which its Congress had already accepted. In Great Britain, Prime Minister Anthony Eden was alleged to have prepared for the invasion of Egypt in 1956 without even consulting his own cabinet, let alone the House of Commons.

The constitutional authority of the executive in foreign affairs, though similar in scope, is exercised somewhat differently in parliamentary and presidential systems. Technically all executive authority in a parliamentary government, including foreign affairs, is vested in the head of state; the crown in Britain, the crown through the Governor General in Canada. In practice, however, the head of state performs only formal, symbolic, and ceremonial roles. Effective authority is exercised by the prime minister as the head of government in consultation with the cabinet. Although politically the prime minister bears the ultimate responsibility for the conduct of the country's foreign relations, the cabinet as a whole becomes a party to this responsibility in keeping with the principle of collective responsibility.

In presidential systems, the chief executive or the president performs a dual role. As head of state, he or she is the nation's representative and spokesperson in foreign affairs and performs all the symbolic and ceremonial roles such as welcoming foreign dignitaries visiting the country and receiving the credentials of diplomats from other countries. As head of government, he or she exercises effective political authority in all aspects of foreign affairs—civil, military, and diplomatic. The cabinet merely assists.

Ministry of Foreign Affairs

Though the primary authority for the conduct of foreign affairs rests with the head of government, it is usually delegated to a member of the cabinet designated variously as minister of foreign affairs, minister of external affairs, or secretary of state, depending on historical circumstances. Normally he or she is a senior minister in the cabinet, who directs the department or ministry of foreign affairs, advises the head of government, and frequently wields considerable influence. His or her role in foreign affairs will vary with the extent of the direct involvement of the head of government or other cabinet or military leaders.

A minister for foreign affairs works with the aid of several specialized agencies and presides over a vast and elaborate hierarchy of administrative personnel and career diplomats. The general pattern of organization of a foreign office consists of:

1. Sections looking after foreign affairs with specific geographical areas of the world.
2. Sections that look after relations with international agencies.
3. Sections dealing with information, public relations, and cultural activities.
4. Sections dealing with matters relating to foreign aid and international development.

The size and importance of each section depends, of course, upon the extent of national involvement in the various facets of international relations.

TECHNIQUES OF PROMOTING FOREIGN POLICY

Diplomacy

Diplomacy is the technique whereby representatives of states conduct negotiations with a view to resolving conflicts and enhancing international cooperation.[1] Historically, the use of diplomacy since Roman times can be divided into three periods,[2] the first of which dates roughly from the end of the Roman Empire to the Renaissance and is designated as the period of unorganised diplomacy. There was little official or persistent relationship between states except for negotiating an end to war or the arranging of an interdynastic matrimonial alliance.

The second stage in the development of diplomacy stretches from the Renaissance to the end of World War I. This period witnessed the rise of nation-states and the development of a persistent pattern of interaction between them. It gave rise to a class of professional negotiators and diplomats. These negotiators acted within the framework of certain principles which in turn brought into existence a widely accepted code of diplomatic protocol and behaviour. This period is known as the period of old diplomacy, whose hallmark was the element of strict secrecy shrouding both negotiations and their outcome in the form of treaties, agreements, or alliances.

The third or modern period of diplomacy began at the end of World War I. The experience of the war had brought into focus the fact that secret arrangements between states, very often unbeknown to third parties directly affected by them, could create serious crises in international relations. It was felt that if international negotiations were con-

---

[1] See Harold Nicolson, *Diplomacy* (London: Oxford University Press, 1950).

[2] See R. B. Mowat, *Diplomacy and Peace* (New York: Robert McBride & Co., 1936), p. 15.

ducted openly and their outcome publicly announced, states would be hesitant to indulge in practices which might lead to serious international consequences. The leading exponent of this view was United States President Woodrow Wilson, who advocated the principle of "open covenants of peace openly arrived at" and that "diplomacy shall proceed always frankly and in the public view."[3] Wilson, however, soon realized that this was a difficult objective to achieve, and he modified his principle to suit his behaviour and participated in secret negotiations at Paris in 1919.

Two aspects of open diplomacy which can be traced back to the Paris Peace Conference of 1919 are the ideas of summit diplomacy and multilateral diplomacy. A peace conference was a gathering of representatives of states for the purpose of negotiating a peace settlement. Instead of professional diplomats, however, several states were represented by their head of state or government. Summit diplomacy downgraded the role of professional diplomats by initiating discussions at a higher level of national decision making. It did not by any means imply that the role of the professional diplomat had come to an end, but his or her role in subsequent years came to be increasingly shared by presidents, prime ministers, foreign ministers, and special negotiators. A summit meeting had certain self-evident advantages. It enabled those responsible for framing policy to conduct negotiations. It saved time and promoted greater flexibility through face-to-face negotiations between policy makers. Since then, but especially since the end of World War II, summit and minisummit negotiations have become a fairly common practice. It may hopefully lead to a situation where, through frequent meetings, heads of states and governments may develop a better knowledge and trust of each other and develop a relationship more conducive to successful international negotiations and harmony. It is also possible that the practice may well result in greater discord and disagreement due to personality clashes.

International negotiation at highest levels of decision making has also been encouraged by the revolution in communication and transportation which facilitates visits and personal contacts between heads of state and governments. The hotline between Moscow and Washington, the telephone connection in the White House in Washington and the prime minister's residence in Ottawa, the direct line between the White House and Number Ten Downing Street (in London), and other means of instant contact have revolutionized diplomacy.

Multilateral negotiations, a second aspect of open diplomacy, consist of conferences and meetings between representatives of many

---

[3] President Woodrow Wilson, "The Fourteen Points" (Address to a joint session of the Congress of the United States, January 8, 1918).

countries who try to reach agreement on matters of common concern. Very often, however, such conferences are transformed into brawling matches between national leaders as has been evidenced in meetings of the United Nations General Assembly and Security Council. Former Soviet Premier Khruschev's shoe-pounding on his desk and mutual recriminations between Israeli and Arab delegates are classic examples.

Open diplomacy has, ironically, been paralleled by development of undercover activity. In the older style of diplomacy, embassies and their staffs did not normally engage in espionage. It was considered to be beneath the dignity of professional diplomats. In modern diplomacy, espionage is considered to be a part of the normal operations of an embassy, and states make no attempt to hide this fact. Espionage is sometimes accompanied by subversion and sabotage. A more insidious aspect of modern diplomatic practice is to sow seeds of discord between the people of a state and its government. This is done widely through radio and press propaganda, and also by embassies and diplomatic missions which promote friendship societies "to cover the knaves who recruit the fools"[4] as it were.

Propaganda

In modern times the use of propaganda to distort and misrepresent the image of one's opponent in international affairs has become an important and accepted part of government activity. All states—great and small, dictatorial and democratic alike—use this method for the promotion of national interest and the achievement of their foreign policy goals. It has been repeatedly said that the essence of modern international politics is the struggle for the minds and loyalties of people. It is felt that more can be gained by manipulating public opinion than by striking physically at opponents through war. Propaganda is directed at opinion formation and political socialization. It aims to "influence opinion and conduct . . . in such a manner that the persons who adopt the opinions and behaviour indicated do so without making any definite search for reason."[5]

The chief devices used in the course of communication by propagandists fall in the following categories:

---

[4] Lord Vansitart, "Decline of Diplomacy" *Foreign Affairs* 28, no. 2 (January 1950): 183–34.

[5] C. F. Bartlett, "Aims of Political Propaganda" in *Public Opinion and Propaganda*," ed. Daniel Katz & Associates (New York: Holt, Rinehart & Winston, 1962) p. 64. Also, B. S. Murty, *Propaganda and World Public Order* (New Haven: Yale University Press, 1968).

1. *Name Calling:* The technique of giving any idea a bad label. The intention is to make the listeners reject and condemn the idea without examining the evidence.
2. *Glittering Generalities:* The technique of associating something with a "virtue word" with the intention of persuading the listener to accept and approve the thing without examining the evidence.
3. *Transfer:* The technique of associating the authority, approval, and prestige of some person or thing in order to make the latter acceptable to the listeners. In the reverse process, one "transfers" the authority, aversion, and disapproval of something or someone to another person or object to encourage the listeners to reject or disapprove it.
4. *Testimonial:* The technique of having some respected or hated person say, or so to attribute, that a given idea or program is good. Conversely, to have some respected or hated person say, or so to attribute, that a given idea or program is bad.
5. *Plain Folks:* The technique of trying to convince listeners that the propagandist and his or her ideas are good because they are "of the people," the plain folks.
6. *Card Stacking:* The technique of selecting and using facts or falsehoods, illustrations or distractions, and logical or illogical statements in order to present the listeners with the best or the worst possible case for an idea, program, person, or product.
7. *Band Wagon:* The technique of employing the theme, "Everybody . . . at least all of us . . . is doing it." By so presenting the situation, the propagandist attempts to convince listeners that all members of a group to which the listener belongs are accepting his or her program and the listener, too, therefore, should follow the crowd and "jump on the band wagon."

Propaganda as an instrument of foreign policy has its limits. It cannot substitute an alien set of values for an existing one. Propaganda can neither alter basic institutions, satisfy physical needs, nor secure a permanent substitution of words for deeds. At the same time, however, it can do a number of things which may not directly achieve policy objectives, but can pave the way for such achievement through an intelligent combination of propaganda and action. Propaganda can confuse the enemy, damage his or her morale, and put him or her on the defensive.

Economic Techniques

Economic factors may play a dual role in international politics as both goals and means. A foreign policy may aim to achieve economic goals through political action or, on the other hand, economic goods and services may be employed as a means for the satisfaction of political objectives. Economic techniques seek indirectly to promote policy objectives as opposed to the directness of diplomacy. While diplomacy involves face-to-face contact between representatives of states, economic methods are aimed at the total population of one country in the hope that popular reaction generated by them might oblige its decision makers to modify their actions to conform with the desires of the other party.

Economic techniques may be used to persuade other state systems to behave in a more congenial fashion or to coerce them into desired policy positions. This was seen, in recent years, in the imposition of an oil embargo by the Arab countries on the West, including the United States and Japan, following the Arab–Israeli War of 1973. The Arabs argued that economic and military aid by the industrialized countries to Israel had enabled it to defeat the Arabs in successive wars, to occupy their territory, and to adopt an intransigent attitude toward the settlement of the "Palestine question." The denial of vitally needed oil supplies was intended to force Israel's friends to change their policies and adopt a more friendly attitude towards the Arabs. Haunted by the spectre of collapsing national economies brought about by a continued scarcity of oil, many of the Western governments, including the United States, indeed modified their policies toward Israel and expressed increased support for the Arab cause. Gradually, the oil embargo was lifted. But the threat of its reimposition continues, if a settlement in the Middle East acceptable to the Arabs is not soon found.

It should be noted that, unlike diplomacy, economic techniques cannot be regularized as a steady and constant instrument of foreign policy. Their effectiveness is generally dependent upon the economic and political position of the countries involved and the nature of the situation. For example, one could hardly emphasize the effectiveness of economic means in the relationship between the United States and the Soviet Union. On the other hand, each has employed economic techniques to influence the smaller and underdeveloped nations. States in a strong economic and political position are able to offer or withhold more of what is needed by others; those in a weak position have little to give. An exception to this pattern, however, are weak states with a monopoly of certain goods and services in high demand, such as those countries which possess vast deposits of oil or rare minerals.

Foreign Aid

Following the end of World War II international society moved into a revolutionary era marked by the end of imperialism and colonialism.

The large number of independent countries created since then are infused with an ardent desire to develop their resources for the good of their peoples and the betterment of their economy. The world also witnessed the emergence of an ideological conflict between the Soviet Union and the Western powers. The professed aim of the Soviet Union was to promote the long-awaited "dictatorship of the proletariat," a development which would endanger Western economic interests and political security. The Soviet Union promised to use all available methods to reconstruct the world in its image. The Western powers responded with a wide variety of measures to "contain" this threat.

Between these two forces were placed the newly emergent nations. They were in dire need of economic development, social progress, and political stability. These circumstances inspired the development of the "new statecraft" in which foreign aid has been used as an economic instrument of foreign policy.[6] The United States and the Soviet Union traded economic assistance for political and military support.

Foreign aid generally consists of money and/or goods, though certain trade arrangements may in themselves also contain an element of aid. Aid may be designated as economic assistance or defence support. Economic assistance consists of aid used to strengthen the economy of the recipient. It is usually provided within the context of projects such as dams, highways, and urban development works. Defence support was the inevitable outgrowth of the formation of regional military organizations. It is intended to compensate a country for expenditures incurred in maintaining the degree of military preparedness required by the regional organization or demanded by the senior partner in the alliance. The psychology behind this course of action is that alliances give the rival great powers much needed military and political support in their global strategy against each other. Aid in the form of defence support is also offered as an incentive for others to join alliances.

Foreign aid, in most cases, is a *quid pro quo* arrangement between the donor and the recipient. The donor country normally expects political and military favours in return for aid. This, indeed, is especially the case with the great powers. A popular misconception is that foreign aid is based on some idealistic principle of social justice which makes it a moral responsibility of the economically advanced countries to assist the underdeveloped countries. In fact, foreign aid in modern international politics is a calculated act of high policy, except perhaps where it is offered to victims of natural disaster or people ravaged by warfare. Even then, aid may have its political overtones. In 1970 the Soviet Union was accused of using its mercy flights to earthquake victims in Peru as a means of gathering air reconnaissance information about Canadian and U.S. military deployments along the Atlantic coast.

---

[6] See George Liska, *New Statecraft* (Chicago: University of Chicago Press, 1960).

The politics involved in foreign aid transactions often provoke resentment, resistance, and retaliation between states caught in the donor-recipient relationship. Very often the recipient feels irked by the restrictions attached to foreign aid, by the favours expected in return, by the feeling that these impinge upon its political freedom, and by the psychologically offensive feeling of being at the receiving end of the line. Equally often, the donor is piqued at what it considers to be a lack of gratitude on the part of the recipient, or the pursuit of a two-faced policy, if political and military favours to the desired extent are not forthcoming in return for the aid received.

One could make an exception to this general operative pattern in the case of foreign aid from states that are considered to be middle powers, such as Canada, Belgium, Italy, and others. Obviously, their political stake in the establishment of a donor-recipient relationship is not as high on the scale as that of the great powers. In fact, the middle powers may themselves be at the receiving end in relation to a great power, or, at best, be among its political clientele. Aid from such states is relatively small in amount and may be motivated by a certain degree of humanitarian considerations. While they may not be instigated by the same political considerations as the great powers, they are, nonetheless, usually inspired by hopes of promoting foreign trade, enhancing national prestige, promoting national security, and maintaining a "positive" and reputable posture in world affairs.

Basic Objectives of Foreign Policy

A foreign policy consists of a set of ranked objectives which a government seeks to achieve in its relations with others. These goals differ from government to government depending upon their perceptions of their ability to successfully achieve them. There are some which are sought by all, irrespective of other considerations.

Territorial Integrity and Political Independence

Two common and interrelated foreign policy objectives are the maintenance of territorial integrity and political independence. Territorial integrity exists when a government is able to maintain control of the territory over which it claims jurisdiction. Political independence exists when this jurisdiction is unchallenged. Territory consists not only of land surface but the air space over it as well as coastal waters. Territorial integrity also means that revolutionary ferment (generated either internally or encouraged from outside and which threatens to break up a state's territory or poses threats of regional secession), must be contained and suppressed. Instigating secession is regarded as treason punishable by death in several countries.

The Nigerian Civil War of 1967–70, in which the central government of Nigeria successfully suppressed a threat of secession by the break-away state of Biafra, is indicative of the extent to which governments are willing to go to maintain their jurisdiction. Efforts by other countries to bring about a reconcilation between the warring factions and to send food and medical relief supplies to the Biafrans were stoutly opposed by the Nigerian Government as outside support to the rebels and thus interference in its internal affairs. Secessionist movements in Canada, on the other hand, have been treated as legitimate as long as they depend upon the mobilization of popular support and operate according to accepted constitutional patterns of behaviour, as has the Parti Québécois. The Front de Libération du Québec (FLQ) was outlawed when it resorted to terrorism. Whether the federal government would resort to the use of force to thwart a unilateral secession by Quebec is another question, although historical precedent elsewhere, the vigour of its response to the FLQ in the events of 1970, and popular support for the government would tend to give an affirmative answer.

The question of Canadian sovereignty over the Arctic is another example of a country's concern to maintain its territorial integrity. The Arctic has been traditionally regarded as a part of Canada. In recent years, the discovery of vast deposits of oil and attempts of certain U.S. interests to navigate Arctic waters aroused fears that Canadian sovereignty over the Arctic might be challenged. The demand for a positive declaration of sovereignty is an expression of the desire to emphasize to the world that the Arctic is a part of Canadian territory and its violation will not be acceptable.

National Security

Closely tied to the objective of territorial integrity and political independence is that of national security. It implies an atmosphere in which a state can exist free from threats to its independence and survival. Since there can be no guarantee of absolute security for any state, governments seek the highest degree of security which is reasonably attainable.

The ongoing debate in Canada over the extent of foreign and, particularly, American investment in the economy is really a debate over a national security issue. Over the years, many of the natural resources in the United States have been harnessed into the service of its economy, while, in contrast, a large part of Canadian resources have lain dormant due partly to a lack of capital and partly to a shortage of trained personnel and technology. The potential of Canada and the economic adventurism of American business has resulted in a tremendous flow of American capital and personnel across the 49th parallel, especially in the decades since World War II. Ordinarily, perhaps, this would not have posed a problem but for the fact that most of the principal offices of American firms with investments in Canada are located in the United States. Corporate policies are determined not by the subsidiaries but by their principals across the border. From a purely economic point of view, even this may be overlooked, but the intimate relationship between economics and politics creates complications. U.S. subsidiaries in Canada have been directed by their principals across the border not to sell their products to certain countries against whom the U.S. government has imposed a trade embargo, though Canada has not. These principals do so under pressure from the U.S. government which demands compliance with the Trading with the Enemy Act. This complicated politicoeconomic situation has, on several occasions, resulted in a conflict of interest between the Canadian government on the one hand and American investors on the other.

The extent of American capital investment in Canada has inspired the revival of economic nationalism. Many Canadians feel that the increasing American takeover of Canadian business should be prevented; flow of American capital into Canada should be restrained; limitations should be imposed on the expatriation of profits from Canada to the United States; U.S. firms should be required to sell more of their stocks to Canadians; and a larger number of Canadians should be hired at the managerial level to work in Canadian subsidiaries. There are others who advocate outright nationalization of all American investments in Canada. These economic nationalists fear that if restrictions are not placed on U.S. investments in Canada, the country will, in the not too distant future, become, at worst, the 51st state of the United States. At best, such extensive foreign control of our natural resources, productive process, and general investment can seriously undermine national security if the foreign investors decide to use their economic control as levers for securing political and military concessions.[7]

National security is also sought through the maintenance of adequately equipped and trained armed forces. The mere possession of a large army or an abundance of weapons or both is, however, not sufficient. The 30-year history of the Arab–Israeli conflict offers an excellent proof of this. The Arabs, who outnumber the Israelis both in

---

[7] See A. E. Safarian, *Foreign Ownership in Canadian Industry* 2d ed. (Toronto: McGraw–Hill, 1973). Kari Levitt, *Silent Surrender: The Multinational Corporation in Canada* (Toronto: Macmillan, 1970). Abraham Rotstein, *Precarious Homestead* (Toronto: New Press, 1973).

armed forces and armaments, have been able to record only one victory, more psychological than military, in 1973, due mainly to the qualitative superiority of the numerically inferior Israeli forces. Quantity and quality are of equal importance to military force if it is to provide reasonable assurances of national security. Personnel have to be trained in the proper use and handling of equipment and maintained in a state of constant readiness premised on a long-range plan of offence and defence. Unless military establishments are maintained on such a basis, they will not be much more effective in providing national security than a rag-tag volunteer force.

National Interest

"National interest" is a very nebulous and vague term. Ordinarily, it means those factors, forces, and needs that are vital to the security and welfare of the nation. The term is loose enough to include practically any set of economic, political, military, or other factors, however remotely or intimately connected they may be to national security. A determination of what does and does not constitute national interest can sometimes be one of the most unprincipled, unscrupulous, and arbitrary decisions made in the determination of foreign policies. European subjugation of Asia and Africa in the 18th and 19th centuries was undertaken in the national interest. Hitler demanded *Lebensraum* (living space) and helped to ignite the fires of World War II in the cause of national interest; the United States fought a war half way around the world in Vietnam in its national interest; Indians and Pakistanis have remained at odds with each other over Kashmir for over a quarter of a century each to protect its national interest; and Rhodesia and South Africa practice systematic racial discrimination each in its national interest. Briefly, national interest has been asserted as being equivalent to national security so that anything that even remotely bears upon national security falls under the umbrella of this term.

CONDITIONING FACTORS OF FOREIGN POLICY

A government, in formulating its foreign policy, must take into consideration not only the goals it wishes to achieve, but also those basic facts of existence which limit or extend its ability to act in a particular manner and determine its status in the international society. They consist of such domestic factors as the geographic location of a state, its population, resources, ideological orientation, and political beliefs. External conditioning factors may be summed up in the existence of international law and the application of the concept of "power" in international relations.

Geographic Factors

Geographic factors are of significance in the determination of a country's foreign policy goals. The study of these factors and their effect on the state is referred to as geopolitics. Geopolitics was popularized in post-World War I Germany which sought geographic justification for national political goals. As a result of its manipulation by Nazi Germany, the term has been largely discarded and replaced by the concept of political geography. It implies

The delineation and exploration of conflict areas, internal political spatial variation of large nations, territorial viability of small national and developing states, the distribution and interaction of political philosophies, ideologies, processes, behaviour and problems.[8]

Geographic factors which condition the determination of foreign policy goals are many and varied. The size of a state, topography, climate, and location are of importance. Proximity to a large and powerful state, especially if relations are not cordial, is also a conditioning factor. The nature and length of the states' borders, too, have a bearing on the formulation of foreign policy.

Location is an important factor in the determination of a state's military policy. Insular states have land areas surrounded by water and their military organizations are generally oriented towards the maintenance of naval power. Great Britain and Japan are two examples of insular countries which played a major role in world affairs in the 19th and the first half of the 20th centuries because their naval forces dominated the seas and oceans around the globe. Countries such as Germany and the Soviet Union have tended to build large and powerful land forces. A country such as the United States, because of its location, has had to develop a more integrated strategy for national security.

Population

The size of a country's population as a determinant of foreign policy goals should be fairly obvious. A large population may mean a large work force to perform the tasks needed to further foreign policy goals. However, this is not always the case. Work force does not mean simply a head count of the population but specifically includes skilled labour and technicians who are capable of performing the necessary tasks. Population is, therefore, a resource like many others, which needs to be properly managed and adequately trained. Most of the major nations of the world, such as the United States, the U.S.S.R., Germany,

---

[8] Allen S. Schneider et al., *A Dictionary of Basic Geography* (Boston: Allyn & Bacon, 1970) p. 157. Also, pp. 87–88.

and Japan, have large work forces as well as large populations because they have successfully harnessed their human resources. On the other hand, others such as India, Indonesia, and Pakistan, despite large populations, have an inadequate work force.

Nevertheless, the size of the population is a significant contributor to the capability of a state to promote its goals. Nazi Germany, Fascist Italy, and Imperial Japan all sought to encourage a higher birthrate so as to obtain workers for their expansionist ambitions. The size of the Chinese populations has a lot to do with the posture and statements emanating from Peking. The teeming millions cause concern among China's neighbours about their prestige and influence as well as their territorial integrity. The rate of population growth is also an important consideration. A reasonable rate of growth offers a reservoir of workers for the future; a declining rate denies that prospect while an excessive rate generates other external and internal problems. A further aspect of the population factor is the presence of racial, ethnic, cultural, and linguistic minorities and their role in the internal politics of the state.

Economic Resources

National economic resources consist of natural resources as well as industrial and agricultural productivity. In this age of interdependence, no state is totally self-sufficient. Some, due to the nature of their geography and the availability of natural resources, enjoy an advantage over others in the production of particular goods and services. The extent of the demand for these goods determines the extent of the dependence of others upon the producer. Obviously then, the more economically dependent a country is upon others, the less free it is to determine and pursue its own goals. By the same token, this freedom of action and decision is enhanced by the degree of balance between the availability of raw materials and its industrial and agricultural productivity.

Economic resources are of vital importance to national security. Dependence upon others for the supply of necessary armaments weakens security and undermines strategy. It is indispensable for the maintenance of effective national security that a government be able to produce and stockpile at least its basic armament needs, anticipate and estimate its future needs, and endeavour to seek its requirements from outside sources through favourable trade agreements. The ability to secure needed goods and services is enhanced by the amount and variety of them which a country is able to offer in return. Several other economic factors have a bearing on a state's foreign policy and its position in the international society. They include such things as foreign trade, the balance of payments, strength and stability of the national currency in the world market, intergovernmental loans and debts, and foreign investment.

Nationalism and Internationalism

Nationalism and internationalism are two opposing forces which bear substantially upon foreign policy goals. Nationalism impels a people to look inwards, to consider their interests first—an attitude which may generate international tension and result in conflict and wars. Internationalism, on the other hand, inspires them to look outwards, to consider the interests and welfare of others, and to adopt flexible attitudes. A nation should seek to fulfill its interests in a manner so as to contribute to the progress and prosperity of humanity as a whole since it, after all, is only a part of humanity and cannot long prosper if the whole is diseased and debilitated. This, of course, is not to deride nationalism or to suggest that it should be sacrificed or even subordinated to internationalism; it simply means that a coordinated pattern of interaction between the two is more conducive to the reduction of international tension and maintenance of peace. The pursuit of internationalism has been most obvious in Europe since 1945 where geographic, military, and economic problems have contributed to bringing the European states closer together. Several successful attempts at European cooperation, wherein the countries think less in terms of a state and more in terms of a European community, have been made in the post-World War II period.

In Asia and Africa, nationalism was inspired by hatred and fear of foreign rule. They had been largely onlookers of the progress of modern industry and technology without appreciably benefitting from it. Under colonial rule, their energies had been suppressed, initiative discouraged, and participation limited in the formulation and execution of official policy. The net result was that when the peoples of these areas became immersed in nationalism, and once they succeeded in gaining independence, they elevated the state to a level which had been common in Europe prior to World War II. Fear of the foreigner and suspicion of his or her motives acted as powerful forces against the generation of a spirit of internationalism. In many cases, internationalism has implied not much more to them than the obligation of the Western world to help in their development without legitimately demanding or even expecting anything in return.

Ideology

The foreign policy of a state reflects its national goals and values which are conditioned by the political, economic, social, and cultural environment in the society. An ideology is a set of integrated and persistent principles which provide sanction for political leadership and action. It is, therefore, logical that governments which are ideologically oriented should not only seek ideological justification for their foreign policy goals but also couch them in ideological jargon.

The role of ideology as a determinant of foreign policy is a subject of some controversy. Those who believe that ideology influences foreign policy point out that ideology establishes and conditions the basic goals which countries seek to achieve. It can be argued, for instance, that the U.S.S.R. dominates Eastern Europe and promotes its influence elsewhere in order to bring about the extension of the international socialist commonwealth. The Soviet military intervention in Hungary in 1956 and in Czechoslovakia in 1968 may be explained in these terms; they were an attempt to defend socialism (of the Soviet variety) in countries where it had already been established against "bourgeois reactionary" enemies of the people. The Brezhnev Doctrine, enunciated by the first secretary of the Communist party of the U.S.S.R., Leonid Brezhnev, following the Soviet military occupation of Czechoslovakia, spells out very clearly this linkage between ideology and foreign policy. It asserts "the right of the Soviet Union to determine whether socialism was in danger in any country of the 'socialist commonwealth' and take whatever measure deemed proper to set things right. It is not necessary for any authority to request help . . . ."[9]

Ideology may also be considered a smokescreen used to conceal the real motives behind foreign policy. Mussolini used the Fascist ideology, including a nostalgia for the glories of the Roman Empire, to justify the expansionist behaviour of his government. More recently, the conflict between China and Soviet Union, which, according to the Chinese, is the result of Soviet deviation from traditional Marxist–Leninist ideology, can well be considered as politically motivated. It is a dispute that has been generated by basic differences in the Soviet and Chinese interpretation of world events and each other's actions: (1) Chinese desire to become the vanguard of communism in Asia and undermine Soviet influence there, (2) China's attempts to reduce its dependence upon the Soviet Union for its national security by developing its own nuclear capability, and (3) by old territorial and border disputes between the two countries.

Imperialism and Colonialism

"Imperialism" and "colonialism" are two words in modern political vocabulary which are very loosely used. The ideas associated with

---

[9] Robert G. Wessen, *Soviet Foreign Policy in Perspective* (Georgetown, Ont.: Irwin–Dorsey Ltd., 1969), p. 382.

them generally stand condemned and the words are used more as epithets than as a description of policy. Great powers use these terms to criticize their rival's policies with which they do not agree; the new countries of Asia and Africa use them continually to condemn policies of the great powers which do not meet their approval; and the New Left uses them indiscriminately to criticize any and every aspect of world politics which does not conform with its conceptions.

Both terms are very old. Imperialism was known at the dawn of recorded history. In fact, much of what is generally called "history" concerns the rise and fall of empires. Imperialism is the process of acquiring, often through the use of force, additional territories by an independent state. These territories have generally been part of other states. The largest empires known in history have been the British and the French of the 20th century, the Spanish in the 18th century, the Mongolian in the 13th century, the Roman in the 2nd century, and the Persian in the 5th century, B.C.

Colonialism is also an old concept. The Greeks were the most enterprising colonists of the pre-Christian era, sending out small groups of people to many corners of the Mediterranean and the Black seas in order to form new settlements. It was in this manner that the Phoenicians created Carthage, which disputed the control of the Mediterranean basin with Rome in the third century B.C. During the Crusades in the Middle Ages, European princes supported a number of religio-political orders which sought to establish small colonies of people in what is now northeastern Poland and the Lithuanian S.S.R. and in Palestine. In modern times colonialism and imperialism have merged with the colonizing of imperial territories in North and South America, North and South Africa, and Australia. The far-flung European empires served as vehicles for the resettlement of over 100 million Europeans in the largest migration in human history.

The motives for imperialism and colonialism have been many and varied. British imperialists justified their nation's policies in the name of the "White Man's Burden," meaning thereby that Western civilization was superior to all other civilizations and it was the moral responsibility of the Europeans to carry the fruits of this civilization to the inferior peoples of Asia and Africa. Lenin, in his work of the same name, called imperialism the highest stage of capitalism.[10] He posited that imperial powers sought colonies so that their economic resources could be utilized for the benefit of the capitalistic interests in the home country.

The era of imperialism and colonialism in its classical form came to

______

[10] V. I. Lenin, *Imperialism: The Highest Stage of Capitalism* (New York: International Publishers, 1939).

an end following World War II. The process of decolonization or the termination of European domination over the peoples of Asia and Africa resulted in the grant of independence to most colonies. But the unhappy and servile experience of imperial domination had generated a feeling of intense aversion toward the imperial powers. On becoming independent, the new nations were inclined to be doubtful and suspicious of the motives of the former imperial powers and wary of developing intimate economic and political relations with them for fear that they might attempt an imperial revival.

Imperialism in the traditional sense has been replaced, in the minds of many, with what is known as neocolonialism, or, more correctly, neoimperialism. This is a by-product of the protracted struggle between the United States and the Soviet Union (Cold War). Both have sought allies and friends through treaty relationships, supporters for their position in world assemblies, and military bases in foreign lands. The establishment of such relationships involves advance commitments and an infringement of the freedom of decision and action of the weaker parties to this relationship. While technically the parties in these relationships may be considered sovereign and independent, politically they are subservient to the senior partner. It is argued that the position of small nations in this situation is, in reality, that of satellites of the great and powerful nations.

One manifestation of the fear of neocolonialism has been the adoption of a policy of nonalignment by many of the newly independent countries. It is motivated by the desire to maintain an independent posture in international relations and make policies and decisions uninfluenced by outside sources. The Cold War has been viewed as basically a conflict between the United States and the U.S.S.R. in which the contenders would not hesitate to undermine the interests of small nations if it suited their purposes. The nonaligned countries contend that their approach to issues is determined by the merits of the case rather than a predisposition toward one side or the other. Being tied to one of them through alliance or treaties or by following a pro-Western or a pro-Soviet policy would widen the scope of the conflict and add to international tension. Peace, they argue, will not be achieved through alignment with one power bloc or the other but through the pursuit of an independent approach to issues such as the maintenance of national and individual freedom and the elimination of racial discrimination. Instead, they seek to act as mediators between the contending forces.

International Law

A set of rules, laws, and norms is essential for maintaining order in a national society. So also is one necessary for maintaining order in the international society even if no "international system" exists. This body of rules, laws, and norms which serves to limit the sovereignty of states in the international society is called *international law*. Oppenheim defines it as that "body of customary and treaty rules which are considered legally binding by States, in their intercourse with each other."[11] Another scholar defines international law as that body of laws which is "applicable to states in their mutual relations and to individuals in their relations with states."[12]

The existence of international law, like national law, has long been recognized though Hugo Grotius, a Dutch scholar, was the first to write a treatise on it entitled *On The Law of War And Peace* published in 1628. Several scholars following Grotius were stimulated by his thinking and their endeavours resulted in a number of other works on the subject. Grotius is, nonetheless, regarded as the father of modern international law.

International law may be divided into three areas: law of peace, law of war, and law of neutrality. The law of war seeks to regulate and control the conduct of war by countries by attempting to define a legal state of war and by delineating conditions under which war may be conducted. Under the latter fall such things as the rights and duties of belligerents, treatment of prisoners of war, the position of humanitarian groups and institutions operating on or near the front—hospitals, churches—and prohibition of genocide.

The law of peace seeks to provide a pattern of acceptable behaviour for governments in their normal relations with each other. It deals with such matters as territorial integrity, political sovereignty, and peaceful means for the settlement of international disputes. The rights and immunities of diplomatic personnel, conditions governing the grant or withdrawal of diplomatic recognition, sanctity, and validity of international treaties are also included in it.

The law of neutrality rests on the basic belief that a condition of neutrality imposes certain responsibilities on a state, the most important of which is that the neutral state should not give any direct or indirect assistance to those at war. At the same time, it is the responsibility of the belligerents to respect the neutrality of a state and not to violate it without just cause.

A distinction should be made between international law and international legislation. International law, as explained earlier, refers to that body of rules which govern the intercourse of states with each other. Most international law is customary in that it results from usage

---

[11] Oppenheim, *International Law: A Treatise,* 8th ed., edited by H. Lauterpacht (London: Longman's Green, 1955), pp. 4–5.

[12] Phillip C. Jessup, *A Modern Law of Nations.* (Hamden, Conn.: Archon Books, 1968), p. 17.

and conventions which have become accepted as more or less binding. Matters relating to diplomatic immunity and protocol and coastal waters are examples of customary international law. International legislation simply means that duly concluded treaties between states ratified in accordance with their constitutional processes assume the form of law. Provisions of these treaties are equally binding upon their governments as well as their nationals. Labour conventions sponsored by the International Labour Organization (ILO), genocide conventions under the Geneva Agreement of 1948, and the United Nations Declaration of Fundamental Human Rights are examples of international legislation.

POWER IN INTERNATIONAL RELATIONS

International relations result from the convergence of the foreign policies of sovereign and equal states who endeavour to maximize their advantage and enhance their power in relation to others. Power is both the product of the environment of a country as well as its ability to use the resources available to it. A country may be weak because it has few resources and a small population or it may be weak and have great resources and a large population. Others may be strong because of their strategic positions, leadership, or the skill and determination of their citizens. Egypt has 15 times the population of Israel and considerably more resources, yet has suffered three disastrous military defeats at the hands of the smaller state. Turkey has been coveted by the Russians for centuries because of the former's control of the only outlet from the Black Sea, yet, the smaller and weaker country has been able to use this geographic power to continually frustrate Russian ambitions by allying itself with stronger opponents of Russian expansion. The billions of dollars held in Western banks by Arab oil interests represent a form of power. Withdrawal of these funds could be disastrous to the economy of many countries.

Obviously, power is related to the effective use of natural and social factors and not to their mere existence. Power is the ability to influence the behaviour of another government in accordance with one's own ends and, therefore, rests on a complex calculation involving resources, their efficiency, and a determination to put them to use. This last fact may be most dramatically illustrated by the long and frustrating Vietnamese wars, where the overwhelming forces and resources of first the French and then the Americans availed them little in return.

Balance of Power

Power, then, is born of the relationship between two or more parties in which each attempts to influence the behaviour of others to suit its own purposes. It does not remain constant nor is its increase or decline absolute; it is always relative. This relativity is in itself a limiting factor upon the use of power, since it implies that not only are there stronger and weaker parties in a given relationship but that each realizes its respective position. This realization on the part of the weaker party naturally encourages it to meet this disparity through whatever means possible, in order to establish a situation where its goals will not be completely submerged in the drives of the stronger party. Such a situation is called a balance of power and acts as the critical limiting factor on the behaviour of governments within the international arena.

There are a number of variants of the balance of power concept. It may refer to a situation in which the power of one state or a group of states is literally balanced by or equivalent to the power of others, for example, a state of power equilibrium. When for instance, people read in the newspapers that a balance of power exists between the United States and the Soviet Union, it means that the power of one is countered and balanced by the roughly equivalent power of the other so as not to allow either a decided advantage.

Second, balance of power may refer to a situation in which there is no literal balance but there is stability. When, for instance, the U.S. government says that any massive supply of Soviet military hardware to the Arabs would necessitate the supply of similar U.S. hardware to Israel to maintain the balance of power in the Middle East, it, in effect, means that the existing disequilibrium between Israel and the Arabs would need to be maintained in order to deter the latter from undermining and threatening Israel's political existence.

Balance of power may also refer to any distribution of power irrespective of its particular condition. Just as the words "rich" and "poor" refer to a person's economic status without indicating how rich or poor he or she is, so also balance of power could refer to any prevailing pattern of power distribution irrespective of whether it is balanced or imbalanced. When, for instance, it is said that Canada's withdrawal from NATO would disturb the existing balance of power in Europe, the reference is to the nature rather than to the extent of the change.

States have several alternative methods at their disposal through which they seek to maintain a balance of power. A common method of maintaining a balance is to form alliances and conclude treaties of security guarantees and military assistance. Alliances aim to pool the resources of their members against an actual or an imaginary enemy. During the interwar years, France sought to promote a balance of power against Germany by seeking security guarantees from Britain and the United States and concluding treaties of guarantee and military assistance with Belgium, Poland, Czechoslavakia, Yugoslavia, and

Romania. In the post–World War II period, alliances have assumed the form of regional military organizations such as the North Atlantic Treaty Organization (NATO) and the Warsaw Treaty Organization commonly referred to as the Warsaw Pact.

The effectiveness of an alliance depends upon the goodwill of its members. Very often the major powers in an alliance, uncertain of the loyalty of an ally, may decide to seek additional assurance by intervening in its internal affairs. Politically, this may be achieved by strengthening or undermining a particular government in order to keep it in power or replace it with a more cooperative one. Militarily, a threat of invasion is often sufficient if the victim has nowhere else to turn. The objective is to either force the recalcitrant government to adhere to the obligations of the alliance or to overthrow it and establish a more friendly and obliging government.

As long as war remains the ultimate instrument for the settlement of disputes between nations, armament will continue to be important in promoting a balance of power. Attempts on the part of one state to increase its armaments may provoke similar action elsewhere. It is natural that a government would not wish to see a potential enemy possessing a military advantage. By seeking to maintain a balance or to preserve or erase military advantages, governments may be instrumental in starting an armaments race.

A cruder way of maintaining balance of power is the temporary or permanent seizure of territory of a weak and small state by a major power, generally through military occupation. Such an act gives to the major power a tactical or strategic advantage by bringing it within closer striking distance to its enemy, by establishing military bases, or by drawing a military cordon around the adversary. Such an advantage tips the balance of power in favour of the state seizing territory. During World War II, for instance, Soviet and British forces occupied Iran so as to preempt a pro-Nazi take-over which would have given Germany a strategic proximity to the southern borders of the Soviet Union. For over a decade the Israeli refusal to withdraw its forces to its pre-1967 borders, without a peace treaty being concluded with the surrounding Arab states, has been motivated by similar considerations. Seizure of territory motivated by balance of power considerations was a common occurrence during the era of imperialism. European powers seized colonies on the grounds that if they did not, their rivals might do so, and thereby alter the balance of power.

A *buffer state* is a relatively small and weak nation located between two contending states which acts as a wedge between them, since neither of the rivals would be willing to allow the other to annex the additional territory for fear of tipping the balance of power against them. Buffer zones are considered to be a useful way of not only keeping the competing forces separated but also maintaining the independence of the small nation. The latter, of course, depends upon the continued acceptance of the buffer by the parties. Historically, Poland has served as a buffer between Russia and Germany and the small and mountainous kingdom of Afghanistan served as the buffer between British India and Czarist Russia.

Finally, another way of maintaining a balance of power is through the technique called divide and conquer. Competing states endeavour to wean away each other's allies, not necessarily to win them over to their side but to detach them from the other and neutralize them. This does not directly add to the power of the seducer but it does decrease the power of the other side. Current policies of both the major powers in world politics are channeled in this direction.

There was a time in the 1950s when nonalignment was considered as immoral by both sides and there was a general feeling that a country which is not on one side is necessarily on the other. With the growing popularity of nonalignment in Asia and Africa, both the United States and the Soviet Union recognized in it a means of preventing the other from gaining allies among the nonaligned countries. They not only accepted nonalignment but indirectly encouraged it. The United States and the Soviet Union endeavour, often successfully, to neutralize each other's allies in return for assistance in one form or another.

Balance of Terror

A new, though related phrase, "the balance of terror" has been coined to reflect the international distribution of power in the nuclear age. The balance of power concept was based on the understanding that a state with a definite power advantage on its side may be able to win victory in war. Discovery of nuclear energy and the awesome arsenal of weapons developed in its wake has led to a situation where a state with an advantage of nuclear weapons on its side may win a war, but the fruits of victory would not be worth the price. As long as only one side had a monopoly over nuclear weapons, it kept the other terrorized and prevented it from making aggressive moves that may lead to an all-out war. When both sides gained possession of nuclear weapons, they terrorized each other and the whole world. This restrains them from the pursuit of policies that may turn out to be explosive. Paradoxically, the effective guarantee of peace as well as the danger of war today appear to lie in the possession of nuclear weapons by the major powers.

The ideas of massive retaliation, limitation on the testing of nuclear devices, and preventing their proliferation are corollaries of the balance of terror. Massive retaliation implies that major powers should concentrate on developing their capacity to retaliate more than their capacity to strike. The fear of nuclear retaliation would deter a state from making the first strike. Limitations on nuclear testing are designed to restrict the development of newer and more powerful nuclear weapons. Preventing their proliferation is motivated by the fear that the larger the number of countries which possess nuclear weapons, the greater will be the danger of their being used and plunging the entire world into a nuclear holocaust. Such a spread of nuclear weapons has recently gained momentum with the explosion of a nuclear bomb by India and the publicly stated determination of a number of states, such as Argentina, to develop their own.

A common desire on the part of both the United States and the Soviet Union, born of the balance of terror, is to prevent the outbreak of smaller wars and control those which cannot be prevented. They are unwilling to be involved in a major war in which chances of an outright victory are remote. A small war may well spread and involve the major powers with little to be gained. The balance of terror not only keeps major powers from going to war with each other but also obliges them to seek satisfaction of their national interests through other means. There has been only one instance since the end of World War II where the two major nuclear powers were involved in a direct confrontation, that being the 1962 Cuban Missile Crisis.

RECOMMENDED READINGS

Beres, Louis René, and Targ, Harry R. *Reordering the Planet: Constructing Alternative Futures*. Boston: Allyn & Bacon, 1974.

Brierly, J. L. *The Law of Nations*. 6th ed. New York: Oxford University Press, 1963.

Burton, J. W. *International Relations: A General Theory*. Cambridge: Cambridge University Press, 1965.

Clarkson, Stephen, ed. *An Independent Foreign Policy for Canada*. Toronto: McClelland & Stewart, Ltd., 1963.

Coplin, William D. *Introduction to International Politics*. 2d ed. Chicago: Rand McNally, 1974.

Deutsch, Karl W. *Analysis of International Relations*. Englewood Cliffs, N.J.: Prentice–Hall, 1968.

Farrell, Barry R. *Making of Canadian Foreign Policy*. Scarborough, Ont.: Prentice–Hall, 1969.

Finlay, David J., and Hovet, Thomas. Jr., *7304: International Relations on the Planet Earth*. New York: Harper & Row, 1975.

Hobson, J. A. *Imperialism: A Study*. London: Allen & Unwin, 1902.

Holsti, K. J. *International Politics*. 2d ed. Englewood Cliffs, N.J.: Prentice–Hall, 1972.

Johnson, E. A. J., ed. *Dimensions of Diplomacy*. Baltimore: Johns Hopkins Press, 1964.

Lerche, Charles O., Jr., and Said, A. A. *Concepts of International Politics*. 2d ed. Scarborough, Ont.: Prentice–Hall, 1965.

Levitt, Kari. *Silent Surrender: The Multinational Corporation in Canada*. Toronto: Macmillan, 1970.

Morgenthau, Hans J. *Politics Among Nations*. New York: A. A. Knopf, 1961.

Nicolson, Harold. *Diplomacy*. London: Oxford University Press, 1950.

Organski, A. F. K. *World Politics*. 2d ed. New York: A. A. Knopf, 1962.

Rosenbaum, Naomi. *Readings in the International Political System*. Englewood Cliffs, N.J.: Prentice–Hall, 1970.

Rotstein, Abraham. *Precarious Homestead*. Toronto: New Press, 1973.

Schuman, Frederick L. *International Politics*. 7th ed. Toronto: McGraw–Hill, 1969.

Schwarzenberger, George. *Manual of International Law*. 4th ed. New York: Praeger, 1960.

Stoessinger, John G. *The Might of Nations*. 4th ed. New York: Random House, 1973.

Strausz–Hupé, Robert, and Hazard, Harry W. *The Idea of Colonialism*. New York: Prager, 1958.

Thompson, D. C. and Swanson, R. F. *Canadian Foreign Policy: Options and Perspectives*. Toronto: McGraw–Hill Ryerson, 1971.

Thordarson, Bruce. *Trudeau and Foreign Policy: A Study in Decision-Making*. Toronto: Oxford University Press, 1972.

13

Towards an International Political System

THE GROWTH of a multitude of limiting factors upon the freedom and sovereignty of states has led in the last century to the constitution of a rudimentary international political system, the actors of which are not individual persons but governments themselves. The creation of alliances and regional organizations has been followed by the realization that some formal decision-making mechanism must be developed to make them effective and satisfactory to all their members. The slow accretion of customs and rules guiding international political behaviour has resulted in an ambiguous and voluntaristic international law. The global interdependence created by technology and communications has led people to see themselves as both national citizens as well as members of the wider human community. The major impulse behind these developments, however, has been the horror caused by wars resulting from the imperfect working of the balance of power principle.

While World War I was still raging, the leaders of the world began to cast about for a better principle on which to organize the relation between nations and create firmer guarantees of world peace and security. The concept of collective security was advanced as a substitute for the balance of power.

COLLECTIVE SECURITY

The idea of collective security was proposed in an embryonic version as early as the 14th century in Dante Alighieri's scheme for the preservation of peace in Europe. Subsequently several Western political thinkers elaborated upon this principle and asserted its usefulness

335

as an effective means for maintaining world peace. Collective security, however, as a principle of international political behaviour, would impinge upon states' sovereignty and circumscribe their freedom to wage war. Governments, therefore, relegated to the bookshelf all projects for preserving international peace through collective security.[1]

It was not until the beginning of the present century that the idea began to gain increasing acceptance with politicians and statesmen. U.S. President Theodore Roosevelt endorsed it in 1902 and again in 1910. He further elaborated upon it during World War I and warned against reliance on balance of power as a means for preserving international peace. At the same time there was a spurt of official and unofficial activity in Europe and North America aimed at developing methods of collective security. President Woodrow Wilson became the first active head of state to not only incorporate the idea as a principle of his foreign policy but also to translate it into political practice.[2] His conviction about the effectiveness of collective security led him to persuade other governments to create an international organization, the League of Nations, to preserve and safeguard international peace and security at the conclusion of World War I. In an address to the U.S. Congress generally known as "The Fourteen Points," in January 1918, Wilson proposed a program, "the only possible program," of world peace, the last item of which suggested "A general association of nations must be formed under specific covenants for the purpose of affording mutual guarantees of political independence and territorial integrity to great and small states alike." Armed with his Fourteen Points, Wilson travelled to Paris to play the role of peacemaker of the world and architect of the Leage of Nations. Since then collective security has become a commonly used, though much distorted and often maligned, concept.

Main Principles and Assumptions

The balance of power is premised on the notion of providing security to one group of states against another; in other words, security of some against some, a kind of selective security. It operates through externally oriented competitive alignments reflecting the belief that a country should join with others to resist aggression only if its own security is affected. The balance of power is valued because it leaves states with considerable freedom to manoeuvre in the pursuit of national objectives.

---

[1] See L. L. Leonard, *International Organization* (Toronto: McGraw–Hill, 1951), chap. 2.

[2] See Inis L. Claude, Jr., *Power and International Relations* (New York: Random House, 1962), chap. 4.

Collective security, on the other hand, is based on the belief that peace and the responsibility for its maintenance is indivisible, that the international society has become so closely knit that a breach of peace in one place threatens international peace in general, that aggression committed and condoned in one part of the world opens the doors to aggression in other places, and that restrictions need to be placed on the ability of countries to wage war. Instead of operating on the basis of externally oriented competitive alignments, they should pool their resources to resist aggression anywhere, regardless of the aggressor or the circumstances. Such an arrangement would then guarantee the security of all states against all states by all the members of the international community.

It is an ostensibly simple scheme for maintaining international peace and tranquility; however, collective security is based on a set of basic assumptions. Its successful implementation as a mode of international behaviour depends on the extent to which these assumptions are sustained by national action and policy.[3]

1. It assumes that interest in resistance to aggression is universal and equal among all countries notwithstanding any other economic or political consideration.

2. It assumes the existence of a universally accepted definition of aggression that would be used to determine which of the parties is the aggressor and action will be taken quickly enough so that the conflict could be prevented from expanding.

3. It assumes that members of the international community are not restricted by other commitments in their freedom and ability to join in whatever action is taken against an aggressor.

4. It assumes a preponderance of power, in contrast to a balance of power, whereby the members' resources in the pursuit of collective action would be so overwhelming that the aggressor would be unable to oppose it. The aggressor's awareness of the actual existence or potential availability of such overwhelming power hopefully would be enough to deter it from committing aggression.

5. Finally, it assumes that if a country is foolhardy enough to persist in aggressive actions despite the overwhelming preponderance of political and military force pitted against it, it will be assuredly vanquished.

It is evident that the last two assumptions are basically correct. Available evidence of the behaviour of states, however, throws some doubt about the validity of the first three.

---

[3] See A. F. K. Organski, *World Politics*, 2d ed. (New York: A. A. Knopf, 1962), pp. 409–19; Inis L. Claude, Jr., *Swords into Plowshares*, 3d ed. (New York: Random House, 1964), chap. 12.

The first assumption is that all countries have equal abhorrence of and interest in resisting aggression, irrespective of all other considerations. Though they may publicly profess equal interest in resisting aggression, the motivations behind foreign policy are many and varied. The concept of national interest, for example, which is a goal of foreign policy, runs counter to the idea of collective security, and a suitable compromise between two such diametrically opposed concepts in international relations has not been easy to find. It is especially true that great powers are often inclined to look the other way if their interests are not directly threatened by an act of aggression and the aggressor is allowed to have his way with the victim.

The second assumption underlines another serious difficulty in the enforcement of collective security. There does not exist a universally accepted definition of aggression. Modern international relations, unlike other periods in the history of the world community, are plagued not only by the problem of military aggression but a wide variety of other types as well: "permissible and impermissible" aggression, economic aggression, psychological aggression, and cultural aggression. Governments disagree not only on the nature of military aggression but also on which particular kinds of action under the other classifications are tantamount to aggression and which are not. Various attempts, first by the League of Nations and then by the United Nations Organization and their numerous committees and commissions, to define aggression and codify acts which could be considered aggressive have been abortive. Many governments argue that a rigid definition of aggression can never be sufficiently comprehensive and, therefore, the determination of what constitutes aggression should be through political consensus rather than on the basis of rigid standards. Though the argument has merit, it overlooks the inherent possibility that a political determination of aggression leaves it open to manipulations and manoeuvrings which may make a mockery of collective security.[4]

Another problem of collective security is that it can be invoked only after an act of aggression has been committed. This reduces collective security to a curative measure aimed at containing aggression and minimizing damage rather than a preventive measure seeking to halt the outbreak of war. This could occur only if it were possible to prejudge the aggressor, which is neither politically wise nor justifiable.

The third assumption is that countries are equally free and able to join in collective action against an aggressor. Despite its interest in resisting aggression, a country may not always be able to do so, since,

---

[4] See B. S. Murty, *Propaganda and World Public Order* (New Haven, Conn.: Yale University Press, 1968); also Julius Stone, *Aggression and World Public Order* (Berkeley: University of California Press, 1958).

for instance, its military force may be committed elsewhere. During the Korean War, France was unable to participate on the side of the United Nations because its forces were committed to the preservation of its colonies in Indochina. Sometimes a government may fear aggression from other quarters and may not find it expedient to send its forces to fight somewhere else. India and Pakistan both professedly found themselves in this position. Each feared aggression from the other and thus excused itself from sending forces to Korea while supporting the UN action there in principle.

Collective security also proposes the utilization of nonmilitary means for the settlement of international disputes. Sanctions, for instance, require that states should sever all diplomatic, economic, cultural, and other relations with an aggressor so as to isolate it from the world community. Peace can also be promoted through pacific settlement of disputes and disarmament. As Inis Claude says: *"Whereas pacific settlement (of disputes) proposes to leave states with nothing to fight about, and collective security proposes to confront aggressors with too much to fight against, disarmament proposes to deprive nations of anything to fight with."*[5]

In summary, one may say that though collective security appears to be a simple, direct, and effective method for preserving peace, its practicality is questionable. Only once since the establishment of the UN has collective security been invoked to punish an aggressor. That was in Korea in 1950, and there is some doubt as to whether enforcement action in Korea taken in the name of collective security was legal or whether it was an attempt on the part of the United States to obtain international sanction for an act of its national policy.[6]

INTERNATIONAL ORGANIZATIONS

The implementation of collective security depends upon the willingness of the international community to organize an institutional framework which would regulate relations between nations. As in national political systems, formal organization provides governments with a mechanism for the resolution of their disagreements and for bringing them together in the pursuit of common interests. At the present, though, international organizations are not supranational bodies and do not possess powers of international legislation. They are voluntary organizations and their effectiveness lies not so much in their constitutional provisions and structural patterns as in the degree

---

[5] See Inis L. Claude, Jr., *Swords into Plowshares*, p. 262. Italics ours.

[6] See Frederick L. Schuman, *International Politics*, 7th ed. (Toronto: McGraw–Hill, 1969), pp. 238–47.

of commitment of their members. They can serve as a framework for preserving world peace and for exploring avenues of international cooperation, but they can also be misused by their members to serve narrow national interests.

It was not until the 19th century that governments agreed to experiment with international organizations. The first political experiment was the Concert of Europe, an arrangement devised by Russia, Prussia, Austria, and Great Britain at the Congress of Vienna in 1815 to conduct European politics and guard against the revival of a Napoleonic regime in France. In the 19th century several other attempts were made, with some success, to establish specialized international organizations. Prominent among them were the Rhine Commission (1815), the Danube Commission (1850), the International Postal Union (1874), the Pan-American Union (1890), and the Permanent Court of Arbitration (1900). The success of the specialized international organizations of the 19th century and the experience of World War I created a general desire for developing an institutionalised arrangement to prevent the recurrence of another world conflagration. Widespread official and unofficial support in Europe and America for the idea of establishing a general international organization and Wilson's program of world peace embodied in his Fourteen points combined to produce a political atmosphere conducive to the birth of the League of Nations.

The League of Nations

The League of Nations was established in 1919 as a quasi-legislative and executive organization to promote international cooperation and achieve international peace and security. As expressed in the preamble of the Covenant, its signatories:

In order to promote international cooperation and to achieve international peace and security, by the acceptance of obligations not to resort to war, by the prescription of open, just and honourable relations between nations, by the firm establishment of the understandings of international law as the actual rule of conduct among Governments, and by the maintenance of justice and scrupulous respect for all treaty obligations in the dealings of organized peoples with one another, Agree to this Covenant of the League of Nations.

The objectives of the League, as expressed in the Covenant, were:

1. To promote world peace and security through organizing for collective action to contain aggression.
2. To seek pacific settlement of international disputes.
3. To formulate a general plan for the reduction of national armaments.

4. To act as protector and guardian of the interests of the non-self-governing territories.
5. To promote international cooperation in economic, social, cultural, and humanitarian matters.

Structures.   The League of Nations was constituted according to the principle of sovereign equality of states. In terms of Article 2 of the Covenant, the League would operate with the help of an Assembly, a Council, and a Secretariat. The Assembly resembled a multilateral conference where every member was represented and each state had one vote. It convened in one regular annual session but special sessions could be convened when the situation so required. It was a forum where states could discuss and deliberate upon matters of common concern.

The Council of the League was originally composed of nine members, but by 1936 its membership had been increased to 11. The five great powers—the United States, Britain, France, Italy, and Japan—were to be permanent members whereas others were nonpermanent members elected by the Assembly from time to time at its discretion. The United States did not join the League of Nations, and its permanent seat was thus left vacant until Germany occupied it in 1926. The distinction between permanent and nonpermanent members of the Council, while theoretically recognizing the sovereign equality of states, underlined the fact that power, and, therefore, responsibility, for maintaining international peace differed between states.

The Secretariat was the administrative organ of the League. It was headed by a Secretary-General with an internationally recruited staff who were considered to be international civil servants. Their main responsibility was to help implement resolutions passed by the League's Council and Assembly and to coordinate the activities of its principal organs and specialized agencies. The Secretary-General of the League of Nations played little or no political role.

Besides these three main organs, the League established a plethora of commissions, committees, administrative bodies, and specialized agencies which looked after particular matters of international concern. The Permanent Court of International Justice (PCIJ), for instance, was the instrument of international adjudication. It was an autonomous body but worked in close association with the world organization.

Evaluation of the League.   The failure of the League of Nations can be attributed to three basic weaknesses. Constitutionally, the Covenant of the League did not outlaw war as an instrument of national policy, it merely imposed certain restrictions on the ability of the members to resort to war. Since war was tacitly recognized, members were less inclined to exhaust the pacific means prescribed by the Covenant for the settlement of disputes. Structurally, the presence of some great powers, and the absence of others, made the League ineffective as an instrument for the preservation of peace on a worldwide basis. The United States never joined; Germany was admitted in 1926 and withdrew in 1933; Japan defected in 1931; and the Sovet Union was admitted in 1934 and expelled in 1939. Politically, the ability of the League to prevent war was dependent upon the cooperation and goodwill of its members; however, the policies pursued by them during the interwar years excluded the possibility of effective cooperation.[7] Added to this was the handicap of the unanimity principle which allowed any state, big or small, to prevent action.

While the League of Nations may have been incapable of achieving its political objectives, it nonetheless made great strides in the promotion of international cooperation in the nonpolitical fields—economic, cultural, technological, and humanitarian. Perhaps its greatest achievement was that of having been the forerunner of an even more ambitious effort to promote international cooperation on a wider scale.

The United Nations Organization

The beginning of World War II in 1939 sounded the death knell for the League of Nations, but faith in the utility of international organizations survived. The experience of the League had pointed out that, given the goodwill and sincerity of its members, it could have been an effective instrument for the maintenance of international peace. Hindsight enabled world leaders to perceive the weaknesses which hampered the League's activities. As the war raged, the feeling grew that a new and more effective organization should be created.

The international organization which came into existence at the end of the war was again the result of American leadership, great power cooperation, and prolonged wartime negotiations. The first move in this direction was made in the Atlantic Charter of 1941 following the conference between Prime Minister Churchill and President Roosevelt. Although the two statesmen did not commit themselves to any specific course of action, their desire to organize the world community was reflected in the following statement:

. . . Since no future peace can be maintained if land, sea or air armaments continue to be employed by nations which threaten, or may threaten, aggression outside of their frontiers, they believe, *pending the establishment of a wider and permanent system of general security,* that the disarmament of such nations is essential.[8]

---

[7] See E. H. Carr, *International Relations between the Two World Wars* (London: Macmillan, 1948).

[8] Italics ours.

Following the Atlantic Charter, the powers undertook a series of intensive and arduous negotiations to frame the basic draft of a world organization. Negotiations held in Moscow in 1943 between the United States, Britain, and the Soviet Union and in 1944 at Dumbarton Oaks outside of Washington, D.C. when China was included, resulted in a preliminary charter draft known as the Dumbarton Oaks Proposals. There was further discussion of the draft between the allies at the Yalta Conference in 1945, and, after some modifications, it was placed in the same year before the United Nations Conference at San Francisco, attended by representatives of 51 countries. The draft was subjected to close scrutiny, many of its proposals were revised, some substantially modified, and, finally, amidst an atmosphere marked by intense bargaining and compromises, the Charter was accepted and the United Nations Organization was created on October 24, 1945. The 51 participants of the San Francisco Conference became the original members of the new world organization.

The Charter of the United Nations is a lengthy document which is more comprehensive and goes into greater detail than the articles of the Covenant. Both are essentially multilateral treaties between signatories who voluntarily accept certain contractural obligations in their relations with each other and solemnly undertake to discharge them. The UN, however, has no machinery at its disposal which could be invoked to enforce its decisions. Its effectiveness, like that of the League of Nations, rests upon the willingness of its members to extend cooperation and provide necessary support to its successful operation.

Principles and Purposes.   After the enumeration of the lofty ideals in the preamble which motivated its formation, the Charter elaborates the purposes of the UN in Article 1. These reflect the general direction of the activities of the organization and the common ends which its members should seek to promote. The primary purposes are to:

1. Preserve and maintain international peace through collective security.
2. Develop "friendly relations among nations based on the respect for the principle of equal rights and self-determination of peoples and to take other appropriate measures to strengthen universal peace."
3. Achievement of "international cooperation in solving international problems of an economic, social, cultural, or humanitarian character, and in promoting and encouraging respect for human rights and for fundamental freedoms for all without distinction as to race, sex, language or religion."
4. To provide a forum "for harmonizing the actions of nations in the attainment of these common ends."

Following the enumeration of its purposes, Article 2 lists the principles which would govern the activities of the organization and the role of its members in pursuit of the purposes of the UN. The Charter requires the members to:

1. Fulfill their obligations contracted under the charter.
2. To settle their disputes by resort to peaceful means.
3. To refrain from the use or threat of force in international relations and to respect the territorial integrity and political independence of other states.
4. To provide all possible assistance to the United Nations in its activities and actions under the Charter and to desist from assisting any state against which the United Nations is taking enforcement action.
5. To desist from interference in the internal affairs of other states.

This last provision has caused many problems due to a lack of definition of the parametres of domestic jurisdiction. States have taken refuge behind this ambiguity by claiming internal jurisdiction over matters which are normally not considered to be so but whose discussion in public is likely to cause political embarrassment. At the same time others have raised matters which are normally considered to be within domestic jurisdiction. In fact, the enumeration of purposes in Article 1 and the statement of principles in Article 2 are so broad in nature and general in verbiage that practically anything can be included or excluded from the purview of the United Nations.

Membership.   The United Nations is organized according to the principle of the sovereign equality of all its members.[9] The Charter, like the earlier Covenant, created two classes of members: original and elected. Original members were the 51 states including the five great powers—China, France, the United Kingdom, the United States, and the Union of Soviet Socialist Republics—who signed the Charter when it was formulated. All other states are elected members.[10]

Qualifications for membership are as ambiguous as they are simple, and thus lend themselves to political manipulations. According to the Charter, membership "is open to all other peaceloving states which accept the obligations contained in the present Charter and, in the judgment of the Organization, are able and willing to carry out these obligations."[11] This could make any state eligible for membership. By the same token, the eligibility of any state could be questioned by its

---

[9] Djura Nincic, *The Problem of Sovereignty in the Charter and in the Practice of the United Nations* (The Hague, Netherlands: Martinus Nijhoff, 1970).

[10] Total membership of the UN in 1975 stood at 138 countries.

[11] Article 2, section 1.

opponents and rivals and its admission blocked. Very often applications for membership or representation of a state in the United Nations have been judged politically rather than legally. The political considerations result from the Cold War and the struggle for power between the United States and the Soviet Union.

A by-product of this political manoeuvring was the unresolved question of China's representation. This was sometimes erroneously referred to as the question of China's admission. In fact, it was a question of who had the right to represent China, which is an original member of the UN. At the time of the signing of the Charter, China was represented by the Nationalist government of Chiang Kai-Shek. After the Communists took over the mainland of China and the Nationalists fled to the island of Taiwan in 1949, the question arose as to which government was legally entitled to represent China. The Communists and their supporters argued that since the Nationalists did not control the mainland they could not represent China abroad. The Nationalists and their supporters countered that theirs was the legally established government of China, that they had signed the charter, and therefore they are the legal representatives of China. Irrespective of the moral niceties of the question, the legal answer remained straightforward; the Communist government was entitled to occupy China's seat in the United Nations. Politically, however, wider issues were involved, and it was thus on political rather than legal grounds that China was represented in the United Nations until 1971 by a government which did not, in fact, govern the country. There have been several other occasions when states were either denied membership for political considerations or their membership delayed until a political accommodation had been reached between the Cold War contestants.

The Covenant of the League of Nations recognized the right of a member to withdraw from the organization "after two years notice of its intention to do so."[12] No such right is recognized by the Charter, although it is understood that the right exists. Indonesia has been the only country to withdraw (in 1965), but returned two years later. Members against whom preventive action has been taken may, however, be suspended and those members who persistently violate the principles of the Charter may be expelled. Finally, a member may be denied its right to vote in the General Assembly if it is in arrears in the payment of its financial contribution and "if the amount of its arrears equals or exceeds the amount of the contributions due from it for the preceding two full years."[13] A crisis occurred in 1965 when the Soviet

---

[12] Article 1, section 3.
[13] Article 19.

Union, France, and several other countries refused to contribute to the United Nations on the ground that decisions under which they were required to contribute funds should have been made by the Security Council rather than the General Assembly. Technically, these countries fell within the purview of Article 19, but since a denial of their right to vote could well have destroyed the UN itself, a diplomatic settlement was devised. Article 19 has not so far been invoked.

Structure and Functions.   The scope of the activities of the United Nations is much broader than was that of the League of Nations, not only in terms of its principles and purposes, but also in matters of structure and functions. Unlike the League, which was composed of three main organs with the PCIJ working in close association with it, the UN is comprised of six main organs: the General Assembly, the Security Council, the Economic and Social Council (ECOSOC), the Trusteeship Council, the Secretariat, and the International Court of Justice (ICJ).

The *General Assembly* of the United Nations resembles a multilateral conference in which each member is represented and has one vote. It convenes in September in a regular annual session which lasts three to four months, but special sessions may be convened when a situation so requires. A large number of the members send their foreign ministers for part of the annual session, and it is not unusual for a head of government or even an occasional head of state to be in attendance. Heads of state visiting the United States are generally invited to address the Assembly if it is in session. Decisions are taken by a majority vote in procedural matters but a two-thirds majority is required in substantive matters. Unlike the League Assembly where the unanimity requirement provided an indirect veto to each member, the General Assembly is free from this encumbrance.

The powers of the General Assembly are broad and it can discuss any matter within the scope of the Charter. It considers and approves the budget of the organization, hears annual reports from other organs and specialized agencies, can initiate studies and make recommendations for the purpose of promoting international cooperation in political, economic, social, cultural, educational, and health fields. In effect, the General Assembly, as the representative body of all its members, is the supervisory and policy-making organ of the United Nations.

The primary responsibility in matters of collective security pertaining to preventive or enforcement action is that of the *Security Council*. Originally composed of 11 members, five great powers were given the status of permanent members and six others were to be elected by the assembly for two-year terms. Decisions on procedural matters required the affirmative vote of any seven members, but decisions on substantive matters called for the affirmative vote of seven members including the concurring votes of the permanent members. The rationale for giving a veto to the permanent members was that substantive matters, which deal largely with the preservation and maintenance of peace and security, not only impose a larger share of the responsibility and contributions upon the great powers, but that there should also be an agreement among the great powers on the action to be taken. This would reduce the likelihood of a direct confrontation between them. In 1963, the General Assembly approved amendments to the Charter which raised the number of nonpermanent members from six to ten and the required minimum affirmative vote from seven to nine for adoption of decisions by the Council.

The primary responsibility of the Security Council is the maintenance of international peace and security. The Council is given wide powers in the areas of pacific settlement of disputes, preventive and enforcement action, regional arrangements, and trusteeship arrangements. It is also responsible for formulating "plans to be submitted to the Members of the United Nations for the establishment of a system for the regulation of armaments."[14]

In pursuance of the purpose of the United Nations to promote international cooperation in economic, social, cultural, and humanitarian matters, the framers of the Charter agreed to establish the *Economic and Social Council* (ECOSOC). The ECOSOC may make or initiate studies to advance international cooperation, to promote respect for and observance of fundamental human rights, convene international conferences on matters within its jurisdiction, and coordinate the activities of the various specialized agencies working in these fields. It may also be called upon to assist the General Assembly and the Security Council in promoting cooperation in nonpolitical areas. Originally, the ECOSOC consisted of 18 members elected by the General Assembly for a three-year term, a third retiring each year. Each member has one vote and decisions are adopted by a majority of those present and voting. By the amendment of 1963, membership of the ECOSOC was increased to 27.

The Charter established an international trusteeship system for the administration and supervision of non-self-governing territories or, as the Charter designates them, "Trust Territories." A trust territory is a former colony placed under the responsibility of the United Nations and administered on its behalf by a designated country. For example, the Pacific Islands, otherwise known as Micronesia, were removed from Japanese control after World War II and designated as a UN trust territory with the United States as the administering authority. A colony, in contrast, is controlled directly by the mother country which owes no obligations to the world organization. The *Trusteeship Council*, operating under the authority of the General Assembly, was to

---

[14] Article 26.

supervise the administration of trust territories. Each administering authority is required to make an annual report to the Trusteeship Council on the state of affairs in the trust territory under its control on the basis of a questionnaire prepared by the Council. The Council, besides considering such reports, accepts petitions from local inhabitants and examines them, makes periodic visits to the trust territories for on-the-spot inspection, and takes action which may be necessary for the discharge of its responsibilities under the Charter.

There is no fixed membership of the Trusteeship Council; it varies in a manner so as to maintain a balance between the states administering trust territories, an equal number of others who are concerned about their administration, as well as those permanent members of the Security Council who are not administering trust territories.

The *International Court of Justice* (ICJ), although a somewhat modified version of the PCIJ, is, in effect, an old wine in a new bottle. The most significant difference is that whereas the old PCIJ was an autonomous body working in close association with the League of Nations, the ICJ is one of the six principal organs of the United Nations. Its structure and functions are patterned on the statute of the PCIJ, which has been incorporated as an annex to the Charter. It serves as the principal instrument of international adjudication.

The *Secretariat* is the principal administrative arm of the UN. The Secretary-General, as the chief administrative officer of the UN, is appointed by the General Assembly on the recommendation of the Security Council. He appoints such other administrative staff as may be required. The Secretary-General is in charge of some 4,000 personnel located at the UN Secretariat in New York City and another 2,500 dispersed around the globe. They are involved in the political, economic, social, and technical operations of the United Nations. Members of the Secretariat are considered to be international civil servants, but due regard is paid to the importance of recruiting the staff on as wide a geographical basis as possible.

Besides administrative responsibilities, the Charter entrusts the Secretary-General with political responsibilities. He may bring to the attention of the Security Council any matter which in his opinion may threaten the maintenance of international peace and security. This, of course, puts the Secretary-General in the midst of the Cold War as well as involving him in the conflicts between smaller states. Despite their attempts at impartiality in terms of their understanding of the job, the first three Secretaries-General have, at one time or another, experienced the displeasure of the superpowers.[15] Charter

---

[15] The three Secretaries-General of the United Nations have been: Trygve Lie, (Norway) 1945–53; Dag Hammerskjoeld, (Sweden) 1953–61; U Thant (Burma) 1961–71. The incumbent Secretary-General, Kurt Waldheim (Austria) took office in January 1972.

provisions aside, the role that a Secretary-General plays in the operations of the United Nations depends, to a large measure, upon the personality of the incumbent.

Evaluation of the United Nations.   The United Nations was formed with a great deal of fanfare and has generated a wide variety of hopes. Consequently, much—perhaps too much—was expected of it. It was hoped that it would, to quote the preamble of the Charter, "save succeeding generations from the scourge of war"; that it would be instrumental in continuing the wartime cooperation between the great powers; that it would become the protector of fundamental human rights and provide succor to persecuted minorities around the world; that it would help promote economic reconstruction and development; and, finally, that it would bring about an end of the seething problems generated by colonialism.

Obviously, this was a tall order. The UN has been unable to resolve, by peaceful means, several serious long-standing disputes between states nor has it been able to bring about any real reduction in national armaments. The misuse of their veto power by the great powers has all but destroyed the effectiveness of the Security Council in maintaining peace. In effect, the record of the UN, like that of the League of Nations, is one of disappointments, frustrations, and failure.

Its greatest success has been to provide a neutral forum where governments can vent their grievances against each other and where they can negotiate; for as long as states continue to talk, war may be put off and the chances of a peaceful settlement always exist. It should not be overlooked that though the UN may have been a failure in its political activities, it has made great strides in promoting international cooperation in other areas of its operations. It has found common interests between nations and brought them together where possible.

REGIONALISM AND REGIONAL ORGANIZATIONS

Article 51 of the Charter of the United Nations reads:

Nothing in the present Charter shall impair the inherent right of individual or collective self-defense if an armed attack occurs against a Member of the United Nations . . .

The UN is based on the concepts of universalism and collective security. However, it was felt that the organization of collective enforcement action would necessarily entail time and effort, and therefore Article 51 was included so as not to circumscribe the ability of states to defend themselves either individually or with the assistance of their friends and allies when attacked. As the article further prescribes, all such measures will be interim until the Security Council has activated collective measures; they shall be reported to the Security Council and the ultimate responsibility for maintaining peace is that of the Council.

Regional organizations may be classified in terms of their orientation. Internally oriented regional organizations are those which look toward the promotion of the interests of their members and to the solution of disputes between them. Externally oriented regional organizations look to the relationship of the whole group with parties outside of it. In terms of Chapter VIII of the Charter, regional organizations were expected to be internally oriented except in cases where collective action by them was sanctioned by the Security Council. The rationale was that regional organizations would be instruments for the settlement of intraregional disputes, and the Security Council would be the instrument of settling interregional problems.

The Charter, however, does not clarify the meaning of "regional arrangements or agencies" and the terms are interpreted in a variety of meanings. In conformity with the geographical definition of "region," regional arrangements would be treaties between states having geographical propinquity with a view to promoting common interests and achieving common objectives. In modern world politics, however, regional arrangements are politically motivated and consist of states with a commonality of political and military objectives irrespective of their geographical location. The creation of regional organizations since 1945 has been guided more by balance of power calculations than by the provisions of the Charter and hence has developed in a direction contrary to the spirit of the Charter. One of the significant problems that has faced the United Nations has been the contradiction in policies and confusion in thinking created by regionalism.

There are many regional organizations in existence serving a variety of purposes. By and large, they belong to one of three categories: military, economic, and political. Regional military organizations are primarily defensively motivated, that is, to strengthen and safeguard the security of their members through mutual action. They include NATO for Western Europe and North America, the Warsaw Treaty Organization for the Eastern European countries, the moribund South East Asia Treaty Organization (SEATO), and the Central Treaty Organization (CENTO). Regional economic organizations are formed for the purpose of coordinating the trade and economic development of their members. Prominent among such organizations are the European Economic Community (EEC), the Council for Mutual Economic Assistance (COMECON) for the Communist countries, and the Latin American Free Trade Association (LAFTA). Regional political organizations are established for the purpose of coordinating international relations within a region and resolving intraregional disputes by peaceful means. One example where a political regional organization has attempted to promote economic development in the region is the Alliance for Progress within the general framework of the Organization of American States (OAS). Besides the OAS, other regional political organizations include the League of Arab States, the Western European Union, the Organization for African Unity, and the Commonwealth of Nations. They seldom have a military motivation and almost never a military infrastructure. Efforts at coordinating and promoting economic development in the region through these organizations may or may not be made, depending upon the prevailing circumstances within the region.

The Commonwealth

It is difficult to explain what the Commonwealth is. It is certainly not a supranational organization through which Britain, as the senior member, determines and controls the affairs of its members, although at one point in its history it operated as such. It is also not a mechanism for the promotion of economic development and resolving disputes between its members, although it was at one point hoped that it would become such an instrument. It is most certainly not a military organization. It is also not an association of the English-speaking peoples of the world, for its members include countries from Asia, Africa, North America, and the down-under countries of Australia and New Zealand. It is a multiracial, multilingual, multicultural association of nations which meets periodically to discuss matters of common interest and explore possibilities of cooperation between its members. Every meeting demonstrates increasing discord and differences of opinion among its members and yet the Commonwealth has so far survived.

The Commonwealth evolved out of British imperalism. When Britain began to acquire colonies around the world, it promised the inhabitants that they would be granted independence as soon as they were ready for it. A great transfusion of British influence into the colonies occurred during the period of its colonial rule, thus creating a wide commonality of interests between them and the mother country. However, British reluctance to grant independence to them led to the American revolution and the demand for independence by the other English-speaking colonies. By 1914 Australia, Canada, New Zealand, and South Africa were granted dominion status.

The concept of dominion status is as difficult to explain as that of the Commonwealth itself. Perhaps the best way to define it is by saying not what it was, but what it was not. Before 1931, dominion status was not independence but only autonomy. Sovereignty over a dominion was vested in the British crown. Dominions were autonomous in the management of certain aspects of their internal affairs but many of the important ones were subject to crown prerogative or approval by the British Parliament in the name of the crown. For example, the Governor General of a dominion was appointed by the British Cabinet and was responsible to it. He could reserve bills passed by dominion legislatures for consideration of the British Parliament; the Parliament could pass laws applying to the dominions; and the highest judicial authority for the dominions was the Judicial Committee of the British Privy Council. In matters of external affairs, defence, and international trade, the crown, through the British Parliament, exercised ultimate authority.

This anomalous and somewhat confusing political arrangement continued until the end of World War I when the dominions, realizing the extent of their contribution to Britain's war efforts, insisted upon the grant of complete independence. As a result of discussions at three Imperial Conferences in 1921, 1923, and 1926, the parties arrived at a formula which was incorporated in the Statute of Westminster passed by the British Parliament in 1931. The preamble of the Statute provided that the Commonwealth was a free association of nations bound by common allegiance to the crown. The dominions were made completely independent in all external and internal matters except where a dominion expressed the wish to retain some of the crown prerogatives. Except for the theoretical and somewhat anachronistic "common allegiance to the crown" mixed with a strong dose of emotional attachment, Britain was left with little control over the affairs of the dominions.

The Commonwealth underwent far-reaching changes in its composition and operation following the end of World War II. The decline of British power at the end of the war and its inability to retain its colonies, combined with the rising tide of nationalism, led to independence for nearly all of them. Despite the acute political tension between Britain, as the imperial country, and the colonies, many of them desired to remain in the Commonwealth after gaining independence. There were certain aspects of the Commonwealth, however, which were politically and emotionally offensive to them. To many Asian countries, the word dominion was offensive, for it contained a suggestion of British domination. They also were unhappy with the idea of "common allegiance to the crown," for to them the crown was a symbol of British imperialism. The nomenclature "British Commonwealth of Nations" was unacceptable for the same reason.

To accommodate these objections, the word "British" was dropped in favour of just The Commonwealth of Nations. Use of the word "dominion" was dropped, except among those who desired to retain it, and members of the Commonwealth could be fully sovereign republics, as are most of the members admitted since 1947. The title of the

Secretary of State for Dominion Affairs, a member of the British cabinet, was replaced by the Secretary of State for Commonwealth Relations. These changes in titles and nomenclature were accompanied by a change in the nature of the Commonwealth. Membership of the new states changed the complexion of the Commonwealth from an association of primarily Anglo-Saxon, English-speaking countries to a multiracial, multilingual, and multicultural Commonwealth. Besides the older dominions (South Africa has since left), membership of the Commonwealth includes such diverse nations as India, Ghana, Tanzania, Nigeria, Cyprus, Jamaica, and Guiana. The heads of Commonwealth governments meet periodically to discuss matters of political and economic interest to them. They do not make decisions and seldom arrive at a consensus. A statement of their joint purpose is, nonetheless, issued following every conference.

The Commonwealth, because of its largely sentimental value, is a living, though not necessarily a going concern. The links which keep these members together are generally intangible. These are the emotional and cultural links between the Commonwealth countries. Many inhabitants of the older dominions are direct descendants of the British and maintain many of the British cultural and political traditions. The newer members have a similar link arising out of their former economic and political associations with Britain. Their legal, constitutional, educational, and administrative systems are patterned on that of Britain. Many of their political leaders and most of their civil and military hierarchy have been educated and trained at Eton, Oxford, and Sandhurst.

RECOMMENDED READINGS

Alker, Hayward R., Jr., and Russett, Bruce M. *World Politics in the General Assembly.* New Haven, Conn: Yale University Press, 1965.

British Information Service. *What is the Commonwealth?* February 1962.

Claude, Inis L., Jr. *Swords into Plowshares.* 3d ed. New York: Random House, 1964.

———. *The Changing United Nations.* New York: Random House, 1967.

Commission to Study the Organization of Peace. *Regional Arrangements for Security and the United Nations: Eighth Report and Papers Presented to the Commission.* New York: Carnegie Endowment for International Peace, 1953.

Eagleton, Clyde. *International Government.* 3d ed. New York: The Ronald Press, 1957.

Goodspeed, Stephen S. *The Nature and Function of International Organizations.* New York: Oxford University Press, 1965.

Haas, Ernst B. "Regionalism, Functionalism and Universal International Organizations." *World Politics* 8, no. 2 (January 1956).

————. *Tangle of Hopes.* Scarborough, Ont.: Prentice–Hall, 1969.

Hertzman, L.; Warnock, J.; and Hockin, T., eds. *Alliances and Illusions: Canada and the NATO–NORAD Question.* Edmonton: M. G. Hurtig Ltd., 1967.

Jacob, Phillip L.; Atherton, Alexine L.; and Wallenstein, Arthur. *The Dynamics of International Organization.* Homewood, Ill.: The Dorsey Press, 1972.

Kay, David A. *The United Nations Political System.* New York: John Wiley & Sons, 1967.

Larus, Joel, ed. *From Collective Security to Preventive Diplomacy.* New York: John Wiley & Sons, 1965.

Nincic, Djura. *Problem of Sovereignty in the Charter and in the Practice of the United Nations.* The Hague, Netherlands: Martinus Nijhoff, 1970.

Plano, Jack C., and Riggs, Robert E. *Forging World Order.* Toronto: Macmillan, 1967.

Sandys, Duncan. *The Modern Commonwealth.* London: Her Majesty's Stationery Office, 1962.

Stoessinger, John C. *The United Nations and the Superpowers.* New York: Random House, 1965.

Taylor, Alastair. *Peacekeeping: International Challenge and Response.* Toronto: Canadian Institute of International Affairs, 1968.

Tung, William L. *International Organization under the United Nations System.* New York: Crowell, 1969.

Wheare, K. C. "Is the British Commonwealth Withering Away?" *American Political Science Review* 44 (September 1950).

Yalem, Ronald D. *Regionalism and World Order.* Washington, D.C.: Public Affairs Press, 1965.

14

Liberalism and Conservatism

By THE TIME of the 16th century, the medieval social and political order in Europe was disintegrating. The growth of cities, the rise of a merchant class, and the increasing consciousness of cultural, social, and political differences among peoples of Europe had strained European society to where it could no longer be contained within the universalist, traditional, and orthodox religious and political institutions. It had functioned on the basis of a rigid system of inherited social status, authoritarian and paternalistic political institutions, and an acceptance of faith as the most desirable faculty of humankind. The growth of commerce throughout Europe and the extension of routes into Asia, the Renaissance in human thought and artistic expression, and the Reformation, which broke the monopoly of faith on European ideas, changed social relationships and theories about them.

The most immediate impact upon political theory was made by the Protestant Reformation. Martin Luther, perhaps unwittingly, opened up a critical political question when he distinguished between people's spiritual lives and their temporal existence. By asserting that an understanding of God's word as written in the scriptures could be achieved without priestly intervention or assistance, Luther undermined the position of the clergy and set the basis for a direct relationship between God and people. He also initiated the movement toward the separation of church and state, for though his emphasis on the freedom and responsibility of the individual was primarily religious, it soon came to serve as religious sanction for economic and political individualism. The English Reformation engineered by Henry VIII, which implicitly asserted the right of a people to devise and profess their own version of Christianity, was another example of the breakdown of religious universalism. The reaction to religious persecutions in much of Europe which followed the Reformation created the belief that people should be free to profess whatever beliefs were compatible with their minds and their consciences.

The Reformation, therefore, signalled the opening of the intellectual floodgates, resulting in a proliferation of political theories since that time. One of the main trends was an increasing emphasis on the role of the individual in society and with it came a variety of theories on how best to organize the political system to serve the interests of the individual while still retaining the order needed for civilized life. This emphasis on the intrinsic worth of the individual is essentially an outgrowth of Christian doctrine, which asserts the equality of people in the eyes of God. The Reformation, by undermining the position of the church hierarchy, forced people to accept responsibility for their actions and this, combined with the emphasis on rationality and creativity that marked the Renaissance, helped to create a radically altered intellectual climate for the discussion and resolution of political issues.

The changes in political ideas which began to take place after 1500 moved in two general directions. First, the rise of commercial powers in Europe worked to the advantage of a number of centralizing monarchs, who were able to create unified domains out of what were formerly patchworks of duchies, baronies, and other fiefdoms. The concepts of divine right and absolute monarchy were created to justify and maintain their power.

The second direction taken in the development of political ideas moved toward the individual and his or her role as a member of society. Instead of reinforcing the union between faith and politics, the idea of the rational individual was emphasized. Thus people would achieve happiness on earth only when they were free to utilize their inherent faculties to their fullest extent. People must be "liberated," that is, free to make political choices of greater or lesser importance.

By the 17th century, absolutism was under attack, especially in England. The justifications for absolute rule—divine right and tradition—were gradually being discredited. There was no longer one universal religion, and so the question as to who could declare validly the existence of divine sanction was proving increasingly difficult to answer. The argument based on tradition took little ingenuity to dispose of since its opponents could make, through reference to certain historic English documents and customs, a counterclaim concerning the limited nature of the sovereign's power. Thus, by 1650 the absolutists were very much on the theoretical defensive. What could be called an attempted rescue mission was carried out by Thomas Hobbes, who on the one hand accepted part of early liberal theory and on the other argued for an absolutist government. Hobbes asserted that there was no half-way point between individual freedom and submission to authority, the latter being a central tenet of conservatism. The reason for an individual's ambivalence lay in Hobbes' pessimistic view of human nature. He argued that people were both rational and selfish and were constantly driven by their desires to seek personal gratification. Though people can determine what is right or wrong for themselves, they are unable to do the same for society as a whole. The net result of this human makeup is that each person is in a constant state of war with other people, and life in this condition is ". . . . solitary, nasty, brutish and short." Reason tells people that the only possibility of survival is through a compromise by which they can maximize their chances of self-gratification and minimize the dangers to their survival. This is possible only through the creation of a sovereign state to which people would surrender their freedom in return for the maintenance of collective order.

Hobbes' view of the nature of people dictated that the leader of this state should be absolute, and that so long as he or she provided physical security, the laws laid down should be obeyed. Individuals or groups were not to be significantly involved in forming public policy, since that was the sovereign's responsibility. This contract between the society and the sovereign would remain in force so long as security was provided; if the sovereign proved to be unable to keep order and peace, then the society would be free to make new arrangements to regain this security. Since the reason for the creation of the sovereign was to provide for personal security, the sovereign could not require any individual to forfeit his or her life unless that individual had broken a clearly prescribed law. Thus, though the decision-making and implementing apparatus was to be absolute and authoritarian in its powers and methods, it was limited by the original terms of the contract.

Hobbes' arguments contained elements of what were later to be known as liberalism and conservatism. He was at once the last great defender of the remnants of the medieval feudal order and the first proponent of the new arguments which were to dominate Western politics until the mid-19th century. From Hobbes it is possible to trace separately the development of liberal theories and the conservative reaction to them.

LIBERALISM

Classical liberal ideals are perhaps given their most lucid expression in John Locke's *Two Treatises of Civil Government* (1690). Locke, like Hobbes, was a social contract theorist and, while he agreed with the latter about the role that human rationality plays in the formation of the state and government, he differed with Hobbes concerning the role of the individual in the organized society. He argued that government was a trust and people were morally self-sufficient to watch over its activities not only in their own interests but also in that of the society at large. These differing conclusions are the product of their differing understanding of human nature. Locke argued that human rationality includes an innate moral knowledge of good and evil. People have the ability to decide not only what is right or wrong for them personally but also what is right or wrong in the larger context of society. To do this, the individual must have unfettered freedom.

The acceptance of Locke's liberal ideas was facilitated by the emergence of a new economic and social order. The ouster of the Stuart kings in 1688 signalled the end of absolutism in England. Both absolutist practice and theory were now discarded. The rising commercial and financial middle classes, conscious of their individualism and believing they possessed the enterprise and initiative which alone could produce creative social activity, espoused liberal ideas in an attempt to secure freedom for their dormant genius. It was natural, therefore, that the concept of the freedom of the individual should spill over from the political into the economic realm.

The major contribution in this direction was made by Adam Smith. He argued in his *Wealth of Nations* (1776) that the maximization of self-interest comes about through a market which operates on the basis of free competition and regulates itself through the laws of demand and supply. Smith posited that the consumption of goods and services is the sole end of production. To achieve the maximum satisfaction of self-interest through consumption, the individual decides what he or she is willing to give away in terms of price in exchange for a product. The producer, in turn, decides what he or she is willing to accept for the product so as to maximize the satisfaction of his or her self-interest. The producer, aware that other sources of supply exist, will not demand an excessive price; the consumer, knowing that other consumers are vying for the same product, will offer to pay a reasonable price. Thus, self-interest would work through the laws of demand and supply to stabilize the price and ensure that these goods and services would continue to be produced as long as the interests of the producer and the consumer coincided. This line of reasoning, in essence, amounted to the acceptance of *laissez-faire* as the focal principle of society's economic activity. The use of the term laissez-faire can be found in the French literature of the middle of the 18th century as an argument against the economic privileges enjoyed by the nobility and the clergy. It was not until the 1820s that laissez-faire came to be used to refer to the three main characteristics of liberal economic theory: a competitive labour market, the gold standard, and free trade.[1]

---

[1] Karl Polanyi, *Great Transformation* (Boston: Beacon Press, 1960), p. 135.

Other theorists, following Adam Smith, addressed themselves to derivations of this general theory, especially in relation to the collective benefits derived from laissez-faire. In his *Essay on Population* (1798), Thomas Malthus attacked the then prevailing belief that society had a duty to provide assistance to those who were unable to find employment in the open competitive market. He argued that society had no such obligation and the unemployed had no right to expect this provision, for it tends to contradict the laws of nature. He asserted that low wages and unemployment were conditions inherent in the lower classes because of their high birth rate. Their misfortunes are thus their own creation and the means of redress are their responsibility. Society and government are without power in this respect. The "Malthusian Doctrine" has been reformulated today to explain the gravity of world overpopulation.

Another derivative concept, still used by economists, is the theory of comparative advantage. In it, the pursuit of individual economic advantage is closely related to the universal good of people. Just as the wealth of a community consists of the accumulation of the wealth of its individuals, so the universal good of the human race is promoted by the progress of different countries. Each country devotes its resources to the production of those goods which are most beneficial to it. It thus distributes labour and capital most effectively and stimulates productivity. This course of activity, in theory, should bind the nations of the world "in one common tie of interest and intercourse." By producing that for which they are best suited and exchanging their products with goods and services produced by others, international trade as well as harmony is stimulated and contributes to the welfare and prosperity of people everywhere. The classical political economist was against governmental interference in this process for, to him, such interference would detract from the progress of the individual, society, and people as a whole.

The emphasis by liberals on free trade continued to mount through the 19th century. The principle of free trade was seen as the panacea for solving the political ills of the world. Liberals were opponents of agricultural protectionism in early 19th-century England and advocated the abolition of all kinds of protective policies in trade and manufacturing imposed by governments. They maintained that laissez-faire would promote the trade of nations far more effectively than the resort to wars, conquests, armaments, or even diplomacy usually adopted for this purpose. Along with comparative advantage, free trade would not only result in increasing material gain for humanity, it would also act as a moral and gravitational force; the interest of expanded trade would inspire countries to set aside their political, racial, and religious differences, thus promoting "eternal peace" and brotherhood. Protectionism in trade would lead to wars for colonial expansion. Colonies are governed in the interest of the imperial power, thereby denying to the colonial peoples the freedom to develop their own future. The removal of protectionism in trade would obviate the need for colonial wars and provide national freedom for colonial peoples. The absence of wars would lead to a reduction of wasteful military expenditure. Part of the money thus saved could be remitted to the taxpayer in the form of reduced taxes; the other part could be used for the provision of free, secular, and universal education. The classical liberal notion of peace through free trade and economic integration provides a theoretical basis for today's common markets in Europe, Africa, and Latin America.

Reform Liberalism

The free enterprise system was not as universally beneficient as its more optimistic proponents had expected. Business competition appeared to be leading to exploitation and monopolistic control, which not only undermined capitalism itself, but also endangered the democratic principle as political power was acquired by a few through their accumulation of great wealth. These problems were discernible in the late 18th century, but their more explicit critics, socialists such as Robert Owen and Karl Marx, emerged in the first half of the 19th.[2] These critics were joined by others who attempted to reform classical liberalism. The modifications were so extensive as to constitute a schism in liberal ranks.

Basically, the evolution of reform liberalism centered around increasing evidence that the maximization of individual happiness did not necessarily result in any common social benefit. Liberals came increasingly to stress the need for positive intervention on the part of the government in order to create conditions whereby each individual could actually exercise his or her own abilities. The existence of this conflict in liberalism was first recognized and discussed by Jeremy Bentham, who stressed for the common good instead of individual maximization.

The dominating feature of Bentham's work was an attempt to construct a good society based on reason. He felt that legal and other social and political traditions should be eliminated if they inhibited this rationalization. He approached the whole legal structure with a critical eye, in effect asking the question as to which laws were truly needed for the promotion of the primary goal as he saw it—the greatest happiness for the greatest number. He argued that laws must be rele-

---

[2] See Chapter 15.

vant, that is, they must have "utility." What is right or wrong for society should be judged according to the principle of the greatest happiness. Bentham claimed that it was possible to make this judgment with mathematical precision. However, though he never succeeded in fully developing his "felicific calculus" to the satisfaction of others, the notion itself has been widely adopted and has been resurrected in contemporary times under the guise of "cost-benefit analysis" and related techniques.

In Bentham's view, a law was useful only if it achieved its desired results in a way which could be adjudged as efficient. If it cost too much to enforce a law, then it was a bad law. In some cases it might be necessary to keep difficult laws on the books, but he felt it not to be a good practice. Laws impose some form of restraint on the actions of members of society so a person's rights may be secured by establishing sufficient penalties to deter others from interfering with them. The protection of property rights and the enforcement of contracts were seen as necessary, not because they constituted inviolable principles, as advocated by many classical liberals, but because they were the only available means for ensuring an orderly and productive distribution of goods and services. By implication, if Bentham had been apprised of a more "efficient" means of achieving the same ends, he would have been quite willing to forgo these devices in favor of others.

Bentham intended to use his utilitarianism to further the cause of the classical liberals; however, his concepts could logically be used to justify an increased role for government as part of liberal theory. Bentham himself noted in 1801:

I have not, I never had, nor ever shall have, any horror, sentimental or anarchical, of the hand of government. I leave it to Adam Smith and the champions of the rights of man . . . . to talk of invasions of natural liberty. . . . . The interference of government [where it will provide the slightest advantage to society] . . . . is an event I witness with . . . . satisfaction. . . . .[3]

His interest in practical rules for the conduct of human society led Bentham away from the stark individualism of the classical liberals. Individual expression had to be balanced with, or even subordinated to, the rights of the majority of society. This line of thought was to be pursued by other reformers.

John Stuart Mill based his ideas on the same utilitarian premise as Bentham. However, he abandoned the egoism and self-interest associated with liberalism in its classical form and argued that the general welfare was a matter of concern for all. He also insisted on the

---

[3] W. Stark, ed., *Jeremy Bentham's Economic Writings* (London: George Allen & Unwin, 1954), pp. 257–58. The difficulty of Bentham's style made it necessary to condense the passage quoted.

value of freedom, integrity, and self-respect quite apart from any utilitarian considerations they might have.

Mill argued in *On Liberty* (1859) that freedom of information and discussion were both intrinsically good as well as necessary for a rational society. He was less optimistic about the potential efficiency of a democratic political system than many liberals, but he felt that it was the only way a civilized society could be built. In a sense he went against pure utilitarianism, since he would not accept any alternative form of government simply because it was shown to be the most efficient means of providing the greatest happiness for the greatest number. At the same time, Mill addressed himself to the question of the role of a majority in a society run on democratic principles. He had no faith in the natural rightness of a majority and was concerned lest a majority become as tyrannical as an aggressive minority.

Other reform liberals took up where Mill stopped. Classical liberalism was accused of having a strong bias favouring the middle class. The liberal problem was viewed as more than one of redressing economic exploitation; the degradation of the exploited individual was spiritual as well as economic, and the former was more important. The classical liberals interpreted freedom as being essentially the absence of restraints upon activity. However, it was quite possible to have the technical freedom to do something and yet not to possess the means. Everyone is free to buy a Rolls-Royce, but not everyone has the money. Many of the political and economic arrangements advocated by liberal theorists deprived most people of any realistic hope for exercising their so-called freedom.

From this, it follows that the role of the government must be expanded. In the earlier liberal tradition, government was primarily an organization designed to provide security for the enjoyment of rights. To reformers, it had to become a positive contributor to freedom by ensuring that individuals are equipped to take advantage of their rights. The government cannot compel people to be fulfilled, but it can make it possible for them to fulfill themselves. Coercion should be replaced by positive policies that emphasize the inherent sociability of people. A healthy community would be one in which each person's claim to his or her rights would be made in recognition of the interests of the larger society. Ultimately this led to the rather ambiguous position of many liberal democrats today, arguing for the need for an integrated and stable society and at the same time attempting to preserve individual freedom.

The 20th century has witnessed further extensions of this line of reasoning, thereby transforming those who now advocate classical liberalism into modern "conservatives." The contributions of John Maynard Keynes to economic thinking have, in application, altered the role that political authority is expected to play in society. He rejected the notions of the existence of any higher governing force, such as Adam Smith's "invisible hand." He did not regard self-interest as enlightened nor the economic system as self-correcting. Writing during the Great Depression of the 1930s, he saw the necessity for state intervention in the economy, the only real questions being the methods and the goals of this action. It was necessary for the government to regulate the economy for the common good, but he doubted that it was necessary or desirable that the government should adopt a socialist formula of direct ownership and management of economic organizations.

John Kenneth Galbraith's criticisms are broader than Keynes as they apply to modern industrial societies, such as those of his native Canada or the United States. He has shown that techniques of production have been mastered and great wealth has been created, but no rationale for it exists. The economy is primarily directed towards the process of producing and selling goods while other tasks go unattended. The individualistic society has been swallowed up by big government, big industry, and big labour, but most people within and without the government pretend not to realize this. Even the educational institutions continue to explain society in mythical terms, which helps only those who control the big institutions.

At the same time, the very bigness of economic organizations is leading to a decline in imagination and innovation as their leaders seek security more assiduously than profit. Thus, Galbraith makes a case for the government to take a stronger hand in directing the distribution of the wealth of the society so that all may share in it. In this way both political stability and a democratic system could be maintained. It is perhaps ironic that liberalism started out with a focus on economic individualism but abandoned that position in favour of large-scale government intervention. This shift makes conservatives, who have adopted the classical liberal's economic theories, wonder how much difference there is between modern liberalism and socialism. Galbraith himself has moved toward a mild form of socialism in his latest writings.[4]

The future thrust of liberalism appears to be away from economic matters, as there appears to be an implicit agreement on the desirability of government intervention in this area. The greatest threat to individuals at present appears to be in the area of self-respect and social self-determination. Thus, there is increased interest in preventing infringements of personal privacy by government or private agencies.

---

[4] J. K. Galbraith, *Economics and the Public Purpose* (Boston: Houghton Mifflin, 1973).

This has become apparent in the concern voiced over the use of sophisticated electronic eavesdropping devices by police and other investigators. A related problem is the collection and use of personal data by private and public organizations. Finally, governments in Europe and North America are gradually altering the positions they once took on legislating private morals and behavior. Advocating the right of individuals to be left alone in the pursuit of their own happiness, a classic liberal tenet, appears to be in fashion once again.

Canadian Liberalism

Liberalism stands for the middle way: the way of progress. It stands for moderation, tolerance, and the rejection of extreme courses, whether they express themselves in demands that the state should do everything for the individual . . . or in demands that the state should do nothing except hold the ring so that fittest survive under the law of the jungle.[5]

This quotation from former Prime Minister Lester Pearson's introduction to J. W. Pickersgill's *Liberal Party* reflects the essence of the liberal tradition in Canada. It is not based upon the ruggedly individualistic and laissez-faire philosophy of the classical liberals; there is little or no tradition of this in Canadian political thinking. Despite the geographic proximity with the United States, where classical liberalism has had its most profound impact, Canada reflects more the reform liberal tradition.

Several reasons may be advanced for the reformist nature of Canadian liberalism. The difficulties experienced in colonizing and developing the northern half of the North American continent have required an approach to individual freedom quite different from that taken in the United States, for instance. A small population, scattered thinly across four thousand miles of wilderness, has continually had to express "liberation" in terms which are more collective than individual. Neither the markets nor the capital resources were large enough to justify the effort of development—unless some guarantees were provided that the whole people would somehow pay, through tariffs or monopolies, for the endeavour.

A second reason for the dominance of reform liberalism arises from the timing of the Canadian expansion. The country began to face the problems of responsible government, economic development, and trade policies only after the classical liberal tradition had been challenged by reform liberalism elsewhere. The formation of factions or parties by liberals, which would challenge the cliques around the colonial governors' offices, came only in the 1820s and 1830s. In En-

---

[5] J. W. Pickersgill, *Liberal Party* (Toronto: McClelland & Stewart, Ltd., 1962).

gland, at the same time, liberal ideas were becoming dominant in politics and the centre of debate appeared to be gradually focussing upon the threat of socialism. In Canadian economics, liberal notions were only slowly being accepted. Indeed, even by the 1870s, there was grave doubt among politicians and economists about the intellectual quality of the work of classical liberals, such as Smith and Ricardo. The tie to the Empire, with its broader economic implications, meant that trade policies were in large part subordinated to British needs, both economic and political. This largely eliminated pressure to formulate independent ideological positions on trade and tariffs until the middle of the 19th century, when the classical liberals' influence had been moderated.

Finally, the introduction of reform liberalism can be seen as a result of the continuing Canadian dependence upon Great Britain in a wider sense than simply through trade. The American Revolution cut off the United States from the full force of the theoretical currents which flowed through Great Britain after 1800. While ideas were exchanged between citizens of the two countries, they did not have similar impacts. As a result, American liberalism generally continued to expand upon the ideas of the classical liberals. Conversely, the colonies that later united to form Canada were more open to reform forces. They also were left, as a result of Imperial ties and the migration of many of the former American loyalist leaders, with a social and political "aristocracy" which combatted liberal ideas throughout the first half of the 1800s. The combination of close intellectual ties to Great Britain and conservative political opposition forced Canadian liberalism to evolve away from that in the United States.

Confederation can be looked upon as both an end as well as a beginning of nation-building. As an end, it provided a national arena for policy and theory, superseding the smaller, weaker colonies of British North America. As a beginning, Confederation and its attendant document, the BNA Act, gave rise to new tensions and conflicts. These strains, which have persisted during the more than a hundred years of Confederation, became the matrix for the development of both Canadian liberalism and conservatism.[6] Responses to these strains may be classified as external and internal concerns. Externally, the major concern centred around the nature of the overall political relationship between Britain and the new confederation. Internally, two major problems had to be tended to: the right political equilibrium in the relations between the federal and the provincial governments, and the political relationship between the French- and the English-speaking communities.

---

[6] C. P. deGlazebrook, *A History of Canadian Political Thought* (Toronto: McClelland & Stewart, Ltd., 1966), p. 156.

External Concerns. The nature of Canadian ties to Great Britain has constituted a matter of major concern to liberal thinkers and political activists since Confederation. One of the earliest to suggest a specific pattern of relationship was Goldwin Smith, who proposed as early as 1863 the conception of Canada as a new nation in the new world. He suggested that Canada should reduce its colonial ties with Britain in order to assume the status of an independent nation while, at the same time, retaining such symbols of the British heritage as dual citizenship, the flag, and other moral and intellectual, rather than political, bonds.

There was started in England, around 1870, a movement for the establishment of an Imperial Federation in which the dominions would relinquish their control over trade to an imperial body. Goldwin Smith staunchly opposed the idea that Canada should surrender control of its trade to any imperial body. He was even more strongly opposed to the underlying idea of the Imperial Federation, namely that Canada might be obligated to defend the interests of the mother country, which close imperial union would imply. To him, both of these would increase Canada's dependence upon Britain and undermine the chance of its ultimate status as an independent nation.

The question of Canadian contribution to imperial defence arose again in connection with the Boer War (1899–1902). The federal government came under intense pressure from the British government, which pressed for increased colonial commitment to the military and naval defense of the Empire. Canadian public opinion was divided on the issue of Canadian participation in the Boer War. Under the direction of Wilfrid Laurier, Canada sent volunteers whom the government paid and equipped, but the government did not undertake any military or naval obligations. The Liberal government maintained the immediate political alliance with Britain without being tied to British policies.

At the Imperial Conferences of 1902 and 1907 Canada, along with the other dominions, was confronted with the proposal for the formation of an Imperial Council and a contribution of ships to the Royal Navy. Laurier declined both to participate in the council and to make any contributions of ships to the Royal Navy. Instead, he indicated that Canada was considering the formation of its own navy, a task which was finally embarked upon in 1910.

The famous editor of the *Winnipeg Free Press,* J. W. Dafoe, has left an indelible mark on the liberal tradition in Canada. His concerns were much the same as those of most other liberals. He did, however, have one advantage over the others; he used his control of the editorial policies of the *Free Press* to propagate his views. Dafoe expanded upon the views of Smith and Laurier in viewing the Commonwealth as an association of free nations bound together by a commonality of ideals and symbols rather than direct political ties. He was an advocate of Canadian cooperation in imperial affairs but emphasized that such actions should emanate not from the proddings of an imperial body but on the strength of national initiative and freedom of action. Canada, he insisted, should determine its attitude on imperial matters according to the merits of the case rather than a predetermined and abject political colonialism. For instance, he did not believe a Canadian government could implement a policy of free trade, though he called for more tariff reductions and free trade than was compatible with the notion of a centralized imperial policy.

The influence of the liberalism of Smith, Laurier, Dafoe, and many others on the question of Canada's ties with Britain has been reflected in the actions of the Liberal governments of recent years. The adoption of the maple leaf emblem as the national flag and the elimination of special political privileges for British subjects are demonstrative of the liberal desire to establish a Canadian identity and lift the country from the status of a remnant of the British Empire. The attempt to establish a Canadian identity independent of Britain is also reflected in such actions as the incorporation of the Queen's Printer into Information Canada, and the renaming the Dominion Bureau of Statistics as Statistics Canada. Finally, the image of the Governor General as the crown's representative has been underplayed by the government and his *de facto* position as the head of the state of Canada has been emphasized.

In recent years the liberal preoccupation with the political connection with Britain has been overshadowed by a perceived threat to the Canadian identity which is embodied in the influence of the United States. Given the present realities, any moves toward freer trade would probably result in an even greater dependence upon the United States. This is viewed by many supporters of the imperial connection as well as the socialists as far more compromising of Canadian independence than the imperial idea had ever been. Canadian liberals have traditionally expressed a degree of admiration for the giant democracy to the south. This, combined with what has become known as "continentalism" in economics, makes it awkward for liberals to contemplate a strong nationalist stance vis-à-vis the United States.

Internal Concerns.   The major internal concerns of liberals have been related to the nature of Confederation and the promotion of individual welfare. Liberals have maintained the position that the union of the vast stretches of territory, comprising the multicultural population found in Canada, could not support the kind of monolithic unity found in more homogeneous cultures. The nature and variety of regional and local interests preclude the development of uniform social policies in many areas by the federal government. Nevertheless, Confederation had produced a political structure which would allow optimal latitude for the expression of local interests, while permitting a reasonable degree of coordination and uniformity in order to project a Canadian identity. The liberals, therefore, took a strong stand against the ascendency of the federal government as envisaged in certain provisions of the BNA Act. They have traditionally opted in favour of allowing considerable autonomy to provincial governments.

The liberal insistence on provincial rights within a loose framework of Confederation has been held responsible by many for fostering separatist tendencies among the provinces. The first overt attempt at separation was made in 1873 at a time when the Liberal government of Alexander Mackenzie had just taken federal office. The Liberals were skeptical of the feasibility of the vast scheme of the Pacific Railway and Mackenzie publicized his view that the railway could not be completed within the stipulated time, by 1880. British Columbians threatened to secede, arguing that the failure to meet this deadline was a violation of the agreement under which they had joined the Confederation. In 1886 Nova Scotia, under the Liberal government of W. J. Fielding, threatened to secede because of disagreements on economic matters with the federal government.

In our own times, responsibility for the rise of separatism in Quebec is laid at the door of liberals. It is argued that the "Quiet Revolution" in Quebec, accompanied by strong assertions of provincial jurisdiction, materialized under the Liberal government of Jean Lesage, which won significant concessions from the federal Liberal government of Lester Pearson. Similar criticism is levelled against Prime Minister Trudeau. Critics point out that Trudeau's efforts at promoting bilingualism, attempting to entrench the rights of Canadians in a constitutional document, his insistence on retaining the cultural diversity of the country and the widespread use of the opt-in opt-out principle in federal-provincial agreements have tended to weaken rather than consolidate Confederation.

Liberal political tradition however, has revolved around the central theme that Canada is one political entity structured on the federal system of government and characterized by the cultural duality of its French- and English-speaking communities. The liberals have insisted that the basic rights of the members of both communities should be guaranteed throughout the country.

Immediately following the establishment of the Confederation, French-Canadian nationalists complained that their interests and identity were being totally submerged by the numerical superiority of the English Canadians, that the federal government had failed to provide adequate satisfaction for their interests and that, therefore, Quebec should withdraw its representatives from Ottawa and demand increasing autonomy for the provincial government, working towards eventual independence. French-Canadian liberals responded to this argument by reiterating the advantages of the Confederation to their community and emphasized the need for maintaining the federal system. While basically accepting the principle of provincial autonomy they pointed out that a strong and forceful French-Canadian presence in Ottawa was necessary in order to assure the rights of their people. They opposed the idea of any special status for Quebec arguing that acceptance of special status would eventually lead to the independence of Quebec, whereupon it would be reduced to the status of a "banana republic."[7]

The liberal concern for the welfare of the individual has been reflected in the reformist traditions imported from Great Britain and the United States. In its Canadian setting, reform liberalism has taken the stance of protecting individuals from the econmic uncertainties of life and from the sometimes malign effects of harsh business practices. Many of the features of the welfare state—medical insurance plans, old-age pensions, unemployment insurance, welfare programs—have been influenced by the thinking of Canada's socialists, but the reforms, whether out of sympathy or electoral pragmatism, have been devised and implemented largely by Liberal governments.

The intertwining of liberal reformism and socialism is more clearly seen in the rise of populist movements in Canada. *Populism* may be defined as a *political movement which attempts to liberate individual producers or workers from the control of larger economic structures.* On the surface, it has much in common both with socialism and the trade union movement: in fact the electoral success of the New Democratic Party is based upon this surface amalgam. But populists are quite different from urban workers. They are generally individual owners of their own means of production—farms and fishing boats, for instance. Populist movements seem to arise when this ownership and its benefits are threatened.

Populist movements have sprung up in all the provinces of Canada. They formed the strength behind the Social Credit movement in Alberta and Quebec; the Progressive movement in Alberta, Saskatchewan, Manitoba, Ontario and Nova Scotia; and the Unionist Party in Newfoundland, to name some of the better-known examples. The major periods of influence of populist movements were 1912–22 and 1934–44. In part, they were born of adverse economic conditions, such as depressions, but they were also impelled to action by governmental and business policies.

The main concern of all populists was to remove the restrictions

---

[7] See Ramsay Cook, *Maple Leaf Forever* (Toronto: Macmillan, 1971).

placed upon individual producers by large economic structures. Most often these were structures which controlled credit (banks) and the transportation and sale of goods (railroads and wholesalers). All populist theories advocated three levels of action to change the practices of these structures. First, there were attempts to deal with problems by pressuring governments and businesses through the formation of "unions." One of the first such movements within the present boundaries of Canada, was the Fishermen's Protective Union in Newfoundland (1911). It was followed by the United Farmers of Alberta and similar organizations in most provinces.

The second level of action, taken when it became obvious that pressure was not enough, was to take over the provincial government through the ballot box. The populists could then try to legislate reforms in their favour. Often this proved impossible as the economic structures under attack were governed by federal law. The federal disallowance of Social Credit legislation in Alberta in the 1930s, which would have affected banking and the money supply, is a case in point.

Finally, all the populist movements accepted the necessity of building consumer-owned structures which would parallel ones deemed oppressive. A variation on cooperatives was the nationalization of services and structures. At this point, the distinction between reform liberals and socialists becomes vague, though it must be noted that populists said little about public ownership or control of farmland or fishing boats. The individual "capitalist" is still to be maintained.

The most durable populist theories have been those of the cooperative commonwealth and social credit. The former has exercised considerable influence upon Canadian socialism.[8] The latter as a movement has had an impact upon Alberta and British Columbia, where Social Credit parties governed for many years, and upon northwestern Quebec, which has supported a federal Social Credit party for 15 years, and, marginally, a provincial wing as well.

The main concern of the social credit movement has been the alleviation of many of the economic ills affecting individuals by a manipulation of credit and the money supply. Social Credit theory was expressed at length in the early 20th Century by C. W. Douglas. He noted that recessions and depressions seemed to be caused by an imbalance between the value of what workers produced and what they were paid. This is similar to Marx's theory of surplus value. Douglas felt that the difference, or unearned income, was being siphoned off by the financiers, with the result that periodically there was an oversupply of goods relative to purchasing power. This resulted in layoffs, unemployment, and bankruptcies, until the balance was restored. Social

---

[8] See Chapter 15.

welfare and economic growth could be best served by distributing this unearned income to the people by means of a government-declared social dividend.

The combination of government control of credit and a regular social dividend greatly appealed to prairie farmers during the Depression of the 1930s. In Alberta, it was championed by a popular radio evangelist, William Aberhart, who quickly built a political party on its ideas. Social Credit dominated Alberta from 1935 until 1971. It did not spread to Saskatchewan because of some tactical blunders by the party leadership. Instead, the Cooperative Commonwealth Federation maintained its leadership of the populist movement there. The combination of a depressed area and a dramatic leader, Réal Caouette, seems to underlie the success of the *Créditiste* movement in northwestern Quebec since 1960.

Outside the areas of concern discussed above, Canadian liberals have not attempted to enunciate abstract normative political prescriptions. In general, they have come to accept active participation of government as a means for the solution of social problems. The economic and political elite prefers to use the power of the government for the purpose of developing and controlling the economy rather than accepting the principle of unfettered private enterprise and a competitive market economy as advocated by the classical liberals. The liberals have found this to be a safe compromise in the face of challenges from the conservative right and socialist left. Instead of individualism, free competition, and laissez-faire, they have adopted the principles of social reform, public ownership of certain sectors of the economy, and the welfare state.

CONSERVATISM

The word *conservative* was derived from the French "conservateur," a name used to designate a group of French writers and political leaders who sought the revival of prerevolutionary conditions after the fall of Napoleon. The essence of conservatism is the attempt to defend an existing social order, regardless of its orientation, against efforts to change it. Conservatives try to preserve those essential values which they feel have proven themselves to be useful to society in the past and seek to apply precedents and experience to the problems of the present.

Liberals emphasize the essential rationality of people and argue that people should be liberated from the artificial and unnatural restraints imposed by society in order to rationally pursue their happiness in which lies also the common good. Conservatives, in contrast, agree with Hobbes' pessimistic view of the nature of people—that people's dispositions are basically selfish and that, unless restrained by coercive power, they will be selfishly preoccupied with the satisfaction of their needs at the expense of others.

This attitude, however, should not be taken to mean that conservatism implies a complete rejection of the concepts of individual freedom and social change. Conservatives insist that they primarily question the wisdom of change for its own sake, especially rapid change, which threatens to alter the established and traditional values of society. They claim to be more discerning and discriminating, favouring deliberate and gradual change whose consequences may be foreseen. They oppose social experimentation. Conservatism, by and large, must be seen more as a state of mind than a coherent doctrine.

Classical Conservatism

The first major assault on liberalism was aimed at Locke's theory of reason and natural law. It questioned the basic foundations of liberalism. Locke had contended that people had the inherent capacity to distinguish between right and wrong and that their reason directs them to act according to that which is right, based on the principles of justice. Locke called these principles the laws of nature. David Hume, in his *Treatise of Human Nature* (1740), questioned the existence of such laws, arguing that though reason can indicate how to achieve certain ends, it cannot discover whether these are good or bad. People's reason is therefore a tool used to serve their passions. The desirability of a particular thing or goal is determined by the preferences of the individual and not necessarily by its intrinsic worth. People's sense of right and wrong comes not from their "nature," but through human conventions which are the product of the collective experience of society. Experience tells them that the satisfaction of their interests is inextricably tied to the survival of society. They must, out of necessity, subject themselves to social authority, bind themselves by laws, and be guided by the wisdom of collective experience. Only then can the integrity of social life be maintained and the organic nature of society preserved. Emphasis on individual freedom, natural law, and human reason would be disruptive to the social order. Hume's insistence that behaviour, or experience, generates values in human affairs has proven to be durable. His work also constitutes a philosophical basis for the behavioural study of politics.

The conservative emphasis on experience was strengthened by the eloquence of Edmund Burke, who was a politician and a member of the British House of Commons for nearly 30 years around the end of the 18th century. He supported the American revolutionaries because they were, in effect, fighting for the liberties of English people and were thus struggling within the mainstream of British political experience. The French revolutionaries, on the other hand, had destroyed the traditional institutions and values in their search for liberty, equality, and fraternity and, having stepped out of the political mainstream, they were opposed by him.

Burke agreed with Hume that the laws of morality could not be determined by logic. A rational person, he argued, is not governed by abstract reasoning, but by experience. Burke did not oppose reason *per se* but only abstract reason divorced from experience. Politics, according to him, is a practical science, and the suitability and qualifications of rulers are not determined by how much abstract reason they can muster but the degree of practical wisdom they command. To do that which is right is not a matter of instinct but of sound, experienced judgment. People's rationality, divorced from the wisdom of the past, would not automatically lead them to do the right thing. Burke also criticized the liberal concept of liberty, arguing that its limits could not be prescribed by abstract reason since only the experience of a society can determine what measure of rights are proper for a given culture. Rights cannot be prescribed by laws; they are an evolutionary product of social growth.

Burke argued further that the social contract was an attempt on the part of liberals to find a simple and logical explanation to the complex phenomena of the development of society. Society may be a contract, he conceded, but not in the sense of a partnership which can be dissolved according to the whims of the parties. It is an indissoluble and perpetual contract in which everyone is assigned duties and responsibilities which they must fulfill. People are temporary and perishable; society is permanent and self-perpetuating. It is a partnership between those who are dead, the living, and those yet to be born. It is not an invention of human reason or desire but the product of an evolutionary process shaped by God's will and should be treated with more reverence than the theory of the social contract would concede. The organic nature of society makes it larger and more enduring than the individual, and therefore the integrity of communal life must be maintained against changes and assertions of individual freedom which might undermine social unity. The interests of the society transcend those of the individual.

This view of society and government did not imply an opposition to reform. Burke opposed reformers such as the French revolutionaries, who sought to destroy existing values and institutions, and start anew. This to him was clearly neither desirable nor feasible, since society could not exist in complete separation from the past. Reforms which seek to better and improve an existing system are desirable, but revolution posing as reform should be rejected.

The views of John Locke as the precursor of classical liberalism, and those of Edmund Burke as the prophet of orthodox conservatism, offer contrasts which run through the entire history of the development of the two theories. Locke posited that the foundations of state and society were laid by a social contract; Burke saw society as an organic whole produced by historical forces and God's will. Locke argued that the social contract could be terminated; Burke posited that the contract, if there indeed was one, was indissoluble. Locke viewed individuals as equal and enjoying equal political rights; Burke recognized their inherent inequality and their differing roles in society. Burke disagreed with Locke concerning the making of decisions. Locke advocated reason as the guiding light in the making of decisions; Burke emphasized the importance of prudence and criticized abstract theorizing. Locke's liberalism emphasized the concept of inalienable natural rights; Burke conceded that though men must have rights, the duties imposed upon them by society must be emphasized as well. Rights and duties are interrelated in both approaches; the difference is one of emphasis.

Classical conservatism, unlike liberalism with its universal abstractions, has always been closely tied to the cultural context in which it has developed. On the European continent, conservatives had to contend with the abrupt shift from absolutist theory to doctrines of popular sovereignty as a result of the French revolution. This was the context of continental conservatism, not that of traditional rights and parliamentary democracy which underlay English conservative ideas.

The French Revolution was seen by European conservatives as satanic and the product of intellectual arrogance instigated by Locke and the liberals. It was a threat to the very foundations of Christian civilization. Religion must be revived so as to defend society against the torrent of liberal errors which were misleading humanity.

Constitutionalism and its attendant attribute of mass franchise could not place the best people in positions of power. It undermined effective authority, led to the rule of demagogues, and resulted in social conflict. Society is composed of unequal individuals falling into different classes, orders, and groups, each performing differing functions in order to sustain society. Hierarchy and differentiation are an inherent characteristic of organized society, since some are meant to rule while others are expected to obey. To resist the authority of those in power is to resist God, the creator of people and of human differences.

Classical conservatism changed its orientation as the 19th century progressed. Burke's affinity for tradition and an orderly, somewhat aristocratic, parliamentarism gave way to new orientations which were based, naturally enough, upon the retention of those liberal tenets which were being attacked and discarded as the century wore on. Classical liberal ideas constituted the new bastion of conservatism.

This new orientation in conservatism was reflected in the writings of Herbert Spencer who merged classical liberalism with biology just about the time when Darwin's theory of evolution became well known. Spencer's works were very popular for a time and have had a continuing impact in the United States; however, Canadian enthusiasm for his *social darwinist* conservatism waned by the end of the 19th century. Spencer claimed to have succeeded in discovering a total explanation of nature and society. This claim was based on the two major themes in his political thought: the theory of evolution and radical individualism. Spencer believed that by applying the laws of biology, he could unify all knowledge. The unifying element was the principle of evolution; society evolved like a human organism and, he optimistically prophesied, evolution was inevitably accompanied by progress.

Spencer exhibited an intense hostility to government, which, he argued, is a social evil and decays as civilization advances. The lesser the influence of government in society, the more progress the society will make. Government, according to him, was incidental to society, not essential to it. He totally repudiated the idea that government legislation has any benefit for the people. On the contrary, it only serves to restrict the activity of individuals and to deny them the natural right of doing as they wished, even to the point of making blunders. Making mistakes is necessary and is inherent in people; it is no business of government to protect people from themselves. Competition is the indispensable prerequisite for progress, since the fittest will survive and the weak and ill-adjusted will perish. Though he was not against sentiments of love, sympathy, and tolerance, he maintained that their proper place is in the family and not in the society. The family existed to provide succor to the weak and the young; the role of society should be to reward the strong.

Spencer opposed government intervention in any aspect of social life. He argued that to encourage the people in the belief that their condition could be ameliorated by government action leads to disillusionment, discontent, and possibly revolution. It suppresses their initiative and enterprise and produces a citizenry of grownup babies. He took issue with the most fundamental principle of the welfare state— that it is the duty and responsibility of the government to ameliorate social suffering. Suffering is inherent and is produced by a malfunction in human nature. To ameliorate suffering through artificial government action, is, therefore, against the basic constitution of human nature. Spencer's support of laissez-faire goes far beyond that advocated by the classical liberals. Needless to say, his ideas were far from those of the reform liberals, who were his contemporaries.

Spencer's basic distrust of government impelled him to warn that while some kinds of coercive governments were dissolving, new kinds were evolving. He distrusted democracy, feeling that it would result in mob rule and tyranny of the majority. The only method of preventing that was to confine the role of the government to merely the enforcement of contracts, a task which included the prevention and control of crime and violence.

Spencer is seen as a conservative partly because of his view of society as a social organism. His individualism was in fact necessary to an application of the theory of evolution. It was not seen as a "liberating" force by him, but instead as an integral element of the natural processes of social life. His view of society resembled more that which Hobbes saw as preceding the social contract, than that of the liberals such as Locke and Smith.

One of the most widely known contemporary conservatives is the unsuccessful Republican Party candidate for the U.S. presidency in 1964, Senator Barry Goldwater. Goldwater's campaign marked the most coherent contemporary effort to install a vigorously conservative national government. It has been suggested that one of the reasons for his defeat at the polls was this staunch conservatism which alienated the middle and the working class among the voters. In his widely read *Conscience of a Conservative*, Goldwater put forward a conservative program of political action for the United States. The central theme of his program is the preservation of individual freedom. He is very concerned with the extension of the power and authority of the U.S. federal government which, in his view, poses the threat of extreme centralization. He would, therefore, limit the authority of the federal government to such matters of overall national importance as defence, maintenance of law and order, administration of justice, and facilitating free trade by eliminating restrictive regulations. All other political power should revert to the state and local levels where it rightfully belongs. Agriculture subsidies to farmers should be discontinued in favour of a competitive market economy. He advocated the imposition of restrictions on trade union activity and the withdrawal of any form of government participation in the economy. In foreign affairs, he advocated a permanent state of military preparedness by the United States to take action against Communist governments which may be vulnerable, as well as providing overt encouragement for the people to overthrow others.

Romantic Conservatism

One of the forces which contributed to the reaction against the French revolution was that of romanticism. Originally, romantic emotional images were used to oppose the rationalism of the liberals. After 1800 romanticism came more and more to be seen as a conservative instrument. The romantic conservatives were obsessed with visions of moral decay and corruption, feeling that the modern bourgeois state, with its rationalist and materialist values, constituted a low point in the moral history of the human race.

As a reaction to corrupt modernity, German and English writers, among others, began to develop political theories based upon the supposed virtues of semimythical peoples and governments. They rejected the classical conservatives' concern for gradual reform and tradition in favour of the resurrection of political relationships which either were long dead or had existed only in their imaginary reconstructions of the past.

Glorification of the State. German romantic conservatism centered around the revival of the *volk*, a collective notion of the people. Novelists and philosophers of the early 19th century popularized this national ideal by reminding Germans of the exploits of the Germanic tribes against the Roman Empire. The *volk*, in its barbaric form, exemplified to many a pure moral state from which the German people had declined over the centuries. Civilization and Christianity had worked to divide the *volk* into petty, warring states which were easily manipulated by outsiders. The advocacy of abstract rationalism by the French revolutionaries was seen as another instrument acting to divide Germans at the individual level. Not only was the German nation divided into weak principalities but individuals were alienated from its spirit by the use of reason.

The call to revive the *volk* came from many parts of the German intellectual community after 1800. The Romantics argued that an individual by himself or herself cannot be expected to think, act, and exist for himself or herself totally separate from the larger society. A rational life consists of submerging one's individual identity with that of the society and striving for the greater glory of the whole of which one is a part. An irrational life, on the other hand, is one in which the individual's thoughts and actions centre around the satisfaction of personal interests. The state is the only entity which works for the continuous development of the higher purpose of human existence, the promotion of human values. The individual alone, motivated primarily by selfish desires, can do very little.

The most elaborate theory in this vein was proposed by the philosopher, G. W. F. Hegel. He attempted to explain the process of history through an analytical concept of *dialectical idealism*. Hegel conceived the entire span of human history to be the product of a movement of a vast force of ideas. However, no idea (thesis) ever contained the absolute truth. On the contrary, inherent within every idea is its own opposition or contradiction (antithesis). The resultant clash created a new idea (synthesis), which is either the product of a fusion of the original ideas or the development of a totally new outlook. This process Hegel called the dialectic and he used it to explain the thrust of history (see Chapter 15, for Marx's use of the dialectic).

Hegel's dialectical idealism reflects both upon the individual as well as the society to which he or she belongs. History, according to him, is a vast stage upon which the recurring phenomena of the clash of ideas unfold. Individuals and societies are nothing more than the unwitting tools through which ideas and their clash is manifested. Human beings, therefore, have little control over the movement of history; the best they can do is to submerge their individual identities in that of the group or nation to which they belong, which, in turn, is possessed by the historical idea of the time. The nation creates the traditions and the institutions in which the individual lives and his or her primary obligation is to pay unflinching obeisance to its political manifestation, the state. Political genius consisted in identifying one-self with a principle, which he felt was the state. The classical liberals engulfed the individual and the individual's role in society in some-thing of an aura of political glamour; Hegel did the same with the state. To him, what is real is rational; the state was the only reality and, therefore, the only rationality. He rejected the social contract theory and the doctrine of natural rights, claiming that the state was not the creation of individual wills but of the forces of history. There could be no such thing as natural rights, since rights are the product of one's relationship to the social organism. They are prescribed by the historical needs of the state.

Hegel's notions of political rule were authoritarian. He favoured the personal rule of outstanding, charismatic individuals—the heroes of history. Such individuals are inspired by historical forces, motivated by a missionary spirit, and propelled by the force of their destiny to carry the state forward to its full glory. He favoured absolutism and advocated the concentration of all political power in the office of the monarch. He rejected the notion of the separation of executive and legislative power, since, he argued, the executive agencies are ulti-mately responsible for the implementation of laws, and they should work out the details of the laws according to their discretion.

Hegel repudiated the notion that international law governs the relations of states with each other. The state is a law unto itself and is the only vehicle for the expression and promotion of the interest of the citizenry. War and conflict are the natural outcome of the dialectical process of the unfolding of history. Only those states which are motivated by their own strength have any place in history; they are the leading, dominating nations. All others are carried away by the forces of history and forgotten.

Rise of the Hero. The glorification of the state and the enhancement of collective action were not the only possible instruments for overcoming the almost despairingly corrupt modern world. To some the concept of the hero, the great and authoritarian leader, appeared to be attractive. The hero would at once represent the highest inspirational and moral qualities of people and demonstrate the complete falsehood of the liberal tenets of individual rationality and equality.

Thomas Carlyle helped to popularize the heroic myth of the romantic conservatives in England. He based his ideas on the premise that a satisfying life is impossible on this earth, and therefore the liberal goal of promoting the happiness of the individual and the utilitarian concept of promoting the greatest good of the greatest number were both idiotic. Life to Carlyle is a constant scramble in which people must continually labour. Free trade results in selfish people accumulating wealth and esteem through unfair practices which then set the tone for society, thereby corrupting it. To keep society moral, he advocated governmental interference in, and control of, the economy. To Carlyle, the individualist liberty advocated by the liberals results in a struggle in which only the fittest survive. True liberty consists of people finding the path to lesser misfortune through the strong and autocratic guidance of heroes. These superior and wiser people should have complete liberty to rule as long as they obey God, providence, destiny, and the law of nature. Individuals will find liberty only through accepting their guidance; military discipline should be imposed in all walks of life.

Carlyle is considered a popularizer of British imperialism. He lauded Anglo-Saxon qualities, argued for their world hegemony, and posited that, as the superior race, they had inherited the earth. He extended the principle of the struggle for existence to the struggle between nations long before the advent of social darwinism.

Friedrich Nietzche is perhaps best known for his atheistic utterance, "God is dead." There are, however, other aspects of his philosophy which have exercised far-reaching political and social influence. As one writer says:

His rhetorical and melodramatic stress on egoism and cruelty, his contempt for ordinary human life and disregard for law, his glorification of struggle and ruthlessness, and his conviction that the society in which he lived was decadent, were to spread like a blight over the early twentieth century.[9]

The statement "God is dead" was a scathing condemnation of Christian society as Nietzche saw it. The Christian world pays only lip service to Christian morality; it had rejected the Christian religion. This rejection, however, was only the first step in the decaying process of the Christian civilization, which will be followed by further destruction, revolution, and terror. The only way to escape this crisis was to be found not by going back to God but through the pursuit and exercise of political power.

Once the force of the Christian faith as the light that guides people through the chaotic existence of this world has been expended, new guidance will be provided by an heroic "superman." This new person will be motivated by "voluptuousness, passion for power, and selfishness." This person will be treacherous, cruel, cunning, and totally devoid of any sympathy for other people. His one great quality, which places him above other people, will be his courage, which will enable him to fight fate and redeem the past. His courage will enable him to withstand suffering and pain with joy. He will know how to live and how to die. Only then will the futility of life be transformed into purpose and meaningfulness. In keeping with this idea of the superman, Nietzche eulogized warriors. His heroes were Caesar and Napoleon—Lincoln was a weakling and a compromiser. Nietzche advised his superman to make fighting his work and victory his peace. The warrior should never compromise but go forward with unflinching courage in the pursuit of his objective. To Nietzche it is not the cause which justifies war but war which hallows the cause. Power, to him, was its own justification.

It is obvious that conservatism, like liberalism, has taken a dual path. On the one hand, it has taken the form of modern conservatism and remained within the democratic mainstream while objecting to liberal tendencies towards complete egalitarianism and its willingness to frequently rearrange social and governmental relationships. On the other hand, a divergent strain has moved to an organic theory of the state, a strong attachment to the nation and its traditions, and a tendency to romanticize the charismatic leader. Its more extreme form shades off into the romantic nationalism of the sort that has bred a number of radical movements, fascism being a prime example.

---

[9] John Bowle, *Politics and Opinion in the 19th Century* (London: Jonathan Cape, 1966), p. 372. First published 1954.

Canadian Conservatism

The conservative principle, then, is the assertion that the chief political good is stability, the existence of order in the state and society. The order intended, however, is not order inspired by authority from without but order arising from equilibrium reached among the elements of society by usage, not an order mechanically contrived, but one resulting from growth from within.[10]

The above statement on the nature of conservatism made by the Canadian historian, W. L. Morton, reflects the major thrust of the political thinking of conservatives in this country. In content it parallels the interests and emphasis of the liberals in that attention tends to be focussed on specific external and internal concerns rather than upon abstract normative principles.

External Concerns. Conservatives have shared with liberals the continuing preoccupation with the posture of Canada's relations with Britain and the United States. They have tended to rely upon the British connection as a counter to the growing influence of the United States. While sharing the liberal concern with developing and maintaining a Canadian identity, they have advocated its development within the framework of the ties with Britain. Conservative politicians such as Joseph Howe, John A. Macdonald, Robert Borden, and John Diefenbaker and intellectuals such as the two George Grants, grandfather and grandson, have taken essentially this position.

Conservatives have tended to view the Empire and its successor, the Commonwealth, as constructive institutions which provided protection for the smaller nations and a framework for their development and progress. As a complement of this faith in the practical value of the Empire and the Commonwealth, many conservatives believe it to be a standard-bearer of Christian morality and ethics. Added to this is a pronounced attachment to what is called the "British way," the traditions and values of the mother country. To many conservatives, this complex of religious and traditional values is the last barrier to the growth in Canada of Marxism, American influence, and a decline in moral values. In some cases, the Commonwealth has been seen as the basis for a third force to counter the ever-increasing political hegemony of the United States and the Soviet Union.

As a consequence of these beliefs, conservatives vigorously advocated the evolution of an imperial foreign policy at a time when Canadian governments under Liberal leadership were opposing the creation of any institutional framework which would tie Canada too

---

[10] W. L. Morton, "The Conservative Principle in Confederation," *The Queen's Quarterly* 71 (Winter 1964–65): p. 529.

closely to British policies. Conservatives voiced vehement opposition when the Laurier government balked at the suggestion of providing assistance to Britain in the Boer War. They fiercely criticized the Naval Service Bill of 1910, which established an independent Canadian navy in preference to contributing ships to the British navy. More recently, conservative attitudes towards a national flag (1964) and the introduction of new metric standards of measurement reflect the romantic attachment to the British heritage. They are understandably unhappy at the British policy of economic, and conceivably political, integration with Western Europe, in preference to its former ties with the Commonwealth.

Conservatives in this country have advocated protectionism and a high tariff designed to counter increasing American economic influence in Canada. Within the old Imperial and Commonwealth contexts this meant preferential access to overseas markets as well as easier access by Britain to the Canadian market. The National Policy of Macdonald, with its commitment to the building of the Pacific Railway, was an early manifestation of the drive to build an independent economy within the context of the Empire.

Internal Concerns.   Many observers feel that Canada is essentially a conservative society not favourably disposed to widespread reformism and experimentation in economic, social, or political life. This innate reluctance to change has been suggested as the main reason for maintaining the British connection. The British influence is viewed as a stabilizing factor in the continuity of Canadian religious, educational, social, and political institutions. It is also perceived as the feature which most distinguishes Canada from the United States. Americans established their political system through revolution; Canadians followed an evolutionary path. The basic structure and procedures of the major organs of government clearly demonstrate the influence of Britain through the retention of the monarchy, the parliamentary system, and the Empire. It was an attempt to create in British America a new nation which should be, in Macdonald's phrase, "a subordinate kingdom" in the Empire.

There are other aspects which reflect this traditionalism. The BNA Act contains no declaration of the rights of people in the French or the American tradition. Instead, reliance for the protection of these rights was placed in the parliamentary traditions of Britain. As Edward Blake said of the BNA Act, "a single line imported in the system, that mighty and complex and somewhat indefinite aggregate called the British constitution."[11] Again, following British practice even while adopting

---

[11] Blake is referring to the Preamble of the BNA Act: "With a constitution similar in principle to that of the United Kingdom," see C. P. de Glazebrook, *History of Canadian Political Thought,* p. 140.

a federal system, the fathers of Confederation reversed the American arrangement and placed residual powers under the authority of the federal rather than provincial governments. The federal authority was further enhanced by vesting in the crown the right to disallow provincial legislation. While the Americans had sought to decentralize political power, the Canadians maintained its centralized character in conformity with British practice. There is little in the BNA Act or conservative thinking of the time that could be called innovative with the possible exception of the adoption of the federal system to circumvent some of the problems raised by the vastness of the country and the presence of the French minority.

The conservative preoccupation with unity, when confronted with the reality of the French-Canadian minority, has led to the growth of two diverging opinions on the subject. There is the position of the diehard Anglophone who in fact pursues a logic similar to that of the American melting-pot idea. There can be only one language and one basic culture, the English. The French are a conquered people and have been well treated. They should, in this view, accept their fate and assimilate. At no time should the government of Canada fall into the trap of appeasing separatist sentiments. Many of Canada's current problems in this area are seen as the result of a too-soft approach by Liberal governments of the past and present. For instance, the Ontario conservative D'Alton McCarthy, in a speech in 1889, expressed these sentiments, arguing that Canada was a British country and that it was necessary to make the French-Canadians British in sentiment and to teach them the English language. Macdonald disavowed McCarthy and his statement, but the sentiments, nonetheless, still persist.[12]

The other opinion is held by the more moderate among the conservatives who, while accepting the cultural duality of the Canadian society, are unwilling to extend it to the political realm. They concede that the French-Canadian community should be provided with legal and constitutional safeguards for its language and culture. They would not, however, accept French Canada and Quebec as being the same and refuse to grant Quebec any status other than that provided all provinces in the Confederation.

The Canadian conservative, like his liberal counterpart, has a different orientation to the role of the government in the economy than is found in the United States. The American conservative is inclined to view government intervention in the economy with great hostility. For Canadians, the government has been, from the earliest days of Confederation, a necessary partner in the development of the economy, the Pacific Railway and the National Policy being examples of this. There are in Canada several crown corporations, such as the Canadian Na-

---

[12] Ibid., pp. 164–65.

tional Railways, Air Canada, and the provincial hydros, which in the United States would be privately owned. Many of these "nationalized" economic enterprises are creations of Conservative governments.

Generally speaking, political parties in Canada do not operate in accordance with the principles normally associated with liberalism and conservatism. Our political parties are now largely opportunistic, and philosophical distinctions are, at best, of secondary importance.

RECOMMENDED READINGS

Bowle, John. *Politics and Opinion in the 19th Century*. London: Jonathan Cape, 1966 (first published 1954).

Brinton, Crane. *English Political Thought in the 19th Century*. New York: Harper & Brothers, 1962.

Bullock, Allan, and Shock, Maurice. *The Liberal Tradition from Fox to Keynes*. London: Oxford University Press, 1967.

Christian, William, and Campbell, Colin. *Political Parties and Ideologies in Canada*. Toronto: McGraw–Hill Ryerson, 1974.

Cook, Ramsey. *The Maple Leaf Forever*. Toronto: Macmillan, 1971.

————. *The Politics of J. W. Dafoe and the Free Press*. Toronto: University of Toronto Press, 1963.

Creighton, Donald. *Canada's First Century*. Toronto: Macmillan, 1970.

Glazebrook, C. P. de. *A History of Canadian Political Thought*. Toronto: McClelland & Stewart, Ltd., 1966.

Goldwater, Barry. *The Conscience of a Conservative*. Kentucky: Victor Publishing Co., 1960.

Grant, George. *Lament For a Nation*. Toronto: McClelland & Stewart, Ltd., 1965.

————. *Technology and Empire: Perspectives on North America*. Toronto: House of Anansi, 1969.

Greene, T. M. *Liberalism: Its Theory and Practice*. Austin: University of Texas Press, 1957.

Hallowell, John M. *Main Currents in Modern Political Thought*. New York: Henry Holt & Co., 1953.

Hearnshaw, F. J. C. *Conservatism in England*. London: Macmillan, 1933.

Hobhouse, Leonard T. *Liberalism*. New York: Oxford University Press, 1968.

Horowitz, Gad. *Canadian Labour in Politics*. Toronto: University of Toronto Press, 1968.

Kirk, Russell. *The Conservative Mind*. Seattle: University of Washington Press, 1951.

————. *A Program for Conservatives*. Chicago: 1954.

Macpherson, C. B. *Political Theory of Possessive Individualism*. London: Oxford University Press, 1962.

Marchak, M. Patricia. *Ideological Perspectives on Canada*. Toronto: McGraw–Hill Ryerson, 1975.

Morton, W. L.   *The Canadian Identity.* Toronto: University of Toronto Press, 1961.

————. *The Kingdom of Canada.* Toronto: McClelland & Stewart, Ltd., 1963.

Pickersgill, J. W.   *The Liberal Party.* Toronto: McClelland & Stewart, Ltd., 1961.

Trudeau, P. E.   *Approaches to Politics.* Toronto: Oxford University Press, 1970.

Underhill, Frank H.   *In Search of Canadian Liberalism.* Toronto: Macmillan, 1961.

Viereck, Peter.   *Conservatism.* Princeton, N.J.: Van Nostrand, 1956.

15

Socialism

TO UNDERSTAND SOCIALISM in its many variations and to comprehend the reasons for its widespread appeal, it is necessary to examine its origins as well as its contemporary content. A socialist theory, loosely defined, depicts people as basically sociable and cooperative animals, whose interests are best served by a political and economic system which strengthens these instincts. The "bourgeois" theories discussed in the previous chapter assume the opposite—that people are basically aggressive and acquisitive and that a political system which channels and controls this competitive instinct is necessary.

Any discussion of the various socialist theories poses a number of problems. Some arise from the mistaken idea that the theories have a common source, such as Karl Marx; other problems stem from the confusion created by various groups as they advanced their claims to the possession of the authentic socialist theory. To the uninitiated, the problem of distinguishing socialism from communism is a most troublesome one. Communism is simply a variety of socialism. To a convinced liberal or conservative, the difference may not appear to be of any real importance, but it has always been of great significance to socialists and communists themselves. Much of the confusion over these terms is created by the fact that many Marxists do not regard themselves as communists, as it is understood in the light of the examples set by the Soviet Union and Communist China. At the same time there are many socialists who do not have any special affection for Karl Marx, though he is the source of truth to virtually all who call themselves communists. It is thus possible to make a distinction between socialists who are Marxists and those who are not. The leading examples of radical Marxist socialism, commonly labelled as communism, are the parties in the Soviet Union and Communist China and several other smaller groups such as the Trotskyites.

The major competing groups of socialists are those commonly referred to as democratic socialists. In most Western European and North American countries, this group is made up of a blend of Marxists, trade unionists, and reformers. The Canadian New Democratic Party falls into this group as do the Labour Party of Great Britain and the social democratic parties in Scandinavia and West Germany, to name a few. The United States is the only major Western democracy that does not have an active and sizable democratic socialist party. These parties are as varied as are the communist parties, but the major distinction between them and the communist, other than the question of fidelity to Karl Marx, is the acceptance of parliamentary democracy as the appropriate means of attaining their goals. Democratic socialists have accepted the democratic method as a matter of principle; the communists, if they accept it at all, usually do so as a matter of expediency.

Utopian Socialism

One of the main sources of socialist theory has been the Judeo-Christian tradition of concern with social welfare. However imperfectly practiced, the ideals of this tradition have served, and continue to serve, as a standard by which the performance of political systems may be judged. Modern socialism can be traced to the Christian ideals of love of neighbour and the sharing of material possessions. As with the earliest proponents of liberal theories, the earliest "socialists" firmly rooted their ideas in religious soil.

The most notable example of early religious socialism, or communalism is that of the Anabaptist movement. The Anabaptists felt that the Reformation had not gone far enough. They called for a church in which membership was voluntary and whose basic principles came from the New Testament. They disagreed with both the Catholics and the Lutherans on the need for a state church. This was tantamount to rejecting political authority in the 1500s and the Anabaptists were persecuted throughout Europe for their beliefs. Their emphasis upon Christian love led them into pacifism, for which they have been persecuted nearly everywhere during wartime. The Mennonite and Hutterite communities throughout Canada trace their history back to this movement. One of the reasons for their immigration into Canada was the assurances made to them that they would not be subject to military service.

The emphasis of the Anabaptists upon fellowship, or the cooperative nature of people, led them to develop and maintain a special lifestyle based upon rural communities centered around small churches. Depending upon the Christian radicalism of the various

Anabaptist groups, today's descendants may live in communally held farm colonies on the Prairies or in private homes in the suburbs of middle-sized cities of central and western Ontario.

Besides the Anabaptists, others attempted to develop theoretical principles which would allow people to live together peacefully. Private property, the basis of liberal theory, was the point of attack by some since they considered it the key to human conflict. Sir Thomas More was one of the earliest such theorists. In his book *Utopia* (1515), he advocated a communal lifestyle based upon a group of agricultural communities of limited size where private property would not exist. Greed would be banished because the society would provide all that its residents need to sustain themselves in comfort. A century later a group known as the "Diggers" was involved in an actual experiment in communal living. They were significant only insofar as they have often been taken as reflecting a longing for communalism among the lower classes of society. They argued that the money system and the existence of private property had corrupted people. Such a system was not a natural, or at least inevitable, result of people's nature or of uncontrollable natural or social forces. The Digger experimental agricultural commune was ended by the intervention of their neighbors and the troops.

These examples illustrate how old are the ideas that people could live without private property and that they should share with and care for others. The French Revolution and the concurrent industrial revolution created favourable circumstances for the proliferation of similar theories and experiments in the first half of the 19th century. The French Revolution both reflected and accelerated the process of disintegration of the old order in France and produced a number of socialist theorists, who tried to evaluate the impact of industrialism and suggest ways in which modern people could live in harmony with each other.

Some, such as Charles Fourier, felt that peace could be achieved only by the rejection of industrialism. Generally described as slightly mad, Fourier was a strong believer in the existence of a fixed nature of people. To him, human nature was based on 12 basic drives, or passions, which it was necessary to liberate from the inhibiting effects of contemporary society. He regarded the emergent capitalist economic system as wasteful and destructive, though he recognized its productive capabilities. Like many early socialists, he adhered to the romantic idea of a small self-sufficient community, organized on the communal style even to the extent of a common kitchen. In such a society, where 2,000 was envisioned as the practical upper limit of population, the spirit of cooperation would be so pervasive that even the most menial and disagreeable tasks would be willingly performed.

The methods by which the community was to be established and the fruits of its labour distributed betrays Fourier's fascination with certain aspects of the capitalist system. All who joined were to invest in the community and the profits were to be divided in an exact proportion of $5/12$ to labour, $4/12$ to capital, and $3/12$ to talent. He envisioned the communal government as being very simple and democratic with elected officials. In fact, little government would be needed as all would be well without it. In this sense a Fourierist community would be virtually anarchistic in practice, with so little structure as to hardly constitute a recognizable political unit. Fourier's prescriptions were followed by a number of people in France and especially in the United States. Many of the communities were short-lived, but there were some relatively successful ones and this orientation was much in vogue during the 1840s among the intellectual and literary circles of the New England states.

During the 1960s there was a revival of interest in communalism of the agrarian type advocated by Fourier. This interest was based upon a similar rejection of contemporary society, especially of the apparently "dehumanizing" character of industrial and urban life. Many of these communes are far more loosely structured than that which Fourier might have considered desirable; in fact they frequently appear closer to an anarchist model. Not only is the urban commercial life rejected, but also its "artificial" qualities, whether they be in the form of food additives, fashion fads, or social arrangements. Emphasis is generally placed upon close relations within the commune and a detachment from the world outside of it. Some contemporary writers suggest that society in general is constantly moving into new relationships and that the pace of these changes is dramatically accelerating. These changes put an emphasis on personal performance and mobility as the key to success, and this necessarily involves frequent breaking of personal, geographic, and organizational ties. Many individuals are unwilling or unable to adapt to the lifestyle of the contemporary society and therefore seek a return to the traditional spirit and security of the old society by attempting to establish self-sufficient communes.[1]

The opposite approach, an attempt to envision a large-scale industrial socialist society, was made by Henri de Saint-Simon, an eccentric French nobleman who spent a good deal of his life involved in efforts to reform society. He had some elements in common with Fourier, especially the negative reaction to the progress of the capitalist system as it then existed. Saint-Simon was convinced that reason and science could be brought to bear on society's problems. New economic and social organizations would have to provide for more than material

---

[1] See issues of the journal, *The Futurist;* also, Alvin Toffler, *Future Shock* (New York: Random House, 1970), and *The Eco-Spasm Report* (New York: Bantam Books, 1975).

wants if society in the future was to be acceptable. Saint-Simon even went so far in this direction as to advocate a new religion designed specifically for this purpose which would substitute a worship of progress and science for more traditional theology.

Saint-Simon was one of the first organization theorists. His goal was to define the type of organization that would put an end to the upheavals of his time, and he came to the conclusion that the two key forces which must be taken into account were science and industry. Society would have to be restructured to give predominance to managers and technocrats if the general welfare of society in an industrial age was to be enhanced. Saint-Simon argued that if the material wants of society were satisfied then the masses would be happy, thus sidestepping the possible conflict between his essentially technocratic and hierarchical system and the egalitarian and democratic sentiments of much of the population. The key to the question of possible abuse of power by the technocrats was that they would be acting in a scientific way, basing their decisions on an accurate perception of the problems and the realistic means available to solve them. In their endeavours they should be left virtually unhindered; government as popularly known would have no significant role. The community would be organized in such a way that cooperation, based on scientific management, would become the order of the day.

In many respects, his arguments may be used even today as a rationale for a government of experts rather than politicians.[2] An oft-stated version of this sentiment in contemporary times is that such matters as defence or monetary affairs should be a matter for the professionals and that politicians should not participate in these areas. This overlooks the obvious point that experts often disagree with each other and that some group has to assume the responsibility for making the decisions, and that it is also possible for experts to come to perfectly "logical" and "scientific" conclusions that are simply not practical in human terms. Such a proposition also overlooks the fact that even the experts are human and are likely to suffer from sundry errors, misconceptions, prejudices, and special interests which may intentionally or otherwise taint or distort their objectivity.

Robert Owen offered a solution which incorporated aspects of industrialism with communal ideals. He was a very successful English business leader as well as a political eccentric. His basic view was that people are shaped by their environment, a view conflicting with that of Fourier, for instance, who assumed the basic character of people to be

---

[2] Formulations and criticisms of the managerial revolution have been with us for forty years. See Friedrich Hayek, *The Road to Serfdom* (Chicago: University of Chicago Press, 1964); Milovan Djilas, *The New Class* (New York: Praeger, 1957); and J. K. Galbraith, *The New Industrial State* (Boston: Houghton Mifflin, 1967).

fixed. To Owen, people's characters were always shaped by those around them; what one becomes is the result of one's environment and socialization. Owen then proceeded to argue that if people are shaped by their environment then it is wrong to insist that individuals are responsible for their situation. He felt that the assumption of conventional religion that people bear a moral responsibility for their own actions was itself the basis of the origin of evil. As a result of this assumption, people fall under the power of the clergy, who have taken upon themselves the right to define what is right and wrong. Christian morals were pictured by him as being based on fear and repression, for the clergy sets impossible standards which no human being can attain, and then hands out rewards and punishments on this basis. The result, in Owen's view, is that such a system forces people to be hypocrites, for they must constantly adjust the irreconcilable differences between this arbitrary morality and reality.

Owen argued for a considerable degree of human freedom—a freedom of ideas and speech, which should be virtually absolute. Freedom of action, however, was seen as necessarily limited in those situations in which others might be hurt by one's exercise of freedom. The ideal society projected by Owen was organized to cope with the realities of the industrial age—it was to be an industrial town run according to his environmentalist principles. An actual community, New Lanark in Scotland, was set up along Owenite lines and was a success in comparison to other such experiments in the 1800s. Owen's environmentalism and concern for human individuality were expressed in his ideal of a system of education in which the children were free to learn as and when they wished. In essence, he was relying upon the natural curiosity of children as the mainspring of the educational system.

In his advocacy of this new society, Owen was forced to come to grips with the industrial age and in so doing he was put in the position of having to judge the rightness of the system that had made him wealthy. He found a great deal wrong with the economic system in England and came to the conclusion that it was the fault of the system itself. The economics of competition so beloved by capitalists was in his view an economics of waste, and this, combined with the stupidity of government and the irrationality of religion, resulted in the system producing far less than was possible or desirable. The system emphasized buying cheap and selling dear and was governed by no restraints in the interests of the general community. The end result, he felt, was inferior goods, badly made with automatic waste. The conventional capitalist was being stupid, for in paying workers subsistence wages he or she was restricting his or her own potential market. In this respect Owen foresaw the development of the attitude among many capitalists that a wider market, and greater long-run profits, could be created by a generally higher wage level.

Owen, in criticizing the economic system, did not spare the institutions and classes which sought to protect the status quo. He regarded lawyers as a total waste and military people and clergy as of even less social value. His view of landlords and rentiers was that they were the worst form of economic parasite. In his own ideal society there would be no role or place for any of them; his society would be hierarchically organized, one in which education and experience would determine who would be the decision makers. The system would be a benevolent patriarchy in which it was recognized that individuals were not literally equal, but in which all were given the chance to be what they could. Conventional politics was of little interest to him, and he parted company with the emerging British trade union movement in the 1830s over their insistence on trying to remake the system by conventional political means or by strikes.

Among the so-called Utopian Socialists of the first half of the 19th century, Owen was perhaps the most practical, but the workers for whose benefit he was attempting to work grew increasingly attracted to the trade union approach to their problems. Owen himself had hoped that his experiment at New Lanark would be so successful that it would recommend itself to his fellow capitalists. The working conditions which obtained in New Lanark would be regarded with horror today insofar as working hours are concerned, but they were quite humane by the standards of the day. His fellow capitalists remained unconvinced, and ultimately Owen lost interest in this idea and began to explore other possibilities. He was at heart an experimenter and never attracted the kind of consistent following that many other reformers in Britain did. He exemplified an aspect of English socialism that set it apart from continental socialism—its experimental and pragmatic character as opposed to the tendency to see things in absolutes. This did not arise from a lack of conviction or passion, but rather from a different frame of mind in expressing them.

MARXIAN SOCIALISM

Karl Marx has emerged from the intellectual ferment of 19th-century Europe as the most important contributor to modern socialist theory. Born in the Rhineland region of Germany, he had personally experienced discrimination and capricious authority in the form of the anti-Jewish bias of the Prussian government. His early career took him into journalism, and he was at one time a reporter and editor for a reformist Rhineland newspaper. In the 1840s he began to show signs of adopting a radical political position, a shift which became definitive after he moved to Paris and began associating with German exiles and other radicals resident there at the time. Forced to move to Brussels, Marx became involved with organizing workers' groups.

The year 1848 was one of upheaval throughout Europe, with Paris being the centre of this activity. A series of revolts occurred in many cities, though most were readily suppressed. Marx himself took no active part in them, though he wrote the now famous *Communist Manifesto* in this context. The manifesto, while it does not represent the full range of Marx' ideas, provides as succinct a statement of them as is to be found. His later, and longer, works are more difficult to read and open to conflicting interpretations. From the summer of 1849 to his death in 1883 he spent most of his time in England writing his major work, *Das Kapital.*

A number of theorists influenced Marx, the best known of these being Friedrich Hegel. Marx borrowed the dialectic from Hegel, but put it to a different use. The dialectic was originally a mechanical debating process invented by the classical Greeks. In its original form it was a means of uncovering truth through a process of step-by-step questions and answers. Hegel argued that concepts contain within themselves their own contradictions or opposites. An opposite can be deduced from the nature of the original concept and used to arrive at a new and more perfect understanding. This process of thesis (original concept), antithesis (its opposite), and synthesis (the resolution of the conflict of opposites) for Hegel formed a triadic pattern with each synthesis becoming a new thesis and the whole process repeating itself. Its relevance for politics was that it could be used to analyze and explain the process inherent in human history. The process was one in which each presumably settled concept would automatically give rise to a contradiction, forcing thinkers to constantly be on the intellectual move to higher and higher planes.

Marx appropriated Hegel's dialectic view of history and used it as a means of explaining human history in the way he saw it. To Marx, an idea or spirit was not the primary force in the evolutionary process of society, but rather the economic system and, more specifically, the question of who owns the tools of production. Marx's theory, in its concentration on the economics of the industrial state, deviated from many of the "utopian" socialists, especially those who wished to go back to a simpler agrarian life. To Marx, this was not possible, and the critical need of the time was to understand how the industrial society in its capitalist form developed and what its future was. The dialectic provided the means of discovering truth and formed the framework for analysis.

In his economic thinking, Marx borrowed heavily from the various classical economists and liberals so important to the development of

FIGURE 15–1
The Dialectic Process

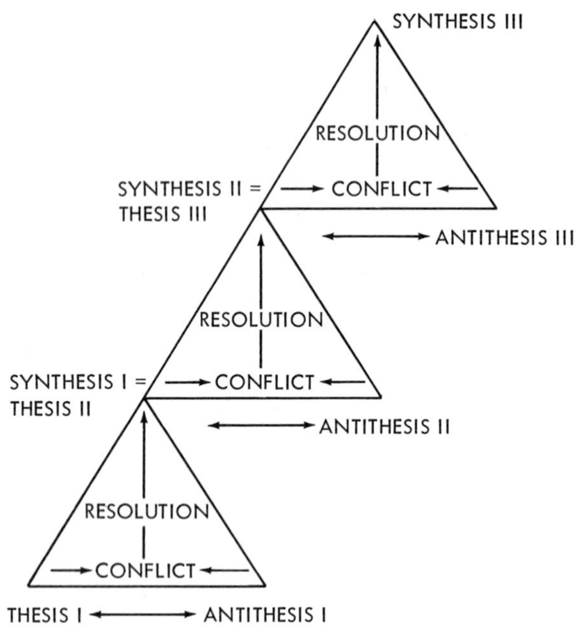

contemporary conservatism and liberalism. He became increasingly abstract and "scientific" as time went on, but his works were always directed at the nature of society, its current state, and its historical background. The key to understanding Marx's ideas is his premise that social change is the result of a disharmony between the material forces of production and the relations of production. The former consist of land, labour, and capital and the latter are the legal and institutional arrangements regarding control over their use. As technology develops, the techniques of production change while the institutional framework lags behind. The resultant tension creates social transformation. The process is inevitable so long as society continues to develop and change at the technological level while the relations of production continue to reflect the arrangement of the material forces of production of an earlier time. The dialectic is the tool used to identify and understand social changes. In Marx's view, the primitive agrarian economy gave way to the slave economy, and that to the feudal economy, and the feudal economy to the bourgeois. The bourgeois economy was, like its predecessors, inevitably creating and unleashing the forces that would ultimately destroy it, and the outcome of that conflict would be the socialist economy.

Marx is a proponent of economic determinism, that is, the position that economic realities shape society. In Marxist terms, the economic system, specifically the modes and relations of production, shape the rest of society including its values, beliefs, and religion. The whole range of social and political institutions is a superstructure dictated by the nature of the economic foundations. Thus, the behavioural phenomena that have been emphasized in this text would be regarded as of little significance by an orthodox Marxist. They would be viewed simply as a result of the fundamental economic reality, a symptom rather than a cause. To treat social ills, a Marxist must go back to the basic economic relationships.

The argument that changes in the means of production will result in a tension between them and the relations of production, a tension which will ultimately force sweeping changes on society, is a logical line of reasoning that has recommended itself to Marxists and non-Marxists alike. The dialectic is, in fact, superfluous to the basic argument. To most non-Marxists the notion that progress comes only from the tensions between opposites (thesis-antithesis) is regarded as simplistic. It is one thing to posit that progress comes from a creative tension between forces in society and quite another to argue that this tension is always bipolar and that there is only one possible result. The dialectic, if one accepts it, does however give to Marxist predictions the element of inevitability. This certainty about the future is clearly one of the reasons why Marxism, of whatever variety, has such an appeal to those who wish to see fundamental changes in society. Not only does Marxism offer a coherent explanation of the forces at work in society, it also reassures the individual believer about the future and of the ultimate value of belief and work whether or not he or she lives to see its fruition.

Marx's analysis led him to believe that the downfall of the capitalist economic system was inevitable. In his view, the old feudal system, based essentially on land, gave way to a commercial system as the result of the growth of a commercial middle class primarily urban in character. The emergence of trading and industrial enterprises put a premium on the availability not of land, but of the tools of production and the capital needed to acquire and operate them. The commercial middle class, which grew out of the feudal system, overthrew it, an assertion which explained the French Revolution. As the new capitalist system matured, it would require both increasingly large amounts of capital and a concentration of the tools of production in order to maintain competitive efficiency. The most critical result of this economic revolution was the emergence of an urban proletariat or working class. The demands of competitive efficiency would require the physical concentration of the new working class into cities, and the basic economies of the system would require that those in control buy cheap and sell dear. The new urban proletariat would thus be under-paid and chronically exploited.

This view of the rationale for the capitalist system was not new with Marx, since earlier liberal economists had recognized its outlines. Marx extended this analysis. Whereas some of the earlier liberal theorists assumed that the proletariat would get its fair share in the selling of its "commodity," its labour, Marx argued the more pessimistic proposition that the working class would be paid as little as possible. The price paid for labour bore no necessary relationship to the value of the product; the difference between what was paid in wages and what the product was worth to the capitalist was referred to as *surplus value*. Surplus value in Marxist terms is the source of capitalist profits. Many of the original proponents of capitalism assumed that wages would be equitable, but to Marx the profit motive forces the capitalist to do otherwise. The capitalist is not an evil person *per se*; but is as trapped by the system as the worker is.

Marx argued that the capitalist system *must* impoverish the proletariat, and inevitably undermine its own original source of power, the middle class. As capitalist enterprises required an increasing concentration of capital and resources to remain effective, the number of individuals who benefitted from them would be reduced and increasing numbers of the middle class would be forced down into the proletariat. Besides, by concentrating workers in industrial cities, such as Paris and London, the capitalists were making it possible for the working class to find its identity. Previously, the exploited had been too dispersed to be important, but now, through their geographic concentration and with the ideological aid of a communist party, they would be able to comprehend the nature of the system and participate in the process of its overthrow. It was the responsibility of this party to make the workers aware of their historical role and to prepare them for the revolution and the power that would come to them afterwards.

Marx also took the position that the loyalties that mattered were class loyalties rather than those based on nation, religion, or ethnic group. It is one of the ironies of history that, though it is based on the concept of a struggle between the proletariat and the bourgeois, Marxist theory derived its most effective proponents from middle-class backgrounds. Marx and Lenin themselves were the clearest examples of this phenomena. The concept of class as the meaningful division in society naturally has been opposed by those who regard the nation or ethnic group as the most important identity. The tendency to identify along national lines also helps to explain many of the tensions within various Marxist groups, and the appeal of nationalism constantly plagues those who prefer to think in terms of a global proletariat engaged in class warfare. Subsequent Marxist theorists have offered different solutions to the dilemma, but in doing so the question of the primacy of economic factors has been brought into question.

Marx never clearly settled the question of the kind of society which would follow the revolution. He regarded the state, as we know it, as the result of the rise of private property and its laws and institutions as simply corollaries to the dominance of the propertied class. Marx clearly expected the rise of the proletariat to signal the end of the dialectic process; the resultant society would be the high point and end of human development. If the logic of the dialectic is in fact ironclad, then it is equally logical to argue that this new society should produce its own tensions, its own thesis-antithesis conflict, and be thus forced to move on to yet another level of development. By making the choice to end the dialectic process with the classless society following the proletarian revolution, Marx deviated from the logic which he himself applied to other systems and societies.

When the proletariat came to power, a new society was to be progressively created and all vestiges of bourgeois society were to be eliminated. This new egalitarian society would by definition be without exploitation. There would be a period of transition, called the *dictatorship of the proletariat,* during which the evils of the capitalist system would be eliminated. After this, there would be no further need for governmental institutions in the usual sense and the state would "wither away." In the long run Marx saw the emergence of a free, egalitarian society similar to the anarchist societies proposed by certain of the early "utopian" socialists and by his contemporary rivals, the Anarchists.

Dissent from Marxism has often taken the form of a challenge to economic determinism. Modern investigations into such diverse areas as anthropology, psychology, and sociology offer strong evidence that the factors influencing human affairs are numerous and that they vary with the situation. Many have come to regard Marx's insights into the exploitative nature of the capitalist system as quite valuable, but far too simplistic.

The question of the inevitability of the revolution has also divided socialists, with non-Marxists tending to argue that such devices as strong trade unions, popular political movements within the system, and pressure groups could force the system into being equitable. This is not the same as the position taken by some Marxists that a revolution can be made by parliamentary methods, for the former assumes the retention of a modified form of capitalism. Marx himself would have none of this.

The events of the century since Marx have both contradicted and supported aspects of his theory as an explanation of political and economic reality. The capitalist system has not survived in its mid-19th-century form, but neither has it perished in a general revolution. It has instead been reformed, partly through the technology which Marx recognized as part of the process of change, and partly through specific changes in the rules of the economic and political games.

Marx stated that political power comes from economic power and has no independent reality. The many reforms in the actual operations of the economic system brought about by political means are taken by many as evidence that Marx was in error on this point. Both the welfare state and various democratic socialist states are based on the exercise of political power to alter economic realities. The Marxist would argue that the basic realities of the system have not been changed—that power still lies with the owners of the means of production and that the working class is still getting the worst of the deal. But it has become increasingly difficult for the Marxists to hold their own against the reformers of capitalism, as the middle class continues to grow in size and prosperity. Further, the organized portion of the working class continues to find various means of gaining a larger share of economic benefits in the industrially advanced countries, and it was in these countries where Marx said the revolution was supposed to begin.

SOVIET COMMUNISM

In understanding the impact of Marxism upon the 20th century, it is necessary to turn to those who translated his rather complex and abstract theories into a program for action. One such person was Lenin. Marx himself was primarily a theorist, uncomfortable in dealing with groups and abrasive to the point of vindictiveness. Lenin was the reverse, a man of action quite capable of working with people to build a revolutionary movement, and yet concerned enough with theory to add a number of important concepts to Marxism. It is not that Lenin was any easier to get along with if one was in opposition to him, but rather that he was capable of organizing people to a degree which Marx was not. Lenin was clearly one of the world's great revolutionaries.

Lenin (born Vladimir Ilich Ulianov) was of middle-class background, his father being a school superintendent. His older brother was arrested for plotting to assassinate Czar Alexander III and was hanged. Lenin himself later turned to Marxism and found himself exiled to Siberia as a political prisoner. He fled Russia in 1899 and became involved with a group of exiled Russian Marxists. By 1907 Lenin found himself largely in control of the Social Democratic Party, as the Russian Marxists were then known. Lenin remained in exile until 1917, when the German government found it expedient to help him reenter Russia. They were gambling that his presence would add to the problems of an unstable Russian government, which was at war with Germany. They were right.

Lenin began to organize a coup d'état against the provisional government that had been formed following the revolution in March 1917. The provisional government, led by moderate socialists, found itself unable to fulfill its military commitments to the Allies and also meet the increasing demands for economic and social reforms at home. It lost ground steadily, pressured by the right as well as the left. Lenin made a successful bid for power on November 7, 1917. Once in control of the government, he found himself faced with the need to end the Russian participation in World War I, which he did early in 1918. He also had to stave off those who would undo his revolution. Several foreign powers intervened and at one point the communists were in dire straits militarily. Lenin, with the brilliant assistance of Leon Trotsky, was gradually able to turn the tide.

Leninism

Before his assumption of power, Lenin made a number of contributions to Marxist theory. One of his major concerns was the role of the Communist party. Marx had never clearly defined the limits of the Communist party's activity or its authority as an organization. Lenin took up where Marx had left off and argued that the revolution would come about through the activities of a highly organized, disciplined, limited group, a "vanguard of the proletariat." This vanguard party was to have considerable flexibility in terms of tactics, but its lines of authority were to be exact and demanding. Lenin felt that the average worker and peasant was in no position to understand the true nature of the forces at work. A trained and dedicated party could lead the proletariat to an understanding of their true place and role. The party's ideological purity must be retained. Those Marxists who advocated a softer or more indirect approach to the problem, were regarded as "revisionists," who diluted the role of the party to little more than a plaything, a bourgeois political faction. In his various writings Lenin vigorously attacked such ideological opponents within the Marxist movement.

One of the acute theoretical problems with which Lenin had to wrestle was the place of Russia in the Marxist system. His rivals in the Social Democratic Party argued that the proletariat was far too weak to make a revolution, that Russia was so backward that it had yet to undergo the bourgeois revolution and enter the capitalist stage. Until that occurred, the proletarian revolution would have to be put off. Trotsky argued otherwise—that the two revolutions could in fact be run together and the capitalist stage short-circuited. While the former was a more orthodox Marxist view, the latter was more appealing for the obvious immediate practical possibilities it offered. Lenin in effect set out to do the latter, while at times appearing to be in favour of the former. As subsequent events were to show, Lenin was correct in his assessment of the practical situation and its possibilities, even if it meant sidestepping one of the basic points of Marxist theory. Practicality aside, some orthodox Marxists felt that Lenin was simply an opportunist who took control through a peculiar circumstance and fashioned something that looked legitimate, but was not. The claim that the two revolutions, bourgeois and proletarian, could be telescoped into such a short period was regarded by many as a heresy.

A third contribution made by Lenin was the development of a Marxist interpretation of imperialism. The need for such an exposition arose from the fact that the proletariat of many nations, including those ostensibily organized in self-conscious movements, joined in support of the efforts of their respective countries in World War I. This ran counter to the tenet that the proletarians have no country, only their class. And it was especially discouraging that the leaders as well as rank-and-file gave in to the enthusiasm of nationalism.

Lenin argued that a small minority of countries were exploiting the rest of the world; the imperialists were getting fat on the labour of the proletariat and the peasants under their domination. With the huge profits that resulted from such exploitation, the capitalists were able to subvert the working class in the imperialist countries, thus dulling their sensibilities toward their brethren in the exploited lands. This view of the world economy was not new to Lenin; he borrowed much of his thesis on the subject from a non-Marxist English scholar, J. A. Hobson. Lenin saw that the extension of control and exploitation to new lands was part of the dialectic process. He argued that these expanding and aggressive empires must ultimately come into conflict with each other. By extending their imperial domains the capitalists had forestalled revolution at home, but this process of expansion had finally brought the empires themselves into mutual conflict.[3]

Lenin, as a successful revolutionary, had to face a problem never seriously confronted by Marx. As the leader of a political organization governing a major country, it fell to him to deal with the question of the role of the state in a socialist revolution. Lenin approached the question of the future role of the state by asserting that it is so intertwined with the capitalist system that it must, and will, be destroyed by the revolution. What emerges is a situation where the proletariat takes over the powers of the state and uses them to secure the revolution. The reality of power and strong opposition to the com-

---

[3] See Chapter 16.

munist vision of the future meant that in practice the state had to be retained as an organizing and repressing instrument, only this time it was to be in the interests of the people. It was the "dictatorship of the proletariat."

Much of the rest of the world watched Lenin's success with fascination or horror. To many socialists, Marxists and non-Marxists alike, it seemed that the future for which they had worked for so long might be just around the corner. The communists, in their initial enthusiasm, welcomed other attempts at revolution—the abortive Spartacist revolt in Germany and the ill-fated Bela Kun regime in Hungary (1919) being the best examples. The opponents of this apparently expanding revolution took steps to repress radical movements in their own countries. The repression of the Winnipeg General Strike (1919) was partially a result of the fear of a similar event occurring in Canada. So were the infamous "Palmer Raids" against radicals and aliens carried out by the United States Attorney General at about the same time.

Lenin's impact on the worldwide socialist movement was positive in that he proved it possible to make a revolution. It was negative in that it further divided the socialist movement. Socialist movements outside of Russia had to decide which course to follow—that set by the Russian communists or a more moderate course. The debate rent the movement and within a few years most Socialist parties had split into at least two camps, a pro-Russian "Communist Party" and independent socialist groups.

Stalinism

The work of Lenin had in many ways only begun when he was wounded in an assassination attempt. From 1921 on his health declined and he took a less active political role. The two key figures who emerged in this period were Leon Trotsky and the then little-known Stalin. Joseph Stalin was the General-Secretary of the Communist Party at the time of Lenin's death in 1924, and there is good evidence that Lenin and others were increasingly uncomfortable with his control of such a powerful position. Whatever the truth, Stalin was clearly bent upon gaining power. In a series of manoeuvres, Stalin gradually eroded the basis of Trotsky's power, and by the late 1920s had exiled him to Siberia.

Just as the seizure of power by Lenin and the subsequent drive of the Russian communists for leadership of socialist movements around the world split these movements, so Stalin's drive for power following Lenin's death produced the same results. In its wake a number of additional theoretical ideas were put forth. During the last three years of Lenin's life, the use of *democratic centralism* as the guiding principle of the Communist Party was applied with increasing rigor. The term sums up Lenin's ideas concerning rigid lines of authority within the revolutionary party and, simply put, it bound party organizations to accept decisions of leaders higher up in the party hierarchy. During Lenin's lifetime, policy debates were frequently quite spirited and Lenin's authority continued to rest to a considerable extent on his prestige and persuasive powers. Stalin was a different sort altogether and his penchant for intrigue put the notion of democratic centralism in a very different light. By the late 1920s, Party decisions by deliberation became unknown.

In his bid to eliminate Trotsky from the Party, Stalin opposed Trotsky's proposal to continue the efforts at revolution abroad. Stalin took a position designed to appeal to Russian nationalism by emphasizing the building of "socialism in one country." Stalin claimed that a socialist economy could be built in a country like Russia by political means, given the availability of resources, natural and human. This appeal was designed to capitalize upon the war-weariness of the average Russian, the natural tendency to think of the national situation first, and the growing feeling that the world revolution was not just around the corner.

To promote the new socialist state, Stalin argued that since the workers owned the factories and controlled the state, there could be no exploitation, even when forced farm collectivization and industrialization began with the First Five-Year Plan in 1928. That he was busily engaged in shaping an economic system by political means, a logical contradiction of orthodox Marxism, was glossed over. For many orthodox Marxists this confirmed the feeling that the Russian Revolution was not legitimate. Trotsky's supporters, still active if not numerous, have continued to this day to contest the political left with the Stalinists in many non-Communist countries, providing yet another split among Marxists.

The emphasis on socialism in one country also signalled the abandonment of the internationalist aspect of Marxism as it had been understood previously. Stalin pursued the goal of control over Communist parties abroad as vigorously as he had at home, and many were rent by bitter disputes, creating further disillusionment among the original sympathizers with the revolution. The assumption that the success of communism was dependent upon the support of the working classes of the industrial nations was reversed and the future of the revolution was now tied firmly to the success of the Russian experiment and its leadership.

Chinese Communism

China would appear at first glance to be an unpromising place for a communist revolution, being even more agrarian and rural than Russia had been in 1918. As the success of the Russian Revolution became obvious in the early 1920s, an effort was made to copy its example in China. Mao Tse-tung was one of the few early Chinese communists to see that the notion of an uprising led by the urban proletariat would be futile. It was attempted anyway in 1927 with the help of the *Comintern* (Communist International) and its failure confirmed Mao in his convictions. He then began the task of rebuilding the party as a revolutionary party based upon the peasantry rather than industrial workers. In making this break with the Russian formula, Mao had to forgo much of the support that he might have otherwise anticipated.

Like most of the major leaders of the Communist movement, Mao Tse-tung was born of a middle-class family. He became increasingly aware of China's degraded and exploited position in the early years of this century and was attracted to Marxism as both an explanation and a guide to action. Mao found it necessary to formulate a theory which would allow for the operation of a Marxist revolutionary movement in a rural, nonindustrial environment. Lenin's interpretation of imperialism as the last stage of capitalism served as the basis for the Maoist alterations in the basic Marxist theory. Mao argued that it was best to attack the imperialists at the periphery of their power, which would dictate an agrarian revolution. In this situation, the proper makeup of a communist party had to be as much military as political. It should take up the side of the peasants in their struggles against their exploiters. By befriending the peasants, the communist party would gradually rob the established government of its ability to rule. It would become in effect an alternate government. This formula has proven itself valuable in a number of situations outside China, most notably in Cuba in the 1950s and in Indochina since 1950. A government that cannot maintain the allegiance of the countryside is in grave danger, and not infrequently the governments in underdeveloped countries are incompetent, corrupt, and vicious. This formula for revolution has been tried elsewhere with less success, but it continues to exert a broad appeal for would-be revolutionaries everywhere outside the industrial world.

This revision of the role of the party to fit underdeveloped countries was coupled by Mao to the more traditional concept of the party as the disciplined political vanguard. After their victory in 1949, the Chinese communists, under Mao's leadership, carried the role of the party as the reshaper of society to new heights. On the one hand, they virtually deified Mao, his world-famous "little red book" having become the only source of inspiration and constructive action in China. On the other hand, a great *cultural revolution* was unleashed in China in 1967 which was designed to uproot all outdated ideas and to eliminate bourgeois remnants. The "Red Guards," a student-youth militia, mounted a massive campaign which reached into all parts of China. They attempted to overhaul various party, government, and commercial agencies and, in the process, caused considerable disruption of normal activities. The core idea of the cultural revolution was to restore the early fervour of the communists by removing and exiling officials who had become too bureaucratic and overbearing. It is probably the most impressive example of a mass socialization drive ever launched anywhere. Such a drive is a logical, if not necessarily obligatory, outcome of the concept of the party as the vanguard of the revolution. In spite of this overly exaggerated role, the Chinese party still adheres to the concept of the eventual withering away of both state and party when its work is done.

The most obvious and important example of dissension among the communist powers is that between China and the Soviet Union. The background for this is complex, and is based in part on Sino-Russian political enmity reaching back to the period of Russian expansion to the Pacific. The ideological gap between Chinese and Russian communism is based in part upon their different revolutionary experiences. In addition, China has looked upon the Russian policy of coexistence with the West, devised in the late 1950s, as an abandonment of the true communist position of hostility towards capitalist powers. Ironically Sino-Soviet tensions have led to a tactical reversal in this area, as China has moved into the international sphere in the 1970s.

The liberalization of the Soviet Union under Khruschev's leadership (1958–64) was regarded by China as a dilution of the authority of the party. The Yugoslav and Czechoslovakian experiments were also condemned on similar grounds. At the same time, the Chinese took issue with Russia's intervention in Czechoslovakia in 1968 as a transgression against a friendly, if errant, party. As the Chinese claim to fear Russian incursions into their territory, they have cultivated friendly ties with the Communist governments in Albania and Romania which have sought to reduce Russian influence upon them while still maintaining party discipline. The tensions within the communist movement which have resulted from this split have badly strained, and in some cases fractured, communist parties in other countries. In India, for instance, there are at least six rival communist parties, some aligned with the U.S.S.R., some with China, and some independent.

Reform Communism

In the years following World War II, a number of communist states were established in Eastern Europe, most on the strength of the victorious Russian army. Two exceptions to this case were Yugoslavia and Albania. The unique course followed by the former in recent years is an example of yet another variation of the many possibilities contained within communism.

The Yugoslav Communist Party was the major force in the country at the end of World War II. Tension with the U.S.S.R. began to build when Stalin tried to bring Yugoslavia into the same relationship with Russia as existed with most of Eastern Europe. A break finally came in 1948, when Stalin found that he could not prevent Tito from going his own way just as he had been unable to prevent Tito from independently taking to the field against the Germans in 1943.

The first years of the Tito regime were as harsh as those of any of its East European contemporaries. As the danger of either a counter-revolution from the right, separatist movements, or a pro-Russian coup receded, the regime began to relax its controls. Tito turned increasingly to the West for military as well as economic aid and began to promote trade and tourism with them. These increasing contacts brought a number of problems into focus, especially in the economic area. The usual practice of central control of the economy, characteristic of communist governments, proved to be an increasing handicap in furthering economic development. The need for economic changes provoked a wider reform impulse, and a policy of decentralization was announced in the early 1960s.

The key to the reform drive has been a decentralization of economic decision making. Basic guidelines are still set by the party at the centre, but the workers' and managers' councils at the plant or shop level ostensibly determine what is to be produced, at what price, and for what market. For this to be effective, there is a need for a fairly sophisticated local organization and work force, and this seems to be the intention. Though the concept of the party as the vanguard of society is not abandoned, its detailed control over economic life has been surrendered in the quest for efficiency and productivity.

Tito's brand of communism also stands out as an example of national communism. This runs counter to the traditional theory that communism and the class conflict know no national boundaries, but he argued that each nation develops to a different degree in a different setting and thus must be treated accordingly. Any attempt to enforce a rigid orthodoxy is a refusal to recognize reality. Thus, Tito, like the Russian and the Chinese, has adapted Marxist theory to fit his own case.

In 1968 the Czechoslovakian government attempted to devise a "socialism with a human face." It was at once an attempt to decentralize the economy in a manner similar to that of Yugoslavia, as well as to limit the role of the party in noneconomic matters. It was characterized by the lifting of restrictions on the press, interest groups, and individual freedoms to an extent far surpassing anything in Yugoslavia. It was clearly the most radical series of moves undertaken by any incumbent communist government in Europe. The experiment was ended when the U.S.S.R. and its allies invaded the country, supposedly at the behest of a rival, but more "legitimate," faction of the party.

The latest movement toward a type of reform communism appears to be a part of the electoral strategy of the Italian Communist Party. Long isolated on the left wing of the political spectrum, the party has gained in popularity as successive centre-left governments of the country have floundered from crisis to crisis. The party's leadership has adopted a moderate stance on issues related to governmental reforms and international affairs which has made it nearly the most popular party in the country.

ANARCHISM

The anarchists have been a much maligned group of theorists and activists. An anarchist movement as such did not emerge until the 19th century, and it has often been associated in the public mind with communism and socialism. One of the reasons for this confusion is that communism as outlined by Marx and his disciples is presented in terms of a revolution followed ultimately by an anarchist society. The anarchists themselves were frequent and bitter opponents of the Marxists, partly because of their rejection of organization, even in the revolutionary effort. Anarchists are probably better classified as a variety of utopian socialists rather than Marxists. At heart, the movement has been more a moral than a political phenomenon.

It is perhaps ironic that the anarchists, like the Marxists, owe a heavy intellectual debt to the theorists of capitalism and liberal democracy. Had not the liberal theoreticians of the 17th and 18th centuries produced the doctrines of human equality and natural rights, the basis for much of the later "radical" theories would have been lacking. The classical liberal notion that there was a natural harmony in the world that would permit most human activities to be carried through successfully without serious government intervention was an important component as well. In addition, the idea that people are rational and capable of making correct and intelligent decisions without the help of a political authority is a major point in anarchist theories. These ideas were not narrowly construed in the fashion common to the classical liberals, but were taken by the anarchists as grounds for assuming that if people were truly sociable animals then they needed neither government nor property. The anarchists attacked the capitalist economic system, stating that property and the desire to protect and extend one's control over it were the root of political oppression. Both must be eliminated to make it possible for people to fulfill their logical destinies.

Michael Bakunin attempted in the 1860s to take the disparate anarchist ideas existing at the time and to develop a coherent and scientific theory from them. He argued that people have undergone an evolutionary development and that in their earlier stages they were guided by their animal instincts and needed the discipline that property and government could provide. People had now evolved to the point where their further progress is being impeded by these institutions. Property had been needed to stimulate people's interest in their material well-being, government was required to protect property, and religion provided necessary psychological comfort and security. Now, even the most thoroughgoing reforms of contemporary institutions in the form of parliaments, universal suffrage, and legal rights will not permit people's further development. In spite of them, the political system would continue to protect the property holders and no amount of democratic tinkering could alter its essentially oppressive nature.

Bakunin saw governments as oppressive in that they rule by compulsion rather than by persuasion. To him the only morally good and justifiable act is one which is *voluntary*, and until people are liberated so that they may act voluntarily they will not reach their full potential. Any act done out of compulsion was regarded by him as having no moral value whatsoever and political authority exercised through compulsion he saw as intrinsically negative and degrading. It is degrading to those compelled, and corrupting for those who are in a position of power because the natural cooperative character of the people is compromised.

Private property, which is the initial rationale for the creation of political authority, is supported and perpetuated by it long after its useful historical function has been served. Bakunin felt that the few who command the economic heights do so at the expense of the millions who toil; again the holders of power are corrupted by their power and those subject to it are degraded and exploited. Religion is used to sanction these arrangements as well as to provide comfort of a sort to the exploited. Marx had made the observation that religion was the opiate of the people, and most anarchists agreed.

The most difficult point for an anarchist to navigate is the necessary connection between this theory and the requirements of successful revolution. The Marxists adopted the highly organized revolutionary party as their vehicle while other socialists preferred the mass parliamentary party. Neither possibility is logically open to the anarchists, for even an organization of anarchists, if it were to have any real impact, would have to be able to mobilize and coordinate people in an authoritative manner. The anarchist is in the position of having to rely on voluntary effort stimulated by reason and persuasion. Various schemes were devised for executing the revolution, and though violence was recognized as inevitable, Bakunin was not an enthusiast for such measures.

The ultimate society envisioned by Bakunin was of the voluntaristic and cooperative style common to many different types of socialism. Distinctions based upon class, race, and religion would all disappear and, in place of laws and compulsion, voluntary associations would provide such organization as was needed. With the end of private property, each individual would be accorded his or her rightful share of the social wealth. Any needed organizations would spring up naturally and last only so long as they were needed. Thus, the anarchist rejected the notion of a highly organized revolutionary party and also of the need for any formal organizations after the revolution. Instead of revolution and social rebuilding from above as advocated by the Marxists, the revolution and the new society would spring up from the masses. The various anarchist associations might federate into large units, potentially involving the whole of Europe and the world, but they must always remain voluntary.

After the death of Bakunin the anarchists became even less organized than before. There was a tendency for some of them to opt for individual actions which could only be described as terrorism. Having accepted the idea that existing organizations should be destroyed, the techniques of riot and assassination were employed with the intent of shattering them. The activities of these "propagandists of the deed" helped to create the image in the popular mind of anarchists as a group of murderers and bomb-throwers. Anarchist violence was especially notable during the 1880s and 1890s.

The theories of anarchism were tied to the natural sciences by Peter Kropotkin. Like Bakunin, he was a Russian of good family who was hostile to the backward and oppressive Czarist regime and extended this hostility to authority in general. He was a naturalist who was concerned with integrating anarchist theories and scientific knowledge, especially with the theories growing from the writings of Charles Darwin. Just as certain conservatives looked to Darwin to give scientific justification for class-structured societies, so Kropotkin used these same ideas concerning evolution to give a new vitality and validity to anarchism.

Kropotkin argued that the laws of evolution were valid both for animals and people, individually and collectively. It was not a question of philosophy, but of scientific fact. The natural course of human evolution could be affected by the activities of people and it could be diverted from its path by ignorance and selfishness. It might well take a violent event to break this pattern and allow human evolution to return to its normal path.

Kropotkin then went on to argue that the view that those who see evolution and progress as depending upon competitiveness were in error, for those who survived were the ones who developed the facility for cooperation among their own kind. People's progress had been blocked by organizations that, in his view, had no historical justification. People had lived without organization at one time and could do so again. Kropotkin, like Marx, felt that political authority was simply the product of economic class; the possessors of economic power used it along with religion to protect themselves. The system did not act in the interest of the masses of workers and peasants, and never could. The postrevolutionary society Kropotkin foresaw was similar to that which Bakunin suggested—one of voluntary associations which could operate on a basis of equal respect for all individuals and would rely upon persuasion and reason rather than law or compulsion. The facts of life, material, psychological, and spiritual, would compel virtually everyone into association with his or her fellows, but, again, these organizations would be the result of needs expressed from below rather than through dictation from above.

Kropotkin believed that this society was inevitable; that the natural process of evolution required that this end be reached. Instead of the dialectic which Marx used to impart an aura of inevitability, Kropotkin used the scientifically accepted theory of evolution, with his own rather individualistic interpretation. That this evolution was inevitable was as certain to Kropotkin as the fact that the logjam created by political authority, private property, and religion could be smashed only with the dynamite of revolution. The important point was not that the revolution would be violent, but that, once over, the natural inclinations of people would assert themselves. At heart, Kropotkin was an eternal optimist where human nature was concerned.

World War I dealt anarchism its harshest blow. Anarchists were dismayed as their leaders, including Kropotkin, rallied to the side of their homelands. The idealistic association with humanity was submerged by nationalist militarism. After the war, the remnants were largely absorbed into the Communist parties. A small "international" was left to carry on the anarchist ideal. Now, almost forgotten, its office in Stockholm carries on.

Syndicalism

A theory related to anarchism which found considerable popularity around the turn of this century was that of syndicalism. Born of the same antagonism to established economic and political organizations as other radical 19th-century theories, syndicalism was created as the result of the adaptation of anarchistic ideas by trade union (syndicate) leaders. Anarchism found its supporters in France, as did Marxism, but from the 1890s syndicalism became the dominant radical sentiment. The main distinction between syndicalism and communism lies in the rejection of the format of the revolutionary party and supplanting it with the concept of the labour union as the revolutionary vehicle. It was also posited that the union be the basic organization of the post-revolutionary society.

The syndicalists felt that both the reformist and revolutionary socialists overlooked the basic social fact that economic classes not only differ in economic interests but in the institutions and ideas which naturally emerge from these differences. In essence, both in terms of standards and organizations, what is right and appropriate is relative to class.

In this frame of reference, the labour union became the distinctive organization of the working class, though not as it is known in the British or American "bread and butter" sense. The typically middle-class methods of bargaining and electoral politicking were felt to be inappropriate to unions. Potentially the most effective weapon should be that characteristic union tactic, the strike. The strike envisioned by the syndicalists was to be a *general strike* which would paralyze the whole of society and force the economic and political power holders into submission. Individual strikes were to be a proving and training ground for the general strike. The notion of the general strike was not new, but its adoption as *the* technique gave syndicalism its distinct character. The idea of the general strike was further elevated by Georges Sorel, who argued that the promise of the strike and all that would go with it were especially important in order to give fervour to the cause. This "myth" of the general strike may or may not have been significant as a concept to other syndicalist leaders, but it does highlight the central role of this technique.

The syndicalists also looked to the use of other means of effecting change, such as sabotage. Their direct-action approach studiously ignored normal political channels as they regarded the state and its institutions as the enemy and thought in terms of a worldwide proletariat. The messy and unpleasant image projected by the political ineptitude of the French Third Republic, and the latter's hostility to labour organizations, probably accounted for much of this bias. Syndicalism was influential in various other countries, especially in Spain in the 1920s and 1930s, but nowhere did it reach the staying power it enjoyed in France. In Canada it was a significant factor, for instance, in Prairie unionism and British Columbia politics after World War I, but soon died out. Only its major tactic, the general strike, has remained to haunt governments.

Since the late 1960s, there has been renewed interest in anarchist and syndicalist solutions to society's problems. Probably the best example of this is the Paris Strike of 1968, in which workers and students tied up Paris, and most of France, for days on end in something approximating a general strike. One of the supposedly revolutionary groups which was notable for its nonparticipation was the French Communist Party, an evasion that alienated many young French revolutionaries. The options advocated by them include the concept of the permanent revolution as derived from Trotsky, the utilization of the general strike as the revolutionary medium as suggested by Sorel, and a simple assault upon authority in the style of Bakunin and Kropotkin. No clear new ideology for the New Left emerged, though ideological questions were debated passionately, generally with schismatic results. A similar revival took place elsewhere, including North America. In the United States, racism and the Vietnam war served to catalyze the New Left there, and literally dozens of radical groups proliferated. One of the better known was the Students for a Democratic Society (SDS), which was formed in 1963 as an aggressive quasi-anarchist reform group. An SDS splinter body, the "Weathermen," resurrected the notion of terrorist bombing. The 1970s may well be seen as a decade of anarchist and terrorist bombing, much like the later years of the 19th Century.

DEMOCRATIC SOCIALISM

The various reform impulses exemplified by the socialism of Owen and Fourier, among others, did not disappear with the emergence of Marxist socialism and anarchism. Marx himself was ambiguous as to whether violent revolution is necessary, and he addressed himself to the question of participation within established parliamentary systems on more than one occasion.

During the 19th century a variety of democratic-socialist theories emerged, creating the tension which still exists between those socialists who followed Marx and those who did not. Of the major European socialist movements, the British has been the most consistently non-Marxist. Its history consists of an amalgam of ideas and movements; British socialists at various times became enamoured of Owen's theories of trade union reformism and ultimately, and most significantly, with the reform socialism of the Fabians.

Fabian Socialism

The last third of the 19th century saw the formation of a variety of socialist groups in Britain dedicated to remaking British society. In 1884, a group of intellectuals who had been politically active for a number of years formed the Fabian Society. The group set out to convince the British middle class that a reform socialism should be instituted. The society generally developed the character of an educational and activating organization. It was never intended as a political party, but rather served as a vehicle for introducing Britons to the virtues of socialism. They avoided involvement in the intricacies of theory and committed themselves to showing the ethical and scientific imperatives for socialism and making specific proposals as to how it might be put into effect. Later they established a formal research organization and became affiliated with the Labour Party. Its members were prolific writers and produced quantities of pamphlets and articles as well as books. Many, such as George Bernard Shaw, were recognized literary figures who could command an audience among the middle class in a way that no labour spokesperson or revolutionary agitator could.

The Fabians' technique of argument parallels to some extent that of the Marxists. They also looked to history to prove their points, but used it in a different manner. It was their contention that history demonstrated a steady movement toward both democracy and socialism. The growth of large-scale industry had not only created an urbanized working class, it had also destroyed the individualism and free competition of the earlier form of capitalism. Society was faced with two alternatives if individualism and democracy were to be preserved: either the large-scale enterprises would have to be broken up with a consequent loss in productivity, efficiency, and living standards, or the economic institutions would have to come under the control of the general population. The Fabians, having accepted material progress as a goal, logically opted for the latter course. In addressing themselves to the question of the source of value in the economic system, they argued that society in general, not any one group, creates what is of value. Logically, society as a whole should control the results of this productivity. They thus rejected the Marxian notion that the working class is alone the source of value, while at the same time agreeing with the Marxist that the landlord, capitalist, or investor makes his or her fortune largely on the productivity of society as a whole. They avoided talking in terms of class and talked in terms of society gradually acquiring control over the means of production and distribution so that all its members might share fairly in the social wealth.

The Fabians looked to the democratic state as the means of bringing about these changes. They shared a widespread 19th-century faith in the usefulness of the state as the instrument of change, arguing that certain specific reforms could remedy the shortcomings of the existing system. In their commitment to reform they amassed vast amounts of data to prove their arguments, and their intellectual energy and productivity made them invaluable allies of the British Labour Party as it sought to gain respectibility. The Labour Party to this day exhibits the pragmatic, problem-solving orientation of the Fabians in spite of occasional bursts of rhetoric and the activities of a radical minority to the contrary.

Continental Democratic Socialism

Democratic socialism on the European continent took on a different character from that in Britain. The strongest Socialist party prior to World War I was the German Social Democratic Party, and it was here that the "revision" of Marxist theory first emerges. The German party implicitly accepted the value of the parliamentary approach to power, in that it had contested for elections. In the last years of the 19th century a Party leader, Edouard Bernstein, began to challenge the orthodox Marxist theories and in so doing embroiled continental socialism in a debate which in various forms lasts to this day.

Bernstein began his revisions publicly in 1896 by arguing that Marx's labour theory of value which, simply put, says that the worker does not receive full value for his or her work, was an inadequate basis for a truly scientific socialism. He also assaulted Marx's theory of economic determinism by arguing that as a person progresses he or she acquires an increasing ability to shape the future through his or her own faculties.

Bernstein's criticism was sharpest when he refuted Marx's belief in the inevitability of the collapse of capitalism. Bernstein perceived that the middle class was expanding rather than contracting. Further, the working class was neither growing nor developing into Marx's monolithic prerevolutionary proletariat. He then argued that socialists should accept these facts and try to make the democratic system work for the society rather than the capitalists. The socialists could expect support from many middle-class elements who, for different ideological reasons, would be concerned about the same problems of concentration or economic power and its abuses by the capitalist.

The revisionists continued to accept the notion that the capitalist system is inherently exploitative and that it inevitably would be replaced. They saw the working class as the really exploited group and argued that democratic procedures should be used; if they were not available, then revolution was the only logical course of action.

An implicit side-effect of revisionism in Europe was the emphasis it put on the national political system. Socialist energies were to be directed at the institutions of one's own country, international socialist brotherhood notwithstanding. The antinational bias of orthodox Marxism was rejected, though the meaning of this rejection was not driven home until World War I. At the outbreak of the war the socialist parties of Europe rallied to the various national causes, and the unity of the proletariat, so long cultivated by Marxists, evaporated in the nationalist fervour of the war. There were individual holdouts, but party after party supported the war in the name of the homeland.

Post-World War I revisionists have continued the lines of thought of the pre-war years. They have rejected Marxian doctrines one after another; the dialectic, economic determinism, class warfare, and the need for revolution. Their gradualism is reflected in their emphasis on such controversial areas as nationalization and on dealing first with those areas where true competition has largely disappeared. Confiscation is regarded as inappropriate, and adequate compensation should be a matter of policy. Trade unions should be given a bigger role in their areas of interest, and income should be redistributed through various fiscal and tax devices. There is a rejection of the classical liberal idea that the general good flows from individual competitiveness, and the faith in people's basic sociability is still a part of socialist thought. Factors other than economic, such as history, race, and culture, are important determinants of the content of a society and must be taken into account in both theoretical and practical endeavors. Whatever skepticism socialists may have for the state when it is in the hands of the capitalists, they retain their optimism about their ability to make it work in the interests of all people when given the chance.

The Internationals

One of the enduring "myths" of socialist movements has been the international nature of economic systems and classes. Socialism inherited from classical liberalism a "world-view"; it was transmitted by Tom Paine (see Chapter 16) in his book *The Rights of Man* through the French Revolution to all parts of Europe and Asia. Part of his vision, the natural right to self-determination, forms a basis for nationalist ideologies today. Another part, the notion that *all* people should enjoy equal rights and access to the world's goods, inspired trade unionists and socialist writers to international perspectives.

This idea was seized upon and expressed more fully by the utopian socialists and by Marx, whose slogan, "Working men of the world unite! You have nothing to lose but your chains!" still has a powerful impact. In 1864, a group of British and French trade-unionists were instrumental in creating the International Workingmen's Association, with headquarters in London. Marx was invited as a representative of German workers and socialists. His literary talents soon gave him the most powerful voice in the organization.

The association soon became known as the International, later the First International. It was a loose federation of groups in many European countries and the United States. Their political orientation included anarchism, Marxist socialism, English trade-union ideals, Christian socialism, freemasonry, and utopian socialism. Few were Marxists in any real sense, but the First International proved to be the vehicle for the spread of Marx's ideas among labour unions and activist intellectuals.

The First International reached its zenith in the years before the Paris Commune in 1871. It was blamed by European governments for devising and coordinating massive strikes in 1868 and 1870 and was seen as the force behind the revolutionary commune.

The First International fell apart as a result of a struggle for control between the Marxists and the anarchists, led by Bakunin, in 1872. Two competing "internationals" were formed and both collapsed in the mid-1870s.

The Second International was formed as a result of an international conference called by various Marxist groups in Paris in 1889. The Second International had no organizational structure through the first decade of its existence. Instead the socialist parties subscribing to its tenets met every year or two to pass joint resolutions.

The Third International, called the Communist International (COMINTERN), was formed in March 1919 in Moscow. Thirty-five socialist parties were represented. At the next congress, in 1920, representation was national, with 36 delegations accredited. From the first the Comintern was under close Russian supervision. Lenin was determined to eliminate parliamentary and national socialism from its delegations. A series of resolutions was passed which proclaimed revolutionary socialism and an acceptance of Soviet Russian leadership. National parties would be accredited to the Comintern as they accepted the resolutions. In nearly every socialist party, a split occurred between those who accepted the Comintern and those who rejected it. This split led to the formation of separate Communist Parties in 1921–22. These were judged by the Comintern to be the "true" heirs of Marx and the First International.

Throughout the 1920s and 1930s, the Comintern, and through it the non-Russian Communist parties, were increasingly made subservient to Soviet Russian needs. The Soviet state was defined by Stalin as the "homeland" for all communists. The professional revolutionaries who had formed the Comintern institutions were replaced by bureaucrats who translated the Soviet "line" into directions for the foreign Communist parties. The Communist Party as a whole was transformed into a single, coordinated world party. Its member sections were forced to perform interesting gyrations as the Soviets and the Nazis varied their relationship in the years just before and after the outbreak of World War II. When the Comintern proved embarrassing to the Soviet-

Western alliance after 1941, it was disbanded. Since its demise in 1943, relations between Communist parties in all parts of the world have tended to disintegrate. Most of them now owe little or no voluntary allegiance to the Soviet leadership.

Canadian Socialism

The origins of socialism in Canada are diffuse. As in other countries, the more radical wing of the 19th-century Canadian labour movement inclined toward socialism. Others, affected by the spread in Great Britain of "the social gospel," moved toward socialism out of religious principles. A large proportion of socialist adherents came to Canada as immigrants and passed along its tenets to their children. Finally, many native-born Canadians moved to socialism as a result of their activity in the populist movements discussed in the previous chapter. The amalgamation of these elements into a reasonably large democratic socialist movement and a much smaller communist party has produced a domestic socialism with its own distinctive elements.

Most of the labour movement in Canada has traditionally been non-socialist. Its tactics and organization have closer ties to American methods, which have been restricted to agitation for better pay and working conditions, than to the British fusion of labour and socialism. Only in the last two decades have the labour movement and the socialists reached general political agreement, and that only at the cost of most socialist dogma.

However, a fraction of the Canadian labour movement has always been attracted to socialism. The first groups of any importance were formed as Canadian branches of the Independent Labour Party, an organization founded in Great Britain in 1893. There was also considerable contact between labour socialists in Canada and American socialist movements. The most important was the expansion of the International Workers of the World (IWW), a mass union with anarchist and socialist leanings, into the Canadian West after 1905. This union was especially strong among British Columbia labour unions and Alberta miners until World War I. The IWW, or "wobblies," as its members were called, advocated the use of the general strike to change the conditions of society. The Winnipeg General Strike of 1919 recalled to the minds of politicians the militancy and aims of the IWW, though it was not responsible for the strike. Fear of a "wobbly" takeover intensified the reaction of the government to the strikers.

The influence of religion on Canadian socialism has been continuous and heavy. Many of the democratic socialist leaders in Canada have been ordained ministers or priests. The cliché that socialism is somehow "godless" is not only wrong, but runs counter to an important element of Canadian socialism. The main source of religious inspiration to socialists has been called "the social gospel." Christian teaching, especially the command to love one's neighbour as oneself, has moved some clergy and faithful in all the Christian churches to advocate socialism as a means of providing for the dignity and equality of all people. The moralistic posture of socialism, standing as it does for cooperation among people, has continued to appeal to Christians upset by poverty and injustice. To paraphrase a statement made about British socialism, Canadian socialism owes *more* to Methodism than to Marx.

Marxian socialism, in all its varieties, is probably more closely tied to immigration, especially from Finland and Eastern Europe, than to any spread of ideas. Some emigrants from the then Russian and the Austro–Hungarian Empires came to Canada in order to avoid political persecution. They had become socialists in response to the political and economic backwardness of these empires and continued their interests in radical politics after their arrival in North America. The nature of early socialist parties in Canada was affected by this immigrant influence. These immigrant socialists remained in concentrated pockets of population and maintained a lively contact with European socialist theories and developments. There was also some contact with American Marxists.

The fourth major source of Canadian socialist ideas and action were the populists, including the cooperative movement. The populists, a brand of reform liberals, tended to find themselves pushed into socialism as their attempts to reform politics and economics failed. Interest in the control of banks and transportation firms blended into a call for their outright ownership by the government, in order to forestall future abuses. William Irvine, a leader of the United Farmers of Alberta, wrote *Farmers in Politics* (1920). In it he tended to see farmers as a separate economic class. He advocated a corporative system of representation at the federal level, so as to ensure that the interests of farmers would be conveyed by their representatives. He also advocated a system of cooperatives and relied upon the message of the social gospel to appeal to the farm community.

Most of the populists elected to Parliament in the 1920s under the banner of the Progressive Party were eventually absorbed by the Liberal Party. The same situation occurred in Newfoundland, where a socialist named Joey Smallwood eventually led the Liberal Party and the people of the colony into Confederation with Canada in 1949. Smallwood had worked for the American Socialist Party during the 1920s and later was a cooperatives organizer in Newfoundland.

The cooperative movement has long been associated in the minds of Canadians with socialism. The greatest strength of the movement has been on the Prairies, in areas often dominated by socialist or social-democratic politics. Its tenets have formed part of the theoretical basis of the major democratic socialist party, the Cooperative Commonwealth Federation (1933–61). But the movement itself has also been strong in areas which have been largely impervious to socialist politics: Quebec, the Maritimes, and small-town Ontario.

In the beginning the cooperative movement had some ties with the Independent Labour Party and the labour movement. As the cooperatives spread, however, their large financial assets proved tempting to all types of socialist and communist organizations. Eventually, in order to protect itself, the Cooperative Union of Canada withdrew from any kind of political involvement.

The theory underlying the cooperative movement was one of unbridled faith in all forms of cooperation. It could reform all of society. It would replace selfish individualism with a new outlook, one of concern for and assistance to all the members of society. The result would be a more efficient and just economic system within a utopian cooperative commonwealth. There would be no revolution—only a gradual replacement of capitalist enterprises by more efficient and attractive cooperatives.

The cooperative movement headed in different directions in various parts of the country after 1920. In Nova Scotia, Father James Tomkins and his cousin Father Moses Coady gradually transformed the extension service of St. Francis Xavier University into a centre for the organization of cooperatives. Its reputation spread throughout the Maritimes, and for that matter the world, and is known as the "Antigonish movement."

In Quebec, as in Nova Scotia, the Catholic Church sponsored cooperatives and credit unions to ameliorate the lot of poor farmers and fishermen. In Ontario, the Cooperative Union of Canada fought a long battle with the Communist Party of Canada for control of the many cooperatives run by Ukranian and Finnish groups in the northern mining towns. It was not until 1931 that the cooperatives were free from political interference. In Saskatchewan and Alberta, the social goals of cooperatives dovetailed with those of populist reformers, with the result that cooperatives were seen as the economic alternative to bank, railroad, and grain storage corporations. Cooperatives, especially in Saskatchewan, became big businesses.

The diversity of the wellsprings of socialist thought in Canada led to a welter of organization channels. Early socialism was characterized by a multiplicity of tiny "parties," with factions continually splitting and merging to form new and more diverse organizations. The most important of the early parties were the Independent Labour Party, which eventually produced much of the leadership of the Cooperative

Commonwealth Federation (CCF), and the Socialist Party of Canada, part of whose leadership helped to form the Communist Party of Canada, which is now the oldest extant socialist organization in the country.

The Socialist Party of Canada (SPC) was formed in British Columbia in 1904 and had most of its strength in the West. It was primarily Marxist in bent. After 1907, a split occurred between the moderates, whose "socialism" included such reforms as state control of liquor, abolition of property qualifications for voting, and state management of natural resources, while the more militant Marxists advocated revolution against the capitalist system. The radicals retained control of the party and the moderates left to form the Social Democratic Party. The Social Democratic Party joined other socialist parties in the Second International, though it was not an important member. Both groups were dependent upon urban labour for support and appealed especially to Eastern European immigrants.

Communism

The SPC was ruined in 1920 by another split, this time over the issue of joining the Comintern. When the leadership hesitated over the conditions laid down by Lenin, the more radical of this already radical group deserted the SPC to found the Workers Party of Canada, which became the Communist Party of Canada (CPC) in 1923.

The CPC never really succeeded in breaking out of its ethnic mould, as it was being dominated from the first by English and Canadian leaders. However, the vast majority of its membership has been derived from Finnish, Ukranian, and other Eastern European groups. Originally the CPC included separate language sections, but these were abolished after the Comintern began to insist that it become a "national" party based on class rather than ethnic lines. The Stalin-Trotsky feud which broke out after Lenin's death led to a number of purges within the CPC, and resulted in part of the original leadership forming a Trotskyite organization which, though always miniscule, has remained in operation to this day.

The original CPC theoretical perspective saw Canada in the role of a British and American colony. In the Leninist view, the CPC was obliged to promote a nationalist-communist revolution which would sunder Canadian political and economic ties with these countries. The CPC therefore came out for the abolition of the BNA Act and the establishment of a Canadian Peoples' Republic. The Senate was to be abolished, mass industrial unions created, and most importantly American capital penetration was to be stopped. In 1925, this was heady stuff indeed.

From 1927 until 1956, the CPC (sometimes under different names) was content to take Moscow's lead in domestic and foreign questions. Theoretical perspective shifted away from the view of Canada as a colony to one of Canada as an exporter of capital, an exploiting capitalist nation in its own right. Much emphasis was put on disciplined "units," or cells, of the party capturing other labour or political organizations and turning them into communist fronts. By and large this never really succeeded, though the cooperatives in the 1920s, and the mass industrial unions of the 1930s and 1940s had great difficulty in eliminating communist influence. The various democratic socialist parties, having had the closest contact with communist tactics since the 1920s, were almost always staunchly opposed to the CPC, though their nonsocialist opponents often tended to lump them together.

The high point of communist influence in Canada came after the attack by Germany on the U.S.S.R. in 1941. Suddenly, after years of opposition to Canada's participation in rearming with and then fighting for "imperialist forces" against the Germans (who were Soviet allies), the communists came out as super-patriotic. They opposed strikes which would cut defence production, rallied to the flag, and formed cooperative associations with politicians of all stripes, even to the point of supporting some Liberal and Conservative candidates in elections.

After the war their influence began to decline and has never really recovered. The arrival of a new wave of Central and East European immigrants, who were anti-Nazi and anti-Communist, shook the ethnic base of the party. Affluence and the increasing integration of old immigrant families deprived the CPC of support and/or dispersed the ghetto blocs whose votes had provided some electoral success. Only in Quebec, where the CPC could draw upon the spread of Marxism from postwar France, did it make any headway. This was short-lived as many of the Francophones left the party in the late 1950s.

The most telling blow to the CPC was the Russian destalinization campaign in 1955–58. The revelation that Stalin was a wartime blunderer and mass murderer who manipulated communist parties for his own benefit, destroyed the faith of many communists in their leadership and in the work they were doing. The CPC was left with a hard-core rump whose policies were increasingly becoming outmoded and ridiculed.

The main plank in communist ideas about Canada has been the merger of nationalism with radical socialism. Communists were among the earliest to object to American cultural and economic penetration. They advocated a national flag a decade before the Liberal Party adopted the idea. On the other hand, the evolution of Canadian society has left the CPC behind. The party has dragged behind on the "left" issues of women's liberation, abortion, student power, and Quebec separatism. As a result, the far end of the radical spectrum has been taken over by the "Maoist" Communist Party of Canada (Marxist-Leninist), which rejects the leadership of Moscow and by the "Trotskyite" League for Socialist Action. The radical left is as split and as powerless as it ever was.

Democratic Socialism

Numerically much larger and more effective than the communist movement in Canada has been that of democratic socialism. Even its sociological and theoretical roots are different. Where the communists depended upon an ethnic amalgam which tended to idealize the Soviet state, the democratic socialists came from populist and labour circles, which were ethnically more varied. Their theoretical roots were found in religious principles and the cooperative ethic.

The rise of democratic socialism in Canada to a third force may be traced to the populist upsurge on the Prairies at the beginning of the 20th century. Though this movement was blunted electorally by World War I, in the early 1920s farmer groups assumed power in Alberta and Ontario and a large Progressive contingent was elected to Ottawa. At the same time, a few members of the Independent Labour Party were also elected from Western urban areas. Once in Parliament, these two groups tended to work together, though it never really proved feasible to generate a united farmer-labour movement in their respective constituencies.

Most of the Progressives were gradually and methodically absorbed by the Liberals. A left-wing faction, led by the labour socialist J. S. Woodsworth, a former Methodist minister, became the "Ginger Group," which maintained a separate identity throughout the 1920s. Though small in number, the Ginger Group was able to gain reforms in labour and pension laws. The Ginger Group also managed to keep alive ideas of cooperation, credit control, and concern for the unemployed in an era when few but the communists took any stand on these points.

As the Depression came and worsened, the idea of developing a farmer-labour coalition around socialist principles seemed feasible. Canada's labour parties began to unite as early as 1929. The organizers of a left-wing conference in 1931 decided to extend invitations to farmer groups as well as to labour unions. In 1932 representatives of these two sectors met in Calgary and agreed to form the Cooperative Commonwealth Federation (CCF). The eight points of the CCF program included economic and social planning, socialization of banks and credit, security of land tenure for farmers, maintenance and development of welfare legislation, health insurance, and assistance to cooperatives.

In that same year a group of Toronto and Montreal intellectuals formed the University League for Social Reconstruction (ULSR). It was self-consciously modelled upon the British Fabian Society and was meant to provide the intellectual backbone for the CCF. Its members helped draft the Regina Manifesto (1933) which served as the basic program for the party until 1956.

The Regina Manifesto covered the eight points of the Calgary program, but went beyond them to include proposals for the reform of the BNA Act, the safeguarding of individual freedom, the regulation of foreign trade, and the nationalization of key utilities and industries. In general, the Manifesto's supporters:

. . . aim to replace the present capitalist system, with its inherent injustice and inhumanity, by a social order from which the domination and exploitation of one class by another will be eliminated, in which economic planning will supersede unregulated private enterprise and competition, and, in which genuine democratic self-government, based upon economic equality will be possible.

The uncompromising socialism of the Regina Manifesto soon began to upset the populists. The United Farmers of Ontario deserted the movement in 1934, the Saskatchewan CCF downplayed socialism after 1936, and the United Farmers of Alberta left the CCF in 1939. By 1940, the main agricultural bastion of the CCF was in Saskatchewan; the focus of the party had largely shifted to urban labour, and the mass industrial unions formed in the late 1930s paralleled the American labour movement.

It is obvious that the CCF was not Marxist. Its major planks were designed to end class strife rather than feed on it. It was moralistic and Christian in outlook and reflected the general North American presumption that there was wealth enough for all, only if it were properly used and shared.

The electoral heyday of the CCF came during World War II, when it formed the government in Saskatchewan and came close to doing so in Ontario. After the war its fortunes declined and the party stagnated, although many of the social reforms it advocated were adopted by pragmatic Liberal governments. By the 1950s it was apparent that a new approach had to be devised and a new structure agreed upon. In a conference in Winnipeg in 1956, a new declaration was made, superseding the Regina Manifesto.

While much of the rhetoric remained the same, the Winnipeg Declaration was even more vague in its program and principles. The uncompromising socialism of the Regina Manifesto disappeared. As well, the key reliance upon social and economic planning was downplayed, partly because of the times. Where there was a need to rationalize and increase production in 1933, during the Depression, by 1956 the primary concern was over the distribution of the fruits of the expanding postwar economy. Nationalization of industry was succeeded by the advocacy of the welfare state in CCF priorities.

Structurally, the CCF was torn between its dual loyalty to farmers and labour. Its doctrines and leadership were predominantly labour-oriented, while its main bloc of support came from the Prairie farms. As the industrial unions grew in Ontario and Prairie cities, they were looked upon with suspicion by farmers. Far from having interests in common, the two groups often worked at cross-purposes. The farmer wanted cheap machinery and manufactures, which could only be produced by low-wage workers; the unions wanted cheap food and tariff protection, both of which worked against the farmers' position. The tension was not really resolved until 1957–58, when, with the great sweep of Diefenbaker in the West, farm power inside the CCF was severely curtailed. The electoral defeat simply underscored the declining importance of farmers in the Canadian population. At the same time, the craft and mass unions moved closer to each other and to the CCF, even though there never had been an arrangement for the formal participation of unions in the CCF structure, as exists in the British Labour Party.

After two years of discussions within party ranks, a decision was made to form a new party. This time, instead of a federation of small populist and labour parties, the "new party" was formed from the top down, like its liberal and conservative counterparts. Room was made for union organizations to be represented and party doctrine was further watered down to stress Keynesian economic controls and a concern over government control over production and resources. The New Democratic Party (NDP) was founded in 1961, and the CCF was dissolved.

A decade later, this new alignment appeared to have paid dividends. The NDP assumed power in Manitoba, Saskatchewan (after losing in 1964), and British Columbia. In the 1972 federal elections, its electoral gains helped to give the party the balance of power in the House of Commons. Although it lost this advantage in the Liberal sweep of 1974, the party gained the status of Offical Opposition in Ontario in the 1975 provincial election. Most of these gains came as a result of an election strategy which focussed upon a criticism of government's performance, a mild nationalistic stance, and an insistence upon reforms which would benefit the less-favoured in society. Only in British Columbia was socialist ideology truly expounded and incorporated into government policy. It would appear to many that this course of action was largely responsible for the NDP defeat in the 1975 provincial election.

The latest ideological challenge to affect the CCF/NDP came in 1969, with the formation of the "Waffle" group at a party conference in Winnipeg. The Waffle was a movement on the left wing of the NDP which stressed that Canadian socialism and nationalism had identical interests:

Capitalism must be replaced by socialism, by national planning of investment and by public ownership of the means of production in the interests of the Canadian people as a whole. . . . [To] pursue independence seriously is to make visible the necessity of socialism in Canada.[3]

The Waffle called for the restoration of socialism to the NDP program; in a sense it was a revivalist movement within the party.

The Waffle threatened, and was threatened by two groups. On its right was the main body of the NDP, interested in reform and the welfare state rather than doctrinaire socialism. It had also been sympathetic to national independence since its beginnings in the CCF. But the potent combination of the two not only frightened the party leadership but threatened to destroy the CCF/NDP's difficult comeback attempt to respectability and electoral success. The unions, especially, would not accept the possible economic consequences of nationalizing Canadian branch plants. The Waffle resolution was defeated in 1969. In 1971, the Waffle put up a candidate, James Laxer, for the leadership of the NDP, who nearly defeated the "establishment's" choice. By 1972 the Waffle was served with an ultimatum by the Ontario NDP to disband or leave the party. Refusing to disband, it became the Movement for an Independent Socialist Canada (MISC).

The second threat came from a sister movement, the New Left. This was an extension of the socialist-anarchist movement which rose during the 1960s in the United States. The New Left favoured Canadian nationalism insofar as it was another obstacle in the path of American policy. The New Left was fundamentally internationalist in outlook, awaiting the socialist revolutions which would bring all people together. The Waffle, while socialist as well, was uncompromisingly nationalist. It was not particularly interested in furthering the cause of the international socialist revolution. However, once it had been expelled from the NDP, it tended to lose its original supporters. Parts of the New Left movement, various Marxists, and others took their place and a new debate opened up within MISC over the importance of nationalism vis-à-vis socialism. Factionalism again,

---

[3] "The Waffle Manifesto," quoted in Virginia Hunter, "Why I Left the Waffle," *Canadian Forum* 649 (March 1975), p. 17.

as it had so often before in other socialist groups, split the group in late 1974, and it may be said to have collapsed.

RECOMMENDED READINGS

Abella, Irving. *Nationalism, Communism and Canadian Labour*. Toronto: University of Toronto Press, 1973.

Apter, David, and Joll, James, eds. *Anarchism Today*. London: Macmillan, 1971.

Avakumovic, Ivan. *Communist Party in Canada: A History*. Toronto: McClelland & Stewart, Ltd., 1975.

Berlin, Isaiah. *Karl Marx*. New York: Oxford University Press, 1959.

Burnham, James. *The Managerial Revolution*. Bloomington, Ind.: Indiana University Press, 1962, first published 1941.

Carew Hunt, R. N. *The Theory and Practice of Communism*. 2d ed. New York: Macmillan, 1957.

Cherwinski, W. J. "Bibliographical Note: The Left in Canadian History, 1911–1969." *Journal of Canadian Studies* 54, no. 4 (November 1969): 51–60.

Coker, Francis. *Recent Political Thought*. New York: Appleton-Century-Crofts, 1934.

Deutscher, Isaac. *Stalin*. New York: Vintage, 1960.

Djilas, Milovan. *The New Class*. New York: Prager, 1957.

Drachkovitch, M. *Revolutionary Internationals 1864–1943*. Stanford: Stanford University Press, 1963.

Durkheim, Emile. *Socialism and St. Simon*. Yellow Springs, Ohio: Antioch, 1958.

Epp, Frank A. *The Mennonites in Canada 1786–1920*. Toronto: Macmillan, 1974.

Fischer, Louis. *The Life of Lenin*. New York: Harper & Row, 1964.

Fox, Paul. "Early Socialism in Canada." In *Political Process in Canada*, edited by J. H. Atchison. Toronto: University of Toronto Press, 1963, pp. 78–98.

Fried, Albert, and Sanders, Ronald. *Socialist Thought*. Garden City: Anchor Books, 1964.

Galbraith, J. K. *The New Industrial State*. Boston: Houghton Mifflin, 1967.

Hayek, Friedrich. *The Road to Serfdom*. Chicago: University of Chicago Press, 1968.

Horowitz, Gad. *Canadian Labour in Politics*. Toronto: University of Toronto Press, 1968.

Jackson, John. *Marx, Proudhon and European Socialism*. London: Oxford University Press, 1957.

League for Social Reconstruction. *Social Planning for Canada*. Toronto: T. Nelson and Sons, Ltd., 1935.

Lewis, David. *Louder Voices: The Corporate Welfare Bums*. Toronto: James Lewis & Samuel, 1972.

Lipset, Seymour M. *Agrarian Socialism: The Cooperative Commonwealth Federation in Saskatchewan*. Berkeley: University of California Press, 1950.

MacPherson, Ian. "The Cooperative Union of Canada and Politics, 1909–1931." *Canadian Historical Review* 54, no. 2 (June 1973): 152–74.

McNaught, Kenneth. *A Prophet in Politics: A Biography of J. S. Woodsworth*. Toronto: University of Toronto Press, 1959.

Manuel, Frank E. *The New World of Henri de Saint Simon*. Cambridge, Mass.: Harvard University Press, 1956.

Mills, C. Wright. *The Marxists*. New York: Dell, 1962.

Roussopoulous, D., ed. *The New Left in Canada*. Montreal: Our Generation Press, 1970.

Sabine, George. *A History of Political Theory*. New York: Holt, Rinehart & Winston, 1961.

Wolin, Sheldon. *Politics and Vision*. New York: Little, Brown & Co., 1960.

Woodcock, George. *Pierre Joseph Proudhon*. London: Routledge and Kegan Paul, 1956.

———. *Anarchism*. Cleveland, Ohio: Meridian, 1962.

Young, Walter D. *Anatomy of a Party: The National CCF: 1932–61*. Toronto: University of Toronto Press, 1969.

Zakuta, Leo. *A Protest Movement Becalmed: A Study of Change in the CCF*. Toronto: University of Toronto Press, 1964.

16

Nationalism

OF ALL THE IDEOLOGIES developed and employed during the last two centuries, those derived from nationalist theories have tended to dominate. Conservatives, liberals, socialists, and communists alike have all succumbed to the appeal of the nation-state and incorporated the concept into their ideologies. The theories underlying nationalist ideologies are of a character which allows nationalism to be compatible with many elements of other ideologies, so that with modifications communism, for instance, could become "national communism" and liberalism "national liberalism."

Nationalism has been defined as *"a fusion of patriotism with a consciousness of nationality."*[1] Both are associated with a concern for the community of which the individual is a member. Patriotism may be defined as *an attachment for a community and its territory and a willingness to defend it against external threats*. These sentiments may be focussed upon a single city, as the citizens of Greek city-states were wont to do, or it may be focussed upon a large agglomeration of territories and peoples, as under the Roman Empire.

The concept of nationality has been developed only since medieval times. Previously, people defined their membership in political groups on the basis of who ruled them or upon distinct blood ties, as in tribalism. Other characteristics, such as religion, were also used as an indicator of group identity. The modern use of the term "nation" began simply as an indication of a person's place of origin. The nation was later seen as an entity in itself, composed of individuals who historically share a common ancestry, language, possibly religion, culture, and historical experiences. The nation has also become identified

---

[1] Carleton Hayes, *Nationalism: A Religion* (New York: Macmillan, 1960), p. 2. Italics ours.

with a certain territory, or fatherland, and patriotism has been invoked to impel individuals to attach their loyalities and their lives to its fate.

Modern nationalism appeared following the collapse of the universalist culture which dominated Europe during the Middle Ages. Religion, language, history, and to a great extent culture, were seen as European rather than national throughout these times. Politics was based on locality and much of Europe was divided into a host of petty principalities coexisting with a universalist organization known as the Holy Roman Empire. Latin was the universal medium of communication; use of the vernacular was left to the peasants and merchants. Religion was organized from Rome; the higher clergy constituted a partial check upon the activities of the princes, and the Pope and the Holy Roman Emperor contested for continental hegemony.

This nonnational order began to crumble as cities and states grew in organization and strength. Vernacular languages began to replace Latin as literacy ceased to be the preserve of the clergy. The invention of the printing press gave new impetus to national languages as the written word became available to a wider market which could not, or would not, learn Latin as a second language. Scholars returning from Arab lands brought with them the ideas of the ancient Greeks and Romans which had been all but forgotten in Europe during the Middle Ages. Niccolo Machiavelli, writing around the beginning of the 16th century, addressed himself to the political problems of Italian princes, in Italian, and suggested that rulers could build a commitment among their populations to their states through positive practical action. Legal acts and pronouncements in both France and England were ordered to be disseminated in the vernacular in the interests of clarity; this movement both tended to erase the importance of Latin and to supplant local dialects, thus helping to forge linguistic unity in these countries.

The 16th century also saw the decline of the universalist church as most of northern Europe broke away from the religious domination of Rome. A series of religious wars resulted in the increasing subordination of church organizations, in both Protestant and Catholic areas, to local political rulers. Partially this was due to the churches' need for physical protection, but the disarray caused by the battles also allowed these rulers to gain an advantage over the clergy while they were preoccupied with theological and other disputes. Popular literacy was further advanced in Protestant areas as the result of the emphasis upon individual communication with God, which was based upon the ability to read God's word as set out in the Bible.

These developments shattered medieval universalism, and the new states of Europe became increasingly differentiated from each other in terms of government, religion, language, and in the reconstruction of the past. The concept of sovereignty, introduced by Bodin in the 17th century, reinforced these differentiations, as each state was seen to be an entity whose rulers could dispose of its component individuals and their property as they saw fit.

EUROPEAN NATIONALISM

The critical convergence of ideas which led to the first modern conception of nationalism occurred in 17th-century England. With the accession of Cromwell to power in the English Commonwealth, the revolutionary leaders saw themselves as agents in the formation of a "new Israel" and the English people under Puritan guidance as another "chosen people." Their religion, with its undertones of personal equality, was harnessed to politics in order to justify the overthrow of the monarchy. The "chosen people" had taken power into their own hands. The sovereignty of the ruler, assumed as part of the theory of divine right, and the sovereignty of the state, were merged into the sovereignty of the people, or nation. This new concept of popular sovereignty became the instrument through which nationalism could be justified and harnessed for political purposes. Cromwell (1657) is quoted as saying that God had two great concerns in the world. One is religion ". . . the other thing cared for is the Civil Liberty and Interest of the Nation. . . . If anyone whatsoever think the Interest of Christians and the Interest of the Nation inconsistent or two different things, I wish my soul may never enter into their secrets!"[2]

The concept of popular sovereignty was not necessarily dependent upon religious nationalism, as subsequent events were to prove. During the period 1650–1800, attempts were made to dissociate political liberties and citizenship from religious belief. They were motivated by a desire to avoid the injustice, intolerance, and inter-group conflict which accompanied a government-enforced religious orthodoxy. It was argued that a difference existed between natural or divine and positive law. Natural law was universal and could be perceived through reason and the use of reason was therefore incumbent upon all peoples. People-made law might differ from nation to nation in particulars, but in all cases it, too, must conform to a rational outline. Good government was in the divine interest. Such government rested upon the union of the people and upon liberty; therefore the good, or patriot, king or queen must have the free acclaim of a united people.

The 18th century produced a number of scientists, historians, and philosophers who were committed to the use of reason to establish the outline of natural forces. Physics, biology, and the whole range of applied sciences, or technology, benefitted from rational thought and it

---

[2] Hans Kohn, *Idea of Nationalism,* (New York: Macmillan, 1944), p. 175.

was felt that the advances in the physical sciences could be duplicated in the social sciences by the application of the same approach. In this way bad government could be supplanted by better government developed by people studying human activity in a rational manner.

The most important contributors to the concept of nationalism during this period were the Frenchmen Montesquieu and Voltaire. They were members of the French middle and upper classes and enjoyed considerable fame and wealth during their lives. Both, to differing degrees, reacted to the political ills of continental Europe and especially to the alliance of church and state in France. Within this context each gave substance to a form of nationalism which differed appreciably from that developed in England before 1700.

Montesquieu, in his *The Spirit of the Laws* (1748), asserted that variations in climate and geography have helped to determine the nature of the customs and forms of government of each land. This flew in the face of previously accepted theory that such differences were due to the will of God or to the sinfulness of people. Montesquieu was in effect asserting the existence of social laws and their interdependence with physical laws. His ideas tended to tie the cultural existence of a people to the territory which they inhabit and not to some form of active heavenly intervention. This suggested that "national" differences were both purposeful and deep-seated.

Voltaire, in his histories and other writings, complemented Montesquieu's ideas on nationality. More than anyone else, he introduced the concept of reason into political action, mainly by showing the historical damage caused by irrational and evil rulers. He was no revolutionary; on the contrary, much of his time was spent in corresponding with the nobility and monarchs of the mid-1700s. For the most part, Voltaire and his associates contributed more to the continuing destruction of the universalist edifice than to its replacement with a new idea. They set the tone for the development in Western Europe and North America of a liberal nationalism, which would liberate people and unite them at the same time, all under the banner of calm reason.

After 1775, the concept of nationalism was subjected to further change by two men whose works served to propagandize the unity of nationalism and revolution. One, Jean-Jacques Rousseau, was a contemporary and an enemy of Voltaire. His major work was finished by 1770, but its impact was not felt until 1790. The other, Thomas Paine, was an Englishman who influenced the ideas of both the American and French revolutions.

Rousseau, like Voltaire, was one of the great writers of the 18th century although he had almost no formal education and derived his steady income from copying musical scores. His ideas were generally inconsistent and often illogical, but he was gifted with the capacity to evoke feeling in his novels and essays. At the height of the rationalists' assault on the existing order, his writings created a great impact, and he found himself opposed by the rationalists for his emotional orientation and opposed by the church and nobility for his penchant for promoting unorthodox ideals. In short, Rousseau allied nonrational concepts with the social goals of the rationalists, for which he received the hatred of both groups.

Rousseau posited that government was formed as a result of a contract between individuals to subordinate themselves to the whole for the common good. This was not an especially new idea. Rousseau's contribution was the notion of the "general will," which suggested that the unit created by the contract had an existence which was different, and perhaps greater, than the sum of its parts. Rousseau broke with the ideas of the old regime by incorporating the contract into his theories and thus rejected divine right. He also rejected the rationalists' view by positing that the whole community or nation had a prior claim to the life and action of the individual. In contrast, the liberal nationalists felt that the nation existed in order to uplift the lives of its component individuals and was in fact subordinate to their interests. Rousseau further suggested that government was the servant of the general will and if it should somehow abuse its trust, it should be replaced through revolution. The church and school were seen as instruments of the general will and the task of each was to promote patriotism throughout the nation. Rousseau had merged elements of popular sovereignty, revolution, nationality, and patriotism into one attractive package. His style and approach appealed primarily to the literate and pious middle classes and it was here that he apparently had his greatest influence. The upper class, which was to be swept away after 1789, was more interested in the clash between the sophisticated rationalists and the orthodoxy of the old regime.

Rousseau's vision of a group of people who existed in a state of nature yet made a contract which bound them into a superior entity may be seen as romantic nationalism. Its first application was in Corsica, an island off the French coast in the Mediterranean Sea, where a revolutionary government had freed it in 1755 from the control of Genoa. The government of Corsica asked Rousseau to draw up a constitution for it in 1764, but a French invasion in 1768 ended this project.

With the "social contract" in mind, Rousseau proposed that every citizen should sign a solemn and irrevocable pledge of himself—"body, goods, will and all my powers"—to the Corsican nation.[3]

---

[3] Will and Ariel Durant, *Rousseau and Revolution* (New York: Simon & Schuster, 1967), p. 204.

Rousseau's original impact on the development of the French Revolution came not from his political ideas in *The Social Contract* but from his novels, *Héloise* and *Émile*. These were read extensively by the literate middle class and intellectuals, who were affected by the romantic elements in his writing. Pilgrims flocked to his tomb outside of Paris and the ideals expressed in his novels were compared with the amoral life of the royal court and the aristocracy. Rousseau's concerns for equality and liberty were also echoed by those who were to be in the forefront of the movement of 1789. Only as the revolution progressed did its leaders begin to take notice of his political writings. These were then carried by the revolutionary armies throughout Europe, providing other groups with a basis for national liberation.

Thomas Paine was, for the most part, self-educated and, until he migrated to the American colonies in 1774, at the age of 37, was a failure at such diverse undertakings as corset-making, writing, tax collecting, marriage, and business. In Philadelphia, he was offered the editorship of a magazine and found his true calling as a journalist and publicist. He wrote *Common Sense* in 1776 in order to encourage Americans to declare their independence from England. The pamphlet's circulation ran to a hundred thousand copies and was also translated and disseminated in France.[4] He assisted in the drafting of the 1778 constitution of Pennsylvania, which had a significant impact upon French ideas. The constitution provided for universal suffrage, a unicameral legislature, and religious freedom. At the time of the French Revolution, Paine was acclaimed by the National Assembly and in 1793 was elected a deputy. Much of his time between 1789 and 1793 was taken up in the defence of the revolution, especially against the writings of Edmund Burke. Paine's *Rights of Man* caused so much unrest in England that he was convicted of sedition *in absentia*. Paine was nearly executed in France during the Terror and later served as an advisor of sorts to Napoleon, and after 1802 to President Jefferson. He died destitute in 1809.

Common Sense and the *Rights of Man* were, like Rousseau's writing, more important for their emotional impact than for specific ideas. Paine's greatest contributions were the merging of the rationalist ideas of natural law and the primacy of knowledge with those of equality and self-determination. Along with Rousseau he was responsible for the propagation of the idea of national liberation among a wider strata of society than had hitherto been touched by it. In this sense they not only added to nationalist theory but also helped create nationalist ideologies. Nationalist thought after Rousseau was

---

[4] In Canada today, an equivalent circulation would be well over a million copies; a number no domestic political tract could hope to reach.

primarily oriented around the romantic outlook, Paine's rationalist orientation being absorbed by it, except in the United States. Only the Marxist revisionists a century later attempted to construct any nationalist theory on rational grounds.

The success of the French revolutionary armies in Europe spread the nationalist idea throughout the area. Much of this was a result of a demonstration effect; nationalistic soldiers fought better and endured more, so the opponents of Napoleon began to evoke national feeling among their peoples in order to withstand him. The idea also spread because of the political activities of the French. In Egypt, their sponsorship of archaeological research aroused the first stirrings of national identification. Along the Dalmatian coast in what is now Yugoslavia, the French encouraged the revival of Slav languages and in western Germany their dissolution of most of the 300 petty principalities enabled many Germans to envision a united Germany. The termination of the Holy Roman Empire during this time also ended the major universalist political fiction which had held back national feeling in Germany for centuries.

The origins of German nationalism paralleled to some degree those of the French; however, the rationalist orientation, which dominated French ideas until Rousseau, was almost nonexistent. As in France, the original concern of German thinkers was for individual liberty. Later, this concern was reformulated as national liberation in response to foreign threats and conquest. Since Germany was broken up into a multitude of political units, German writers also had to concentrate on popularizing the theme of political unity. Rousseau alone became the guiding light and German nationalism developed along romantic lines.

Johann Herder is commonly accredited with giving the first major impetus to German nationalism. He lived in East Prussia and later in Latvia in the late 1700s. Herder's main interest was the collection and publication of folk songs, which led him to certain ideas on the nature of national identity—that each nationality was in some unfathomable fashion unique and that individuals could only find meaning and expression in life through the medium of their nationality. Further, nationality could be traced through folk origins and could be expressed only through language. A nationality, therefore, is an organic whole and not susceptible to rational analysis. It also has nothing to do with the existence of a state, which is but an artificial political device. Supranational ideas and institutions such as universal Christianity and the Holy Roman Empire were also contrary to the reality of the unique nationalities of Europe.

The uniqueness also extended to the connection between nation and state, for each nation accepted different forms of state control and makeup as its unique history and combination of values dictated. England was a constitutional monarchy, France a secular republic, and Germany required something else. The Prussian authoritarian state could perhaps serve as a model. In it, the individual, as a product of the nation, should be prepared to subordinate himself or herself to the agent of the nation, the state. From this vision, the totalitarian state could easily follow.

The German nationalists who followed Herder were also affected by patriotism in a pan-German sense and tried to show that the German people were superior to their neighbours by tracing German identity back to the barbarian tribes which overthrew the western Roman Empire. A case was made that the English, French, Spanish, and Italians were basically bastardized Germans and that only in Germany did the true genius of the "race" lie.

The spirit of romantic nationalism was dulled after the defeat of Napoleon in 1815, when the monarchs of Austria, Prussia, and Russia entered into the Holy Alliance, which was designed to restore royalty to France and to maintain the territorial status quo in Europe. The west German states, though fewer in number, were resurrected, the Dalmatian provinces and northern Italy were restored to Austrian domination, and the Poles were once more subjugated. Popular revolts in Naples and Spain were put down in 1820–21 and plans were made to restore the newly independent South American states to Spanish rule.

A greater threat to the maintenance of these nonnational states was the struggle by Greek nationalists to free themselves from Turkish domination after 1820. The Greek cause was given great publicity throughout Europe, where it was seen as an attempt to restore the freedom and democracy of classical Greece. In a sense, the struggle was the first "war of national liberation." Neither Russia nor Austria had any love for the Turks, but their fear of incipient nationalist feelings among the minorities in their empires restrained them in aiding the Greeks. Only after the English had been prompted, for reasons of domestic politics and international advantage, to support Greek independence, was the Russian government forced to also support it for fear of discrediting its claim to be the defender of the Orthodox faith. The Holy Alliance eventually collapsed in 1848, undermined by nationalistic strains.

Modern Italian nationalism was also inspired by the French Revolution. In contrast to German nationalism, which was stimulated by opposition to Napoleon, Italians regretted the end of Napoleonic rule primarily because the restored monarchical rulers were worse. Secret societies were formed throughout the peninsula and an abortive revolt was undertaken in southern Italy in 1820. Like Herder, the Italians saw Europe as a continent of nations but felt that the uniqueness of these nations lay in the roles they were assigned in history at any given stage in the progress of humanity. Italy, of course, was to play a central role in this drama as the harmonizer between German thought, French action, and English commerce. Before Italy could play its role, the country had to be united and cleansed of the remnants of tradition and privilege. A democratic republic must be formed from the disunited monarchical and religious fragments. Italy was finally united in 1860, but not as the nationalists had hoped. Instead, it was united under a constitutional monarchy with limited suffrage.

Nationalism in Eastern Europe was born as the result of a history of local struggles with Germans to the west, Turks to the south, and Mongols to the east. It was also stimulated by the development of a literary interest in Slavic folk culture in imitation of Herder's work in Latvia. The implicit claim of the Orthodox church to represent the tradition of the Byzantine church also contributed to a feeling of pan-Slavism which only gradually evolved into specific nationalisms. There was some attempt to relate nationalism to specific political forms, but the only common denominator appeared to be the need for some sort of state organization and an assertion of the validity of na-tional self-determination. The conflict between tradition and privilege on the one hand and liberal nationalism on the other, which had racked England in the 1600s and France in the 1700s, was missing in Eastern Europe. Nationalism was effectively harnessed by the semifeudal landowners and aristocracies as a support for their political systems.

The Socialist Reaction

As the 20th century opened, the major opposition to nationalist ideologies was not the tradition and privilege found a century earlier but a new derivation of rationalism, Marxist socialism. Marx's theories had been predicated upon a rational and assertedly scientific basis. Nationalism and the nation-state were seen as devices used by the ruling classes, regardless of their traditional or economic background, to keep the mass of people quiet and obedient. Nationalism was "false consciousness" insofar as it did not promote proletarian uprisings. The *Communist Manifesto* (1848) proclaimed as much in the cry: "Work-ers of the world unite! You have nothing to lose but your chains!"

Political movements based on Marx's ideas arose in all of the na-tions of continental Europe and played a significant role in the politics of France and Germany. Elsewhere political movements remained rather small and powerless until the 1900s. During the last half of the 19th century most of these movements were united under two succes-sive Internationals, which brought them together and coordinated their actions and theories. Other more radical Marxist splinter groups remained aloof from the International but sympathized with the internationalist concept inherent in Marxian socialism. All of them were seen as antinational and hence traitorous groups by liberal and conservative nationalists alike. To some degree this hindered their growth but did not really threaten their existence.

Socialists responded in three ways to the question of nationalism during the first two decades of the 20th century. Some splinter groups were formed, especially in Germany and in parts of the Austro–Hungarian Empire, which were primarily nationalist, though they incorporated socialist ideals within their goals. These national-socialist movements were the precursors of post-World War I organizations, such as the German National Socialist Workers' (Nazi) Party which Adolf Hitler used for his rise to power.

Most European socialists moved by 1900 toward parliamentary participation in France, Germany, Italy, and Austria–Hungary. They gradually absorbed nationalist outlooks, to the extent that by 1914 the majority of the membership of such parties enthusiastically supported their national positions in the World War.

A more radical fringe maintained its aloofness from the war and incurred the displeasure of the national authorities in all of Europe. The Bolsheviks belonged to this fringe and their leadership remained in exile in Switzerland until the first Russian revolution in 1917.

RADICAL NATIONALISM

As early as 1780 the national idea was shared by two opposing philosophical camps, the rationalists, or liberals, and the romantics. The rationalists tended throughout the next century and a half to approve of nationalism, while keeping a wary eye upon this idea, since they were concerned about the unity of people. To the rationalists, nationalism has remained an element of human life, but one which should be subordinate to the needs of people as a whole.

Romantic nationalists have tended to occupy the other half of the spectrum. Some managed to merge conservative views with romanticism and produced an amalgam which allowed for democratic forms and political activism without essentially contesting the social relations and ideals brought forward from the past. Where these modifying forces were destroyed or absent, the romanticists developed radical forms of nationalism. Radical nationalism, where all social relations are subordinated to the needs and whims of the nation or its agent, the nation-state, is based upon an extrapolation of the ideals of such men as Rousseau and Herder. We know these forms as fascism and national socialism. While the terminology of these "isms" has for the most part been discarded since 1945, radical nationalism itself continues to be a factor elsewhere in the world.

The radical nationalists who dominated Italy and Germany especially through much of the period between the two world wars have been commonly labelled as fascists, a term derived from the name of the Italian variety. The word itself refers to the Roman "fasces," a bundle of sticks tied together with an axe in the centre, representing the strength of justice. The origins of fascist theory differed according to the nation in which it developed and, except for the common idea that the nation was the end and justification of all, expressed itself in different, national forms. In effect there are different "fascisms."

There were no fascist movements of any noteworthy size before the end of World War I. It was mistakenly believed that a German defeat in that war would make the world safe for democracy. In reality, it made the world safe for nationalism by destroying the only major multinational empires, Austria and Russia, and ending, temporarily, the supranational ambitions of Germany. Five years after its end, antidemocratic fascism dominated Italy and was making serious inroads into other states in Europe.

Italy

Italian fascism was constructed out of a strange amalgam of romantic nationalism and radical Marxism. Fascist theory was never really defined until after the movement had gained control of the Italian state, so that its antecedents and the history of the movement are of critical importance.

Benito Mussolini, later the fascist leader, was an active revolutionary socialist before World War I. He tended to emphasize revolution over socialism and was instrumental in 1912 in breaking the hold of the "parliamentarians" over the Socialist Party. His work during the next two years as editor of the socialist newspaper helped to solidify the revolutionary and internationalist wing of the Party, indirectly contributing to the founding of the Italian Communist Party after World War I. Mussolini, prior to 1914, was heavily contemptuous of the Italian nationalist movement.

Mussolini's commitment to an activist socialism grew out of his interest in Marxism and a feeling that life was action, which to Mussolini was perfectly compatible with the notions of class warfare and revolution. The conflict between action and socialism, which first suggested itself in an attack upon the parliamentary Socialists in 1912, arose in a more definitive form with the beginning of World War I. At the beginning of the conflict, in August 1914, he was adamantly opposed to Italian or at least socialist intervention, but gradually the activist in him overcame the socialist and he came out for alliance with the Allies against the Central Powers, which had attacked small Serbia and overrun neutral Belgium. This led to the loss of his editorial position and later to a severance of his links with the socialists. Throughout the war he propagandized on behalf of Italian participation, entered the army and was wounded in action. By 1919 he had become a left-wing nationalist and had lost all influence with the socialists.

Mussolini's evolution continued. He opposed Bolshevik Russia because the leaders had been assisted by the Germans and had made peace with them in 1918. He moved away from the socialists after the failure of their "revolution" in 1919–20 and the resurgence of the parliamentarian wing of the Party. He was casting about for a revolutionary instrument when a band of Italian romantic nationalists occupied Fiume, a town on the Yugoslav side of the Adriatic Sea which Italians felt should be theirs.

The call of the "liberators" of Fiume for national revival and Italian expansionism gave Mussolini the orientation he needed. By the end of 1920 his Fascist "action squads" had begun to destroy socialist newspaper offices and disrupt meetings. His opposition to the socialists was based upon the conflict between nationalism and internationalism. All other political and economic arrangements became secondary and subject to change as the need or opportunity arose. In this manner fascism moved from the political left to the political right. It was supported by conservative nationalists and military leaders, absorbed their energies, and moved beyond to a radical and authoritarian nationalism.

Fascist theory was only developed after Mussolini came to power. The main attempt of fascist theoreticians was to show that their ideas represented a valid counterforce to liberal nationalism. They emphasized the organic nature of the Italian nation, thus overcoming individualism with its attendant liberal and democratic qualities. Second, fascism recognized the historic mission of the nation; Italy was associated with the glories of the Roman Empire and in the future would develop a new spiritual, if not physical, empire. The Italian genius lay in the combination of thought and action, a sentiment which was used both to justify the fascist accession to power without a fixed ideology and to prepare Italians for further ideological and political shifts as historical circumstance might warrant.

The nation existed as a spiritual manifestation of the people, but this manifestation was also accompanied by that of the state. Fascist theory is unclear about the relationship between these two ideas, since the state at one point arises from the existence of the nation in the collective mind, whereas elsewhere the nation is pictured as depending for its existence upon the state. At any rate, the state becomes the concrete manifestation of national will and, as such, enjoys a claim to totality: "All is in the State and for the State; nothing outside the State, nothing against the State." The state therefore binds all together and leads the nation to its destiny.

The nation also produces heroes from time to time who arise to lead it to higher degrees of existence. These heroes, of whom Mussolini was one, are able through their special insight to penetrate to the essence of reality for correct solutions to national problems and have the courage to transform that thought into appropriate action. Since these heroes are especially gifted, their actions might not be comprehensible to the rest of the nation, but they must be obeyed.

Fascism is best known as an Italian movement, but the idea spread to other parts of Europe as well. Hitler was impressed with Mussolini's success and in 1923 tried to imitate his example by fomenting an uprising in Munich, which proved abortive. Other movements were created in Greece, Romania, Poland, Hungary, Austria, Finland, Spain, and Belgium in Europe and Brazil and Argentina in South America. For the most part these movements were small but dangerous. Only in some of the more backward countries of Central Europe and in those occupied after 1939 by the fascist powers did they achieve any success. The Spanish Falangist regime, which had fascist leanings and ties with Italy and Germany, was created only through the assistance of these powers in a long civil war.

Germany

German radical nationalism, more than any other to date, has realized the fear that

. . . the idea of the nation is one of the most powerful anaesthetics that man has ever invented. Under the influence of its fumes the whole people can carry out its systematic program of the most violent self-seeking without being in the least aware of its moral perversion . . .[5]

German nationalism, as we have seen, was mainly influenced by romantic and conservative ideals in the 19th century. In this respect the national ideology resembled the Italian and, like Italy, World War I both heightened German national feeling and deprived it of satisfaction at the conclusion of hostilities. Though the postwar Weimar Republic was led by the Social Democrats, it was increasingly dominated by conservatives and militarists who chafed under the restrictions imposed by the victorious Allies. It was in this atmosphere of conservative nationalism that Adolf Hitler and his Nazi Party began their political careers and achieved power.

---

[5] Rabindranath Tagore, *Nationalism* (1917), p. 57, quoted in Rudolf Rocker, *Nationalism and Culture*, 2d ed. (London: Freedom Press, 1946), p. 252.

German radical nationalism may be traced back to Herder's concept of the folk and the extension of this concept into the realm of the state. Fredrich Ludwig Jahn, for instance, carried the concept of the folk to an early extreme. He developed a hatred of things French during the occupation of Germany in 1806–13 and, in searching for an alternative to the French Revolution and its works, adopted the folk as his image of things German. Jahn's *German Folkdom* (1810) emphasized the notion of folkdom as the unconscious force which has shaped all history. The uniqueness of each folk meant that each must live alone, apart from all others. Jahn was not above advocating the creation of a wilderness barrier between France and Germany so as to ensure German purity from French ideas. The German folk, Jahn felt, is the only true basis for a state, and consequently Germany must be united under one state. In order to keep the folk pure, education must be oriented toward German ideas, and in order to realize its potential, the Germans must acquire a predominant place among the folks of the earth.

Jahn and his successors emphasized the spiritual and physical relationship inherent in the folk concept. A folk consisted of people in mystical communion with each other and their environment. Jahn dressed throughout much of his life in primitive garments, once lived in a cave, and encouraged studied boorishness in order to demonstrate the primitive essence of the German *volk*. He has been called "the first storm trooper."[6]

A French conservative, Joseph Arthur Gobineau, added the concept of race to the complex of German radical nationalist thought. In his *Essay on the Inequality of the Human Races* (1853–55), Gobineau attempted to uncover the causes of the decline of civilizations. He hypothesized that the collapse of empires and cultures was due to racial degeneration rather than to economic decline or class conflict. To some degree he was expanding on the environmental ideas popular around 1750 with such men as Montesquieu and adapting these ideas to a primitive idea of evolution. Gobineau suggested the existence of three human races—white, yellow, and black—which began and evolved independently of each other. Each race has its own physical and psychological characteristics, which were most pronounced when the stock was pure. He naturally attributed the "best" characteristics to the white race and went on to suggest that the decline of major (white) civilizations had been due to interbreeding among the races during the height of these civilizations. His racial theories applied to the early 19th century justified a conservative, aristocratic, orientation

---

[6] Peter Viereck, *Metapolitics: Roots of the Nazi Mind* (New York: Capricorn Books, 1965), chap. 4. (Originally published 1941).

since those who rule must come from a superior race. The French Revolution, by destroying the aristocracy, was leading to the decay of civilization, since class lines and hence blood lines were intermingled in its wake. Gobineau's ideas were not well known in Germany until the 1890s, but they did influence the central figure in the development of German radical nationalism, Richard Wagner.

Wagner is known throughout the world more for his music than for his political ideas. His work was one of inspiration rather than theoretical construction. Part of his career was spent dabbling in politics and political writings, but his greatest fame and influence came through his operas. During the 1848 revolts in Germany, he developed an appreciation for the romantic forms of nationalism and became enamoured with the concept of the folk and with the life of the fields and forests. These ideals were subsequently expressed in his operas, which eulogized the historic nordic folk, their gods, legends, and their primitive environment. In his operas he also featured great leaders and helped to popularize the idea of the folk king, who not only leads but incarnates the very essence of the folk. Wagner brought together all the disparate strands of German folk nationalism, pan-German feeling, pagan religion, antisemitism, the leader or *fuehrer* principle, and the concept of the folk-state. Wagner's son-in-law, Houston S. Chamberlain, was the foremost German race theorist at the turn of the century. In 1900, Chamberlain published his *Foundations of the Nineteenth Century,* in which he outlined world history in a Darwinian mould. His thesis was that history consisted of the records of a bitter evolutionary struggle in which weak races fell before the stronger. Most of the world at present consisted of the leftovers of this struggle—"a chaos of peoples"—and only two races remained pure, the Teutonic and the Jewish. These two races, because of their purity, naturally were stronger than the mongrelized rest of the world, but their essential natures differed. The Teutonic race, which Chamberlain saw in almost as broad terms as Gobineau's white "Aryans," were responsible for all that was great and good in humanity. All great and creative people were of Teutonic background and, where their names and ancestry might be considered as placing them outside this rule, an investigation into their backgrounds and into the distorted languages of their names would invariably show their Teutonic origins. The Jewish race, on the other hand, were the epitome of all that was evil. Chamberlain arrived at this conclusion as a result of his investigations which showed Jewish influence in important capitalist and socialist circles, both of which he abhorred. Since large-scale capitalism and all socialism were evil, it followed that those who controlled them, such as the Rothschilds and Marx, were also evil. Further, since history, according to Chamberlain, was racial, it was logical to see these people as representatives of their "race" and to ascribe to this race the evil characteristics of these ideas.

Chamberlain's twisted logic and his pseudo-science provided the perfect rationale for the defeat of Germany in World War I. Since the folk of that country were "pure," they naturally should have won the war against the decadent Allies. That they lost was not due to their inferiority, but because the mortal enemies of the Teutonic race, the Jews, "stabbed Germany in the back." The preponderance of socialists in the successor regime to the empire, the Weimar Republic, only served to "prove" this allegation. Hitler and other radical nationalists felt that a second war with the Allies would prove successful only if the Jews were first neutralized.

Hitler and Mussolini were similar in that both produced writings that expressed some fascist thought, but Hitler was in fact heavily indebted to an associate, Alfred Rosenberg, for ideas. Rosenberg's major ideas were first outlined in 1917, though they were not published until 1930 in his *Myth of the Twentieth Century*. The myth of the 20th century is the myth of blood, or race. This, not democracy or liberal nationalism, was to be the principle on which people would act and for which they would fight. He asserted that races are the building blocks of history and that the nation is only the political expression of the race. A state which is not based upon a race is soulless and deserves no loyalty.

Rosenberg's racism paralleled that of Chamberlain in that he saw history as a succession of racial struggles. The victors, he asserted, must retain their innate superiority by imposing themselves as a conquering class which must never interbreed with its inferiors. Since the Aryan race, which Rosenberg felt was pure only in its Germanic variety, was innately superior, it would eventually dominate and other races would be its permanent slaves. This superiority extended to morals and spiritual values, so that one should not expect the Aryans to act according to the common and inferior standards of the rest of the world.

The *carte blanche* for the Aryan race was especially necessary in the 20th century in order to combat the latest threat to the uplifting of world civilization. By liberating all races and classes, Rosenberg felt that the French Revolution let the Jews out of their ghettos and into positions of control in the capitalist and communist countries. He saw them as being conspirators, a method opposed to good Aryan aggression and contemptible because of it. The Jews were seen by him as setting class against class, faith against faith, and people against people in their drive for world domination. Marxism, for instance, was predicated upon the class struggle in order to break down national unity—Rosenberg therefore identified it as tactic in a larger race war and therefore to be stamped out by the true representatives of the German folk, the Nazi organization.

Rosenberg was one of Hitler's earliest allies and was instrumental in the formulation of much of his leader's *Mein Kampf* (My Struggle). He was appointed editor of the Nazi paper, *Volkischer Beobachter* (The Folkish Observer) and served as the chief Nazi ideologue until the collapse of Germany in 1945. He was subsequently executed by the Allies following the Nuremberg Trials in 1946.

Nazi fascism differed from the Italian variety in that it emphasized the idea of the race whereas the Italians tended to worship the all-powerful state. In a sense the Nazi orientation was more mystical, the Italian more organizational. Nazi fascism was also global in scope whereas the Italians dreamed mainly of a resurrection of the Roman Empire.

AMERICAN NATIONALISM

The events which gave birth to the United States and its environment led to a form of nationalism which is unique and somewhat anachronistic today. Nationalism has generally grown out of an increasing awareness of a common language and culture among a group. The United States is a country peopled almost entirely by immigrants of widely divergent ethnic and religious traditions. Thus American nationalism does not fit the usual pattern and the concept of folk, or the bond of common ancestry, is useless in this context.

The United States shares, with a number of other countries, the English language and culture. The circumstances which surrounded the establishment of a separate political system two centuries ago resulted in the severing of many of the ties with the then existing British political tradition. Other successor states to the British Empire evolved directly out of that tradition, even though for many of them, such as India or Nigeria, the English language and culture were of marginal importance. All of the countries that emerged from the Empire have naturally begun the process of movement away from the inherited values. American nationalism, growing out of revolution against the British tradition instead of evolution from it, has developed in a way quite distinct from any of the other successor states.

One aspect of this distinctive development was that the Americans opted for a new political system based on theories of federalism and separation of powers, then not widely known or appreciated. In seeking to curb executive power they borrowed from a British tradition that had surfaced during the period of the English Civil War. They maintained at the time that they were in fact simply asserting the ancient rights of English people dating back to the Magna Charta, rights that the Imperial government was deliberately ursurping. The political structures thus created were to be the vehicle not only for the maintenance of independence but also for the prevention of any usurpation of these ancient rights by an American government. Thus the concept of a strictly limited government was built into the structure as well as the theory of American politics. This is in direct contrast to the mainstream of the British tradition which emphasizes the supremacy of the legislature. The American Constitutional document became the venerated symbol of the new nation and the rights of its citizens.

Finally, as if to thoroughly frustrate the models of the romantic and radical nationalists, there is no common American religion, nor is there an historically defined American "border," which has had to be defended from onslaughts by outsiders. A German romantic poet who visited the United States in the 1820s vented his frustrations thus:

One should not think that the American loves his fatherland or that he has a fatherland. Every single individual lives and works in that republican association because, and only as long as, his private fortunes are secured by it. What we call a fatherland, is here only an insurance company for one's property . . . . The state is not for him a spiritual or moral institution, a fatherland, but only a material convention.[7]

Lenau's confusion is excusable, since American nationalists developed their ideas largely from factors opposite to those used elsewhere.

It was noted in Chapter 14 that liberal ideas began to be discussed with some seriousness toward the middle of the 18th Century. This was the same period when the English colonists in America began to reassess their relationship with the government in London. The liberal notion that the state should serve the needs of the individual was used as a justification for rebellion in 1776.

The idea of individual liberation remained as one of the fundamentals of American nationalism. It was invoked by the antislavery forces in the North prior to and during the American Civil war and by President Woodrow Wilson during World War I when he stated that American intervention was necessary in order to make the world safe for democracy. It has also played an important role in American involvement in the Cold War in which the United States is portrayed as the bulwark of freedom arrayed against the forces of communism and collectivism.

One of the problems of combining liberalism with nationalism is their incompatibility when the limits of the nation are discussed. Liberalism too easily slips into universalism, that is, *all* people should be free, while nationalism is much more restricted and particular.

---

[7] Hans Kohn, *American Nationalism* (New York: Macmillan, 1957), p. 73. (Quoting the poet, Nikolas Lenau.)

American nationalism, because of its liberal base, has had to be defined continually both in the particular American context as well as the larger world context. In this sense it is not unlike the Stalinist identification of the Russian nation with the communist role of world revolution.

The exporting of "Americanism" was given its first boost by the process of uniting the colonies, first during the Revolutionary War and later under a new constitution in 1789. Unity was arrived at freely: there was no Imperial government in London to legislate a union as was the case with the Canadian Confederation. The accomplishment of uniting the states seemed proof that other lands could establish or join unions of free people.

The idea that the United States had a mission to bring liberation to other parts of the world was eventually called Manifest Destiny. It was the duty of the nation to bring to the rest of North America, and elsewhere, the light of liberation, by force if necessary. The first period of this expansionism, 1832–60, included the invasion of Mexico and the annexation of the Republic of Texas, as well as the establishment of a number of new states within the territory of the union. A group of radical Democrats formed the "Young America" movement to promote expansion. Primary education was dominated by McGuffey's *Eclectic Reader,* which preached the virtues of America to the immigrant children, while Herman Melville and Walt Whitman began to extol American virtues in prose and poetry.

Manifest destiny reached a new peak of intensity in the 1880s and 1890s and culminated in the annexation of Hawaii, the acquisition of Puerto Rico and the Philippines as a result of success in the Spanish–American War (1898), and the fomenting of the secession of Panama from Colombia to facilitate the building of the Panama Canal. As a result of victory in the Spanish–American War, the United States became the dominant power in the Caribbean and Central America. This enthusiasm for the liberation of other peoples was dampened when it became clear, especially with the guerrilla war fought by native nationalists in the Philippines, that many of the "liberated" also resented their new masters.

Since World War I, the universalist side of American nationalism has been torn between the practical need to make the world safe for the international expansion of American business and an instinctive sympathy for anticolonial movements in Africa and Asia. The tension between universalism and particularism has been in evidence most recently in the decade-long debate over the meaning and nature of America's role in Indochina.

A third aspect of American nationalism has been the polyglot nature of the American people. In part, the development of the United States can be seen as a practical manifestation of the liberal notion that free individuals can and will cooperate in the best interests of the whole people. People of all languages, religions, and races could come together in a new land and work to create a new state and a new people. To this idea of the "melting pot" was added that of the "frontier." In 1893, Frederick Jackson Turner wrote a short paper on "The Significance of the Frontier in American History." He argued that the frontier was at that time finally closed in, but during the preceding century the lure of open spaces and the pressures to survive on the edge of civilization had moulded a new people and a new way of life. As this view became popular in the 1900s, American nationalism gained further identity from qualities which were opposite to those used elsewhere to define a nation—diverse ancestries and mobility.

It is not easy to categorize American nationalism. It could be seen as a variety of liberal nationalism, which declined elsewhere with the end of the Napoleonic regime in 1815. It also could be likened to the Soviet Russian nationalism, an "internationalist" national creed. But these are not really satisfactory. A unique set of historical and physical circumstances have produced its identity and one must see it in that context.

ASIAN AND AFRICAN NATIONALISM

Outside of Europe and the American continents, the national idea was weak or nonexistent as late as 1914. Only Japan, which had begun a process of rapid economic development and promotion of national interests after 1868, could be said to be an exception. Other areas of the world contained people who were determined to throw off foreign rule or influence, but these individuals acted largely in a reactionary sense. They opposed outside rule but did not effectively articulate a national consciousness.

African and Asian nationalist ideas grew out of their experience with imperialism, especially that surge of European expansion after 1870, which brought most of these continents under different types of foreign domination. Reaction to foreign interference in local cultural, economic, and political patterns constituted the central element in the nationalism which appeared throughout these areas. The formation by the imperial powers of relatively integrated colonial governments, which later could be identified as nations, was a second element. The colonial units themselves then provided an anchor for imported nationalist theory. A third element, whose importance varied from area to area, was the traditional complex of cultural and economic orientations and ideas. Where these were strong, as in China, India, and the Arab lands, they were incorporated into nationalist ideas and were used to justify and promote nationalist activity. The existence of these elements in concrete terms helped to forge new varieties of nationalism.

Three critical incidents in the rise of nationalist ideologies in the non-Western world occurred in the first quarter of this century. First, the Japanese victory over the Russians in 1905 proved to Asians that a European nation could be defeated by Asians if the latter adapted themselves to modern conditions. Nationalist modernizers in all parts of the world looked to this victory as an example and a hope.

A second incident occurred after World War I when Allied leaders made statements about the sanctity and desirability of popular self-determination. The principle of self-determination was over a century old by then, but its espousal by the colonial masters of the world reverberated throughout their empires. Colony after colony sent delegations to Versailles where the Peace Treaty ending World War I was being negotiated, pleading for the application of self-determination to their areas.

The third critical incident was the Russian Revolution, which led to the injection of Marxian socialism into the nationalist theories developing in Asia and Africa. It resulted in the development of a nationalist and socialist regime in Russia and helped to popularize Lenin's ideas on imperialism and national liberation.

Upon taking power in Russia, the Bolsheviks worked out a new nationalist policy, partly to satisfy stresses inside Russia and partly to assume the leadership of the radical elements in the European socialist parties. Within Russia a number of theoretically sovereign but federated republics were created, as well as numerous autonomous republics and regions. These were then united in the Union of Soviet Socialist Republics (U.S.S.R.), a supranational grouping of states. Within the U.S.S.R., local languages and certain historical cultural aspects of life were encouraged in each republic or region, while other aspects, less suited to a secular, modern existence were suppressed. This encouragement of a partial nationalism within a supranational union was an attempt to harness this powerful idea for the benefit of international socialism.

The U.S.S.R. also moved to reestablish the Socialist International by constituting a Communist International (Comintern), grouping together all those parties whose commitment was still to proletarian revolution and internationalism. The establishment of the Comintern marked the splitting of most socialist parties after 1920 into one which was socialist, parliamentarian, and nationalist, and another which was radically socialist, antiparliamentarian, internationalist, and pro-

Soviet. Again the internationalist organizations were persecuted for their lack of national feeling.

The need to build up the U.S.S.R. as a bastion of radical socialism became apparent once the hope of revolutions in the rest of Europe similar to that in Russia died. A policy of "socialism in one country" was adopted, which saw the increasing subordination of both internal and external communist organizations to the needs of the U.S.S.R. as a unit. This trend was increased after the Nazi onslaught in 1941, and appeals to Russian patriotism grew during what is now called the Great Patriotic War (1941–45). The inability of the U.S.S.R. to submerge national identities and feelings in Eastern Europe after the war underlined the fact that international communism was becoming more "national."

What Rousseau did for nationalism in the 19th century, Lenin did in the 20th century. His book *Imperialism, the Highest Stage of Capitalism* (1916), is one of the critical works of the century, not for its intrinsic merits, but for the inspiration it has provided to the nationalists of Asia, Africa, and Latin America. Lenin favoured the struggles of the nationalists in many parts of the world because he saw in their success the possibility of hastening the global socialist revolution.

Nationalism in Europe had eroded the traditional regimes and formed the basis for much capitalist growth. In Europe this growth reached the stage where it should spark the socialist revolution, but, according to Lenin, this did not happen because of the ability of Western capitalists to expand into Asia and Africa. These continents were being exploited by Europe and North America in order to use profitably their surplus capital and to alleviate the conditions of the working class in their own countries. Lenin in effect posited the existence of two types of countries, capitalist and proletarian, instead of sticking closely to Marx's global classes.

It was logical to the Asian and African nationalists, then, that any blow struck at the imperial powers and the corporations behind them would be of benefit to mankind. The U.S.S.R., through the Comintern, pledged to help nationalist movements, regardless of their ties to communism, since national liberation by itself was a step toward revolution. As a result of this doctrine, nationalists found global justification for their work; they found an apparently disinterested ally in the U.S.S.R., and the communists gained *entrée* into nationalist movements all across the underdeveloped part of the world. The communists' direct influence has been blunted in most countries, but their support has resulted in the merging of nationalism with local brands of socialism nearly everywhere.

China

The first significant national movement found in a "colonial" area arose in China just before 1900. Though this country was never completely absorbed into a foreign empire during the era of imperial expansion (1870–1900), many important bases and provinces were detached from it and foreign powers exercised a number of humiliating privileges elsewhere. Chinese nationalism was largely confined to the literate middle class, but its strength was sufficient to sweep away the millenial royal institutions in favor of a national republic in 1911.

In 1905, a revolutionary league was founded on the bases of nationalism, democracy, and socialism. It opposed the ruling Manchu dynasty as well as the imperial powers. Democracy meant a struggle against traditional Confucian ideals, replacing them with a bill of rights, personal equality, and republican institutions. Socialism was not that of the Marxian variety, but consisted of an adaptation of some odd single-tax theories to China. A revolution in 1911 established a republic but failed to restore Chinese unity. The nationalists became embroiled in a revolutionary struggle against the warlords, who had succeeded the Manchus. They worked in tandem with the communists, although there was little sympathy for Leninst ideas.

The ideas of the Chinese nationalists were hardly original or profound but they affected nationalism throughout East Asia. They were introduced to the native peoples in Indochina, Thailand, Malaya, and Indonesia by expatriate Chinese populations.

India

Indian nationalism before World War I developed within the context of the British liberal tradition. The Indian National Congress worked originally for administrative reform and elements of home rule within the British Empire. After World War I, Indian nationalists began to advocate "swaraj," or political independence, instead of autonomy. They suggested the use of political agitation, such as demonstrations, and noncooperation as the major means for achieving independence. It had to be achieved by struggle if it were to be of any value. They were hardly revolutionaries; on the contrary, it was felt that good government required the development of moral virtues in the Indian people, which must come out of their Hindu traditions. India should be independent and "good" at the same time. The British had provided much that should be retained, but their rule was now unnecessary.

Mohandas K. Gandhi influenced the whole of Indian society—not just the political or, more narrowly, the nationalist aspects of it. He returned to India in 1915 from an extended stay in South Africa where he had become disillusioned with British democracy and institutions. Like others, he attempted to merge independence, reform, and Hindu ideals into a force which would revive India. His philosophy arose from his Indian background and was only marginally affected by outside forces and ideas. In practice, Gandhi made use of Western devices by using the communications links and literacy promoted by the English to build a mass following throughout the country. He became the leader and the symbol of the Congress and the symbol of its ultimate goal, the creation of an independent state of India. Gandhi saw the genius of India in its half-million villages and built his political ideals around village life. He felt that materialism and machinery led to evils among people and tried to show the way to a more spiritual life by the rejection of all but local cottage crafts, simple, austere living, and the development of a decentralized, democratic state. His tactics were basically those of noncooperation, nonviolence, and civil disobedience. Eventually, after more than a quarter century, India gained independence in 1947. Indian nationalism today is a composite of Hindu ideals and socialism. In its nature, it is different from the traditional European nationalism, which was based upon a community of language, culture, religion, and social customs. In a country with a multiplicity of religious, linguistic, and regional cultural variations, Indian nationalism rests largely upon a community of interests among its varied population and opposition to imperalism, its relations with China, and enmity with its neighbour, Pakistan.

The Middle East

The countries of the Middle East have been more affected by European nationalist theories than any other part of Asia. Napoleon's invasion of Egypt in 1798 inspired the beginnings of nationalism there. Later, national feeling was stimulated among the Christian Arabs of Lebanon by the successful revolt of Greece against the Ottoman Empire, which also controlled the whole of the Arab lands except for the desert interior of the Arabian peninsula. Turkish students brought back ideas of liberal nationalism into Constantinople, the capital of the Empire. A revolt in Egypt, led by Colonel Arabi, led to the occupation of the Nile by the British in 1881, setting back Egyptian and Arab nationalism. Then, such liberal modernizers as Mustafa Kamil and Saad Zaghulul sparked the formation of the nationalist Wafd Party. Egypt received nominal autonomy in 1922 and Iraq in 1923.

The Ottoman Empire was dismembered by the victorious Allies, the Ottomans having entered the war on the side of Germany and

Austria. Plans were also made to divide up the Turkish heartland in the process, but in a series of stunning military battles, a Turkish general, Mustafa Kemal, later called Ataturk, crushed an invading Greek army and bluffed the allied forces out of Turkey proper. Ataturk, still the model for many national modernizers, then set about reforming the country by decree. He abolished the Empire and created a Turkish Republic, disestablished the Islamic religion, eliminated a number of socioreligious customs, formed a single governing party, and brought industrialization into Turkey. His methods were antithetical to those of Gandhi in India.

A third strain of nationalism introduced into the Middle East considerably complicated the situation after World War II. This was Zionism, or Jewish nationalism. Zionism was popularized by Theodor Herzl throughout Europe in the last decade of the 19th century. Herzl and his followers carried the romantic concepts of nationalism past the territorial folk idea of the Germans into an act of creating a nation-state where none had really existed. The Zionists were committed to the migration of Jews from their homes in Europe, Africa, and Asia to a new territory which would be their own. At one point, consideration was given to an offer of land in Uganda in East Africa, but their real interest lay in Palestine, the historical "promised land" of Moses. Politically, Zionism was modernizing and, eventually, socialist. Zionists began emigrating to Palestine after 1900 and by the 1930s formed a considerable minority. At this point Zionism ran into nascent Arab nationalism and the continuing crisis of the Middle East was born.

The clash between Zionism and Arab nationalism has led to an evolution in Arab thinking. Basically the reformist and modernizing ideas of the early nationalists have been discarded for an amalgam of traditionalism and radical socialism. Since 1952, the date of the Egyptian Revolution, the ideal of pan-Arab nationalism, based partly upon religious and linguistic feelings and upon socialist theories adapted from France and the U.S.S.R. has been predominant. Zionism and its creation, Israel, have served to bring all Arabs, from Iraq to Morocco, together in spirit, if not into a permanent political union.

CANADIAN NATIONALISM

Nationalism in Canada has been characterized by two processes; a search for a common identity among its many ethnic groups and the development of two national ideologies. To a great extent these processes have generated and, at the same time, are the result of each other's existence. Much thought has been devoted to uncovering the roots of a common Canadian identity, which has been complicated by an increasing awareness that the roots of such an identity are found in dual and to some degree antithetical concepts.

Both of these interpretations are founded upon versions of the garrison mentality. Running throughout our history since the 18th century have been two, not one, nationalist impulses. First there has been the French-speaking Canadians' commitment to *la survivance* in the face of the vast English-speaking majority in North America. Second, there is the English-speaking Canadians' desire to survive as a people separate from the United States.[6]

The dual roots of nationalism in Canada are found in the historical myths of French and English settlement of the Great Lakes–St. Lawrence area. The French settlers came first but found themselves, after 1759, under English political control. English settlers then came as a small minority of "conquerers" whose numbers were later swelled by refugees from the American War of Independence.

Nationalist ideas filtered into Lower Canada from the United States and France. As early as 1794, revolutionary agents were sent to Canada to rouse French Canadians against Great Britain by suggesting to them the idea of their own republic on the banks of the St. Lawrence. Such attempts met with little success, however; it was not until the second decade of the 19th century that French and American liberal nationalism began to influence French Canadians.

Nationalist ideas first developed in Lower Canada when a small group of professionals formed the *Patriote* Party in 1827. They were concerned with developing Lower Canada along the lines taken by the revolutionaries in France three decades earlier. They tried to introduce the ideas of liberty, progress, economic development, and science into the area. In 1834 the St. Jean Baptiste Society was founded to hold banquets and meetings to promote these liberal ideas. It was also concerned with the development of national feeling in Lower Canada and devised a flag and a motto, "Our institutions, our language, and our laws." The flag resembled the French tricolor to some degree, and the emblem adopted by the society was the maple leaf. These liberal nationalists were also affected by English ideas of the period and they associated the development of a French-Canadian nation with democratic principles and a parliamentary form of government. Liberal nationalism was discredited for many years following the abortive attempt at rebellion made by a fraction of the *Patriote* movement in 1837. Its leaders were arrested or fled into exile; the St. Jean Baptiste Society was suppressed until 1842 and newspapers supporting *Patriote* ideas were closed for some time.

---

[6] Ramsay Cook. *The Maple Leaf Forever* (Toronto: Macmillan of Canada, 1971).

After 1840, nationalism in Lower Canada took a more conservative turn. An alliance of professionals and clergy produced an orientation which included cooperation with English authorities and a campaign against French-Canadian liberals. The failure of the 1837 revolt demonstrated to some *Patriotes* that the needs of French Canadians could only be served within the British monarchical system and that they could only maintain their identity by providing assistance to those English politicians willing to bargain with them. Active cooperation of this sort dominated Lower Canadian nationalism until 1885 and has remained significant to the present.

Internally the Catholic clergy adopted the nationalist concept in order to reinforce the tie between Lower Canada and Catholicism. French Canadians were seen as the bearers of Catholicism to the new world and as its protectors until the materialist English colonists would come to their senses and adopt its tenets. Conservative Catholics in Europe opposed nationalism because of its liberal ties and its threat to the independence of the church; but in Lower Canada it was found to be an effective safeguard against Protestant and English encroachment. Elements of liberal nationalism remained, especially in the *rouge* political faction and in the St. Jean Baptiste Society.

Upper Canada was originally settled largely by Loyalist refugees who had suffered from the effects of American nationalism. It was not until the successes of the War of 1812 that their descendants developed a firm sense of their own identity separate from both the English and Americans. By the 1830s, the myth of the United Empire Loyalists (UEL) as people of high principle, preferring starvation and exile to the acceptance of republican ideas, was being embellished. This was reinforced by the importation of the "sturdy yeoman" concept from England which was then used to reinterpret the War of 1812. General Brock's success in 1812 at the head of a body of militia was, during the 1840s and 1850s, compared to the defense of Thermopylae. Darwinian concepts were later introduced into the UEL myth to prove that natural selection had been at work during the American Revolution, sifting the high-principled and superior colonists from the rabble, toughening them and their children in a bleak northern climate in order to produce the highest species of people. This process of natural selection also ensured that the greatest device for human freedoms, embodied in the British constitutional and monarchial tradition, would be preserved on the American continent until the mass of colonists, Catholics and republicans alike, would come to their senses and adopt its tenets.

The growing respectability of political liberalism in England and on the European continent after 1830 had its effects upon Canadian political thought, including nationalism. The concepts of economic growth and progress, free trade, and technological development especially affected Upper Canada, with its immigrant population and its American heritage. The restlessness of Upper Canada and the defensiveness of Lower Canada were combined in Confederation in 1867.

The first two decades of the existence of the Canadian state established Upper Canadian, now Ontarian, nationalism as the "official" national ideology of the country. Ontarian ideas came increasingly to dominate the orientations of those who came from Europe as immigrants to fill the West. The small outcroppings of French Canadians which existed in northern Ontario, Manitoba, and the Northwest Territories (then Saskatchewan and Alberta) were also neutralized by the "official" ideology. This became apparent in the two Riel Rebellions (1870 and 1885), and Quebec nationalism thereafter grew increasingly conservative and defensive. The need for a "Fortress Quebec" became even more compelling as "religion" collapsed before "technology" in the Saskatchewan valley.

As Ontarian nationalism became the official Canadian nationalist ideology under Mowat, Macdonald and Mackenzie, it acquired new elements. Writers and journalists became fired with expansionary visions, and saw the development of a Canadian state which would rival the United States in transcontinental breadth. The Canada First movement was begun by a disparate group of English Canadians who were concerned with the development of a Canadian nationality which would lend cohesion to the new state and give it some influence within the British Empire. Canada First was based upon the UEL tradition with certain additions and modifications. The successful attempt of the North in the U.S. Civil War to impose its values on the South was seen as an indication of the aggressive nature of the dominant American culture. U.S. industrialism and equalitarian democracy were an attraction for some Canadians and therefore a threat to the existence of the new country. Others in the group enhanced the myths of the 1840s, perceiving the British constitution as the epitome of freedom, and the traditions and moderation of Canadian society as an example to the world.

Another element of the new Canadian nationalism was a mild racism. The people of the north, it was felt, were tough, strong and hardy, due to the rigours of the climate. Only those who were superior came to Canada and stayed. Less hardy people and dissolute races from the warmer climes soon left for the United States. Though there was always some mention of the French-Canadians as descendants from Norman and hence Teutonic stock, the main emphasis was upon the desirable qualities of new immigrants from the British Isles, Germany, and Scandinavia. The racists were disconcerted later by the great migration from Central Europe, which by no definition was "Nordic."

Some Canadians began to be concerned about their place in the British Empire and suggested that eventually the Empire must be composed of an alliance of nations. Others resurrected the republican notions of the rebels of 1837 and asserted that Canada deserved independence. More grandiose writers felt that the size of Canada would make it the most populous of the British states, and would eventually result in a shift in the center of gravity of the empire from Europe to North America. This was easily merged with the moral antipathy towards the United States as well:

. . . (Canada) is Imperial in herself, we sons of her think, as the number, the extent, and the lavish natural wealth of her Provinces, each not less than some empire of Europe, rises in our minds. . . . Her valley of the Saskatchewan alone, it has been scientifically computed, will support eight hundred millions. In losing the United States, Britain lost the *smaller* half of her American possessions . . .[7]

Toward the end of the century, this early nationalism gave way to a movement to create an Imperial Federation. The imperialist concept, built upon a vision of a populous and prosperous Canada assisting the empire in bringing civilization and British freedom to the world, influenced domestic and foreign policy through World War I. To some, the French Canadians were included in those to be "saved" by the Empire; to others the "Norman connection" and the misguided, though sound, conservatism of an agrarian, peasant Quebec were compatible with the imperial dream.

The first crisis between Quebec and the rest of Canada occurred in 1885, when Louis Riel was hanged for treason. This event was seen in Quebec as the triumph of the modified English nationalism in the West. A second crisis arose in the late 1890s as the victory of 1885 was finalized in the repression of French in the Manitoba schools. At the same time, the imperial dream was given life through Canadian partipation in the Boer War. Laurier's involvement in both decisions represented an attempt by moderate liberal French Canadians to ally themselves with the imperial concept, but to the conservative nationalists in Quebec, Laurier's decisions only reinforced the idea that provincial autonomy was necessary for cultural survival.

After 1885, one wing of Quebec nationalists pushed for increasing provincial autonomy as a defence against the threat posed by the imperialists. They stressed the development of agriculture in spite of the exhaustion of available land and increasing urbanization, tried to defend French-speaking minorities outside of Quebec, and demanded recognition of French as an official language of the country. A second wing was led by Henry Bourassa after 1896, whose Nationalist League, while oriented towards liberalism, was of an anti-Laurier

---

[7] W. D. Lighthall, *Songs of the Great Dominion* (London: Walter Scott, 1889), p. 22.

variety. Bourassa stressed the need for Canadian nationalism, but felt that it could not be compatible with imperalism if it included the Québécois. He was also concerned with the influence of the United States upon the whole of the country. While Bourassa attacked the imperialists within Canada, he also worked against the conservative nationalists inside Quebec. He founded the newspaper *Le Devoir* to disseminate his views and supported the formation of trade unions, even though they were opposed by the clergy because of their Marxist bent in Europe and their materialist orientation in the United States.

The Conscription Crisis of 1917 was the climactic triumph of the Canadian imperialists, but the conscription of French Canadians to serve in the armed forces also marked the revival of nationalism in Quebec. After 1917, nationalism in Canada as a whole moved slowly toward the idea of independent nation-state, while in Quebec, racialist and extreme-conservative views were pushed. The *Action Francaise,* whose title, if not ideology, paralleled the major french fascist group, was formed in 1917. Colonization of new farmland was encouraged, small business as opposed to English capitalism was advocated for French Canadians living in cities, cooperatives and Catholic trade unions were seen as compatible with the French character. Finally, the ideals of corporatism were advocated for Quebec. French-Canadian nationalism began to incorporate new progressive ideas only as the church's stand on economic and social problems changed with the Depression. At the political level, however, they were suppressed as Maurice Duplessis and his Union Nationale took power in the mid-1930s and did not emerge again until 1960. French-Canadian nationalism outwardly remained conservative, defensive, and oriented toward provincial autonomy.

From 1920 on, nationalism in the rest of Canada began a long campaign for the acceptance of an independent Canadian nation-state. An independent Canada would continue to act as an integral part of the British Commonwealth since it was a "British nation," bound to the mother country by linguistic and moral ties although freed from contractual political obligations to it.

The version of Canadian nationalism which stressed its British ties remained the "official" ideology as long as Prime Minister W. L. Mackenzie King was active in politics, but new ideas arising out of the Depression and World War II saw Canada move toward a more independent stance. The Depression encouraged many writers, including the Canadian socialists who founded the CCF, to include economic affairs as part of a nationalist creed. They were joined in this respect by the economic nationalists in the Conservative Party who had inherited the National Policy of Macdonald. The postwar weakness of Great Britain and the gradual dissolution of the empire encouraged an independent foreign policy. The combination of economic and political factors resulted in the nationalist focus shifting from British imperialism to a wariness about American domination.

The nationalist concern over the influence of the United States has been largely limited to two areas; the Canadian economy and what might be broadly called cultural identity. Canadian nationalists have only marginally examined Canadian–American relations in the broader international context. They have generally assumed that the otherwise vexatious problem of geographical proximity to the United States is something of an advantage in dealing with the rest of the world. The focus of nationalism has therefore been upon the impact of "the American Way of Life" in Canada itself.

The problem of maintaining a Canadian economy somewhat separated from that of the United States has faced politicians and thinkers since before Confederation. Macdonald's National Policy was designed to spur the development of a national economy through the protection of domestic industries and the extension of their markets to the Maritimes and the West. But, by the 1950s, the problem became one of control rather than tariff protection. American corporations accepted and eventually used the Canadian tariff wall. They formed subsidiaries, thereby increasing manufacturing in Canada. The problem then became one of devising a way to control these new and desirable organizations, so that they would function as "good corporate citizens" and not simply as profit-centres in a multinational framework.

The Report of the Royal Commission on Canada's Economic Prospects (1957) served to publicize the problem. The report noted that while foreign investment should be encouraged, it was becoming too concentrated in its directions. Technologically based industries and resource industries were heavily foreign dominated. Further, foreign investment was being used to acquire equity in corporations, to own parts or all of them, instead of being used as loan capital, which did not require ownership. The Chairman of the Royal Commission, a prominent Liberal politician, Walter Gordon, began to speak and write about this problem of foreign ownership. He felt that the loss of economic independence implied by a rising level of foreign ownership would inevitably lead to a loss of political independence. The old remedy, tariff protection, now was serving as a shield for multinational operations to hide their activities and should be lowered. Instead, increased government control of the Canadian economy should become the cornerstone of a new national policy. Gordon tried to implement some of his ideas when he became finance minister in 1963, but for a number of reasons he was not successful.

From a more conservative vantage point, George Grant pessimistically noted in his *Lament for a Nation* (1965) that Canada forms a necessary part of a total North American economy. The centralizing impact of American technology and economic practices make it virtually inevitable that Canada will be absorbed into the United States. Only the maintenance of a unique national culture and political philosophy and the creation of a planned economy might serve to reverse the process.

One of Gordon's decisions as finance minister during this period was to set up a Task Force on the Structure of Canadian Industry. Its chairman, Mel Watkins, became the leading socialist exponent of economic nationalism after the Report of the Task Force was made public in 1968. The socialist argument crystallized in 1969 around the so-called Waffle movement and its slogan, "an independent socialist Canada." Canada could not be independent of the United States unless its economy was broken away from the American-dominated multinational complex. This could only be done through the development of nationalized industries or crown corporations as a substitute for foreign subsidiaries. The Waffle acted as an internal NDP pressure group until it was expelled two years later. But it had served its purpose, for the NDP had been moved to a more vocal commitment to nationalism. Its commitment helped, in turn, to move Liberal policy makers during the period of Liberal minority government (1972–74) into a more nationalistic stance.

The debate over the economy also engendered discussion about the nature of the Canadian identity. Economic ties had naturally extended into the area of the media, with American newspapers, magazines, films, and radio and television productions being imported into Canada in large quantities. Actions were taken by the government throughout the 20th century to restrict ownership of Canadian media to citizens, but these relatively small organizations did not have the resources to compete with imported materials. Only as nationalist feeling arose among writers, artists, and performers was there any significant movement to generate stable domestic cultural "industries." During the past decade feature films have been subsidized, advertising expenditures have been redirected to Canadian publications, and content regulations have been introduced into broadcasting. These and other measures have been designed to generate higher quality cultural activities and greater exposure to them.

A "Quiet Revolution" in Quebec, which had its beginnings in the postwar era, was promoted by the provincial Liberal Party after it took over power from the conservative nationalists in 1960. The Quiet Revolution generated a new nationalist trend in the province which was broadly based upon a liberal strand of thought which went back to the *Patriotes* of 1837. It emphasized the need for education, secularism, industrialization, and general modernization. The liberation of the

Québécois population was to be accomplished through the positive use of state power. In their enthusiasm to "catch up" with the rest of the country, the definition of provincial authority was expanded beyond the limits accepted in Confederation, giving rise to jurisdictional conflicts. Quebec frustrated the country by such measures as vetoing the total patriation of constitutional amending powers in 1971, which was a Canadian nationalist goal, and the federal government frustrated Quebec in its attempts to develop international links relative to matters under its authority.

The new Quebec nationalists also revived an earlier concept, that of the political separation of Quebec from the rest of Canada. Separatism is not new, having been advocated by French revolutionary agents in 1794. It also underlay the 1837 rebellion and later constituted part of the conservative nationalists' visions for Quebec, expecially after the imperialists seemed to be completely victorious. In the 1920s the vision of a French Catholic state of "Laurentia" was advocated as a means of protecting the values of the people.

The separatism of the 1960s was generally not of a conservative variety, however. For the moderates, the existence of an independent state of Quebec was seen as a precondition for the extension of prosperity to all parts of the province. For the revolutionaries, it was a by-product of a Marxist revolution in Quebec.

Quebec nationalism bears many similarities to its counterparts in the areas of the world under former colonial domination. In 1960, the publication of *Les Insolences du Frère Untel,* by Jean –Paul Desbiens, popularized the use of idiomatic French, or *joual,* in the media. Quebec was given its own "language." Folksingers began to resurrect the musical styles of the old French colony, and adapted them to modern tastes. Broadcasters and newspapermen, such as René Lévesque and Pierre Bourgault, began to devote their talents to explaining the nationalist/separatist idea. Finally, the writings of Frantz Fanon, especially his *The Wretched of the Earth,* were brought to Quebec and formed a bridge between the ideals of independence and of socialism. Quebec was seen as another, though less bloody, colonized nation like Algeria. Fanon pointed out that socialism was necessary if a newly independent state wished to avoid permitting an indigenous elite to become a new oppressor.

In 1960, Marcel Chaput and others formed the *Rassemblement pour l'Indépendance Nationale* (RIN), which advocated the creation of an independent Quebec. Later, the separatist ranks were joined by Lévesque, the most active promoter of the positive use of state power in the 1960–66 Quebec Liberal government. Lévesque brought the RIN and other separatist groups, ranging from conservatives to Marxist socialists, together in 1968 to form the Parti Québécois. This party advocates separatism to be followed by an economic association between Quebec and Canada, resembling that of the European Common Market. Domestically, Lévesque's program is oriented toward a version of social democracy not unlike that of the NDP or European social democratic parties. The shadowy *Front de Libération du Québec* (FLQ) rejected the electoral politics of the PQ in favour of a revolutionary type of socialism. The ideology of the FLQ and the more radical Marxists has tended to lack coherence, there being no agreed-upon set of tenets outside of independence and some form of revolutionary socialism. Outbursts of terrorism began in 1963 and reached a climax in October 1970 with the kidnappings of James Cross and Pierre Laporte, the latter being subsequently murdered. There is considerable doubt as to the permanence of the FLQ, in spite of the assertion in 1970 by the federal government that its existence was a serious threat to peace and unity in the country. The FLQ label was adopted by different groups between 1964 and 1970. Since 1970 no reports about the existence of the FLQ have been heard.

A third outgrowth of the Quiet Revolution are the federalists, most conspicuously led by Pierre Trudeau, who aim to forge a Canadian identity which reflects liberal principles while at the same time incorporating French-Canadian interests within the framework of Confederation. This group's primary concern is the integration of the two trends of nationalism which have existed since the 1830s into a pan-Canadian idea.

Both nationalisms in Canada appear to be gathering force in the 1970s. While separatist violence in Quebec has largely disappeared since 1970, the more subtle process of internal examination and reform has gone on. The use of the French language has been strengthened by legislation affecting both the schools and the workplace. The Parti Québécois, while being prevented from a significant share of power in the province, has increased its appeal in two elections. Popularization of nationalist ideals through the media, especially films and books, has increased. Leander Bergeron's Marxist cartoon-pamphlet *Le Petit Manuel d'Histoire du Québec* has approached in Quebec the relative circulation enjoyed by Tom Paine's *Common Sense* on the eve of the American Revolution.

In English-speaking Canada, a similar process of internal examination is just beginning. Nationalist literature, ranging from the potboilers of Richard Rohmer to the studied nationalist seriousness of Margaret Atwood's *Survival,* are evidence of this trend. Some appreciation of regionalism as a Canadian virtue has begun to be seen in the media and in the structures of the bureaucracy as the federal government has begun to move towards decentralization of its operations. Federal-provincial conflicts over energy supplies, especially oil and gas, have increased the awareness of regionalism as part of a Canadian identity.

RECOMMENDED READINGS

Akzin, Benjamin. *State and Nation.* London: Hutchinson University Library, 1964.

Berger, Carl. *Sense of Power: Studies in the Idea of Canadian Imperialism, 1967–1914.* Toronto: University of Toronto Press, 1970.

Binder, Leonard. *Ideological Revolution in the Middle East.* New York: John Wiley & Sons, 1964.

Brown, D. Mankenzie. *The National Movement: Indian Political Thought from Ranade to Bhave.* Berkeley: University of California Press, 1965.

Carsten, F. L. *The Rise of Fascism.* Berkeley: University of California Press, 1967.

Cecil, Robert. *The Myth of the Master Race: Alfred Rosenberg and Nazi Ideology.* New York: Dodd, Mead, 1972.

Cook, Ramsay. *French-Canadian Nationalism.* Toronto: Macmillan of Canada, 1969.

————. *The Maple Leaf Forever.* Toronto: Macmillan of Canada, 1971.

Deutsch, Karl. *Nationalism and Social Communication.* Boston: Massachusettes Institute of Technology Press, 1966.

Doob, Leonard. *Patriotism and Nationalism: Their Psychological Foundations.* New Haven, Conn.: Yale University Press, 1965.

Dyck, Harvey, and Krosby, H. Peter, eds. *Empire and Nation.* Toronto: University of Toronto Press, 1969.

Emerson, Rupert. *From Empire to Nation.* Boston, Mass.: Beacon Press, 1962.

Fairbank, John K.; Reichauer, Edwin O.; and Craig, Albert M. *East Asia: The Modern Transformation.* Boston: Houghton Mifflin, 1965.

Grant, George. *Lament for a Nation.* Toronto: McClelland & Stewart, Ltd., 1965.

Hagy, J. W. "Quebec Separatists: The First Twelve Years." *Queen's Quarterly* 76, no. 2 (Summer 1969): 229–39.

Hayes, Carlton J. H. *Essays on Nationalism.* New York: Russell and Russell, 1966, originally published 1926.

————. *Nationalism: A Religion.* New York: Macmillan, 1960.

Hofstadter, Richard. *The Progressive Historians.* (New York: A. A. Knopf, 1968).

Kohn, Hans. *Idea of Nationalism.* New York: Macmillan, 1944.

————. *American Nationalism.* New York: Macmillan, 1957.

————. *Nationalism: Its Meaning and History.* Princeton, N.J.: Van Nostrand, 1955.

————. *The Age of Nationalism.* New York: Harper & Row, 1966.

Lenin, V. I. *National Liberation, Socialism and Imperialism.* Selected writings by V. I. Lenin. New York: International Publishers, 1968.

Masur, Gerhard. *Nationalism in Latin America.* New York: Macmillan, 1966.

Nolte, Ernst. *Three Faces of Fascism*. Toronto: New American Library of Canada, 1969.

Potter, David, and Manning, Thomas G., eds. *Nationalism and Sectionalism in America*. New York: Holt, Rinehart & Winston, 1949.

Royal Institute of International Affairs. *Nationalism*. London: Oxford University Press, 1939.

Russell, Peter, ed. *Nationalism in Canada*. Toronto: McGraw–Hill, 1966.

Smiley, Donald. *The Canadian Political Nationality*. Toronto: Methuen & Co., 1967.

Smith, A. D. "Ideals and Structure in the Formation of Independence Ideals." *Philosophy of the Social Sciences* 3, no. 1 (March 1973): 1–17.

———. "Theories and Types of Nationalism." *Archives Europeenes de Sociologie* 10, no. 11 (1969).

Szymanski, Albert. "Fascism, Industrialism and Socialism: The Case of Italy." *Comparative Studies in Society and History* 15, no. 4 (Oct. 1973): 395–404.

Tipton, C. Leon, ed. *Nationalism in the Middle Ages*. New York: Holt, Rinehart & Winston, 1972.

Viereck, Peter. *Metapolitics: The Roots of the Nazi Mind*. New York: Capricorn Books, 1965, originally published 1941.

Name Index

A

Aberhart, William, 122, 371
Alexander the Great, 4
Alexander III (Czar), 398
Allende, Salvador, 45
Almond, Gabriel, 21, 56, 58, 61–62
Arabi, (Colonel), 450
Aristotle, 1, 2, 4–5, 14, 19, 151, 256
Arnstein, Sherry, 289
Atwood, Margaret, 460
Austin, John, 275–76

B

Baar, Carl, 276
Bagehot, Walter, 162
Bakunin, Michael, 406–9, 411, 415
Barrett, David, 122–23
Bennett, W. A. C., 65, 67, 122
Bentham, Jeremy, 1, 258, 360–61
Bergeron, Leandre, 460
Bernstein, Edouard, 413
Bertrand, J. (Premier), 123
Blake, Edward, 382
Blum, Leon, 299
Bodin, Jean, 18, 155, 429
Borden, Robert, 381
Bourassa, Henri, 455–56
Bourassa, Robert, 150
Bourgault, Pierre, 459
Brezhnev, Leonid, 325
Broadbent, Edward, 126
Brock, Isaac (General), 453
Buddha, Gautama, 1
Burke, Edmund, 161, 372–75, 432

C

Caesar, Julius, 380
Caouette, Real, 371
Carlyle, Thomas, 379
Chamberlain, Houston, 441–42
Chaput, Marcel, 459
Chiang Kai-shek, 345
Christ, 273
Churchill, Winston S., 342
Cicero, 1, 153
Claude, Inis L., Jr., 339
Coady, Moses, 418
Confucius, 1–2
Cromwell, Oliver, 155, 429
Cross, James, 460

D

Dafoe, John W., 366–67
Dante, 335
Darwin, Charles, 375, 408
Davey, Keith (Senator), 214, 216
Davis, William, 65
de Gaulle, Charles, 46, 84, 116
Desbiens, Jean-Paul, 459
Deutsch, Karl W., 21, 22
Diefenbaker, John, 120, 122, 158, 195, 205, 381, 423
Dirksen, Everett M. (Senator), 227
Djilas, Milovan, 109
Dodd, Thomas (Senator), 228
Douglas, C. W., 370
Douglas, T. C., 126, 161
Downs, Anthony, 351
Drybones, Joseph, 158, 275–76

Dubcek, Alexander, 110
Duplessis, Maurice, 456

E–F

Easton, David, 21
Eden, Anthony, 309, 311
Fanon, Frantz, 459
Faure, Edgar, 185
Fielding, W. J., 368
Ford, Gerald F., 227, 310
Fourier, Charles, 388–89, 411
Franco, Francisco (General), 81

G

Galbraith, J. K., 363
Gandhi, Mohandas K., 273, 449–51
Glassco, J. Grant, 240–41
Gobineau, Joseph, 440–41
Goldwater, Barry (Senator), 113, 376
Gordon, Walter, 194, 457–58
Grant, George, 381, 457
Grant, George (Rev.), 381
Grazia, Alfred de, 2
Grotius, Hugo, 256, 328

H

Hagen, Everett E., 39
Hammurabi (King), 262
Hegel, Georg Friedrich, 1, 377–78, 393
Henry VIII, 355
Herder, Johann, 433–36
Herzl, Theodore, 451
Hitler, Adolf, 17, 19, 44, 48–49, 60, 98,
    111, 153, 273, 287–88, 302, 321, 436,
    439, 442–43
Hobbes, Thomas, 1, 19, 291, 356–57, 371,
    376
Hobson, J. A., 400
Hoffer, Eric, 299
Holmes, J. T., 279
Howe, Joseph, 381
Hume, David, 372–73
Hunter, Guy, 39
Hyneman, Charles, 2

I

Ibn Khaldun, 1
Ibn Rushd (Averroes), 1
Ibn Sina (Avicenna), 1
Irvine, William, 417

J

Jahn, Friedrich Ludwig, 440
James, I., 152

Jefferson, Thomas, 157, 432
John (King), 154
Johnson, Andrew B., 224
Johnson, Lyndon B., 87–88, 227
Johnstone, John C., 63–64, 70

K

Kamenka, Eugene, 297
Kamil, Mustafa, 450
Kautilya, 1–2
Kemal, Mustafa (Ataturk), 451
Kennedy, John F., 83, 93, 227, 293
Keynes, John Maynard, 362–63
Khan, Ayub (Field Marshal), 142
Khruschev, Nikita, 404
King, Martin Luther, 93
King, W. L. MacKenzie, 456
Koestler, Arthur, 302
Kornberg, Alan, 217–20
Kropotkin, Peter, 408–9, 411
Kuhn, Thomas, 13
Kun, Bela, 401

L

La Follette, Robert (Senator), 112
Laporte, Pierre, 93, 460
Laurier, Sir Wilfrid, 119, 366–67, 382, 455
Laxer, James, 424
Lenau, Nikolas, 444
Lenin, V. I., 105, 153, 273, 302, 326, 396,
    398–403, 415, 419, 448
Lesage, Jean, 149, 368
Levesque, Rene, 123, 459–60
Lewis, David, 126
Lincoln, Abraham, 380
Locke, John, 1, 19, 155, 357–58, 372, 374,
    376
Lougheed, Peter, 122
Louis XIV, 152
Luther, Martin, 355

M

McCarthy, D'Alton, 383
McCarthy, Joseph (Senator), 228
Macdonald, John A., 381–82, 454, 456
McGee, Dárcy, 93
McGovern, George, 113
Machiavelli, Niccolo, 1–2, 4, 428
McIlwain, Charles, 153
Mackenzie, Alexander, 368, 454
McWhinney, Edward, 276, 280
Madison, James, 166
Malthus, Thomas, 359
Mao Tse-tung, 153, 304, 403

Marx, Karl, 1, 299, 360, 370, 378, 386–87, 392–400, 406–7, 409, 411, 413–15, 435, 441, 448
Melville, Herman, 261, 445
Mencius, 1
Mill, John Stuart, 1, 161, 361–62
Montesquieu, Baron de, 155, 163, 430, 440
More, Sir Thomas, 388
Morton, J. D., 272, 381
Mowat, Sir Oliver, 454
Mussolini, Benito, 44, 48, 153, 293, 325, 437–39, 443

N

Nagel, Stuart, 264
Napoleon, 246, 303, 371, 380, 432–34
Nasution (General), 295
Necker, Jacques, 299
Nehru, Jawaharlal, 273
Newton, Sir Isaac, 13
Niemoller (Pastor), 49
Nietzsche, Friedrich, 379–80
Nixon, Richard M., 84, 103, 189, 195, 223–24, 227, 263, 309
Nkrumah, Kwame, 44
Novotny, Antonin, 110

O–P

Orwell, George, 51
Owen, Robert, 360, 390–92, 411
Paine, Thomas, 141, 413, 430, 432–33, 460
Pearson, Lester, 141, 159, 196, 364, 368
Peck, S. R., 279
Pickersgill, J. W., 364
Plato, 1–2, 4, 10, 14, 151, 255–56
Pritchett, C. Herman, 279

R

Rankovic, Aleksander, 109
Richert, Jean-Pierre, 71
Riel, Louis, 273, 293, 454–55
Robarts, John, 149
Roblin, Duff, 161
Rohmer, Richard, 460
Roosevelt, Franklin, 342
Roosevelt, Theodore, 336
Rosenberg, Alfred, 442–43
Rousseau, Jean-Jacques, 1, 19, 430–33, 436, 448
Rovet, E., 279
Russell, Peter, 279

S

St. Augustine, 1
St. Thomas Aquinas, 1
Saint-Simon, Henri de, 389–90
Schubert, Glendon, 279
Schwartz, Mildred, 67
Shaw, George Bernard, 412
Shirer, William, 252
Smallwood, Joseph, 417
Smiley, Donald, 160
Smith, Adam, 155, 358–59, 361, 363, 376
Smith, Goldwin, 366, 367
Socrates, 1, 273
Sorel, Georges, 410–11
Spencer, Herbert, 375–76
Stalin, Josef, 48–49, 105, 153, 401–2, 419
Stolypin, P., 299

T

Tito, Josip Broz, 109, 405
Tomkins, James, 418
Trotsky, Leon, 105, 273, 399, 401–2, 411, 419
Trudeau, Pierre Elliott, 4, 149–50, 159, 187, 194, 368, 460
Turgot, A. R., 299
Turner, Frederick Jackson, 446

V

Van Loon, Richard, 21
Verba, Sidney, 56, 58, 61–62
Voltaire, F., 430

W–Z

Wagner, Richard, 441
Wallace, George, 112–13
Washington, George, 157
Watkins, Mel, 458
Weber, Max, 244–45
Wells, H. G., 83
Wheare, K. C., 166, 170
Whitman, Walt, 445
Whittington, Michael, 21
Williams, Phillip, 196, 239
Wilson, John, 67–68
Wilson, Thomas Woodrow, 4, 313, 336, 444
Wittfogel, Karl, 41
Woodsworth, J. S., 421
Zaghlul, Saad, 450

Subject Index

A

Administration, 237–52; *see also*
  Bureaucracy
  civil service, 180–81, 241–42
  controls over, 208, 237, 251–52
    activity, 28–29, 249–51
    finance, 247–48
    personnel, 240, 246–49, 251
  divisions in, 245–47
  and revolution, 302–4
  secrecy in, 232
Advisory boards, 198, 234–35
Afghanistan, 332
Africa, 39, 164, 321, 324, 326-27, 351, 360,
  446, 448, 450–51
Albania, 404
Alberta, 67–68, 122, 150, 264, 283, 369–71,
  417–18, 422, 454
Algeria, 46
Anabaptists, 387–88
Anarchism; *see* Socialism
Argentina, 246, 333, 439
Asia, 39, 164, 189, 283, 321, 324, 326–27,
  351–52, 446–58, 450–51
Assassination, 93, 293, 408
Atlantic Charter, 342–43
Atlantic Provinces, 64–65, 120–21
Australia, 130, 153, 166, 168, 326, 351
Austria, 340, 417, 434, 436–37, 439, 351
Authoritarian systems; *see* Political sys-
  tem, types

B

Babylon, 245
Balance of power, 329–32

Belgium, 130, 163, 318, 330, 438–39
Brazil, 246, 439
British Columbia, 65, 67–68, 121–22, 150,
  161, 198, 368, 370, 410, 416, 423–24
Budget, 187, 245
  audit, 248
  fiscal year, 247
  planning programming budgeting sys-
    tem (PPBS), 177, 239–40, 248
Buffer state, 331
Bureaucracy, 100–103, 232, 241, 243–48,
  251–52, 285, 390
  representativeness of, 242–43
Burma, 286

C

Cabinet; *see also* Canada; France; Germany, Federal Republic of; Italy; Japan; Leadership; USSR; United
  Kingdom; *and* United States
  composition of, 190–91, 193–97
  executive-legislative relations, 200–203
  origins of, 189–90
  political party in, 184–95
  rule implementation, functions in,
    237–41
    coordination, 238–39
    exercise of administrative powers,
      239–40, 249, 251–52
    insulating administration, 239
  rule-making, functions in, 189–97
Cambodia, 300, 305
Canada
  administration, 100–102, 187–88, 190–
    91, 194, 197, 233–34, 236, 241–43,
    247–49, 251–52, 311, 367, 460

Canada—*Cont.*
  administration—*Cont.*
  advisory boards, 198, 234–35
  bilingualism program, 243, 368
  auditor-general, 207–8, 248
  Crown corporations, 197, 240, 246,
      383–84
    Air Canada, 383–84
    Canadian Broadcasting Corpora-
        tion, 84, 246
    Canadian National Railways, 197,
        246, 383–84
    Information Canada, 118, 232, 367
    Public Service Commission, 208,
        237, 248–49
    Regulatory boards, 240, 267
    Royal Canadian Mounted Police
        (RCMP), 168
  armed forces, 97, 317, 330, 366, 382
  Bill of Rights, 158–60, 276
  cabinet, 146, 163, 186–89, 190–96, 198,
      210, 216, 234, 247, 252
  Confederation, 141–45, 166, 171, 274,
      276, 283, 285, 365–69, 383, 417,
      445, 454, 459
  conferences
    Charlottetown, 142
    Dominion-Provincial, 29, 141, 149,
        159, 172
  constitution, 141, 143, 145, 147–50, 167,
      170–72
    British North America Act, 141–45,
        147–49, 158, 162, 167–69, 171–72,
        209–10, 267–68, 274, 285, 365,
        368, 382–83, 419, 422
  courts, 262–64, 272
    Exchequer Court, 267
    Federal Court, 267
    Supreme Court, 149, 158–59, 266–67,
        272–75, 279
  electoral processes, 128, 131, 133–37
  flag debate, 119, 180, 367, 382, 420
  foreign investment, 67, 120–22, 319–20,
      367, 382, 419–20, 424, 456–57
  foreign policy, 318, 381
  French Canada; *see* Quebec
  functions
    interest aggregation, 134, 215, 219
    interest articulation, 34–35, 83–84, 93,
        96, 100–104, 194, 234–35, 288
    political socialization, 69–70, 72, 74,
        217–18, 458
    rule adjudication, 97–98, 255–56, 258,
        262–64, 266, 273–74
    rule making, 179–80
    rule implementation; *see*
        administration
  Governor-General; *see* Head of state

Canada—*Cont.*
  Head of state, 163, 183
    Governor-General, 146, 163, 169,
        183–86, 188, 198, 204, 213, 247,
        311, 352, 367
    Lieutenant-Governor, 169, 185
  House of Commons; *see* legislature of
  legislature of, 25, 100–101, 146–47,
      149–50, 158, 162, 184–85, 188,
      200–201, 203, 205, 207, 210–22,
      226, 268, 421
    House of Commons, 25, 121, 135, 146,
        150, 188, 192, 204–5, 210–18,
        221–22, 228, 234, 247–48, 423
    committees, 178–79, 207, 212–14
    relations with executive, 169, 210–
        12, 214–15
    relations with head of state, 185
    representation, 161, 210–11, 219–20
    membership, 216–22
    Senate, 25, 146, 150, 203–4, 209–10,
        213, 215–16, 221–22, 419
  Lieutenant-Governor; *see* Head of state
  nationalism, 120–21, 366–68, 381, 424–
      25, 451–61
  Parliament; *see* legislature of
  political culture, 55, 57, 59–68, 177, 382,
      458
  political parties, 118–25, 188, 218–19;
      see also Quebec
    Communist Party, 129, 418–21
    Communist Party (Marxist-Leninist),
        129, 421
    Cooperative Commonwealth Federa-
        tion (CCF); *see* New Democratic
        Party
    Liberal Party, 104, 118–24, 127, 129,
        132, 135, 187, 192, 195, 198, 205,
        218, 278, 366–69, 383, 411, 420–
        23, 458–59
    New Democratic Party (NDP), 73,
        104, 118, 121–22, 126–27, 129,
        132–35, 198, 218, 283, 369–71,
        387, 418–19, 421–424, 456, 458,
        460
    Parti Québécois, 123–24, 285, 319,
        459–60
    Progressive, 417, 421
    Progressive-Conservative (PC), 104,
        118, 120–22, 127, 129, 132, 135,
        161, 205, 218, 278, 382–84, 420,
        423, 456
    Ralliément Créditiste, 122–23, 134,
        218, 371
    Social Credit, 73, 122–23, 129, 132,
        134, 283, 369–71
    Socialist Party of Canada, 419
  political system, 22, 293, 351

Canada—*Cont.*
  Prime Minister, 17, 184, 187–89, 198
    Prime Minister's Office (PMO), 189,
      192
    Privy Council, 146, 185–87
      Privy Council Office (PCO), 186–87,
        189, 192
    public opinion, 83, 89, 366
    Riel rebellions, 296, 454
    Royal Commission
      functions of, 198–99
      on Biculturalism and Bilingualism,
        171
      on Canadian Economic Prospects,
        457
      on Government Operations (Glassco
        Commission), 240–41
    Statute of Westminster, 274, 352
    Supreme Court; *see* courts
    Task Force on the Structure of Canadian
      Industry, 458
    Treasury Board, 186–87, 193, 247–48,
      252
    United Empire Loyalists, 453–54
    Waffle, 424, 458
    War Measures Act, 160, 293
Canada First, 454
Canadian Labour Congress, 121
Cape Breton Island, 68
Capitalism, 358–60, 362–63, 369–70,
    388–89, 391–98, 400, 406, 412–14,
    418, 420, 424
Carthage, 326
Central Treaty Organization (CENTO),
    350
Ceylon; *see* Sri Lanka
Chad, 295
Change, 282–91; *see also* Revolution *and*
    War
  dynamics of, 282–84
  and economic development, 283–84,
    394–95
  and technology, 38–39, 283–84
  types of, 292
    conspiracy, 42, 293–95
    evolutionary, 284–91, 372, 394, 412
    rebellion, 42, 112–13, 170, 293–96
    revolution, 296–301, 394–95
    turmoil, 292–93
  and violence, 291–305
Chief executive; *see* Executive
Chile, 45, 295
China, 1, 17, 41–42, 73, 248, 302, 304, 323,
    325, 343–45, 386, 402–5, 446, 449–450
Citizen participation, 165, 288–91
Class; *see* Social class *and* Socialism
Collective security, 335–39, 343
Colombia, 445

Colonialism, 296, 316–17, 324–27, 360,
    419, 445–46, 448–49, 452, 459
Comintern; *see* Socialist Internationals
Committees; *see* Legislature
Common Market; *see* European Economic
    Community
Commonwealth, 22, 163, 184, 264, 274–
    75, 351–53, 366–67, 381–82, 456
Communism; *see* China; Czechoslovakia;
    France; Hungary; Italy; Socialism;
    USSR; *and* Yugoslavia
Concert of Europe, 340
Confederation; *see* Canada
Congress of Vienna (1815), 340
Conservatism, 356, 362–63, 371–84
  Canadian, 365, 371, 381–84, 453, 456
  classical, 372–76
  romantic, 376–80
Constitution, 140–55, 169–71, 308
  amending of, 146–51, 167, 274, 459
  definition, 140
  distribution of powers, 164–65, 167–68
  evolution of, 151–55
  and federalism, 165–70
  and representative government, 160–61
  and rights, 156–60
  and secession, 170–72
Constitutionalism, 23, 28–29, 141, 155–69,
    374
Conversion process; *see also* Rule adjudi-
    cation; Rule implementation; *and*
    Rule making
Corporatism, 209, 417, 456
Corsica, 431
Coup d'état, 293–95, 299–300, 303, 399
Crime, 16, 268, 271
  classes of
    indictable, 268
    sedition, 273
    summary, 268
    treason, 273
  definition, 268
Crise de régime, 293, 295, 303
Crown corporations; *see* Canada
Cuba, 302, 304, 403
  and missile crisis, 323
Cyprus, 353
Czechoslovakia, 110, 325, 330, 404–6

D

Danube Commission, 340
Democratic systems; *see* Modern demo-
    cratic systems; Political systems; *and*
    Traditional democratic systems
Denmark, 117, 163, 250
Dialectic, 378, 393–94, 397, 400, 409, 414
Diggers, 388

Diplomacy, 312–14
Distribution of powers; *see* Constitution
Divine Right, 19, 152, 154, 183, 356, 358,
    429

E

Eastern Europe, 84, 435, 448
Economic determinism, 394–395, 397–98,
    413–14
Egypt, 41, 245, 309, 311, 329, 433, 450
Elections, 128–38; *see also* Canada, elec-
    toral processes *and* United States
    electoral system
    functions of, 129–30
    in nondemocratic systems, 130, 295
England; *see* United Kingdom
Ethiopia, 42, 45
European Economic Community (EEC),
    180, 324, 350, 382, 460
Executive; *see* Administration; Cabinet;
    Head of government; *and* Head of
    state
Executive-legislative relations, 162–64,
    200–203, 308–12

F

Fascism, 44–47, 209, 325, 380, 436–50; *see
    also* Modern nondemocratic systems
    German, 44–46, 437, 439–43
    Italian, 44–46, 48, 323, 437–39, 443
    Spanish, 45–46, 439
Federalism, 109, 165–70, 408, 445
    cooperative, 168–69
    and court structures, 167
Federation of Rhodesia and Nyasaland,
    170
Federation of West Indies, 170
Federations of West and Equatorial Africa,
    170
Finland, 250, 439
Foreign aid, 316–18
Foreign policy, 308, 312–29
    factors in, 321–29
    objectives of, 318–21
    techniques of, 312–18
France, 39, 137, 152, 161, 190, 239, 250,
    293, 299, 302–3, 326, 330, 340–41,
    344, 346, 358, 371, 382, 389, 409, 414,
    428, 430–36, 452, 459
    army, 46, 98, 339, 433
    cabinet in, 185, 239
    Conseil d'État, 251
    constitutions, 141, 165
    interest articulation in, 84
        interest groups in, 99
    legal system, 262, 264–65

France—*Cont.*
    legislatures, 200–201, 206, 432
    political culture, 53
    political parties, 115–17, 237, 411
    Republic
        Fifth, 53, 117, 142–43, 158
        Fourth, 45–46, 115–16, 143, 185, 190,
            196, 200–201, 237, 239
        Third, 17, 185, 299, 410
    Revolution, 17, 44, 53, 256, 297–300,
        303, 373–74, 377, 388, 395, 432,
        434, 440–42
    Vichy regime, 300
Functions; *see* Political system
Fusion of powers; *see* Executive-
    legislative relations *and* Parlia-
    mentary systems

G

General strike; *see* Strikes
General will, 431
Gerrymandering, 136
Geneva Agreement on Genocide (1948),
    329
Germany (and Germans), 17, 19, 54–61,
    244, 330, 332, 377, 392, 398–99, 414,
    433–40, 493, 450–51, 454
    Federal Republic of, 143, 147, 158, 166,
        194, 196, 236, 250–51, 307, 387
        interest aggregation in, 114, 413
        political culture of, 54–61
        rule adjudication in, 264–65, 273–74
    Nazi Germany, 49, 60, 98, 252, 257, 288,
        301, 322–23, 331, 405, 420, 436, 438
        Nazi party of, 108, 111, 125, 439, 443
    Weimar Republic, 44, 60, 141, 287–88,
        322, 341–42, 400, 439, 442
Ghana, 44, 353
Government (definition), 3
Government party, 201
Great Britain; *see* United Kingdom
Greece (and Greeks), 1–2, 4–5, 151, 255–
    56, 326, 427–28, 434, 439, 450–51
Guiana, 353

H

Hawaii, 445
Head of government, 163–64; *see also*
    Leadership
Head of state, 163–64, 237–38; *see also*
    Leadership
    functions in rule-making, 182–85
Holy Alliance, 434
Holy Roman Empire, 428
Hungary, 325, 401, 439

I

Ideology, 49, 283, 299, 324–25
Imperialism, 38–39, 42, 44, 316–17, 321,
    325–27, 331, 351, 365–67, 379, 381,
    420, 434, 437–38, 443, 446, 455–56
    Leninist theory of, 326, 400, 403, 447–
        48
India, 36, 163, 273, 323, 332–33, 339, 353,
    443, 446, 449–51
    constitution of, 141–44, 147, 169
    political parties in, 404
        Congress Party, 296, 449–50
    and political theory, 1
Indochina, 339, 403, 445, 449
Indonesia, 115, 295, 323, 449
Interest aggregation, 27, 107–38, 200, 235;
        see also Political parties
    definition of, 27, 107
    functions of, 107, 111, 114–15
    in nondemocratic systems, 111
    in totalitarian systems, 108–10
Interest articulation, 27, 76–105, 235, 287,
    298, 301; *see also* Canada; France;
    Italy; USSR; United Kingdon; *and*
    United States
    active, 92–105, 288–91
        functions of, 27
        and government agencies, 97–98,
            100–102, 285
        leadership of, 104–5
        and media, 103
        organized interest groups, 96–105,
            107, 289, 405
        techniques, 99–105
        types of, 76–77, 98–99
    unorganized, 43, 93–96, 99, 235, 408,
        410–11, 460
    passive; *see* Public opinion
International Labour Organization (ILO),
    329
International law, 7, 18, 327–29, 335–38,
    378–79
International organization, 7, 339–53
International Postal Union, 340
International relations, 6–7, 308, 329–33
    definition, 308
Internationals; *see* Socialist Internationals
International Workers of the World (IWW),
    416
Iran (Persia), 196, 326, 331
Iraq, 450–51
Ireland, 142–43
Israel, 17, 141, 163, 203, 294, 316, 329–31
Italy, 81, 99, 201–2, 206, 293, 303, 318,
    307, 323, 341, 434, 436
    political culture, 54, 58–63
    political parties, 116–17

Italy—*Cont.*
    political parties—*Cont.*
        Christian Democratic Party, 62,
            80–81, 116
        Communist Party, 62, 117, 406, 437
        Socialist Party, 437–38

J

Jamaica, 353
Japan, 42, 45, 143, 165, 194, 196, 250, 257,
    294, 316, 322–23, 341–42, 347
Judicial review, 268, 274
    in Canada, 274–75
    and centralization, 276–77
    and natural law, 257
    types of, 275
    in United States, 257
Jurisprudence, 258–60
Jury, 264–65

L

Laissez-faire, 358–59, 371, 376
Laos, 305
Latin America, 39, 81, 144, 164, 262, 295,
    326, 360
Law, 16, 254–55, 357, 360–61, 372; *see
    also* Crime *and* Rule
    definition, 254
    integration role of, 255
    science of, 259
    types of, 255–58, 262, 265
Leadership
    bureaucratic, 245
    as cabinet, 162, 189–90, 193
    in democratic systems, 125–28
    election, 164
    as head of government, 163, 183, 187–
        89, 311
    as head of state, 163, 182–83, 311
    as hero, 319–80, 439, 441
    as monarch, 151–53, 162, 186, 356, 378
    origins, 186–90
    in rebellion, 295–96
    recruitment, 73–74
    in revolution, 299
    in totalitarian systems, 109–10
League of Arab States, 350
League of Nations, 309, 336, 338, 340–42,
    345–46
Lebanon, 194, 209, 294, 450
Legal system, 260–68
    attorney, 263
    court, 266–67
        behavior, 276–80
    judges (magistrates, justices), 263–64
    jury; *see* Jury
    law; *see* Law

Legal system—*Cont.*
  roles of, 261
  trial, 262–63, 272–73, 302
Legislature; *see also* Parliamentary sys-
      tems; Presidential systems; *and vari-*
      ous country headings
  electoral factors, 133–38
  evolution, 199
  executive-legislative relations, 162–64,
      200–205
  functions of, 28
    administrative oversight, 208
    catharsis, 206
    communication, 205–6
    deliberation, 207–8
    information-gathering, 206–7, 213–14,
      216, 309–10
    legitimization, 204–5
    representation, 160–61, 208–10,
      219–20
  membership of, 208–11, 226
  role-playing in, 25
Legitimacy, 54, 104, 183–85, 188, 204–5
Liberalism, 357–71, 374, 376, 380, 387,
      396, 444
  Canadian, 364–71, 375, 383–84, 452–54,
      458–60
  classical, 357–60, 365, 375, 378, 393–94,
      406, 414
  reform, 360–65, 369–70
Lithuania, 326
Lobbyists, 96, 102–3, 235
Lower Canda, 452–54

M

Magna Charta, 145, 154, 156, 443
Malta, 17
Malaysia, 194, 449
Management by objectives (MBO),
      251–52
Manitoba, 64, 68, 121–22, 127, 132, 134,
      150, 161, 198, 241, 265, 369, 423,
      454–55
Maritime Provinces, 55, 118, 120, 194,
      204, 418, 457
Marxism; *see* Socialism
Media, 82–85, 106, 128, 132–33, 138,
      231–32, 308, 315, 459–60
Mexico, 58–62, 111–12, 445
Middle East, 83, 262, 294, 446–47, 450
Modern democratic systems, 36–38, *see*
      also Canada; United Kingdom; *and*
      United States
  definitions, 36
  interest groups in, 37–38
  nature of democratic process, 34, 38,
      153–54, 165, 208, 362, 387, 413

Modern democratic systems—*Cont.*
  public opinion, 37
  subsystem autonomy, 34, 36–37
Modern nondemocratic systems, 44–51,
      378, *see also* Fascism *and* Totalitarian
      systems
  class alliances, 46
  contrasted with democratic systems, 34,
      37
  interest aggregation
    and interest groups, 47
    and political parties, 47
  interest articulation, 300
    socialization, 47–48, 206
    public opinion, 78
  military, 45–46
  political culture, 54
  rule implementation
    administration, 47
    police, 47
  rule-making, 198
    legislatures, 47, 206
  and subsystem autonomy, 45
Monarchy; *see* Leadership
Mongolia, 326, 435
Morocco, 46, 239, 451

N

Nation, 427–28
National interest, 321
National liberation, 432, 434, 444–45
National security, 319, 321, 323
Nationalism, 324, 352, 400, 409, 414, 420,
      427–61
  American, 432, 443–46, 453
  Asian and African nationalism, 446–51
  Canadian, 120–21, 366–68, 381, 424–25,
      451–61
  and Communism, 405, 421, 427
  definition, 427
  English, 429–35
  European, 429–35
  French, 431–32, 435
  German, 377, 433–34, 439–43
  Greek, 434
  and imperialism, 434, 438, 445
  liberal, 430, 432, 436, 438, 444–45, 450,
      452, 427, 444
  and modern nondemocratic systems, 46,
      434
  and racism, 434, 440–43, 454
  radical, 436–43, 444
  romantic, 430–34, 436, 444
  Russia (and USSR), 402, 446–48
  and socialism, 435
Nationality, 427
Nauru, 17

Nepal, 33
New Brunswick, 143–44, 150, 171, 194
New Left, 326, 389, 411, 424
New Zealand, 146, 250, 351
Newfoundland, 150, 204, 369–70, 417
Nicaragua, 239
Nigeria, 170, 295, 319, 353, 443
North Atlantic Treaty Organization (NATO), 330–31, 350
Northwest Territories, 243, 265, 276
Norway, 117, 294
Nova Scotia, 121, 143–44, 150, 171, 368–69, 418

O

Ombudsman, 208, 249–51
Ontario, 64, 67–68, 119–21, 134, 149, 161, 171, 193–94, 204, 236–37, 241, 289, 369, 383, 388, 418, 421–24, 454
Opposition party, 201–2, 205, 207, 286, 423
Organization for African Unity, 350
Organization of American States, 351

P

Pakistan, 142–43, 170, 321, 323, 339, 456
Palestine, 17, 294, 316, 451
Panama, 445
Pan-American Union, 340
Paris
  commune, 415
  peace conference, 313
  strike of 1968, 411
Parliamentary systems, 137, 161–63, 181–82, 200–202, 233, 239, 308–9, 311, 407; *see also* Canada; France; Italy; *and* United Kingdom
Patriotism, 427–28
Permanent Court of Arbitration, 340
Permanent Court of International Justice, 341, 346
Peru, 317
Philippines, 445
Poland, 293, 326, 330, 332, 439
Police; *see* Rule implementation
Policy, 175–81
  analysis, 176–78, 187
  process, 176–81, 197–98, 232, 241
Political culture, 23, 39–40, 53–68, 261, *see also* Canada; Germany; Italy; Legitimacy; Mexico; Unted Kingdom; *and* United States
  definition, 23
  types of, 56–57, 67
Political justice, 272–74, 302, 455

Political justice—*Cont.*
  and amnesty, 274
Political parties, 107–29; *see also* China; Czechoslovakia; Italy; Mexico; Spain; USSR; United Kingdom; United States; *and* Yugoslavia
  and administration, 237, 404
  definition, 107
  finances, 128–29
  functions of, 107–8, 118, 399, 403–5, 408, 410
  leadership of, 125–28
  and legislature, 200–201
  and media, 108, 128, 132
  organization of, 124–25, 399, 401–2, 415, 420, 447–48
  party systems, 62–63, 108
    Canadian, 118–25
    multiparty, 114–18
    one-party, 108–12
    two-party, 112–14
Political recruitments, 26
Political science
  approaches to the study of, 1–2, 13–15, 20–22
  definition of, 2–3
  normative aspects, 9–11, 373, 395
  and other social sciences, 7–9
  scientific aspects, 11–13
  specialization within, 4–7
Political socialization, 26, 69–74, 130, 314, 391, 407, 431
  agents of, 69–73
  in Canada, 69–70, 72, 74, 132–33
  and recruitment, 73–74
  definition, 69
Political system, 20–31; *see also* Change; Parliamentary systems; *and* Presidential systems
  boundaries of, 23
  capability, 38–39, 42, 286–87, 296–97, 304
  definition, 22
  feedback, 23, 282–83, 285, 288
  functions, 25–30; *see* Interest aggregation; Interest articulation; Rule adjudication; Rule implementation; *and* Rule making
  inputs, 23, 283, 287, 297
  international, 335
  load, 287–88, 291, 296
  maintenance of, 286–88, 302
  outputs, 23, 283
  roles; *see* Roles
  and the state, 20
  structures, 24–25, 30
  types, 33–51; *see also* Modern democratic systems; Modern nondemo-

Political system—*Cont.*
  types—*Cont.*
      cratic systems; Traditional demo-
      cratic systems; *and* Traditional
      nondemocratic systems
Political theory, 4–5
  conservative, 371–84
  liberal, 357–71
  nationalist, 427–61
  socialist, 386–425
Popular sovereignty, 153–55, 374
Populism, 369–70, 416–18, 421
Portugal, 295, 303
Power
  definition, 3
  in international relations, 329–33, 337
Prairie Provinces, 55, 120–21, 194, 388,
    410, 418, 421, 423
Presidential systems, 138, 164, 199, 201–3,
    239, 308–9, 311
Prince Edward Island, 68, 150, 203
Propaganda, 314–15
Proportional representation, 134
Prussia, 340, 392, 433–34
Public opinion, 77–92, 314
  definition, 23, 77
  determinants of, 78–85
  and media, 82–85
  surveys, 77, 85–92
Puerto Rico, 445

Q

Quebec, 55, 61, 64–65, 68–70, 119–23,
    135, 149–50, 171–72, 185, 193, 195,
    204, 211, 262, 266, 276–77, 285, 292,
    368–69, 383, 418, 420–21, 455, 458–59
  political parties, 123, 236, 285, 293, 319,
    370–71, 452–53, 456, 458–60

R

Rebellion; *see* War, civil
Regionalism; *see* Regional organizations
Regional organizations, 335, 349–53
Representation; *see* Bureaucracy *and*
    Legislatures, membership of
Representative government, 160–161,
    165; *see also* Legislature *and* Parlia-
    mentary system
Responsible government, 162–163; *see*
    also Legislature *and* Parliamentary
    system Revolt; *see* War, civil
Revolution, 56, 285, 291, 296–301, 374,
    407
  and administration, 302–4

Revolution—*Cont.*
  American 44, 156, 256, 297, 303, 365,
    373, 432, 443, 445, 452–53, 460
  definition, 297
  English, 44, 297, 358
  French, 17, 44, 53, 256, 297–300, 373–
    74, 377, 388, 395, 432, 434, 440–42
  Marxist ideas of, 397–405, 411, 414, 419,
    424
  mechanics of, 298, 305
  Russian, 44, 60, 299, 301, 399, 402, 447
  and totalitarian systems, 48
Rhine Commission, 340
Rhodesia, 321
Rights
  Bill of; *see* Canada; United Kingdom;
    and United States
  fundamental, 156–60, 368–69, 373, 444
  natural, 19–20, 156, 378, 406
Riots, 292, 294–95, 303, 408
Roles, 24–25, 285, 300
  definition, 24
  role conflict, 25, 237
  role playing, 16–17, 57
  role system, 24
Roman Empire, 1, 153, 256, 312, 325–26,
    377, 427, 433–34, 438, 443
Romania, 330, 404, 439
Rule
  and policy, 175–76
  definition, 175
  as law, 254–55
Rule adjudication; *see also* Judicial re-
    view; Jury; Law; Legal system; *and*
    Political justice
  definition, 254
  functions of, 235
    interpretation, 29
    reinforcement of political culture,
      261–62, 272
    structures; *see* Legal system
Rule implementation, 28, 231–252; *see*
    also Administration
  definition, 28, 231
  subfunctions, 102–4, 231–36
    communication, 231–33
    enforcement, 235–23
    facilitation, 198, 233–35
    police, 39–40, 231, 235–36, 270–72
    RCMP, 168, 233, 236
  in totalitarian systems, 237
Rule making, 28, 175–29, 374; *see also*
    Cabinet; Head of government; Head
    of state; Legislature; *and* Policy
  definition, 28, 187
  and democratic systems, 181
  and nondemocratic systems, 181
Russia; *see* USSR

S

St. Jean Baptiste Society, 452–53
Saskatchewan, 68, 121–22, 150, 161, 198, 237, 241, 369, 371, 418, 422–23, 454
Saudi Arabai, 33
Scandinavia, 201, 250, 307, 387, 454
Secession, 68, 170–72, 285, 295, 318–19, 383, 405, 459
Self-determination, 414, 447
Separatism; *see* Secession
Serbia; *see* Yugoslavia
Social contract, 19–20, 357, 373–74, 376, 378, 431
Social class, 394–96; *see also* Socialism
Social credit, 370–71
Social Darwinism, 375–76, 379, 408, 453
Social Gospel, 416–17, 422
Socialism, 34, 360, 363, 386–425
  anarchism, 389, 406–7, 410–11, 415–16
    and Marxists, 397
    and New Left, 389
  communism, 34, 283, 386–87, 406
    Canadian, 416, 419–21
  democratic socialism, 387, 398, 411–14
    Canadian, 367, 369–71, 410, 416–19, 421–25
    European, 413
    Fabian, 411–413, 422
    and nationalism, 413, 436, 448, 451, 459
    and populism, 369
  Marxian, 325–26, 370, 381, 386–87, 392–406, 411–15, 417, 419–20, 422, 435–37, 442–43, 447–49, 459–60
  syndicalism, 409–11
  Trotskyite, 386, 402, 411, 421
  utopian, 387–92, 406, 414–15
Socialist Internationals, 403, 414–16, 419, 435–36, 447–48
Society, 16
South Africa, 56, 286, 321, 326, 351, 353, 450
South East Asia Treaty Organization (SEATO), 311, 350
South Vietnam, 305, 309–10
South Yemen, 305
Sovereignty, 18, 155, 307, 319, 327, 335–36, 351, 357
Soviet Union; *see* USSR
Spain, 18, 326, 434, 439
  civil war, 45
  Falange (fascist) Party, 111
Sri Lanka, 165
State, 16–20, 308
  definition, 17
  essential elements of, 17–18, 307, 321–24, 329, 397

State—*Cont.*
  glorification of, 377–79
  origins of, 18–20
  and political system, 20, 438–39
State of nature, 19–20
Strikes, 180–81, 273, 292–93, 401, 410, 415–16, 420
Structures; *see* Political system
Survey research, 54, 68, 77, 85–92
Sweden, 117, 165, 203, 250
Switzerland, 147, 158, 166, 169, 190, 263
Syndicalism; *see* Socialism
System; *see* Political system
Systems analysis; *see* Political science, approaches to the study of

T

Tanzania, 250, 353
Territorial integrity, 318–19
Terror, as a political weapon, 301–2, 304
  terrorism, 293–94, 319, 460
Thailand, 42
Totalitarian systems, 48–51, 434
  contrasted with other authoritarian systems, 48
  and interest articulation, 300, 405
  and leadership, 49
  and political parties, 50, 302, 304, 401–2, 405
  and political socialization, 48, 50, 404
  and revolution, 48, 299–300, 403–4
  and rule adjudication, 302
  and rule implementation, 50, 237
  and rule making, 401
  and technology, 48–49
  and terror, 51
Trade unions; *see* Interest articulation, organized, *and* Socialism
Traditional democratic systems, 36
Traditional nondemocratic systems, 38–44, 283
  administration in, 198
  capability of, 38–39, 42
  and elections, 43
  as hydraulic societies, 41
  and ideology, 39
  inputs, 40
  interest articulation in, 40, 43, 94–95, 296
    interest groups, 40
    military as interest group, 41–42
  outputs, 40–41
  as peasant societies, 39
  political culture, 39–40, 64
  socialization, 39–40
Treaties, 309–10
  of Versailles, 309

Trotskyites; *see* Socialism
Tunisia, 46, 165
Turkey, 42, 287, 329, 434–35, 450–51

U

USSR (Union of Soviet Socialist Republics), 17, 84, 109–10, 262, 273, 283, 301–3, 316–17, 322, 327, 329–33, 340, 342–46, 381, 386, 398–99, 404–5, 417, 420, 434, 437–38, 447–48, 451
  administrative controls, 251
  cabinet, 190–91, 196
  constitution of, 141, 147, 157, 166, 170
  economic plans, 402
  ideology, 39, 325
  interest articulation in, 235
  legislature, 210
  political parties,
    Communist Party (CPSU), 35, 108, 325, 401
      Bolsheviks, 302–3, 436
  political socialization in, 34–35, 73
  revolution, 44, 60, 299, 301, 399, 402, 447
Unitary government, 164–65
United Kingdom, 33, 39, 84, 119, 131, 137, 152, 154–55, 160–61, 163, 165, 167, 184, 297, 308–9, 311, 322, 326, 330–31, 340–41, 343–44, 351–53, 356, 358–59, 364–66, 369, 377, 379, 381–82, 390–91, 393, 414–15, 452–56
  administration, 190, 192, 237, 240
  Bill of Rights, 145, 155
  cabinet of, 194, 196, 239–40
  constitution, 141, 143, 145–46, 158
  legal system, 256, 258, 264, 273–74
  legislature, 145, 147–48, 154–55, 162, 165, 199–200, 205, 212, 226, 274, 352
    House of Commons, 180, 199–200, 213, 372–73
    House of Lords, 203
  Northern Ireland, 92, 294
  parliamentary commissioner, 250
  party system, 114, 121, 180, 387, 412–13, 416, 423
  political culture, 54, 58–63
  Privy Council, 186, 274, 276, 352
  socialism, 391–92, 411–13, 416–17
United Nations, 311, 329, 338–39, 342–49
  Charter of, 343–44, 349–50
  membership, 18, 22, 344–46
  organs of
    Economic and Social Council, 346–47
    International Court of Justice, 346, 348
    Secretariat, 346, 348
    Trusteeship Council, 346–48

United Nations—*Cont.*
  Security Council, 346–47, 349–50
United States, 39, 120, 166, 185, 288, 307–10, 316, 319–22, 327, 329–30, 332–33, 339, 341–47, 364–65, 367, 369, 375, 381, 383, 389, 411, 432, 452–54, 457–58
  administration, 190–92, 197, 200, 236–37, 239–40, 250, 309, 317, 376, 401
  Bill of Rights, 157, 382
  civil war, 112–13, 444, 454
  Constitution, 141–44, 147, 155, 157–58, 166, 168, 202, 209, 310, 444–45
  Declaration of Independence, 156–57, 296
  electoral system, 112–13, 134, 137, 165
  executive
    Presidency, 188–89, 195, 200–202, 223–24, 227, 247, 275, 293, 309, 313, 336, 340, 342, 376, 432
    cabinet, 194–96
  interest articulation, 84–85, 93, 96, 235, 416, 422
  interest aggregation, 134
    political parties, 112–20, 127–28, 226–28
  judiciary, Supreme Court, 29, 88–90, 144, 256, 263–65, 273–76, 279
  legislative-executive relations, 223–27, 443
  legislature, 155, 166, 203, 208, 226
    Congress, 147, 188, 200–202, 218, 221–29, 310, 336
      committees of, 178, 207–8, 213–14, 223–26
      House of Representatives, 200, 210, 222–27
      Senate, 155, 200, 204, 209–10, 222, 227–28, 263, 309
  political culture, 58–63, 382
  political socialization, 73–74
  public opinion polls, 87–90
  revolution, 44, 156, 256, 297, 303, 365, 373, 432, 443, 445, 452–53, 460
  socialism in, 112, 387, 417, 424
  Watergate scandal, 62, 85, 128, 189, 223
University League for Social Reconstruction, 422
Upper Canada, 454
Uruguay, 294
Utilitarianism, 258, 360–62

V

Vietnam, 62
Violence, 291–305, 408
  and change, 288, 297
  definition, 291
  and system maintenance, 284, 288, 291

W

War
  Algerian, 304
  Biafran, 295, 319
  Boer, 366, 382, 455
  civil, 42, 112–13, 170, 293–96, 299–300,
      319, 393, 441, 444, 452, 454, 459
  and conservatism, 379–80
  economic, 315–16
  of 1812, 453
  First World, 244, 312, 335–36, 340, 352,
      398–400, 409–10, 413–14, 436–39,
      442, 444, 447, 449–50, 455
  Indochinese, 83, 310
    Vietnam, 62, 223, 257, 304, 321, 328,
      411
  Israeli-Arab, 294, 316, 320–21
  Korean, 310, 339

War—*Cont.*
  law of, 328
  and liberalism, 360
  revolutionary, 304–5, 403, 445, 452–53
  Spanish-American, 445
  Second World, 98, 137, 192, 209, 241–
      42, 257, 310, 313, 316, 320–21, 324,
      327, 331, 333, 342, 352, 404–5, 415,
      422, 448, 456
Warsaw Pact, *see* Warsaw Treaty Organi-
    zation
Warsaw Treaty Organization, 331, 350
Western European Union, 350

Y

Yugoslavia, 109–10, 250, 230, 404–5, 433,
    438
Yukon Territory, 243, 264

*This book is set in 10 and 9 point Caledonia,
leaded 2 points. Chapter numbers are 36-
point Bodoni Italic #175A and chapter titles
are 24 point Bodoni Italic #175A. The size of
the type page is 27 by 45½ picas.*